DIRECTORY OF
AMERICAN LIBRARIES
WITH GENEALOGY OR
LOCAL HISTORY COLLECTIONS

DIRECTORY OF AMERICAN LIBRARIES WITH
GENEALOGY
OR
LOCAL HISTORY COLLECTIONS

Compiled by

P. William Filby

SR *Scholarly Resources Inc.*
Wilmington, Delaware

The paper used in this publication meets the minimum requirements of the
American National Standard for permanence of paper for
printed library materials, Z39.48, 1984.

© 1988 by Scholarly Resources Inc.
All rights reserved
First published 1988
Printed and bound in the United States of America

Scholarly Resources Inc.
104 Greenhill Avenue
Wilmington, Delaware 19805-1897

Library of Congress Cataloging-in-Publication Data

Filby, P. William, 1911-

    Directory of American libraries with genealogy or local history collections / compiled by
P. William Filby.
       p.   cm.
    Includes index.
    ISBN 0-8420-2286-4 : $75.00
    1. Genealogical libraries—United States—Directories.
2. Historical libraries—United States—Directories. 3. Genealogy—
Library resources—United States—Directories. 4. Local history—
Library resources—United States—Directories. 5. United States—
Genealogy—Library resources—Directories. 6. United States—History,
Local—Library resources—Directories. I. Title.
Z675.G44F56 1988
026.973'025—dc19   87-37109
                                                 CIP

**A Sample Questionnaire is located
on the inside back cover of this volume.**

Contents

Contents

Sample Questionnaire for the
Directory of American Libraries
with Genealogy or Local History Collections
Part 1

1. DAYS AND HOURS OPEN TO THE PUBLIC.

2. NAME OF THE HEAD OF YOUR GENEALOGY OR LOCAL HISTORY SECTION.

3. APPROXIMATE NUMBER OF BOOKS BY LANGUAGE IN YOUR GENEALOGY OR LOCAL HISTORY SECTION.

4. APPROXIMATE NUMBER OF MANUSCRIPT COLLECTIONS CONCERNING GENEALOGY OR LOCAL HISTORY IN YOUR LIBRARY.

5. APPROXIMATE NUMBER OF REELS CONCERNING GENEALOGY OR LOCAL HISTORY IN YOUR MICROFILM COLLECTION.

6. WHAT GEOGRAPHICAL AREAS DOES YOUR COLLECTION COVER?

7. DO YOU ANSWER QUESTIONS BY TELEPHONE OR LETTER CONCERNING GENEALOGY OR LOCAL HISTORY?

8. IS THERE A QUALIFIED GENEALOGIST ON YOUR STAFF?

9. IS THERE A CHARGE FOR THE USE OF YOUR LIBRARY?

10. DO YOU LEND BOOKS FROM YOUR GENEALOGY OR LOCAL HISTORY COLLECTION?

11. DO YOU LEND MICROFORMS FROM YOUR GENEALOGY OR LOCAL HISTORY COLLECTION?

12. IS THERE A PUBLISHED GUIDE TO YOUR HOLDINGS?

13. LIST ANY UNPUBLISHED INDEXES OR OTHER GUIDES TO YOUR COLLECTION.

14. HAVE YOU A LIST OF PROFESSIONALS WHO WILL RESEARCH FOR A FEE?

15. IS YOUR COLLECTION ON OCLC? IS YOUR COLLECTION ON RLIN?

**A Sample Questionnaire is located
on the inside back cover of this volume.**

Part 2

Please indicate which of these publications your library owns. If your holdings of any series are incomplete, please note this at the end of the title (e.g., vols. 4-10 only).

BOOKS & SETS

1. **Biography and Genealogy Master Index.** 2d. ed., 8v., 1980. Suppls., 1981-86.
2. **D.A.R. Lineage Books.** v. 1-166, 1890-1921.
3. Filby, Meyer, & Lower, **Passenger & Immigration Lists Index.** 3v., 1981. Suppls., 1982-86.
4. Filby, **Philadelphia Naturalization Records.** 1982.
5. Glazier & Tepper, **Famine Immigrants.** 7v., 1983-86.
6. Gregory, **American Newspapers, 1821-1936.** 1937.
7. Hinshaw, **Encyclopedia of American Quaker Genealogy.** 7v., 1936, or reprint 6v., 1969.
8. **International Genealogical Index.**
9. Jetté, **Dictionnaire généalogique des familles du Québec.** 1983.
10. Kaminkow, **Genealogies in the Library of Congress.** 2v., 1972.
11. Kaminkow, **Genealogies in the Library of Congress.** Suppls., 1972-76, 1977.
12. Kaminkow, **Genealogies in the Library of Congress.** Complement, 1981.
13. Kaminkow, **U.S. Local Histories in the Library of Congress.** 4v., 1973.
14. Kaminkow, **U.S. Local Histories in the Library of Congress.** Suppl. & Index, 1975.
15. New York Public Library, **Dictionary Catalog of the Local History and Genealogy Division.** 18v., 1974.
16. New York Public Library, **U.S. Local History Catalog.** 2v. & Suppl., 1974.
17. Newberry Library (Chicago), **Genealogical Index.** 4v., 1960.
18. Rider, **The American Genealogical-Biographical Index.** 1952- .
19. Rietstap, **Armorial général.** 2v., 1950, 1972; Illustrations, Rolland, 6v., 1903-26, 1967. Suppls., 1904-54, 1969-71.
20. St. Louis Public Library, **Heraldry Index.** (Gambrill), 4v., 1980.
21. Sibmacher, **Grosses and Allgemeines Wappenbuch . . .** 9v., 1605-1961(?).
22. Swierenga, **Dutch Emigrants . . . 1835-1880.** 1983.
23. Swierenga, **Dutch Immigrants . . . 1820-1880.** 2v., 1983.
24. Tanguay, **Dictionnaire généalogique des familles canadiennes.** 7v., 1871-90, or reprint, 1967.
25. Tanguay, **Dictionnaire généalogique des familles canadiennes.** Leboeuf: Complément, 2v., 1975-77.
26. U.S. Bureau of the Census, **Bureau of the Census, Heads of Families at the First Census, 1790.** 12v., v.d.

PERIODICALS. Quote numbers held if partial run (e.g., v. 14- , 1861-).

1. **The American Genealogist,** 1- , 1922- .
2. **Canadian Genealogist,** 1- , 1979- .
3. **Detroit Society for Genealogical Research Magazine,** 1- , 1937- .
4. **The Genealogical Helper,** 1- , 1947- .
5. **Genealogical Periodical Annual Index,** 1962-69, 1974- .
6. **Genealogists' Magazine** (Society of Genealogists, London), 1- , 1925- .
7. Jacobus, **Index to Genealogical Periodicals.** 3v., 1858-1953, v.d.
8. **National Genealogical Society Quarterly,** 1- , 1912- .
9. **New England Historical and Genealogical Register,** 1- , 1847- .

A Sample Questionnaire is located
on the inside back cover of this volume.

Introduction

As a former librarian, as well as a current author and compiler of several major genealogical reference works, I often receive questions about the availability of the published and unpublished materials to which I refer. These questions have led me to believe that there is a substantial need for a publication that will offer genealogists, historians, librarians, and those individuals seeking their family history information on where genealogy and local history collections are located, what they contain, and how they may be accessed. The *Dictionary of American Libraries with Genealogy or Local History Collections* is the first of its kind and is designed to save invaluable time for both the researcher and the librarian.

The *Directory*, which lists over 1,500 libraries in the United States and Canada, is arranged alphabetically by state and city. Among other information, it includes library name, address, and telephone number; days and hours open to the public; lending policies; the head of the genealogy or local history section; size and contents of collections pertaining to genealogy or local history; whether there are published or unpublished guides or indexes to the collections; and major genealogical reference works and serials owned.

Chosen from the *American Library Directory*, Mary K. Meyer's *Genealogical Societies in the U.S.A. and Canada*, various R. R. Bowker library mailing lists, as well as from leading magazines in the field and individual suggestions, over 4,000 questionnaires were sent to U.S. and Canadian libraries. The two-part questionnaire was compiled with the aid of several prominent genealogists. The fifteen questions in Part 1 request information designed to give the researcher basic information about a particular library and what genealogy or local history collections it holds. Part 2 provides a select checklist of twenty-six books and sets, in addition to nine periodicals, to determine which reference works a library contains that may be of special interest to the researcher. The numbered questions in Part 1 and the numbered lists in Part 2 correspond to the numbered responses following the name and address of each library. For the researcher's convenience, sample questionnaires have been placed following the table of contents and on the inside back cover of the volume.

In constructing a questionnaire, it is difficult to avoid misunderstandings completely, and, despite our care and preliminary testing, ambiguity crept into several questions. For instance, some public libraries replied that they had no genealogy or local history holdings simply because there was no separate section housing these collections. This may be true, but one would assume that a library with 100,000 volumes would contain a considerable collection of city, county, and state local histories. In such cases this proved to be disappointing, but it was outweighed by those questionnaires revealing large collections previously not generally known.

Most responses to Question 3, which asked the approximate number of books by language contained within a library's genealogy or local history collection, were answered carefully and completely. However, several libraries chose merely to state "All" or "Some." Confusion also arose over the phrasing in Question 8. Libraries often had qualified genealogists on their staff, although not necessarily certified. Therefore, this question was sometimes left blank because of the ambiguity of the term "qualified." Finally, the answer to Question 15, although applicable to all North American libraries, mostly remained unanswered by Canadian respondents.

With the closing date for the submission of all questionnaires extended to October 5, 1987, many libraries still responded too late for inclusion in the *Directory*. It is hoped that, if a second edition is published, these libraries will be added, as will others that either failed to answer or for some reason did not receive a questionnaire. Of the over 1,500 replies, 128 came from Canada, with an outstanding 62 from Ontario. (See Total Library Counts by State and Province.)

The index in this volume contains a list of all libraries that hold significant out-of-state collections and is divided by state, region and ethnic group, province, or country to which a collection pertains. The index is designed to allow the researcher to find whether a library in Austin, Texas, might house, for instance, a genealogy or local history collection on Alabama, New England, Germany, or the Cherokee Indians. Index entries are arranged alphabetically by state or province. The *Directory* also includes all those libraries that returned questionnaires but stated that they did not hold genealogy or local history collections.

Finally, a word about the Church of Jesus Christ of Latter-day Saints, which maintains a library system under the jurisdiction of its local ecclesiastical leaders. Each of the Family History centers has on microfiche a catalog of microfilm that can be obtained on loan from the Family History Library. Those interested in determining the locations of Family History centers are invited to write to the Family History Library, 35 NW Temple Street, Salt Lake City, Utah 84150.

P. William Filby
Former Director, Maryland Historical Society
Fellow of the Society of Genealogists, London
Fellow of the National Genealogical Society

Acknowledgments

I am most grateful to the following leading genealogists whose suggestions and cooperation helped to develop the questionnaire that made the *Directory* possible: Gunther E. Pohl, Mary K. Meyer, Dorothy M. Lower, Thomas Jay Kemp, J. Carlyle Parker, Judith E. Reid, Terrence M. Punch, Wiley Roger Pope, Lloyd DeWitt Bockstruck, George and Elizabeth Hancocks, and Carol Willsey Bell. Many of the above remained in contact to answer further questions as the project unfolded, particularly Judith Reid at the Library of Congress; Thomas Kemp of the Pequot Public Library, Connecticut; and, in Canada, Terrence Punch and Brenda Merriman. Much credit also must go to all those libraries that answered the questionnaire, and I thank them.

The *Directory* could not have been successful without the enthusiastic support of Daniel C. Helmstadter, president of Scholarly Resources, and the close attention to detail and expert supervision of Carolyn Travers, project editor. Also, I am indebted to Ann Aydelotte, Barbara Beidler, Mildred Hanlin, Cindy Klosowski, Amy Rashap, and Barbara Segal who combined their organizational, editing, proofreading, and computer skills to provide invaluable assistance throughout the many stages of production.

Finally, I wish to express my gratitude to Jerry Kightlinger, Doris Chaney, Linda Redmond, and Maryianne Fincham at the post office in Savage, Maryland, for their patience in handling the thousands of pieces of mail involved with this project.

P.W.F.

Key to Abbreviations

G	genealogy
G/LH	genealogical/local history
ILL	interlibrary loan
LH	local history
MS	manuscript, Mississippi
MSS	manuscripts
N/AN	not answered
N/AP	not applicable
N/AV	not available
NC	no charge, North Carolina
OCLC	On-Line Computer Library Center
RLIN	Research Libraries Information Network
SASE	self-addressed stamped envelope
suppl(s)	supplement(s)
tel	telephone

Total Library Counts by State and Province

UNITED STATES

Alabama	13	Montana	7
Alaska	4	Nebraska	7
Arizona	10	Nevada	2
Arkansas	9	New Hampshire	11
California	87	New Jersey	46
Colorado	13	New Mexico	7
Connecticut	29	New York	77
Delaware	3	North Carolina	41
District of Columbia	5	North Dakota	8
Florida	26	Ohio	88
Georgia	27	Oklahoma	11
Hawaii	5	Oregon	13
Idaho	5	Pennsylvania	46
Illinois	65	Rhode Island	5
Indiana	43	South Carolina	17
Iowa	20	South Dakota	9
Kansas	17	Tennessee	15
Kentucky	13	Texas	51
Louisiana	22	Utah	11
Maine	8	Vermont	10
Maryland	30	Virginia	45
Massachusetts	74	Washington	13
Michigan	40	West Virginia	10
Minnesota	16	Wisconsin	33
Mississippi	22	Wyoming	3
Missouri	24		

CANADA

Alberta	12	Ontario	62
British Columbia	13	Prince Edward Island	3
Manitoba	6	Quebec	10
New Brunswick	3	Saskatchewan	5
Newfoundland	1	Yukon Territory	1
Nova Scotia	12		

UNITED STATES

**A Sample Questionnaire is located
on the inside back cover of this volume.**

ALABAMA

ANNISTON

Public Library of Anniston and Calhoun County, Alabama Room, 108 E 10th St, PO Box 308, 36202
Tel: 205-237-8501

1. M-F, 9:30-5; Sa, 12-4; Su (winter only), 2-5
2. Janice Yates Earnest
3. English, 7,000
4. 15
5. 7,000
6. Southeastern US, especially AL state, GA
7. Tel & letter: yes, NC for brief queries except for copies and postage
8. No
9. No
10. No
11. No
12. No. Forthcoming in 1988
13. *Guide to the Genealogical Holdings of the Alabama Room; Guide to the Manuscript Holdings of the Alabama Room*
14. N/AN
15. No
Books & Sets: 2(v.1–70),3,7, 10–12,22,23,26
Periodicals: 1,4(partial),7,8

AUBURN

Auburn University, Ralph Brown Draughon Library, Mell Street, 36849
Tel: 205-826-4500

1. Su-Sa, 85 1/4 hrs/week (Special Collections)
2. Gene Geiger, Special Collections
3. English, 1,478
4. None
5. 2,781 (US Bureau of the Census MS tapes on microfilm)
6. Southeastern US
7. Tel & letter: yes, NC
8. No

9. No
10. No
11. No
12. No
13. N/AN
14. No
15. OCLC: yes
Books & Sets: 1–7,10–14,17,19,26
Periodicals: 1,4,5,7,8

BIRMINGHAM

Birmingham Public Library/ Linn-Henley Library for Southern Research, 2100 Park Place, 35203
Tel: 205-226-3665

1. M-T, 9-8; W-Sa, 9-6; Su, 2-6
2. Mary Bess Paluzzi
3. English, 56,000; 6,000 bound periodicals
4. N/AN
5. 12,500
6. Southern US
7. Tel & letter: no
8. No
9. No
10. No
11. No
12. *Genealogical Research in the Tutwiler Collection of Southern History and Literature*, $2
13. No
14. Yes
15. OCLC: in process ABJ
Books & Sets: 1,2(incomplete), 3–7,10–14,16–19,22,23,26
Periodicals: 1(incomplete),4,5,7–9

Samford University, Harwell G. Davis Library
Special Collection Department, 800 Lakeshore Drive, 35229
Tel: 205-870-2749

1. M, 8am-9pm; T-F, 8-4:30
2. Elizabeth C. Wells
3. English, 25,000+
4. 6,000
5. N/AN

6. Primarily AL and the Southeast; Ireland, especially Counties Cork and Kerry
7. Tel: no; letter: yes, minimum $10
8. Yes
9. No
10. Limited borrowing policy
11. Yes
12. Yes (partial)
13. Information indexes— Subject index to MSS also includes listing of MS collections and newspaper holdings
14. Yes
15. No
Books & Sets: 2–7,10–14,17,19, 22,23,26
Periodicals: 1,3–5,7–9

DOTHAN

Houston-Love Memorial Library, 212 W Burdeshaw St, PO Box 1369, 36302
Tel: 205-793-9767

1. M,T, 9-9; W-F, 9-6; Sa, 9-1
2. Yvonne Cooper, Reference Librarian
3. English, 2,225
4. None
5. 223 (5 microfiche)
6. Primarily AL, GA
7. Tel: yes, NC; letter: yes, NC, with $1 minimum/copy
8. No
9. No
10. No
11. No
12. No
13. *Wow: Have You Got Ancestors*, $5.75
14. No. Refer to Southeast Alabama Genealogical Society
15. No
Books & Sets: 2,3,5,7,10–12,26
Periodicals: 4,8

FLORENCE

Florence-Lauderdale Public Library, 219 North Wood Ave, 35630
Tel: 205-764-6563

1. M-Th, 9-7; F-Sa, 9-6; Su, 2-6
2. Staffed with volunteers
3. English, 1,000 (plus 1,000 books on the Civil War in the Genealogy-Local History Room)
4. 1,000
5. 250
6. AL, TN, VA, GA, NC, SC, the Southeast
7. Tel: no; letter: yes, NC
8. William Q. Hill
   Mildred Kimbrough
   Alice Locker
   Pat Mahan
   Alfred McCroskey
   Derrell A. Russel
9. No
10. No
11. No
12. No
13. Microfilm, newspaper, and cemetery collections; Family File, Russellville Collection, Kennedy-Douglas Collection
14. No
15. Belongs to Library Management Network
Books & Sets: 26
Periodicals: 4,9, *Southern Genealogical Index;* library receives over 150 titles of genealogical periodicals through its exchange program, most titles continuous since 1980

GADSDEN

Gadsden-Etowah County Public Library, 254 College St, 35999
Tel: 205-547-1611, ext 66

1. M-Th, 9-8; F, 9-6; Sa, 9-5
2. Barbara Reed
3. English, 3,600
4. N/AP
5. 10,000
6. Southeast; lower New England
7. Tel: yes, NC; letter: yes, NC for brief queries, with SASE
8. Bette Sue McElroy
9. No
10. No

11. No
12. No
13. List of family histories; list of Alabama county holdings
14. Yes
15. N/AN
Books & Sets: 10–12
Periodicals: 4

HUNTSVILLE

Huntsville-Madison County Public Library, 915 Monroe St SW, PO Box 443, 35804
Tel: 205-532-5940

1. Labor Day-May 31: M-Th, 9-9; F-Sa, 9-5; Su, 1-5; June 1-Labor Day: M-Th, 8-8; F-Sa, 8-5; Su, 1-5
2. Annewhite Thomas Fuller
3. English, 4,300; German, 5
4. 10
5. 4,000
6. US east of Mississippi River; TX, LA, AR, MO, IA, MN
7. Tel: yes, NC; letter: yes, 15¢/copy
8. Alexandra Baird
   Annewhite T. Fuller
   Margaret H. Henson
   Ranee G. Pruitt
9. No
10. Yes, duplicates only
11. Yes, duplicates only
12. No
13. None
14. Yes
15. No
Books & Sets: 1–5,7,10–13,19,26
Periodicals: 1,4,5,7–9

MOBILE

Mobile Public Library
Special Collections,
701 Government St, 36602
Tel: 205-438-7093

1. M-Sa, 9-6
2. Robert J. Zietz
3. English, 15,000; German, a few; French, 20-30
4. Uncounted
5. 5,230 microfilm reels; 1,100 microfiche
6. Eastern colonies and states, the Southeast, Southwest, Gulf Coast, Midwest
7. Tel: yes, NC, if brief; letter:

yes, $2 minimum
8. No
9. No
10. No
11. No
12. No
13. Card catalog
14. Yes
15. OCLC: AMP
Books & Sets: 2–7,10-14,19,24-26
Periodicals: 1(v.39–,1963–),4 (v.13–,1959–),8(v.36–, 1948–),9

MONTGOMERY

Alabama Department of Archives and History
624 Washington Ave, 36130
Tel: 205-261-4361

1. M-F, 8-5; Sa, 9-5
2. David K. Brennan
3. N/AN
4. N/AN
5. N/AN
6. Primarily AL; also south-eastern states
7. Tel & letter: yes, NC
8. No
9. No
10. No
11. No
12. No
13. N/AN
14. Yes
15. No
Books & Sets: 2,3,6,7,10,19,26
Periodicals: 1,4,6-9

PHENIX CITY

Chattahoochee Valley Community College
2606 Savage Dr, 36867
Tel: 205-297-4981

1. M-Th, 8am-9pm; F, 8-5; Su (except summer), 2-6
2. Estelle B. Owen
3. English, 3,200
4. 50
5. 672
6. Southeastern states, New England
7. Tel: yes, NC; letter: yes, NC for brief queries
8. No
9. No
10. No
11. No

12. No
13. None
14. No
15. No
Books & Sets: 3,5(v.1),7(v.1), 10,26
Periodicals: 4,5(1978),9(index v.1–50)

TUSCALOOSA

Tuscaloosa Public Library
1801 River Road, 35401
Tel: 205-345-5820

1. M-Th, 9-9; F, 9-5; Sa, 2:30-5; Su, 2:30-6
2. Glen A. Johnson
3. English, 1,800. Vertical file relating to Tuscaloosa (city and county), AL in general
4. Numerous collections of local club and organization minutes
5. 40 reels of census (chiefly AL); 240 reels of *Tuscaloosa News*, 1967–
6. AL, chiefly Tuscaloosa and surrounding counties; VA, NC, SC, GA
7. Tel: yes, NC, when time permits; letter: yes, 10¢/copy
8. Glen A. Johnson
9. No
10. No
11. No
12. No
13. None
14. Yes
15. No
Books & Sets: 2
Periodicals: 4(1966–)

VALLEY

H. Grady Bradshaw-Chambers County Library and Cobb Memorial Archives
Highway 29, 36854
Tel: 205-768-2161

1. M-F, 10-6; Sa, 10-5
2. Miriam Ann K. Syler
3. English, 450
4. 150
5. 12
6. Chattahoochee Valley: Chambers County, AL, Troup and Harris Counties, GA; some surrounding counties
7. Tel & letter: yes, NC with SASE
8. No
9. No
10. No
11. No
12. No
13. Inventory list, card file
14. Yes
15. No
Books & Sets: 2(v.43–52, 1903–18),26(NC,SC)
Periodicals: 4(partial to 1977, 1977–86),8(v.69–72 incomplete)

ALASKA

ANCHORAGE

**Anchorage Municipal Libraries,
Z. J. Loussac Public Library**
3600 Denali St, 99503
Tel: 907-261-2975

1. M-Th, 12-9; F,Sa, 10-6;
Su, 12-6
2. Robert C. Williams, Head of
Reference and Readers' Services
3. English, 1,000
4. None
5. AK census, 1900, on film;
10+ drawers microfiche on G/LH
6. US in general; some Europe
7. Tel: no; letter: yes, NC from
out of state
8. No
9. No
10. No
11. No
12. No
13. N/AN
14. No
15. No
Books & Sets: 1,2(partial),
3,10–12,17,19,26
Periodicals:4(v.26–,1972–),
5(v.15–, 1976–),9

FAIRBANKS

**Fairbanks-North Star Borough
Public Library,** 1215 Cowles St,
99701
Tel: 907-452-5177

1. T,W, 10-9; Th,F, 10-6; Sa,
10-5; Su (except summer), 1-5
2. None
3. English, 692
4. None
5. 140
6. No specific area covered
7. Tel & letter: yes, NC for
brief queries
8. No
9. No
10. No
11. No
12. No
13. N/AN
14. Yes. Refer to local genealogy association
15. No
Books & Sets: 1,3,6,7,10,11,26
Periodicals: 8(to 1977)

JUNEAU

Alaska Historical Library
PO Box G, 8th Floor, State
Office Bldg, 99811
Tel: 907-465-2925

1. M-F, 9-5
2. Phyllis J. DeMuth, Librarian
3. N/AV
4. N/AV
5. N/AV
6. Alaska; some Arctic and
Yukon
7. Tel & letter: yes, NC
8. No

9. No
10. No
11. Yes
12. No
13. Various finding aids with
name sections; newspaper clippings; some Alaska-Yukon
cemetery records
14. No
15. No

KENAI

Kenai Community Library
163 Main Street Loop, 99611
Tel: 907-283-9215

1. M-Th, 8:30-8; F, 8:30-5;
Sa, 10-5
2. Emily Deforest
3. English, 400
4. None
5. 20
6. Entire US
7. Tel: no; letter: yes, NC
8. No
9. No
10. Yes
11. No
12. No
13. None
14. No
15. WLN: code AKKe
Books & Sets: 3,10,11,26
Periodicals: 4,8

ARIZONA

FLAGSTAFF

Flagstaff City-Coconino County Public Library
300 W Aspen, 86001
Tel: 602-779-7670

1. M-Th, 10-9; F-Sa, 10-6; Su, 1-4
2. John Irwin
3. English, 300; German, 10
4. None
5. 50
6. AZ, the Southwest in general
7. Tel & letter: yes, NC
8. N/AN
9. No
10. No
11. No
12. No
13. Selected bibliography
14. No
15. RLIN: AzF
Books & Sets: 3,5,10–17,22,23, 26(VA only)
Periodicals: 4,5,7,8(v.74–, 1986–)

KINGMAN

Mohave County Historical Society Library, 400 W Beale St, 86401
Tel: 602-753-3195

1. M,T,W, 10-3; other days and hours by appointment
2. Mona Cochran
   Karin Goudy
3. English, 800
4. N/AN
5. N/AN
6. Mohave County, AZ, the Southwest
7. Tel: yes, NC; letter: yes, $10/hr; free (but not unlimited) to members of Historical Society

8. No
9. No
10. No
11. No
12. No
13. Card catalog
14. No
15. No
Books & Sets: 3,5
Periodicals: 4,8

MESA

Mesa Arizona Branch Genealogical Library
464 E 1st Ave, 85204
Tel: 602-964-5934

1. M,F, 9-5; T-Th, 9-9; Sa, 9-3
2. Benner A. Hall
3. English, 14,000; German, 50; some Danish, French, Swedish
4. 13,500
5. 26,000
6. US, Canada, Denmark, England, Germany, France, Sweden
7. Tel & letter: yes, NC
8. Yes
9. No
10. No
11. No
12. No
13. Family group records and pedigree sheets
14. Yes
15. N/AN
Books & Sets: 2–5,7,8
Periodicals: 1,4,8,9

PHOENIX

Arizona State Library, Genealogy Library, Archives and Public Records, 1700 W Washington, State Capitol, 85007
Tel: 602-255-3942

1. M-F, 8-5
2. Linda S. McCleary
3. English, 11,000; German, 5
4. None
5. 100
6. New England, South, Midwest, most of US; some German, Irish, French resources
7. Tel: yes, NC; letter: yes, 15¢/copy, plus postage and handling
8. Linda S. McCleary
9. No
10. No
11. No
12. *Arizona Department of Library, Archives and Public Records, Genealogy Library Shelflist,* $7.50 ($2.50 for each of 6 suppls)
13. *Arizona Newspapers on Microfilm, Guide to Delaware Archives, Guide to Pennsylvania Archives, Publishing Your Family History Bibliography*
14. Yes
15. RLIN: AZP since 1982
Books & Sets: 1–7,10–14,18,23,26
Periodicals: 1,3–5,7–9

Phoenix Public Library-Central Library, 12 E McDowell, 85004
Tel: 602-262-6451

1. M-Th, 9-9; F-Sa, 9-6; Su, 1-5
2. Jeanne Schnurstein
3. English, 28,000
4. 1
5. None
6. All, especially US, with focus on AZ and Indian heritage
7. Tel: no; letter: yes, for short queries related to AZ, plus 10¢/copy
8. No
9. No

10. Yes, 2-week loan
11. No
12. No
13. N/AN
14. No
15. OCLC: yes
Books & Sets: 1–6,10–12,19,23,26
Periodicals: 4(v.22–)

PRESCOTT

Prescott Public Library
215 E Goodwin, 86301
Tel: 602-445-8110

1. M,F,Sa,10-5:30; T,W,Th, 10-9
2. James Christopher
3. N/AN
4. None
5. None
6. N/AN
7. Tel: no; letter: yes, NC
8. No
9. No
10. No
11. No
12. No
13. N/AN
14. No
15. N/AN
Books & Sets: 3,10–12
Periodicals: 4

SCOTTSDALE

Scottsdale Public Library
3839 Civic Center Plaza, 85251
Tel: 602-994-2476; 994-2179

1. M-Th, 9-7; F,Sa, 9-5; Su, 1-5
2. Heather Goebel, Reference Coordinator; Mario Klimiades, Southwest Librarian
3. English, G, 40, LH, 25
4. Included in #3
5. N/AP
6. Scottsdale, AZ state

7. Tel: yes, NC; letter: yes, NC for brief queries
8. No
9. No
10. Yes, few titles on Scottsdale local history
11. No
12. No
13. None
14. No
15. OCLC: AZD
Books & Sets: 1
Periodicals: 4

SUN CITY WEST

R. H. Johnson Library
(houses library of the Sun City Genealogical Society),
13801 Meeker Blvd, 85375
Tel: 602-584-2405

1. T-Sa, 10-4
2. Rex K. Moorhead
3. English, 800
4. 10
5. N/AN
6. US; small collections on Great Britain, Germany, Canada
7. Tel & letter: yes, NC
8. Yes
9. No
10. No
11. No
12. *Library Book List*, $5
13. N/AN
14. No
15. No
Books & Sets: 3(missing 1986,1986 suppls),5(v.1–2),26
Periodicals: 1(v.34–,1958–),3 (v.41–,1977–),4,5,7,8 (v.42–, 1954–),9(v.120, 1966–)

TUCSON

Tucson Public Library
200 S 6th Ave, 85701
Tel: 602-791-4062

1. M-Th, 9-8:45; F,Sa, 9-4:45; Su, 1:30-4:45
2. Anne Denny
3. English, 1,900
4. None
5. 610
6. US
7. Tel & letter: yes, NC, limited service; charge for copies
8. No
9. No
10. No
11. No
12. No
13. N/AN
14. No. Refer to Arizona State Genealogical Society
15. OCLC: AZT
Books & Sets: 2(v.1–163),3(no suppls),6,7,10,11,19,26
Periodicals: 1(1965–83),4(1951–), 6(1981–),7,8(1940–),9(1959–84)

YUMA

Arizona Historical Society, Century House Museum
240 Madison Ave, 85364
Tel: 602-782-1841

1. T-Sa, 10-4
2. Mark Santiago
3. English, 100
4. 20
5. None
6. Lower Colorado River; Yuma, LaPaz Counties, AZ; Imperial County, CA
7. Tel & letter: yes, NC
8. No
9. No
10. No
11. No
12. No
13. N/AN
14. No
15. N/AN

ARKANSAS

EL DORADO

Barton Library, E 5th &
N Jefferson Sts, 71730
Tel: 501-863-5447

1. M,W,F, 9:30-5:30; T,Th,
1-9; Sa, 1-5
2. Nancy Arn, Librarian
3. English, 500
4. 171
5. 194
6. Primarily the South; some
northern states
7. Tel: yes, NC for brief
queries; letter: yes, NC except for
copies
8. Dorathy Boulden
9. No
10. No
11. No
12. No
13. N/AN
14. No. Refer to Genealogical
Society
15. No
Books & Sets: 2(v.43–109),3(3 v.,
1981),11
Periodicals: 4(1950–),8(1964–67),
9(1952–53)

FAYETTEVILLE

Fayetteville Public Library
217 E Dickson St, 72701
Tel: 501-442-2242

1. M-Sa, 9-5
2. Grace W. Keith
3. English, 2,400
4. 1
5. 490
6. US, England, Scotland,
Ireland, Canada, Wales, Germany
7. Tel & letter: yes, NC
8. Grace W. Keith
Helen M. Brannan

9. No
10. No
11. No
12. No
13. *Genealogical Bibliography,
Fayetteville Public Library*
14. Yes
15. N/AN
Books & Sets: 2(v.1–126),3,5,7
(3 v. only),10–14,26
Periodicals: 1(1980–84),4,5,7,8

FORT SMITH

Fort Smith Public Library
61 S 8th St, 72901
Tel: 501-783-0229

1. Genealogy Room: M,W-Sa,
9-5:30; T, 9-9; microfilm collection: M-Th, 9-9; F,Sa, 9-5:30
2. Wanda J. Karrant
3. English, 5,000
4. Approx 1,000 family files
5. 2,000
6. AR and the South; entire US
7. Tel: yes, NC; letter: yes, $5/
hr or $2.50 minimum plus copies
8. Wanda J. Karrant
9. No
10. No
11. No
12. No
13. N/AN
14. No
15. OCLC: FSM
Books & Sets: 2,7(v.1, 3–6),26
Periodicals: 4

HELENA

Phillips County Library
623 Pecan St, 72342
Tel: 501-338-3537

1. M-Sa, 9-5
2. N/AN

3. English, N/AN
4. N/AN
5. N/AN
6. Phillips County, AR state
7. Tel: yes, NC; letter: yes, NC
except 20¢/copy
8. No
9. No
10. Yes, in-house use only
through ILL
11. No
12. No
13. N/AN
14. No
15. No

HOPE

Hempstead County Library
Fifth & Elm Sts, 71801
Tel: 501-777-4564

1. M, 12-9; T-F, 9-6
2. Nell Jones, Librarian
3. English, 150 (500 in
Arkansas Collection)
4. None
5. 11
6. No real specifics. Genealogy section added in 1986
7. Tel: no; letter: yes, NC.
Refer to Hempstead County
Genealogical Society
8. No
9. No
10. No, not from genealogy
section; Library lends from
Arkansas Collection
11. No
12. No
13. No
14. No
15. No
Books & Sets: 2(v.78)
Periodicals: 4(partial)

JONESBORO

Craighead County-Jonesboro Public Library, 315 W Oak St, 72401
Tel: 501-935-5133

1. M-W, 9:30-8:30; Th,F, 9:30-6; Sa, 9:30-5
2. Rusty Dancer, Reference Librarian
3. English, 5,000
4. 3,000
5. 500
6. AR state; TN, MS, GA, VA, MO, IL
7. Tel & letter: no
8. No
9. No
10. No
11. No
12. No
13. N/AN
14. Yes
15. N/AN

LITTLE ROCK

Central Arkansas Library System, 700 Louisiana St, 72201
Tel: 501-370-5952

1. T-Sa, 9-4
2. Bill Kastanotis, Head of Reference Services
3. English, 7,500: 3,900 G,

3,600 AR history, cataloged separately
4. None
5. None
6. G, 50 states; history, AR state
7. Tel & letter: yes, NC except for copies. Refer to Arkansas Genealogical Society, which owns half of Library's genealogical collection
8. No
9. No
10. No
11. No
12. No
13. Card catalog
14. Yes. Refer to Arkansas Genealogical Society
15. OCLC: AKD
Books & Sets: 1–4,6–8,10–12,17, 18,22,23
Periodicals:1(partial),4(partial),8 (partial),9(partial)

PINE BLUFF

Pine Bluff and Jefferson County Library System, 200 E 8th, 71601
Tel: 501-534-4802

1. M-Sa, 10-5
2. N/AN
3. English, 8,000
4. 500
5. 1,250

6. VA, TN, SC, NC, AR, AL, TX
7. Tel: no; letter: yes, NC for brief queries
8. Yes
9. No
10. No
11. No
12. No
13. Local index
14. Yes
15. No
Books & Sets: 2–5,7,8,10–15,17, 18,20,22,23,26

WASHINGTON

Southwest Arkansas Regional Archives, Box 134, 71862
Tel: 501-983-2633

1. M,W-Sa, 9-4; Su, 1-5
2. N/AN
3. English, 500
4. 50
5. 2,500
6. 12 counties in southwest AR
7. Tel: yes, NC; letter: yes, NC for brief queries
8. No
9. No
10. No
11. No
12. No
13. *Southwest Arkansas Regional Archives,* free
14. Yes
15. N/AN

ARCADIA

Arcadia Public Library
20 W Duarte Rd, 91006
Tel: 818-446-6589

1. M-Th, 10-9; F,Sa, 10-6
2. Janet Sporleder
3. English, 100; LH clipping files, scrapbooks, photographs
4. N/AN
5. 130: local newspaper
6. Arcadia, local history
7. Tel: no; letter: yes, NC
8. No
9. No
10. Yes, some books, 2-week loan
11. No
12. No
13. In-house index to LH collection
14. No
15. No
Books & Sets: 1,3
Periodicals: 4

ARCATA

Humboldt State University Library (Humboldt County Collection), 95521
Tel: 707-826-3419

1. M,Th, 9-5, 6-9; T,W,F, 9-5; Su, 1-5
2. Erich F. Schimps
3. English, LH, 1,500
4. LH: 100
5. LH: 200
6. Del Norde, Humboldt, Trinity Counties; major emphasis, Humboldt
7. Tel: yes, NC, brief requests only; letter: yes, NC except for copies

8. No
9. No
10. No, through ILL only
11. No
12. No
13. Subject guide to pamphlet/clippings file; subject/name guide to photos; partial index to *Union* (newspaper), 1977-84
14. No
15. OCLC: CHU
Books & Sets: 6

AUBURN

Auburn-Placer County Library
350 Nevada St, 95603
Tel: 916-823-4391

1. M,F, 10-6; T,W,Th, 10-9; Sa, 9-1
2. James R. Hickson, Reference Librarian
3. English, 280
4. 5
5. 12 (including census, DAR cemetery records)
6. US
7. Tel: no, except simple "yes"/"no" response; letter: yes, if brief
8. No
9. No
10. No
11. No
12. No
13. 1984 shelf list; index to local county history (in 2 vols)
14. No. Refer to Placer County Genealogy Society
15. No
Books & Sets: 3,7,10,12,13,19,26
Periodicals: 4

BERKELEY

Berkeley Public Library
2090 Kittredge St, 94704
Tel: 415-644-6648

1. M-Th, 10-8; Sa, 10-6; Su, 1-5
2. Diane Davenport
3. N/AN (all books in English)
4. Oral histories: approx 40 transcripts
5. None
6. Berkeley, CA
7. Tel & letter: yes, NC
8. No
9. No
10. No
11. N/AP
12. No
13. Card catalog
14. No
15. No

BURBANK

Southern California Genealogical Society Library, 122 S Golden Mall (Rear), PO Box 4377, 91503
Tel: 818-843-7247

1. M,W-Sa, 10-4; T, 10-9; 1st, 2d Su, 10-4
2. Jan Jennings, President, SCGS; Brian C. Smith, Chairman, Library Committee
3. English, 5,850
4. 16 file drawers, arranged geographically; 20 file drawers, arranged by family name
5. Approx 30
6. US; some world
7. Tel & letter: yes, NC for brief queries; research at $5–$10/name by SCGS members
8. Yes
9. No, but donations requested

10. No
11. No
12. No
13. Author/title shelf list
14. Yes
15. No
Books & Sets: 3–5,7,9,24–26
Periodicals: 1(1947–, incomplete),
3(1954–, incomplete),4(1948–,
incomplete),5(1962–65,1976–85),
7,8(1912–36, incomplete; 1942–),
9(1847–)

BURLINGAME

Burlingame Public Library
480 Primrose Rd, 94010
Tel: 415-342-1037

1. M-F, 9-9; Sa, 9-6; Su, 1-5
2. Allen Testa, Reference
Librarian, Local History
3. No estimate. Collection
primarily clipped newspaper
articles, other miscellaneous
materials
4. N/AN
5. None
6. Burlingame, San Mateo
County, San Francisco Bay region,
CA state
7. Tel & letter: yes, NC
8. No
9. No
10. Yes, 3-week loan
11. N/AP
12. No
13. Index to local history
14. No
15. N/AN
Periodicals: 4(2 years & current
year)

CARLSBAD

Carlsbad City Library
2600 Elm Ave, 92008
Tel: 619-438-5614

1. M-Th, 9-9; F,Sa, 9-5
2. Ray F. Brookhart
3. English, 12,200 titles,
15,400 volumes
4. Draper, Corbin, Turner,
Holingsworth, Torrey, Cape Cod

5. 570
6. US, Canada
7. Tel & letter: yes, NC except
for copies
8. Yes
9. No
10. No
11. No
12. No
13. None
14. No
15. OCLC: 80% CCP
Books & Sets: 3–5,6,9–14,18,
22–24,26
Periodicals: 1,3(1969–82),
4(1960–),5,7,8(1912–),9(1947–)

CARMEL

Harrison Memorial Library
PO Box 800, 93921
Tel: 408-624-4629

1. M-Th, 9-9; F,Sa, 9-6;
Su, 1-5
2. Tamara Hennessy
3. English, 1,500+
4. LH: 500, plus clipping file
5. LH: 70
6. LH: Carmel, Carmel Valley,
Big Sur; G: geographically
dispersed
7. Tel: yes, NC for brief
queries; letter: yes, NC
8. No
9. No
10. Yes, 5-day loan for reference books, 2-week or 4-week loan
for others
11. No
12. No
13. Index to local history file
14. No
15. No
Books & Sets: 3
Periodicals: 4

CARMICHAEL

**Capitol Area Joint Genealogical
Library,** Genealogy Room,
Carmichael Regional Library,
5605 Marconi Ave, 95608
Tel: 916-483-6055

1. M, 12-9; T, 10-9; W, 10-6;
Th, 12-9; F, 1-5; Sa, 1-5
2. Mary Pitts, Librarian, Root
Cellar; Lorraine Lineer, Librarian,
Genealogical Association
3. English, 3,000; German, 1
4. N/AN
5. 8 film, some fiche
6. US, Canada, some Europe;
Special Collection of the Sacramento City/County Library on
California
7. Tel: no; letter: yes, NC. Paid
researchers available, with SASE
8. Root Cellar and Genealogical Association of Sacramento
members (see explanation below)
9. No
10. No
11. No
12. *Capitol Area Joint Genealogical Library Shelf List 1985* and
1986 Supplement, $4
13. Surname roster, Bible
records, index to unpublished MSS
14. Yes
15. No
Books & Sets: 2(partial),3,5,11,
22,26(partial)
Periodicals: 4,5(partial),7,8(v.1–
72),9(partial)
The Library is sponsored by three
groups: Root Cellar, Sacramento
Genealogical Society; Genealogical Association of Sacramento; and
the Sacramento City/County
Library System. The Carmichael
Regional Library, where the
collections are located, is a part of
the Sacramento City/County
System. Each sponsor retains
ownership of its collections.

CHICO

**California State University,
Meriam Library,** 1st & Hazel Sts,
95929
Tel: 916-895-5862

1. M-F, 8-5 during semester;
changes during breaks
2. William A. Jones
3. Not known

4. 150 (Northeastern CA)
5. 1,000
6. Northeastern CA
7. Tel & letter: yes, $10/hr
8. No
9. No
10. No
11. Limited lending policy
12. Some guides
13. Too many to list
14. No, but will research for a fee
15. OCLC: yes
Book & Sets: 6,11

COLUSA

Colusa County Free Library
738 Market St, 95932
Tel: 916-458-7671

1. M,F, 10-5; T-Th, 10-9
2. Reference Desk
3. English, 177
4. None
5. 284 rolls: local newspapers, census; 2 sets microfiche: Sutro Library listings
6. CA state; various other states
7. Tel: yes, NC; letter: yes, $5/ name for births, deaths, marriages
8. No
9. No
10. No
11. No
12. No
13. George Zumwalt Collection of over 10,000 names
14. No
15. RLIN: CNSG (only items owned by Library)
Periodicals: 4(incomplete)

CORONA

Corona Public Library
650 S Main St, 91720
Tel: 714-736-2386

1. M,T,Th, F, 10-9; W, 10-5; Sa, 1-5; Su (except June-Sept), 1-5
2. Gloria Scott
3. English, 100
4. N/AN

5. 402: newspapers
6. Southern CA
7. Tel: no; letter: yes, NC with research limited to 30 minutes of staff time, plus 10¢/copy
8. No
9. No
10. No
11. No
12. No
13. On-line catalog
14. No
15. OCLC: JQL
Periodicals: 4

DOWNEY

Downey City Library
11121 Brookshire Ave, 90241
Tel: 213-923-3256

1. M-Th, 10-9; F,Sa, 10-5
2. Joyce Melbinger
3. English, 50
4. None
5. 30
6. Downey, CA
7. Tel & letter: yes, NC
8. No
9. No
10. Yes
11. No
12. No
13. None
14. No
15. No
Periodicals: 4(1950–)

EL SEGUNDO

El Segundo Public Library
111 W Mariposa Ave, 90245
Tel: 213-322-4121

1. M-Th, 9-9; F, 9-6; Sa, 9-5
2. Barbara L. Kirby
3. N/AN
4. 50
5. 58 plus microfiche
6. El Segundo, US, some Europe
7. Tel: no; letter: yes, NC
8. No
9. No
10. Yes

11. No
12. No
13. N/AN
14. No
15. No
Periodicals: 4(1967–69, 1971–),8(1982–),9(1968–78, 1982–)

EUREKA

Eureka-Humboldt County Library, 636 F St, 95501
Tel: 707-445-7284

1. M,Th-Sa, 10-5; T,W, 10-9
2. Maggie Nystrom
3. English, 3,000
4. None
5. 1,100
6. CA counties of Humboldt, Del Norte
7. Tel: yes, NC; letter: yes, NC except 10¢/copy
8. No
9. No
10. Yes, duplicates only
11. No
12. No
13. Several indexes
14. No
15. No
Books & Sets: 2(incomplete), 3(incomplete),6,10–13,26
Periodicals: 1(1922–77),4(1966–), 8(1928–78)

FORTUNA

Redwood Genealogical Society
PO Box 645, #5 Park, 95540
Tel: N/AN

1. W, 9-11
2. Ruth Teasley, Librarian
3. English, 5,000
4. N/AN
5. 10
6. "Everywhere"
7. Letter: yes, NC
8. No
9. No
10. Yes, to members only
11. Yes, to members only
12. No

13. In process of indexing Humboldt County books
14. No
15. No
Books & Sets: 2(several copies)
Periodicals: 4,8

FRESNO

Fresno County Free Library
2420 Mariposa, 93721
Tel: 209-488-3195

1. M,T, 9-9; W,F, 9-6; Th, 12-9; Sa, 1-5
2. Local History Librarian
3. English, 14,000
4. None
5. 1,500
6. Fresno County, CA state
7. Tel: yes, NC; letter: yes, NC except 10¢–25¢/copy
8. No
9. No
10. Yes
11. No
12. No
13. Selective indexes of local newspapers
14. Yes
15. OCLC: JQR (partial)
    RLIN: CFCG (partial)
Books & Sets: 2(v.44–128),3,6, 10–14,19,26
Periodicals: 4

GLENDALE

Sons of the Revolution Library
600 S Central Ave, 91204
Tel: 818-240-1775

1. M, 12-8; Th-Sa, 10-4
2. John R. Justice
3. English, 40,000; German, 20
4. N/AN
5. None
6. US
7. Tel: no; letter: yes, charges depending upon work required
8. John R. Justice
9. No
10. No
11. No

---

12. No
13. N/AN
14. Yes
15. N/AN
Books & Sets: 2,5,7,17,26
Periodicals: 1,4,7–9

HANFORD

Kings County Library
401 N Douty, 93230
Tel: 209-582-0261

1. M,T, 10-9; W,Th, 12-8; F,Sa, 12-5
2. Joyce H. Hall, Head, Reference Dept
3. English, 500
4. None
5. 18
6. LH: Kings, Tulare Counties, CA
7. Tel & letter: no
8. No
9. No
10. Not those on genealogy
11. No
12. No
13. N/AN
14. No
15. N/AN
Books & Sets: 1,3(no suppls),9,10
Periodicals: 4(1972–)

HAYWARD

Chabot College, South County Community College District
25555 Hesperian Blvd, 94545
Tel: 415-786-6764

1. M-Th, 7:45am-10pm; F, 7:45-5; Sa, 9:30-2
2. N/AN
3. English, 12–14 on Hayward and Alameda County
4. N/AN
5. N/AN
6. Alameda and Contra Costa Counties, San Francisco
7. Tel & letter: no
8. No
9. No
10. Yes, to enrolled students only

---

11. No
12. No
13. N/AN
14. No
15. OCLC: CAB

Hayward Area Historical Society, 22701 Main, 94541
Tel: 415-581-0223

1. M-F, 11-4; Sa, 12-4
2. Bernard Golumb
3. English, 15-20; German, 1; Danish, 2
4. 20
5. 4
6. Hayward, Castro Valley, San Lorenzo
7. Tel: N/AN; letter: yes, $10/hr
8. No; two volunteers
9. Donations accepted
10. No
11. No
12. No
13. N/AN
14. Yes
15. No

LA MESA

Irish Family Names Society
PO Box 2095, 92041
Tel: 619-466-8739

1. Not open to the public
2. William P. Durning, Director
3. English, 290; other, 10 (Gaelic, Spanish, French)
4. 50
5. None
6. Ireland. Society's objective is discovery of Irish family relationships prior to translation of Gaelic surnames into English
7. Tel & letter: yes, NC for brief queries with SASE. No personal research done
8. W. P. Durning
9. Not open to the public
10. No
11. No
12. No
13. *A Guide to Irish Roots*;

three *Newsletters* per year.
Discoveries published in book
form when complete
14. No
15. No

LA VERNE

**University of La Verne, Wilson
Library,** 2040 Third St, 91750
Tel: 714-593-3511, ext 4300

1. Academic year: M-F, 8-5;
summer: M-F, 8:30-4:30, except as
posted
2. N/AN
3. English, 100+
4. N/AN
5. N/AN
6. PA Germans, Church of the
Brethren
7. Tel: no; letter: yes, 15¢/
copy
8. No
9. No
10. No (not genealogy books)
11. No
12. No
13. N/AN
14. No
15. OCLC: CLV
Books & Sets: 6,10–13

LIVERMORE

**Livermore-Amador Genealogical
Society Library,** Livermore
History Center, East Room, Old
Carnegie Library, 3rd & K Sts,
PO Box 901, 94550
Tel: N/AN

1. W-Su, 11:30-4
2. N/AN
3. English, 350
4. N/AN
5. N/AN
6. Mainly US
7. Tel: no; letter: no, but will
put in our *Quarterly* at $1/request
8. Yes; in the club, not on staff
9. No
10. Yes, to members only
11. No
12. Yes, to members only

13. N/AN
14. No
15. No
Periodicals: 4(most),5(1977–85),
6(some),7, 8(1975–),9(some)

LOMPOC

Lompoc Public Library
501 E North Ave, 93436
Tel: 805-736-3477

1. M-Th, 10-9; F,Sa, 10-5;
Su, 1-5
2. N/AN
3. English, 100
4. 3
5. 6
6. Lompoc Valley
7. Tel & letter: yes, NC
8. No
9. No
10. Yes, 3-week loan
11. Yes, 3-week loan
12. No
13. N/AN
14. No
15. No
Books & Sets: 3,10,19
Periodicals: 4(1982–)

LONG BEACH

**Long Beach Public Library and
Information Center,** 101 Pacific
Avenue, 90815
Tel: 213-437-2949

1. M, 10-8; T-Sa, 10-5:30;
Su, 1-5
2. LH: Doug Kermode; G:
volunteers from local genealogy
society
3. English, LH, 2,000, G, 850
4. None
5. 301: newspapers
6. Long Beach, CA state; US
7. Tel: yes, NC for brief
queries; letter: yes, $3 for obituar-
ies or LH when person has exact
dates
8. Robert E. Brasher, Volunteer

9. No
10. Yes, 3-week loan
11. No
12. No
13. Typed in-house guide
14. No
15. OCLC: CLB
Books & Sets: 1,3–5,7,17,26
Periodicals: 3,4,6,8,9

LOS ANGELES

**Los Angeles Public Library,
History and Genealogy Dept**
630 W Fifth St, 90071
Tel: N/AN

1. Closed on account of fire
until summer 1988
2. Michael Kirley
3. English, 39,887; German,
510; French, 560; Spanish, 260;
Danish, 100; Dutch, 100; Swedish,
50; Italian, 25; Polish, 20; Portuguese, 20
4. 21,500
5. 5,254 microfilm; 16,617
microfiche; 1,387 microcards
6. US, Canada, Europe,
Hispanic America
7. Tel: yes, NC; letter: yes, NC
except for copies
8. Darell Brown
Michael Kirley
Arthur Reynolds
9. No
10. No
11. No
12. Ellen C. Barrett, *A Catalogue of Printed and Manuscript
Genealogies Available in the
Genealogy and Local History
Division of the Los Angeles Public
Library,* 1965 (out of print)
13. Darell Brown, *A Bibliography of Printed and Published
Census Records, Land Grants
and Voter Lists;* Irwin L. Stein,
*Preliminary Finding List of Coats
of Arms to Accompany Surnames
Listed in Smith's Dictionary of
American Family Names;* L. W.
Van Kersen, *Index to Coats of
Arms in Historisch-Biographisch-
ers Lexikon der Schweiz.* Also a

family history index on cards (66 catalog drawers), a local history index (24 drawers), and a coat-of-arms index (18 drawers); in the California Room, a CA subject index (120 drawers) and a CA biography index (168 drawers)
14. Yes
15. OCLC: LPUG
    RLIN: CLAG
Books & Sets: 1–26
Periodicals: 1–3,4(v.4–, 1950–), 5–9

University of California at Los Angeles, University Research Library, 405 Hilgard Ave, 90024-1575
Tel: 213-825-1201

1. M-Th, 8am-11pm; F, 8-6; Sa, 9-5; Su, 1-10. Variations on holidays, summer, and between quarter sessions
2. No separate G/LH section
3. English, N/AP; German, N/AP; other, N/AP
4. N/AP
5. N/AP
6. N/AN
7. Tel & letter: no, except for holdings information
8. No
9. No
10. Yes; borrower must purchase a Library card, or through ILL
11. No
12. No
13. N/AN
14. No
15. OCLC: CLU
Books & Sets: 1,5,6,9,13,18,22,26
Periodicals: 9
"The library does not collect genealogy as such, but many items acquired to support the University's research and teaching programs in history and other fields would, of course, be of value to genealogists."

MERCED

Merced County Library
2100 O St, 95340
Tel: 209-385-7597

1. M-Th, 9-9; F,Sa, 9-6
2. Catherine McCullough
3. English, 2,400 (G: 300)
4. None
5. 60, exclusive of newspapers
6. Merced County, CA state; US
7. Tel: no; letter: yes, NC except 10¢/copy
8. No
9. No
10. Yes, G books, through ILL; LH books do not circulate
11. No
12. No
13. Index to the *Merced Sun/ Star*, 1977–
14. No
15. OCLC: MCF
Books & Sets: 3,4
Periodicals: 4(1977–)

MILL VALLEY

Mill Valley Public Library
375 Throckmorton Ave, 94941
Tel: 415-388-2190

1. History Room: M-Th, 10-12, 2-4, 7-9; F, 10-12, 2-4; Sa, 2-4
2. Joyce Crews
3. N/AN
4. 100 oral histories on tape, and transcribed
5. *Mill Valley Record* (weekly newspaper), 1907–
6. Mill Valley, Marin County
7. Tel & letter: yes, NC for brief queries
8. Mary Minton
9. No
10. No
11. No
12. No
13. Card catalog
14. No
15. OCLC: MLV (partially)
    CNBG: MVY (partially)
Periodicals: 4(1975–)

MODESTO

Stanislaus County Free Library
1500 I St, 95350
Tel: 209-571-6821

1. M-W, 1-9; Th,Sa, 10-5
2. None
3. English, 500
4. None
5. 50
6. Stanislaus County, CA state
7. Tel & letter: no
8. No
9. No
10. No
11. No
12. No
13. None
14. Yes
15. No
Books & Sets: 3–6,10–14,17,22,23
Periodicals: 4,7–9

MONROVIA

Monrovia Public Library
321 S Myrtle Ave, 91016
Tel: 818-358-0174

1. Winter: M-W, 10-9; Th-Sa, 10-5; summer: M, 10-9; T,W, 10-6; Th-Sa, 10-5
2. None
3. English, 50
4. N/AP
5. Reels of local newspapers, late 1800s–
6. City of Monrovia
7. Tel & letter: yes, NC
8. No
9. No
10. No, not from LH
11. No
12. No
13. N/AV
14. No
15. No

MONTEREY

Monterey History and Art Association, O'Donnell Library
Box 805, 93940
Tel: 408-372-2608

1. W,F,Sa,Su, 1-4
2. Martha Bentley (volunteer)
3. English, 1,500
4. Clippings and miscellaneous
5. None
6. Monterey (City), Monterey Peninsula
7. Tel & letter: yes, NC
8. No; limited photocopy at cost
9. No
10. No
11. No
12. No
13. Card file
14. No
15. No

MONTEREY PARK

Bruggemeyer Memorial Library
City of Monterey Park,
318 S Ramona Ave, 91754
Tel: 818-307-1333

1. M-W, 12-9; Th,F, 10-6; Sa, 10-5
2. Brian C. Smith, Assistant City Librarian
3. English, less than 100
4. 3
5. Local newspaper (*Monterey Park Progress*) on microfilm, 1918–
6. Monterey Park, San Gabriel Valley, all CA to some extent
7. Tel & letter: yes, NC except 10¢/copy plus postage
8. Brian C. Smith
9. No
10. Yes, except reference vols. Postage, insurance both ways; 3-week loan. No charge to other metropolitan cooperative library system members
11. No
12. No
13. Index to *Monterey Park Progress* under way
14. Yes
15. OCLC: MEY
Books & Sets: 3(no suppls), 19(1950,1972 only)

NAPA

Napa City-County Library
1150 Division St, 94559-3396
Tel: 707-253-4235

1. M,T,F, 10-5:30; W,Th, 10-9; Sa, 10-5
2. N/AN
3. English, 1,400
4. None
5. 480
6. Napa County, CA
7. Tel: yes, NC; letter: yes, NC except 10¢/copy with SASE
8. No
9 No
10. No
11. No
12. *Napa City-Co. Library Local History Indexer's Manual*, $8
13. Ongoing indexing project for Napa County newspapers, at present indexed for name and subject 1850–1900 and 1973–
14. Yes
15. OCLC: yes
    RLIN: yes
Books & Sets: 1,3,6,10–12,18,19
Periodicals: 4

Napa Valley Genealogical and Biographical Society
2977 Solano Ave, Suite G, 94558
Tel: 707-226-9889

1. T,W, 10-4; Th, 10-9 (except 3d Th, 10-4); 2d, 4th Sa, 10-2
2. Virginia Brumage Wakeman, Librarian
3. English, 3,000
4. 150
5. 50
6. Napa County, US; England, Canada
7. Tel: no; letter: yes, charge varies
8. Yes
9. Yes, $3/day for nonmembers
10. No
11. No
12. No

13. *Marriages and Deaths of Napa County, CA*
14. No
15. No
Books & Sets: 2,3,24–26
Periodicals: 1,4,6,8,9 (all broken sets)

NEVADA CITY

Nevada County Library, Nevada City Branch, 211 N Pine St, 95959
Tel: 916-265-1407

1. M,T,W,F, 11-6; Th, 11-8
2. Dorothy Boettner
3. English, all
4. None
5. 530 (gold-mining era newspapers)
6. Nevada County, CA
7. Tel & letter: no
8. No
9. No
10. No
11. Yes, microfilm of old newspapers through ILL
12. No
13. Selected reading list
14. No
15. N/AN

Searls Historical Library
214 Church St, 95959
Tel: 916-265-5910

1. M-Sa, 1-4
2. Edwin L. Tyson
3. English, LH, 2,000
4. LH: 1,600; more than 200,000 documents, pamphlets, reports, and vertical file material
5. N/AN
6. Nevada County, CA state, from 1849 Gold Rush through WWII
7. Tel & letter: yes, NC
8. N/AN
9. No, but donations welcome
10. No
11. No
12. No
13. N/AN
14. Yes
15. No

NORTH HIGHLANDS

Krans-Buckland Family Association Library
PO Box 1025, 95660-1025
Tel: 916-332-4359

1. By appointment only
2. Joyce Buckland
3. English, 1,500; German, 15; French, 12; Swedish, 10; Danish, 6
4. 1: northern Sacramento County pioneers
5. 400
6. In order of number of books: England, Canada, CA, Germany, Sweden. Specialties are British Isles and Sacramento County
7. Tel: yes, NC; letter: yes, NC, but donations appreciated
8. Joyce Buckland
9. Donations requested
10. No
11. No
12. No, but one is due out in 1988
13. Subject list of books on the British Isles; unpublished list of CA holdings
14. Yes
15. No
Books & Sets: 3,8,24,25
Periodicals: 2(1981–),4(1974–),6 (1982–)

OAKLAND

East Bay Genealogical Society Library (together with Society of Mayflower Descendants)
405 14th St, 94619
Tel: 415-451-9599

1. M, 8-4
2. Lois J. Kline
3. English, 40
4. None
5. None
6. General US
7. Tel: yes, NC; letter: yes, NC except for copies
8. No
9. Yes, donation to Mayflower library

10. No
11. No
12. No
13. List of holdings with monthly updates in EBGS *Newsletter*
14. No
15. N/AN
Books & Sets: 25
Periodicals: 4(1971–)

Oakland Public Library
125 14th St, 94612
Tel: 415-273-3281

1. M-Th, 10-8:30; F,Sa, 10-5:30
2. R. T. Ragsdale
3. English, 800
4. None
5. None
6. "All"
7. Tel & letter: yes, NC
8. No
9. No
10. No
11. No
12. No
13. N/AN
14. No
15. No
Books & Sets: 1–3,7,10–14,26
Periodicals: 4(1984–),9(1944–)

Society of Mayflower Descendants in the State of California
405 14th St, Terrace Level, 94612
Tel: 415-451-9599

1. M, 8-4
2. Oliver S. Hayward, Librarian
3. English, 3,000
4. Folger Collection of 50,000 families of Pilgrims' descendants
5. 12
6. CA; Northeast
7. Tel & letter: yes, donations accepted
8. Edith Thomas
9. Yes, donations accepted
10. No
11. No
12. No
13. Index to Folger Collection
14. No

15. N/AN
Books & Sets: 10,24–26
Periodicals: 1(v.51–),4,7–9

OCEANSIDE

Oceanside Public Library
615 Fourth St, 92054
Tel: 619-439-7330

1. M-Th, 9-8:45; F,Sa, 9-5:45
2. Deborah Polich, Head of Adult Services
3. English, 1,000
4. None
5. Microfiche of local *Blade Tribune* newspaper, 1975–84; subject card file of *Blade Tribune*, 1975–
6. Oceanside, San Diego County, CA state
7. Tel: yes, NC for local history questions; no queries regarding genealogical research; letter: yes, $5
8 No
9. No
10. No
11. No
12. No
13. Subject index to local *Blade Tribune* newspaper, 1975–
14. No
15. RLIN: CCPG
Books & Sets: 3

ONTARIO

Ontario City Library, Model Colony History Room
215 East C St, 91764
Tel: 714-988-8481

1. T-Sa, 1-5
2. Judith L. Evans
3. English, LH, 2,500
4. LH: 30
5. 5 census tapes for Ontario Township, 1860–1910; microfilm of local newspapers, 1883–
6. Ontario, CA state, and west end of San Bernadino County
7. Tel & letter: yes, NC except for copies
8. No

9. No
10. No
11. No
12. No
13. Card catalog
14. No
15. OCLC: ONT (partial)
Books & Sets: 1

OROVILLE

Butte County Library
1820 Mitchell Ave, 95966
Tel: 916-538-7642

1. T, 10-5; W, 2-9; Th, 2-5;
F, 10-5; Sa, 10-4
2. Nancy Brower
3. English, 400
4. N/AN
5. 600 (mostly newspapers)
6. Northern Sacramento Valley
7. Tel: no; letter: yes, NC
8. No
9. No
10. Yes; most items 2-week
loan for in-library use only
11. Yes, newspaper film only;
3-week loan for in-library use only
12. No
13. N/AN
14. No
15. OCLC: JQI
    RLIN: CNSG
Books & Sets: 2(v.1–60), 3(3 v.,
1982,1983 suppls only),4,10–13,26
Periodicals: 4(1977–)

PALM SPRINGS

Palm Springs Public Library
300 S Sunrise Way, 92262
Tel: 619-323-8294

1. M-Th, 9-8; F, 10-5:30; Sa,
9-5:30; summer: M-W,Sa, 9-5:30;
Th, 9-8; F, 10-5:30
2. Suzanne Sutton, Reference
Coordinator
3. English, 800
4. None
5. 50
6. New England, Middle
States, South and Southwest,
Midwest, Colonial America,

British Isles, Germany. Various
ethnic groups
7. Tel & letter: yes, NC
8. No. Refer to Palm Springs
Genealogy Society
9. No
10. Yes, duplicates only
11. No
12. No
13. Card catalog; lists of
monthly acquisitions
14. No
15. OCLC: yes
Books & Sets: 3,5,22,26
Periodicals: 4,6–9

PALOS VERDES

Palos Verdes Library District
650 Deep Valley Drive,
Rolling Hills Estates, 90274
Tel: 213-377-9584, ext 51

1. M,W, 1-4:30, and by
appointment
2. Lenore M. Blume
3. English, 74
4. 2
5. 1
6. Palos Verdes Peninsula of
Los Angeles County
7. Tel & letter: yes, NC
8. No
9. No
10. No
11. No
12. No
13. N/AN
14. No
15. OCLC: some
Books & Sets: 1,3,11
Periodicals: 4

PASADENA

**Pasadena Historical Society
Research Library**
470 W Walnut St, 91103
Tel: 818-795-3002

1. T,Th, 1-4 (closed Aug); first
and last Su of each month, 1-4
2. Dorothy B. Welles
3. English, 1,600
4. 40

5. None
6. Pasadena and environs
7. Tel & letter: yes, suggested
donation of $10/hr
8. No
9. No
10. No
11. No
12. No
13. Collections: Pasadena Black
History, Tournament of Roses,
Scrapbook, Manuscript, Photo-
graphic Albums, Periodicals, Map,
Printed Ephemera
14. No
15. No

PLACERVILLE

El Dorado County Library
345 Fair Lane, 95667
Tel: 916-626-2561

1. T-Th, 10-8; F,Sa, 10-5
2. Constance M. Rael
3. English, 170; French, 1
4. None
5. 204
6. US, Europe
7. Tel & letter: no
8. No
9. No
10. Yes, in-library use only and
through ILL
11. Yes, through ILL
12. No
13. Card catalog
14. Yes
15. No
Books & Sets: 3
Periodicals: 1(v.52),8(v.68–
73),9(v.109–37)

PORTERVILLE

Porterville Public Library
41 W Thurman Ave, 93257
Tel: 209-784-0177

1. Genealogy: M-Sa, 9-5;
Local History: M-Th,10-12
2. Melanie Wells
3. English, 2,000
4. N/AN
5. G: 20; LH: local newspaper

on microfilm, 1911–
   6. G: US, Europe; LH: Tulare County, CA state
   7. Tel & letter: yes, NC
   8. N/AN
   9. No
   10. No
   11. No
   12. No
   13. N/AN
   14. No
   15. No
Books & Sets: 10–12,26
Periodicals: 4

REDWOOD CITY

Redwood City Public Library
881 Jefferson Ave, 94063
Tel: 415-369-3738

   1. M-Th, 10-9; F,Sa, 10-5; Su, 1-4
   2. Sarah Sheehan
      Jean Thieverage
   3. English, 60
   4. Schellens Collection: 100 vols of newspaper articles covering Redwood City, San Mateo County
   5. Schellens Collection also available in microfiche
   6. Redwood City, San Mateo County
   7. Tel: no; letter: yes, NC
   8. No
   9. No
   10. Some; most books in reference collection
   11. No
   12. No
   13. Index to Schellens Collection; also, subject index to LH holdings
   14. No
   15. No

RICHMOND

Richmond Public Library
325 Civic Center Plaza, 94804
Tel: 415-620-6561

   1. M-Th, 9-9; F,Sa, 9-6; Su, 1-5
   2. Emma Clark, Head, Reference Dept

   3. English, 100
   4. LH: 15; G: 1
   5. Local newspapers only; will obtain census films by ILL
   6. Contra Costa County, Richmond, CA state; general background books in European, Hispanic, and black American research
   7. Tel: yes, NC; letter: yes, NC except for duplicating orders over 5 pages, 15¢/copy
   8. Peggy Jo Zemens
   9. No
   10. Yes, 28-day loan
   11. No
   12. No
   13. Occasional genealogical bibliography handouts; index to National Genealogical Society *Journals*
   14. No
   15. RLIN: CRPG
Books & Sets: 1,26
Periodicals: 4(1985–),8(incomplete 1912–70)

ROSEVILLE

Roseville Public Library
225 Taylor St, 95678
Tel: 916-781-0231

   1. M-Th, 9-9; F, 9-6; Sa, 9-5; Su, 1-5
   2. None
   3. N/AN
   4. N/AN
   5. Local newspaper, Roseville *Press Tribune*
   6. Roseville, CA
   7. Tel: yes, NC. Regarding obituaries: will send copies if patrons can provide exact day and year, with SASE; letter: yes, NC
   8. No
   9. No
   10. No
   11. No
   12. No
   13. N/AN
   14. No
   15. N/AN
Books & Sets: 3,7(missing v.4),10
Periodicals: 4

SACRAMENTO

California State Library, California Section
914 Capitol Mall,
PO Box 942837, 94237-0001
Tel: 916-445-4149

   1. M-F, 8-5
   2. Richard Terry
   3. English, 75,000; German, less than 100
   4. "Premier in the state"
   5. 100,000
   6. All CA, some NV (mining and Gold Rush)
   7. Tel & letter: yes, NC
   8. Reference librarians
   9. No
   10. Yes, to state employees; not to general public except through ILL
   11. Yes, 12 reels of microfilm per request, 5-week loan, shipped third class. Policy same as #10, either ALA form and EMS
   12. Small pamphlets; collection too comprehensive for major guide
   13. Too numerous to list
   14. Yes
   15. RLIN: CCSG
Books & Sets: 1,2,6,10,12–14

California State Railroad Museum Library
111 I St, 95814
Tel: 916-323-8073

   1. T-Sa, 1-5
   2. Ellen Schwartz, Librarian; Blaine P. Lamb, Archivist
   3. Imprints of National Railway Publications Company
   4. Early records of Central Pacific, Southern Pacific, Western Pacific railroads; Lima Locomotive Works construction drawings; papers of Pacific Coast chapter of Railway and Locomotive Historical Society; Hardy, Kneiss, Merritt, and Stein railroad collections. Also, portrait file; Pullman Company glass negatives
   5. N/AN

6. Western US, with emphasis on CA, NV
7. Tel & letter: yes, NC
8. No
9. No
10. No
11. No
12. No
13. *California State Railroad Museum Library*, flyer
14. No
15. No

SALINAS

Monterey County Library
26 Central Ave, 93901
Tel: 408-424-3244

1. M-F, 8-5; by appointment only
2. Ruth Forsberg
3. English, 30
4. N/AN
5. 6
6. Monterey County, CA state
7. Tel & letter: yes, NC
8. No
9. No
10. No
11. No
12. No
13. None
14. No
15. No

SAN ANDREAS

Calaveras County Museum and Archives Library, PO Box 1281, 30 N Main St, 95249
Tel: 209-754-4203

1. Archives: W, 1-5; Th,F, 8:30-5
2. Lorrayne Kennedy, Archivist
3. English, 150
4. 50
5. None
6. Calaveras County, CA
7. Tel & letter: yes, $6/hr
8. Judith Cunningham, Museum Director; Lorrayne Kennedy, Archivist

9. No
10. No
11. No
12. No
13. N/AN
14. No
15. No

SAN BERNARDINO

San Bernardino County Library
104 W 4th St, 92415
Tel: 714-387-5719

1. M-F, 8-5
2. Marjorie Merritt
3. English, 1,200+
4. 100+
5. None
6. Southern CA, CA state; US
7. Tel & letter: yes, NC
8. No
9. No
10. Yes, to other libraries
11. No
12. No
13. In-house bibliography
14. Yes
15. OCLC: CBL
Books & Sets: 1,3,7,19,24
Periodicals: 4(1981–)

SAN DIEGO

San Diego Historical Society
Research Archives, 1649 El Prado, Balboa Park, 92101
Tel: 619-232-6203

1. W-Sa, 10-4
2. Richard W. Crawford, Archivist/Historian
3. English, 250 linear ft
4. 20
5. N/AN
6. San Diego County
7. Tel: no; lettter: yes, NC
8. No
9. Yes: $1/day for nonmembers
10. No
11. No
12. *Guide to the Public Records Collection*

13. Computer indexes to various collections: wills, court records, tax lists
14. Yes
15. No

San Diego Public Library
820 E St, 92101-6478
Tel: 619-236-5834

1. M-Th, 10-9; F,Sa, 9:30-5:30
2. Mary Allely
3. English, 3,670 (half of collection on permanent loan from DAR)
4. None
5. 125
6. 13 original colonies, eastern states (1,000 vols)
7. Tel: no; letter: yes, minimal charge and 20¢/copy
8. No
9. No
10. No
11. No
12. No
13. None
14. No. Refer to Mormon Genealogical Library, 3705 10th Ave, San Diego, 92103
15. OCLC: yes
Books & Sets: 1–7,10,13,14, 16–19,24,26
Periodicals: 1(v.9–12, 1932–36, v.31, 1955–),4(v.4–37 microfiche, v.34– microfilm),5,6(1979–, broken earlier issues),7,8(v.43, 1955–),9(1874–)

SAN FRANCISCO

California Genealogical Society Library, 300 Brannan St, 94142
Tel: 415-777-9936

1. T,W,Th, 9-4; Sa, 10-3
2. Bette Gorrell Kot, Librarian
3. English, 30,000; German, several
4. 15
5. 2,500
6. Mostly US, British Isles
7. Tel: yes, NC (limited); letter: yes, $20 minimum, up to 2 hrs

8. Mary C. Sweetman
Bette G. Kot
9. Yes: $5/day, nonmembers
10. No
11. No
12. No
13. N/AN
14. Yes
15. No
Books & Sets:2,3,7,8,10,11,13,
14,18,26
Periodicals: 1(v.1,v.9–),4,5,7–9

**California State Library, Sutro
Library,** 480 Winston Dr, 94132
Tel: 415-731-4477

1. M, 10-9; T-Sa, 10-5; closed
state holidays
2. Clyde Janes, Supervising
Librarian
3. English, 60,000
4. Few
5. 25,000
6. Mostly US, with exception
of CA (kept at State Library main
branch in Sacramento); some
England, Canada, Mexico
7. Tel & letter: yes, NC
8. Frank J. Glover
9. No
10. Yes, primarily to CA
libraries, occasionally to out-of-
state libraries, according to ALA
guidelines
11. Yes, primarily to CA
libraries; books on microfilm to
out-of-state libraries occasionally
12. *The Sutro Library Family
History and Local History Subject
Catalogs*; *Local History and
Genealogy Resources of the
California State Library and Its
Sutro Branch*
13. *New Arrivals in American
Local History and Genealogy*, a
quarterly available if requested on
letterhead of library or genealogical society
14. No
15. RLIN (much of Sutro
catalog is included in State Library
catalog, which is going on RLIN)

Books & Sets: 2–5,7,8,10,11(no
1977),13,17–19,22–24,26
Periodicals: 1,3(incomplete), 4,5,
6(v.12–15 only),7–9

SAN JOSE

**San Jose Public Library,
California Room**
180 W San Carlos St, 95113
Tel: 408-277-4867

1. M, 6-9; T-Sa, 2-5
2. Julie Pifer
3. English, 18,000; Spanish,
over 100
4. None
5. 60
6. City of San Jose, Santa
Clara County, San Francisco Bay
area, CA state (major areas and
events)
7. Tel: yes, NC; letter: yes, NC
except for copies, $3 minimum up
to 3 pages, 40¢/page thereafter
8. No
9. No
10. No
11. No
12. No
13. N/AN
14. No
15. OCLC: SJPC (presently
being encoded)
Periodicals: 4 (1961–)

SAN LEANDRO

**San Leandro Community
Library, Californiana Room**
300 Estudillo Ave, 94577
Tel: 714-577-3491

1. M-Th, 10-9; F, 10-5:30;
Sa, 10-5
2. Pat O'Meara
3. English, 5,700. LH:
Californiana Collection
4. None
5. 14
6. San Leandro area, CA state
7. Tel: yes, NC for brief
queries; letter: yes, NC
8. Janet Prince
9. No

10. Yes, except for Californiana
Collection
11. No
12. No
13. Genealogy book lists; card
catalog to Californiana Collection
14. No. Refer to Hayward Area
Genealogical Society, East Bay
Genealogical Society, Oakland
Genealogy Library
15. No
Books & Sets: 6
Periodicals: 4(1978–),5(v.14–17)

SAN MATEO

**San Mateo County Historical
Association,** College of San Mateo
Campus, 1700 W Hillsdale Blvd,
94402
Tel: 415-574-6441

1. M-Th, 9:30-4:30; Su, 12:30-
4:30
2. Marion C. Holmes,
Archivist
3. English, LH, 1,018
4. LH: 337 MSS; G: no
estimate
5. LH: 101
6. San Mateo County
7. Tel & letter: yes, NC
8. No
9. No
10. No
11. No
12. No
13. *La Peninsula*, guide to
Library's publications; indexes of
1860, 1870 censuses of San Mateo
County
14. No
15. No

SAN RAFAEL

**Marin County Library,
Anne Kent California Room**
Civic Center, 94903
Tel: 415-499-7419

1. M,W,Th,F, 10-6; T, 10-8:30
2. Jocelyn A. Moss
3. English, 3,500
4. 100

5. 100
6. CA, with emphasis on San Francisco Bay area
7. Tel & letter: yes, NC
8. No
9. No
10. No
11. No
12. No
13. Bibliography of Marin County books, 1977
14. Yes
15. OCLC: yes
    RLIN: yes

San Rafael Public Library
1100 E St, 94904
Tel: 415-485-3121

1. M-Th, 10-9; F,Sa, 10-5
2. N/AN
3. English, LH, 142. Clippings from *Marin Journal*, *Independent Journal*, started in 1960
4. N/AN
5. *Marin Journal*, 1861–1949
6. Marin County
7. Tel & letter: yes, NC
8. No
9. No
10. No
11. No
12. No
13. Bibliography of Marin County history
14. No
15. OCLC: (since 1979)
    RLIN: (since 1979)

SANTA ANA

Santa Ana Public Library, Santa Ana History Room
26 Civic Center Plaza, 92701
Tel: 714-647-5280

1. T,Th,Sa, 2-6
2. Anne Harder
3. English, 600
4. 20
5. Unknown; held in Media Section of Library
6. Orange County, CA

7. Tel: yes, NC; letter: N/AN
8. No
9. No
10. No
11. No
12. No
13. Biography Index, Non-Book Index, Santa Ana Building and Business Index, finding aids for Chamber of Commerce and City of Santa Ana collections
14. No
15. OCLC: JRT
Books & Sets: 1,10,11 (located in Reference Section, not in Santa Ana History Room)
Periodicals: 4(1975–) (also located in Reference Section)

SANTA BARBARA

Santa Barbara Public Library
40 E Anapamu St, PO Box 1019, 93102
Tel: 805-962-7653

1. M-Th, 10-9; F,Sa, 10-5:30; Su, 1-5
2. N/AN
3. English, G, 200; LH, many more
4. N/AN
5. 6 reels of Santa Barbara County census microfilm, 1850-1910. *Santa Barbara News Press* on microfilm, 1937–; incomplete holdings from 1955 of other Santa Barbara newspapers
6. Santa Barbara area
7. Tel & letter: yes, NC
8. No
9. No
10. No
11. No
12. No
13. N/AN
14. No
15. N/AN
Books & Sets: 2(incomplete),3, 10–12,26
Periodicals: 4(1970–),8(v.54–58, misc issues),9(v.67-86)

SANTA CLARA

Santa Clara Central Library
2635 Homestead Rd, 95037
Tel: 408-984-3236

1. M-F, 9-9; Sa, 9-6; Su, 1-5
2. No one staff member, but active genealogical society
3. English, 4,200; German, 1; Spanish, 1
4. 20
5. 1,300 plus 1,812 microfiche
6. New England states, other US, England, and some books and guides for European and other countries
7. Tel: yes, NC; letter: yes, $10/hr. Refer to Santa Clara County Historical and Genealogical Society, at above address
8. No
9. No
10. Yes: duplicate copies circulate
11. No
12. *The Santa Clara Collection: A Title List of the Genealogical Materials at the Santa Clara Public Library*, $12.95 (from Ann Alder, 647 Hudson Dr, Santa Clara, CA 95051)
13. N/AN
14. Yes
15. N/AN
Books & Sets: 1,3–7,10–13,15, 17(microfilm guide),19,23, 24(microfilm),26
Periodicals: 1,3(v.24–, 1961–), 4(current issues; microfiche ordered by Genealogical Society), 5,6(v.21, 1985),7,8(v.35, 1947–),9

SANTA CRUZ

Genealogical Society of Santa Cruz County Library, Branciforte Branch Public Library
230 Gault St, 95062
Tel: 408-426-7054

1. M, 12-9; T-Th, 10-9; F,Sa, 10-5

2. Jean Adams Wells, Society's Library Coordinator
3. English, 3,000
4. 25: family histories, genealogies
5. 111
6. US; Canada, England, Wales, Scotland, Ireland, Germany, Barbados, Scandinavia, other foreign countries
7. Tel: no; letter: yes, $1 for brief queries, $10/hr for record searching. Write to Genealogical Society of Santa Cruz County, PO Box 72, Santa Cruz, CA 95063
8. No
9. No
10. No
11. No
12. No
13. Card catalog; 152-page catalog, updated as new material is accessed
14. No
15. No
Books & Sets: 3(with suppl 1987), 5,7(6 v.,1969),10–12,23,26
Periodicals: 1(v.1–53,54–, 1922–), 4(v.25–, 1971–),5(v.1–4,13–, 1962–65, 1974–),7,8(v.59–, 1971–),9(recent years)

University of California at Santa Cruz, McHenry Library, Special Collections, Santa Cruz Collection, 95064
Tel: 408-429-2076

1. School year: daily, 10-12, 1-4; quarter break and summer: closed except by appointment
2. Rita Bottoms
3. English, 750
4. 300 local prestatehood documents
5. None
6. Santa Cruz County
7. Tel & letter: yes, NC
8. Judy Steen, Reference Librarian, UCSC Library
9. No
10. No

11. No
12. No
13. *Santa Cruz Local History Subject Index; Genealogy: University Library, University of California, Santa Cruz* (1987), free
14. No
15. OCLC: yes
Books & Sets: 1,3,6,13–14

SANTA ROSA

Sonoma County Library
Third & E Sts, 95404
Tel: 707-545-0831

1. M-Th, 9:30-9; F,Sa, 9:30-6; Su, 2-6
2. Winifred Swanson, Genealogy; Audrey Herman, Local History
3. English, LH, 1,100, G, 1,500
4. 7,700 photos, 1,700 maps
5. LH: 2,000; G: 300
6. LH: Sonoma County; G: CA state, New England, the South. How-to guides for other states and foreign countries
7. Tel & letter: yes, NC for brief queries
8. Audrey Herman
   Winifred Swanson
9. No
10. Yes, reference books overnight; books to other libraries through ILL
11. Yes, to other libraries through ILL
12. No
13. North Bay Cooperative Library System microfiche catalog
14. Yes
15. OCLC: NOB (few titles)
    RLIN: CNBG (since 1978)
Books & Sets: 1,3–7,10–14,19, 22,23,26
Periodicals: 1(v.52–, 1976–), 2(v.3–, 1981–),4(1952–, partial), 5(1962–65,1975–),7,9(v.83–, 1929–)

SONORA

Tuolumne County Genealogical Society Library, 158 W Bradford Ave, 95370
Tel: 209-532-6317

1. T-Th,Sa, 10-4
2. Delores Cole
3. English, 900; Spanish, 5
4. 50
5. 75
6. Tuolumne County, CA state; "the world"
7. Tel: yes, NC; letter: yes, donations accepted
8. Metta Schafft
   Gloria Lucas
9. No
10. No
11. No
12. Yes
13. N/AN
14. Yes
15. N/AN
Books & Sets: 1–3,8,10–12,15, 16,26
Periodicals: 1,4–6,8,9

Tuolumne County Library
480 Greenley Rd, 95370
Tel: 209-533-5507

1. M,W, 10-9; T,Th,F, 10-6; Sa, 10-5
2. Joan Rutty
3. English, 450
4. 2 or 3
5. 175 reels of local newspapers
6. Tuolumne County, Calaveras County
7. Tel & letter: yes, NC
8. No
9. No
10. No
11. No
12. No
13. None
14. No
15. OCLC: TUO (except local history)

SOUTH SAN FRANCISCO

South San Francisco Public Library, Grand Avenue Branch Library, 306 Walnut Ave, 94080
Tel: 415-877-8533

1. M-F, 1-4
2. Kathleen Kay, Local History
3. English, 15
4. 86 oral history indexes, transcripts (primarily Italian, German families); files on several individuals
5. 40: local newspaper, *Enterprise Journal*, 1895–
6. South San Francisco, neighboring cities; San Mateo County. Emphasis on local industry
7. Tel: yes, NC for brief queries; letter: no
8. No
9. No
10. No
11. No
12. No
13. List of oral history collection; card catalog
14. No
15. N/AN

STOCKTON

Haggin Museum, Alameda May Petzinger Library of Californiana, 1201 N Pershing Ave, 95203-1699
Tel: 209-462-4116

1. By appointment only, T-Sa, 1:30-4:30
2. Tod Ruhstaller, Curator of History
3. English, 250, primarily LH
4. 25–50
5. None
6. Stockton, Central Valley, CA state; the West
7. Tel: no; letter: yes, NC
8. No
9. No

10. No
11. N/AP
12. No
13. N/AV
14. No
15. No

Stockton-San Joaquin County Public Library, 605 N El Dorado St, 95204-1999
Tel: 209-944-8221

1. M,W,Th, 10-9; T,F, 10-6; Sa, 10-5
2. Isabel Benson
3. English, G, 850
4. LH: 2
5. 275: census, CA local histories; 2,800: local newspapers
6. Local area, US
7. Tel & letter: yes, NC except 10¢/copy; 25¢/copy, microfilm
8. Karen Ramos
9. No
10. Yes: limited number of books and microfilm rolls are available for loan to other libraries for in-library use
11. Yes: newspaper microfilm available for loan to other libraries for in-library use
12. No
13. Stockton newspapers index, 1850–; Stockton newspapers obituary index, 1850–, incomplete
14. Yes (nonprofessionals)
15. OCLC: CSP
Books & Sets: 2(incomplete),3,4, 6,7,10–13,19,26
Periodicals: 1(v.38–59, 1962–83), 4(v.2–, 1948–),5,7,8(v.5–71, 1916–83), 9(v.104–, 1950–)

University of the Pacific Libraries, Holt-Atherton Center for Western Studies, 95211
Tel: 209-946-2404

1. M-F, 9-5; other times, by appointment
2. Thomas W. Leonhardt, Dean of Libraries; Daryl Morrison, Special Collections Librarian
3. English, 40,000

4. 230, related to CA history (1,200 linear ft)
5. 464, including Plains and Rockies section of the Cox Library of Local History (252) and John Muir Papers (35)
6. Stockton, San Joaquin Valley, CA state; trans-Mississippi West
7. Tel & letter: yes, $5/hr after first 15 minutes
8. No
9. No
10. No
11. Yes, 2-week loan
12. No
13. Bibliographic Reference Series and Index to Manuscript Collections; subject card file to 30,000-photograph collection
14. No
15. RLIN: CUPG (since 1982)
Books & Sets: 6

TORRANCE

Augustan Society Library
1510 Cravens Ave, 90501
Tel: 213-320-7766

1. T-F, 10-4; Sa, 11-4
2. Chris Velline
3. English, 14,000–15,000; German, 100; Spanish, Italian, Scandinavian, French, Dutch, 500 total
4. 40 linear ft
5. None
6. Europe, Near East, North and South America, some Asia and Africa
7. Tel & letter: yes, NC; charge if extensive request
8. Yes
9. Donation of $5 accepted for two visits
10. Yes; to other institutions through ILL and to members
11. N/AP
12 Catalogue #1, $2.70; Catalogue #2, $1; acquisitions continued in *Genealogical Library Journal*
13. List of books kept by librarian by subject or family

14. Yes
15. No
Books & Sets: 1(1981–86 suppls),
3(1982–86 suppls only),5–7,
19,22–26
Periodicals: 1,4–9

TULARE

Tulare Public Library
113 North F St, 93274
Tel: 209-688-2001, ext 435

1. M-W, 10-7; Th, 10-9
2. Donna D. Benson, Genealogy Librarian
3. English, 3,836; French, 9
4. None
5. 2,982 reels; 3,084 microfiche titles
6. Local area, US
7. Tel: yes, NC; letter: yes,
$1.25 plus Xerox per letter
8. N/AN
9. No
10. No
11. No
12. No
13. 3 county histories have
every-name indexes; 1880 and
1900 census for Tulare County on
index cards
14. No
15. No
Books & Sets: 2,3,5,7,10,11(no
suppls),12–14,18,19,24,26
Periodicals: 1(v.24,42–44),3
(broken set),4(1955–),5,6
(v.16–18),7,8(12 v., scattered
dates),9(v.100–13,124–26,138, &
incomplete v.)

TURLOCK

**California State University,
Stanislaus Library**
801 W Monte Vista Ave, 95380
Tel: 209-667-3233

1. M-Th, 7:30am-11pm;
F, 7:30-5; Sa, 9-5; Su, 1-9
2. J. Carlyle Parker
3. English, 1,000
4. None

5. 200
6. Central CA, New England
7. Tel & letter: yes, NC
8. J. Carlyle Parker
9. No
10. Yes, 3-week loan
11. Yes, 3-week loan
12. *Genealogy in the Central
Association of Libraries: A Union
Catalog,* 1981 (out of print)
13. Local History Biographical
Card Index (to 12 histories of
Calaveras, Mariposa, Merced, San
Joaquin, Stanislaus, and Tuolumne
Counties)
14. Yes
15. OCLC: CTU
Books & Sets: 6,10–14

VISALIA

**Tulare County Free Library
System, Annie Mitchell History
Room,** 200 W Oak St, 93291
Tel: 209-733-6954

1. History Room: W, 11-5, 6-8
2. Mary Anne Terstegge
3. English, 3,000+
4. George Stewart Collection
(Sequoia National Park and CA
National Guard)
5. 14. Visalia Branch at same
address has all old local newspapers on microfilm
6. Tulare County, San Joaquin
Valley, Sequoia National Park
7. Tel: yes, NC; letter: yes, NC
except 15¢/copy
8. N/AN
9. No
10. No
11. No
12. No
13. Card catalog and card
vertical file index, plus detailed
indexes to 3 old county/San
Joaquin Valley histories
14. No
15. N/AN
Books & Sets: 10–12,14
Periodicals: 4(for current 2 years)

WHITTIER

Whittier Public Library
7344 S Washington Ave, 90602
Tel: 213-698-8949

1. M-W, 10-9; Th,F, 10-6;
Sa, 10-5
2. Cynthia Birt
3. English, 500–1,000
4. N/AN
5. None
6. Whittier, CA history
7. Tel: yes, NC if ready
reference; letter: yes, NC except
for copies
8. No
9. No
10. No
11. No
12. No
13. N/AN
14. No
15. OCLC: General collection,
not reference
Books & Sets: 6,7,10–14,19,26
Periodicals: 4,7

WOODLAND

Yolo County Library
373 N College St, 95695
Tel: 916-666-8005

1. 7 public branches and
archives: hours, collections vary
2. N/AN
3. English, small collection
4. N/AN
5. 225
6. Yolo County, Sacramento
Valley, CA
7. Tel & letter: yes, NC
8. No
9. No
10. No
11. Yes, request on ALA form;
require insurance on return
12. No
13. Guides and finding aids for
Archives Collection are in final
stages of preparation
14. Yes
15. OCLC: soon

Books & Sets: 13,14
Periodicals: 4(1972–)

YORBA LINDA

Yorba Linda Public Library
18262 Lemon Dr, 92686
Tel: 714-777-2873

1. M-Th, 9-9; F,Sa, 9-5
2. Diane Schwarzmann
3. English, LH, 500; G, 100
4. None
5. None
6. LH: Yorba Linda, Orange County; early CA history
7. Tel: LH, yes, NC; G, no; letter: no
8. No

9. No
10. No
11. No
12. No
13. None at this time
14. No
15. No
Books & Sets: 3
Periodicals: 8(1986–)

YREKA

Siskiyou County Library
719 4th St, 96097
Tel: 916-842-5256

1. M-W, 9-8; Th,F, 9-6; Sa, 10-5

2. K. Fueston
3. English, 1,000
4. None
5. 500
6. Siskiyou County, CA state; US
7. Tel & letter: yes, NC
8. No
9. No
10. Yes
11. Yes
12. No
13. Microfilm newspaper and census listing
14. No
15. OCLC: CIY
Books & Sets: 10–12,26
Periodicals: 4

COLORADO

AURORA

Aurora Public Library
14949 E Alameda Dr, 80012
Tel: 303-695-7450

1. M-Th, 10-10; F,Sa, 10-6;
Su, 12:30-6
2. Mary K. Ayers, Information
Services Librarian
3. English, 640
4. None
5. None
6. General materials on states,
CO, Aurora
7. Tel: no; letter: yes, NC
8. No
9. No
10. No
11. N/AP
12. No
13. N/AN
14. No
15. OCLC: yes
Books & Sets: 3–5,22
Periodicals: 4(1950–74,1982–),
5(1976–),7

BOULDER

**Carnegie Branch Library for
Local History (Boulder Genea-
logical Society Collection)**
PO Drawer H, 80306
Tel: 303-441-3110

1. T,Th,F,Sa, 11-5; W, 1-9
2. Lois Anderton, Librarian/
Archivist
3. English, 4,000
4. 1,430 linear ft of MSS,
photo collections
5. 15
6. CO, Boulder County,
Boulder
7. Tel: yes, NC; letter: yes, NC
except for copies

8. Boulder Genealogical Society genealogist
9. No
10. No
11. No
12. No
13. Card catalog
14. No
15. No
Books & Sets: 2,3,7(v.1,2,3,6 of
reprint),26
Periodicals: 1(v.59–61),4(v.13–),5,
7,8(v.53–),9(v.125–)

COLORADO SPRINGS

Pikes Peak Library District
20 N Cascade, 80903 (mailing
address: PO Box 1579, 80901)
Tel: 303-473-2080, ext 251

1. M-Th, 10-9; F,Sa, 10-6
2. Ree Mobley, Local History
and Genealogy Librarian
3. English, 8,000; German, 5;
French, 5
4. 3
5. 2,500 (CO census, genealogy books, city directories,
newspapers)
6. US; strong areas include
MA, GA, TN, KY, MD, VA, PA
7. Tel & letter: yes, NC except
for copies: 10¢/8x10, 20¢/8x14 or
8x17
8. Mary M. Davis
9. No
10. No
11. No, except for Colorado
Springs *Gazette, Gazette
Telegraph*. Newspapers are loaned,
5 reels/3-week loan
12. No
13. N/AN
14. Yes. Refer to members of
Pikes Peak Genealogy Society
15. No

Books & Sets: 2–7,10–14,17,
20,22,23,25,26
Periodicals: 1,4,5,7–9

DENVER

**Colorado Historical Society,
Stephen H. Hart Library**
1300 Broadway, 80203
Tel: 303-866-2305

1. T-Sa, 10-4:30
2. Katherine Kane, Director of
Public Services and Access
3. English, 40,000
4. 1,300
5. 28,000
6. CO
7. Tel & letter: yes, NC except
for copies
8. No
9. No
10. No
11. No
12. No
13. *Guide to Manuscript Collections; Guide to Oral Histories*
14. Yes
15. OCLC: DNH (books only)

Denver Public Library
1357 Broadway, 80203
Tel: 303-571-2190

1. M-W, 10-9; Th-Sa, 10-5:30;
Su, 1-5
2. Joanne E. Classen, Genealogy Collection Specialist
3. English, 19,990; German, 5;
French, 5
4. 20 (6 MS boxes)
5. 3,500, including census
6. Emphasis on states east of
Mississippi River, but also on 48
states, England, Scotland, Ireland,
Germany

7. Tel & letter: yes, NC
8. N/AN
9. No
10. Yes: in-library use only, limited loan period
11. No
12. *Denver Public Library Genealogy Division Catalog* (1985), $20, on microfiche
13. *Guide to the Genealogy Collection of the Denver Public Library*
14. Yes
15. OCLC: DPL
Books & Sets: 1–7,9–14,17–19, 23–26
Periodicals: 1,3–5,6(v.7,v.10–), 7,8(v.14, 1925–),9

GRAND JUNCTION

Mesa County Public Library
530 Grand Ave, 81502
Tel: 303-243-4442

1. M-W, 12-9; Th-Sa, 10-5
2. None
3. English, 100
4. 5–10
5. 20
6. CO state
7. Tel: no; letter: yes, $1 handling charge plus 25¢/copy
8. No. Refer to Mesa County Genealogical Society
9. No
10. No
11. No
12. No
13. N/AN
14. Yes
15. OCLC: DMP
Periodicals: 1,4

GREELEY

Greeley Public Library, Colorado History Collection
919 7th St, 80631
Tel: 303-353-6123, ext 392

1. M-Th,9-9; F,Sa, 9-5
2. Shirley Soenksen, Reference Librarian

3. English, 2,000 books/ pamphlets
4. N/AN
5. 475 reels of *Greeley Tribune*
6. Greeley, Weld County, CO. Some general history of the West
7. Tel & letter: yes, NC for local residents only; otherwise $5/ request, plus 10¢/copy
8. No
9. No
10. Yes, if circulating copies are available
11. No
12. No
13. N/AN
14. No. Refer to local genealogical society
15. No
Books & Sets: 2(v.1–127, incomplete)

Greeley Public Library, German-Russian Collection
919 7th St, 80631
Tel: 303-353-6123, ext 392

1. M-Th, 9-9; F,Sa, 9-5
2. Shirley Soenksen, Reference Librarian
3. English, 775; German, 125. Most actual family histories are in Lincoln, NE, so Library has mostly social/cultural history of the German-Russians
4. N/AN
5. None. Refer to American Historical Society of Germans from Russia Archives in Lincoln, NE
6. US, Russia, Canada, Latin America
7. Tel & letter: yes, NC for local residents only, otherwise $5/ request, plus 10¢/copy
8. No
9. No
10. Yes, through ILL: 4-week loan. Borrowing library must pay return postage; limit 3 requests/ patron
11. No
12. *Bibliography of the AHSGR Archives and Historical Library*

(Greeley, CO, 1981), $7. Available only from Lincoln, NE
13. N/AN
14. No. Refer to local genealogical society
15. No
Books & Sets: 2(v.1–127, incomplete)

Weld Public Library
2227 23rd Ave, 80631
Tel: 303-330-7691

1. M-Sa, 9-6
2. Reference Librarian
3. English, 1,200; German, 10; Norwegian, 2
4. None
5. 10
6. US, Europe
7. Tel & letter: yes, NC if brief request
8. No
9. Yes, for out-of-county residents
10. Yes, through ILL
11. No
12. No
13. Brief outline used at a seminar
14. Yes
15. N/AN
Books & Sets: 2(1966 index, 1921 index only),3,4,7(v.1–6),26
Periodicals: 1(very few),4(almost complete),8(very few),9(ca 10 years)

LAKEWOOD

Lakewood Library, Jefferson County Public Library
10200 W 20th Ave, 80215
Tel: 303-232-7004

1. M-Th, 10-9; F,Sa, 10-5; Su, 12-5
2. None
3. English, 1,500
4. None
5. 15
6. North America; Europe
7. Tel: no; letter: yes, NC for brief queries
8. No

9. No
10. Yes, 3-week loan
11. No
12. In progress
13. N/AN
14. No
15. No
Books & Sets: 3,4,9,10
Periodicals:1(v.38–),4(1967–85),
5(1969,1974–78),7,8(1962,1969–76,
1980–81,1983–84),9(v.117–)

LONGMONT

Longmont Public Library
409 Fourth Ave, 80501
Tel: 303-651-8470

1. M-Th, 9-9; F,Sa, 9-6
2. Beatrice Malchow, Library
Director
3. English, 500
4. 200
5. 650
6. Longmont, St. Vrain Valley
7. Tel & letter: yes, NC
8. No
9. No
10. Yes; no charge on circulating copies
11. Yes; duplicate newspaper reels
12. No
13. Newspaper indexes since 1879
14. Yes

15. OCLC: CNL
Books & Sets: 3
Periodicals: 4,5,7

LOVELAND

Loveland Public Library
300 N Adams, 80537
Tel: 303-667-4040

1. Sept-May: M-Th, 10-9; F,Sa, 10-5; June-Aug: M-Th, 9-8; F,S, 9-5
2. Linda Vasenius, Reference Librarian
3. English, 100; German, 2; Swedish, 2
4. None
5. 200 reels, various Loveland newspapers: *Reporter, Herald, Register*
6. Larimer County
7. Tel: yes, NC; letter: yes, charge, with SASE
8. Betty Wickam (volunteer)
9. No
10. Yes, unless rare or out of print; 4-week loan through ILL
11. No; will send copies at 10¢ each
12. No
13. N/AN
14. Yes
15. No
Periodicals: 4

PUEBLO

Pueblo Library District
100 E Abriendo Ave, 81004
Tel: 303-543-9601

1. M-Th, 9-9; F,Sa, 9-6
2. Charles Turner, Reference Dept Head; Ronda Gettel, Genealogy
3. English, 3,000; German, 1; French, 1
4. N/AN
5. 1,200: G; 500: local newspaper
6. Pueblo area, CO state; New England states, midwestern states
7. Tel: no; letter: yes, NC for brief queries
8. Noreen Riffe
9. No
10. No
11. Yes; one reel of local newspaper at a time, 4-week loan
12. *Pueblo Library District's Genealogy Holdings List* (computer generated), $5
13. N/AN
14. Yes
15. OCLC: CQA
Books & Sets: 2–5,7,10–14,17–18, 19(1950,1972 only),20,22,26
Periodicals: 1,3,4(incomplete), 5(v.1–8,15–),7–9

CONNECTICUT

BRANFORD

James Blackstone Memorial Library, 758 Main St, 06405
Tel: 203-488-0884

1. M-F, 9-8; Sa, 9-5 (July-Aug; Sa, 9-12)
2. Betty M. Linsley, Assistant Librarian
3. English, 700
4. 12 linear ft
5. 8
6. Branford, North Branford, New Haven County
7. Tel: yes, NC for short queries; letter: yes, NC except 15¢/copy
8. No
9. No
10. No
11. No
12. No
13. Finding lists for Manuscript Collection
14. Yes
15. No
Books & Sets: 3,26
Periodicals: 1(1940),9(missing v.14–20, 1860–66)

BRIDGEPORT

Bridgeport Public Library
Historical Collections,
925 Broad St, 06610
Tel: 203-576-8192

1. M-Sa, 9-5; Su, 1-5; closed Sa, Su from Memorial Day to Labor Day
2. Mary K. Witkowski, Assistant Head
3. N/AN
4. 300
5. N/AN
6. City of Bridgeport, Fairfield County
7. Tel & letter: yes, $5/search plus copies
8. No
9. No
10. No
11. No
12. No
13. *A Brief Guide to Historical Collections*, free
14. No
15. OCLC

BRISTOL

Bristol Public Library
5 High St, PO Box 730, 06010
Tel: 203-584-7747

1. Bristol History Room: M-Th, 8:30-1, or by appointment; Library: M-Th, 8:30-8; F,Sa, 8:30-5
2. Sharon Krawiecki
3. English, 3,500
4. 100
5. None
6. Bristol, Hartford County, CT state
7. Tel & letter: yes, NC
8. No
9. No
10. No
11. No
12. No
13. Special Collection, Bristol Room, index; birth/death index, 1871–74, 1916, 1917, 1981–; marriage index
14. Yes
15. No
Books & Sets: 2,3,26(New England states)
Periodicals: 9

CHESHIRE

Cheshire Public Library
104 Main St, 06410
Tel: 203-272-2245

1. M-Th, 10-9; F,Sa, 10-5
2. Reference Librarian
3. English, 200
4. None
5. None
6. Cheshire, Wallingford, New Haven, Meriden, Guilford, Weathersfield, Waterbury, Litchfield, CT history
7. Tel & letter: no
8. No
9. N/AN
10. No
11. No
12. No
13. N/AN
14. No
15. No

COS COB

Historical Society of the Town of Greenwich
39 Strickland Rd, 06807
Tel: 203-869-6899

1. T,Th, 10-2
2. Meriweather Schmid, Genealogy; William Finch, Jr., Local History
3. English, 150
4. No estimate
5. None
6. Greenwich, Fairfield County
7. Tel & letter: yes, NC
8. Yes
9. No
10. No
11. No
12. No

13. N/AN
14. No
15. N/AN

DANBURY

Danbury Public Library
70 Main St, 06810
Tel: 203-797-4527

1. M-Th, 9-9; F,Sa, 9-5; Su, 1-5
2. Barbara K. Blanchard
3. English, 500
4. 25
5. 20
6. Greater Danbury area, Fairfield County
7. Tel: no; letter: yes, NC except 10¢/copy
8. No
9. No
10. No
11. No
12. No
13. N/AP
14. No
15. No
Books & Sets: 26

Danbury Scott-Fanton Museum and Historical Society
43 Main St, 06810
Tel: 203-743-5200

1. T-F, 10-5; Sa,Su, 2-5
2. Lucye Boland
3. English, 188; Portuguese, 1
4. 18
5. None
6. LH: Fairfield County; G: Danbury
7. Tel & letter: yes, NC for brief queries, otherwise $5/hr
8. No
9. No
10. No
11. N/AP
12. No
13. N/AN
14. Yes
15. No
Books & Sets: 1,26(only PA,MA,VT,RI,VA,MD,SC)

EAST HADDAM

Rathbun Free Memorial Library, 36 Main St, 06423
Tel: 203-873-8210

1. T,W,F, 10-5; Th, 10-8
2. Martha T. Monte
3. English, 400
4. 50
5. 100
6. East Haddam, Haddam, Moodus, East Hampton, Colchester, Lyme, Old Lyme; also, extensive CT history collection
7. Tel: yes, NC; letter: yes, charge
8. Dr. Karl Stofko
9. No
10. No
11. No
12. No
13. N/AN
14. No
15. No
Books & Sets: 2,26

FARMINGTON

Farmington Library
Box 407, 6 Monteith Dr, 06034
Tel: 203-673-6791

1. M,T,Th, 9-9; W, 10-9, F, 9-5:30; Sa, 9-5 (summer, 9-1)
2. Ann J. Arcari
3. English, 500
4. 100
5. N/AP
6. Farmington, CT, and daughter towns: Bristol, Avon, Plainville, Berlin, Burlington
7. Tel: yes, NC; letter: yes, NC except for copies and mailing
8. No
9. No
10. No
11. N/AP
12. No
13. N/AN
14. Yes
15. No

GLASTONBURY

Welles-Turner Memorial Library, 2407 Main St, 06033
Tel: 203-659-2733

1. M-F, 9-9; Sa, 9-5 (closed July–Aug)
2. Barbara Bailey, Reference Librarian
3. English, 10
4. None
5. None
6. Glastonbury-Wethersfield
7. Tel & letter: yes, NC
8. No
9. No
10. No
11. N/AP
12. No
13. N/AN
14. Yes
15. No

GREENWICH

Greenwich Library
191 W Putnam Ave, 06830
Tel: 203-622-7900

1. M-F, 9-9; Sa, 9-5; Su, 1-5, except summer
2. Louise Gudelis
3. English, 3,000
4. 460 oral history transcripts
5. 50
6. Greenwich; surrounding communities
7. Tel & letter: yes, NC; ready reference only; minimum charge for photocopies
8. No
9. No
10. No
11. No
12. No
13. Tom Kemp, *Genealogies in the Greenwich Library;* Oral History Index; computer catalog
14. Yes
15. OCLC: GRN
Books & Sets: 1,3,5,10–14,18,26
Periodicals: 4(1986–),7,9(1847–)

HARTFORD

Connecticut Historical Society
1 Elizabeth St, 06105
Tel: 203-236-5621

1. Labor Day-Memorial Day: T-Sa, 9-5; closed Sa in summer
2. Judith Ellen Johnson
3. English, 12,500
4. 716 linear ft
5. 500 (Library also acquiring Holbrook Vital Records for MA on microfiche as they become available)
6. CT, New England, some NY, OH, PA
7. Tel: yes, NC; letter: yes, plus 25¢/copy and 75¢ for postage
8. Judith Ellen Johnson
9. No
10. Yes, to members only
11. No
12. *Connecticut Historical Society Loan Collection Catalogue* (1987), $5
13. Card catalog
14. Yes
15. OCLC: CTH (partially)
Books & Sets: 2-7,10-14,16-18, 26
Periodicals: 1,3(v.3-45),4(v.13-), 5,7,8(lacking v.27),9

Connecticut State Library, Archives, History, and Genealogy Unit, 231 Capitol Ave, 06106
Tel: 203-566-3692

1. M-F, 8:30-5; Sa, 9-1
2. Theodore O. Wohlsen
3. English, 22,000; German, 100
4. 300
5. 4,000
6. CT and bordering states; New England; other areas from and to which CT people migrated
7. Tel & letter: yes, NC for brief queries; cannot undertake research
8. No
9. No
10. Yes, duplicate copies of post-1901, through ILL
11. Yes, duplicates and secon-

dary sources only, through ILL
12. Guides to court, church, and probate records and to archives: out of print, but will photocopy
13. Card catalogs for family and local histories; aids to MS and microfilm collections
14. Yes
15. OCLC: CZL (partial)
Books & Sets: 1-7,9-14,18-19, 24,26
Periodicals: 1,3-5,7-9

MADISON

E. C. Scranton Memorial Library, 801 Boston Post Rd, Box 631, 06443
Tel: 203-245-7365

1. M,T,Th, 9-5:30; W,F, 9-9; Sa, 9-5. Summer: closed F at 5:30; closed Sa at noon
2. Marcia Sokolnicki
3. English, 550
4. Vertical file of ephemeral local history materials, but very few MS materials
5. 200: local newspapers
6. Histories of CT towns, CT state; genealogies and miscellaneous materials re adjacent towns, especially Guilford, Clinton, New Haven
7. Tel & letter: yes, NC, but only quick questions
8. No
9. No
10. No
11. No
12. No
13. Card catalog; card index to file
14. No
15. No
Books & Sets: 26 (reprint of 1908 ed)

MERIDEN

Meriden Public Library
105 Miller St, 06450
Tel: 203-238-2348 (Reference)

1. M-Th, 10-9; F, 10-5; Sa, 9-5; closed Sa in summer

2. Louise L. Cowing
3. English, 1,100
4. None
5. None
6. CT state, New England
7. Tel: no; letter: yes, $3/half-hour for brief queries
8. No
9. No
10. No
11. No
12. No
13. N/AN
14. No
15. No
Books & Sets: 1(v.2-6,8-13, v.75-98, 1894-98, 1924-28), 5(v.1-3), 26
Periodicals: 1(v.1-7, v.13-, 1922-31, 1936-),9

MIDDLETOWN

Godfrey Memorial Library
134 Newfield St, 06457
Tel: 203-346-4375

1. M-F, 9-4; closed most holidays and vacations
2. N/AN
3. English, 15,000; other, several
4. Less than 20
5. 50
6. Most of US
7. Tel: no; letter: yes, $10/hr
8. Yes
9. No, but donations accepted
10. No
11. No
12. No
13. Card catalog
14. N/AN
Books & Sets: 2(incomplete),3,4, 5(v.1-4),18,26
Periodicals: 1(incomplete), 4(incomplete),7,9

NEW BRITAIN

New Britain Public Library
20 High St, 06051
Tel: 203-224-3155

1. M,T,Th, 9-9; W,F,Sa, 9-5

(closed Sa July–Aug); Su (Oct-May), 1-5

Local History Room: M, 1-9; T, 9-6; W, 1-5; Th, 9-5; F,Sa, 9-5 (alternate weeks)

2. Arlene C. Palmer
3. English, 1,000; other, some Polish, Swedish
4. Few
5. 30, mostly US Census 1800–1900 for New Britain
6. New Britain; surrounding area; CT state
7. Tel: yes, NC; letter: yes, NC except 10¢/copy
8. No
9. No
10. No
11. No
12. No
13. *The Burritt Collection* (Elihu Burritt, 1810–79)
14. No
15. No
Books & Sets: 3,19,26(CT,MA)
Periodicals: 9(1896–1907,1923)

NEW HAVEN

New Haven Colony Historical Society, Whitney Library
114 Whitney Ave, 06510
Tel: 203-562-4183

1. T-F, 10-4:45
2. Ottilia Koel
3. English, 25,000; German, few; some French, Ukrainian, Yiddish
4. 100
5. 500
6. New Haven, CT state; New England; US
7. Tel: yes, NC for brief queries; letter: yes, $10
8. Arthur Reinhart, Assistant Librarian
9. Yes, $2/day
10. No
11. No
12. No
13. A guide (folder), free. MS collections reported to *NUCMC*
14. Yes
15. No

Books & Sets: 2–3,5–7,10–13,17, 18,26
Periodicals: 1,3–5,7–9

NORWICH

Otis Library, 261 Main St, 06360
Tel: 203-889-2365

1. N/AN
2. Joanna L. Oudin, Head, Reference Dept
3. English, 1,600
4. None
5. No microfilm, but 300 microcards
6. Norwich area, southeast CT
7. Tel & letter: yes, NC
8. No
9. No
10. No
11. No
12. Guide to various sources in the region was published in 1982: *Genealogical & Local History Resources in the New London County Libraries,* James R. Benn, ed. Available from SECLA, Avery Point, Groton, CT 06340
13. Card catalog
14. Yes
15. No
Books & Sets: 3(1980 ed),18,26
Periodicals: 1, 4(1968–),5,7–9

OLD SAYBROOK

Acton Public Library, 60 Old Boston Post Road, 06475
Tel: 203-388-2037

1. M-Th, 12-8:30; F,Sa, 9-5
2. N/AP
3. English, 150
4. 30
5. None
6. CT state
7. Tel: no; letter: yes, NC
8. No
9. No
10. Yes, 2-week loan, renewable
11. No
12. No
13. N/AN

14. No
15. No

RIDGEFIELD

Ridgefield Library and Historical Association
472 Main St, 06877
Tel: 203-438-2282

1. Historical collection: by appointment. Library: M,T,W,F, 10-6; Th, 10-9; Sa, 9-5; Su (Sept-May), 1-5
2. Anita T. Daubenspeck, Director
3. English, 3,000 (includes pamphlets, photographs, documents)
4. 2,000
5. 60
6. Ridgefield; Fairfield County; some CT state and Westchester County, NY
7. Tel: yes, NC; letter: yes, NC unless photocopy is over 10 pages
8. No
9. No
10. No
11. No
12. No
13. Card catalog
14. No
15. No

SOUTHPORT

Pequot Library
720 Pequot Ave, 06490
Tel: 203-259-0346

1. Summer (July 4–Labor Day): M,T,Th,F, 9-5:30; W, 9-8:30; Sa, 9-1; winter: M,W, 9-8:30; T,Th,F, 9-5:30; Sa, 9-5; Su, 2-6
2. Thomas Jay Kemp
3. English, 35,000
4. 10
5. 300: film; 9,000: fiche
6. CT, New England, NY, Northeast, eastern US
7. Tel & letter: yes, NC
8. Thomas Jay Kemp

9. No
10. Yes, some from local history collection; none from genealogy section
11. No
12. *Catalogue of the Monroe, Wakeman and Holman Collection of the Pequot Library...in the Yale University Library* (1960), $15; T. J. Kemp, "Genealogies in Connecticut Libraries and Historical Societies: A Union List"; new acquisitions listed quarterly in *Connecticut Ancestry*; annotated guide to serial holdings
13. N/AN
14. No
15. RLIN: yes
Books & Sets: 1–6,8,10–12,26
Periodicals: 1,3–5,7–9

SOUTH WINDSOR

South Windsor Public Library
1550 Sullivan Ave, 06074
Tel: 203-644-1541

1. M-Th, 9-9; F,Sa, 9-4:30 (hours change in summer)
2. N/AN
3. English, 150
4. N/AN
5. N/AN
6. South Windsor
7. Tel: N/AN; letter: yes, NC for brief queries
8. No
9. N/AN
10. No
11. No
12. No
13. N/AN
14. N/AN
15. N/AN

STAMFORD

Ferguson Library, One Public Library Plaza, Broad & Bedford Sts, 06904
Tel: 203-964-1000

1. M-F, 9-9; Sa, holidays, 9-5:30; Su (Sept-June), 1-5
2. Robert J. Belletzkie

3. English, 3,500
4. None
5. 200+
6. CT, NY, New England; some Old Northwest, US, world
7. Tel: no; letter: yes, NC except 10¢/copy plus postage
8. Robert J. Belletzkie
9. No
10. No
11. No
12. No
13. N/AN
14. No
15. No
Books & Sets: 1–7,8(US, Canada, England),9–14,19,24,26(New England only)
Periodicals: 1,4,5,7–9

STRATFORD

Stratford Library Association
2203 Main St, 06497
Tel: 203-259-6605

1. M-Th, 10-8; F,Sa, 10-5
2. Lynne A. Perrigo
3. English, 1,275
4. Less than 5
5. None
6. Stratford; CT state; New England
7. Tel: yes, for brief queries; letter: yes, NC except for copies
8. No
9. No
10. No
11. No
12. No
13. In-house bibliography in process
14. No
15. OCLC: SSA
Books & Sets: 26
Periodicals: 1(5 years),4,9

WALLINGFORD

Wallingford Public Library
200 N Main St, 06492
Tel: 203-265-6754

1. M-F, 10-9; Sa, 10-5 (fall, winter, spring)

2. Reference Librarian
3. English, 800
4. None
5. 26
6. Wallingford, New Haven County; some for whole state of CT
7. Tel & letter: yes, NC
8. No
9. No
10. No
11. No
12. No
13. N/AN
14. No
15. No
Books & Sets: 3

WATERBURY

Silas Bronson Library
267 Grand St, 06702
Tel: 203-574-8222

1. M,W, 9-9; T,Th,F, 9-5:30; Sa, 9-5
2. None
3. English,"all"; French, approx 10
4. 550; 3,000 pamphlets
5. None
6. Waterbury, CT state; some New England, NY
7. Tel & letter: yes, half-hour search free, then $15/hr
8. No
9. No
10. No
11. No
12. No
13. Card catalog
14. No. Refer to Connecticut Society of Genealogists, Glastonbury
15. No

WEST HARTFORD

West Hartford Public Library
20 S Main St, 06107
Tel: 203-236-6286

1. M-F, 9-9; Sa (winter), 9-5, (summer), 9-1

2. Thomas Kilfoil, Reference Librarian
3. English, 500
4. None
5. None
6. CT state; some New England
7. Tel & letter: no
8. No
9. No
10. No
11. No
12. No
13. N/AN
14. No

15. OCLC: WHP (partial)
Books & Sets: 3,26(CT only)
Periodicals: 9

WILTON

Wilton Library, 137 Old Ridge-field Road, 06897
Tel: 203-762-3950

1. M,T,W,F, 9-5:30; Th, 9-9; Sa, 9-5; Su (Oct -Apr), 1-5
2. Carol Russell, Curator
3. English, 50
4. 300
5. None
6. Wilton; some Fairfield County; few CT state
7. Tel: yes, NC; letter: yes, NC except for copies
8. No
9. No
10. No
11. N/AP
12. No
13. Index to Wilton History Room and its materials
14. No
15. N/AN

DELAWARE

DOVER

Delaware State Archives
Hall of Records, 19901
Tel: 302-736-5318

1. T-F, 8:30-4:15; Sa, 8:00-3:45
2. Joanne A. Mattern, Deputy State Archivist
3. English, 4,000; French, 6
4. 275
5. 30
6. DE, with materials from MD, NJ, PA
7. Tel: yes, NC; letter: yes, but do not research for patrons
8. No
9. No
10. No
11. No, but available for purchase at nominal fees
12. *Preliminary Inventory of the Holdings of the Delaware State Archives*
13. Checklists in Research Room
14. Yes
15. No
Books & Sets: 2,26

WILMINGTON

Hagley Museum and Library
PO Box 3630, 19807
Tel: 302-658-2400

1. M-F, 8:30-4:30; 2d Sa each month, 9-4:30
2. No G/LH sections. Imprints reference librarian, ext 227; Manuscripts and Archives reference archivist, ext 330
3. Unable to define G/LH collection within Imprints or Manuscripts and Archives Depts. Subject areas are: business and industrial history, development of technology, DE Valley business records. Special collections include Du Pont Company and family publications and papers
4. See above
5. 1,450 reels of census data
6. American economic and business history with emphasis on mid-Atlantic region
7. Tel & letter: yes, NC, but limited staff time available
8. No
9. No
10. No; reference collection for on-site use; ILL on limited basis, applied for on ALA-approved ILL forms, 1-month loan
11. No, as above
12. John B. Riggs, *A Guide to Manuscripts in the Eleutherian Mills Historical Library*, $10. Supplements, 1966–75, $15
13. In-house finding aids
14. No. Refer to Historical Society of Delaware
15. OCLC: DEH
Books & Sets: 1,6

Historical Society of Delaware
505 Market St, 19801
Tel: 302-655-7161

1. M, 1-9; T-F, 9-5
2. Barbara E. Benson
3. English, 6,000; Flemish, 2; French, 3; Swedish, 2
4. 1,000
5. 300
6. DE state; some MD, PA
7. Tel & letter: yes, NC for brief queries; $10 for basic surname search
8. Barbara Benson
   Ellen Peterson
   Constance Cooper
9. No
10. No
11. No
12. No
13. Card catalog
14. Yes
15. No
Books & Sets: 2,3,5,6,26(MD,PA, CT,SC,VA)
Periodicals: 5(v.13–23),7–9

DISTRICT OF COLUMBIA

WASHINGTON, DC

Columbia Historical Society
1307 New Hampshire St NW,
20036
Tel: 202-785-2068

1. W,F,Sa, 10-4; Th, 12-4
members only
2. Lawrence Baume, Curator
of Collections
3. English, 12,000
4. 380
5. N/AP
6. Washington, DC, metropolitan area
7. Tel & letter: yes, NC for
catalog search only; $20 research
fee
8. No
9. No
10. No
11. No
12. *Guide to Research Collections*
13. Finding aids in MS and
photo collections
14. Yes
15. No
Books & Sets: 6

**Daughters of the American
Revolution Library**
1776 D St NW, 20006-5392
Tel: 202-879-3229

1. M-F, 9-4; Su, 1-5; closed
federal holidays and Su before
holiday
2. Eric G. Grundset, Library
Director
3. English, 85,000; German, 5
4. 200,000 files of MS
material
5. 300: Seimes Microfilm
Collection
6. US (from settlement to early

20th century); Canada
7. Tel: yes, NC; letter: yes, NC
except for copies
8. Yes
9. Yes, $5/day for non-DAR
members; $3 on Sundays
10. No
11. No
12. *DAR Library Catalog: V. 1:
Family Histories and Genealogies;
V. 2: State and Local Histories and
Records*
13. DAR Library Analytical
Card Index; specialized card
indexes on various states and
subjects
14. Yes
15. No
Books & Sets: 2–5,7,10–14,
18(partial),24,26
Periodicals: 1,3–5,7–9

**Library of Congress, Local
History and Genealogy Reading
Room,** General Reading Rooms
Division, 10 First St SE, 20540
Tel: 202-287-5537

1. M-F, 8:30am-9:30pm;
Sa, 8:30-5; Su, 1-5
2. Judith P. Austin
3. English, over 100,000;
other, material in all Western
languages as well as Oriental,
Greek, Slavic
4. Over 100
5. Over 1,000 (no census
records)
6. US, British Isles, Germany;
worldwide
7. Tel & letter: yes, NC
8. Yes
9. No
10. No
11. Yes; duplicates only
12. J. A. Babel, *Lest We Forget:
A Guide to Genealogical Research*

in the Nation's Capital (1982);
*Library of Congress Publications
in Print; National Union Catalog,
Pre-1956 Imprints* (754 v. including supp); *Guide to the Library of
Congress; Special Collections in
the Library of Congress; Geography and Map Division; Rare
Book Division;* and five important
guides to local history and genealogy by Marion J. Kaminkow, ed.
(items 10–14 listed below under
Books & Sets)
13. Consult *Library of Congress
Publications in Print* for guides to
specific collections
14. No. Refer to Board for
Certification of Genealogists
15. N/AN
Books & Sets: 1–7,9–24,26
Periodicals: 1–3,4(lacks
1973–74,1977),5–9

**Martin Luther King Memorial
Library, Washingtoniana
Division,** 901 G St NW, 20001
Tel: 202-727-1213

1. Sept–mid-June: M-Th, 9-9;
F,Sa, 9-5:30; Su, 1-5; June–Aug:
M,Th, 9-9; T,W,F,Sa, 9-5:30
2. Roxanna Deane
3. English, 14,000
4. None
5. DC newspapers, census,
city directories
6. DC area
7. Tel: yes, NC for limited
research; letter: yes, NC except
15¢/copy with $1 minimum
8. No
9. No
10. No
11. No
12. No
13. N/AN
14. No

15. N/AN
Books & Sets: 1,3,10–12,19,26
Periodicals: 4,7

National Archives and Records Administration, 8th & Pennsylvania Ave, NW, 20408
Tel: 202-523-3218

1. Main research rooms: M-F, 8:45am-10pm; Sa, 8:45-5:15; closed federal holidays. Business hours of building: M-F, 8:45-5:15

2. No specific G/LH sections. Direct inquiries to Reference Services Branch, National Archives and Records Administration, Washington, DC 20408. Tel: 202-523-3218

3. Most materials are not in book form. The NARA collection does not relate to genealogy as much as it relates to federal archives. Researchers of family history are interested in archival records rather than in published books

4. NARA does not solicit MS collections, except for the several presidential libraries. The vast majority of holdings are archival records of the federal government, arranged primarily by agency of origin, and then by the agency's filing system. Finding aids at several levels provide access to these records

5. 65,000 rolls in 3 primary categories: federal population census schedules, military service and pension application files, and passenger arrival records. This figure continues to grow and represents only a narrowly defined number of rolls used primarily for family history research. Over 150,000 rolls of microfilm are produced by NARA, and many other rolls conceivably could have family history value, given the right circumstances. For example, a researcher with an ancestor who was a consular representative in a foreign country will be interested in microfilm publications of the consular post records during the time that the ancestor served with that post

6. US plus Department of State and related records covering diplomatic relations with most foreign countries

7. Tel & letter: yes, NC. NARA will not perform research for individuals. Copies of some records (military service, pension application, census, passenger arrival) can be requested by mail through the use of a form and will be supplied for a fee. Direct inquiries to Reference Services Branch at the address and telephone listed in #2

8. No. To contact the consultant staff familiar with records held by NARA, use the address and telephone listed in #2

9. No, except for copies

10. No

11. Yes, through the Census Microfilm Rental Program

12. Those listed below are most relevant to family history research. Guides: *Guide to the National Archives of the United States* (general guide to all NARA archival holdings); *Guide to Genealogical Research in the National Archives* (revised); *Black History: A Guide to Civilian Records in the National Archives; The Confederacy: A Guide to the Archives of the Confederate States of America; The Union: A Guide to Federal Archives Relating to the Civil War; Guide to Records in the National Archives Relating to American Indians.* Census publications: *Federal Population Censuses, 1790–1890; 1900 Federal Population Census; The 1910 Federal Population Census* Select catalogs of microfilm publications: *American Indians; Black Studies; Genealogical & Biographical Research; Immigrant & Passenger Arrivals.* For prices, contact Publications Sales Branch, National Archives and Records Administration, Washington, DC 20409. Tel: 202-523-3164

13. Unpublished indexes and other guides are too numerous to list. For a specific area, contact Reference Services Branch at the address and telephone listed in #2

14. No

15. No

FLORIDA

BARTOW

Polk County Historical and Genealogical Library
PO Box 1719, 33830-1719
Tel: 813-533-5146

1. M-F, 8:30-5; closed last F of every month, legal holidays
2. LaCona Padgett, Librarian; Kathleen M. Greer, Assistant
3. English, 10,000; German, 1; Spanish, 1
4. Vertical files on individual families
5. 3,000–4,000
6. FL state; NC, SC, WV, VA, GA, KY, TN, AL, LA, MS, TX, AR, MD
7. Tel: no; letter: yes, NC except 25¢/copy. Refer extensive work to paid researchers
8. No
9. No
10. No
11. No
12. No
13. N/AN
14. Yes
15. No
Books & Sets: 2,3(not all suppls), 26
Periodicals: 1,4,5,7–9

BOYNTON BEACH

Boynton Beach City Library
208 S Seacrest Blvd, 33435
Tel: 305-732-2624

1. M-Th, 9-8:30; F,Sa, 9-5
2. William Coup
3. English, 40
4. 10
5. None

6. Boynton Beach and surrounding area
7. Tel & letter: yes, NC
8. No
9. No
10. Yes, circulating items only to card holders; 2-week loan, limit 3 books/subject
11. No
12. No
13. Card catalog
14. No
15. No

BRADENTON

Manatee County Central Library, 1301 Barcarrota Blvd, 33507
Tel: 813-748-5555

1. M-F, 10-9; Sa, 10-5
2. Rose Marie Taylor
3. English, 1,500
4. Eaton Collection (one full room of FL history), Manatee County Historical Collection
5. 50
6. East of Mississippi River, New England, the South; some PA, NY
7. Tel & letter: yes, NC
8. No
9. No
10. No
11. No
12. No
13. Both collections, Manasota Genealogical Society
14. No
15. OCLC: yes
Books & Sets: 2–6,8–14,18,19, 24–26
Periodicals: 1,4,5,7–9

DAYTONA BEACH

Volusia County Library Center
City Island, 32015
Tel: 904-752-8374

1. M,F, 9-5; T,W,Th, 9-9; closed legal holidays
2. Mary Gasparry, Reference Librarian
3. English, 1,000
4. Several in vertical files
5. 28, state census; 3, Hollingsworth card file index; 6, Newberry Library holdings; miscellaneous GA reels, deeds, wills, marriages; local newspaper
6. Northeast, Middle Atlantic, southern states, areas east of the Mississippi; some TX, KY, OH
7. Tel & letter: yes, NC
8. Yes. Refer to Volusia County Genealogical Society
9. No
10. No
11. No
12. Not complete
13. N/AN
14. N/AN
15. OCLC: yes
Books & Sets: 2(some),9–14,17, 25,26
Periodicals: 1–9

FORT MYERS

Fort Myers-Lee County Public Library, 2050 Lee St, 33901
Tel: 813-334-3992

1. M-Th, 9-9; F,Sa, 9-6
2. See Reference Department
3. English, 648
4. None
5. 25: *New England Historical and Genealogical Register*; 35: FL census; 11: other census

6. US east of Mississippi River
7. Tel & letter: no
8. Jessie Richmond Hooper, Volunteer
9. No
10. No
11. No
12. No
13. None
14. No. Refer to local Genealogical Society
15. OCLC: FFL
Books & Sets: 3,7(v.2–6),10–14, 26(lacks NC)
Periodicals: 1(v.43, 1967–, incomplete),2(v.14, 1960–, incomplete), 5(1962–65,1969,1974–81),7,8(v.64, 1976–),9

FORT PIERCE

St. Lucie County Library System, 124 N Indian River Dr, 33450
Tel: 305-461-5708

1. M-Th, 9-8:30; F,9-6; Sa,9-5
2. Allardya A. Hamill
3. English, 350
4. None
5. 816 plus 136 fiche
6. FL, some materials on other states
7. Tel & letter: yes, NC
8. No
9. No
10. No
11. No
12. No
13. *Genealogical Resources in the St. Lucie County Library System*
14. No
15. No
Books & Sets: 1,3
Periodicals: 4(v.30, 1976–),5(v.12, 1982),8(v.74, 1986–),9(v. 140, 1986–)

JACKSONVILLE

Jacksonville Public Library
122 N Ocean St, 32202
Tel: 904-633-3305

1. M, 10-8; T-Th, 10-5:30; F,Sa, 10-6
2. Carol Harris, Florida Curator; Arden Brugger, Genealogy Librarian
3. English, 16,843; Spanish, 20; French, 26; Latin, 1
4. No MS collection; 10 file drawers of historical and family files
5. 6,086
6. FL Collection: Jacksonville area and especially on crown area of FL: Duval, Baker, Nassau, and St Johns Counties. Genealogy Collection: emphasis on southeastern US; also books on 34 states
7. Tel & letter: yes, minimum charge for photocopies, $2 (20¢/ page) with SASE. Not staffed for involved genealogical research but will check indexes and files
8. Arden Brugger
9. No
10. No
11. No
12. No
13. *Florida Times-Union* Index, 1895–1927, 1929–30, 1938–; *Jacksonville Journal* Index, 1925–28
14. Yes
15. OCLC: JPL
Books & Sets: 1(suppl 1981), 2–7,10–14,18,19,23,26
Periodicals: 1,4,5(v.13, 1974–), 6,7,8(v.51, 1963–),9(v.1–59, 1847–1905, v.69, 1915–)

KEY WEST

Monroe County-May Hill Russell Library
700 Fleming St, 33040
Tel: 305-294-8488

1. Florida Reference Room: M-Sa, 9-5
2. Thomas Hambright
3. English, 3,500; Spanish, 40
4. None
5. 1,383
6. FL, the Caribbean
7. Tel & letter: yes, NC
8. No

9. No
10. No
11. No
12. No
13. Catalog card file
14. No
15. No
Books & Sets: 3,13,14,26
Periodicals: 4,8

LAKELAND

Lakeland Public Library
100 Lake Morton Dr, 33801
Tel: 813-686-2168

1. M-F, 9-5, or by appointment
2. Waneta Sage-Gagne
3. English, 2,500
4. None
5. N/AN
6. Lakeland, Polk County, FL
7. Tel & letter: yes, NC
8. No
9. No
10. No
11. No
12. No
13. N/AN
14. No
15. No

LIVE OAK

Suwannee River Regional Library, 207 Pine Ave, 32060
Tel: 904-362-5779

1. M, 8am-9pm; T-F, 8-5:30; Sa, 8-4
2. N/AN
3. English, 75
4. N/AN
5. 120
6. Mostly FL, some GA
7. Tel & letter: yes, NC
8. No
9. No
10. Yes, but some titles are not lent
11. No
12. No
13. N/AN
14. No
15. No

MIAMI

Miami-Dade Public Library
101 W Flagler St, 33130-1504
Tel: 305-375-2665, ext 8354

   1. M-W,F,Sa, 9-6; Th, 9-9;
Su (Oct-May), 1-5
   2. Renee Pierce
   3. English, 6,500
   4. None
   5. 11,850
   6. US, Great Britain
   7. Tel & letter: yes, $2.50
minimum/copies
   8. No
   9. No
   10. No
   11. No
   12. No
   13. None
   14. No
   15. OCLC: DZM
Books & Sets: 1–6,7(v.2–5 only),
10–14,17,18,19(2 v., 1950 only),
23,26
Periodicals: 1,3,4,5(v.1–4 only),
7–9

NAPLES

Collier County Public Library
650 Central Ave, 33940
Tel: 813-262-4130

   1. M-Th, 9-9; F,Sa, 9-5
   2. None
   3. English, 150
   4. None
   5. US Census for FL only
   6. New England, the South, FL
   7. Tel: no; letter: yes, NC
   8. No
   9. No
   10. No
   11. No
   12. No
   13. N/AN
   14. No
   15. No
Books & Sets: 11–14,26
Periodicals: 4,9

ORLANDO

**Orange County Library System,
Genealogy Department,** 101 E
Central Ave, 32801
Tel: 305-425-4694, ext 380

   1. M-F, 9-9; Sa, 9-6; Su, 1-5
   2. Eleanor Crawford
   3. English, 20,000; German, a
few; other, a few
   4. Beatrice Brown Commander
Collection (southern material)
   5. 2,631 (5,000 reels on order)
   6. US with emphasis on New
England, NY, and the South
   7. Tel: yes, NC; letter: yes, NC
except for copies
   8. Yes
   9. No
   10. Yes; small "how-to"
collection circulates, but pre-1900
material does not
   11. No
   12. No
   13. Obituary index to *Orlando
Sentinel*, 1961–
   14. Yes
   15. OCLC: ORL
Books & Sets: 1–7,10–14,17–19,
26
Periodicals: 1,2,3(v.2–8,16–22,
35–36,45–),4(v.9, 1955),5,6(v.16,
1970–),7–9

PALATKA

**Putnam County Library System,
Palatka Public Library,** 216 Reid
St, 32077
Tel: 904-329-0126

   1. M,W,Th, 9-6; T, 9-9; F, 9-5;
Sa, 9-1
   2. Jo Waterhouse
   3. English, 300
   4. 2
   5. 75–100
   6. Southern states
   7. Tel: yes, NC (limited);
letter: yes, NC
   8. No
   9. No
   10. No
   11. No

   12. No
   13. In-house bibliography
(copies available to public)
   14. No
   15. N/AN
Books & Sets: 3,5,10–12
Periodicals: 4,5,7,8,

PENSACOLA

**Lelia Abercrombie Historical
Library-Pensacola Historical
Museum,** 405 S Adams St, 32501
Tel: 904-433-1559

   1. M-Sa, 9-4:30
   2. Norman Simons, Curator
   3. English, 2,000; Spanish, 10
   4. 100 Hollinger boxes;
genealogy vertical files, local
history files
   5. 120
   6. Escambia County, FL,
especially Pensacola and metropolitan Santa Rosa County
   7. Tel: yes, NC; letter: yes, NC
for brief queries; otherwise $5/hr
with 2-hr minimum
   8. Yes
   9. No
   10. No
   11. No
   12. No
   13. Typescript index and
calendar; card catalog
   14. Yes
   15. No

West Florida Regional Library
200 W Gregory St, 32501
Tel: 904-435-1763

   1. M-Th, 8-8; F,Sa, 8-5
   2. Dolly Pollard
   3. English, 1,500
   4. None
   5. 850
   6. Mostly Southeast: VA, NC,
SC, GA, FL, AL, also PA. Ex-
panding rest of Southeast, North
Central, and Northeast, with focus
still on the South. Also building
collection on Creek Indian
(eastern) genealogy
   7. Tel: no; letter: yes; cannot

do research but will give requests to volunteer, who charges fee

8. No
9. No
10. No
11. No
12. In process
13. N/AN
14. Yes
15. No

Books & Sets: 3,7(v.3),10,11,13,14,22,23,26
Periodicals: 1(v.52–54),4,8(v.65,68–70)

PORT CHARLOTTE

Port Charlotte Public Library
2280 Aaron St, 33952
Tel: 813-625-6470

1. M-W, 9-9 (M nights only during summer); Th, 1-5; F,Sa, 9-5
2. John Kavanagh, President; Joyce Hoffman
3. English, 420
4. None
5. None; Port Charlotte rents films from State Library
6. US
7. Tel & letter: yes, NC
8. No
9. No
10. No, but patrons may make copies
11. N/AP
12. Genealogy Society of Port Charlotte's newsletter, *Geneagram*, contains bibliography of library's collection
13. Card catalog
14. No
15. No

Books & Sets: 3,5,22
Periodicals: 4,8

SAINT PETERSBURG

St. Petersburg Public Library
3040 8th Ave N, 33713
Tel: 813-893-7928

1. M-Th, 9-9; F, Sa, 9-5:30
2. Caroline W. Everett

3. English, G, 748; 2,500, FL material; Spanish, few in FL collection
4. N/AP
5. 330: census; 39: Spanish land grants (FL)
6. Tampa Bay, FL state (LH); US, southeastern states (G)
7. Tel: yes, NC for brief queries; letter: yes, $2 minimum
8. No
9. No
10. No
11. No
12. No
13. N/AN
14. Yes
15. No

Books & Sets: 2,26
Periodicals: 1(1959–70),3(1970–72,1984),4(1955–79,1982–),7(1932–64),8(1960–),9(broken set)

SARASOTA

Selby Public Library
1001 Boulevard of the Arts, 33577
Tel: 813-951-5501

1. M,T,Th, 9-9; W,F,Sa, 9-6
2. Staffed by Genealogical Society volunteers
3. English, 1,700
4. 20, includes Jessop and Northrop books
5. None
6. US, Australia, Canada, England, Germany, Holland, Ireland, Scotland, Sweden, Wales, Barbados
7. Tel: no, if it involves research; letter: no
8. Yes
9. No
10. No
11. No
12. *Genealogical Holdings in Selby Library Genealogy Room* (publication of the Genealogical Society of Sarasota), $3 donation plus $1.20 postage
13. N/AN
14. No
15. N/AN

Books & Sets: 2,5,19,26(most indexes)
Periodicals: 1(incomplete),4,5,7–9

STARKE

Bradford County Public Library, 105 E Jackson St, 32091
Tel: 904-964-6400

1. M, 9-8; T-Th, 9-5; F, 9-5; Sa, 9-2
2. Arnold D. Weeks, Jr.
3. English, 80
4. N/AP
5. 145 reels, 100 fiche
6. Southeast US, especially GA, FL, SC
7. Tel: no; letter: yes, NC for brief queries, with SASE
8. No
9. No
10. Yes, but not genealogy books
11. No
12. No
13. N/AN
14. No
15. No

Books & Sets: 26
Periodicals: 4

TALLAHASSEE

Florida State Archives, Genealogy Collection, Division of Library and Information Services, R. A. Gray Bldg, 500 S Bronough St, 32399-0250
Tel: 904-487-2073

1. M,W,Th, 8-5; T, 8-8; F, 8-1
2. Richard Roberts, Public Services Section
3. English, 6,000
4. 400
5. 4,500
6. US, with emphasis on southeastern, mid-Atlantic, and New England states
7. Tel: no; letter: yes, NC except 25¢/copy
8. No
9. No

10. Decision on loan policy is pending

11. No

12. *Genealogy and Local History: A Bibliography*, $9 plus $2 postage

13. *Index to County Records, Index to 1845 Statehood Election Returns*

14. Yes

15. OCLC: FBA

Books & Sets: 2–5,7,10,11,17–19, 22,23,26

Periodicals: 1,3–5,7–9

State Library of Florida, Division of Library and Information Services (Local History Collection), R. A. Gray Bldg, 500 S Bronough St, 32399-0250
Tel: 904-487-2651

1. M-F, 8-5
2. Beverly Byrd, Florida Collection
3. English, 10,000; Spanish, 15-20, and French, 10-15 (early accounts of discovery, exploration, colonization)
4. 105
5. 887
6. FL, all areas and counties
7. Tel & letter: yes, NC (local history only)
8. No
9. No
10. Yes, if 2 copies are owned by State Library
11. No
12. No
13. *Reference Index* (subject/ geographic areas) and *Biography Index*
14. Yes
15. OCLC: FAB
Books & Sets: 1

TAMPA

Tampa-Hillsborough County Public Library System, Special Collections Department
900 N Ashley St, 33602
Tel: 813-223-8865

1. M-Th, 9-9; F, 9-6; Sa, 9-5
2. Joseph Hipp
3. N/AN
4. N/AN
5. N/AN
6. Original 13 colonies, southeastern US
7. Tel & letter: yes, NC
8. No
9. No
10. No
11. No
12. No
13. N/AN
14. Yes
15. N/AN
Books & Sets: 1–7,10–15,17–19, 22,24–26
Periodicals: 1,4–6,8,9

TITUSVILLE

North Brevard Public Library
2121 S Hopkins Ave, 32780
Tel: 305-269-7323

1. M-W, 9-9; Th,Sa, 9-5; F, 12-5
2. Verna G. Langlais
3. English, 900+
4. 8
5. 105
6. North America, Europe, Great Britain, Australia, China, Guatemala, Haiti, Japan
7. Tel: yes, NC; letter: yes, NC except 25¢/page copy charge for more than 3 pages
8. Nancy Sieck, volunteer, 1 day/week
9. No
10. Limited policy
11. Yes, in-county only
12. In-house publication, *Genealogy at the North Brevard Library*
13. N/AN
14. No
15. OCLC: Yes
Books & Sets: 2(v.42–125,160), 3(all plus 1987),4,7,8(microfiche), 10–12,26
Periodicals: 1(to 1982 only), 2(1980–82),3(v.39–48),4(v.23,25,

1969,1971,1974),8(1912,1914; v.56–59,63),9(1958–60,1966–)

WEST PALM BEACH

Historical Society of Palm Beach County, Palm Beach County Public Library, 3650 Summit Blvd, 33406
Tel: 305-471-1492

1. M-Th, 10-4; F, 10-1
2. Nan Dennison, Director
3. English, 500
4. N/AN
5. 20 oral history
6. Palm Beach County
7. Tel: yes, NC; letter: yes, plus copies and postage
8. No
9. No
10. No
11. No
12. No
13. N/AN
14. Yes
15. No

Palm Beach County Genealogical Society Library, 100 Clematis St, PO Box 1746, 33402
Tel: 305-832-3279

1. M-Sa, 10-5
2. Herbert C. Gee
3. English, 8,000; German, 2; Spanish, 8
4. Several hundred
5. 325
6. Southern states, New England, PA, Midwest
7. Tel: yes, NC; letter: yes, NC except for copies
8. N/AN
9. No
10. No
11. No
12. In preparation
13. N/AN
14. No
15. No
Books & Sets: 2,3,5,7(6 v. only),8, 19,26
Periodicals: 1,3(misc issues to 1980),4(1952–),5,7,8(1946–),9

GEORGIA

ALBANY

Dougherty County Public Library, 300 Pine Ave, 31701
Tel: 912-431-2900

1. M, 10-9; W, 10-4, 6-9;
F, 10-4; Sa, 1-4
2. James F. Forsyth, Genealogical Reference Librarian
3. English, 4,200
4. 350
5. 1,200, mostly 1820–1910 census
6. Primarily southeastern US
7. Tel & letter: yes, NC except for copies
8. James F. Forsyth
9. No
10. No
11. No
12. No
13. None
14. Yes
15. No
Books & Sets: 2(incomplete),3,
5(v.1–4),26
Periodicals: 4(1966–),8(1960–)

AMERICUS

Lake Blackshear Regional Library, 307 E Lamar St, 31709
Tel: 912-924-8091

1. M-Sa, 9-6; T, 9-9
2. N/AN
3. English, 4,000
4. 150
5. 1,000 (includes 525 GA courthouse records for 20 counties); 4,500 microfiche (Genealogy and Local History Collection, 1st installment)
6. GA state; SC, NC, VA, MD, PA, AL, TN
7. Tel: yes, NC; letter: yes,

charge for time and photocopies
8. No
9. No
10. No
11. No
12. No
13. Card catalog
14. No
15. No
Books & Sets: 1–3,7(v.1, NC only),10–14,26(11 v.)
Periodicals: 1(v.43–45),4(v.31–), (v.66–)

ATLANTA

Atlanta-Fulton Public Library
One Margaret Mitchell Square, 30303
Tel: 404-688-4636, ext 212, 292

1. M, 9-6; T-Th, 9-8; F, 9-6;
Sa, 10-6; Su, 2-6
2. Janice W. Sikes, Curator;
Joyce E. Jelks, Assistant Curator
3. English, 8,000; French, 3
4. None
5. 700–800 microfilm, 791 microfiche
6. Migratory route from New England through southeastern US to Texas; concentration on GA
7. Tel: no; letter; yes, NC except 10¢/copy
8. No
9. No
10. No
11. No
12. No
13. N/AN
14. Yes
15. No
Books & Sets: 1–4,6,7(v.1–6),
10–13,15–19,26
Periodicals: 1(1982–85),4(v.2–),5,
8(v.66–73, 1977–85),9

Atlanta Historical Society
Library, 3101 Andrews Dr NW, 30305
Tel: 404-261-1837, ext 109

1. M-F, 9-5:30; Sa, 9-5
2. Anne Salter, Librarian;
Bill Richards, Department Head;
Nancy Wight, Research Associate;
Don Rooney, Library Assistant
3. English, 17,000 on GA and Atlanta history, 300 on family history, 100 county histories, as well as city directories
4. 800
5. 18 reels of 1900 US Census that includes Atlanta and area counties
6. GA, with special emphasis on Atlanta
7. Tel & letter: yes, NC
8. Yes
9. No
10. No
11. No
12. *Guide to the Manuscripts Collection of the Atlanta Historical Society* (out of print). Copies available from gift shop
13. Card catalog, MS catalog, visual arts catalog, architectural drawings catalog
14. Yes
15. No
Books & Sets: 2,3

Genealogical Center Library
15 Dunwoody Park Rd, #130, 30338 (mailing address: Box 88100, 30356-8100)
Tel: 404-393-1135

1. M,W,Th, 10-3; T, 10-3, 7-9pm
2. Diane Dieterle
3. English, 10,000
4. 5

5. None
6. US, mainly GA, VA, IL, KY
7. Tel: yes, NC; letter: yes, NC, with SASE
8. Diane Dieterle
9. Yes, $2/day, or $20/year membership
10. Yes, $2/book only to library members; 2-week loan
11. N/AP
12. *Book Collection Catalog*, $5; included with membership
13. 37,000-name *Index to Indexes*, compiled from names which appear 10 or more times in the indexes of Library's books
14. No
15. No
Books & Sets: 1,3,5,26
Periodicals: 1,3–5,8,9

Georgia Department of Archives and History, Search Room
330 Capitol Ave, SE, 30345
Tel: 404-656-2350

1. M-F, 8-4:15; Sa, 9:30-3:15. Closed on Confederate Day, Memorial Day, and other national holidays
2. Sandra J. Boling
3. English, 20,000; German, 3; French, 13 (includes Louis Pierre d'Hosier, *Armorial Général de la France*, 11 vols)
4. 1,000
5. 30,000 rolls microfilm; 1,500 cards microfiche
6. Southeastern US, East Coast from MD southward, some New England
7. Tel: yes, NC, for general inquiries only about holdings; letter: yes, $1/copy, $2 minimum
8. No
9. No
10. No
11. No
12. Robert S. Davis, Jr., *Research in Georgia, with Special Emphasis on the Georgia Department of Archives and History*, 1981. Not an official publication, and Library does not sell it

13. N/AN
14. Yes
15. No
Books & Sets: 1,2(v.1–128, 134–40,150–51),3–6,7(v.1–3, 1969),9–13,16,18,26
Periodicals: 1(v.40–41,53–), 4(v.1–12 misc issues, 13–),5,7(rev ed, Boyer, 1983),8,9(v.4,79–80, 90,92–, various loose issues)

AUGUSTA

Augusta-Richmond County Public Library, 902 Greene St, 30901
Tel: 404-821-2600

1. M-F, 9-9; Sa, 9-5:30; Su, 2-5:30
2. Alice O. Walker
3. English, 2,000
4. None
5. 240
6. GA primarily
7. Tel: yes, NC; letter: yes, NC except for copies
8. Alice O. Walker
9. No
10. No
11. No
12. No
13. *Georgia Genealogy and Local History in the Augusta Regional Library; Genealogy, Local History, and Heraldry Books in the Augusta Regional Library*
14. No
15. No
Books & Sets: 3,7(1 v.),12,18, 26(3 v.)
Periodicals: 4(incomplete)

CANTON

Sequoyah Regional Library
400 E Main St, 30114
Tel: 404-479-3090

1. M,W,F, 9-5:30; T,Th, 9-8; Sa, 9-4
2. Joan Adams, Director
3. English, 120
4. None
5. 115

6. Primarily GA, all counties (books); census and newspapers of the region on microfilm. Library serves Cherokee, Gilmer, and Pickens Counties
7. Tel & letter: no. Requests are answered with list of qualified genealogists who will research for small fee
8. No
9. No
10. No
11. No
12. No
13. N/AN
14. Yes
15. No

CARROLLTON

West Georgia Regional Library
710 Rome St, 30117
Tel: 404-836-1325

1. M,Th, 9-8; T,W,F, 9-5:30; Sa, 9-4:30
2. Roni Willis
3. English, 1,000
4. N/AN
5. 1,000
6. GA state; parts of AL, SC, NC, VA, TN
7. Tel & letter: yes, NC
8. No
9. No
10. No
11. No
12. No
13. N/AN
14. No
15. No

CLARKESVILLE

Northeast Georgia Regional Library, Jefferson at Green St, PO Box 378, 30523
Tel: 404-754-4413

1. M, 9-8; T,W,Th,F, 9-5; Sa, 9-1
2. Emily Anthony
3. English, 650
4. Extensive file of family histories

5. 300
6. Southeastern US
7. Tel: yes, NC; letter: yes, NC except 15¢/copy
8. No
9. No
10. No
11. No
12. No
13. N/AN
14. Yes
15. No

COLUMBUS

Bradley Memorial Library
1120 Bradley Dr, 31995
Tel: 404-327-0211

1. M-Th, 9-9; F,Sa, 9-6; Su, 1:30-6:30
2. Brady Wilson
3. English, 3,000
4. N/AN
5. 1,000
6. All states; emphasis on colonial days
7. Tel: yes, NC for information only; letter: yes, NC except for copies
8. N/AN
9. No
10. No
11. No
12. No
13. N/AN
14. Yes
15. N/AN
Books & Sets: 2,3,5,7,10,11,19, 26(incomplete)
Periodicals: 1,4,8,9

DALTON

Dalton Regional Library
310 Cappes St, 30720
Tel: 404-278-4507

1. M,W,F, 9-6; T,Th, 9-8; Sa, 9-5
2. Eugenia Cavender, Director; Martha Hoole, Reference Librarian
3. English, 3,000
4. None

5. 200
6. Whitfield, Murray, Gordon, Catoosa Counties; northwestern GA; GA state
7. Tel & letter: yes, NC, on a limited basis
8 No
9. No
10. No
11. No
12. No
13. N/AN
14. No
15. No
Books & Sets: 3,6,7,19

DOUGLAS

Satilla Regional Library
701 E Ward St, 31533
Tel: 912-384-6450

1. M-F, 8-5:30; Sa, 9-1
2. Winifred Merier Gourley
3. English, 800
4. 1,000
5. 900
6. AL, FL, GA, KY, NC, SC, PA, TN, TX, VA
7. Tel: no; letter: yes, charge depends on information needed
8. Winifred Merier Gourley
9. No
10. No
11. No
12. No
13. N/AN
14. No
15. No
Books & Sets: 3(no suppls),7(v.1 only),26
Periodicals: 4(1967–),8(1978–)

FITZGERALD

Fitzgerald-Ben Hill County Library, 123 N Main St, 31750
Tel: 912-423-3642

1. M,W,F, 9-6; T,Th, 9-8; Sa, 9-5
2. Barbara MacDonald
3. English, 1,000
4. N/AN
5. 733

6. GA
7. Tel: no; letter: yes, $10 out-of-county fee/year
8. J. Sara Laidler
9. No
10. Yes, with valid Ben Hill County library card
11. No
12. No
13. Card catalog, lists of county-related information
14. Yes
15. No
Books & Sets: 3
Periodicals: 4(1972–77),8(v.74, 1985)

JONESBORO

Clayton County Library System Headquarters, 865 Battlecreek Rd, 30236
Tel: 404-478-5143

1. M-Th, 9-9; F,Sa, 9-6
2. N/AN
3. English, 800
4. None
5. 75
6. GA state, especially Clayton, Henry, Fayette Counties; some NC, SC, VA, MD
7. Tel: yes, NC; letter: yes, NC except for copies
8. No
9. No
10. No
11. No
12. No
13. None
14. No
15. No
Books & Sets: 3,5
Periodicals: 4(1977–),8(1985–), 9(incomplete)

LAFAYETTE

LaFayette-Walker County Library, PO Box 707, 305 S Duke St, 30728
Tel: 404-638-2992

1. M,W,F, 9-6; T,Th, 9-8; Sa, 9-5

2. None; librarians will assist
3. English, 1,000+
4. None
5. 300
6. GA, SC, NC, TN primarily
7. Tel: no, but will answer general questions; letter: yes, NC except 15¢/copy. Refer to Historical Society for detailed queries
8. No
9. No
10. No
11. No
12. No
13. None at this time
14. No. Refer to Historical Society
15. No
Books & Sets: 2,7(v.1),26(5 v.)
Periodicals: 4,5(v.15, 1976), 8(some back issues)

MACON

Washington Memorial Library
1180 Washington Ave, 31201
Tel: 912-744-0820/0821

1. M, 9-9; T-Sa, 9-6
2. Willard L. Rocker, Chief of Genealogy
3. English, 15,000+; German, 6
4. N/AN
5. 5,000
6. Area east of Mississippi River, with emphasis on 13 original colonies. Foreign collection on England, Ireland, Scotland, Wales; general books on German research
7. Tel: yes, NC for general questions; letter: yes, NC except 20¢/copy with SASE
8. Amateur genealogists or certified librarian
9. No
10. No
11. No, but will make copies if pages are specified; 20¢/copy
12. No
13. N/AN
14. No
15. No
Books & Sets: 2–5,7,10–14,19,23, 26
Periodicals: 4–9

MARIETTA

Cobb County Public Library
30 Atlanta St SE, 30060
Tel: 404-423-2333

1. M,Th,F,Sa, 10-6; T,W, 10-9:30
2. Steven R. Bedworth
3. English, 4,000; French, 6
4. None
5. 1,120
6. Marietta, Cobb County, GA; southeastern US
7. Tel & letter: yes, NC except 15¢/copy with SASE
8. No
9. Yes, $10 for nonresident borrower's card (State of GA only)
10. No
11. No
12. *List of Genealogical Materials in the Cobb County Public Library System* (not available for purchase)
13. Listing of subjects in Cobb County and GA vertical files; card file of historical holdings; listing of GA historical materials
14. Yes
15. No
Books & Sets: 2(broken set),3–5, 7(v.1, NC),9–13,26
Periodicals: 4(v.18,1964–),5,7, 8(v.22, v.46–)

MILLEDGEVILLE

Georgia College, Ina Dillard Russell Library, 231 W Hancock St, 31061
Tel: 912-453-5573

1. M-Th, 7:30am-10pm; F, 7:30-5; Sa, 1-5; Su, 2-10
2. Nancy Davis Bray
3. English, 150
4. 10
5. None
6. Primarily GA, especially Baldwin, Putnam, Wilkinson, Washington, Hancock, and Jones Counties
7. Tel: yes, NC; letter: yes, NC except for copies

8. No
9. No
10. No
11. N/AP
12. No
13. N/AN
14. No
15. No
Books & Sets: 6

MOULTRIE

Moultrie-Colquitt County Library, 204 5th St SE, 31768
Tel: 912-985-6540

1. M-Sa, 8:30-5:30; T, 8:30-8
2. Melody S. Jenkins
3. English, 5,000
4. None
5. 452
6. Southwestern GA
7. Tel: yes, NC; letter: yes, NC except for copies
8. No
9. No
10. No
11. No
12. No
13. N/AN
14. No
15. No
Books & Sets: 2
Periodicals: 4

PERRY

Houston County Public Library
1201 Washington Ave, 31069
Tel: 912-987-3050

1. M,W-Sa, 9-6; T, 9-9
2. N/AN
3. N/AN
4. 260
5. 45
6. Houston County, GA state
7. Tel: yes, NC; letter: yes, NC except 15¢/copy
8. No
9. No
10. No
11. No
12. No
13. N/AN

14. No
15. No

ROME

Sara Hightower Regional Library (Special Collections)
606 W First St, 30161
Tel: 404-291-7568

1. M-Th, 9-9; F, 9-6; Sa, 9-5
2. Jacqueline D. Kinzer, Curator
3. English, 8,000
4. 2
5. Local/Misc, 90; pre-1940 newspapers, 65; census, 320
6. Rome, Floyd County, GA state; the Southeast; Cherokee Indians
7. Tel: yes, NC; letter: yes, $2 minimum
8. Yes
9. $10/year for out-of-region patrons to charge out materials; no charge for in-house use
10. No
11. No
12. No
13. Pamphlet: *Abbreviated Guide to Historical and Genealogical Collections and Information*
14. No
15. No
Books & Sets: 2,3,5,7,11
Periodicals: 4,5,7–9

SAVANNAH

Chatham-Effingham-Liberty Regional Library, 2002 Bull St, 31499-4301
Tel: 912-234-5127

1. M-Th, 9-9; F, 9-6; Sa, 10:30-6; Su, 2-6
2. Janet C. Langford
3. English, 3,000+
4. 1
5. 804+; also, 224 years of local newspaper, indexed, 1763–
6. GA state; southeastern states

7. Tel & letter: yes, NC except for copies
8. No
9. No
10. Yes
11. No
12. No
13. *Genealogical Sources—Georgia Collection*
14. Yes
15. OCLC: GSC partially
Books & Sets: 3,4,10,11,26(incomplete)
Periodicals: 4(1977–84),8(1981–)

Georgia Historical Society
501 Whitaker St, 31499
Tel: 912-651-2128

1. M-F, 10-5; Sa, 9-1
2. Kaye Kole, Genealogy Committee Chairman
3. Collections are intermixed, not separate, and therefore uncounted
4. In 300-500 Hollinger boxes
5. 300 plus census
6. GA, the Southeast
7. Tel: yes, NC, if short answer, otherwise request in writing; letter: yes, NC except $5 minimum for copies
8. Kaye Kole and George Mulholland, qualified volunteer genealogists
9. No
10. No
11. No
12. No
13. Collections have "working folders": item-by-item descriptions
14. Yes
15. OCLC: soon
    RLIN: soon
Books & Sets: 3,5,7,26
Periodicals: 9

STATESBORO

Statesboro Regional Library
Main St South & Grady, 30458
Tel: 912-764-7573

1. M-Sa, 8:30-5:30
2. Henrietta Royal
3. English, 4,000

4. 650
5. 250
6. GA, SC, NC, VA
7. Tel: yes, NC except 10¢/copy; letter: yes, NC
8. Henrietta Royal
9. No
10. No
11. No
12. *Statesboro Regional Library System: A Bibliography of Holdings in Genealogy in all Branches*, $25
13. N/AN
14. Yes
15. No
Books & Sets: 10,26
Periodicals: 4

VALDOSTA

South Georgia Regional Library
300 Woodrow Wilson Dr, 31602
Tel: 912-333-5285/6

1. M-Th, 10-9; F,Sa, 10-5:30; Su, 2:30-5:30
2. Roddelle Folsom, Director
3. English, 1,775
4. None
5. 376: Valdosta *Daily Times*
6. Mostly GA state; some SC, NC, VA
7. Tel & letter: yes, NC
8. No
9. No
10. No
11. No
12. No
13. Card index of names; card catalog
14. No
15. N/AN
Books & Sets: 2,3

VIDALIA

Ohoopee Regional Library, John E. Ladson, Jr., Genealogical and Historical Foundation Library Branch, 119 Church St, 30474
Tel: 912-537-8186

1. M-F, 9-1, 2-6; Sa, 10-1
2. Emilie K. Hartz

3. English, 11,500
4. None
5. 2,600
6. All states, but primarily New England, mid-Atlantic; VA, NC, SC, GA, TN, KY
7. Tel & letter: no
8. No
9. No
10. No
11. No
12. *Family Histories in the John E. Ladson, Jr., Historical and Genealogical Foundation Library,* $25
13. N/AP
14. No
15. No

Books & Sets: 2(incomplete),7,10, 26(10 v.)
Periodicals: 4(1957–),8(incomplete),9(1847–1976)

HAWAII

HONOLULU

Bishop Museum Library
1525 Bernice St, 96817
Tel: 808-848-4147

1. M-F, 10-3; Sa, 9-12, except holiday weekends
2. Marguerite K. Ashford, Head Librarian
3. Collection totals 90,000 vols. Some G/LH materials are also in Hawaiian and in other Pacific islands languages
4. 2,500 cu ft
5. 50
6. Hawaii, Pacific islands
7. Tel & letter: yes, NC
8. No
9. No
10. No
11. No. Copies made by the Genealogical Society of Utah are available for purchase through them
12. *Dictionary Catalog of Bernice P. Bishop Museum Library* (9 vols & 2 suppls)
13. In-house inventories and finding aids, including one summarizing genealogical holdings
14. No
15. No

Hawaiian Historical Society
560 Kawaiahao St, 96813
Tel: 808-537-6271

1. M-F, 10-4
2. Barbara Dunn
3. English, 11,000; Hawaiian, 1,000
4. 21 linear ft
5. Primarily newspapers
6. Hawaii, the Pacific (Polynesia)

7. Tel: yes, NC; letter: yes, $5/request, which covers some copying
8. No
9. No
10. No
11. No
12. No
13. Card catalog
14. No
15. No

Hawaii State Archives
Iolani Palace Grounds, 96813
Tel: 808-548-2355

1. M-F, 7:45-4:30, except state and federal holidays
2. No separate section
3. English, 3,700; Hawaiian, some
4. 450
5. 1,000
6. Hawaiian Islands
7. Tel & letter: yes, NC for brief queries; otherwise, $5/hour
8. No
9. No
10. No
11. No
12. No
13. Various indexes and finding aids
14. No
15. No

Hawaii State Library
478 S King St, 96813
Tel: 808-548-4165

1. M,W,F,Sa, 9-5; T,Th, 9-8
2. Sandra Ann Kolloge, Language, Literature, and History Section; Proserfina Strona, Hawaii and Pacific Section
3. English, 5,000; Korean, 1
4. None

5. 60-75 rolls
6. Collection of local DAR chapter once housed in this library, related to early American immigrants. Collection now includes basic materials for immigrants to the US from a number of areas. The Hawaii and Pacific Section houses several items related to Hawaiians' genealogy as well as items available from the US Archives, census records, etc.
7. Tel & letter: yes, NC except 25¢/copy
8. No
9. No
10. Some guides and handbooks, which circulate on 2-week loan, with one renewal allowed
11. No
12. *Genealogical Sources in the Hawaii and Pacific Section of the Hawaii State Library: A Bibliography*
13. In-house computer catalog
14. Yes
15. No
Books & Sets: 1,2(index only),3–5, 7,10–13,17–19,22–24,26
Periodicals: 1(1973–84),4(1972–), 5,7,8(1982–),9

LAIE

Brigham Young University, Joseph F. Smith Library
Kulanui St, 96744
Tel: 808-293-3878

1. M-Th, 7am-11pm; F, 7am-9pm; Sa, 9-3
2. Reference librarian
3. English, 100; German, 15
4. 250+
5. 50+
6. England, US, Hawaii, Germany

7. Tel & letter: yes, NC
8. No
9. No
10. Yes

11. No
12. No, all holdings retrieved from on-line catalog
13. N/AN

14. No
15. OCLC: yes
Books & Sets: 1,3,5,19
Periodicals: 1,4,8

IDAHO

BOISE

Boise Public Library
715 S Capitol Blvd, 83702
Tel: 208-384-4076

1. T,W,Th, 10-9; F, 10-6;
Sa, 1-5; Su (Sept-May), 1-5
2. William J. Wilson, Librarian, Pacific Northwest Room
3. English, 6,100
4. N/AN
5. 7 rolls, Boise City Directory
6. Boise, Ada County; ID, OR, WA, MT
7. Tel & letter: yes, NC except for copies
8. No
9. No
10. No
11. No
12. Western Library Network
13. Card index (topics) to Idaho Pamphlet file; card index (subject) to articles published in Pacific Northwest magazines
14. No
15. No, WLN: IdB
Books & Sets: 26

Idaho State Historical Society, Genealogical Library
325 W State St, 83702
Tel: 208-334-2305

1. M,Th,F, 9-5; T,W, 9-9
(closed evenings July, Aug)
2. Frieda O. March
3. English, 7,700; German, 3
4. Many
5. 1,200
6. US, England, some Switzerland and Germany
7. Tel & letter: yes, $5/request
8. Frieda O. March

9. No
10. No
11. No
12 In progress
13. N/AN
14. Yes
15. No
Books & Sets: 2,3,5,7,8,10–12, 15,16,18,24–26
Periodicals: 1,3–5,7–9

KETCHUM

Community Library, Regional History Department, 415 Spruce Ave North, PO Box 2168, 83340
Tel: 208-726-3493

1. M,W, 9-5; T,Th-Sa, 1-5
2. Ginger Piotter
3. English, 12
4. Oral histories, 375; photographs, 3,707; MSS, 661
5. 101 reels, newspaper collection
6. Wood River Valley, mid and southeastern ID
7. Tel: yes, NC; letter: yes, NC except 15¢/copy
8. No
9. $5 deposit returnable after 6 months for library card (no charge for Regional History Dept)
10. Yes, through ILL only
11. No
12. No
13. N/AN
14. No
15. No

MOSCOW

University of Idaho Library
83843
Tel: 208-885-6534

1. 40 hrs/week
2. N/AN
3. English, German, N/AP
4. N/AP
5. N/AP
6. ID, Pacific Northwest
7. Tel & letter: yes, NC
8. No
9. No
10. Yes, through ILL
11. Yes, through ILL
12. No
13. N/AN
14. No
15. No
Books & Sets: 1,3,6,10–14

REXBURG

Ricks College, McKay Library
525 S Center (mail address), 83440
Tel: 208-356-2376

1. Winter: M-F, 7am-10pm;
Sa, 10-6; summer: M-Th, 8-8;
F, 8-5
2. Blaine R. Bake
3. English, 15,000; German, 50
4. 1,000
5. 10,000
6. US, with emphasis on western US, ID state
7. Tel & letter: yes, NC
8. Blaine R. Bake
   Neal Southwick
9. No
10. Yes
11. No
12. No
13. N/AN
14. No
15. N/AN
Books & Sets: 1,3–8,10–14,16,17, 19,22,23,26
Periodicals: 1,3(1954–),4–9

ALTON

**Alton Area Historical
Society Research Library**
121 E Broadway, 62002
Tel: N/AN

1. Th-Su, 1-4 (and by appointment)
2. Sister Mary Ursula Diebold, OSU (618-465-9112)
3. English: 1 ref; other, alphabetical vertical file
4. 20+ scrapbooks on families
5. N/AN
6. Greater Alton area, including Bethalto, Brighton, East Alton, Wood River
7. Tel & letter: yes, donations accepted
8. Sister Mary Ursula Diebold, OSU
9. No, but donations accepted
10. No, but policy is being considered
11. N/AN
12. No
13. N/AN
14. No
15. No

**Haynor Public Library District,
Main Library,** 326 Belle St, 62002
Tel: 618-462-0651

1. M-Th, 8-8; F, 8-5; Sa, 9-5; Su (Sept-May), 2-5
2. Katherine Bouman, Adult Services Librarian
3. English, 1,400
4. 10
5. 437 (407 of *Alton Evening Telegraph*, 1836–)
6. Alton, IL; surrounding communities in Madison County

7. Tel: yes, NC for brief queries; letter: yes, $5/hr, $1/copy
8. No
9. No
10. No
11. No
12. Lewis & Clark Library System, *Where to Dig It Up: A Genealogy and Local History Guide Book* (1982)
13. Indexes to *Alton Evening Telegraph*, 1836–1933, 1980–85
14. No
15. No
Periodicals: 4(1965–),8(1968–72, 1978–81, incomplete),9(v.49–72, incomplete)

ARLINGTON HEIGHTS

**Arlington Heights Memorial
Library,** 500 N Dunton Ave, 60004
Tel: 312-392-0100

1. M-F, 9-1; Sa, 9-5; Su, 12-5
2. Nancy E. Bodner
3. Total 4,000
4. None
5. 100 (also have microfiche)
6. US, primarily IL and surrounding states. Some foreign; mostly basic guides to research
7. Tel & letter: N/AN
8. N/AN
9. No
10. Yes
11. No
12. No
13. N/AN
14. N/AN
15. OCLC: JBL
Books & Sets: 1,3–13,16,21,23,24
Periodicals: 1,3–5,8,9

BARRINGTON

Barrington Area Library
505 N Northwest Highway, 60010
Tel: 312-382-1300

1. M-Th, 9-9; F,Sa, 9-5; Su, 1-5
2. Mila Bryan, Head, Adult Services; Nancy Allan, Reference Librarian (Genealogy)
3. English, 200
4. Lines Collection: MS history of Barrington, genealogies, lists of cemetery inscriptions
5. 29 reels of US censuses, 1840–1910, of Barrington and portions of Cook, Lake, Kane, and McHenry Counties; 1 reel of unpublished history of Barrington
6. Barrington area of northeastern IL; Cook, Lake, Kane, and McHenry Counties; Chicago and other suburbs
7. Tel: yes, NC; letter: yes, minimal charge with SASE
8. No
9. No
10. No
11. No
12. *Genealogy: Adult Services Bibliography IX* (22 pp); *Genealogy Update* (2 pp); price = copying (10¢/page) and postage
13. Surname index to Barrington genealogies
14. Yes
15. No
Books & Sets: 1,10–12,17,26 (ME,MA,NH,RI,VT,CT)
Periodicals: 4(1978–)

BELLEVILLE

Belleville Public Library
121 E Washington St, 62220
Tel: 618-234-0441 (ask for Archives)

1. M-Th, 9-9; F,Sa, 9-5
(shorter hours in summer)
2. Lou Ann James
3. English, 1,500; German, 7;
classical languages, some
4. 50, plus more than 100
group sheets in binders
5. 1,100; microfiche of births
and marriages
6. Belleville, St. Clair County,
IL; states east of Mississippi River;
Great Britain, Germany, some
Europe
7. Tel: no, unless brief; letter:
yes, $10/hr plus copies and postage
8. No
9. No
10. Yes
11. No, but will make copies at
50¢/sheet
12. *Bibliography of the
Archives Collection*, $8 ($10 by
mail prepaid); *Bibliography of the
Archives Collection Supplement I*
($10, $12 by mail prepaid)
13. Card files: obituaries from
Belleville newspapers (1940–52,
incomplete to 1980, 1980–), St.
Clair County burials, name and
subject index to Belleville newspapers articles (1840–1940), index to
East St. Louis newspapers
(1865–1936)
14. Yes
15. No
Books & Sets: 2(v.1–6,15–17,19,
21,43–49,54–55,57–129,133–34,
136,140–43,146,148,150–52,
154–66),3,26(8 v. only: CT, MA,
NC,PA,VA,RI,SC,VT)
Periodicals: 4(microfiche: v.4–15,
1950–61; magazines: v.16,17,19,
20–35,36,37–40),7(1 v.),8(v.66)

**St. Clair County Historical
Society Library**
701 E Washington St, 62220
Tel: 618-234-0600

1. M-W,F,Sa, 12-3; Su, 2-4;
closed Th
2 Cleo Ford
3. English, 50
4. 20
5. N/AP

6. St. Clair County, IL state
7. Tel & letter: no
8. No
9. No
10. No
11. No
12. No
13. None
14. No
15. No

BELLWOOD

Bellwood Public Library
600 Bohland Ave, 60104
Tel: 312-547-7393

1. M-Th, 9:30-9; F, 9:30-6;
Sa, 9:30-4
2. Adult Services Librarian
3. English, 30
4. N/AN
5. N/AN
6. Bellwood, IL
7. Tel & letter: yes, NC
8. No
9. No
10. No
11. N/AN
12. No
13. N/AN
14. No
15. No
Periodicals: 4(1968–80)

BLOOMINGTON

**Bloomington-Normal
Genealogical Library**
201 E Grove St, 61701
Tel: 309-827-0428

1. T-Su, 1-5
2. N/AN
3. English, 2,000; German, 1
4. 2,000
5. 25
6. IL, eastern states
7. Tel: yes, NC; letter: yes, $5
8. No
9. No
10. Yes, to members of Genealogical Society
11. No
12. No

13. Two shelf lists
14. No
15. No
Books & Sets: 5(v.1–6)
Periodicals: 4,8,9

Bloomington Public Library
205 E Olive St, PO Box 3308,
61702-3308
Tel: 309-828-6091

1. M-Th, 9-9; F,Sa, 9-5; Su,
1-5 (Sept-May)
2. Lois Wood
Mary Wilkins
3. English, 4,000
4. None. Library has clippings
file that contains newspaper clippings on local history as well as
pamphlets, brochures, letters: 66 ft
5. 1,080
6. Bloomington-Normal,
McLean County, IL
7. Tel: no; letter: yes, $1/first
copy, 10¢/page thereafter; 25¢/
microfilm copy
8. No
9. No
10. Yes, selected titles through
ILL
11. No
12. *Leafing Out the Family
Tree,* free of charge
13. Card catalog index of local
newspaper
14. No
15. OCLC: yes
Books & Sets: 3,16,26

CANTON

**Parlin-Ingersoll Library, Fulton
County Historical and Genea-
logical Society Collection**
205 W Chestnut St, 61520
Tel: 309-647-0328; 647-0771,
Dr. Bordner

1. M-Sa, 9-6; Su, 12-4
2. Dr. Marjorie R. Bordner,
President, Fulton County Society
3. English, 600
4. 10
5. 50

6. Fulton County, Spoon River country, IL
7. Tel: no; letter: yes, $5/hr plus copy and postage costs
8. Betty Gibboney
9. No
10. No
11. No
12. No
13. N/AN
14. Yes
15. N/AN
Books & Sets: 3,7
Periodicals: 4(1970–),8(1970–)

CARTERVILLE

Shawnee Library System
Greenbriar Rd, 62918
Tel: 618-985-3711

1. M-Th, 8:30-8; F,Sa, 8:30-5
2. Judy Tippy, Special Collections Librarian
3. English, 6,450
4. None
5. 1,688 (mostly IL federal census)
6. Extreme Southern IL; KY, IN, NC, SC, TN, VA; some PA, OH, IN; southeastern US, East Coast, MO, AR, OK (Cherokee)
7. Tel & letter: no
8. No
9. No
10. Yes, $5/title to out-of-state borrowers
11. Yes, same as above. IL federal census loaned only to Southern IL libraries. Microfiche: will search and copy early land records, index to Adjutant General's Report
12. *Combined Bibliography of the Genealogy Collection* (1976, out of print), and *Supplement I* (1980), $7. Cumulative catalog in progress
13. New acquisitions shown in *Newsletter* of the Genealogy Society of Southern Illinois (c/o John A. Logan College, Carterville, 62918)
14. Yes
15. OCLC: IUI

Books & Sets: 1(no suppls), 2(v.43–83, incomplete),3–5,7, 10–14, 17,18(v.1–45,74–146),22, 23,24(l v. only),26
Periodicals: 1(v.34, 1958–), 4(1969–72,1973–),5(1963–),7, 8(1956–),9(index only)

CHICAGO

Newberry Library
60 W Walton St, 60610
Tel: 312-943-9090

1. T-Th, 11-7:30; F,Sa, 9-5
2. David T. Thackery
3. English, 100,000+
4. 1,000+ vertical file items
5. 10,000+
6. LH: US, Canada, British Isles; transcriptions of local records: New England, mid-Atlantic states, Midwest, South, Gulf states, eastern Canada, some British Isles; G: continental Europe, primarily on heraldry and nobility
7. Tel: yes, only queries re holdings; letter: yes, NC for brief queries, donations welcome
8. Yes
9. No, but $10 donation requested
10. No
11. No
12. In progress
13. N/AN
14. Yes
15. OCLC: IBV (post-1977 acquisitions only)
Books & Sets: 1–26
Periodicals: 1–9

CHICAGO HEIGHTS

Chicago Heights Free Public Library, 15th & Chicago Rd, 60411
Tel: 312-754-0323

1. M,T,W, 9-9; Th,F,Sa, 9-5
2. Barbara Paul
3. English, 50
4. 10
5. 100
6. City of Chicago Heights;

Bloom Township
7. Tel: no; letter: yes, $2 per immigration/naturalization record found; charge for copies
8. No
9. No
10. No
11. No
12. No
13. Obituary index to *Chicago Heights Star*, 1906-69, 1975–; index to naturalization petitions, City Court of Chicago Heights, 1900-40
14. No
15. No

DANVILLE

Danville Public Library
307 N Vermilion St, 61832
Tel: 217-446-7420 (ask for Archives)

1. M,T, 5:30-8; W, 9-12; Th, 9-1; F, 12-3:30; Sa, 9-5:30
2. Phillip Cohee
3. English, 2,000
4. N/AN
5. 1,800
6. Vermilion County, IL state; IN, OH, PA, VA, NY, NJ, KY
7. Tel: yes, NC for brief queries; letter: yes, NC except 15¢/copy
8. No
9. No
10. No
11. No
12. No
13. N/AN
14. No
15. No
Books & Sets: 2,3,5,7,10–14
Periodicals: 4,5,7,8,9(none after 1985)

DECATUR

Decatur Genealogical Library
355 N Main St, PO Box 2205, 62526
Tel: 217-429-0135

1. M, 10-8:30; W,Sa, 10-4
2. Carolynne Jean Cearlock, Librarian

3. English, 4,000
4. 35
5. 311
6. US; some foreign
7. Tel: no; letter: yes, $3/member, $5/nonmember
8. Rosella Vohs
9. Yes, $1/day for nonmembers
10. Yes, to members only
11. No
12. *Decatur Genealogical Library Holdings*
13. Card catalog
14. Yes
15. No
Books & Sets: 2–5,7,8,26
Periodicals: 1–5,8,9

Decatur Public Library
247 E North St, 62523
Tel: 217-428-6617, ext 135

1. M, 1-3, 6-8; W, 10:30-12, 1-3; Sa, 10:30-12, 1-3
2. Jerald A. Merrick
3. English, 200+
4. Oral histories: 85
5. 1,920, mostly newspapers and some census
6. Decatur, Macon County; contiguous counties in IL state
7. Tel: prefer letter or visit; letter: yes, fee revision in process
8. No
9. No
10. No
11. No
12. No
13. Card catalog; *Decatur Herald & Review*, news and obituary indexes; small booklists
14. No. Refer to local genealogical library
15. No
Books & Sets: 26
Periodicals: 4

Macon County Historical Society Library, 5580 North Fork Rd, 62521
Tel: 217-422-4919

1. Office: M-F, 8-4; Museum, T-F, 1-4, also Sa,Su

2. N/AN
3. English, 1,335 (528 relate to local area, 807 to 19th or early 20th century); German, 6–10
4. 750
5. None
6. Macon County, IL state
7. Tel: no; letter: yes, NC
8. No
9. No
10. No
11. N/AP
12. No
13. Card catalog for books and pamphlets
14. No
15. No

DE KALB

De Kalb Public Library
309 Oak St, 60115
Tel: 815-756-9568

1. M-F, 9-9; Sa, 9-5; Su, 1-5 Sept-May
2. Urla M. Golden
3. English, 900
4. None
5. N/AN
6. DeKalb County
7. Tel: no; letter: yes, $1 minimum for copies, $5 minimum for research
8. No
9. No
10. Yes, through ILL
11. No
12. No
13. N/AN
14. No
15. No
Books & Sets: 3,4,7,10,12
Periodicals: 3(1963–65),4(1961–), 9(1981–83)

DUNDEE

Dundee Township Library
55 Barrington Ave, 60118
Tel: 312-428-3661

1. M-Th, 9-9; F,Sa, 9-5:30
2. Abbey LaVell, Local History

3. English, 255
4. None
5. 139
6. Dundee Township and immediate area
7. Tel & letter: yes, NC
8. No
9. No
10. No
11. No
12. No
13. N/AN
14. No
15. No

EDWARDSVILLE

Southern Illinois University at Edwardsville, Archives, Lovejoy Library, 62026
Tel: 618-692-2665

1. M-F, 8:30-4:30
2. Louisa Bowen
3. English, 5,000; German, 200; other, 5,000 (mostly Slavic and East European-American imprints)
4. 100
5. 200
6. Southwestern IL, IL state; greater St. Louis, MO, Mississippi Valley
7. Tel: no; letter: yes, NC except for copies
8. No
9. No
10. Yes, through ILL
11. No
12. *Guide to Research Collections* (1971), $5
13. *National Inventory of Documentary Sources in the U.S.*, Part 4
14. No
15. OCLC: IAT
Books & Sets: 1,3(1981),6,17
Periodicals: 9(1940–75)

ELGIN

Gail Borden Public Library District, 200 N Grove Ave, 60120
Tel: 312-742-2411

1. M-Th, 9-9; F,Sa, 9-5:30;

Su, 2-5; summer: M, 9-9; T-Sa,
9-5:30
   2. Jan Halvorsen
   3. English, 2,500
   4. Vertical file of unpublished
family histories
   5. 84
   6. US, with emphasis on IL,
PA, KY, OH, NY
   7. Tel & letter: no
   8. No
   9. No
   10. No
   11. No
   12. No
   13. N/AN
   14. Yes
   15. No
Books & Sets: 1,2(incomplete),3,
4,7(v.7),10–14,18,26(PA,CT,
MD,NC,SC,NY only)
Periodicals: 4(v.14, 1960 incomplete),5(1962 incomplete),7,
8(v.51, 1963; v.56, 1968; v.66,
1978),9(incomplete)

ELMHURST

**Library of Chicago Genealogical
Society,** 129 Berteau Ave, 60126
Tel: 312-834-7491

   1. Open to Genealogical
Society members only
   2. Mildred R. Smith
   3. English, 250
   4. None
   5. None
   6. US
   7. Tel & letter: yes, NC to
members
   8. N/AN
   9. No charge to members
   10. Yes, to members only,
4-week loan
   11. N/AP
   12. No
   13. Quarterly for members lists
updates
   14. Yes
   15. No

ELMWOOD PARK

Elmwood Park Public Library
4 Conti Parkway, 60635
Tel: 312-453-7645

   1. M-Th, 9-9; F, 9-6; Sa, 9-5
   2. Russell Parker
   3. English, 40
   4. None
   5. None
   6. Elmwood Park, Chicago,
Leyden Township, IL
   7. Tel & letter: yes, NC
   8. No
   9. No
   10. Yes; reference copies may
go out for 2 days
   11. No
   12. No
   13. N/AN
   14. No
   15. No

EVANSTON

Evanston Public Library
1703 Orrington Ave, 60201
Tel: 312-866-0305

   1. M-Th, 9-9; F, 9-6; Sa, 9-5;
Su, 1-5
   2. Martha Quinn, Head,
Reference Dept
   3. English, 1,000
   4. None
   5. 25 black oral history tapes
   6. Evanston, IL
   7. Tel & letter: yes, NC except
$2 up to 5 copies, then 50¢/copy
   8. No
   9. No
   10. No
   11. No
   12. No
   13. Card catalog, computerized
on CLSI
   14. No
   15. OCLC: IHE
Books & Sets: 1,6,10–12,26

FLORA

**Cumberland Trail Library
System,** 12th & McCawley, 62839
Tel: 618-662-2679

   1. M-F, 7:30-5:30
   2. Leigh Ann Smith
   3. English, 100
   4. None
   5. 30
   6. Southern IL
   7. Tel & letter: yes, NC
   8. No
   9. No
   10. Yes
   11. Yes
   12. Yes, but no longer in print;
photocopies only
   13. N/AN
   14. No
   15. OCLC: IEZ
Books & Sets: 10–14

FRANKLIN PARK

**Franklin Park Public Library
District,** 10311 W Grand Ave,
60131
Tel: 312-455-6016

   1. M-Th, 9-9; F,Sa, 9-5;
Su, 1-5
   2. Mark Johnson
   3. English, 50
   4. None
   5. 6
   6. Franklin Park, Leyden
Township, Cook County, Chicago
metropolitan area
   7. Tel & letter: yes, NC
   8. No
   9. No
   10. Yes, 4-week loan
   11. No
   12. No
   13. None
   14. No
   15. No
Books & Sets: 3
Periodicals: 4(1978–)

FREEPORT

Freeport Public Library
314 W Stephenson St, 61032
Tel: 815-235-9606

1. M-Th, 9-9; F, 9-6; Sa, 9-5; Su, 1-4
2. John Locascio
3. English, 500
4. None
5. 800
6. Freeport, Stephenson County, northwestern IL
7. Tel & letter: yes, charge for copies or time
8. No
9. No
10. Yes, through ILL
11. Yes, microfilm of local newspapers through ILL
12. No
13. Index to births, deaths in Freeport newspaper
14. Yes
15. No
Books & Sets: 2(incomplete), 19(2 v., 1950,1972),26
Periodicals: 4(1968–),9(1900–49, 1969–)

GENEVA

Geneva Public Library District
127 James St, 60134
Tel: 312-232-0780

1. M-F, 9-9; Sa, 9-5
2. Jeanne Hintze
3. English, LH, 200
4. None
5. Census, newspapers
6. IL state
7. Tel & letter: no
8. No
9. No
10. Yes, 4-week loan
11. No
12. No
13. N/AN
14. Yes
15. No
Books & Sets: 2

GLENVIEW

Glenview Public Library
1930 Glenview Rd, 60025
Tel: 312-729-7500

1. M-F, 9-9; Sa, 9-5; Su, 2-5 (Sept-May)
2. Sally E. Morris, Reference Librarian
3. English, 500
4. 50; many brief family histories
5. 30, census; 50, local newspapers, 1930–; 5, Kennicott Papers
6. US, with emphasis on Midwest, especially Chicago area, Glenview
7. Tel & letter: yes, NC
8. No
9. No
10. No
11. No
12. No
13. Card catalog
14. No
15. No
Books & Sets: 3,10,11
Periodicals: 4(1977–),8(1969–71)

GRANITE CITY

Granite City Public Library
2001 Delmar Ave, 62040
Tel: 618-452-6238

1. Sept-May: M-Th, 9-9; F,Sa, 9-5; June-Aug: M,W, 9-9; T,Th-Sa, 9-5
2. Jeanette L. Kampen, Assistant Director
3. English, 550
4. None
5. 360: federal census; 250: Granite City newspapers
6. IL state; TN, KY, VA, NC, PA
7. Tel: yes, NC; letter: yes, charge for staff time and copies
8. No
9. No, but charge of $25/yr for nonresident library card
10. Yes, 2-week loan; some reference books, 1–3 days

11. No
12. No
13. "Granite City Public Library Bibliography of Genealogy and Local History"
14. No
15. No
Books & Sets: 3(lacks 1985–86 suppl),10,12,26(NC,PA,VA)
Periodicals: 4(v.36–, 1982–), 8(v.71–74, 1983–86)

GURNEE

Warren-Newport Public Library, 224 N O'Plaine Rd, 60031
Tel: 312-244-5150

1. M-Th, 9-9; F,Sa, 9-5
2. T. Sievers, Information Services Dept
3. English, 150
4. 5
5. None
6. Warren Township, Newport Township; Lake County, IL
7. Tel & letter: yes, NC
8. No
9. No
10. No
11. No
12. No
13. *Local History Index*
14. No
15. OCLC: JED

HARVEY

Harvey Public Library
155th St & Turlington Ave, 60426
Tel: 312-331-0757

1. M-Th, 9-8; F,Sa, 9-5
2. JoAnn Aufden-Kamp
3. English, 25–30
4. None
5. Local newspaper, 1935–
6. City of Harvey
7. Tel & letter: yes, NC
8. No
9. No
10. No
11. No
12. No

13. N/AN
14. No
15. N/AN

HARWOOD HEIGHTS

Eisenhower Public Library District, 4652 N Olcott Ave, 60656
Tel: 312-867-7828

1. M-Th, 10-9; F, 10-6; Sa, 10-5
2. N/AN
3. None
4. Six pamphlet file drawers of clippings on Harwood Heights, Norridge, Norwood Park Township (Cook County)
5. N/AN
6. N/AN (see #4)
7. Tel & letter: no
8. No
9. No
10. No
11. No
12. No
13. None
14. No
15. No

HOMEWOOD

Homewood Public Library District, 17900 Dixie Hwy, 60430
Tel: 312-798-0121

1. M-F, 9:30-9; Sa, 9:30-5
2. None
3. English, 20-25
4. None
5. Local newspaper on microfilm (1985–), but no index available
6. Homewood, Flossmoor, Cook County
7. Tel & letter: yes, NC
8. No
9. No
10. Yes, 4 weeks through ILL; 3 weeks to local or reciprocal library card users
11. N/AP
12. No
13. N/AN

14. No
15. OCLC: JNG (after July 1986)

KANKAKEE

Kankakee Public Library
304 S Indiana Ave, 60901
Tel: 815-939-4564

1. M-Th, 9-9; F, 9-6; Sa, 9-5
2. Karen Burden
3. English, 1,000+; German, 13
4. None
5. 700
6. Kankakee County, IL; east of Mississippi River
7. Tel: yes, NC; letter: yes, NC except 20¢/copy
8. No
9. No
10. No
11. No
12. Yes
13. N/AN
14. No
15. N/AN
Books & Sets: 2–5,22,24–26
Periodicals: 1(v.35–45),4(v.16–24, 1962–70; v.27, 1973–),5(1974–),7, 8(v.46–49,v.69–, 1958–61,1981–), 9(v.110–12, 1956–58, v.117–25, 1963–71)

LAKE VILLA

Lake Villa Public Library District, 1001 E Grand Ave, 60046
Tel: 312-356-7711

1. M-Th, 9-9; F,Sa, 9-5
2. Julianne Trychta
3. English, 20
4. 30
5. None
6. Northwestern Lake County, IL
7. N/AN
8. N/AN
9. N/AN
10. N/AN
11. N/AN
12. N/AN

13. N/AN
14. N/AN
15. N/AN

LIBERTYVILLE

Cook Memorial Public Library
413 N Milwaukee Ave, 60048
Tel: 312-362-2330

1. M-Th, 9-9; F,Sa, 9-5; Su, 1-5
2. Nelda W. Willming, Genealogy; Eileen Kloberdanz, Local History
3. English, 1,500; German, 1
4. 75
5. 50
6. Lake County, IL; states bordering Mississippi River
7. Tel: yes, NC; letter: yes, donation requested (Lake County Genealogical Society members answer letters)
8. Nelda W. Willming
9. No
10. No
11. No
12. No
13. None at this time
14. No
15. OCLC: JED
Books & Sets: 2(incomplete & fragile),3–5,7(3 v.: NC,NY,OH), 8,10–14,26
Periodicals: 1(v.11,21,39–, 1934, 1945,1963–),3(v.16–19,21–, 1952–55,1957–),4(v.7,8,9,10–, 1953–55, 1956–),5(1962–65, 1967–69),7, 8(incomplete),9(incomplete)

LINCOLNWOOD

Lincolnwood Public Library District, 4000 W Pratt Ave, 60646
Tel: 312-677-5277

1. M-F, 10-5
2. Ruth Whitney
3. English, all
4. N/ AN
5. N/AN
6. Lincolnwood only; mainly photographs and oral history
7. N/AN

8. No
9. Yes, for photocopies
10. No
11. No
12. No
13. N/AN
14. No
15. No

LYONS

Lyons Public Library
4209 Joliet Ave, 60534-1597
Tel: 312-447-3577

1. Winter: M-F, 10-9; Sa, 10-4; call for summer hours
2. Winifred Koukol
3. English, 740
4. None
5. 15
6. IL state; New England, PA
7. Tel & letter: yes, NC
8. No
9. No
10. Yes, through ILL
11. Yes, through ILL
12. No
13. N/AN
14. No
15. No
Books & Sets: 3–5,10(1976–86), 11,12,23
Periodicals: 4,5

McHENRY

McHenry Public Library District, McHenry County Genealogical Society
1011 N Green St, 60050
Tel: 815-385-0036

1. M-Th, 10-8:30; F,Sa, 10-5
2. Beth Nickels
3. English, 2,000
4. None
5. 9 reels of census
6. IL state and counties, especially McHenry. Some US and foreign countries
7. Tel & letter: yes, NC
8. No. Refer to local genealogists
9. No

10. No
11. No
12. No
13. Bibliography of holdings on microcomputer is in progress
14. Yes
15. No
Books & Sets: 3,5,8
Periodicals: 4(1979–),7, 9(1970–76)

MORRIS

Morris Public Library
604 Liberty St, 60450
Tel: 815-942-6880

1. M-F, 10-9; Sa, 10-4
2. Deborah Trotter
3. English, 250
4. 300
5. 244
6. Grundy County, IL; Ireland, Norway, England, Poland, Germany, Scotland
7. Tel & letter: yes, NC
8. No
9. No
10. Yes, 2-week loan
11. No
12. No
13. Index to local newspaper, 1855-80; tombstone transcriptions from Grundy County cemeteries
14. No
15. No

NAPERVILLE

Nichols Library
200 W Jefferson Ave, 60540-5351
Tel: 312-355-1540

1. M-F, 9-9; Sa, 9-5; Su, 1-5 (Sept–May)
2. Margaret A. Brown
3. English, 250
4. None
5. 193, local newspapers; 9, federal census of local townships; 2, St. John's United Church of Christ records; 8, minutes of Naperville City Council, 1857–1981
6. Naperville, Lisle Township,

Naperville Township, DuPage County
7. Tel: no; letter: yes, NC except for copies and postage
8. No
9. No
10. No
11. No
12. No
13. N/AN
14. No
15. No
Books & Sets: 1(suppls),26
Periodicals: 4

OAK LAWN

Suburban Library System
Reference Service, 9444 S Cook Ave, 60453
Tel: 312-423-7110

1. M-Th, 9-9; F,Sa, 9-5
2. Linda Ameling
3. English, 98%; German, 2%
4. None
5. None. Census microfilm for IL located at SLS Headquarters, Burr Ridge, IL
6. IL primarily, with some VA, KY, OH; some Germany
7. Tel & letter: no
8. No
9. No
10. Yes, 2-week loan
11. N/AP
12. No
13. None
14. No
15. OCLC: IED
Books & Sets: 3–5,9–12,16, 18,24(v.1 only)
Periodicals: 1(1983–84),4(1980–), 5(1984),7,8

OAK PARK

Oak Park Public Library
834 Lake St, 60301
Tel: 312-383-8200

1. M-F, 9-9; Sa, 9-5; Su (Sept-May), 1-5
2. William Jerousek
3. English, 675

4. None
5. 200
6. Oak Park, IL
7. Tel & letter: yes, charge for time, postage, and copies
8. No
9. No
10. No
11. No
12. No
13. N/AN
14. No
15. OCLC: IUO
Books & Sets: 1–3,19
Periodicals: 4

OTTAWA

Starved Rock Library System
900 Hitt St, 61350
Tel: 815-434-7537, ext 109

1. M-F, 8-5; only to librarians and 1 or 2 patrons at a time
2. Richard E. Goach
3. English, 5,000; ultrafiche of Library of American Civilization covers early local history
4. None
5. 2,664 microfiche titles; 691 ultrafiche; 100 microfilm
6. IL; IL city directories; eastern original states; PA, NC, NY, MA, NJ
7. Tel: no; letter: yes, NC for member libraries
8. Richard E. Willson
9. No
10. Yes, through ILL
11. Yes, through ILL
12. No
13. N/AN
14. Yes
15. OCLC: yes
Books & Sets: 3,4,5(v.1–3),7, 10–14,26
Periodicals: 1(v.56),4(1980–),5, 7,8(v.68),9(v.127–)

PALOS HILLS

Green Hills Public Library
8611 W 103rd St, 60465
Tel: 312-598-8446

1. M-F, 9-8:30; Sa, 9-5 (except June-Aug: Sa, 9-3)
2. Darline Filis
3. English, 35
4. Few
5. 27 (Chicago City Directory, 1880–1929)
6. Hickory Hills, Palos Hills, IL; some surrounding areas
7. Tel & letter: yes, NC
8. No
9. No
10. Yes, 2-week loan for anyone holding SLS card
11. No
12. No
13. None
14. No
15. No
Periodicals: 4(v.29–40, 1975–85)

PARK FOREST

Park Forest Public Library
400 Lakewood Blvd, 60466
Tel: 312-748-3731

1. M-Th, 10-9; F, 10-6; Sa, 9-5; Su, 2-5
2. Gretchen Falk, Head, Reference Dept
3. English, 75
4. N/AN
5. 80 reels of Park Forest newspapers
6. Southern Cook County, Will County; Park Forest history, 1948–
7. Tel & letter: yes, NC
8. No
9. No
10. Yes, from genealogy holdings only
11. No
12. No
13. N/AN
14. No
15. No
Books & Sets: 19

PEKIN

Pekin Public Library
301 S 4th St, 61554-4284
Tel: 309-347-7111

1. M-Th, 9-9; F, 9-6; Sa, 9-5; June-Aug: M-Th, 9-8; F, 9-6; Sa, closed
2. Laurie Hartshorn
3. English, 120
4. Vertical file and clippings
5. 193
6. Tazewell County, IL, and surrounding counties
7. Tel & letter: yes, NC except 10¢/copy
8. No
9. No
10. No
11. No
12. No
13. N/AN
14. No
15. N/AN

QUINCY

Quincy Public Library
526 Jersey St, 62301
Tel: 217-222-0226

1. Sept-May: M-Th, 9-9; F,Sa, 9-6; Su, 1-5; June-Aug: M, 9-9; T-Sa, 9-6
2. Carolyn Jensen, Head, Reference Dept
3. English, 660; German, 12
4. None
5. 1,500
6. Adams County, IL state; IL Bounty Lands; US, Canada, England, Wales, France, Germany, Ireland, Poland, Norway, Scotland, Sweden, Switzerland
7. Tel: yes, NC; letter: yes, fee for research. Refer to Great River Genealogical Society
8. No
9. No
10. No
11. No
12. No
13. Surname card file; notebook listing for genealogical and family histories
14. Yes
15. OCLC: IDQ (partial after 1978)

Books & Sets: 2,3(1981 only),
5(3 v.),10–14,26(6 v.)
Periodicals: 4

ROCKFORD

Rockford Public Library
215 N Wyman St, 61101
Tel: 815-965-6731, ext 263

1. M,T,W,F, 9-12,1-6; Th,
12-5,6-9; Sa, 1-5
2. John L. Molyneaux
3. English, 7,000+; Swedish,
German, French, scattered volumes
4. None
5. 850
6. IL; US east of Mississippi
River, especially areas that supplied immigrants to northern
Illinois
7. Tel: no; letter: yes, $5/hr
plus copies
8. John L. Molyneaux
9. No
10. No
11. No
12. No
13. Obituaries from Rockford
newspapers, 1840s, 1850s, 1860s;
obituaries from Rockford *Cru-
sader*, 1950–57 (Afro-American)
14. Yes
15. OCLC: JBO
Books & Sets: 1–7,10–14,17–19,
22–24,26
Periodicals: 1(v.17–, 1940–),4,7–9

SAINT CHARLES

St. Charles Public Library
District, 1 S Sixth Ave, 60174
Tel: 312-584-0076

1. M-Th, 9-9; F, 9-6; Sa, 9-5;
Su, 1-5 (except summer)
2. Marilyn Stewart
   Laura Haule
3. English, 410
4. None
5. 109
6. Kane County, IL state
7. Tel & letter: yes, NC
8. No. Refer to local genealogy group

9. No
10. Yes, 3-week loan
11. No
12. No
13. Card catalog
14. Yes
15. No
Books & Sets: 3
Periodicals: 4(1977–),8(1985–)

SOUTH HOLLAND

**South Suburban Genealogical
and Historical Society Library**
PO Box 96, 320 E 161st Place,
60473
Tel: 312-333-9474

1. M,F, 10-4; T, 1-9; W, 10-4,
7-9; Sa, 11-4
2. Alice DeBoer
3. English, 4,200; German, 3;
Dutch, 6
4. MSS cataloged as printed
material
5. 65
6. Early American records,
Atlantic seaboard to MS; local
history of northeast IL, northwest
IN
7. Tel: yes, NC; letter: yes, NC
for brief queries, otherwise $5/hr
8. Joellen Johnson
   Paula Molak
9. No, but donations welcome
10. No
11. No
12. Computer catalog in
progress
13. Periodical list; pamphlet file
subject list; index to *Quarterly*
contents
14. No
15. No
Books & Sets: 2(incomplete),3,7,
8,10,17,22,23
Periodicals: 1(v.41–47, 1965–71),
3(v.31–, 1968–),4(v.8–, 1954–,
some missing),5(v.15–24),
8(v.44–72, 1956–84, some
missing),9(v.113–, 1959–)

SPRINGFIELD

Illinois State Archives
Capitol Complex, 62756
Tel: 217-782-4682

1. M-F, 8-4:30; Sa, 8-3:30
2. Lowell M. Volkel, Head,
Reference Dept
3. English, 500
4. Thousands of state government documents
5. 10,000
6. IL state
7. Tel & letter: yes, NC except
for copies
8. Lowell M. Volkel
9. No
10. No
11. No, but microfilms of some
records are loaned by Illinois State
Library (see next entry)
12. *Descriptive Inventory of the
Archives of the State of Illinois*,
$20
13. N/AN
14. No. Refer to Illinois State
Genealogical Society
15. No

Illinois State Historical Library
Old State Capitol, 62701
Tel: 217-782-4836

1. M-F, 8:30-5
2. Janice Petterchak
3. English, 162,000; German,
175
4. 9.5 million
5. 63,000
6. IL; also IN, KY, MD, MA,
NJ, NY, NC, OH, PA, SC, TN, VA
7. Tel & letter: yes, NC for in
state; out of state, $5 for initial
search
8. Yes
9. No
10. Yes, through ILL if Library
has duplicate
11. Yes, through ILL
12. No
13. N/AN
14. No. Refer to State Genealogical Society
15. OCLC: JFK

Books & Sets: 1–5,7,10–12,14,17, 18,19(incomplete),24,26
Periodicals: 3,4(broken set),5,8,9

Illinois State Library, Centennial Bldg, Room 350, 62756
Tel: 217-782-5430

1. M-F, 8-4:30
2. None
3. No estimate
4. Draper Manuscript Collection
5. No estimate
6. IL state, Northwest Territory
7. Tel & letter: no
8. No
9. No, except for photocopies
10. Yes, duplicates only, 4–6 weeks, via OCLC or through ILL
11. Yes, 4-week loan
12. No
13. "Facts–Genealogical Resources," flyer
14. No
15. OCLC: SPI
Books & Sets: 1,3(no suppls),6, 10–12,14,26
Periodicals: 1,4(v.26, 1972)

Lincoln Library-Sangamon Valley Collection, 326 S 7th St, 62701
Tel: 217-753-4910

1. M-Th, 9-9; F, 9-6; Sa, 9-5
2. Edward J. Russo
3. English, 700
4. None
5. 200
6. Central IL; VA, KY
7. Tel & letter: yes, NC except for copies
8. No
9. No
10. Yes, through ILL if Library has more than one copy
11. No
12. No
13. Obituary index to Springfield newspaper; name indexes to various books
14. No

15. OCLC: ILM
Books & Sets: 3,5,7,10,26
Periodicals: 1(1972–),4(1969–), 8(1970–)

STREAMWOOD

Poplar Creek Public Library
1405 S Park Blvd, 60107
Tel: 312-837-6800

1. M-Th, 9am-9:30pm; F,Sa, 9-5; Su, 12-5
2. N/AP
3. N/AN
4. N/AN
5. N/AN
6. IL local areas
7. Tel & letter: yes, NC
8. No
9. No
10. Yes, 3-week loan
11. N/AN
12. No
13. Card catalog
14. No
15. N/AN
Books & Sets: 3,4,26(MD)
Periodicals: 4

SULLIVAN

Moultrie County Historical and Genealogical Research Library
117 E Harrison, 61951
Tel: 217-728-4085

1. M,Sa, 1-5
2. Sue Durbin
3. English, 3,000
4. 150
5. 200
6 Midwest, especially IL
7. Tel: yes, NC; letter: yes, NC for members only; charge for nonmembers
8. Gertrude Dixon
   Sue Durbin
9. No
10. Yes, to members only
11. Yes, to members only
12. No
13. Card file
14. Yes
15. N/AN

Books & Sets: 26
Periodicals: 1(incomplete),4

URBANA

University of Illinois Library, Illinois Historical Survey Library 346, 1408 W Gregory Dr, 61801
Tel: 217-333-1777

1. M-F, 9-5
2. N/AP
3. English, 12,000; German, 100
4. No estimate
5. No estimate
6. IL state
7. Tel & letter: yes, NC
8. Josephine F. Moeller, Library Assistant
9. No
10. No, not from Survey Library
11. No
12. Maynard Brichford et al., *Manuscripts Guide to Collections at the University of Illinois at Urbana-Champaign,* Part II, $15
13. Josephine F. Moeller, "A Select Guide to Genealogical Research Sources in the University of Illinois Library at Urbana-Champaign" (1986); Diane F. Carothers, "A Genealogical Guide to the University of Illinois Bookstacks," *Champaign County Genealogical Society Quarterly* 4 (Winter 1982)
14. No
15. OCLC: UIU
Books & Sets: 1,3–7,9–14,17–19, 21–24,26
Periodicals: 4,5,7–9

Urbana Free Library, Champaign County Historical Archives, 201 S Race St, 61801
Tel: 217-367-4025

1. M-Sa, 10:30-4:30; Su, 1-5
2. James A. Edstrom
3. English, 5,100
4. 50
5. 1,830

6. East central IL
7. Tel: yes, NC; letter: yes, NC for first hour, $7.50/hr thereafter
8. No
9. No
10. No
11. No
12. No
13. Name index
14. Yes
15. No
Books & Sets: 2–7,10,13,14,26
Periodicals: 1,3(1950–),4(1950–), 5,7,8(1956–),9

VANDALIA

Evans Public Library
215 S 5th St, 62471
Tel: 618-283-2824

1. M-F, 10-8; Sa, 9-5; Su (Sept-May), 2-4
2. Agnes Grubaugh, Librarian, Fayette County Genealogy Society
3. English, 500. Library of Fayette County Genealogy Society
4. N/AN
5. 200
6. Fayette County, IL; some IN, OH, KY, NC, SC
7. Tel & letter: no
8. No
9. No
10. No
11. No
12. No
13. N/AN
14. Yes
15. No
Books & Sets: 3

WATSEKA

Iroquois County Genealogical Society, 103 W Cherry, 60970
Tel: 815-432-5675 (ask for Genealogy)

1. M-F, 1-4
2. N/AN
3. English, 1,000
4. 50

5. 320
6. Iroquois, adjoining counties, IL; counties, states in migration pattern of Iroquois County settlers
7. Tel: no; letters: yes, NC, but donations appreciated
8. Yes
9. No
10. No
11. No
12. No
13. N/AN
14. No
15. No
Books & Sets: 3
Periodicals: 4,5(v.16 only),7, 9(v. 69–71,81,82, 1965–67, 1977–78)

WHEATON

Wheaton Public Library
225 N Cross St, 60187
Tel: 312-668-1374

1. M-F, 9-9; Sa, 9-5; Su, 1-5 (Sept-May)
2. Marjorie Herlache Peters
3. English, 1,500; German, 4; French, 8
4. None
5. 15
6. DuPage County, surrounding counties, IL; states east and immediately west of Mississippi River; some Europe and Canada
7. Tel: no; letter: yes, NC except for copies
8. Marjorie Herlache Peters
9. No
10. No
11. No
12. *Genealogical Holdings of the Wheaton Public Library: A Subject Guide*, free
13. N/AN
14. Yes
15. OCLC: JAD
Books & Sets: 3–7,9–14,17, 19(2 v. set only),22,24,26
Periodicals: 1(v.55–, 1979–), 4(v.14–, 1960–),5(v.1–4,13–, 1962–65,1974–),7,8(v.54–61,75–, 1966–73,1985–),9(v.106–, 1952–)

WILMETTE

Wilmette Public Library
1242 Wilmette Ave, 60091
Tel: 312-256-5029

1. M-F, 9-9; Sa, 9-5; Su, 2-5 (during school year)
2. Rosella O'Reilly
3. English, 40
4. 30
5. 300 reels of *Wilmette Life*
6. Wilmette, IL
7. Tel & letter: yes, NC
8. No
9. No
10. Yes, books circulate, pamphlet files do not
11. No
12. No
13. N/AN
14. No
15. No

WILMINGTON

Will-Grundy County Genealogical Society Library
Wilmington Township Library, 201 S Kankakee St, 60481
Tel: 815-476-6719 (Wilmington Township Library)

1. M,T,Th, 10-8:30; W,F,Sa, 10-4
2. Andrew Bale, Society Librarian
3. English, 500+
4. None
5. 100
6. Will and Grundy Counties, IL
7. Tel: no; letter: yes, NC
8. No
9. No
10. No
11. No
12. No
13. N/AN
14. No
15. No
Books & Sets: 5(v.1 only)

WINNETKA

**Winnetka Public Library
District,** 768 Oak St, 60093
Tel: 312-446-7220

1. M-Th, 9-9; F,Sa, 9-5; Su,
1-5 (during school year)
2. Margaret M. Hamil
3. English, 6,000; German, 1
4. 700
5. 265; 7 titles in microfiche

6. US east of Mississippi
River; MO, IA, MN; also Nova
Scotia, lower Canada, Barbados
(areas leading into eastern US)
7. Tel & letter: yes, NC
8. Elizabeth White
Connie O'Kieffe
Dorothy Thompson
Harriet Hodge
9. No
10. Yes, "how-to" titles
circulate. Most genealogy material,

classified as reference, does not
circulate
11. No
12. No
13. N/AN
14. Yes
15. OCLC: IWE & JED
Books & Sets: 1,2,3(suppl through
1985),4,5,7,10–14,17,19,26
Periodicals: 1,3–5,7–9

INDIANA

ANDERSON

Anderson Public Library
111 E 12, 46016
Tel: 317-641-2442

1. M-Th, 9-9; F,Sa, 9-5:30;
Su, 1-5 (library closed for lunch
11-12 M-Sa)
2. Howard I. Eldon
3. English, 12,000
4. 250
5. N/AN
6. All US; some foreign
countries
7. Tel: yes, NC for brief
queries; letter: no
8. Howard I. Eldon
9. No
10. No
11. No
12. No
13. N/AN
14. Yes
15. OCLC: APL IND
Books & Sets: 3,13,14,26
Periodicals: 4,7

BEDFORD

Bedford Public Library
1323 K St, 47421
Tel: 812-275-4471

1. M-Th, 9-8; F,Sa, 9-5; Su,
1-5
2. Starr DeJesus
3. English, 700
4. 97
5. 321
6. Lawrence and nearby
counties
7. Tel & letter: yes, NC
8. No
9. No
10. Yes, duplicates only
11. No

12. No
13. N/AN
14. No
15. No

BLUFFTON

**Bluffton-Wells County Public
Library**, 223 W Washington,
46714
Tel: 219-824-2315

1. M-Th, 9-8; F, 9-6; Sa, 9–5,
(Sept-May), 9–12
2. Barbara Elliott
3. English, 1,500
4. 1,000
5. 500
6. Mainly Wells County, IN
state; OH, MI, KY
7. Tel: yes, NC; letter: yes,
charge for time and copies
8. N/AN
9. No
10. No
11. No
12. No
13. N/AN
14. Yes
15. OCLC: IWM
Periodicals: 4,6

COLUMBUS

**Bartholomew County Public
Library**, 5th & Lafayette Sts,
47201
Tel: 812-379-1266

1. M-Th, 8:30am-9pm; F,Sa,
8:30-6
2. Reference staff
3. G: approx 640 titles; Indiana
Collection: approx 1,300 titles;
LH: approx 50 titles
4. Unable to answer
5. 70: 22 titles

6. IN, KY, OH, New England,
NJ, NY, PA, MD, VA, WV, NC,
SC
7. Tel & letter: yes, NC except
for copies
8. No
9. No
10. Not generally
11. No
12. In-house list
13. *Genealogical Material in
the Bartholomew County Library*
14. Yes
15. No
Books & Sets: 3,7,10–12,26
Periodicals: 4

CRAWFORDSVILLE

**Crawfordsville District Public
Library**, 222 S Washington,
47933
Tel: 317-362-9493

1. M-F, 9-9; Sa, 9-5
2. Tom Day
3. English, 3,000
4. 1,500
5. 700
6. Montgomery County, surrounding counties in IN; some VA,
KY
7. Tel: yes, NC for brief
queries; letter: yes, $5/hr
8. Karen Zach
9. No, except for copies
10. No
11. No
12. No
13. ALSA bibliography, *Locations of Works in Libraries in an 8-
County Area;* index of persons and
firms in Montgomery County; indexes to census records, marriages,
births, deaths, cemeteries
14. Yes
15. OCLC: partial

Books & Sets: 3,7
Periodicals: 4

CROWN POINT

**Crown Point Community
Library,** 214 S Court St, 46307
Tel: 219-663-0270

1. M-Th, 9-8; F,Sa, 9-5
2. Frances McBride
3. N/AN
4. 4–5
5. Census, 2 years of local
weekly newspaper on microfilm
6. Crown Point, Lake County,
IN state
7. Tel: yes, NC; letter: yes,
charge for time
8. Frances McBride
9. No
10. No
11. No
12. No
13. Card catalog; access to
DAR records of cemeteries in Lake
County
14. No
15. No
Periodicals: 4(1984–85)

EAST CHICAGO

East Chicago Public Library
2401 E Columbus Dr, 46312
Tel: 219-397-2453

1. M-Th, 9-8; F,Sa, 9-5:30
2. Julia B. Timmer
3. English, 5,000; Spanish, 250
4. 200
5. None
6. IN state, East Chicago
7. Tel & letter: yes, NC
8. No
9. No
10. No
11. No
12. No
13. N/AN
14. No
15. No
Books & Sets: 3,20,26

ELKHART

Elkhart Public Library
300 S Second St, 46516
Tel: 219-522-5669

1. M-Th, 9-9; F,Sa, 9-6
2. Marsha J. Eilers, Associate
Director of Reference Services
3. English, 525
4. None
5. 75 census reels; 630 newspaper reels
6. Elkhart County, surrounding
counties, IN state, areas east of IN
7. Tel: no; letter, yes, NC except for copies. Minimal searching
done
8. No
9. No
10. No
11. No
12. No
13. None
14. No
15. OCLC: IEB
Books & Sets: 3,7(v.1–5,7)
Periodicals: 4(v.22–, 1968–),
9(v.114–18,120–21,125–, 1960–
63,1965–67,1971–)

EVANSVILLE

**Evansville-Vanderburgh
County Public Library**
22 SE Fifth St, 47708
Tel: 812-428-8218

1. Sept-June: M-W, 8:30-7;
Th-Sa, 8:30-5:30; June-Sept:
M-Sa, 8:30-5:30
2. Judith Hanefeldt, Head,
Reference Dept
3. English, 2,000; Library also
has a deposit genealogy collection
of the local DAR chapter, of
limited access to the general public
4. N/AN
5. 1,300 reels of local newspapers; 60 reels of local history,
census, obituaries
6. Evansville, Vanderburgh
County, IN state
7. Tel & letter: yes, NC except
for copies

8. No
9. No charge to residents or
reciprocal borrowers
10. No
11. No
12. No
13. Index to 18 standard history
volumes:*Vanderburgh County,
Indiana, Index of Persons, Businesses, Organizations, Etc.*; card
file index to local newspapers,
1972–
14. No
15. OCLC: partially
Books & Sets: 26
Periodicals: 4(1983–)

FORT WAYNE

**Allen County Public Library,
Fred J. Reynolds Historical
Genealogy Department**
900 Webster St, 46802
Tel: 219-424-7241, ext 2242

1. M-Th, 9-9; F,Sa, 9-6; Su,
1-6 (Labor Day-Memorial Day)
2. Michael B. Clegg
3. English, 125,000; German,
500; French, 500
4. Library does not collect
MSS per se but has some on fiche
and in book form
5. 100,000 microforms
6. US, Canada; England, Scotland, Wales, Ireland
7. Tel: yes, NC for short
requests; letter: yes, $3/letter and
20¢/copy
8. Yes
9. No
10. No
11. No
12. Guide forthcoming in 1988
13. N/AN
14. Yes
15. OCLC: IMFG
Books & Sets: 1–19,21–26
Periodicals: 1–9

FRANKFORT

**Frankfort Community Public
Library,** 208 W Clinton St, 46041
Tel: 317-654-8746

1. M-Th, 9-8; F,Sa, 9-5
2. Helen E. Grove
3. English, 650
4. 50
5. 400
6. IN, VA, New England; some KY, OH
7. Tel: yes, with charge for extensive research; letter: yes, NC except 15¢/copy
8. Helen E. Grove
9. No
10. Yes
12. No
13. Bibliography
14. No, other than Mrs. Grove
15. OCLC: XFP
Books & Sets: 2,26 (6 v.)
Periodicals: 4(partial),8(partial), 9(partial)

FRANKLIN

Franklin College
501 E Monroe, 46131
Tel: 317-736-8441, ext 266

1. Hours vary with school year
2. Mary A. Medlicott
3. English, 10,000; French, 5
4. 3
5. 10
6. IN state; Northwest Territory
7. Tel & letter: yes, NC
8. No
9. No
10. Yes, 30-day loan, through ILL
11. No
12. Catalog of David Demaree Banta Indiana Collection, $5 including postage
13. In-house indexes
14. Yes
15. OCLC: IFC
Books & Sets: 6

Franklin-Johnson County Public Library, Madison at Home Ave, 46131
Tel: 317-738-2833

1. M-Th, 9:30-8; F,Sa, 9:30-6
2. Trudy Bender

3. English, 800
4. None
5. 443
6. Johnson County, IN state, some US
7. Tel: no; letter: yes, NC
8. No
9. No
10. No
11. No
12. No
13. N/AN
14. Yes
15. OCLC: IFJ
Books & Sets: 2(v.22–32,40–53), 26(NC,PA,VA)
Periodicals: 4(1959–83)

Johnson County Historical Museum, 150 W Madison St, 46131
Tel: 317-736-4655

1. T-F, 10-12, 1-4; Sa, 10-3; Su,M, closed
2. Kay L. DeHart, Curator
3. English, 400
4. 300
5. None
6. Johnson County, IN; KY, NC, SC, OH, PA, VA, NY
7. Tel & letter: yes, NC except 10¢/copy
8. No
9. No
10. No
11. N/AP
12. No
13. Index to Johnson County histories
14. Yes
15. No
Periodicals: 4(v.21–26, 1968–72)

GARY

Gary Public Library
220 W 5th Ave, 46402
Tel: 219-886-2484

1. M-Th, 9:30-8; F,Sa, 9:30-5
2. No head
3. English, 1,500
4. WPA files; *Gary Post Tribune* index

5. *Gary Post Tribune,* 1908–; *Crown Point Register,* 1972–79
6. Gary, Calumet region, northwestern IN
7. Tel: yes, rarely; letter: yes, NC for limited search
8. No
9. No
10. No
11. No
12. No
13. *Gary Post Tribune* index, 1910–
14. No
15. N/AN

INDIANAPOLIS

Indiana Historical Society
315 W Ohio St, 46202
Tel: 317-232-1879

1. M-F, 8-4:30; Sa, 8:30-4 Sept-May, except holidays
2. Robert K. O'Neill, Director; Leigh Darbee, Head, Reference Dept
3. English, most; German, 30; French, 200
4. No estimate
5. No estimate
6. IN, Midwest, especially during Old Northwest territorial period
7. Tel & letter: yes, NC except for copies
8. No
9. No
10. No
11. Yes, for selected microfilm of MS collections and county histories
12. *A Guide to the Manuscript Collections of the Indiana Historical Society and Indiana State Library,* $25
13. Computerized (in-house) index to architectural drawings and photographs. Books and MSS being cataloged on the OCLC system
14. No
15. OCLC: XHS

Indianapolis-Marion County Public Library, Social Sciences Division, PO Box 211, 46206
Tel: 317-269-1733

1. M-F, 9-9; Sa, 9-5; Su, 1-5
2. Lois Laube, Social Sciences Division
3. English, 1,000 (including 130 years of Indianapolis city directories)
4. 78 file drawers of local newspaper clippings
5. City directories on microfilm
6. Indianapolis, IN state
7. Tel & letter: yes, NC except $1/copy
8. No
9. No
10. Yes, through ILL
11. No
12. No
13. Authority file by individual name for Afro/Americans in biographical clipping file; authority file by street address for Indianapolis houses and buildings
14. No
15. OCLC: IMD
Books & Sets: 1,6

Indiana State Library
140 N Senate Ave, 46204
Tel: 317-232-3689

1. M-Sa, 8-4:30; closed Sa, June-Aug
2. William O. Harris
3. English, 47,000; German, 600; Latin (mainly Catholic church records), 400; French, 400; Spanish, 25
4. 65 major collections plus 80 drawers of vertical files
5. 30,000
6. IN, OH, KY, TN, Eastern Seaboard states; some other US; Great Britain, Germany
7. Tel & letter: yes, NC
8. Diane Weimer Sharp
9. No
10. No
11. No
12. Carolynne L. Miller,

Indiana Sources for Genealogical Research in the Indiana State Library (1984), $20
13. Two-page guide, free
14. Yes
15. OCLC: ISL
Books & Sets: 1–7,10–24,26
Periodicals:1,3–5,6(v.18–, 1976–), 7–9

JEFFERSONVILLE

Jeffersonville Township Public Library, 211 E Court Ave, PO Box 1548, 47131
Tel: 812-282-7765

1. M-Th, 9-9; F, 9-5:30; Sa, 9-5
2. Stephen Day
3. English, 500
4. 50
5. 147
6. Primarily Clark County, IN state, and other states
7. Tel: yes, NC for short questions; letter: yes, NC except 25¢/copy
8. Yes (volunteers)
9. No
10. No
11. No
12. No
13. In-house list, catalog cards
14. Yes
15. N/AN
Books & Sets: 1,3
Periodicals: 4 (1974–)

KOKOMO

Kokomo-Howard County Public Library, 220 N Union, 46901
Tel: 317-457-3242

1. M-Th, 12-5,7-9; F, 12-5
2. Margaret Cardwell
3. English, 2,560
4. 1: research on Greentown Glass
5. 1,765
6. IN, OH, KY
7. Tel & letter: yes, NC except 15¢/copy. Letter queries preferred
8. Margaret Cardwell

9. No
10. No, but if a certain page is needed, Library will photocopy
11. No
12. No
13. Bibliographies
14. Yes
15. OCLC: IHP
Books & Sets: 3,7,10–12,26
Periodicals: 4(v.26–, 1972–),5,7, 8(v.60–, 1972–),9(v.127–, 1973–)

LAFAYETTE

Alameda McCollough Library, Tippecanoe County Historical Association, 909 South St, 47901
Tel: 317-742-8411

1. T-F, 1-5; 3d Sa of each month except Dec, Jan; closed Jan
2. Nancy Weirich, Librarian
3. English, 5,000+
4. 100+
5. 575
6. Tippecanoe County, surrounding IN counties
7. Tel: yes, NC for limited queries; letter: yes, $10/surname or hourly charge
8. Yes (experienced volunteers)
9. No
10. No
11. No
12. No
13. Not at the present time
14. No
15. No
Books & Sets: 2,3,5,26

Tippecanoe County Public Library, 638 North St, 47906
Tel: 317-423-2602

1. M-Th, 9-9; F,Sa, 9-5; Su, 1-5
2. Cindy Mitchell
3. English, 3,000
4. None
5. 92
6. Tippecanoe County, city of Lafayette, Wabash River Valley, IN state
7. Tel: yes, NC; letter: yes, $3

8. No
9. No
10. No
11. No
12. No
13. None
14. No
15. OCLC: XWE
Books & Sets: 10,11

LAPORTE

LaPorte County Public Library
904 Indiana Ave, 46350
Tel: 219-362-6156

1. M-Th, 9-9; F,Sa, 9-6
2. James D. Cline
3. English, 651
4. None
5. 970
6. IN, Midwest, US
7. Tel: no; letter: yes, NC
except 15¢/copy
8. No
9. No
10. Yes, to other libraries, 4-week loan. Reference books do not circulate
11. No
12. *LaPorte County Public Library Genealogy Collection Master List,* no charge
13. N/AN
14. No
15. OCLC: some IMQ
Books & Sets: 3,10,11
Periodicals: 4(1976–),8(1983–)

LOGANSPORT

Logansport-Cass County Public Library, 616 E Broadway, 46947
Tel: 219-753-6383

1. M-F, 9-9; Sa, 9-5
2. N/AN
3. N/AN
4. N/AN
5. Census on microfilm; local newspapers from 1865
6. Cass and Miami Counties, IN state
7. Tel & letter: no

8. No
9. No
10. No
11. No
12. No
13. N/AN
14. Yes
15. N/AN
Books & Sets: 3,10,11

MADISON

Madison-Jefferson County Public Library, 420 W Main St, 47250
Tel: 812-265-2744

1. M-Th, 9-8; F,Sa, 9-6
2. Dennis Babbitt
3. English, 1,950
4. Library does not differen-tiate between books and MSS
5. 1,024
6. Madison; Jefferson County; Scott, Jennings, Switzerland, Ripley Counties, IN state; KY, some OH, VA, PA, MD, NC, SC
7. Tel & letter: yes, NC except 25¢/copy with SASE
8. No
9. No
10. No
11. No
12. No
13. N/AN
14. No
15. No
Books & Sets: 2,3,6,10–12,17,26
Periodicals: 4(incomplete),9

MENTONE

Bell Memorial Public Library
306 N Broadway, PO Box 368, 46539
Tel: 219-353-7234

1. M-Sa, 9-5
2. Eileen Bowser
3. English, 100
4. 50–60 pamphlets, folders; county histories; indexed obitu-aries, 1885–
5. Local newspapers, 1885–1986

6. Kosciusko, Fulton, Miami, Marshall, Wabash Counties in IN
7. Tel: yes, NC; letter: yes, $1/query
8. No
9. No
10. No
11. No
12. No
13. N/AN
14. No
15. No
Books & Sets: 2
Periodicals: 4

MISHAWAKA

Mishawaka-Penn Public Library
209 Lincoln Way E, 46544
Tel: 219-259-5277

1. Winter: M-F, 9-9; Sa, 9-6; summer: M-Th, 9-9; F, 9-6; Sa, 9-1
2. Olga Nazaroff
3. English, 500
4. None
5. 600
6. IN state; some OH, PA
7. Tel & letter: yes, NC except 25¢/copy
8. No
9. No
10. No
11. No
12. No
13. N/AN
14. No
15. OCLC: IMP
Books & Sets: 1,8
Periodicals: 4

MOUNT VERNON

Alexandrian Public Library
115 W 5th St, 47620
Tel: 812-838-3286

1. M-Th, 9-8; F,Sa, 9-5; Su, 1-5
2. Don W. Barlow
3. English, 300
4. N/AN
5. 235
6. Posey County, southern IN and IL, western KY

7. Tel: no; letter: yes, NC
8. No
9. No
10. No
11. No
12. No
13. N/AN
14. No
15. N/AN
Books & Sets: 3

MUNCIE

Muncie Public Library
301 E Jackson St, 47305
Tel: 317-747-8200

1. M-F, 9-9; Sa, 9-6
2. Reference librarian
3. N/AN
4. None
5. 1,600
6. Muncie and Delaware County, IN
7. Tel: no; letter: yes, SASE requested; photocopy minimum $1, additional copies 25¢
8. No
9. No
10. No
11. No
12. Newspaper holdings listed in John Miller, *Indiana Newspaper Bibliography*
13. Mimeographed lists of reference, "how to do it," county histories, newspaper holdings
14. Yes
15. OCLC: IMU
Books & Sets: 1–3

NEW ALBANY

New Albany-Floyd County Public Library, Stuart Barth Wrege Indiana History Room
180 W Spring St, 47150-3692
Tel: 812-949-3527

1. M-Th, 9-8:30; F,Sa, 9-5:30
2. Benita K. Mason
3. English, 4,500
4. 700 genealogy folders (family names research); 1,400

vertical file folders (local, state history)
5. 343: newspaper (mostly local); 469: census; 73: local records
6. Floyd County, surrounding counties in IN; IN state; nearby states
7. Tel & letter: yes, NC except for copies and postage. Prefer written inquiries
8. No
9. No
10. No
11. No
12. No
13. Mimeographed bibliography of genealogical holdings ($1 plus postage); index to Floyd County items in microfilmed New Albany newspapers, 1849–1935; name index to family (genealogical research) folders; name index to many Floyd County cemeteries
14. Yes
15. No
Books & Sets: 1(v.3–5),3(v.1–3 only, no suppls),4,6,7,10,11,13, 14,26
Periodicals: 4

NEWBURGH

Newburgh-Ohio Township Public Library, 23 W Jennings St, 47630
Tel: 812-853-5468

1. M-F, 11-8; Sa, 11-4
2. Janet Weideman
3. English, 1,500
4. Not counted
5. 75
6. Warwick County, IN; IN state; other US. Have most Unigraphic county history reproductions
7. Tel & letter: yes, NC for brief queries
8. Yes
9. No
10. No
11. No
12. No

13. In-house guides
14. No
15. No
Periodicals: 4(1959–81),9(scattered)

NEW CASTLE

New Castle-Henry County Public Library, 376 S 15th St, 47362
Tel: 317-529-0362

1. M-Th, 8am-9pm; F,Sa, 8-5
2. Marjorie J. Johnson
3. English, 5,000
4. None
5. 1,000
6. Henry County, IN state
7. Tel & letter: yes, NC except 10¢/copy
8. No
9. No
10. No
11. No
12. No
13. None
14. No
15. No

NOBLESVILLE

Noblesville-Southeastern Public Library, One Library Plaza, 46060
Tel: 317-773-1384

1. M-Th, 9:30-8:30; F,Sa, 9:30-5:30; Su hours to be implemented fall 1987
2. Beverly Jean
3. English, 1,500
4. None
5. N/AN
6. Hamilton County, IN
7. Tel & letter: yes, NC
8. No
9. No
10. No
11. No
12. No
13. None
14. Yes
15. No

Books & Sets: 3
Periodicals: 4(1973–86)

PORTLAND

Jay County Public Library
131 E Walnut St, 47371-2192
Tel: 219-726-7890

1. M-F, 9-8; Sa, 9-5
2. None
3. English, 200
4. 25
5. 200
6. Jay County
7. Tel: no; letter: yes, $5/hr
8. No
9. No
10. No
11. No
12. No
13. N/AN
14. Yes
15. No
Books & Sets: 2,3,7
Periodicals: 4

RICHMOND

Morrisson-Reeves Library
80 N 6th St, 47374
Tel: 317-966-8291

1. Sept-May: M-Th, 9-9; F,Sa, 9-5:30; June-Aug: M-Sa, 9-5:30
2. Carol McCafferty, Head, Reference Dept
3. English, 500
4. None
5. 1,200
6. Wayne County and contiguous IN and OH counties; IN, OH, US
7. Tel & letter: yes, NC except 10¢/copy plus postage
8. No
9. No
10. No, although some local county histories are available for checkout through ILL
11. No
12. No
13. Card index to local newspapers; mimeographed booklet describing genealogy holdings

14. Yes
15. OCLC: INR
Books & Sets: 2(v.1,37–40,42–65, 107–66),2(3 v., 1981 only),7,13, 14, 26
Periodicals: 4(v.31–, 1977–),7(rev ed, 1983)

SHELBYVILLE

Shelbyville-Shelby County Public Library, 57 W Broadway, 46176
Tel: 317-398-7121

1. M-F, 9-7; Sa, 9-5
2. Margaret Hamilton, Director
3. English, 350
4. Vertical files
5. 28 census reels; also Forest Hill Cemetery; Shelbyville newspaper, 1854–
6. Shelby County, surrounding counties; surrounding states
7. Tel: no; letter: yes, NC except 15¢/copy with SASE
8. No
9. No
10. No
11. N/AN
12. No
13. Index of Shelby County names, persons, firms
14. Yes
15. No
Periodicals: 4

SOUTH BEND

South Bend Public Library
122 W Wayne St, 46530
Tel: 219-282-4625

1. M-Th, 9-9; F,Sa, 9-6; Su (Oct-Apr only), 1-5
2. Sarah Betts
3. English, 2,500
4. None
5. 700
6. Northern IN, some OH, PA, NY, New England
7. Tel: yes, NC for limited service; letter: yes, NC
8. No

9. No
10. No
11. No
12. No
13. *Index to the South Bend Tribune; Necrology Index to South Bend Tribune,* 1930–
14. Yes
15. OCLC: yes
Books & Sets: 1–3,5,10–12,17,26
Periodicals: 4,5,7–9

SULLIVAN

Sullivan County Public Library
100 Crowder St, 47882
Tel: 812-268-4957

1. Winter: M-Th, 9-8; F, 9-6; Sa, 9-5; June-Aug: M-F, 9-6; Sa, 9-4
2. Sara Richards
3. 80
4. Included with books
5. 750
6. Sullivan County, IN
7. Tel & letter: no
8. No
9. No
10. No
11. No
12. No
13. N/AN
14. Yes
15. N/AN

TERRE HAUTE

Vigo County Public Library
Special Collections,
One Library Square, 47807
Tel: 812-232-1113, ext 212 or 292

1. M-Th, 9-9; F, 9-6; Sa, 9-5; Su, 1-5 (closed Su Memorial Day–Labor Day)
2. Nancy Sherrill, Genealogy; Susan Dehler, Archives
3. English, 7,500
4. Surname files, 28,092 items; Community Affairs File, 260,890 items; Community Deposit Collections (Archives), 180 items
5. 3,490 reels: census, Terre Haute newspapers, courthouse records

6. Terre Haute, Vigo County, Wabash Valley (counties bordering Wabash River in IN, IL), IN state
7. Tel & letter: yes, NC except 10¢/copy and postage
8. Nancy Sherrill
9. No
10. Yes, duplicates only
11. Films of newspapers of which the Library has negatives are loaned. Only 3 rolls can be borrowed at one time and must be insured, $20/roll
12. No
13. Special Collections brochure; bibliographies on holdings for IN counties: Vigo, Greene, Sullivan, Parke, Vermillion, Clay, Owen, Putnam
14. Yes (interested amateurs)
15. OCLC: IVC
Books & Sets: 2,3(3 v., 1981 only),4–7,10,11(1972–76),12,26
Periodicals: 1(v.56–, 1980–), 3(v.45–, 1982–),4(v.12–17,23–, 1959–63,1967–),5,7,8(v.26, 1938), 9(v.134, 1980)

TIPTON

Tipton County Public Library
127 E Madison, 46072
Tel: 317-675-8761

1. M-W, 10-8; Th-Sa, 10-5:30
2. Janine Parks
3. English, 700
4. 75
5. 340
6. KY, TN, VA, WV, OH, PA, IN
7. Tel: yes, NC; letter: no
8. Donna Ekstrom
9. No
10. No
11. No
12. No
13. *Genealogy Handbook for the Tipton County Public Library*; surname index of obituaries from local newspaper
14. No

15. No
Books & Sets: 7(v.3,5),26(8 v.)
Periodicals: 4,8

VALPARAISO

Valparaiso Public Library
107 Jefferson St, 46383
Tel: 219-462-0524, ext 8

1. M-F, 9-9; Sa, 9-5
2. Mary K. Patterson, Librarian, Genealogy Dept
3. English, 10,000; German, 4
4. Original MSS are in Old Jail Museum, Valparaiso
5. 2,000 reels of microfilm; 1,300 reels of microfiche
6. New England, NY, PA, NJ, DE, MD, DC, WV, VA, NC, SC, GA, TN, KY, OH, IN, IL, MI, WI, IA, MO, KS
7. Tel: yes, NC; letter: yes, $2.50–$5
8. No
9. No
10. No
11. No
12. Yes, no charge
13. Indexes to: Porter County cemeteries, death records (1884–1959), marriages (1836–1920), obituaries (1980–), births (1884–1919), wills (1839–80), naturalizations (1854–1955), and census (1850–1910). Also, abstracts of Porter County newspapers (complete from 1847–1900)
14. No, but Library has list of nonprofessionals who will do research
15. No
Books & Sets: 2,3,5–8,10–12, 17–19,22,23,26
Periodicals: 1,3–5,7–9

WABASH

Wabash Carnegie Public Library, 188 W Hill St, 46992
Tel: 219-563-2572

1. M-Th, 9-8; F,Sa, 9-6; summer: M-Sa, 9-6
2. Library Director
3. N/AN
4. Over 1,000 books and bound pamphlets
5. 45-50
6. Wabash County, adjacent Miami, Huntington, Kosciusko Counties, IN state; Tuscarawas County, OH, OH state; some KY, PA, VA
7. Tel & letter: yes, NC except if request involves extensive research: $3-$10
8. Gladys Harvey
9. Yes, Library card charge to nonresidents
10. No
11. No
12. No
13. N/AN
14. Yes
15. No
Books & Sets: 2

WARSAW

Kosciusko County Genealogy Research Library, PO Box 1071, 46580
Tel: 219-267-1078

1. F-Su, 1-4
2. Kenneth Fawley
   Caroline Fawley
3. English, 300
4. 100
5. 100
6. Kosciusko County, IN state, surrounding areas
7. Tel: no; letter: yes, with costs and donation
8. No
9. No
10. No
11. No
12. Partial guide to holdings; not available
13. Extensive alphabetical newspaper extraction file
14. Yes
15. No
Periodicals: 4,5,8

IOWA

AMES

Ames Public Library
515 Douglas Ave, 50010
Tel: 515-233-2115

1. M-Th, 9-9; F,Sa, 9-6; Su, 1:30-5 (closed Su June-Aug)
2. Roy Kenagy, Assistant Director; Mike Quinn, Information Services
3. English, 300
4. N/AN
5. 300
6. Midwest, IA, US
7. Tel: yes, NC for limited requests; letter: yes, NC except for copies
8. No
9. No
10. No
11. No
12. No
13. N/AN
14. No
15. OCLC: UIB
Books & Sets: 3(1981–82)
Periodicals: 4(1965)

CARROLL

Carroll Public Library
118 E 5th St, 51401
Tel: 712-792-3432

1. M-F, 12-8:30; Sa, 9-5
2. Gordon S. Wade
3. English, 175
4. 2
5. 200
6. US, with emphasis on Midwest, East, South
7. Tel: no; letter: yes, $5 minimum payable in advance
8. No
9. $20/year
10. No

11. Yes; limit of 4 reels per time sent only to other libraries
12. No
13. N/AN
14. No
15. N/AN
Books & Sets: 3,5

CEDAR FALLS

Cedar Falls Public Library
524 Parkade, 50613
Tel: 319-266-2629

1. M-F, 9-9; Sa, 9-5
2. None
3. English, 50
4. None
5. 180 reels of old Cedar Falls newspapers (1860–1903, 1910–12, 1922–68, 1969–83)
6. Black Hawk County, IA
7. Tel: yes, NC; letter: N/AN
8. No
9. Yes, $20/year for out-of-county residents
10. No
11. No
12. No
13. None
14. No
15. No
Books & Sets: 10

CEDAR RAPIDS

Cedar Rapids Public Library
500 First St SE, 52401-2095
Tel: 319-398-5123

1. M-Th, 9:30-9; F,Sa, 9:30-5; Su, 1-5
2. None
3. English, 600
4. None
5. 250
6. Cedar Rapids, IA state

7. Tel & letter: no
8. No
9. No
10. Yes, to local patrons only
11. No
12. No
13. None
14. No
15. OCLC: IWR
Books & Sets: 1–5,7,10,12,14, 17,26

DAVENPORT

Davenport Public Library
321 Main St, 52801
Tel: 319-326-7902

1. M,T, 10-8:30; W-Sa, 10-5:30
2. David E. Montgomery, City Archivist and Supervisor of Special Collections
3. English, 5,300+; German, 25–30
4. None
5. 2,000 reels, Davenport newspapers; several hundred microfiche, IA State Census, Davenport maps; 200 reels, genealogical records
6. Davenport and Scott Counties, eastern IA, IA state; western IL; general genealogical collection covers many eastern and midwestern states
7. Tel: yes, NC; letter: yes, NC with SASE
8. Certified genealogists on a volunteer basis
9. No
10. No
11. Yes, 2 weeks through ILL
12. No
13. N/AN
14. No
15. OCLC: IOS

Books & Sets: 1–3,6,7,10–13,26
Periodicals: 4(1969–),9

DES MOINES

Public Library of Des Moines
100 Locust, 50308
Tel: 515-283-4259

1. M-Th, 9-9; F, 9-6; Sa, 9-5; summer: Th,F, 9-6
2. Shirley Shisler
3. English, number N/AV
4. None
5. None
6. Des Moines, Polk County, IA
7. Tel: yes, NC for brief queries; letter: yes, NC
8. No
9. No
10. No
11. No
12. No
13. Card file index to *Des Moines Register & Tribune* includes obituaries
14. Yes
15. OCLC: IOU
Books & Sets: 3,6,10–12,26(NH, VT,MD only)

DUBUQUE

Carnegie-Stout Public Library
11th & Bluff Sts, 52001
Tel: 319-589-4227

1. Winter: M-Th, 10-8; F, closed; Sa, 10-5; Su, 1-5; summer: M,W, 10-8; T,Th,F, 10-6; Sa, 9-5
2. None
3. English, 1,500
4. None
5. 400: local newspapers
6. IA, Dubuque County and city specifically
7. Tel: yes, NC; letter: yes, NC except $1/copy
8. No
9. No
10. Yes, duplicates only
11. No
12. No

13. In-house indexes to *Dubuque Telegraph Herald* and to area WWII servicemen
14. No. Refer to Genealogical Society
15. OCLC: KAY (some)
Books & Sets: 2,3,10–12
Periodicals: 4

ELGIN

Elgin Public Library
250 Center St, 52141
Tel: 319-426-5313

1. T,F, 1-5; W, 9:30-11:30, 1–5; Sa, 9-3
2. Norma Wilson
3. English, 20
4. 6
5. 32
6. Fayette and Clayton Counties, IA
7. Tel & letter: yes, NC
8. No
9. No
10. Yes
11. No
12. No
13. N/AN
14. No
15. No

FORT DODGE

Fort Dodge Public Library
605 1st Ave N, 50501
Tel: 515-573-8168

1. Winter: M-Th, 8:30am-9pm; F,Sa, 8:30-5:30; summer: M-Sa, 8:30-5:30
2. N/AN
3. English, 250
4. None
5. 450
6. Fort Dodge, Webster County
7. Tel & letter: yes, NC
8. No
9. No
10. Yes, duplicates only
11. Yes
12. No
13. N/AN

14. No
15. No
Periodicals: 4

IOWA CITY

State Historical Society of Iowa, Bureau of Library/Archives, Iowa City, 402 Iowa Ave, 52240
Tel: 319-335-3916

1. T-Sa, 9-4 (last T of each month, 6-9pm)
2. Karen Laughlin, Reference Librarian
3. English, 82,000; German, 50; other, 100
4. 4,000 linear ft
5. 13,500, newspapers; 3,000, census and other films
6. IA; Midwest; eastern and southern states
7. Tel: yes, NC for limited requests, for lengthy requests a letter is required; letter: yes, NC for history questions, for genealogical questions $5/half hour for non-IA residents and $3/half hour for IA residents
8. No
9. No
10. No, except for duplicate copies through ILL, $1/2-week loan
11. Yes, newspaper film and duplicate census records available through ILL: $1 fee/2 film rolls for 2-week loan
12. *Bibliography of Iowa Newspapers, 1836–1976*, out of print
13. *Population Census on Microfilm in the State Historical Society of Iowa Library*, free on request; *Major Genealogical Sources in the State Historical Society of Iowa Library*, free on request
14. Yes
15. OCL: CIOQ
Books & Sets: 2–7,10–14,17,22, 23,26
Periodicals: 1(v.40, 1964–),3(v.19, 1955–),4(v.13, 1959–),5,7,8(v.47, 1959–),9

KEOKUK

Keokuk Public Library
210 N Fifth St, 52632
Tel: 319-524-1483

1. M-Th, 9:30-9; F,Sa, 9:30-6
2. Shirley Dick, Director
3. English, 700
4. 100
5. 434
6. Area surrounding Keokuk: southeast IA, northeast MO, western central IL
7. Tel & letter: yes, NC
8. No
9. No
10. No
11. No
12. No
13. *Bibliography of Genealogical Materials for the Tri-State Area*
14. Yes
15. No
Books & Sets: 2(v.1–125, v.1,2 index),3,26
Periodicals: 4(v.20–, 1966–87)

MARSHALLTOWN

Marshalltown Public Library
36 N Center St, 50158
Tel: 515-754-5738

1. Sept-May: M-Th, 9-7:30; F,Sa, 9-5; Su, 1-4; June-Aug: M-Sa, 9-6; closed Su
2. Melissa Hauelka
3. English, 1,480
4. 105
5. All copies of local newspaper
6. Marshall County, central IA
7. Tel: yes, NC for brief requests; letter: yes, $2–$10 for staff time and microfilming
8. No. Refer to Central Iowa Genealogical Society
9. No
10. No
11. Yes, to other libraries through ILL
12. No
13. N/AN

14. Yes
15. OCLC: just starting
Books & Sets: 2(v.1–128),3,7(v.2)
Periodicals: 4(1975–86)

MUSCATINE

Musser Public Library
304 Iowa Ave, 52761
Tel: 319-263-3472

1. M-Th, 10-9; F, 10-6; Sa, 10-4
2. Barbara Bublitz
3. English, 600+
4. N/AN
5. 760, includes Muscatine newspapers from 1840, county censuses, city directories
6. Muscatine County, IA state; census indexes for nearby states, Midwest, New England
7. Tel: yes, NC for brief requests; letter: $5/hr plus 25¢/copy
8. Two experienced genealogists
9. No
10. No
11. No
12. No
13. N/AN
14. No, but help is available
15. N/AN
Books & Sets: 3,26
Periodicals: 4(1978–),8(1980–)

OAKLAND

Eckles Memorial Library and Botna Valley Genealogical Society, 207 S Highway, 51560
Tel: 712-482-6668

1. M,Th, 1-5; T, 9-12, 1-5; F, 7-9pm; Sa, 1-5
2. Any member of the Genealogical Society available
3. English, no count
4. N/AN
5. 84 reels, Pottawattamie County census and newspapers
6. Pottawattamie County, surrounding IA counties
7. Tel & letter: yes, $5/hr

8. No, but members of Genealogical Society are available
9. No
10. No
11. No
12. No
13. Obituary file of small towns in east Pottawattamie County
14. Yes
15. No
Periodicals: 4

ONAWA

Onawa Public Library
707 Iowa Ave, 51040
Tel: 712-423-1733

1. Genealogy Dept: M,T, 12:30-4:30; Th,F, 12:30-4
2. Ariel E. Wonder
3. English, "great number"
4. 45 family history books
5. 21: census; 81: newspapers
6. Monona, Woodbury, Harrison Counties
7. Tel & letter: yes, NC
8. Ariel E. Wonder
9. No
10. No
11. No
12. No
13. Over 5,000 original probates of wills; area newspapers, 1869–; church, school histories of area; Monona County marriages, 1856–80; record of death certificates, 1880–1922; over 10,000 newspaper obituaries
14. No. Refer to Onawa Genealogical Society
15. N/AN
Books & Sets: 1,2(13 v.),8
Periodicals: 4,5

ORANGE CITY

Northwestern College, Ramaker Library, 101 Seventh St, 51041
Tel: 712-737-4821

1. M-Sa, 8am-midnight
2. Cornelia B. Kennedy
3. English, 35; Dutch, 15
4. Approx 50 folders of church records, family histories

5. 50
6. Marion County, northwest IA; southeast SD
7. Tel: no; letter: yes, NC
8. No
9. No
10. Yes, 3-week loan
11. No
12. No
13. Untitled inventory
14. Yes
15. OCLC: IOO
Books & Sets: 22,23

OTTUMWA

Ottumwa Public Library
129 N Court St, 52501
Tel: 515-682-7563

1. Winter: M-Th, 9-9; F,Sa, 9-6; summer: M-W, 9-6; Th, 9-9; F,Sa, 9-5
2. Mary Ann Lemon
3. English, 2,200
4. N/AN
5. 76
6. Southern, central, southeastern IA
7. Tel: yes, NC for brief queries; letter: yes, $1/copy
8. No
9. No
10. No
11. N/AN
12. No
13. Index to Iowa Collection
14. Yes
15. No
Books & Sets: 2,3
Periodicals: 4

SIOUX CITY

Sioux City Public Library
705 Sixth St, 51105-1998
Tel: 712-279-6179

1. M-Th, 9-9; F,Sa, 9-5; Su (Sept-May), 1-5

2. Susan K. Hunting, Information Services Coordinator
3. English, 5,000; Swedish, 1. Library recently acquired extensive holdings of Martha Washington Chapter of the DAR and Woodbury County Genealogical Society; now being accessioned
4. Some cataloged into collection
5. 1,200, mostly newspapers, 1857–
6. LH: "Siouxland"; Sioux City, IA. G: mainly original states, then west to IA
7. Tel & letter: yes, NC for general questions only. Refer to Woodbury County Genealogical Society
8. No
9. No
10. No
11. No
12. No
13. N/AV
14. No
15. OCLC: IWP
Books & Sets: 2,3(1982 only),10, 11,26
Periodicals: 1(1978–),4(1985–),7

TOLEDO

Tama County Historical Museum Library
200 N Broadway, 52342
Tel: 515-484-6767

1. W-Sa, 1-4
2. Joan J. Bidwell, President, Tama County Tracers Genealogical Society
3. English, 3,000; German, 45
4. 500
5. 1,000
6. Tama County, other IA counties; OH, IN, IL, PA, NY, MD, MA, VA, NC, SC, CT, NJ, VT

7. Tel: no; letter: yes, $5/hr plus expenses
8. Joan J. Bidwell
9. No
10. No
11. No
12. No
13. Brochures may be obtained by sending large SASE
14. No
15. N/AN
Books & Sets: 7,8
Periodicals: 4,8(1970–),9(1970–)

WATERLOO

Grout Museum of History and Science, 503 South St, 50701
Tel: 319-234-6357

1. Winter: T-F, 1-4:30; Sa, 1-4; summer: T-F, 10-4:30; Sa, 1-4
2. Jan Taylor, Museum Archivist
3. English, 600
4. Approx 80 items for Black Hawk County, IA
5. None
6. Black Hawk County, northeastern IA, IA state; other US; some Europe
7. Tel & letter: yes, NC except for copies
8. No
9. No
10. No
11. No
12. *Holdings of the Northeastern Iowa Genealogical Society, Grout Museum Library,* $1.25, and Appendix I, $.50
13. None
14. No. Refer to Northeastern Iowa Genealogical Society
15. No
Books & Sets: 2,7(NJ & PA v. only),26
Periodicals: 4(current 2 years),7

DODGE CITY

Kansas Heritage Center, PO Box 1275, 1000 Second Ave, 67801
Tel: 316-227-2823

1. M-F, 8-5
2. Jeanie Covalt
3. English, 135
4. None
5. 465 reels of area newspapers, Ford County census
6. Southwestern KS
7. Tel & letter: yes, $7.50/hr plus copies
8. No
9. Yes, small out-of-city resident fee
10. Yes, only to KS residents, with fee plus shipping. Many books are reserve only
11. Yes, only to KS residents, with small fee plus shipping
12. No
13. N/AN
14. No
15. No

EMPORIA

Emporia Public Library
110 E 6th, 66801
Tel: 316-342-6524

1. M-Th, 9-8; F,Sa, 9-6; Su, 2-5; Memorial Day-Labor Day: closes at 6 on M,T,Th
2. Roger Carswell
3. English, 500
4. None
5. 500
6. Lyon County, US
7. Tel & letter: yes, NC for simple searches; otherwise $2–$5/hr plus copies
8. No
9. No

10. Yes, books not in reference collection on 2-week loan through ILL
11. No
12. No
13. N/AN
14. No
15. No
Books & Sets: 3,5,7(v.1 only),26
Periodicals: 1(v.9–20,24–50, 1932–44,1948–74),4(1961–), 8(1932–58,1980–),9(v.92–96, 1938–42)

HAYS

Fort Hays State University, Forsyth Library, 600 Park St, 67601
Tel: 913-628-4431

1. M-F, 8-4:30; closed during University vacations
2. Esta Lou Riley
3. English, 2,225; German, 56; other, 4
4. Less than 5 MSS
5. 89, plus US Censuses for Kansas; State of Kansas censuses
6. Ellis County, western KS, KS state
7. Tel & letter: yes, NC for general questions, no research
8. No
9. No
10. Yes, but only if in general collection
11. No
12. No
13. N/AN
14. No
15. OCLC: KFH
Books & Sets: 1,6,10,11,13,14,16

Hays Public Library, Kansas Room, 1205 Main, 67601
Tel: 913-625-9014

1. M-Th, 9-9; F, 9-6; S, 9-5
2. Mary Ann Thompson
3. English, 560; German, 5–10
4. Collection of 25 Record Center Boxes
5. 307
6. Ellis County, KS state; Volga-Germans
7. Tel: yes, NC; letter: yes, NC except 10¢/copy
8. Mary Ann Thompson
9. No
10. No
11. No
12. No
13. N/AN
14. Yes
15. OCLC: yes
Books & Sets: 3–5,10–12,26
Periodicals: 1(1979–),4(1978–), 5(1962–69,1974–80),7,8(1963–), 9(1978–)

LAWRENCE

Lawrence Public Library
707 Vermont, 66044
Tel: 913-843-3833

1. M-F, 9:30-9; Sa, 9:30-6; Su, 1:30-5:30
2. Cecilia Jecha May, Head, Reference Dept
3. English, 700. Also, 900 books of the DAR, Douglas County Genealogical Society collections
4. None
5. 528
6. Lawrence, Douglas County, KS state
7. Tel & letter: no
8. No
9. No
10. Yes, through ILL
11. No
12. No

13. Card catalog; shelf lists for DAR, DCGS collections
14. Yes
15. No
Books & Sets: 1–3,7(v.3 only),10, 11,13,14
Periodicals: 4,9

LEAVENWORTH

Leavenworth Public Library
417 Spruce, 66048
Tel: 913-682-5666

1. M-Th, 9-9; F,Sa, 9-5
2. N/AN
3. English, 2,500
4. Approx 10
5. 200
6. City, county, state, some surrounding state materials
7. Tel: yes, NC; letter: yes, $5/hr for questions handled by genealogical researchers
8. No
9. No
10. No
11. No
12. No
13. N/AN
14. No
15. N/AN
Books & Sets: 2,3(no suppls), 26(6 v.: NY,MA,RI,NH,ME,VT)
Periodicals: 2(1980–; partial copies, or 2 of each),4,9(1915, 1916,1972–83)

LIBERAL

Liberal Memorial Library
519 N Kansas, 67901
Tel: 316-624-0148

1. M-Th, 9-8; F,Sa, 9-5
2. None
3. English, 125
4. None
5. Unknown
6. Southwestern KS
7. Tel & letter: yes, NC
8. No
9. No
10. No
11. No

12. No
13. None
14. No
15. OCLC: some
Books & Sets: 2(3 v.),3,10
Periodicals: 4,8

NORTON

Northwest Kansas Library System, 408 N Norton, 67654
Tel: 913-877-5148

1. M-F, 8-5
2. Linda Keith, Reference
3. English, 250
4. None
5. None
6. Northwestern KS, US, parts of Europe
7. Tel & letter: yes, NC
8. No
9. No
10. Yes, only through member system libraries
11. N/AP
12. No
13. *Genealogy Collection* bibliography, free on request
14. No
15. OCLC: KKV (shared holding symbol with 2 other library systems)
Books & Sets: 3,7(v.1, 1978), 10–12,26

OLATHE

Olathe Public Library
201 E Park St, 66061
Tel: 913-764-2259

1. M-Th, 10-9; F,Sa, 10-5; Su, 1-5
2. Mary Jo O'Brien, Reference Librarian
3. English, 300
4. 1. Genealogical materials on surname Stewart
5. 100: local newspapers, 1864–; 14: KS census, 1925
6. Mostly US
7. Tel & letter: yes, NC
8. Yes
9. No

10. No
11. No
12. No
13. None
14. No
15. No
Books & Sets: 3,7,10–12
Periodicals: 4,5,7

OSKALOOSA

Jefferson County Genealogical Society, Research Center, Highway 59, Old Jefferson Town, 66066
Tel: 913-863-2070

1. M, 7pm-8:30pm; Sa, 1-5; Su, 1:30-5
2. Karen Heady, Librarian
3. English, 664
4. 1,700 periodicals
5. 300
6. Jefferson County, KS; other KS and MO counties; other US; some England, Europe
7. Tel & letter: yes, NC for brief queries
8. No
9. No
10. Yes, 2-week loan to Society members
11. No
12. No
13. None
14. Yes
15. N/AN
Books & Sets: 8(US,Canada,most Europe)
Periodicals: 4(1971–)

SHAWNEE MISSION

Johnson County Library
8700 W 63rd St, Box 2901, 66201
Tel: 913-831-1550

1. M-Th, 9-9; F, 9-6; Sa, 9-5; Su, 1-5
2. N/AP
3. English, 3,000
4. None
5. 50
6. Eastern US, Southeast,

Midwest, Central Plains, British Isles
    7. Tel & letter: yes, NC for local history only
    8. Volunteers only
    9. No
    10. No
    11. No
    12. No
    13. N/AP
    14. Yes
    15. No
Books & Sets: 1,3,4,6,7,10,11,13, 14,19(6 v.1903–26 only),26
Periodicals: 1(v.48–, 1972–), 4(v.36–, 1982–),5(1976–),7(v.1,3), 8(v.48–, 1965–),9(v.134–, 1980–)

TOPEKA

Kansas State Historical Society Library, 120 W 10th, 66612
Tel: 913-296-4776

    1. M-F, 9-5; Sa, 8-12 except for holiday weekends
    2. No section heads
    3. English, 23,675 (does not include KS material)
    4. 13
    5. 2,060 out-of-state census film
    6. KS; areas providing majority of KS settlers, such as MO, OH, IN, IL, PA; New England
    7. Tel: no; letter: no, except for holdings information. Queries answered on holdings for non-KS material
    8. Reference librarians
    9. No
    10. No
    11. No
    12. N/AN
    13. Several unpublished indexes to KS biographical sketches and necrologies
    14. Yes
    15. No
Books & Sets: 2–8,10–14,17,18, 22–24,26
Periodicals: 1,3–5,7–9

Topeka Genealogical Society Library, 2717 Indiana Ave, 66605
Tel: 913-233-5762

    1. W, 1-4; Th, 1-4; Sa, 1-4; 1st & 3d Th, 5:30-8:30
    2. Katy Matthews, Librarian
    3. English, 1,700; German, 1. Also, periodicals, 200 titles, approx 2,000 bound vols
    4. 2
    5. 1
    6. US, Canada, Europe
    7. Tel & letter: yes, NC
    8. N/AN
    9. Yes, $1/visit to nonmembers; free to members
    10. Yes, 4-week loan, to members only
    11. No
    12. No
    13. Card index, shelf list
    14. Yes
    15. No
Periodicals: 3–5,8,9

Topeka Public Library
1515 W 10th St, 66604
Tel: 913-233-2040

    1. M-F, 9-9; Sa, 9-6; Su (during school year), 2-6
    2. Warren E. Taylor
    3. English, 1,900; French and German, several
    4. Several boxes of family papers
    5. 10, plus complete run of local newspapers
    6. Emphasis on KS
    7. Tel: no; letter: yes, charge depends on search time and number of copies
    8. No
    9. No
    10. No
    11. No
    12. No
    13. Obituary index of *Topeka State Journal* newspaper, 1906–26
    14. Yes
    15. OCLC: KTP
Books & Sets: 3–7,10,12,18,19, 24,26

Periodicals: 4(v.17–),9(v.100–11, v.128–)

WHITE CITY

Morris County Genealogical Library, Box 114, 3rd & Grant Sts, 66872
Tel: 913-349-2987

    1. F, 1-4
    2. Reference librarian
    3. English, 300
    4. 25
    5. 5 microfilm; microfiche collection
    6. US, some foreign countries
    7. Tel & letter: yes, NC
    8. Sue Metcalfe
       Carole Price
    9. No
    10. No
    11. No
    12. No
    13. Morris County: part of federal census (1900), marriage records (1854–87), tax roll (1870), all county cemeteries
    14. Yes
    15. No
Books & Sets: 2(1968)
Periodicals: 4(1955–)

WICHITA

Midwest Historical and Genealogical Society
PO Box 1121, 67201
Tel: 316-264-3611

    1. Tu,Sa, 9-4; 2d Sa each month, 9-12:30
    2. Jerry Ann Stout, Librarian
    3. English, 2,630
    4. 2,630 [*sic*]
    5. 50
    6. US; some foreign
    7. Tel: yes, NC for brief queries; letter: yes, NC except for copies and postage
    8. No, all volunteers
    9. Yes, either by membership ($10/yr) or $1/day
    10. No
    11. No

12. In progress
13. N/AN
14. No
15. No
Books & Sets: 3(1986 only), 26(incomplete)
Periodicals: 3(v.25–, 1961–), 4(v.4–41),5,8(incomplete 1943–83),9(incomplete 1907,1950–)

Wichita Public Library
223 S Main, 67202
Tel: 316-262-0611, ext 262

1. M-Th, 8:30am-9pm; F,Sa, 8:30-5:30; Su, 1-5
2. Marsha Stenholm
3. English, 16,000; German, 2; French, 5; Swedish, 2; Welsh, 1
4. None
5. 2,500
6. KS, states east of KS
7. Tel & letter: yes, for basic reference service only. No research for individuals by either letter or phone
8. No

9. No
10. No
11. No
12. No
13. None
14. Yes
15. OCLC: KFW
Books & Sets: 2–5,7,10–12, 18,23,26
Periodicals: 1,3(v.19–26, 1955–62),4(v.6–, 1952–),5(v.1–8,13,14), 6(scattered issues),7,8(v.6–, 1917–),9(except v.127,128)

ASHLAND

**Boyd County Public Library
(Minnie Winder Genealogy and
Local History Collection)**
1740 Central Ave, 41101
Tel: 606-329-0090

1. M-F, 9-9; Sa, 9-6
2. James C. Powers, Assistant
Director
3. English, 2,475
4. N/AP
5. 1,543
6. KY, VA, WV, NC, PA,
some New England states
7. Tel & letter: yes, NC
8. James C. Powers
9. No
10. Yes, within state through
ILL
11. Yes, within state through
ILL
12. No
13. N/AN
14. No
15. No
Books & Sets: 2(v.86,121,125,126,
152,160),3,5(v.1 only),7,10,11,13,
14,18(v.1–45),26
Periodicals: 4(1959–),5,7,8(v.55–,
1957–)

BOWLING GREEN

**Western Kentucky University,
Kentucky Library, 42101**
Tel: 502-745-6263

1. M-F, 8-4:30; Sa, 9-4:30
2. Constance A. Mills
3. English, 3,000
4. 1,275. Separate unit in
Western KY University Dept of
Library Special Collections: Manu-
scripts/Folklife Archives

5. 1,720
6. South central KY, KY state;
some southeastern US
7. Tel & letter: yes, NC except
15¢/copy
8. No
9. No
10. No
11. No
12. No
13. *Researcher's Guide* (1-sheet
introduction), family file index,
card catalog
14. Yes
15. No
Books & Sets: *1,6,7,10,11,*13,
*14(*located in WKU main
library)
Periodicals: 1(v.43–, 1967–),
4(v.4–10,39–, 1950–56,
1985–),8,9(v.117–, 1963–)

COVINGTON

Kenton County Public Library
5th & Scott Sts, 41011
Tel: 606-491-7610

1. M-Th, 10-9; F, 10-6; Sa,
10-5
2. Charles D. King
3. English, 5,000; German, 30
4. 35
5. 4,500
6. Kenton, Campbell, Boone
Counties in depth; KY state
7. Tel: yes, NC; letter: yes,
hourly rate plus copies
8. Charles D. King
9. No
10. No
11. No
12. No
13. "Suggested Sources for
Genealogical Research in the
Kenton County Public Library";
newspaper index, 1835–1919;

obituaries, 1835–1912; births,
1878–1912
14. Yes
15. OCLC: KCE
Books & Sets: 2(v.1–54),3–6,
10–14,26(VA only)
Periodicals: 4(1972–)

FLORENCE

Boone County Public Library
7425 US 42, 41042
Tel: 606-371-6222

1. M-Th, 9-9; F,Sa, 9-5
2. Patricia Yannarella, Adult
Services Librarian
3. English, 300
4. None
5. 300
6. Boone County; some KY
state
7. Tel & letter: yes, NC
8. No
9. No
10. Yes, 2-week loan
11. No
12. N/AN
13. "Genealogical Sources at
Boone County Public Library,"
6-page typescript
14. Yes
15. No
Periodicals: 4(1980–)

FRANKFORT

**Kentucky Department for
Libraries and Archives,
Public Records Division**
300 Coffee Tree Rd, 40602
Tel: 502-875-7000

1. M-Sa, 8-4:15
2. James Prichard
3. English, 750
4. 1

5. 20,000
6. KY, VA, NC, OH, PA, MD, SC, IN, MO, TN
7. Tel & letter: yes, NC except for copies
8. James Prichard
9. No
10. No
11. No
12. No
13. Typescript guide to KY state archives
14. Yes
15. No
Books & Sets: 6
Periodicals: 4(1965–77),5, 8(1974–)

Kentucky Historical Society Library, 300 Broadway, Old Capitol Annex, 40602
Tel: 502-564-3016

1. M-Su, 8-4:30
2. Anne McDonnell
3. English, 60,000
4. 1,000 cu ft
5. 10,000
6. KY and surrounding states
7. Tel: no; letter: yes, NC for brief queries
8. Yes
9. No
10. No
11. No
12. No
13. N/AN
14. Yes
15. No
Books & Sets: 2–8,10–19,26
Periodicals: 1,3–9

HARLAN

Foot Prints Publications and Research, PO Box 1498, 40831
Tel: 606-573-6958, M-Sa, 9-3

1. By appointment only
2. Holly Fee
3. English, 200+

4. 20 ft of files
5. 10–12 reels
6. Southeastern KY, related areas
7. Tel: brief inquiries only; letter: brief inquiries w/SASE
8. Holly Fee
9. No, but contributions appreciated. Copying charges
10. No
11. No
12. No
13. None
14. Yes
15. No
Periodicals: 4(partial),8(partial), 9(partial)

LEXINGTON

Lexington Public Library, Kentucky Room, 251 W Second, 40507
Tel: 606-231-5520

1. M-Th, 9-9; F,Sa, 9-5; Su, 1-5
2. Robin Rader
3. English, 4,000
4. 10
5. 2,300
6. Lexington, KY state
7. Tel & letter: yes, NC except for copies, $1 plus 15¢/page, or 20¢/microfilm reader-printer copy
8. No
9. No
10. No, but several Lexington and KY history books are available through ILL
11. No
12. No
13. Local History Index: card file to local newspapers. Also, 2 leaflets: *Resources for Genealogists: Kentucky Reference Collection*; *Kentucky Reference Collection*
14. Yes
15. No
Books & Sets: 1,10–14,26(NH,VT, NC,PA,MD,VA)
Periodicals: 4(v.34–),8(v.74–)

University of Kentucky, Margaret I. King Library
Department of Special Collections and Archives, 40506-0039
Tel: 606-257-8611

1. M-F, 8-4:30; Sa, 8-12; Su, 2-5 (closed Su when University not in full session)
2. B. J. Gooch
3. English, 6,400
4. 600–700 different record groups (including LH/G, ecclesiastical)
5. 12,000
6. KY, TN, VA, WV, OH, IL, MO, IN, NC, SC, NJ, PA, MD
7. Tel & letter: yes, NC for brief queries
8. B. J. Gooch
9. No
10. Yes
11. Yes
12. In progress
13. Guide to manuscript collection; guide to LH/G materials; guide to Kentuckiana Manuscript Collections
14. Yes
15. OCLC: KUK
Books & Sets: 1,3(suppls 1982– 84),5,6,13,17,18,26(PA,MD, VA,NC)
Periodicals: 9

MAYSVILLE

Mason County Museum
215 Sutton St, 41056
Tel: 606-564-4659

1. T-Sa, 10-4
2. Margaret G. Kendall
3. English, 1,000
4. "Family files" from A-Z
5. 339
6. Mason, Bracken, Fleming, Robertson Counties in KY; Adams, Brown, Clermont Counties in OH
7. Tel: no; letter: yes, NC except for copies

8. Margaret G. Kendall
9. Yes, $1.25/visit or $12 annual membership
10. No
11. No
12. No, desk guide only
13. N/AP
14. No
15. No
Books & Sets: 2,3,5,26
Periodicals: 4,7,8(1960–)

MURRAY

Murray State University, Forrest C. Pogue Special Collections Library, 42071-3309
Tel: 502-762-6152

1. M-W, F, 8-4:30; Th, 8-8; Sa, 10-3. Variable hours during summer and university breaks
2. Keith M. Heim
3. English, 8,000; 4,000 bound periodicals
4. 1,300 Hollinger boxes of papers of congressmen, public officials, families; extensive vertical files
5. 6,000
6. KY, TN; states from which settlers came, especially VA, NC, SC, IL; also GA, MD, PA, MO
7. Tel & letter: yes, NC for limited questions
8. No, but Library has professional historian

9. No
10. No
11. No
12. Brochure
13. Card catalogs
14. Yes (experienced researchers)
15. OCLC: KMSU
Books & Sets: *1,2(partial),3,4, 5(v.1–5),*6,7,10–14,17,19(2v., 1950,1972),26 (*located at main campus library)
Periodicals: 4,5(1962–65,1974–), 7,8

OWENSBORO

Owensboro-Daviess County Public Library, 450 Griffith Ave, 42301
Tel: 502-684-0211 (Kentucky Room)

1. M-F, 9-9; Sa, 9-6; Su, 2-5. Kentucky Room closes 12-1 for lunch
2. Sheila E. Heflin
3. English, 9,000
4. 200
5. 1,800
6. KY, VA, WV, PA, MD, TN, NC, SC, southern IN, southern IL, small area of MO
7. Tel & letter: yes, NC for brief requests except 10¢/copy or 20¢/microfilm copy plus postage
8. No
9. No

10. No
11. No
12. No
13. Obituary listings from *Owensboro Messenger* (1920, 1930–81, 1985–); over 100 years of microfilmed Owensboro newspapers
14. Yes
15. No
Books & Sets: 2,7,10,17,26
Periodicals: 4(1967–86),5,7, 8(1942–79),9(1945–50)

PADUCAH

Paducah Public Library
555 Washington St, 42001-1199
Tel: 502-442-2510

1. M-F, 10-9; Sa, 10-6; Su, 2-6
2. Barbara Dubber
3. English, 1,600
4. 2
5. 200
6. KY, TN, VA
7. Tel & letter: yes, NC
8. No
9. No
10. No
11. No
12. No
13. N/AN
14. Yes
15. No
Books & Sets: 3,10,11,17,26
Periodicals: 4(1980–82)

LOUISIANA

ALEXANDRIA

Rapides Parish Library
411 Washington St, 71301
Tel: 318-445-2411

1. M-W,F,Sa, 9-6; Th, 9-8
2. Reference Department
3. English, 550
4. N/AP
5. 800
6. LA, southern states
7. Tel: no; letter: yes, $1/minimum for copies
8. No
9. No
10. Yes, but not reference books
11. No
12. No
13. Partial bibliography
14. Yes
15. No
Books & Sets: 11

BATON ROUGE

East Baton Rouge Parish Library, Centroplex Branch
120 St. Louis St, PO Box 1471, 70821
Tel: 504-389-4690

1. M-Th, 8-7; F,Sa, 9-6; Su, 2-6
2. Sylvia Walker
3. English, 6,000; French, 12
4. Figure not available
5. 8,500
6. Southern states
7. Tel & letter: yes, NC if brief
8. No
9. No
10. Yes, duplicates only
11. No
12. No
13. *Bibliography of Louisiana Titles in Centroplex Genealogy*

Collection; Periodic Lists of New Books in the Centroplex Library Genealogy Collection
14. Yes
15. OCLC: LEB6 (LA Genealogy), LEB7 (General Genealogy)
Books & Sets: 2(incomplete), 3–5,9–14,22–26
Periodicals: 4,5(1962 only),7, 8(1978–),9(1986–)

Louisiana State Library
760 Riverside North, PO Box 131, 70821
Tel: 504-342-4914

1. M-F, 8-4:30; closed holidays
2. Harriet Callahan
3. English, 3,500; German, 5; French, 10
4. 600
5. 3,800
6. LA, the South, US
7. Tel: yes, NC; letter, N/AN
8. No
9. No
10. Yes, from LA Section but not from Genealogy Section
11. Yes, at $2.50/roll
12. *Searching for Your Ancestors on Microfilm*, free brochure
13. N/AN
14. Yes
15. OCLC: LSLW (LA Genealogy), LSIG (Genealogy)
Books & Sets: 3,5–7,10–13,17, 19,23–26
Periodicals: 8(v.1–62, 1912–74), 9(1963–69)

EUNICE

Louisiana State University at Eunice, LeDoux Library
PO Box 1129, 70535
Tel: 318-457-7311, ext 64

1. M-Th, 7:30-7; F, 7:30-5
2. James L. Forester
3. English, 4,500; German, 10; French, 50
4. 3 (LA colonial documents)
5. 100
6. Southeastern states; LA, Quebec, Nova Scotia
7. Tel & letter: yes, NC for limited requests
8. James L. Forester
9. No
10. Yes, through ILL. Rare and LA materials may be restricted
11. No
12. *Genealogical Resources, Bayouland Library System*, $12.50. Available from Bayouland Library System, 301 W Congress St, Lafayette, LA 70501
13. Index to Eunice area cemeteries
14. No
15. No
Books & Sets: 3,7,24–26
Periodicals: 4

FRANKLINTON

Washington Parish Library System, 825 Free St, 70438
(Bogalusa Branch: 304 Ave F, Bogalusa, 70427)
Tel: Franklinton: 504-839-5336; Bogalusa: 504-735-1961

1. Franklinton: M-F, 10-5; Sa, 10-1; Bogalusa: M, 10-6; T-F, 10-5; Sa, 10-3
2. Franklinton: Veronica Westbrook, Circulation; Bogalusa: Alecia Applewhite, Branch Assistant
3. English, 360 (Franklinton), 150 (Bogalusa)
4. None

5. Franklinton: 171; Bogalusa, 100

6. Franklinton: LA, SC, MS, MD, NC, GA; Bogalusa: LA, MS, SC, GA, TN

7. Tel: yes, NC (Franklinton), no (Bogalusa); letter: yes, NC except 20¢/copy

8. No
9. No
10. No
11. No
12. No
13. N/AN
14. No
15. No

HOUMA

Terrebonne Parish Library
424 Roussell St, 70360
Tel: 504-876-5861

1. M-Th, 9-8; F,Sa, 9-5
2. Dorotha Horvath, Genealogical Assistant
3. English, 2,700; French, 50
4. N/AN
5. 385
6. Lafourche Interior (Lafourche, Terrebonne, and Ascension Parishes); LA, southern states
7. Tel: yes, NC for limited requests; letter: yes, NC
8. Dorotha Horvath
9. No
10. Yes, duplicate copies
11. No
12. *Genealogical Resources Catalog*, $15. Available from Bayouland Library System, 301 W Congress St, Lafayette, LA, 70501
13. Index of the *Houma Courier* for births and deaths, computer index of cemeteries of Terrebonne Parish
14. No
15. No
Books & Sets: 1,3,10–12,24,25
Periodicals: 4

LAFAYETTE

Lafayette Parish Public Library
301 W Congress, 70506
Tel: 318-261-5787

1. Winter: M-Th, 9-9; F,Sa, 9-5; summer: M-W, 9-7; Th, 9-9; F, 9-5; Sa, 9-4
2. Jane Dillion
3. English, no estimate; French, no estimate
4. N/AN
5. N/AN
6. N/AN
7. Tel & letter: yes, NC
8. No
9. No
10. Yes, lend local history only
11. No
12. No
13. N/AN
14. Yes
15. OCLC: LFY
Books & Sets: 3,9
Periodicals: 4(1974–),8(1985–)

LA PLACE

St. John the Baptist Parish Library, 1334 W Airline Highway, Riverlands Shopping Center, 70068
Tel: 504-652-6857

1. M-Th, 8:30am-9pm; F,Sa, 8:30-5:30
2. Mary L. Duhe
3. N/AV
4. N/AV
5. 123
6. St. John the Baptist Parish, LA state
7. Tel & letter: yes, NC for brief queries except 10¢/copy
8. No
9. No
10. Yes, duplicates only, through ILL
11. No
12. No
13. N/AN
14. No
15. No

Books & Sets: 3,10–14,24–26
Periodicals: 8

LEESVILLE

Vernon Parish Library
301 E Courthouse St, 71446
Tel: 318-239-9522

1. M,W,F,Sa, 8-5:30; T,Th, 8-7:30
2. N/AN
3. English, N/AN
4. 800
5. 420
6. LA, AL, MS, GA, VA; some TX
7. Tel: no; letter: yes, for history questions, not genealogy
8. No
9. No
10. Yes, through ILL for in-house use only
11. Yes, through ILL only
12. No
13. N/AN
14. No
15. No
Books & Sets: 3

LUTCHER

St. James Parish Library
Rt 1, Box 32-C, 70071
Tel: 504-869-3618

1. M-Th, 8:30-6; F, 8:30-5; Sa, 8:30-1
2. Kenneth P. Neal, Reference Librarian
3. English, 155; German, 4
4. None
5. 88
6. Southeastern, southwestern, northern LA; LA river parishes; East Texas, southern MS
7. Tel & letter: yes, NC
8. No
9. No
10. Yes
11. No
12. No
13. St. James Parish Collection
14. No

15. No
Periodicals: 7

MARKSVILLE

Avoyelles Parish Library
101 N Washington, 71351
Tel: 318-253-7559/7550

1. M,T,Th,F, 8-5; W, 9-6; Sa,
9-1
2. Susan Guidry, Associate
Librarian
3. English, 1,668; French, 20
4. None
5. 11
6. Avoyelles, Rapides, Point
Coupee Parishes; southern LA
7. Tel: no; letter: yes, 20¢/
copy plus $1 handling fee
8. Susan Guidry
   Elsie Reed (volunteer)
9. No
10. Yes, to Avoyelles residents
only; will send copies of information to nonresidents
11. No
12. No
13. *Avoyelles Parish Genealogy
Collection*: booklet available for
use in genealogy room
14. No professionals, but one
person will research for fee
15. No
Books & Sets: 3,24
Periodicals: 4

METAIRIE

Jefferson Parish Library
3420 N Causeway Blvd, 70010
Tel: 504-833-1771

1. M-F, 9-8; Sa, 9-5
2. N/AN
3. English, 900; French, 17;
Russian, 1
4. None
5. Over 1,000 (includes
newspapers)
6. Canada, Germany, Great
Britain; US and some states: AL,
IL, LA, MO, NY, NC, PA, SC, VA
7. Tel: yes, NC; letter: N/AN
8. Dwight Duplessis

9. No
10. No
11. No
12. *Looking Back at Your Ancestors: A Selected Genealogy
Bibliography*
13. N/AN
14. No
15. OCLC: LMJ
Books & Sets: 1,3,5,19,24,25
Periodicals: 4,8

NAPOLEONVILLE

Assumption Parish Library
Hwy 308 at Franklin,
PO Drawer A, 70390
Tel: 504-369-7070

1. M,W,Th, 8:30-5:30;
T, 8:30-7; Sa, 9-1
2. Mary G. Judice, Librarian
3. French, approx 20
4. 500
5. 120
6. LA state; Canada
7. Tel & letter: yes, NC
8. No
9. No
10. Yes, 2-week loan; 30-day
loan, through ILL
11. No
12. No
13. N/AN
14. Yes
15. No
Books & Sets: 3,24,25

NEW ORLEANS

**Historic New Orleans Collection
Library,** 533 Royal St, 70130
Tel: 504-523-4662

1. T-Sa, 10-4:30
2. Florence M. Jumonville,
Head Librarian, Research Library
3. English, 24,000; German,
10; French, 50; Spanish, 25. Includes pamphlets
4. Held by MS Division
5. Held by MS Division
6. LA, with emphasis on New
Orleans; some Mississippi Valley,
Gulf South

7. Tel & letter: yes, NC except
25¢/copy
8. No
9. No
10. No
11. No
12. *Guide to Research at the
Historic New Orleans Collection,*
free
13. N/AN
14. No
15. No
Books & Sets: 3,6

**Louisiana State Museum,
Louisiana Historical Center
Library,** Old US Mint, 400
Esplanade Ave, 70116 (mailing
address: 751 Chartres St)
Tel: 504-568-8215

1. W-F, 10-4:45
2. Rose Lambert, Librarian
3. Scattered texts in various
languages relating to LH
4. Large MS collection
relating to LA history
5. None
6. LA, with concentration on
New Orleans
7. Tel & letter: yes, NC for
brief queries except for copies
8. No
9. No
10. No
11. No
12. No, but included in L. T.
Cummins and G. Jeansonne, eds.,
*A Guide to the History of Louisi-
ana* (1982)
13. N/AN
14. No
15. No
Books & Sets: 24(7 v., 1871–90)

**New Orleans Public Library,
Louisiana Division**
219 Loyola Ave, 70140
Tel: 504-596-2610

1. M-Th, S, 10-6
2. Collin B. Hamer, Jr.
3. English, 25,000; German,
16; French, 41; Spanish, 24
4. 150

5. 8,000
6. Southeastern US, Canada, Western Europe
7. Tel: no; letter: yes, NC for very limited responses
8. Collin B. Hamer, Jr.
9. No
10. No
11. Yes, but will not lend heavily used titles
12. *Genealogical Material in the New Orleans Public Library,* $4.75
13. N/AN
14. Yes
15. OCLC: LNC
Books & Sets: 1,2(v.1–128),3–6, 9–12,19,22–26
Periodicals: 4(v.15,21–, 1961, 1967–),5,7–9

Tulane University, Howard-Tilton Memorial Library, 70118
Tel: 504-865-5695 (Manuscripts); 865-5643 (LA Collection); 865-5605 (Reference)

1. Manuscripts: M-F, 8:30-5; Sa, 9-1; LA Collection: M-F, 8:30-5; Sa, 10-5; Reference: M-Th, 8:30am-10pm; F, 8:30-5; Sa, 10-5; Su, 1-10
2. Manuscripts: Wilbur E. Meneray; LA Collection: Gay G. Craft
3. English, 250 (LA); French, 30
4. 2,500 dealing with LA families or local history
5. 35
6. LA, southern MS, lower South, South in order of strength of holdings
7. Tel & letter: yes, NC except for copies
8. No
9. No
10. No
11. No
12. No
13. N/AN
14. Yes
15. OCLC: some LRU
Books & Sets: 1–6,7(v.1–6),17,

18(broken set, v.50–),19(partial), 24–26
Periodicals: 1(v.9–13, 1932/33–37),3(1939),4(broken set),5(v.1,4, 8,13–24, 1962,1965,1968,1974–85),6(v.7, 1936),7(broken set, & v.51–, 1963–)

PLAQUEMINE

Iberville Parish Library
1501 J. Gerald Berret Blvd, PO Box 736, 70764
Tel: 504-687-4397; 687-2520; 344-6948

1. M, 8:30-6; T-Th, 8:30-5:30; F, 8:30-5
2. N/AN
3. English, 56
4. 20
5. 50
6. LA state; southern US
7. Tel & letter: yes, NC
8. No
9. No
10. No
11. No
12. No
13. N/AN
14. No
15. N/AN

PORT ALLEN

West Baton Rouge Parish Library, 830 N Alexander, 70767
Tel: 504-343-3484

1. M-F, 9-5:30; Sa, 9-1
2. N/AN
3. English, 400; French, 30. G: mostly Acadian, some French and Spanish Colonial
4. N/AN
5. 30
6. LA state; other southern states
7. Tel & letter: no
8. No
9. No
10. Yes
11. No
12. No

13. N/AN
14. No
15. N/AN
Books & Sets: 3,24,25

SAINT MARTINVILLE

St. Martin Parish Library
105 S New Market St, 70582
Tel: 318-394-4086

1. M,W, 8-8; T, Th,F, 8-5; Sa, 8-noon
2. Marian T. Barras
3. English, 2,096; small amount in French and Spanish
4. 50
5. 681
6. Southern LA
7. Tel & letter: no
8. No
9. No
10. Yes, through ILL
11. Yes, through ILL
12. *St. Martin Parish Microfilm Collection,* $5; *St. Martin Parish Genealogy Collection,* $5
13. N/AN
14. No
15. N/AN
Books & Sets: 2(2 v.),3,10,13, 19,24–26
Periodicals: 4(1981–)

SHREVEPORT

Shreve Memorial Library
424 Texas St, 71101
Tel: 318-226-5890

1. M-Sa, 9-6; Su, 1-5
2. Mignon Morse
3. English, 7,000
4. N/AN
5. 11,000
6. All US states except HI; some foreign countries
7. Tel & letter: yes, NC except for copies and postage
8. N/AN
9 No
10. No
11. No
12. No

13. New-books lists, list of books in order by counties
14. No
15. No

Books & Sets: 1,2(v.1–160),3–5,7, 10–14,18,19,22–26

Periodicals: 1(v.55–60),3(v.47–50),4(v.11–38,39–41),5, 8(v.45–69,71–73),9 (v.54–64,67–69,76–105,107–35; v.1–131 on microfilm)

THIBODAUX

Lafourche Parish Library
303 W 5th St, 70301 (office)
Tel: 504-447-4119 (Thibodaux Branch Library, Reference and Interlibrary Loan Department)

1. M-F, 9-6; Sa, 9-5
2. Cathy McKenzie
3. No accurate counts kept
4. None
5. Over 300 reels
6. LA; some MS; Canada (Acadia)
7. Tel: yes, NC for simple questions; letter: yes, NC except for copies
8. No
9. No
10. No
11. Yes, patron pays postage
12. No
13. N/AN
14. No
15. No

Books & Sets: 24–26

MAINE

AUBURN

Auburn Public Library
49 Spring St, 04210
Tel: 207-782-3191

1. M,Th, 9-8; T,W,F, 9-6; Sa, 9-5
2. Lois C. Wagner, Reference Librarian
3. English, 2,500
4. 25
5. 6
6. Androscoggin County, ME state; some NH, MA
7. Tel & letter: yes, NC except expenses
8. Nancy Taylor (amateur)
9. No
10. Yes, through ILL for in-house use only
11. Yes, through ILL for in-house use only
12. No
13. Family history list, town history list
14. Yes
15. N/AN
Books & Sets: 2(v.16,54,55),18, 19,26
Periodicals: 7,9

AUGUSTA

Maine State Library, Sta #64, Cultural Building, 04333
Tel: 207-289-5600

1. M,W,F, 9-5; T,Th, 9-9; Sa, 11-5
2. Don Wismer, Head, Reference Dept
3. English, 9,000
4. N/AP
5. 375
6. New England, as follows:

comprehensive for ME; strong in MA, NH; basic for VT, RI, CT
7. Tel: yes, NC for brief queries; letter: yes, NC except for copies
8. No
9. No
10. G, no; LH, yes, through libraries only with limit of 2 books per time
11. No
12. No
13. *Genealogy of French Canada, Acadia, & Franco-America at the Maine State Library*
14. Yes
15. OCLC: MEA (75%)
Books & Sets: 1,3,4,6,9–12,18, 19(2v., 1950,1972),24,25
Periodicals: 1(v.19–41,56–), 3(v.46–, 1982–),4(v.26–, 1972–), 5(v.15–, 1976–),6(v.21–, 1983–), 7(1973 rev),8(v.45–, 1957–),9

BRUNSWICK

Curtis Memorial Library
23 Pleasant St, 04011-2295
Tel: 207-725-5242

1. Winter: M-W, 9-9; Th,F, 9-6; Sa, 9-5; summer: M, 9-9; T-F, 9-6
2. N/AN
3. English, 100
4. None
5. 200 (newspapers only)
6. Brunswick and Harpswell, ME
7. Tel & letter: yes, NC
8. No
9. No
10. Yes, through ILL
11. No
12. No
13. "Information Sources on Genealogy at Curtis Memorial

Library," 1 p; "Brunswick History: A Guide to Basic Sources," 4 pp (both free for return postage)
14. No
15. OCLC: CTM

Pejepscot Historical Society
159 Park Row, 04011
Tel: 207-729-6606

1. By appointment
2. Kathy Hudson, Director; Peter Bals, Curator
3. English, "all"
4. 12, plus town records
5. None
6. Brunswick, Topsham, Harpswell, ME
7. Tel & letter: yes, NC
8. No
9. No
10. No
11. No
12. No
13. Card index; genealogical guide to the area
14. No
15. No

LEWISTON

Lewiston Public Library
105 Park St, 04240
Tel: 207-784-0135

1. Winter: M-Th, 9-8; F,Sa, 9-5; summer: M, 9-8; T-F, 9-5; Sa, 9-2
2. Lizette R. Leveille, Reference Librarian
3. English, 800; other, 60
4. None
5. 640 in English (includes reels of local newspapers), 65 in French (local newspaper)
6. ME; some New England;

much on French Canadian sections of Canada, ME

7. Tel: no, unless very brief; letter: yes, $2 reference fee plus copying costs. No extensive genealogical searching
8. No
9. No
10. No
11. No
12. No
13. No
14. Amateurs who concentrate in Franco-American genealogy for modest fee
15. No
Books & Sets: 19,24,26

PORTLAND

Maine Historical Society
485 Congress St, 04101
Tel: 207-774-1822

1. T,W,F, 9-5; Th, 9-7; 2nd Sa of each month, 9-5
2. Margaret J. McCain
3. English, 17,000
4. N/AP
5. 800
6. ME, New England, Great Britain, Maritime Provinces of Canada

7. Tel: G, no, LH, yes, if brief; letter: yes, $10 for brief search
8. No
9. Yes, $2/day
10. No
11. No
12. No
13. *Guide to the Maine Historical Society Library* (informal guide for visitors)
14. Yes
15. No
Books & Sets: 2,3,5,6,18,19,24–26
Periodicals: 1,5,6(1925–67),7–9

WATERVILLE

Waterville Public Library
73 Elm St, 04901
Tel: 207-873-4779

1. Hours on request
2. Richard Sibley
3. English, 50
4. 1
5. None
6. ME, NH, MA
7. Tel: no; letter: yes, NC for simple questions, except 15¢/copy
8. No
9. No
10. No

11. No
12. No
13. N/AN
14. Yes
15. No

YORK

Old York Historical Society Library, 140 Lindsay Rd, 03909
Tel: 207-363-4974

1. T-F, 9-12, 1-5
2. Debra Cunningham
3. English, 4,000
4. 500
5. 60
6. ME, with emphasis on York, York County; some NH
7. Tel: yes, NC; letter: yes, $10/hr
8. Debra Cunningham
9. No
10. No
11. No
12. No
13. "Genealogical Guidebook to York, Maine"
14. Yes
15. No
Books & Sets: 8,26
Periodicals: 9(1895,1906–)

MARYLAND

ANNAPOLIS

Anne Arundel County Public Library, 5 Truman Parkway, 21401
Tel: 301-224-7371

1. M-F, 9-9; Sa, 9-5; Su, 1-5
2. None
3. English, 690
4. None
5. 10
6. Anne Arundel County; other MD counties; MD state
7. Tel & letter: yes, NC
8. No
9. No
10. Yes, except for some items in Maryland Room Collection
11. No
12. Yes, available for in-library use only
13. N/AN
14. No. Refer to Maryland Hall of Records
15. No

Maryland State Archives Library, 350 Rowe Blvd, 21401
Tel: 301-974-3915

1. M-Sa, 8:30-4:30
2. Douglas P. McElrath
3. English, 4,000
4. 800
5. 2,000
6. MD, mid-Atlantic
7. Tel: no; letter, yes, $5 charge
8. No
9. No
10. No
11. Yes, through ILL
12. Yes
13. Catalog
14. Yes

15. No
Books & Sets: 2(incomplete),3,6, 13,26
Periodicals: 9(incomplete)

Maryland State Law Library
Courts of Appeal Building, 361 Rowe Blvd, 21401
Tel: 301-974-3395

1. M,W,F, 8:30-4:30; T,Th, 8:30am-9pm; Sa, 9-4
2. Shirley Rittenhouse
   Michael S. Miller
3. English, 7,000
4. 25
5. 2.200
6. MD; some DE, CT, GA, KY, ME, MA, NH, NJ, NY, NC, PA, RI, SC, TN, VT, VA, WV
7. Tel: yes, NC; letter: yes, NC except for copies
8. No
9. No
10. Yes, only titles in print or duplicate copies; 2–4 week loan
11. Yes, newspapers only
12. *Genealogical Holdings in the Maryland State Law Library,* $3
13. N/AN
14. Yes
15. OCLC: MSI (currently converting)
Books & Sets: 1(1981–84), 3(1982–84),6,7,10–12,26(MD,VA only)
Periodicals: 4(v.25–, 1971–), 5(1962–69),7(3v.)

BALTIMORE

Baltimore County Public Library, Catonsville Area Branch, 1100 Frederick Rd, 21228
Tel: 301-747-3551

1. M-Th, 9-9; F,Sa, 9-5:30; Su, 12-5
2. Evangeline Benner, Branch Manager
3. English, 700
4. 30
5. 50
6. Catonsville area; some southwest Baltimore County communities
7. Tel & letter: yes, NC
8. No
9. No
10. Yes
11. No
12. No
13. None
14. Yes
15. No
Books & Sets: 18,26(MD only)
Periodicals: 4(1979–)

Enoch Pratt Free Library, Maryland Department
400 Cathedral St, 21201
Tel: 301-396-5468

1. M-Th, 10-9 (tel service begins at 9); F,Sa, 9-5; Su (Oct-May only), 1-5
2. Wesley L. Wilson
3. English, 99%
4. None
5. N/AN
6. MD
7. Tel & letter: yes, NC except 15¢/copy
8. No
9. No
10. Yes, through ILL
11. No
12. No
13. N/AN
14. Yes
15. OCLC: MDB
Books & Sets: 3,6,7,17,18,26
Periodicals: 1

Maryland Historical Society
201 W Monument St, 21201
Tel: 301-685-3750, ext 359

1. T-F, 11-4:30; Sa, 9-4:30
2. Francis P. O'Neill
3. English, 20,000; German, 20
4. 150
5. 500
6. Mid-Atlantic states, especially MD; New England, the South
7. Tel: yes, NC for brief queries; letter: yes, $9.50 for brief queries or $20/hr for extended questions, with SASE
8. No
9. Yes, $2.50/day for non-members
10. No
11. Yes, church records, newspapers, and MS collections through ILL
12. *Guide to the Research Collections of the Maryland Historical Society*, $20
13. Card catalog, genealogical card index, index to *Maryland Historical Magazine*
14. Yes
15. No
Books & Sets: 2–7,9–13,16–18, 20,21,26
Periodicals: 1,3–9

BOWIE

Prince George's County Genealogical Society Library
12207 Tulip Grove Dr,
Belair Mansion, 20715
Tel: 301-262-6200

1. W, 10-1; 2d Su, 2-4
2. H. Ivan Rainwater
3. English, 600
4. 25
5. None
6. Prince George's County, MD state; US generally
7. Tel: no; letter: yes, NC except 25¢/copy
8. H. Ivan Rainwater
   Karin Miles
9. No

10. No
11. No
12. *Library Accessions* (books and periodicals), $1
13. N/AN
14. Yes, Society members
15. N/AN
Books & Sets: 3
Periodicals: 4,5,7,8(v.26–, 1938–), 9(incomplete)

CAMBRIDGE

Dorchester County Public Library, 303 Gay St, 21613
Tel: 301-228-7331

1. M,W,F, 10-6; T,Th, 10-8; Sa, 9-5
2. Jean S. Walter
3. English, 2,240
4. 900
5. 150
6. Eastern Shore, with concentration on Dorchester County, MD
7. Tel & letter: yes, NC except for copies, with SASE
8. No
9. No
10. Yes, through ILL, except for books in Maryland Room
11. No
12. No
13. Indexed land records, 1669–1860
14. Yes
15. No
Books & Sets: 2,12

CATONSVILLE

University of Maryland, Baltimore County, Albin O. Kuhn Library and Gallery
5401 Wilkens Ave, 21228
Tel: 301-455-2232

1. M-Th, 8am-11pm; F, 8-6; Sa, 10-4; Su, 1-9
2. Simmona E. Simmons
3. English, 200
4. N/AP
5. 130
6. MD, VA
7. Tel & letter: yes, NC

8. No
9. No
10. Yes, through ILL
11. No
12. No
13. *Genealogy and Local History: A UMBC Library Bibliography* (in-house use only)
14. No
15. OCLC: MUB
Books & Sets: 1–5,9–12,14,15, 21,26

CENTREVILLE

Queen Anne's County Free Library, 121 S Commerce St, 21617
Tel: 301-758-0980

1. M,Th, 9-9; T,W,F,Sa, 9-5
2. Kimberly Baklarz
3. English, 100
4. Collection of Queen Anne's County Historical Society, in two 4-drawer filing cabinets
5. 13
6. Queen Anne's County, MD
7. Tel: yes, NC; letter: yes, NC except 10¢/copy
8. No
9. No
10. Yes, 4-week loan with valid MD library card. No reference books
11. No
12. No
13. Card catalog
14. Yes
15. No
Periodicals: 4(1982–)

COLLEGE PARK

National Trust for Historic Preservation Library
Architecture Library, University of Maryland, 20742
Tel: 301-454-3979

1. M-F, 9-5
2. Sally R. Sims
3. English, 11,500
4. Files of local historic preservation ordinances; 18,500

postcards, 1903–14, covering all states; vertical files on over 400 historic preservation-related subjects and 300 LH-related organizations
5. N/AP
6. Entire US
7. Tel & letter: yes, NC
8. No
9. No
10. No
11. No
12. In progress
13. N/AN
14. No
15. OCLC: in progress

University of Maryland, McKeldin Library, Marylandia Department and Historical Manuscripts and Archives Department, 20742
Tel: 301-454-3035; 454-2318

1. M-F, 8:30-5; Sa, 10-5 (when University is in session)
2. Peter Curtis, Marylandia Dept; Lauren Brown, Historical Manuscripts and Archives Dept
3. English, 45,000; German, 100; other, 100
4. 80
5. 4,000
6. MD
7. Tel & letter: yes, NC. Library does not collect genealogical material and staff does not research
8. No
9. No
10. No
11. Yes, through ILL
12. No
13. Specialized card catalogs, MS collection inventories
14. No
15. OCLC: UMC

DENTON

Caroline County Public Library
100 Market St, 21629
Tel: 301-479-1343

1. M,F, 9-9; T-Sa, 9-5:30

2. Deborah Bennett, Assistant Administrator
3. English, 350
4. Vertical file on local history
5. 144
6. Caroline County, Eastern Shore, MD state
7. Tel & letter: yes, NC except 20¢/copy
8. No
9. Out-of-state fee for library card
10. No
11. Yes, only to other MD libraries
12. No
13. Card catalog
14. No
15. No
Books & Sets: 3,26(MD only)

EASTON

Talbot County Free Library, Maryland Room
100 W Dover St, 21601
Tel: 301-822-1626

1. M,Th, 9-9; T,W,F,Sa, 9-5; summer: M, 9-9; T-F, 9-5; Sa, 9-1
2. Scotti Oliver, Curator, Maryland Room
3. English, 4,000
4. 100: 345 boxes
5. 154
6. Eastern Shore, MD state
7. Tel: yes, NC (won't return long-distance calls); letter: yes, NC except 10¢/copy for Xeroxes over $1, with SASE
8. No
9. No
10. No
11. No
12. *Guardian of Our Maryland Heritage: The Maryland Room, Talbot County Free Library* (1968), $2.50
13. N/AN
14. Yes
15. No
Books & Sets: 3,26(MD,PA,VA)
Periodicals: 7(partial)

ELKTON

Cecil County Public Library
301 Newark Ave, 21921
Tel: 301-398-0914

1. M-Th, 9-9; F,Sa, 9-5
2. Cathy Hurley
3. N/AN
4. None
5. 30
6. Cecil County
7. Tel & letter: refer to Historical Society of Cecil County, Elkton
8. No
9. No
10. No
11. No
12. No
13. N/AN
14. No
15. No

FREDERICK

C. Burr Artz Library
110 E Patrick St, 21701
Tel: 301-694-1628

1. T,W, 1-4; F,Sa, 9-12
2. Kathryn J. Flynn
3. English, 2,000; German, several newspapers
4. 10
5. 425
6. Frederick County, MD state
7. Tel: yes, NC for brief queries; letter: yes, NC with SASE
8. N/AN
9. No
10. Yes, decided on individual basis
11. No
12. No
13. Card catalog, *Local History and Genealogy Handbook*
14. Yes
15. No
Books & Sets: 3–6,9–11,18,26
Periodicals: 7

HAGERSTOWN

Washington County Free Library, Western Maryland Room, 100 S Potomac St, 21740 Tel: 301-739-3250, ext 158

1. M,Th,F, 4-9; T, 9-noon
2. John C. Frye
3. English, 4,250
4. 2,268
5. 141
6. Western MD; adjacent counties in VA, WV, PA
7. Tel & letter: yes, NC
8. No
9. No
10. No
11. No
12. No
13. N/AN
14. Yes
15. No

LA PLATA

Charles County Community College, Southern Maryland Studies Center, PO Box 910, Mitchell Rd, 20646-0910 Tel: 301-934-2251, ext 610

1. Reading Room: M-Th, 8am-10pm; F, 8-4; Sa, 9-4 (hours vary between college sessions); Documents Room: M-F, 1-4
2. Sarah L. Barley
3. English, 2,000
4. 80
5. 285
6. Southern MD: Charles, St. Mary's, Calvert, southern Prince George's Counties
7. Tel: yes, for limited queries, NC except 25¢/copy; letter: yes, NC except 25¢/copy with SASE. Refer to Historical Society of Charles County for research projects
8. No.
9. No
10. No
11. No
12. No

13. *Accokeek Foundation Records, Samuel Ward Collection, Charles County Historic Sites File Index, Maryland: 350th Anniversary Celebration, Charlotte Hall School Collection Card File, Southern Maryland Room Vertical File Index, Southern Maryland Collection: Newspapers on Microfilm* and *Book Collection,* all available for use in Studies Center
14. No. Refer to volunteers from Historical Society of Charles County, $10/hr
15. No
Books & Sets: 3,9,11

Charles County Public Library PO Box 490, Charles & Garrett Sts, 20646 Tel: 301-934-9001

1. M-Th, 9-8; F, 12-5; Sa (closed summers), 9-5
2. Louise C. Crouse
3. English, 300; also, vertical file of pamphlets
4. 15
5. 81
6. Charles County, southern MD
7. Tel & letter: yes, NC except 15¢/copy for over 10 pages
8. No
9. No
10. Yes, to other libraries through ILL
11. No
12. No
13. N/AN
14. No
15. No
Books & Sets: 26
Periodicals: 4

LEONARDTOWN

St. Mary's County Historical Society Library, 11 Court House Dr, PO Box 212, 20650 Tel: 301-475-2467

1. T-Sa, 10-4
2. Hope H. Grace
3. English, 1,000

4. 5
5. 210
6. St. Mary's County principally; Charles, Calvert Counties, MD state; some KY
7. Tel & letter: yes, NC for brief queries, otherwise $10/hr
8. Hope H. Grace
9. No
10. No
11. No
12. *Genealogical Resources,* free
13. None
14. No
15. No

OAKLAND

Ruth Enlow Library of Garrett County, 6 N Second St, 21550 Tel: 301-334-3996

1. M,F, 9:15-8; T-Th, 9:15-5:30; Sa, 9-4
2. Edith G. Brock, Director
3. English, 500
4. None
5. 85 (including local newspaper)
6. Garrett County, MD
7. Tel & letter: yes, NC, with SASE
8. No
9. No
10. Yes, duplicates only
11. No
12. *Western Maryland Material in Allegany and Garrett Libraries*
13. N/AN
14. No. Refer to curator of Garrett County Historical Society Museum (in Enlow Library)
15. No
Books & Sets: 3,26(2 v. only)

REISTERSTOWN

Baltimore County Public Library, Reisterstown Branch Cockeys Mill Rd, 21136 Tel: 301-833-1550

1. M-Th, 10-9; F,Sa, 10-5:30; Su, 12-5

2. Grace Jonke, Branch Manager
3. English, 400
4. None
5. None
6. Reisterstown, Glyndon, Owings Mills communities in Baltimore County
7. Tel & letter: yes, NC
8. No
9. No
10. No
11. No
12. No
13. Partial indexes
14. No
15. No

ROCKVILLE

Montgomery County Historical Society Library
103 W Montgomery Ave, 20850
Tel: 301-340-2974

1. T-S, 12-4; first Su of month, 2-5
2. Jane C. Sween, Librarian
3. English, 1,350
4. Count not available
5. None
6. Montgomery County, adjacent counties, MD state
7. Tel: yes, NC for quick questions; letter: yes, NC but donation requested
8. Jane C. Sween
9. Yes, $1 to nonmembers
10. No
11. N/AP
12. No
13. Card catalog
14. No
15. No
Books & Sets: 3,26(MD only)
Periodicals: 4,8(1961–)

Rockville Regional Library, Montgomery County Public Libraries, 99 Maryland Ave, 20850
Tel: 301-279-1953

1. M-Th, 9-9; F,Sa, 9-5; Su (during school year), 1-5
2. Patricia Burt
3. 600
4. N/AN
5. 80–100, includes MD census reels, local newspapers
6. Montgomery County, MD state
7. Tel & letter: yes, NC for simple queries in local history
8. No
9. No
10. Yes
11. No
12. No
13. N/AN
14. No
15. No
Books & Sets: 3,10,26
Periodicals: 4(1979–)

SAINT MARY'S CITY

St. Mary's College of Maryland Library, 20686
Tel: 301-862-0257

1. N/AN
2. N/AN
3. No estimate. St. Mary's County reference works
4. N/AN
5. No estimate. St. Mary's County deeds (1796–1893), censuses (1820–80, including slaves), Orphan's Court (1807–52), inventories of estates (1795–1829)
6. St. Mary's County during Colonial era, c. 1600–1775
7. Tel & letter: yes, NC
8. No
9. No
10. Yes
11. No
12. N/AN
13. "A Selected Resource Bibliography"
14. No. Refer to St. Mary's County Historical Society Library, Leonardtown
15. N/AN

SALISBURY

Wicomico County Free Library
PO Box 4148,
122-126 S Division St, 21801
Tel: 301-749-5171

1. M-Th, 10-9; F,Sa, 10-5
2. Joanne Doyle, Head of Reference
3. English, 1,000
4. None
5. 704
6. Eastern Shore of DE, MD, VA,with emphasis on Somerset, Wicomico, Worcester Counties, MD; also some MD state, PA, DE, VA, NC, SC, KY, TN, OH
7. Tel: yes, NC; letter: yes, NC except 15¢/copy
8. Yes. Refer to volunteers from Genealogical Society in Maryland Room, Th 1-4
9. No
10. No
11. No
12. No
13. Card catalog
14. Yes
15. No
Books & Sets: 3,7,10,11,13,14, 19,26
Periodicals: 5,7–8

SEVERNA PARK

Ann Arrundell County Historical Society Library
PO Box 836, 21146
Tel: 301-768-5918

1. Th, 10-3
2. Mary K. Meyer
3. English, 1,600
4. 3
5. 15
6. Anne Arundel County, MD state; some NY, PA, VA
7. Tel: yes, NC for brief queries; letter: yes, $5 and up
8. Mary K. Meyer
9. Yes, $1/day for non-members

10. No
11. No
12. No
13. *Index to 1850 Census, Anne Arundel County*
14. Yes
15. No
Books & Sets: 26 (ME,VT,PA, NY,MD)
Periodicals: 1(scattered),3(partial), 4(v.2–, 1947–),6(scattered),7, 8(v.50–71, 1952–86),9(scattered)

SNOW HILL

Worcester County Library
307 N Washington St, 21864
Tel: 301-632-2600

1. M,W, 10-8; T,Th,F, 10-6; Sa, 10-2
2. Louise Ash, Auxiliary Services Assistant
3. English, 200
4. 13
5. 80–85
6. Worcester, Somerset, Wicomico Counties, MD; Accomack County, VA
7. Tel & letter: yes, NC
8. No
9. No
10. No

11. No
12. Guide to William D. Pitts Collection of land survey records, dating to 1677 (in progress)
13. Indexes to Pitts Collection; guide to special collections; genealogy bibliography
14. Yes
15. No

TOWSON

Baltimore County Public Library, Towson Area Branch
320 York Rd, 21204
Tel: 301-296-8500

1. M-Th, 10-9; F,Sa, 10-5:30; Su, 12-5
2. Cornelia M. Ives, Branch Manager
3. English, 650
4. 3
5. 360
6. Towson, Baltimore County, Baltimore City
7. Tel & letter: yes, NC
8. No
9. No
10. Yes, lending policy varies
11. No
12. No

13. Card index to Towson Room Historic Pamphlet file
14. Yes
15. No

WESTMINSTER

Carroll County Public Library
50 E Main St, 21776
Tel: 301-876-6008

1. M-Th, 9:30-8:45; F,Sa, 9:30-5
2. Janet R. Colburn
3. English, 400
4. None
5. 50
6. Carroll, Frederick, Baltimore Counties, MD; some south central, southeastern PA
7. Tel & letter: yes, NC except for copies
8. No
9. No
10. No
11. No
12. No
13. Baltimore/Carroll County joint public libraries catalog
14. Yes
15. No
Books & Sets: 3,5
Periodicals: 4,8

MASSACHUSETTS

ABINGTON

Dyer Memorial Library
PO Box 2245, Centre Ave, 02351
Tel: 617-878-8480

1. M,T,Th,F, 1-5; closed W and holidays
2. N/AN
3. No estimate. Volumes on *Mayflower* descendants, MA soldiers and sailors (Revolution, Civil War), Union and Confederate navies
4. N/AN
5. N/AN
6. N/AN
7. N/AN
8. N/AN
9. No
10. No
11. N/AN
12. No
13. N/AN
14. N/AN
15. N/AN
Periodicals: 9(v.1–138, 1847–1984)

ACTON

Acton Memorial Library
Main St, 01720
Tel: 617-464-9641

1. M-Th, 9-9; F, 9-5; Sa, 9-5 (except July-Aug); Su (Oct-Mar), 2-5
2. Dianne Ryan, Reference Librarian
3. English, 650
4. Less than 5
5. 11
6. Acton Collection: Acton and all other MA communities; genealogy collection: MA, early colonies, New England

7. Tel: no; letter: yes, NC
8. No
9. No
10. Yes, through ILL
11. No
12. No
13. "Genealogy Books" (bibliography)
14. No
15. No
Books & Sets: 1(1984 suppl only), 3(no suppls),26(MA only)
Periodicals: 4(1985–),9(1965–75, 1978–)

AGAWAM

Agawam Public Library
750 Cooper St, 01001
Tel: 413-789-1550

1. M-Th, 9-9; F, 9-6; Sa (closed summers), 9-5
2. N/AP
3. English, 70
4. None
5. None
6. Agawam, Hampden County; limited works on northern CT
7. Tel: yes, NC; letter: no
8. No
9. No
10. No
11. No
12. No
13. N/AN
14. No
15. No

AMESBURY

Amesbury Public Library
149 Main St, 01913
Tel: 617-388-0312

1. M-Th, 10-9; F,Sa, 10-5
2. Margaret Rice (part-time)

3. English, 1,000
4. 500
5. N/AN
6. New England
7. Tel: no; letter: yes, NC except for copies
8. Margaret Rice
9. No
10. No
11. No
12. No
13. N/AN
14. No
15. No
Books & Sets: 26
Periodicals: 9

ANDOVER

Memorial Hall Library
Elm Square, 01810
Tel: 617-475-6960

1. M-F, 9-9; Sa, 9-5; Su, 2-5; closed weekends during summer
2. None
3. English, 750
4. None
5. 135
6. Local
7. Tel & letter: yes, NC except 25¢/copy
8. No
9. No
10. No
11. No
12. *Greater Lawrence: A Bibliography* (1978), $15. Available from the Museum of American Textile History, 800 Massachusetts Ave, North Andover, MA
13. None
14. No
15. No
Books & Sets: 1,26
Periodicals: 9

ATTLEBORO

Attleboro Public Library
74 N Main St, 02703
Tel: 617-222-0157

1. Labor Day–mid-June: M-Th, 9-8:30; F,Sa, 9-5:30; summer: M,W, 9-8; T,Th,F, 9-5:30; closed Sa
2. Greta M. Dow, Reference Librarian
3. English, 2,000; collections of Maine Historical Society, v.1–24; early records of Town of Providence, RI, v.1–21
4. General vertical file
5. 2
6. Attleboro, Norton, Rehoboth; vital records to 1850 of many MA towns, cities
7. Tel: yes, NC; letter: yes, charge
8. No
9. No
10. No
11. No
12. No
13. N/AN
14. No
15. No
Books & Sets: 2(v.1–131)

BEDFORD

Bedford Free Public Library
Mudge Way, 01730
Tel: 617-275-9440

1. M-Th, 9-9; F,Sa, 9-5; Su (Sept-May), 2-5
2. Reference Librarian
3. English, 600
4. None
5. 3
6. Bedford, MA only
7. Tel: no; yes, NC except for copies
8. No
9. No
10. No
11. No
12. No
13. Bedford Collection Index

(guide to uncataloged pamphlets, documents, reports, etc.)
14. No
15. No
Periodicals: 4(1986–)

BELMONT

Belmont Public Library, PO Box 125, 336 Concord Ave, 02178
Tel: 617-489-2000

1. M-Th, 9-9; F,Sa, 9-5; LH collection open M,W,F, 2-4 and by appointment
2. Madaline Marshall, Curator, Belmont Room (LH collection)
3. English, 30
4. Extensive files and archives on Belmont, including Cushing and Homer families
5. Belmont newspapers only
6. Belmont, MA
7. Tel & letter: yes, NC
8. Duane Crabtree
9. No
10. No
11. No
12. No
13. Index to Belmont Room archives in progress
14. No
15. N/AN

BOSTON

The Boston Athenaeum
10 1/2 Beacon St, 02174
Tel: 617-227-0270

1. M-F, 9-5:30; Sa (Oct-May), 9-4
2. Reference Dept
3. English, 5,000
4. 20
5. None
6. New England, US, Great Britain
7. Tel & letter: yes, NC except 25¢/copy
8. No
9. No
10. No
11. N/AP
12. No

13. N/AN
14. No
15. OCLC: some BAT
Books & Sets: 6,10–12,19,24,26
Periodicals: 8,9

Boston Public Library, Social Sciences Department
666 Boylston St, 02116
(PO Box 286, 02117)
Tel: 617-536-5400, ext 261

1. M-Th, 9-9; F,Sa, 9-5; Su (Oct-May), 2-6
2. Edwin G. Sanford, Coordinator of Social Sciences
3. English, 80,000; German, small number; other, several
4. None
5. Hundreds of thousands: 3,300 newspaper titles alone
6. New England for family histories, British Isles for local histories; New England, US, some foreign
7. Tel & letter: yes, NC for short or bibliographical queries. Charge only for copies
8. Yes
9. No
10. Yes, through ILL within MA only
11. No
12. Brief guide
13. Genealogical catalog with analytics; large heraldry catalog; obituary catalog from 1952– (some gaps)
14. No. Refer to New England Historic Genealogical Society
15. OCLC: BRL
Books & Sets: 1–3,5–24,26
Periodicals: 1,4–9

Massachusetts Historical Society
1154 Boylston St, 02215
Tel: 617-536-1302

1. M-F, 9-4:45
2. John D. Cushing
3. English, 30,000
4. LH: 1,000
5. None
6. New England

7. Tel & letter: yes, NC for limited LH search
8. No
9. No
10. LH: no
11. No
12. *Catalog of Manuscripts,* 9 v., $1,250
13. N/AN
14. No
15. OCLC: MAH
Books & Sets: 6,16

Massachusetts Society of Mayflower Descendants
101 Newbury St, 02116
Tel: 617-266-1624

1. Open only to those working on *Mayflower* lineages for membership and to members
2. N/AN
3. English, 3,000
4. 1
5. 200
6. New England
7. Tel: yes, NC for limited requests; letter: yes, 25¢/copy plus postage. Donation appreciated
8. No
9. No
10. No
11. No
12. No
13. Card index to MS collection and lineage papers
14. Yes
15. N/AN
Books & Sets: 8,26
Periodicals: 1,5,9

New England Historic Genealogical Society
101 Newbury St, 02116
Tel: 617-536-5740

1. T-Sa, 9-4:45; closed Sa before Monday holiday
2. George F. Sanborn, Jr.
3. English, 200,000; German, 1,000; French, 1,500
4. 1 linear mile
5. 2,000

6. New England, northeastern US, Midwest, eastern Canada, British Isles, Western Europe
7. Tel: no; letter: yes, $20/hr, limited to members only, with SASE
8. George F. Sanborn, Jr.
   David C. Dearborn
   Gary B. Roberts
   Jerome E. Anderson
9. Yes, $10/day for nonmembers, $3/day for students
10. Yes, $8/order for 3-book limit; 2-week time limit. No limit on number of orders at any one time
11. Yes, same as #10, 3-reel limit
12. *Catalogue to NEHGS Circulating Collection,* 4 vols ($5.95 each plus $1 postage). Three supplements are also available
13. N/AN
14. Yes
15. No
Books & Sets: 1–5,7–14,17–19, 21–24,26
Periodicals: 1–9

State Library of Massachusetts
341 State House, 02133
Tel: 617-727-2590

1. M-F, 9-5
2. N/AN
3. N/AN
4. 25–50
5. 30
6. LH: MA, New England
7. Tel: yes, only to verify holdings; letter: yes, NC
8. No
9. No
10. No
11. No
12. No
13. Unpublished finding aids for MS collections
14. Yes
15. OCLC: yes
Books & Sets: 6,18
Periodicals: 9

BRIDGEWATER

Bridgewater Public Library
15 South St, 02324
Tel: 617-697-3331

1. T, 2-4; Th, 7-9pm; or by appointment
2. Elizabeth L. Gregg, Associate Director, Public Services
3. English, 950
4. None
5. 16
6. Bridgewater, surrounding towns; southeastern MA; MA state
7. Tel & letter: yes, NC except 10¢/copy with SASE
8. No
9. No
10. No, except for some reprints: 3-week loan
11. No, but will send print copies
12. No
13. Card catalog, vertical file
14. No
15. No
Books & Sets: 26

BROCKTON

Brockton Public Library
304 Main St, 02401
Tel: 617-580-7860

1. M-Th, 9-9; F,Sa, 9-5; closed Sa (June-Aug)
2. Lucia Shannon, Head of Adult Services
3. N/AN
4. N/AN
5. *Brockton Enterprise,* 1880–
6. Southeastern MA, MA state
7. Tel: no; letter: yes, NC
8. No
9. No
10. No
11. Yes
12. No
13. N/AN
14. No
15. No
Books & Sets: 2,26
Periodicals: 4,9

BROOKLINE

Public Library of Brookline
361 Washington St, 02146
Tel: 617-730-2369

1. M, 12-9; T-Th, 10-9; F,Sa, 10-5:30; Su, 1-5
2. Deborah Abraham, Head of Reference
3. English, 1,500
4. 500
5. 200
6. Brookline, Norfolk County
7. Tel & letter: yes, NC
8. No
9. No
10. Yes, duplicates only
11. No
12. No (planned for 1989)
13. MS card file; index to *Brookline Chronicle*, 1872–1922, 1947–80
14. No
15. OCLC: BRP in progress
Books & Sets: 1,3,26
Periodicals: 9

CAMBRIDGE

Cambridge Public Library
449 Broadway, 02138
Tel: 617-498-9080

1. M-F, 9-9; Sa, 9-5
2. N/AN
3. English, 5,000, includes pamphlets
4. 3 file drawers; 1 file drawer of typescript WPA Cambridge Genealogy project
5. 250: Cambridge tax records, 1794–1900; city directories, 1848–; Cambridge newspapers
6. New England
7. Tel & letter: yes, NC for brief queries; otherwise, hourly rate
8. No
9. No
10. Yes, 2-week loan, renewable by telephone
11. No
12. No

13. Card catalog index of books in G/LH Room; MS index, partial picture index, inventory list, title card index for materials in Cambridge History Room
14. No
15. No
Books & Sets: 1,2,18(Index, 1942–52),26
Periodicals: 5,7,9

CHELMSFORD

Chelmsford Public Library
Boston Rd, 01824
Tel: 617-256-5521 or 2344

1. M-Th, 9-9; F,Sa, 9-5:30
2. Linda Webb
3. English, 700
4. None
5. 10
6. Chelmsford, MA; southern NH; New England in general
7. Tel & letter: yes, NC except for copies, with SASE
8. Cliff Choquette (part-time)
9. No
10. Yes, several reprints
11. Yes, according to ALA guidelines; 3-week loan
12. No
13. Card catalog
14. No
15. No
Books & Sets: 26(MA only)
Periodicals: 4(current year only), 9(1986–)

CONCORD

Concord Free Public Library
129 Main St, 01742
Tel: 617-369-2309

1. M-F, 9-9; Sa, 9-5; Su, 2-5
2. Marcia E. Moss, Curator
3. English, 1,000+
4. Many, 1635 to present
5. Town records, newspapers, Concord authors
6. Concord
7. Tel: yes, NC for limited

queries; letter: yes, charge for time, copies, and postage
8. Marcia E. Moss
9. No
10. No
11. No
12. No
13. Moss, "List of Holdings"; Wheeler, "Cemetery List"
14. No. Amateur members of Genealogical Round Table
15. No
Books & Sets: 19(partial),26
Periodicals: 1(1971–86),4, 5(v.15–24, 1975–85),9

DANVERS

Peabody Institute Library, Danvers Archival Center
15 Sylvan St, 01923
Tel: 617-774-0554

1. M, 1-7:30; W,Th, 9-12, 1-5; 2d, 4th F of month, 1-5; 1st Sa of month, 9-12, 1-5
2. Richard B. Trask, Town Archivist
3. English, 5,000
4. 250,000
5. 350
6. Salem Village and Danvers, MA
7. Tel: yes, NC; letter: yes, $2
8. Richard B. Trask
9. No
10. No
11. No
12. No
13. *Union Catalog* in Archives
14. No
15. No
Books & Sets: 6
Periodicals: 9

EAST BRIDGEWATER

East Bridgewater Public Library, 32 Union St, 02333
Tel: 617-378-2821

1. M-Th, 10-8; F, 10-5; S, 9-2
2. Joan S. Leland
3. English, 650
4. 10

5. 6
6. MA (vital records to 1850);
Plymouth, Bristol, Norfolk,
Barnstable Counties; towns of
East Bridgewater, Bridgewater,
Brockton, West Bridgewater
7. Tel & letter: yes, NC
8. No. Refer to Plymouth
County Genealogists
9. No
10. No
11. No
12. Not yet
13. Card catalog; handmade
indexes
14. Yes
15. No
Periodicals: 9(1847–82; microfilm
index)

GLOUCESTER

Cape Ann Historical Association
27 Pleasant St, 01930
Tel: 617-283-0455

1. T-Sa, 10-5
2. N/AP
3. English, 90
4. 125
5. None
6. Cape Ann: Gloucester,
Rockport, Magnolia
7. Tel: yes, NC; letter: yes, NC
except 15¢/copy
8. No
9. Yes, $2 museum admission
10. No
11. No
12. No
13. N/AN
14. No
15. N/AN

Sawyer Free Library
2 Dale Ave, 01930
Tel: 617-283-0376

1. M-F, 9-8; Sa, 9-5
(summers, 9-1)
2. Elizabeth Roland
3. English, 500
4. None
5. 400
6. Cape Ann

7. Tel & letter: yes, NC
8. No
9. No
10. Yes, but reference books do
not circulate
11. Yes, to other libraries only
12. No
13. *A Selective Guide to Genealogical Resources: Gloucester
Lyceum and Sawyer Free Library*
14. No
15. No
Books & Sets: 3,26
Periodicals: 9

HAVERHILL

Haverhill Public Library
99 Main St, 01830
Tel: 617-373-1586

1. M-W, 1-9; Th,F, 1-5:30; Sa,
9-5:30; Su 1-5 (Oct-May only)
2. Gregory H. Laing
3. English, 9,500; German, 1
4. 1,500+
5. 50 (federal census for Essex
County, MA, 1800–1910)
6. New England; some NY, NJ
7. Tel: yes, NC; letter: yes, $5
for research
8. Gregory H. Laing
9. No
10. No
11. No
12. No
13. N/AN
14. Yes
15. No
Books & Sets: 2,6,7,18,19(incomplete),24(v.1),26
Periodicals: 1,5,9

HINGHAM

Hingham Public Library
66 Leavitt St, 02043
Tel: 617-749-0907

1. M-Th, 9-9; F, closed; Sa,
9-5; Su (winter only), 2-5
2. Reference Librarian
3. English, minimal
4. N/AN

5. 200: includes local newspaper, 1827–; Bicentennial
Collection
6. Hingham
7. Tel: no; letter: yes, NC
8. No
9. Yes, to nonresidents
10. No
11. No
12. No
13. Hingham Bicentennial
microfilm collection index (to MS
collection of Hingham histories,
business and institutions, churches,
clubs, families, maps, diaries,
wills, deeds)
14. Yes
15. No

HOLYOKE

Holyoke Public Library
335 Maple St, 01040
Tel: 413-534-2211

1. M-Th, 9-9; F, 9-5; Sa, 9-4;
closed Sa, June-Aug
2. None
3. English, 500
4. None
5. None
6. Holyoke
7. Tel & letter: yes, NC except
for copies
8. No
9. No
10. Rarely lend; by permission
of library director only
11. N/AN
12. No
13. N/AN
14. No
15. No
Books & Sets: 2(v.80–146),
24(5 v.),26

LAWRENCE

Lawrence Public Library
51 Lawrence St, 01841
Tel: 617-682-1727

1. M,W,F,Sa, 9-5; T,Th, 9-9
2. Reference staff
3. English, 250

4. 30

5. None. 100 still photos back to 1875

6. Greater Lawrence; northern Essex County

7. Tel: yes, NC for brief queries; letter: yes, $6 minimum

8. No

9. No

10. No

11. No

12. No

13. Local history bibliography (1984)

14. No

15. No

Books & Sets: 2

Periodicals: 4

LEXINGTON

Cary Memorial Library
1874 Massachusetts Ave, 02173
Tel: 617-862-6288

1. M-Th, 9-9; F,Sa, 9-6; Su (except summers), 1-5

2. Elizabeth A. Cross

3. English, 2,200

4. None

5. None

6. Lexington, environs

7. Tel & letter: yes, NC for simple reference questions

8. No

9. No

10. No

11. No

12. *Guide to the Study of Lexington*, no charge

13. Card catalog

14. No

15. OCLC: LEX

Periodicals: 9

LYNN

Lynn Historical Society, Museum and Library, 125 Green St, 01902
Tel: 617-592-2465

1. Research: M-F, 9-4; Sa, 1-4

2. Fay Greenleaf, Administrative Assistant

3. English, 1,500. Essex County probate to 1840, MA vital records to 1850, early New England marriages to early 1700s

4. 368

5. 1 (Quaker marriages)

6. Lynn area; Essex County; some NH, ME

7. Tel: yes, NC; letter: yes, NC except for copies

8. No

9. Yes, $2/day

10. No

11. No

12. No

13. "Manuscript Genealogies"; "Bible and Sampler Listings"

14. No

15. N/AN

Books & Sets: 2(v.6,8–18), 26(2 v. NH)

Periodicals: 9

Lynn Public Library
N Common St, 01902
Tel: 617-595-0567

1. M-W, 9-9; Th, 9-6; F,Sa, 9-5; summer hours differ

2. Kathe Landergan

3. English, 4,000

4. N/AN

5. 50

6. Lynn; Essex County; MA vital records

7. Tel & letter: yes, NC except 10¢/copy

8. No

9. No

10. No, but will make copies

11. No, but will make copies

12. No

13. N/AN

14. No

15. No

Books & Sets: 2,3,5,6,24,26

Periodicals: 9

LYNNFIELD

Lynnfield Public Library
18 Summer St, 01940
Tel: 617-334-5411

1. M-Th, 9-9; F,Sa, 9-5; Su, 2-5

2. Marcia Wiswall Lindberg

3. English, 3,000

4. None

5. 90

6. Eastern MA; ME, NH, CT; Maritime Provinces, Canada

7. Tel: yes, NC for simple requests; letter: yes, charge for copies and postage

8. Marcia Wiswall Lindberg

9. No

10. No

11. No

12. No

13. None

14. No

15. No

Books & Sets: 3,5,6,9–12,13(New England/NY),24,25,26(New England only)

Periodicals: 1(v.42–, 1966–), 4(1976–),5,7,9

MALDEN

Malden Public Library
36 Salem St, 02148
Tel: 617-324-0218

1. M-Th, 9-9; F,Sa, 9-6

2. Information/Reference Staff

3. English, 1,800

4. None

5. 9

6. Malden, MA

7. Tel & letter: yes, NC except 50¢/copy or microfilm prints

8. No

9. No

10. No

11. No

12. No

13. Index to local newspapers

14. No

15. No

Books & Sets: 1

Periodicals: 9

MARLBOROUGH

Marlborough Public Library
35 W Main St, 01752
Tel: 617-485-0494

1. M-Th, 9-8:30; F,Sa, 9-5
2. Ellen Dolan Hayden
3. English, 3,000
4. 50
5. N/AN
6. Marlborough, MA state
7. Tel: no; letter: yes, $5 plus 10¢/copy
8. No
9. No
10. No
11. No
12. No
13. N/AN
14. No
15. N/AN

MARSHFIELD

Ventress Memorial Library
Library Plaza, 02050
Tel: 617-837-5035

1. M-Th, 10-9:30; F,Sa, 10-5:30
2. Nancy A. Mullen
3. English, 200
4. 20
5. 10 reels; 60 microfiche of vital statistics
6. Marshfield, surrounding towns
7. Tel & letter: yes, NC
8. No
9. No
10. No
11. No
12. No
13. Card catalog
14. Yes
15. No
Books & Sets: 26(5 v.)
Periodicals: 9

MELROSE

Melrose Public Library
69 W Emerson St, 02176
Tel: 617-665-2313

1. M-Th, 9-9; F,Sa, 9-5; closed Sa in summer
2. Jane M. D'Alessandro
3. English, 1,000
4. None

5. None
6. New England, especially MA
7. Tel & letter: yes, NC
8. No
9. No
10. No
11. N/AP
12. No
13. N/AN
14. No
15. No
Books & Sets: 2(v.1–88),3(3 v., 1981),10,11(1972–76),26(2 v. New England only)
Periodicals: 4(last 5 years),9

MENDON

Taft Public Library
PO Box 35, Main St, 01756
Tel: 617-473-3259

1. M,W,Th, 1:30-5, 6:30-8; Sa, 10-12; Sa closed (July-Aug)
2. Lorna F. Rhodes, Librarian
3. English, 200–300; French, 2
4. N/AN
5. None
6. Mendon and environs
7. Tel: no; letter: yes, NC except 20¢/copy
8. No
9. No
10. No
11. No
12. No
13. N/AN
14. No
15. N/AN

MILFORD

Milford Town Library
80 Spruce St, 01757
Tel: 617-473-2145

1. M-Sa, 9-9
2. N/AP
3. English, 1,000
4. None
5. 340
6. MA state
7. Tel & letter: yes

8. No
9. No
10. Yes
11. No
12. No
13. List of local newspapers by date
14. No
15. No
Periodicals: 9(1987)

MILTON

Milton Public Library
476 Canton Ave, 02186
Tel: 617-698-5707

1. M-Th, 10-9; F, 9-5:30; Sa, 9-5; Su (Sept-June), 1-5
2. Eileen Piazza
3. N/AN
4. N/AN
5. N/AN
6. Milton, MA (mostly LH, some G)
7. Tel & letter: yes, NC for brief queries
8. No
9. No
10. No
11. No
12. No
13. Index to Milton *Record-Transcript*, 1904–48; to houses still standing, built before 1850
14. No
15. No

NATICK

Morse Institute Library
14 E Central St, 01760
Tel: 617-651-7300

1. M-Th, 9-9; F,Sa, 9-5
2. Carol Coverly
3. English, 400
4. 20
5. 21: vital records; 101: newspapers
6. Natick, Middlesex County, MA state
7. Tel & letter: yes, NC
8. No
9. No

10. No
11. No
12. No
13. "Guide to Natick Historical Reference Books"; "Indexes to Natick Vital Records"
14. No
15. N/AN
Periodicals: 9(1972–)

NEEDHAM

Needham Free Public Library
1139 Highland Ave, 02194
Tel: 617-455-7559

1. Genealogy: M-Th, 9-9; F,Sa, 9-5:30. Local history: by appointment
2. Elizabeth L. Rich
3. English, 900
4. Uncounted MS material on Needham history
5. 67
6. Needham area, eastern MA
7. Tel: yes, NC; letter: yes, NC except 25¢/copy after $1 minimum
8. No
9. No
10. Yes, Genealogy Section only, 1-week loan
11. No
12. No
13. Card index of both genealogy and local history collections
14. No
15. No
Books & Sets: 3,10–12
Periodicals: 9(incomplete)

NEW BEDFORD

Free Public Library
613 Pleasant St, 02740
Tel: 617-999-6291, ext 15

1. M,T,Th-Sa, 9-5; W, 9-9
2. Paul Cyr
3. English, 8,000; French, 350
4. 60
5. 1,300
6. Southeastern MA; New England; Quebec, Maritime Provinces
7. Tel & letter: yes, NC

8. Paul Cyr
9. No
10. Yes, duplicate copies
11. Yes, newspapers, whaling logbooks, some histories
12. No
13. Index of 250,000 whalemen, 1820–1925
14. Yes
15. No
Books & Sets: 2,3,8–10,12,17, 18,24,26
Periodicals: 1,9

NEWBURYPORT

Newburyport Public Library
94 State St, 01950
Tel: 617-462-4031

1. M-Sa, 10-4
2. Dorothy LaFrance
3. English, 4,000
4. 25
5. 165
6. MA, ME, NH
7. Tel: yes, NC for brief queries; letter: yes, $10/research, $2/copying fee
8. No
9. No
10. No
11. Yes, to institutions only
12. No
13. Card catalog
14. Yes
15. No
Books & Sets: 3,5,26
Periodicals: 4(1983–),9(1987)

NEWTON

Newton Free Library
414 Centre St, 02158
Tel: 617-552-7152

1. M-Th, 9-9; F, 9-6; Sa, 9-5; Su, 1-4; summer: same, except Sa, 11-4; Su, closed
2. Gina Flannery
3. English, 3,550
4. 7
5. 230
6. Newton, MA; some New England

7. Tel & letter: yes, NC except for copies
8. No
9. No
10. No
11. No
12. *Newtoniana*
13. Index for Newton newspapers
14. No
15. No
Books & Sets: 1
Periodicals: 4(1984–),9

NORTHBOROUGH

Northborough Free Library
34 Main St, 01532
Tel: 617-393-2401

1. M-Th, 10-8; F,Sa, 10-5
2. None
3. English, 60
4. None
5. None
6. Northborough, local area
7. Tel: yes, NC for simple questions; letter: no
8. No
9. No
10. No
11. No
12. No
13. In-house list of family, town histories
14. No
15. No

NORWELL

James Library
24 West St, Box 164, 02061
Tel: 617-659-7100

1. M-W,F, 2-5; Th, 7pm-9pm; Sa, 9-12
2. Librarian on duty
3. English, 200+. Over 100 vital records of MA towns
4. None. Refer to local Historical Society
5. History of First Parish Church - Unitarian
6. South Shore (area south of Boston)

7. Tel & letter: yes, NC
8. No
9. No
10. No
11. No
12. No
13. N/AN
14. N/AN
15. No

NORWOOD

Morrill Memorial Library
Walpole St, 02062
Tel: 617-769-0200

1. M-F, 9-9; Sa, 9-5; Su, 1-5; closed Sa, Su (July 4-Labor Day)
2. Reference Librarian
3. N/AN
4. None
5. Local newspaper since 1887, with some indexing
6. Town of Norwood
7. N/AN
8. N/AN
9. N/AN
10. N/AN
11. N/AN
12. N/AN
13. N/AN
14. N/AN
15. N/AN

PITTSFIELD

Berkshire Athenaeum, Local History and Literature Services
1 Wendell Ave, 01201
Tel: 413-499-9486

1. M-Th, 10-9; F,Sa, 10-5; July-Aug: M,W,F, 10-5; T,Th, 10-9; Sa, 10-1
2. Ruth T. Degenhardt
3. English, 7,000; French, several; Polish, several
4. Materials not cataloged
5. 875
6. Berkshire County; MA state; New England, neighboring areas of NY; some MI, OH
7. Tel: yes, for brief queries; letter: yes, NC except 25¢/copy
8. Yes

9. No
10. No
11. No
12. No
13. Indexes to several early local histories, to portions of special genealogical collections, to some newspapers
14. Yes
15. No
Books & Sets: 2–6,8–13,16,17, 23–26
Periodicals: 1,4(v.23–),5(1974–),7, 8(v.71–),9

PLYMOUTH

Plymouth Public Library
11 North St, 02360
Tel: 617-746-1927

1. Winter: M-Th, 9-8; F,Sa, 9-5; summer: M-Th, 9-8; F, 9-5
2. Grace E. Karbott, Reference Librarian
3. English, 1,300
4. 200 items
5. 9 filmed books; local newspaper, 1821–
6. Plymouth, South Shore, MA state
7. Tel & letter: yes, NC for brief queries except for copies
8. No
9. No
10. Yes, duplicates only
11. No
12. Guide in progress
13. Card catalog
14. Yes
15. N/AN
Books & Sets: 3,26
Periodicals: 9

READING

Reading Public Library
64 Middlesex Ave, 01867
Tel: 617-944-0840

1. M-F, 9-9; Sa, 9-5:30
2. N/AN
3. English, 1,400
4. N/AN
5. None

6. Reading; Middlesex County
7. Tel & letter: yes, NC, but no in-depth research
8. No
9. No
10. No
11. No
12. No
13. Inventory as of Jan 1984
14. No
15. No
Periodicals: 9(1919–)

ROCKLAND

Rockland Memorial Library
366 Union St, 02370
Tel: 617-878-1236

1. M-Th, 10-8; F,Sa, 10-5; closed Sa in summer
2. None
3. English, 700
4. G: 13 notebooks; LH: 16 notebooks
5. 55: local newspapers
6. Rockland; MA state (military histories, especially Civil War); some New England
7. Tel: no; letter: yes, NC except $1/copy
8. No
9. No
10. No
11. No
12. No
13. Archives card file
14. Yes
15. No

SALEM

Peabody Museum of Salem, Phillips Library, East India Square, 01970-1682
Tel: 617-745-1876

1. M-F, 10-5
2. Gregor Trinkaus-Randall
3. English, 10,000
4. 100
5. 20
6. New England
7. Tel: yes, NC; letter: yes, NC except 25¢/copy

8. No
9. Yes, $3 museum entrance fee
10. No
11. No
12. No
13. Numerous MS registers
14. No
15. No

Salem Public Library
370 Essex St, 01970
Tel: 617-744-0860

1. M-Th, 9-9; F,Sa, 9-5
2. Elizabeth M. Armand, Reference Librarian
3. English, 2,000
4. None
5. 675
6. Salem, MA
7. Tel & letter: yes, NC
8. Elizabeth M. Armand
9. No
10. Yes
11. No
12. No
13. N/AN
14. No
15. No
Periodicals: 9(v.2–33)

SALISBURY

Salisbury Public Library
Elm St, 01952
Tel: 617-465-5071

1. M,T,Th, 9-8; W,F, 9-5
2. N/AN
3. English, 125
4. 30
5. 10
6. MA North Shore, southern NH. Also, vital statistics throughout MA, southern NH, Cape Cod area, Nantucket, Kittery, ME
7. Tel & letter: yes, NC except for copies
8. No
9. No
10. No
11. No
12. No
13. N/AN

14. No. Refer to local specialist in Historical Society
15. N/AN
Periodicals: 9

SCITUATE

Scituate Town Archives
Fiest Parish Rd, 02066
Tel: N/AN

1. M, 10-2
2. Dorothy Clapp Langley, Archivist
3. English, 1,200
4. 500
5. 2: Scituate vital records
6. Town of Scituate, Plymouth County
7. Tel: no; letter: yes, NC
8. No
9. No
10. No
11. No
12. No
13. Town histories at NEHG
14. No
15. N/AN

Scituate Town Library
85 Branch St, 02066
Tel: 617-545-6700

1. M-W, 9-9; Th, 1-9; F, closed; Sa, 9-5; Su (Oct-May), 1-5
2. Adult Services Librarian
3. English, 500
4. Dozen genealogical MSS of varying length
5. None
6. Scituate, Marshfield, Cohasset, Hingham, MA
7. Tel: yes, NC for brief queries; letter: yes, NC except for copies
8. No
9. No
10. No
11. No
12. No
13. None
14. No
15. No

SHARON

Sharon Public Library
11 N Main St, 02067
Tel: 617-784-5974

1. T,W,Th, 9:30-9; F,Sa, 9:30-5:30
2. Reference Librarian
3. English, 150+
4. Numerous files on town families, locations
5. Approx 47: local newspapers
6. Sharon, surrounding towns; MA state
7. Tel & letter: yes, NC except for copies plus postage
8. No
9. No
10. No
11. No
12. No
13. N/AP
14. No
15. No
Books & Sets: 1

SHREWSBURY

Shrewsbury Public Library
609 Main St, 01545
Tel: 617-842-0081

1. M,W,F,Sa, 10-6; T,Th, 10-9
2. Beverly S. Fisher
3. English, 400
4. None
5. N/AN
6. Worcester County, MA state
7. Tel: no; letter: yes, NC
8. No
9. No
10. No
11. No
12. No
13. N/AN
14. No
15. No

SOMERVILLE

Somerville Public Library
79 Highland Ave, 02143
Tel: 617-623-5000

1. M-Th, 9-9; F, 9-6; Sa, 9-3
2. Alix Minton
3. English, 4,500
4. 250
5. 90: mostly of *Somerville Journal*
6. Somerville, MA state; some New England history
7. Tel & letter: yes, NC except for copies
8. Alix Minton
9. No
10. No
11. No
12. No
13. *Annotated Bibliography of the Somerville Collection in the Somerville Public Library*
14. No
15. No
Books & Sets: 26(v.1–6)
Periodicals: 9(1849–1940)

SOUTH NATICK

Natick Historical Society
c/o Bacon Free Library, 58 Eliot St, 01760
Tel: N/AN

1. W, 2-4:30; Sa (Sept-June), 10-12:30
2. Anne K. Schaller, Director
3. English, 350. MA vital statistics to 1850
4. Mostly papers of prominent Natick citizens
5. N/AN
6. Natick, some surrounding towns; MA state
7. Tel: no; letter: yes, charge for time
8. No
9. No
10. No
11. N/AN
12. No
13. None
14. No
15. No

SPRINGFIELD

Springfield City Library
220 State St, 01103
Tel: 413-739-3871, ext 230

1. M-Th, 9-9; F,Sa, 9-5; Su, 1-5
2. Joseph Carvalho III
3. English, 32,000; German, 25; French, 2,000; Latin, 30; Italian, 15; Gaelic, 10
4. 1,500 linear ft of Springfield history; 30 linear ft of New England family genealogies
5. 10,000
6. New England; Quebec; NY; PA
7. Tel: yes, NC; letter: yes, NC except 20¢/copy
8. Joseph Carvalho III, CGRS
9. No
10. No, except for "how-to" books
11. No
12. Listing of Quebec parish records by county and town/city: Norman LaRose and Jacqueline Stagnard, *French Canadian Collection Guide,* 6th ed, 2 vols, $15
13. Springfield Index (500,000 entries citing people, places, institutions, businesses, events)
14. Yes
15. No
Books & Sets: 2–6,7(v.1 only), 8–14,16(no suppl),17–19,24–26
Periodicals: 1,2(v.2–, 1980–), 3(v.11–),4(v.21–, 1967–),5,7–9

SUDBURY

Goodnow Library
21 Concord Rd, 01776
Tel: 617-443-9112

1. M-W, 9-9; Th-Sa, 9-5; Su, 1-5; closed Sa, Su during summer
2. Gordon Arnold, Reference Librarian

3. English, 500
4. N/AN
5. 20
6. Sudbury; Middlesex County; MA state
7. Tel: yes, NC if brief query; letter: yes, NC except 10¢/copy
8. N/AN
9. No
10. No
11. No
12. No
13. *A Selection of Genealogical and Historical Materials in the Goodnow Library* (1983)
14. No
15. No
Periodicals: 1(1979–),9(v.63–68, 72,93–107,109–12,125–)

WAKEFIELD

Lucius Beebe Memorial Library
Main St, 01880
Tel: 617-245-0790

1. M-Th, 1-9; F,Sa, 9-5; closed Sa in summer
2. Charlotte Thompson
3. English, 500
4. 20
5. All MS collections on microfilm
6. Middlesex County
7. Tel: no; letter: yes,NC
8. No
9. No
10. No
11. No
12. No
13. Index to Eaton's *History of Reading*
14. No
15. No
Books & Sets: 2

WATERTOWN

Watertown Free Public Library
123 Main St, 02172
Tel: 617-924-5390

1. M, 9-6; T,W, 9-9; Th, 1-9; F,Sa, 9-5; Su, 1-5; closed Sa, Su (June-Aug)
2. Reference staff
3. English, under 1,000
4. 200
5. Under 10
6. Watertown, MA
7. Tel & letter: yes, NC
8. No
9. N/AN
10. Yes, subject to conditions
11. No
12. No
13. N/AN
14. No
15. OCLC: WAT
Books & Sets: 3
Periodicals: 9

WAYLAND

Wayland Public Library
5 Concord Rd, 01778
Tel: 617-358-2311

1. M-Th, 9-9; F, 9-6; Sa, 10-5; Su, 2-5; closed Sa, Su (June-Sept)
2. Phoebe Homans
3. English, 400
4. None
5. 12
6. Wayland only
7. Tel & letter: yes, NC
8. No
9. No
10. No
11. No
12. No
13. No
14. None
15. No

WENHAM

Wenham Public Library
138 Main St, 01984
Tel: 617-468-4062

1. M,W,Th, 2-5, 7-9; T, 9-12, 2-5, 7-9; F, 2-5; Sa, 10-5 (summer: Sa, 10-1)
2. Cynthia McCue
3. English, 500
4. None

5. None
6. MA, especially Essex County
7. Tel: yes, NC for brief queries; letter: yes, NC except 10¢/copy
8. No
9. No
10. Yes, through ILL
11. No
12. No
13. Card catalog
14. No
15. No

WESTBOROUGH

Westborough Public Library
55 W Main St, 01581
Tel: 617-366-0725, ext 176

1. M,W,F, 10-6; T,Th, 10-9; Sa, 10-5
2. Jacqueline C. Tidman, LH Librarian
3. English, 1,200
4. Several dozen
5. 75
6. Westborough, MA state; New England
7. Tel & letter: yes, NC
8. Jacqueline C. Tidman
9. No
10. No
11. No
12. No
13. Card catalog
14. No
15. No
Books & Sets: 26
Periodicals: 5,9

WESTFORD

J. V. Fletcher Library
50 Main St, 01886
Tel: 617-692-5555

1. M-Th, 10-9; F, 1-5; Sa, 10-5; Su (Jan-Apr), 1-5
2. N/AP
3. English, 1,800
4. 250
5. 20

6. Westford, MA state; southern VT; southern NH
7. Tel: yes, NC; letter: yes, NC except 10¢/copy
8. No
9. No
10. Yes, 3-week loan
11. No
12. No
13. Card catalog
14. Yes
15. No
Periodicals: 9(1903–31)

WESTON

Weston Public Library
356 Boston Post Rd, 01760
Tel: 617-893-3312

1. M,W,Th, 9-9; T, 1-9; F, 9-6; Sa, 9-5; Su 2-5
2. Carol Johnson Shedd
3. English, 70
4. 50
5. None
6. Weston, Waltham, Watertown
7. Tel: yes, NC; letter: yes, NC except 10¢/copy with SASE
8. N/AN
9. No
10. No
11. N/AN
12. No
13. "Reference Sources for Weston History," pamphlet (can be copied for 50¢)
14. No
15. No

WINCHESTER

Winchester Public Library
80 Washington St, 01890
Tel: 617-721-7171

1. M-Th, 10-9; F, 10-5:30; Sa, 10-5:30
2. Linda Rossman, Head, Reference Dept
3. English, 100
4. 1
5. 224

6. Winchester, MA
7. Tel & letter: yes, NC
8. No
9. No
10. Yes, circulating books lent to Library cardholders only
11. No
12. No
13. N/AN
14. No
15. No
Books & Sets: 1

WOBURN

Woburn Public Library
45 Pleasant St, 01801
Tel: 617-933-0148

1. Winter: M-Th, 9-9; F,Sa, 9-5:50; summer: M,W,F, 9-5:30; T,Th, 9-9
2. Gwendolyn S. Fletcher, Reference Librarian
3. English, no estimate
4. 124 boxes of loose MSS; approx 35 vols of bound MSS
5. 75: mostly local newspapers, 1844–. Also, Woburn soldiers from 1700s–1800s, vital statistics, atlases
6. Woburn, Boston, Middlesex County, MA; some NY
7. Tel: yes, NC; letter: yes, NC except 10¢/copy and postage
8. No
9. No
10. No
11. No
12. No
13. Index to Woburn historical collection; indexes of local newspapers, 1844–; guide to MS collection
14. No
15. No

Periodicals: 9(1847–1977)

WORCESTER

American Antiquarian Society
185 Salisbury St, 01609-1634
Tel: 617-755-5221

1. M-F, 9-5, except for legal holidays, 3d W in Oct, F after Thanksgiving
2. Keith Arbour
3. English, 76,000; French, no number given
4. Most re genealogy were transferred in mid-1970s to New England Historic Genealogical Society. Inquiries should be addressed to Curator of Manuscripts
5. 1,550 microfiche; 33 microfilm rolls, excluding newspaper collection
6. US, Canada
7. Tel: no; letter: yes, NC for brief queries, with SASE
8. Marie E. Lamoureux
9. No
10. No
11. No
12. *Dictionary Catalog of American Books Pertaining to the 17th through 19th Centuries* (Greenwood Press), 20 vols
13. N/AN
14. Yes
15. RLIN: MAAR
Books & Sets: 2,3,5–7,9–11, 15,17,24–26
Periodicals: 1,3,4(1962),5(1962–69),7–9

Worcester Historical Museum
39 Salisbury St, 01606
Tel: 617-753-8278

1. T-Sa, 10-4

2. N/AN
3. English, 500
4. N/AN
5. N/AN
6. Worcester only
7. Tel: no; letter: yes, NC
8. No
9. No
10. No
11. N/AN
12. No
13. N/AN
14. No
15. No
Books & Sets: 26

Worcester Public Library
Salem Square, 01608
Tel: 617-799-1655

1. M-Th, 10-8:30; F, 10-5:30; Sa (Sept-June), 9-5:30
2. Nancy E. Gaudette
3. English, 8,700
4. None
5. Censuses, directories, newspapers, vital records
6. New England, with emphasis on Worcester, Worcester County, MA state
7. Tel: yes, NC for brief queries; letter: yes, NC
8. No
9. No
10. No
11. No
12. No
13. N/AN
14. Yes
15. OCLC: yes
Books & Sets: 2(v.1–130, 1890–1917),3–6,10–14,16,18,19,24,26
Periodicals: 4(v.29–, 1975–), 5(1976),7,8(v.65–, 1977–),9

MICHIGAN

ADRIAN

Adrian Public Library
143 E Maumee St, 49221
Tel: 517-263-2161, ext 277

1. M,T,Th, 10-9; W,F, 10-5:30; Sa, 9:30-5:30
2. Jule J. Fosbender
3. English, 500
4. 100
5. 1,000
6. City of Adrian; Lenawee County
7. Tel: no; letter: yes, NC except for copies
8. No
9. No
10. No
11. No
12. No
13. N/AN
14. Yes
15. No
Books & Sets: 26

BATTLE CREEK

Willard Library
7 W Van Buren St, 49017
Tel: 616-968-8166

1. M-Th, 9-9; F,Sa, 9-5
2. Helen Jo Emerson, Reference Head Librarian; Marlene A. Steele
3. English, 9,000
4. 150–200
5. 550
6. Battle Creek, Calhoun County, MI; some NY, OH, and Ontario, Canada
7. Tel & letter: yes, NC except for copies
8. Marlene A. Steele
9. No
10. No

11. No
12. No
13. Ross Coller Collection index; indexes to Battle Creek newspapers, 1840s–1970
14. Yes
15. OCLC: EEW
Books & Sets: 2(v.30–43,51,54),3, 6,7(v.3–5),26
Periodicals: 3(v.17, 1954–),4, 8(various),9(various)

BAY CITY

Bay City Branch Library, Bay County Library System
708 Center Ave, 48708
Tel: 517-893-9566

1. M-Th, 9-9; F,Sa, 8-5; Su (Sept-May), 1-4
2. Mary McManman, Reference Librarian
3. English, 1,600
4. None
5. 1,360
6. MI, especially Bay County
7. Tel & letter: yes, NC except 10¢/copy
8. No
9. No
10. Yes, 4-week loan
11. No
12. No
13. None
14. No
15. OCLC: EZWD
Books & Sets: 10,11,26
Periodicals: 3(v.23–46, 1960–82), 4(v.23–32, 1969–78),8(v.61,62, 1973–74)

BIRMINGHAM

Baldwin Public Library
300 W Merrill St, 48012
Tel: 313-647-1700, ext 27

1. M-Th, 9:30-9; F,Sa, 9:30-5:30; Su, 1-5
2. James Moffet, Head, Reference Dept
3. English, 500
4. None
5. 90
6. Birmingham, Detroit, Oakland County, MI state
7. Tel & letter: yes, NC
8. No
9. No
10. No
11. No
12. No
13. Index to *Birmingham Eccentric* newspaper, 1877–
14. No
15. No
Books & Sets: 1–3,10–12,19
Periodicals: 3,4

CADILLAC

Cadillac-Wexford Public Library, 411 S Lake St, 49601
Tel: 616-775-6541

1. Sept-May: M-Th, 8:30-8:30; F,Sa, 8:30-5:30; June-Aug: M,W, 8:30-8:30; T,Th,F, 8:30-5:30; Sa, 8:30-12:30
2. N/AP
3. English, 60
4. None
5. 26
6. Wexford, Missaukee, and Osceola Counties
7. Tel & letter: yes, NC for brief queries
8. No
9. No
10. No
11. Yes, through ILL
12. No
13. N/AN
14. No

15. OCLC: EZZ
Books & Sets: 3
Periodicals: 4(1980–)

COLDWATER

Branch County Library
10 E Chicago St, 49036
Tel: 517-278-2341

1. M, 10-8; T,W, 9-5; Th, 9-8;
F, 9-5; Sa, 9-4
2. Shirley Pascal
3. N/AN
4. N/AN
5. N/AN
6. Branch County
7. Tel: yes, NC; letter: yes,
$6/hr plus copies
8. No
9. No
10. No
11. No
12. No
13. N/AN
14. Yes
15. No
Books & Sets: 2(incomplete),3
Periodicals: 3(incomplete),
4(incomplete)

COMSTOCK

Comstock Township Library
6130 King Highway, 49041
Tel: 616-345-0136

1. M-Th, 10-9; Fr, 10-6; Sa,
10-4
2. Sandra Capp
3. English, 25
4. None
5. None
6. Mostly Comstock; some
Kalamazoo City and County
7. Tel & letter: yes, NC
8. No
9. No
10. No
11. No
12. No
13. N/AN
14. No
15. OCLC: EXM
Periodicals: 4(1986)

DECATUR

Van Buren County Library
200 N Phelps St, 49045
Tel: 616-423-4771

1. M,W, 9-8; T,Th, 9-6; F, 9-5;
Sa, 9-4
2. Shirley Swift Howe
3. English, 400–600
4. 20–30
5. 60–70: censuses, news-
papers
6. MI, surrounding states;
some eastern states (prior to 1850)
7. Tel: no; letter: yes, NC
8. Shirley Swift Howe
9. No
10. Yes, through ILL
11. No
12. 1978 guide being updated
13. N/AN
14. Yes
15. N/AN
Books & Sets: 7
Periodicals: 4(v.26–)

DETROIT

Detroit Public Library,
Burton Historical Collection
5201 Woodward Ave, 48202
Tel: 313-833-1480

1. M-T,Th-Sa, 9:30-5:30; W,
9-9
2. Alice C. Dalligan
3. 260,000 books, not divided
by language
4. 5,060 ft of MS collections
5. 18,000
6. All states, but principally
Detroit, Old Northwest; eastern
Canada
7. Tel: yes, NC for LH, no for
G; letter: no
8. No
9. No
10. No
11. No
12. *Guide to the Manuscripts of*
the Burton Historical Collection,
$47
13. N/AN
14. Yes

15. OCLC: yes
Books & Sets: 1–14,16–19,22–26
Periodicals: 1–9

FARMINGTON

Farmington Community
Library, Farmington Branch
23500 Liberty St, 48024
Tel: 313-474-7770

1. M-Th, 10-9; F,Sa (during
school year), 10-5
2. N/AN
3. Approx 1,200 titles
4. None
5. None
6. Farmington area, MI state
7. Tel & letter: yes, NC
8. No
9. No
10. No
11. N/AN
12. No
13. Robert Cook indexes to
marriages, deaths in local newspapers, late 1800s–1940s
14. No
15. No
Books & Sets: 3
Periodicals: 3(1963–),4(1987–)

FLINT

Flint Public Library
1026 E Kearsley St, 48502
Tel: 313-232-7111, ext 261

1. M-Th, 11-9; F,Sa, 11-6
2. Roberta Schaafsma
3. English, 9,500; German, 10
4. None
5. 4,500
6. MI, New England, NY, OH,
PA, some Canada
7. Tel & letter: yes, NC except
for copies and postage
8. No
9. No
10. No
11. No
12. *Local History and Geneal-*
ogy Book List (1976), $2; 1987
supplement in press

13. Purdy Surname Index; Genesee County Biography Index; *Flint Journal* Index, subject 1964–81, names 1964–83; obituary indexes for various dates
14. Yes
15. OCLC: EZH (some titles)
Books & Sets: 1,2(incomplete), 3–5,10–12,18,19,22–24,26
Periodicals: 1(v.32–59),2(v.1–3), 3–5,7,8(v.43–71),9

GRAND RAPIDS

Grand Rapids Public Library, Michigan and Family History Department, 60 Library Plaza, NE, 49503
Tel: 616-456-3640

1. M,Th,F,Sa, 9-5:30; T,W, 12-9
2. Gordon Olson
3. English, 30,000
4. 500
5. 3,700 (of which 2,700 are local newspapers)
6. Grand Rapids, Kent County, surrounding counties; MI state; Old Northwest; New England; NY
7. Tel: yes, NC; letter: yes, $10/hr
8. No
9. No
10. No
11. No
12. No
13. N/AN
14. Yes
15. OCLC: EXR (for acquisitions since 1976)
Books & Sets: 2,3,5–7,10–14, 18,19,22–26
Periodicals: 1–5,7,8(1947–),9

HILLSDALE

Mitchell Public Library
22 N Manning St, 49242
Tel: 517-437-2581

1. M-W, 10-8; Th,F, 10-5; Sa, 9-5

2. Research Committee of Friends of Mitchell Public Library
3. English, 300; German, 1
4. Uncounted vertical files of family histories, local histories
5. 297: newspapers; 14: census; 5: church and funeral homes; 22: county records
6. Hillsdale County and nearby counties of MI, OH, IN
7. Tel: yes, NC; letter: yes, $6/hr plus copies
8. No
9. No
10. No
11. No
12. No
13. Various indexes; biographical card file; index search checklist
14. Yes
15. No
Books & Sets: 2(1–100 except 2–5, 40)
Periodicals: 1(incomplete), 3(1961–, few missing),4(last 5 years),9(1926–39)

HOLLAND

Herrick Public Library
300 River Ave, 49423
Tel: 616-394-1400

1. Winter: M-Th, 9-9; F,Sa, 9-6; Su, 2-5; summer: M-Th, 9-9; F, 9-6; Sa, 9-1; closed Su
2. Darlene Winter
3. English, 1,000; Dutch, 40
4. N/AN
5. 1,000 (includes newspapers)
6. Western MI, other US areas with Dutch settlements; Netherlands
7. Tel: yes, NC; letter: yes, contributions requested
8. Darlene Winter
9. No
10. No
11. No
12. No
13. Free handout
14. Yes
15. No
Books & Sets: 3,4,22,23
Periodicals: 3–5

HOWELL

Howell Carnegie Library
314 W Grand River Ave, 48843
Tel: 517-546-0720

1. M-Th, 10-8; F, 12-5; Sa, 10-5
2. N/AP
3. English, 175
4. 25
5. 73
6. Livingston County, MI
7. Tel: no; letter: yes, NC except for copies
8. No
9. No
10. Yes, through ILL
11. No
12. No
13. Bibliography of genealogy collection; list of local newspapers on microfilm
14. Yes
15. OCLC: Mi How QYHAdc
Books & Sets: 2(v.41–112)
Periodicals: 4(current year only),7

IRON MOUNTAIN

Dickinson County Library
401 Iron Mountain St, 49801
Tel: 906-774-1218

1. Winter: M-F, 9-9; Sa, 9-5; Su, 1-4; summer: M-F, 9-8; Sa, 9-1; closed Su
2. None
3. English, 500
4. None
5. Upper Peninsula census, 1830–1910; *Marquette Mining Journal*, 1880–91; local newspaper, 1889–1917, 1921–; *Florence Mining News*, 1881–1900
6. MI, WI
7. Tel & letter: yes, NC
8. No
9. No
10. Yes, duplicates only
11. Yes, only to cooperative
12. No
13. None
14. Yes
15. No

Books & Sets: 3,24
Periodicals: 4(1977–)

JACKSON

Jackson District Library
244 W Michigan Ave, 49201
Tel: 517-788-4316

1. M-Th, 10-9; F,Sa, 10-5:30;
Su (Oct-Apr), 1-5
2. Reference Department
3. English, 2,000
4. None
5. 5,000: all states, 1790–
1820; NY, 1830; MI, 1830–1910
6. Jackson; most of central MI,
some northern MI
7. Tel: no; letter: yes, NC
except for copies over 10 pages
plus postage
8. No
9. No
10. No
11. No
12. No
13. N/AN
14. No
15. OCLC: EEJ (partial)
Books & Sets: 2(partial),
3(1982–85)

KALAMAZOO

Kalamazoo Public Library
315 S Rose St, 49007
Tel: 616-342-9837, ext 245

1. M-Th, 9-9; F, 9-6; Sa, 9-5;
Su (Sept-May), 1-5
2. Catherine A. Larson
3. English, 8,000
4. 100
5. 1,400
6. Kalamazoo County; MI,
Great Lakes states, NY, New
England. Minimal coverage of
eastern Canada, Great Britain,
Germany
7. Tel: yes, NC; letter: yes, NC
except for copies
8. Catherine A. Larson

9. No, for in-house use. Nonresident borrower's card, $81.20
for 1987
10. No
11. No, but most film is dupli-
cated in circulating collection of
Library of Michigan, Lansing
12. No
13. Card catalog; History Room
name and subject indexes; Vital
Records File; other smaller indexes
14. Yes
15. OCLC: EXZ
Books & Sets: 1–5,10–13,17,
19(illustrations only),22,23,26
Periodicals: 1(v.58–, 1982–),
4(hold for last 5 years),5(v.62–67,
1974–),7,8(v.71–, 1983–),9

LANSING

Lansing Public Library
401 S Capitol Ave, 48933
Tel: 517-374-4600

1. Local History Room: T,
11:30-5:30 or by appointment;
Library: M-Th, 9:30-8:30; F, 9:30-
5; Sa, 9:30-4:30. If LH Room is
closed, a reference librarian will
retrieve material for patrons for in-
library use
2. Jane McClary
3. English, 4,000
4. 3 dozen
5. Newspapers only
6. Lansing, Ingham County,
MI
7. Tel & letter: yes, NC
8. No
9. No
10. No
11. No
12. No
13. Card catalog, information
file
14. No
15. OCLC: EEPH2s

Library of Michigan
PO Box 30007,
735 E Michigan Ave, 48909
Tel: 517-373-1593

1. M-F, 8-6
2. Carole C. Callard
3. English, 60,000
4. 370 boxes
5. 63,000 reels
6. MI; Old Northwest; Great
Lakes; New England; NY, PA,
VA, KY, NC; Canada; some
British Isles
7. Tel & letter: yes, NC
8. Carole C. Callard
9. No
10. Yes, only "how-to" guides
11. Yes, only MI newspapers on
microfilm
12. *Sourcebook of Michigan
Census, County Histories, and
Vital Records*, $6
13. None
14. Yes
15. OCLC: EEX
Books & Sets: 1–7,9–19,22–26
Periodicals: 1–9

MANISTEE

Manistee County Library
95 Maple St, 49660
Tel: 616-723-2519

1. Winter: T,W, 10-8:30;
Th,F, 10-5; Sa, 9-2; summer:
M-W, 10-8:30; Th,F, 10-5
2. N/AN
3. English, 50 on Manistee
County, plus 746 on MI and by MI
authors
4. N/AN
5. Local newspapers since
1871 (no index)
6. Manistee County, MI state
7. Tel: no; letter: yes, NC for
brief queries except for copies. Refer to Manistee County Historical
Society
8. No
9. No
10. Yes
11. Yes
12. No
13. N/AN
14. Yes
15. OCLC: (since 1965)

MARQUETTE

Peter White Public Library
217 N Front St, 49855
Tel: 906-228-9510

1. T-Th, 9-9; F,Sa, 9-6
2. Cheryl Hirschi
3. English, 500
4. None
5. 455
6. Marquette, Upper Peninsula
7. Tel: yes, NC for limited queries; letter: yes, NC except for copies and postage
8. No
9. No
10. No
11. No
12. No
13. *Peter White Public Library Genealogy*, free brochure
14. Yes
15. OCLC: EZPA
Books & Sets: 2,3,10,11,13,14,24

MOUNT CLEMENS

Mount Clemens Public Library
150 Cass Ave, 48043
Tel: 313-469-6200

1. M-Th, 9:30-9; F,Sa, 9:30-5:30
2. Deborah J. Mowat, Adult Services Librarian
3. English, 2,000
4. None
5. 500
6. Wayne, Oakland, Macomb Counties, MI; New England, NY, PA, OH; Ontario
7. Tel: yes, NC; letter: yes, NC except for copies
8. No. Refer to local volunteer genealogy group
9. No
10. No
11. No
12. No
13. N/AN
14. No
15. No
Books & Sets: 1–5,10,13,18,23–25
Periodicals: 3,4(1975–),5,7,9

NOVI

Novi Public Library
45245 W Ten Mile Rd, 48050
Tel: 313-349-0720

1. M-Th, 10-9; F,Sa, 10-5
2. Barbara Louie
3. English, 50
4. 5
5. None
6. Novi, Northville, Farmington, Oakland County, Wayne County, Detroit
7. Tel & letter: yes, NC
8. No
9. No
10. Yes, 2-week loan with Library card
11. No
12. No
13. None
14. No
15. No

PORT HURON

St. Clair County Library
210 McMorran Blvd, 48060
Tel: 313-987-7323

1. M, 5:30-8:30; T-Th, 9-12,1:30-4:30
2. Frances Marshall
3. English, 5,414
4. None
5. 83
6. St. Clair County; "thumb area" of MI
7. Tel: yes, NC except for copies; letter: yes, $5 basic fee, $1 for first copy, 25¢ thereafter
8. No
9. No
10. No
11. Yes, newspaper microfilm only, through ILL
12. No
13. N/AN
14. No
15. No
Books & Sets: 2,3
Periodicals: 3(1956–),9(v.80, 82–84)

ROCHESTER

Rochester Hills Public Library
210 W University Dr, 48063
Tel: 313-656-2900

1. M-Th, 9:30-9; F, 9:30-5:30; Sa, 9:30-5
2. Sibyl Burke
3. English, 150
4. None
5. N/AN
6. Detroit, Rochester, Avon Township; Oakland, Macomb Counties
7. Tel & letter: yes, NC
8. No
9. No
10. No
11. No
12. No
13. None
14. No
15. No
Books & Sets: 3,5
Periodicals: 3(5 years & current), 4(5 years & current)

ROYAL OAK

Royal Oak Public Library
PO Box 494, 222 E Eleven Mile, 48068-0494
Tel: 313-541-1470

1. M,T,Th, 10-9; W,F,Sa, 10-6
2. N/AN
3. N/AN
4. None
5. None
6. Royal Oak
7. Tel: no; letter: yes, NC
8. No
9. No
10. No
11. No
12. No
13. N/AN
14. No
15. No
Books & Sets: 1,3
Periodicals: 3

SAGINAW

**Hoyt Public Library,
Eddy Historical Collection**
505 Janes Ave, 48605
Tel: 517-755-0904

1. M-Th, 9-9; F,Sa, 9-5
2. Kate Tesdell, Head, Reference Dept
3. English, 9,000; German, 20; French, 75
4. 25
5. 3,500
6. MI; New England, mid-Atlantic states, colonial South, Midwest; Canada
7. Tel & letter: yes, NC except for copies
8. Anna Mae Thompson Maday
   Peggy Lugthart
9. No
10. Yes, duplicates only
11. No
12. *Genealogy Materials in the Eddy Historical Collection* (1975), out of print; *Supplement* (1979), no charge
13. *A Guide to the Eddy Historical Collection*; *Starting Your Family History*; *Guide to the Eddy Room: Irish Genealogical Resources, Polish Genealogical Resources, Afro-American Roots*
14. Yes
15. OCLC: EZWU
Books & Sets: 1–5,7,9–14,18,19, 22–24,26
Periodicals: 1–5,6(1964–77),7–9

SAINT CLAIR SHORES

St. Clair Shores Public Library
22500 Eleven Mile Rd, 48081
Tel: 313-771-9020

1. Summer: M,W,F, 9-5; T,Th, 1-9; winter: M,W,Sa, 9-5; T,Th, 1-9
2. N/AP
3. English, 3,600; French, less than 10
4. None

5. 10
6. MI and Great Lakes
7. Tel & letter: yes, NC
8. No
9. No
10. No
11. No
12. "Genealogy Sources at the St. Clair Shores Public Library"
13. None
14. No
15. No
Periodicals: 3(v.2, 1938–), 4(1984–)

SAINT JOSEPH

Genealogical Association of Southwestern Michigan
500 Market St, PO Box 573, 49085
Tel: 616-983-7168

1. M-Th, 10-9; F,Sa, 10-6
2. Harold Atwood
3. English, 425
4. None
5. None
6. MI, IN; all US
7. Tel: no; letter: yes, NC except for SASE
8. No
9. No
10. No
11. No
12. No
13. Catalog of LH/G materials for Allegan, Berrien, Cass, Van Buren Counties, MI
14. No
15. No
Books & Sets: 26
Periodicals: 3,4,8,9

Maud Preston Palenske Memorial Library
500 Market St, 49085
Tel: 616-983-7168

1. M-Th, 10-9; F,Sa, 10-6
2. Barbara Troost
3. English, all
4. 1,900 books
5. 222
6. MI, especially St. Joseph and Berrien County

7. Tel: no; letter: yes, NC except for copies and postage
8. No
9. No
10. No
11. No
12. No
13. N/AN
14. No
15. N/AN
Periodicals: 4(1971–)

SAULT SAINTE MARIE

Lake Superior State College, Kenneth J. Shouldice Library
49783
Tel: 906-635-2402

1. Winter: M-Th, 8am-11pm; F, 8-5; Sa, 12-5; Su, 1-11; summer: M-Th, 8am-9pm; F, 8-5
2. N/AP
3. English, LH, 1,400; French, 10–20
4. N/AP
5. N/AP
6. MI state
7. Tel & letter: yes, NC
8. No
9. No
10. No
11. No
12. No
13. N/AN
14. No
15. OCLC: EZL
Books & Sets: 1(1980),3(3 v. 1981)

STERLING HEIGHTS

Sterling Heights Public Library
40255 Dodge Park Rd, 48078-4496
Tel: 313-977-6267

1. M-Th, 9:30-8:30; F,Sa, 9:30-5; closed Sa in summer
2. Julia Santini
3. English, G, 150, LH, 300
4. 5
5. None
6. Sterling Heights, Macomb County

7. Tel & letter: yes, NC
8. Ruth Baker
9. No
10. Yes
11. No
12. No
13. "A Genealogy Pathfinder"; "A Guide to Sterling Heights Municipal Documents" (in progress)
14. No
15. No
Books & Sets: 3,10
Periodicals: 3(1960–),4(1983–)

STURGIS

Sturgis Public Library and Information Center
130 N Nottawa, 49091
Tel: 616-651-7907

1. Winter: M-Th, 9:30-8:30; F,Sa, 9:30-5:30; summer: M,Th, 9:30-8:30; T,W,F, 9:30-5:30; Sa, 9:30-3
2. Jeri Cook
3. English, 1,200
4. None
5. 425
6. MI, IN, OH, NY, PA, MD
7. Tel: yes, NC; letter: yes, charge for copies, minimum $1
8. No
9. No
10. No
11. No
12. No
13. N/AN
14. No
15. No
Books & Sets: 3,7
Periodicals: 3(1971–),4(1975–), 8(1961–)

TAWAS CITY

Iosco-Arenac Regional Library
951 Turtle Rd, 48763
Tel: 517-362-2651

1. M-F, 8-4:30
2. N/AN
3. English, 35
4. 10
5. 40

6. Iosco and Arenac Counties
7. Tel & letter: no
8. No
9. No
10. No
11. No
12. No
13. None
14. Yes
15. No

TRAVERSE CITY

Northwestern Michigan College, Mark Osterlin Library
1701 E Front St, 49684
Tel: 616-922-1060

1. Winter: M-Th, 8am–10pm; F, 8-5; Sa, 9-4; Su, 1-5; summer: M,Th,F, 8:30-4:30; T,W, 8:30am-9:30pm
2. Elaine Beardslee
3. G: English, 500; German, 3; French, 1
4. None
5. G: 122
6. G: North Atlantic states, Midwest, Atlantic Coast, New England
7. Tel & letter: $2 plus postage
8. No
9. No
10. No
11. No
12. L. E. Wallace, *Researching Genealogy in Traverse City at Northwestern Michigan College* (1985), $17.50
13. N/AN
14. Yes
15. No
Books & Sets: 1(1983 suppl),3,5, 7(microfilm),26
Periodicals: 1(1983–84),3(1972–), 4(1955–),6(1975–82),7,8(1956–73, 1976,1978–),9(1924–26,1930–32,1964–67,1981–86)

TROY

Troy Public Library
510 W Big Beaver Rd, 48084
Tel: 313-524-3538

1. M, 1-9; T-Th, 10–9; F,Sa, 10-6; Su (Sept-June), 1-6
2. Marcia Rutledge
3. English, 700
4. None
5. 44
6. US; Canada, United Kingdom, some Germany
7. Tel & letter: yes, NC
8. No
9. Yes, $20 for nonresidents
10. Yes, 3-week loan
11. No
12. No
13. N/AN
14. No
15. OCLC: Some
Books & Sets: 1(part of Bio Base),2(Index only),3,11,26
Periodicals: 3

WHITE CLOUD

Newaygo County Society of History and Genealogy, Evans Historical Collection, 1038 Wilcox Ave, PO Box 68, 49349
Tel: 616-689-6631

1. T,F, 10:30-5:30; Sa, 10:30-2 (hrs subject to change)
2. Ronald Taylor
3. English, 700
4. 825 files, 3 private collections
5. 375
6. Newaygo County, surrounding counties, MI
7. Tel: yes, NC; letter: $8/hr or $1/specific item
8. Ronald Taylor
9. No
10. Yes, through ILL
11. No
12. No
13. *Guide to Research in the Martha E. Mudget Evans Historical Collection*, no charge
14. No
15. No
Books & Sets: 14,22,23

Periodicals: 3(v.32–42, 1969–78), 4(v.19–40, 1965–86),5(1977), 8(v.67–69, 1979–81),9(v.132–35, 141–, 1978–81,1987–)

WYANDOTTE

Bacon Memorial Public Library
45 Vinewood, 48192
Tel: 313-282-7660

1. Oct-May: M-Th, 10-9; F, closed; Sa, 10-5; June-Sept: M-Th, 10-8; F, 10-5
2. Wallace Hayden
3. English, 400
4. 400 scrapbooks; 4,000 photographs; thousands of clippings; 105 years of local newspapers on microfilm, most indexed
5. 200
6. "Downriver" area, especially Wyandotte, Riverview, Trenton, Grosse Ile, Southgate
7. Tel: yes, NC; letter: yes, charge for copies over $1
8. No
9. No
10. No
11. Yes, through ILL
12. No
13. 60,000-card catalog in Local History Room
14. No
15. No
Periodicals: 3(1958–)

YPSILANTI

Ypsilanti District Library
229 W Michigan, 48197
Tel: 313-482-4110

1. M, 10-8; T-Th, 9-8; F,Sa, 9-5:30
2. Paula Drummond, Reference Dept
3. English, 60
4. None
5. None
6. Ypsilanti, MI
7. Tel & letter: yes, NC. Refer to Ypsilanti Historical Society, 220 N Huron, Ypsilanti, MI 48197 (313-482-4990)
8. No
9. No
10. Yes, with Library card: $10 for nonresidents
11. N/AP
12. No
13. None
14. No
15. OCLC: MIY (partial)
Books & Sets: 19(1965)
Periodicals: 4(1982–)

MINNESOTA

AUSTIN

Austin Public Library
201 2nd Ave NW, 55912
Tel: 507-433-2391

1. Winter: M-Th, 8:30am-9pm; F, 8:30-5; Sa, 9-5; summer: M,Th, 8:30am-9pm; T,W,F, 8:30-5; Sa, 9-1
2. No designated head
3. English, 50
4. 5 locally produced family histories, 7 community centennial publications
5. 670
6. Mower County, some nearby counties, MN
7. Tel & letter: yes, NC except for copies
8. No
9. No
10. No
11. No
12. No
13. *Genealogical Resources at Austin Public Library* (bibliography)
14. Yes
15. No
Periodicals: 4(10 years)

Mower County Historical Society, Box 804, 55912
Tel: 507-437-6082

1. Genealogy Room: T,W, Th, 1-4 (summer only, or by appointment)
2. Monica Lonergan, Chairman
3. English, no estimate; other, a few Danish and Norwegian
4. No estimate. All are LH, G
5. None
6. Mower County, some neighboring counties

7. Tel & letter: yes, NC for brief queries, otherwise $4/hr
8. Yes
9. No
10. No, only to members
11. No
12. No
13. None
14. Yes
15. No

CHISHOLM

Iron Range Research Center
Hwy 169 West, PO Box 392, 55719
Tel: 218-254-3321

1. M-Su, 10-5
2. Edward Nelson, Archivist and Assistant Director
3. English, 1,700; German, 4; Finnish, Croatian, Slovenian, 100 each
4. 900
5. 4,400
6. St. Louis County, Itasca County, northeastern MN, MN state
7. Tel & letter: yes, NC except for copies
8. No
9. No
10. Yes, 3-week loan
11. Yes, 3-week loan
12. No
13. Brochures, indexes
14. Yes
15. OCLC: IRR
Books & Sets: 3–5,10,11,22,23
Periodicals: 2,4,5,8

DULUTH

Duluth Public Library
520 W Superior, 55802
Tel: 218-723-3802

1. M,Th, 10-8:30; T,W,F, 10-5:30; Sa (Oct-May), 10-4
2. David Ouse, Head, Reference
3. English, 500; French, 10
4. None
5. 1,000
6. Great Lakes, East Coast states
7. Tel & letter: yes, NC except for copies
8. No
9. No
10. No
11. Yes, through ILL
12. No
13. CLSI computerized catalog
14. Yes
15. No
Books & Sets: 1–3,5(v.1–3),6,7, 10–14,19,22,24,26
Periodicals: 4,5,7,8(1943–53), 9(v.1–15,26–41,62–114,119–20, 122–24,128–)

EDINA

Hennepin County Library, Southdale
7001 York Ave South, 55435
Tel: 612-830-4933

1. M-Th, 10-9:30; F,Sa, 10-5; Su (Oct-Apr), 12-5
2. Julie Setnosky, Senior Reference Materials Librarian
3. English, 200
4. None
5. None
6. MN
7. Tel & letter: yes, NC for brief queries
8. No
9. No
10. No

11. N/AP
12. No
13. N/AN
14. No
15. No
Books & Sets: 1,3,6,10–12,17,
19,24,26
Periodicals: 4(1977–)

MINNEAPOLIS

**Minneapolis Public Library
and Information Center,
Minneapolis History Collection**
300 Nicollet Mall, 55401
Tel: 612-372-6648 (LH),
372-6537 (G)

1. M-Th, 9-9; F,Sa, 9-5:30;
closed summer Sa
2. LH: Librarian, Minneapolis
History Collection; G: Robert K.
Bruce, Department Head, History
and Travel
3. LH: English, 13,000; G:
English, 550 plus county, family
histories; German, 3–5
4. LH: thousands of clippings
and photos; G: N/AN
5. LH: none; G: 23
6. LH: Minneapolis, metropolitan area; G: MN east through
New England into Europe
7. LH: tel & letter: yes, NC;
G: tel: no, except citation; letter:
yes, charge if over 15 minutes
8. LH: yes; G: no
9. No
10. LH: no; G: no, except "how-
to" items
11. LH: N/AP; G: no
12. LH: no; G: no
13. LH: "Discover a Minneapolis Gold Mine," brochure; G:
N/AV
14. LH: yes; G: yes, refer to
Minnesota Historical Society
15. OCLC: MNI
Books & Sets: 1,2(v.1–36, 1910–
80),3,7,10–16,18,19,21,24(v.1,
1969),26(6 microcards)
Periodicals: 4(v.14, 1960–),5,
7(v.1–2)

**University of Minnesota,
Humanities and Social Sciences
Libraries,** 55455
Tel: 612-624-0303

1. Hours vary
2. Relevant materials integrated into Humanities and Social
Science Libraries
3. N/AN
4. N/AN
5. N/AN
6. US; Europe, especially
Scandinavia
7. Tel & letter: yes, NC for
brief queries
8. No
9. No charge for walk-in users;
charge for extensive research for
nonuniversity users
10. Yes, through ILL, not
directly to nonuniversity users
11. Yes, through ILL, not
directly to nonuniversity users
12. No
13. N/AN
14. No
15. OCLC: MNU
    RLIN: MNU
Books & Sets: 1–3,5,6,9,13,
16(suppl 1977, 1983–85),18(48v.),
19(1934,2v., 1926–54, 7v. suppl),
23,24,27
Periodicals: 7(v.1–3, 1932–53),
9(broken set)

MOORHEAD

**Concordia College, Carl B.
Ylvisaker Library,** 56560
Tel: 218-299-3237

1. School year: M-Th, 7:45am-
midnight; F, 7:45am-10:30pm; Sa,
10-5; Su, 12:30-midnight; summer:
M-F, 8-4:30
2. Mary Larson
3. English, 500; Norwegian,
600
4. None
5. Microfilm: 250; microfiche:
150
6. Norway in particular; other

Scandinavian countries, Germany,
England
7. Tel: yes, NC for brief
queries; letter: yes, charge
8. No
9. No
10. Yes
11. No
12. N/AN
13. "Guide to Genealogical Resources in the Carl B. Ylvisaker
Library"
14. No
15. OCLC: TRI
Books & Sets: 3,10–14
Periodicals: 4,5

**Moorhead State University,
Northwest Minnesota Historical
Center,** Livingston Lord Library,
56560
Tel: 218-236-2343

1. M-F, 8-12, 1-5
2. Terry L. Shoptaugh,
Archivist
3. English, 50
4. 150
5. 25
6. Northwest MN area
7. Tel & letter: yes, NC
8. No
9. No
10. No
11. No
12. *Northwest Minnesota
Historical Center Collections*,
not for sale
13. None
14. No
15. OCLC: yes
Books & Sets: 3,6,26

OWATONNA

Owatonna Public Library
105 North Elm, 55060
Tel: 507-451-4660

1. M-Th, 8am-9pm; F,Sa, 9-5
2. Bonnie Krueger, Reference
Librarian

3. English, unknown
4. Several
5. 300+: newspapers since 1868
6. Owatonna, Steele County, MN
7. Tel & letter: yes, NC
8. No
9. No
10. Yes, through ILL only
11. No
12. N/AN
13. N/AN
14. Yes
15. No
Books & Sets: 5
Periodicals: 4(1960–75,1976–)

ROCHESTER

Rochester Public Library
11 First St SE, 55904
Tel: 507-285-8002

1. M-W, 9:30-9; F, 9:30-5:30; Sa, 9-5 winter; 9-1 summer
2. Louise Moe, Reference Librarian
3. English, 200
4. None
5. None
6. US
7. Tel & letter: yes, NC
8. No
9. No
10. No
11. No
12. No
13. None
14. No
15. OCLC: ROC
Books & Sets: 3
Periodicals: 4

SAINT PAUL

Minnesota Genealogical Society Library, 678 Fort Rd, 55104
(mailing address: PO Box 16069, 55116)
Tel: 612-222-6929

1. W,Th,Sa, 10-4; T,Th, 6:30-9:30 pm
2. Alfred Dahlquist
   Jim Warren
3. English, 2,000; French, 500. Also, large inventory of French Canadian marriage *répertoires* from Northwest Territory French & Canadian Heritage Institute
4. A few
5. A few
6. French Canada, US
7. Tel: yes, NC, brief requests on Wednesday only; letter: yes, NC except 15¢/copy
8. No, but many people who do genealogical research
9. No
10. No
11. No
12. No
13. None
14. Yes
15. No
Books & Sets: 5,9,24,25
Periodicals: 1(v.35–58, 1959–82), 2(v.1,6, 1979, 1984),4(v.4–, 1950–),8(v.66–, 1978–), 9(1980–85)

Minnesota Historical Society, Reference Library
690 Cedar St, 55101
Tel: 612-296-2143

1. M-Sa, 8:30-5
2. Patricia Harpole, Chief, Reference Library
3. Library does not separate G/LH from rest of the collection, comprising 400,000 books, pamphlets, other print materials. These include 15,000 family histories
4. 34,000 cubic ft, total MSS; 29,000 cubic ft, total State Archives
5. 35,000
6. US: MN, upper Midwest, Western Reserve; Canada: Manitoba, Ontario, Quebec
7. Tel: yes, NC for general queries only; letter: yes, $1 minimum for copies, plus 10¢–25¢/page
8. All of staff
9. No
10. No

11. Yes, through ILL; $2.50/request, up to 6 reels
12. Small guides to special collections. Request publications catalog for title lists
13. Biography files, Civil War Veterans files, MS inventories
14. Yes
15. OCLC: MHS
    RLIN: MNHV (partial)
Books & Sets: 2–7,10–14,17–19, 24–26
Periodicals: 1–5,7–9

St. Paul Public Library
90 W 4th St, 55102
Tel: 612-292-6307 (Reference Room)

1. M,Th, 9-9; T,W,F,Sa, 9-5:30
2. Larry Hlausa, Librarian in charge of St. Paul Collection
3. English, 3,000. Library does not collect family histories as such. Refer to the Minnesota Historical Society
4. None
5. Several hundred
6. St. Paul, MN
7. Tel & letter: yes, NC for simple reference questions. Fees charged for questions involving considerable research
8. No
9. No
10. No
11. No
12. No
13. *Research Guide to the St. Paul Collection*
14. Yes, list published by Minnesota Historical Society
15. No

SOUTH SAINT PAUL

South St. Paul Public Library
106 3rd Ave N, 55075
Tel: 612-451-1093

1. Daily, 9-6
2. N/AP
3. English, 50
4. N/AN

5. N/AN
6. Dakota County
7. Tel & letter: yes, NC
8. No
9. No
10. Yes, 3-week loan
11. No
12. No
13. N/AN
14. No
15. No
Periodicals: 4(1980–)

WASECA

Waseca-LeSueur Regional Library, 408 N State, 56093
Tel: 507-835-2910

1. M-Th, 9-8:30; F,Sa, 9-5
2. N/AN
3. English, 75
4. None
5. None
6. MN; some New England, Europe, misc

7. Tel & letter: yes, NC
8. No
9. No
10. 3-week loan for non-reference materials
11. N/AP
12. No
13. Microfiche
14. Yes
15. OCLC: yes
Books & Sets: 3
Periodicals: 4

MISSISSIPPI

BROOKHAVEN

Lincoln County Public Library
100 S Jackson St, 39601
Tel: 601-833-3369

1. M-W, 9-6; T,Th, 9-8; F, Sa, 9-5
2. Henry J. Ledet
3. English, 1,000
4. 40
5. 400
6. Southeastern US, concentrating on Lincoln, Lawrence, and Franklin Counties, MS
7. Tel & letter: no
8. No
9. No
10. No
11. No
12. No
13. N/AN
14. Yes
15. No
Books & Sets: 2,3,26
Periodicals: 1,4,5,7

CLARKSDALE

Carnegie Public Library of Clarksdale and Coahoma County, 114 Delta Ave,
PO Box 280, 38614
Tel: 601-624-4461

1. M, 9-8; T-Th, 9-5:30; F, 9-5; Sa, 10-2
2. N/AN
3. English, G, 1,003, LH, 1,200
4. N/AN
5. 92, genealogy; 188, local newspaper
6. Clarksdale, Coahoma County, MS; states east of Mississippi River: VA, SC, NC, GA, AL, MS, TN, AR, LA, KY

7. Tel & letter: yes, NC except for copies: 20¢/letter, 25¢/legal, 30¢/11x17, plus postage
8. N/AN
9. No
10. No
11. No
12. No
13. Card catalog
14. No
15. No
Books & Sets: 2(v.49–61, 64–128),26(PA,NC,SC,VA)
Periodicals: 4(v.15–26, 1961–72), 9(v.111–21, 1957–67)

CLEVELAND

Bolivar County Library
104 S Leflore Ave, 38732
Tel: 601-843-2774

1. M-Th, 9-8 (summer, 9-6); F, 9-5; Sa, 9-5 (summer, 10-2)
2. N/AN
3. English, 1,100
4. None
5. 108: local newspapers, Bolivar County tax rolls
6. Cleveland, Bolivar County, MS; other southern states
7. Tel: yes, NC; letter: yes, NC except 15¢/copy
8. No
9. No
10. No
11. No
12. No
13. Subject card catalog; some titles listed on computer; most titles in Mississippi Union Catalog
14. No. Refer to Mississippi Department of Archives and History, Jackson
15. No
Books & Sets: 26(NC,SC,VA)

COLUMBUS

Lowndes County Library System, 314 N 7th St, 39701
Tel: 601-328-1056

1. M-Th, 9-8; F, 9-5; Sa, 9-3
2. Carolyn Neault
3. English, 5,000
4. 100
5. 200
6. VA, NC, SC, GA, AL, MS, TN, KY; some MA, PA, NJ
7. Tel & letter: yes, NC except 25¢/copy
8. No
9. No
10. No
11. No
12. No
13. N/AN
14. No
15. No
Books & Sets: 2,7,11,26
Periodicals: 8

CORINTH

Corinth Public Library
1023 Fillmore St, 38834
Tel: 601-287-2441

1. M-Th, 9-8; F,Sa, 9-5
2. Mrs. Charles McDonald, Librarian
3. English, 300
4. None
5. None
6. Northeastern MS; southwestern TN
7. Tel: no; letter: yes, NC
8. No
9. No
10. Yes, 2-week loan
11. Yes, 2-week loan
12. No
13. None

14. No
15. No
Periodicals: 4

GREENVILLE

**Washington County Library
System, William Alexander
Percy Memorial Library**
341 Main St, 38701
Tel: 601-335-2331

1. M-W, 9-8; Th,F, 9-6; Sa,
Su, 1-5
2. Information Department
3. N/AN
4. 15
5. 215
6. MS, NC, SC, VA, TN, AL,
GA
7. Tel & letter: yes, NC
8. N/AN
9. No
10. No
11. No
12. No
13. N/AN
14. Yes
15. No
Books & Sets: 1(8 v. set),2,10,11
Periodicals: 4(1965–66, 1968–81),
8(1966–)

GREENWOOD

**Greenwood-Leflore Public
Library**, 405 W Washington,
38930
Tel: 601-453-3634

1. M-Th, 9-8; F,Sa, 10-5
2. Miss Van Dyke Neill
3. English, 3,800
4. 2
5. 350
6. MS, AL, GA, KY, LA,
MD, MA, NJ, NC, PA, SC, TN,
TX, VA
7. Tel: yes, NC for quick
answers; letter: no
8. No
9. No
10. No
11. No

12. *Catalogue of the Genealogical Collection, Greenwood-Leflore Public Library*, out of print; *Supplement to the Catalogue of the Genealogical Collection* (1983), $3
13. N/AN
14. Yes
15. No
Books & Sets: 2(v.28–38,40,45–54),6,10,11,26(MD,ME,MA,NH, NC,PA,SC,VT,VA)
Periodicals: 1(1932–52),4(1973–), 8(1944–84), 9(1847–71,1944–60, 1975–)

GULFPORT

**Gulfport-Harrison County
Library**, 14th St & 21st Ave,
39502
Tel: 601-863-6411

1. M-Th,9-8; F,9-6; Sa, 9-5
2. Alvina E. Bristow
3. English, no estimate;
French, 6
4. None
5. 220
6. South, Southeast, Middle
Atlantic, New England, Northeast,
Midwest
7. Tel & letter: yes, NC
8. No
9. No
10. No
11. No
12. No
13. N/AN
14. No
15. No
Books & Sets: 2(v.48–54),3(46–53),26(CT,KY,MA,MD,NY, NC,PA,VA)
Periodicals: 4(1965–),8(1973–75), 9(1973–74,1982)

HATTIESBURG

**Hattiesburg Public Library
System**, 723 Main St, 39401
Tel: 601-582-4461

1. M,T, 9-8:30; W-Sa, 9-5:30
2. Reference Librarian

3. English, approx 978;
French, 13
4. N/AN
5. Approx 547
6. Southeastern states, including LA, TX
7. Tel: no; letter: yes, NC for
brief queries
8. No
9. No
10. No
11. No
12. No
13. N/AN
14. No
15. No
Books & Sets: 2(v.11,13,17–19,21, 23–166),5,10–12,24,26
Periodicals: 1(v. 52–60, 1976–84), 4(1959–66,1978–),5(1967–75)

**University of Southern
Mississippi, McCain Library
and Archives**, Box 5148,
Southern Station, 39401
Tel: 601-266-5077

1. M-Th, 8am-9pm; F, 8-5; Sa,
10-5; Su, 1-5
2. Betty S. Drake
3. English, 5,000
4. 3,600 files on individual
families in vertical files
5. 4,250
6. Southern states
7. Tel: yes, NC for brief
queries; letter: $2 plus copies and
postage
8. Betty S. Drake
9. No
10. Seldom
11. No
12. Brief summary, distributed
locally
13. Alpha list of soldiers of MS
Territory, War of 1812; alpha list
of MS soldiers in Mexican War.
Most periodicals are indexed by
major family records
14. Yes
15. OCLC: yes
Books & Sets: 1,2(lack only few
volumes),3,7,10–14,17–19,24,26
Periodicals: 4(v.6–, 1952–),
8(v.43–, 1955–),9(v.1–50)

INDIANOLA

Sunflower County Library
201 Cypress Dr, 38751
Tel: 601-887-1672

1. M,W-F, 9-5:30; T, 9-8; Sa, 9-12; Su, 1:30-5:30
2. Anice Powell
3. English, no estimate. Also, 1,025 magazines
4. 75 file folders
5. 87
6. Mainly southern states
7. Tel & letter: yes, NC for brief queries except for copies
8. No
9. No
10. No
11. No
12. No
13. N/AN
14. No
15. N/AN
Books & Sets: 3(3 v. 1981),10–12
Periodicals: 4,7,8

IUKA

Iuka Public Library
204 N Main St, 38852
Tel: 601-423-6300

1. M,T,F, 10-6; W,Th, 10-7; Sa, 10-4
2. Fredda Sanderson, Librarian
3. English, 55
4. N/AN
5. 48
6. Tishomingo County, MS, 1840–1910; KY (1850–) and NY (1800–) population censuses on microfilm
7. Tel & letter: yes, NC
8. No
9. Yes, $10 check-out charge for nonresidents
10. Yes, through ILL
11. No
12. No
13. N/AN
14. Yes
15. N/AN

JACKSON

Mississippi Department of Archives and History, Archives and Library Division, 100 South State, PO Box 571, 39201
Tel: 601-359-1424

1. M-F, 8-5; Sa, 8:30-4:30
2. Anne Lipscomb, Head Librarian
3. English, 38,000, of Mississippiana
4. 1,854
5. 2,000–3,000 counting census; newspapers, military records
6. MS, southeastern US
7. Tel & letter: yes, NC except for copies and postage
8. Vera Richardson
9. No
10. No
11. No
12. *Guide to Official Records,* outdated
13. In-house MS index, official record guide
14. Yes
15. No
Books & Sets: 2–4,6,7,10–12,14, 17,19,26
Periodicals: 8,9

LAUREL

Lauren Rogers Museum of Art Library, PO Box 1108, 5th Ave at 7th St, 39441
Tel: 601-649-6374

1. M, closed; T-Sa, 10-5; Su, 1-4
2. Diane E. Clark
3. English, 3,000
4. 4
5. 223
6. Jones County, MS state; other southeastern states, NY, PA, Northeast
7. Tel & letter: yes, NC except 15¢/copy
8. Diane E. Clark
9. No
10. No
11. No

12. No
13. N/AN
14. Yes
15. No
Books & Sets: 2,7(v.1),10–12, 26(8 v.)
Periodicals: 4(v.33–, 1979–)7,9

McCOMB

Pike-Amite-Walthall Library System, 114 State St, 39648
Tel: 601-684-2661

1. M-Th, 8:30-8; F,Sa, 8:30-5
2. Katherine M. Niemeyer
3. English, 800
4. None
5. 1,000
6. Southern MS counties; parishes over LA line; NC, SC, GA, New England states
7. Tel & letter: yes, NC for brief queries except for copies
8. Katherine M. Niemeyer
9. No
10. Yes, 1-week in-house use
11. Yes, 1-week in-house use
12. No
13. N/AN
14. No
15. No
Books & Sets: 2(v.24–64),3,8(US & Devon, England)

MERIDIAN

Meridian Public Library
2517 7th St, 39301
Tel: 601-693-6771

1. M-Sa, 9-6
2. Carol James
3. English, 675
4. 118
5. 620
6. Mostly MS, AL, GA, Southeast
7. Tel: yes, NC; letter: no
8. No
9. No
10. No
11. No
12. No

13. N/AN
14. No
15. No
Books & Sets: 3,5(v.1–5),7(v.1–6), 26(8 v.)
Periodicals: 4(1966–68,1970–)

NEW ALBANY

Jennie Stephens Smith Library
219 King St, 38652
Tel: 601-534-4331

1. M,W,F, 9-5:30; T,Th, 9-8; Sa, 9-1
2. N/AN
3. English, approx 2,200
4. N/AN
5. 45: census records
6. Southeastern US
7. Tel & letter: no
8. No
9. No
10. No
11. No
12. No
13. N/AN
14. No
15. N/AN
Books & Sets: 2(incomplete), 7(v.1,2),26
Periodicals: 4(1947–66,1970–84), 7(v.1), 8(1914–43,1948–64), 9(incomplete)

PASCAGOULA

Jackson-George Regional Library System
3214 Pascagoula St, 39567
Tel: 601-762-3060

1. M-Th, 9-8; F,Sa, 9-5
2. No specific staff assigned
3. 950
4. N/AN
5. 70: Jackson County records, 1875–1930
6. Jackson County, MS Gulf Coast
7. Tel & letter: no, but letters are forwarded to queries chairman for local Society

8. No
9. No
10. No
11. No
12. No
13. N/AN
14. No
15. No
Books & Sets: 3,26
Periodicals: 4

RIPLEY

Ripley Public Library
308 N Commerce, 38663
Tel: 601-837-7773

1. M,W,F,Sa, 9-5; T,Th, 9-8
2. Tommy Covington
3. English, 400
4. 200
5. 125
6. Tippah County, MS
7. Tel: yes, NC; letter: N/AN
8. No
9. No
10. No
11. No
12. No
13. None
14. No
15. No

TUPELO

Lee County Library
219 Madison St, 38801
Tel: 601-841-9029

1. M-Th, 9:30-8:30; Sa, 9-5
2. N/AP
3. English, 800
4. None
5. 1,000: census
6. MS; Southeast
7. Tel: yes, NC; letter: yes, NC except 15¢/copy
8. No
9. No
10. No
11. No
12. No
13. N/AN

14. No
15. No
Books & Sets: 5,7(v.1),26

UNION

Union Public Library
101 Peachtree St, 39365
Tel: 601-774-8095

1. M-F, 8:30-5:30
2. None
3. English, 100
4. None
5. None
6. Union, Newton County, MS state
7. Tel & letter: yes, NC
8. No
9. No
10. No
11. No
12. No
13. N/AN
14. No
15. N/AN

WASHINGTON

Historic Jefferson College, Mississippi Department of Archives and History
PO Box 100, 39190
Tel: 601-442-2901

1. M-Sa, 9-5; Su, 1-5
2. N/AN
3. English, 27
4. None
5. None
6. Southwestern MS
7. Tel & letter: yes, NC except 25¢/copy plus postage
8. No
9. Donations accepted
10. No
11. No
12. No
13. N/AN
14. Yes
15. No
Books & Sets: 3(no suppls)

MISSOURI

CAPE GIRARDEAU

Cape Girardeau Public Library
711 N Clark, 63701
Tel: 314-334-5279

1. M-Th, 9-9; F, 9-6; Sa, 9-5
2. Martha Maxwell, Library Director
3. English, 1,050; German, 3
4. 30
5. 831, including passenger lists of vessels arriving at New Orleans, 1820–1902
6. Southeastern MO (areas of German settlements), MO state; IL, KY, TN, PA, VA, SC, NC, MD, NJ, OH, IN, LA
7. Tel: yes, NC for brief query; letter: no, refer to local genealogist
8. No
9. No
10. Yes, if in circulating collection; must be requested by another library through ILL
11. No
12. *The Allene W. and Frederic A. Groves Genealogy Resource Center* (rev June 1986), $4
13. N/AN
14. No
15. No
Books & Sets: 2–4,10,12
Periodicals: 4(1976–),7(3v.), 9(1981–)

COLUMBIA

State Historical Society of Missouri
1020 Lowry St, 65201
Tel: 314-882-7083

1. M-F, 8-4:30; Sa, 9-4:30; closed legal holidays, holiday weekends
2. N/AN

3. English, 99.9%; German, .1%
4. 475
5. N/AN
6. MO; states from which Missourians originated: VA, KY, PA; trans-Mississippi West
7. Tel & letter: yes, NC
8. No
9. No
10. LH, yes; G, no
11. Yes, 2 rolls for 2-week loan; $2 fee plus postage
12. *Catalog of Missouri Newspapers on Microfilm at State Historical Society of Missouri*, $10; *Manuscripts: Guide to Collections*, $10 (microfiche copy)
13. Surname index to biographical sections in Missouri county histories before 1950; indexes to *Gateway Heritage, Bulletin, Missouri Life, Missouri Historical Review;* newspaper card indexes; card files to historic sites and to MO Confederate soldiers
14. Yes
15. N/AN
Books & Sets: 3,6,7,10–14, 17–19,24,26
Periodicals: 1(random issues only),4,5,8,9

EAGLE ROCK

Tree Trackers Library
HCR-01, Box 41, 65641
Tel: 417-271-3532

1. By appointment only
2. Phyllis Eldrige Friesner
3. English, 900; Norwegian, 2
4. N/AN
5. No estimate
6. US; some Norway
7. Tel: N/AN; letter: yes, NC, but donation accepted

8. Phyllis Eldrige Friesner; Lois Fertig Crull, Mormon genealogy
9. Yes, donation
10. No
11. No
12. No
13. N/AN
14. No
15. No
Periodicals: 9(1925–32)

HARRISONVILLE

Cass County Public Library
400 E. Mechanic, 64701
Tel: 816-884-6223

1. M,Th, 9-7; T,W, 9-6; F, 9-5; Sa, 9-3
2. Kim Hammontree
3. English, 300
4. None
5. 165
6. Cass County, other MO counties
7. Tel & letter: yes, NC
8. No
9. No
10. No
11. No
12. No
13. N/AN
14. Yes
15. No
Books & Sets: 3,10–14
Periodicals: 4

INDEPENDENCE

Mid-Continent Public Library, North Independence Branch
15616 E 24 Highway, 64050
Tel: 816-252-0950

1. M-Th, 9-9; F, 9-6; Sa, 9-5
2. Martha L. Meyers

3. English, 14,000; German, 5
4. 12 cubic ft
5. 26,000
6. MO; migration routes states into MO: KY, TN, NC, SC, MD, VA; also IL, IN, OH, PA
7. Tel & letter: yes, NC
8. Martha L. Meyers
9. No
10. Yes, only books in AFRA Genealogy Circulating Collection
11. Yes, only to libraries in MO
12. No
13. *Genealogy and Local History Department; Genealogical Resources on Microfilm, Available at the Mid-Continent Public Library, North Independence Branch; Genealogical Resources Available through Interlibrary Loan*
14. Yes
15. OCLC: CMI
Books & Sets: 1,2(v.16–166),3,5, 7,10–14,16,17,19(Rolland, 6 v.), 22,23,26
Periodicals: 1,3–5,7,8,9(v.1–59, 95–, 1847–1905,1941–)

JEFFERSON CITY

Missouri State Archives
1001 Industrial Drive,
PO Box 778, 65101
Tel: 314-751-3280

1. M-F, 8-5; Th, 8am-9pm; Sa, 8:30-3:30
2. Gary Beahan, State Archivist
3. English, 1,000
4. 15
5. 10,000. Includes microfilmed records for 113 (except Gentry) of MO's 114 counties
6. MO state
7. Tel: no; letter; yes, NC except for copies. Must use library's Genealogical Request Form
8. Yes
9. No
10. No
11. No
12. *Missouri Archives Bulletin*;

Guide to County Records on Microfilm
13. *Reel-to-Reel Listing of County Records on Microfilm at the Missouri Archives*, $5 (1 reel); numerous finding aids for census records, tax lists, government records, church records
14. Yes
15. No
Periodicals: 4(partial run, 1980s),8(partial run, 1970s–80s)

JOPLIN

Joplin Public Library
300 Main, 64801
Tel: 417-623-7953

1. M,Th, 9-9; T,W,F,Sa, 9-6
2. Administered by Joplin Genealogical Society, Box 152, Joplin, 64802
3. English, 2,200
4. N/AN
5. 275
6. Primarily MO, KS, AR, TN, OH, KY, VA, IL, NC; material on all except FL, NV, ND, WY
7. Tel & letter: yes, NC
8. Several volunteers
9. No
10. No
11. No
12. No
13. No
14. None
15. No
Books & Sets: 2(v.1–101),3,5, 7(NY,NC),26
Periodicals: 4

KANSAS CITY

Kansas City Public Library, Missouri Valley Room
311 E 12th St, 64106
Tel: 816-221-2685

1. M-Sa, 9-5
2. Marjorie Kinney
3. English, 16,500; German, negligible; other, negligible
4. 44
5. 1,034

6. Emphasis on MO, KY, TN, VA, NC, SC, Middle Atlantic, New England, OH, PA; other US; some Great Britain, Europe
7. Tel: yes, NC; letter: yes, 10¢/copy plus postage and $1 handling charge
8. Virginia Wright
9. No
10. No
11. No
12. No
13. "How to Use the Missouri Valley Room"
14. Yes
15. OCLC: KCP
Books & Sets: 2–5,7,17–19,22, 24,26
Periodicals: 1,3–5,7–9

MARYVILLE

Northwest Missouri State University, Owens Library
64468
Tel: 816-562-1590

1. M-F, 8am-10pm; Sa,Su, 12-4
2. Bob Nedderman
3. English, 500
4. 200
5. 120
6. Northwest MO
7. Tel: no; letter: no, refer to local genealogical society
8. No
9. No
10. Yes, 2-week loan to residents
11. No
12. No
13. N/AN
14. No
15. No
Books & Sets: 6

MOBERLY

Little Dixie Regional Libraries
111 N 4th St, 65270
Tel: 816-263-4426

1. Winter: M,T,Th, 8-8; W,F,Sa, 8-5; summer: M-Sa, 8-5

2. Vacant at present
3. English, 86
4. None
5. Local (Moberly, Higbee) newspapers; censuses of Randolph and Monroe Counties, 1850–1910
6. Randolph and Monroe Counties
7. Tel & letter: no. Refer to local free-lance genealogist
8. No
9. No
10. No
11. No
12. No
13. None
14. Yes
15. No

SAINT JOSEPH

St. Joseph Public Library
Tenth & Felix Sts, 64501
Tel: 816-232-8151

1. M-Th, 9-9; F,Sa, 9-6
2. N/AN
3. English, 450–500
4. None
5. 1,098, local newspaper; 52, census; 18, local city directory
6. MO state; some eastern US; some English, German
7. Tel & letter: no
8. No
9. No
10. No
11. No
12. Partial guide: *A Bibliography of Missouri State and Local History and Genealogy in the Collections of the Grand River Library Conference Members* (1982), compiled in cooperation with Northwest Missouri Library Network. No longer available
13. None
14. No
15. No
Books & Sets: 2,3,11,19(no suppls),26
Periodicals: 3(current 3 years only),9(v.1–123)

SAINT LOUIS

Missouri Historical Society Research Library and Archives
Jefferson Memorial Building,
Forest Park, 63112-1099
Tel: 314-361-1424

1. T-F, 9:30-4:45
2. Peter Michel, Chief Curator, Division of Library and Archives
3. English, 50,000; German, undetermined; French and Spanish, undetermined
4. 1,000: Archives Collection
5. 300+: newspapers, some census
6. St. Louis City and County; MO state; westward expansion into Louisiana Purchase Territory; general family histories; some materials dealing with other states
7. Tel & letter: no
8. No
9. Yes, $5/day to nonmembers; $25/year for research membership, $45/year for full membership
10. No
11. Yes, microfilmed newspapers only (2 reels/request) through ILL
12. *A List of Manuscript Collections in the Archives of the Missouri Historical Society*, $2.50; *In Her Own Write: Women's History Resources in the Library and Archives of the Missouri Historical Society*, $4; *The Lewis and Clark Expedition: A Guide to the Holdings in the Library and Archives*, $2.50
13. Vertical file; information file; archives catalog
14. Yes
15. OCLC: MJE (small portion; no longer using OCLC)
Books & Sets: 7,16,24,26
Periodicals: 7,9

St. Louis County Library
1640 S Lindbergh Blvd, 63131
Tel: 314-961-6462

1. M-F, 8:30 am-9 pm; Sa, 8:30-6
2. Susan Likes, Supervisor, Reference Dept
3. English, 868; German, 1
4. N/AN
5. 1,179
6. St. Louis, St. Louis County, MO state
7. Tel & letter: yes, NC
8. June Sommer
9. No
10. No
11. Yes, to any MO public library
12. "Studying Family Trees: A Guide to Genealogical Research at St. Louis County Library," $1.50
13. Index to MO county histories
14. N/AN
15. No
Books & Sets: 1,3,5-6,10–12, 19(2 v., 1950,1972)
Periodicals: 4(1977–),7

St. Louis Mercantile Library Association, 510 Locust,
6th Floor, 63101
Tel: 314-621-0670

1. M-F, 8:30-4:30
2. Charles E. Brown, Reference Librarian
3. English, 1,250–1,300
4. None
5. None
6. Old South; trans-Mississippi West, with concentration on St. Louis, MO state, adjacent areas in IL
7. Tel & letter: yes, NC for less than 1 hr, otherwise $5/hr
8. No
9. Yes; regular use by nonmembers discouraged, annual membership/$25
10. No
11. No
12. No
13. N/AN
14. No

15. OCLC: SLM (since 1983)
Books & Sets: 19(suppl, Rolland, v.1–7, 1926–54 w/index 1951), 24(1871–90),26
Periodicals: 5(1962),9

SEDALIA

Sedalia Public Library
311 W Third St, 65301
Tel: 816-826-1314

1. Winter: M-Th, 9-9; F, 9-6; Sa, 9-5; summer: M, 9-8; T-F, 9-6; Sa, 9-4
2. N/AN
3. English, 200
4. N/AN
5. 500: newspapers
6. Sedalia, Pettis County, MO
7. Tel: yes, NC; letter: yes, $1 minimum
8. No
9. No
10. No
11. No
12. No
13. None
14. Yes
15. No
Books & Sets: 3(3 v. 1981),10, 13,14
Periodicals: 4(1963–85)

SHELBINA

Shelbina Carnegie Public Library, 102 N Center St, 63468
Tel: 314-588-4472

1. M-Sa, 1-5
2. Gladys G. Powers
3. English, 40
4. 50
5. None
6. Shelby and neighboring counties
7. Tel: no; letter: yes, NC
8. No
9. No
10. No
11. No
12. No

13. Index to all marked graves in Shelby County, MO
14. Yes
15. N/AN
Books & Sets: 2

SPRINGFIELD

Ozarks Genealogical Society Library, PO Box 3494, 65808
Tel: N/AN

1. M-Th, 8:30am-9pm; F,Sa, 8:30-6
2. Fannie Frank, Librarian
3. English, 2,500. Major holdings housed at Springfield-Greene County Library, Springfield
4. 5
5. 365
6. Southwestern MO; states contributing migrations to MO: AL, AR, GA, IL, IN, KY, MD, MO, MS, NY, NC, OH, PA, SC, TN, VA; New England, the South
7. Tel: no; letter: yes
8. All volunteers
9. No
10. No
11. No
12. Yes, for members
13. N/AN
14. No
15. No
Books & Sets: 5,7
Periodicals: 4(1948–),5(1979–82), 7,8(1959–),9(1976,1978–81)

Springfield-Greene County Library, Shepherd Room
Main Library, 397 E Central, MPO Box 797, 65801
Tel: 417-869-4621

1. M-Th, 8:30am-9pm; F, 8:30-6; Sa, 8:30-5
2. Michael Glenn
3. English, 7,000
4. 5
5. 2,100, primarily newspapers, census records
6. Southwestern MO, MO state, Ozarks

7. Tel & letter: yes, $2 plus charge for copies
8. No
9. No
10. No
11. No
12. No
13. Newspaper index (card file); William K. Hall, "Index to Items of Genealogical Interest, 1865–1908, 1943–53"
14. Yes
15. OCLC: MOS

STANBERRY

Gentry County Library
64489
Tel: 816-783-2335

1. M-F, 8-5; Sa, 8-4
2. A. Whittington
3. English, all
4. 20
5. 60
6. Gentry County, other counties in MO
7. Tel: yes, NC; letter: yes, NC except for copies
8. N/AN
9. No
10. No
11. No
12. Yes
13. N/AN
14. No
15. No
Books & Sets: 2,26

TROY

Powell Memorial Library
951 W College, 63377
Tel: 314-528-7853

1. M-Th, 8-7; F, 8-3:30; Sa, 1-5
2. Marcella Pollman
3. English, 260
4. 246 items
5. 53
6. Lincoln County, MO; VA, NC

7. Tel & letter: no
8. No
9. No
10. No
11. No
12. No
13. N/AN
14. Yes
15. No
Books & Sets: 7(v.1)

UNION

Scenic Regional Library
11 S Washington, 63084
Tel: 314-583-3224

1. M-F, 8-6; Sa, 9-3
2. Carolyn Scheer
3. English, 300
4. None
5. 300
6. Franklin, Gasconade,
Warren Counties in MO
7. Tel: yes, NC; letter: yes, NC
except for copies and postage
8. No
9. No
10. No
11. No
12. No
13. *Books on Genealogy and
Local History from Scenic
Regional Library*, $1
14. No
15. No

UNIVERSITY CITY

**St. Louis Genealogical Society
Library, University City Public
Library**, 6701 Delmar, 63130
Tel: 314-727-3150

1. M-F, 9-9; Sa, 9-5; Su, 2-5
2. Gail Thomas
3. English, 3,000; German,
100
4. 200
5. 300
6. MO, IL primarily; all US
7. Tel: no; letter: yes, $5/hr
8. Lorraine Cates
9. No
10. No
11. No
12. *Booklist, St. Louis Genealogical Society*
13. N/AV
14. Yes
15. No
Books & Sets: 1–4
Periodicals: 4,8(broken set),
9(1982–)

WARRENSBURG

**West Central Missouri Genea-
logical Society and Library,
Trails Regional Library**
125 N Holden, 64093
Tel: 816-747-7912

1. Sa, 1-4
2. Nadine Adams, Librarian
(PO Box 435, Warrensburg,
64093)
3. English, 1,150
4. Included in 1,150 books
5. None. Refer to those in
Trails Regional Library
6. MO counties: Bates, Cass,
St. Clair, Henry, Johnson, Lafayette, Benton, Jackson, Pettis,
Saline; MO state; some US

7. Tel: no; letter: yes, charge
for time, copies, and postage
8. No
9. No
10. Yes, to members only; none
by mail
11. No
12. No
13. Card catalog
14. No
15. No
Books & Sets: 2,7(v.1),8,26(5
or 6 v.)
Periodicals: 4,8(broken set),9

WASHINGTON

Washington Public Library
415 Jefferson St, 63090
Tel: 314-239-7779

1. M-W, 8-8; Th,F, 8-6;
Sa, 9-1
2. N/AN
3. English, 40+
4. 10+
5. N/AN
6. Washington, Franklin
County, MO
7. Tel & letter: no
8. No
9. No
10. Yes, 2-week loan
11. No
12. No
13. N/AN
14. No
15. N/AN

MONTANA

BUTTE

Butte-Silver Bow Public Library
106 W Broadway, 59701
Tel: 406-723-8262, ext 377

1. T, 12-9; W, 9-9; Th-Sa, 9-6
2. M. Andersen
3. English, 100
4. None; all MSS stored at Archives
5. 650
6. Southwestern MT, MT state; limited coverage of adjacent areas in WY, ID, the Dakotas
7. Tel & letter: yes, NC usually. Refer detailed queries to private researchers
8. John Hughes
9. No
10. No
11. Yes, Butte newspapers, 3 reels for 10-day loan
12. No
13. Mary Murphy, *Butte, Montana, A Select Bibliography* (ca 1979). On-line access available through Western Library Network
14. Yes
15. No
Books & Sets: 2,3,5,10,13,26
Periodicals: 4

GREAT FALLS

Great Falls Genealogy Society Library, 1400 First Ave North, Room 30, 59401
Tel: Library has no phone

1. T-F, 10-4; Sa, 1-4
2. Blanche R. Rutz, Librarian
3. English, 2,500; German, 6; French, 5; Swedish, 4
4. N/AN
5. 250
6. US, Canada and other countries
7. Tel: N/AP; letter: $5 donation/surname requested
8. No
9. No
10. Yes, to members only, for 2-week loan
11. No
12. No
13. Shelf list; card index by author, title, subject
14. No
15. N/AN
Books & Sets: 3,8,15,26
Periodicals: 1,4,8,9

HELENA

Lewis and Clark Public Library, Lewis and Clark Genealogical Society
120 S Last Chance Gulch, 59601
Tel: 406-442-2380

1. Society: M,Th, 1-3, 7-9; Sa, 10-12
2. Ellie Arguimbau, Genealogy Librarian
3. English, approx 200; German, 2
4. 20
5. None. Have 92-fiche set of LDS Family Registry Index
6. All areas of US; Europe
7. Tel & letter: yes, NC
8. Ellie Arguimbau
9. No
10. No
11. No
12. No
13. N/AN
14. Yes
15. No
Periodicals: 4(1952–)

Montana Historical Society
225 N Roberts St, 59620
Tel: 406-444-2681

1. M-F, 8-5; Sa, 9-4:30; summer: M-F, 8-5
2. Robert M. Clark, Head Librarian; Dave Walker, Reference
3. English, 4,000–10,000
4. G: 1,000 linear ft; LH: much more
5. 13,000, principally state newspapers
6. Predominantly MT; also, 2,500 vols of non-MT genealogical reference for 13 original states and Northeast, with some 400 family histories
7. Tel & letter: yes, NC for brief queries, otherwise refer to contract researcher
8. No
9. No, except for copies
10. Yes, duplicates only
11. Yes, 5 reels maximum for 2-week loan, renewable, with $2 fee. Do not loan census film
12. Newspaper list (paper), $10; map collection (microfiche), $3
13. Index to newspaper obituaries; surname indexes covering biographies, 1864–1957, appearing in subscription histories of state
14. Yes
15. OCLC: MTL, newspapers only
Books & Sets: 2(v.1–128),3(3 v., 1981,1982 suppl),6,26
Periodicals: 3(v.3–36),4(v.6–13), 9(v.77–105)

MILES CITY

Miles City Public Library
1 S Tenth St, 59301
Tel: 406-232-1496

1. M, 10-8; T,Th, 12-8:30; W, 12-5; F, 10-5; Sa, 11-5
2. Linda L. Hieb, Reference/Research Librarian
3. English, 1,900
4. None
5. 158 (newspapers only)
6. MT, some WY
7. Tel & letter: yes, $3–$5/hr plus copies
8. Delores Drennen
9. No
10. Yes, duplicates only
11. Yes, per ALA request form
12. No
13. None
14. Yes
15. No

MISSOULA

Missoula Public Library
301 E Main, 59802
Tel: 406-721-2665

1. Summer: M, 10-6; T-Th, 10-9; F, 10-6; winter: T-Th, 10-9; F,Sa, 10-6
2. Vaun Stevens
3. English, 3,000
4. 12
5. None
6. Western MT primarily; MT state, WY, ID, WA, OR
7. Tel & letter: yes, NC except for copies
8. No
9. No
10. No
11. No
12. *The Montana Historical and Genealogical Data Index*, $7
13. *Missoulian* newspaper index, 1973–
14. No
15. N/AN
Books & Sets: 2(v.27,45–54), 3(3 v., 1981),10
Periodicals: 4(1974–75,1977–),8,9

RONAN

Ronan City Library
203 Main St SW, 59864
Tel: 406-676-3682

1. M,W-F, 2-5; Th,Sa 10-1, 2-5
2. None
3. English, LH, 10
4. LH: 2
5. None
6. Ronan area, MT state
7. Tel: yes, NC; letter: no
8. No
9. Yes, $2/year for adults
10. Yes, 2-week loan
11. N/AP
12. No
13. N/AN
14. No
15. No

NEBRASKA

CRETE

Crete Public Library
305 E 13th, PO Box 156, 68333
Tel: 402-826-3809

1. M,W,F,Sa, 10-5:30; T,Th, 10-7:30; Su (Sept-May), 2-5
2. Margaret Harding
3. English, 500; Czech, several
4. Vertical file materials
5. Newspapers, 1871–1970
6. Saline County, other NE counties, NE state
7. Tel: no, prefer written request; letter: yes, NC (10 pages copied at no cost)
8. No
9. No
10. Yes, through ILL
11. Yes, through ILL
12. No
13. N/AN
14. No
15. No
Periodicals: 4(1976–)

EXETER

Nebraska State Genealogical Library, Route 2, Box 28, 68351
Tel: 402-266-8881

1. (Library, dependent on donations, is housed in a private home until permanent site is found)
2. Rose Marie Hulse
3. English, 5; German, 4; Czech, 8; Turkish, 4; Swedish, 1; Polish, 1; Danish, 1; Dutch, 1
4. 1,000
5. 2
6. NE, family histories; most of US; several foreign countries
7. Tel: no; letter: yes, $5/hr
8. No

9. Yes, postage for book shipping
10. Yes, books are sent through mail to members of Nebraska State Genealogical Society
11. No
12. *Nebraska State Genealogical Society Library Collection*, $3.86
13. N/AN
14. No
15. N/AN
Periodicals: 4

LINCOLN

American Historical Society of Germans from Russia
631 D St, 68502
Tel: 402-474-3363

1. M-F, 8:30-4; Sa, 9-3
2. JoAnn Kuhr, Genealogy Researcher; Mary Rabenberg, Librarian
3. English, 1,218; German, 840; Spanish, Portuguese, Russian, 42
4. No estimate
5. 40 titles
6. Areas in Soviet Union where Germans lived and are living; areas of German immigration from Russia to North and South America, West Germany
7. Tel & letter: yes, NC for brief queries, otherwise $7.50/hr. Genealogical queries answered only for members
8. JoAnn Kuhr
9. No
10. Yes, through ILL
11. Yes, through ILL
12. *Guide* (1981), out of date
13. New acquisitions annotated in quarterly *Journal*
14. No

15. OCLC: yes
Periodicals: 4(1978–83, incomplete)

Nebraska Library Commission
1420 P St, 68508
Tel: 402-471-2045

1. M-F, 8-5
2. N/AN
3. English, 100; German, 1
4. None
5. None
6. NE, general immigration
7. Tel: N/AN; letter: yes, NC
8. No
9. No
10. Yes, 3 weeks outside of Lincoln
11. N/AP
12. On OCLC
13. In-state Union Catalog
14. No
15. OCLC: NBL
Books & Sets: 1,3,6,10–14,26

Nebraska State Historical Society, 1500 R St, 68501
Tel: 402-471-4751

1. M-F, 10-5; Sa, 8-5
2. Sherrill F. Daniels, Director of Reference Services
3. English, 20,000
4. N/AV
5. N/AV
6. NE, Midwest; largest genealogical collection in NE, which includes good source material for entire US
7. Tel: yes, NC for brief questions; letter: yes, $5 minimum
8. Experienced staff members
9. No
10. No, will copy pages for fee
11. No
12. No

13. Reference leaflets available on request

14. Yes

15. OCLC: NHT (small portion)
Books & Sets: 2,3(3v., 1982–85 suppls),4,5(v.1–6),6,7,9,10,11(no suppl),12–14,17(on microfilm), 18,22,23,26
Periodicals: 1,3(scattered issues, 1939–59),4,5,6(1925–1970s),7, 8(incomplete v.3–44, complete v.45–),9

NORFOLK

Norfolk Public Library
308 Prospect Ave, 68701
Tel: 402-644-8711

1. M-F, 10-8; Sa, 10-5; Su (Sept-May), 1:30-4:30
2. N/AN
3. English, 800
4. N/AN
5. 660
6. NE; some materials, including census indexes, for many eastern, midwestern states
7. Tel: no; letter: yes, for requests with specific citations given and no searching needed, copying and postage charges only
8. No
9. No
10. No
11. No
12. No
13. N/AN
14. Yes
15. N/AN
Books & Sets: 2(incomplete),3(no suppls),10–14
Periodicals: 4

OMAHA

W. Dale Clark Library
215 S 15th St, 68102
Tel: 402-444-4840

1. Winter: M-Th, 9-8:30; F,Sa, 9-5:30; summer: M,W,Th, 9-8:30; T,F,Sa, 9-5:30
2. Thomas Heenan
3. English, 7,500
4. N/AN
5. 1,200
6. NE, states east of Missouri River
7. Tel: yes, NC for brief queries; letter: yes, NC for brief queries except for copies
8. No
9. No
10. No
11. No, except local newspapers
12. "Genealogy Services," free
13. N/AN
14. Yes. Refer to local Genealogy Society
15. OCLC: NBO

CARSON CITY

Nevada State Library and Archives, Capitol Complex, 401 N Carson St, 89710
Tel: 702-885-5160

1. M-F, 8-5
2. N/AP
3. English, no estimate. Comprehensive collection of state documents
4. None
5. Microfilm of all NV newspapers
6. Primarily NV
7. Tel & letter: yes, NC for brief queries except for copies
8. No
9. No

10. Yes, duplicates only, through ILL
11. Yes, through ILL, with in-house use only at borrowing library; do not loan census film
12. No
13. Bibliography of representative titles
14. Yes
15. No
Books & Sets: 3(3 v., 1981),6, 10–14

LAS VEGAS

Nevada State Museum and Historical Society, 700 Twin Lakes Dr, State Mail Complex, 89158
Tel: 702-385-0115

1. M-F, 8:30-4:30
2. David Millman
3. English, 500
4. 20
5. 200 old newspapers
6. Southern NV
7. Tel & letter: yes, NC
8. No
9. No; copying charges only
10. No
11. No
12. No
13. Index to following newspapers: *Las Vegas Review-Journal, Las Vegas Age, Pioche Weekly Record*
14. No
15. No

NEW
HAMPSHIRE

BARRINGTON

Barrington Public Library
Community Bldg, Star Route
(Province Lane), 03825
Tel: 603-664-9715

1. M,W, 10-4:30, 7-9; T,Th,
F, 10-4:30; Su, 2-4:30
2. Barrington Historical
Society
3. English, 20
4. None
5. None
6. Strafford County, NH
7. Tel: no; letter, yes, NC
8. No
9. No
10. No
11. No
12. No
13. N/AN
14. No
15. No

CONCORD

**New Hampshire Historical
Society**, 30 Park St, 03301
Tel: 603-225-3381

1. M,T,Th,F, 9-4:30; W, 9-8
2. William Copeley, Associate
Librarian
3. English, 15,000
4. None
5. 100
6. NH, New England, NY
7. Tel: yes, NC; letter: yes,
NC, except $3 minimum copy fee
8. William Copeley
9. Yes, $2/day for non-
members
10. No

11. Yes, through ILL, 4-week
loan
12. *New Hampshire Historical
Society Guide to the Library*, free
brochure
13. Card catalog; biographical
index for NH notables (30,000
cards); 3-v. inventory of NH newspapers; card index of surnames in
Bible records; card index of NH
surnames currently being
researched
14. Yes
15. No
Books & Sets: 2,3(no suppls),6,
9–14,24–26
Periodicals: 1,8,9

New Hampshire State Library
20 Park St, 03301
Tel: 603-271-2144

1. M-F, 8:30-4:30; T (Sept-
May) until 8
2. Stella J. Scheckter, General
Reference Section
3. English, 7,900
4. 15
5. 675
6. New England; other northeastern states
7. Tel: no; letter: yes, NC
8. Yes, volunteer
9. No
10. No
11. No
12. J. W. Dunn, *Genealogical
Sources in New Hampshire* (1987)
13. Card catalog
14. Yes
15. OCLC: NHS (partial)
Books & Sets: 1–3,5–7,9–14,
18,19(no suppls),24,26

Periodicals: 9

**State of New Hampshire,
Division of Records Management and Archives**
71 S Fruit St, 03301
Tel: 603-271-2236

1. M-F, 8-4:30
2. Frank C. Mevers, Director
and State Archivist
3. N/AN
4. 500,000
5. 100
6. NH state
7. Tel: no; letter: yes, NC
except for copies
8. No
9. No
10. N/AN
11. Yes, through ILL
12. *Guide to Early Archives,
c. 1650–c. 1900, at the New Hampshire State Archives* (out of print)
13. Guides and indexes to
various parts of the collection
14. Yes
15. No

DOVER

Dover Public Library
73 Locust St, 03820
Tel: 603-742-3513

1. Winter: M-Th, 9-8:30;
F, 9-5:30; Sa, 9-5; summer: M-W,
9-8:30; Th,F, 9-5:30; Sa, 9-1
2. Anne Crist
3. English, 4,000
4. None
5. 400 reels: old newspapers;
12 reels: census records, Strafford
County, NH, 1810–1910; 9 reels:

Quaker records, Dover, NH, Rev. Enoch Place journals, First Parish Church records

   6. NH, ME, northeast MA

   7. Tel: yes, NC for brief query; letter: yes, NC

   8. No, but several qualified librarians

   9. No

  10. No

  11. No

  12. No

  13. Card catalog in Historical Room

  14. Yes

  15. OCLC: in progress

Books & Sets: 2,3,5,26

Periodicals: 9

EAST SWANZEY

Mt. Caesar Union Library
PO Box 8, 03446
Tel: 603-357-0456

   1. M,W,1-5, 6:30-9; T,Th, 9:30-11:30, 1-5, 6:30-9

   2. Ruth Palm, Director

   3. English, 24

   4. None

   5. None

   6. Cheshire County; Rockingham County

   7. Tel: no; letter: yes, NC except for copies

   8. No

   9. No

  10. No

  11. No

  12. No

  13. None

  14. No

  15. No

HANOVER

Dartmouth College, Dartmouth College Library, 03755
Tel: Reference: 603-646-2560; Special Collections: 603-646-2037

   1. Reference: M-F, 8am-10pm; Sa, 9-6; Su, 1-10 (hours change); Special Collections: M-F, 8-4:30

   2. Robert D. Jaccaud, Genealogy Bibliographer; Kenneth Cramer, Archivist

   3. English, no estimate

   4. No estimate

   5. No estimate

   6. Hanover, Lyme, NH; Norwich, VT; NH, VT states

   7. Tel: yes, NC for brief queries; letter: yes, NC

   8. Robert D. Jaccaud

   9. No

  10. Yes, 4-week loan

  11. Yes, 4-week loan, 6 reels

  12. No

  13. *Passages to Family History: A Guide to Genealogical Research in the Dartmouth College Library*, free

  14. No

  15. OCLC: DRB
     RLIN: NHDG

Books & Sets: 1,3,4,6,7,10–14, 18,19,22–24,26

Periodicals: 7,9

KEENE

Historical Society of Cheshire County Archive Center
246 Main St, PO Box 803, 03431
Tel: 603-352-1895

   1. M-F, 9-4

   2. Alan F. Rumrill

   3. English, 3,000

   4. 100

   5. 40

   6. Cheshire County, southwestern NH

   7. Tel & letter: yes, NC

   8. Alan F. Rumrill

   9. No

  10. No

  11. No

  12. No

  13. *Guide to the Archive Center Collection*

  14. No

  15. No

Periodicals: 4(v.30–)

Keene State College, Mason Library, Preston Collection, 03431
Tel: 603-352-1909, ext 248

   1. Call for information

   2. Robert J. Madden

   3. English, 3,500

   4. None

   5. 60 (census, Sanborn fire insurance maps, Bartlett and Plumer papers), plus local newspapers

   6. NH, especially southwestern area; town histories from nearby VT, MA

   7. Tel: no; letter: yes, NC

   8. No

   9. No

  10. No, but UMI dissertations loaned through ILL for in-library use

  11. No

  12. No

  13. Card catalog

  14. No

  15. OCLC: KNM (recent acquisitions)

Books & Sets: 1,3,6,26(ME, NH,VT,MA)

MANCHESTER

American-Canadian Genealogical Society Library
52 Concord St, PO Box 668, 03105
Tel: 603-622-2883

   1. W, 1-9; F, 10-9; Sa, 9-4

   2. Mark Gauthier, President

   3. French, 3,000

   4. No estimate

   5. 100

   6. French Canada: Acadia, New England, LA

   7. Tel: no; letter: yes, $1/marriage

8. Louis Valliere
9. No
10. No
11. No
12. In progress
13. N/AN
14. No
15. No

Books & Sets: 9,24,25
Periodicals: 2,4,9

**Manchester City Library,
New Hampshire Room**
Carpenter Memorial Building,
405 Pine St, 03104-6199
Tel: 603-624-6550

1. Labor Day–mid-June:
M,T,Th, 9-9; W,F, 9-5; Sa, 9-5;
summer: M,Th, 9-9; T,W,F, 9-6
2. Cynthia N. O'Neil
3. English, 18,000; French,
35+; Greek, 1; Polish, 1
4. None
5. 127
6. NH: state and local history,
biography, genealogy, history of
Amoskeag Corp.; other New
England states; French-Canadian
sources
7. Tel & letter: yes, fee
schedule furnished upon request
8. Cynthia N. O'Neil

9. No
10. No
11. No
12. No
13. Subject clipping file,
Manchester *Union Leader;* card
index, *New Hampshire Profiles,
New Hampshire Times;* scrapbooks
of newsclippings, 1840–1942
14. No
15. OCLC: HSID

Books & Sets: 1–3,6,9,11–14,
18(v.1–13),24,25,26(NH,ME,
NY,CT,VT,RI)
Periodicals:4(v.32–,1978–),5(1962–
65, 1967–69,1974,1985),7,9

NEW JERSEY

BELVIDERE

Warren County Library
Court House Annex, 07823
Tel: 201-475-5361

1. M,F, 8:30-4:30; T-Th, 8:30-8:30; Sa, 9-12
2. N/AN
3. N/AN
4. N/AN
5. 7
6. NJ counties: Warren, Hunterdon, Sussex; Pa counties: Monroe, Northampton
7. Tel & letter: no
8. No
9. No
10. No
11. No
12. Untitled holdings list by shelf list order, $5
13. N/AN
14. No
15. No
Books & Sets: 2

BRIDGETON

Bridgeton Free Public Library
150 E Commerce St, 08302
Tel: 609-451-2620

1. M-Th, 9-9; F, 9-5; Sa, 10-4, (June-Aug), 9-1
2. N/AP
3. English, 1,350
4. Counted as books
5. 334: Bridgeton *Evening News,* 1900–
6. Cumberland County, with emphasis on Bridgeton
7. Tel: yes, NC; letter: yes, NC except for copies
8. No
9. No
10. No

11. No
12. No
13. N/AN
14. Yes
15. No
Books & Sets: 7(v.2)

BURLINGTON

Burlington County Historical Society, Delia Biddle Pugh Library, 457 High St, 08016
Tel: 609-386-4773

1. M-Th, 1-4; W, 10-12; Su, 2-4
2. Mrs. H. T. Pernichief
3. English, 1,500
4. 180
5. None
6. Burlington County and surrounding areas
7. Tel: yes, NC; letter: yes, NC except 20¢/copy
8. Mrs. H. T. Pernichief
9. No, but donation suggested
10. No
11. No
12. No
13. Card catalog
14. No
15. No
Books & Sets: 7
Periodicals: 4(scattered 1976–85)

CAPE MAY COURT HOUSE

Cape May County Historical and Genealogical Society
DN 707, Rte 9, 08210
Tel: 609-465-3535

1. M-Sa
2. Hannah K. Swain
3. N/AN
4. N/AN
5. N/AN

6. Cape May County; South Jersey
7. Tel: no; letter: yes, charge
8. Hannah K. Swain
9. Yes, to nonmembers
10. No
11. No
12. No
13. N/AN
14. Yes
15. N/AN

Cape May County Public Library, Mechanic St, 08210
Tel: 609-465-1042 (Reference)

1. Winter: M-F, 8:30am-9pm; Sa, 9-5; Su, 1-5; summer: M-Th, 8:30am-9pm; F, 8:30-4:30; Sa, 9-5; closed Su
2. Leonard Symanski
3. English, 1,500
4. None
5. 50: local newspapers, local federal census
6. Cape May County, southern NJ, NJ state
7. Tel & letter: yes, NC for limited queries
8. No
9. No
10. Yes, some materials circulate; others are restricted to in-library use
11. No
12. No
13. Jerseyana file kept in Reference Dept
14. No
15. OCLC: CMPA
Books & Sets: 1,3,7

CHATHAM

Library of the Chathams
214 Main St, 07928
Tel: 201-635-0603

1. M-Th, 9:30-9; F, 9:30-6; Sa, 9:30-5; Su, 2-5
2. None
3. English, 500
4. 50
5. 25
6. Chatham, Morris County, NJ
7. Tel: no; letter: yes, NC
8. No
9. No
10. No
11. No
12. No
13. N/AN
14. No
15. No
Periodicals: 4(1984–)

CLARK

Clark Public Library
303 Westfield Ave, 07066
Tel: 201-388-5999

1. N/AN
2. None
3. English, approx 10
4. None
5. None
6. Clark
7. Tel: yes, NC; letter: no
8. No
9. No
10. Yes, 4-week loan
11. N/AP
12. No
13. N/AN
14. No
15. No

EAST ORANGE

East Orange Public Library
21 S Arlington Ave, 07018
Tel: 201-266-5613

1. M-Th, 9-9; F, 10-6; Sa, 9-5; Su, 1-5
2. J. Robert Starkey
3. English, 600
4. None
5. None
6. East Orange

7. Tel & letter: yes, NC
8. No
9. No
10. No
11. No
12. No
13. N/AN
14. No
15. OCLC: (post-1983)
Books & Sets: 6

EDISON

Edison Public Library
340 Plainfield Ave, 08817
Tel: 201-287-2298

1. Winter: M-F, 9-9; Sa, 9-5; summer: M-W, 9-9; Th,F, 9-5
2. Barbara Espenschied, Acquisitions Librarian
3. English, 100+
4. None
5. None
6. Edison (formerly Raritan) Township; Middlesex County, NJ
7. Tel: no; letter: yes, NC
8. No
9. No
10. Yes, most books circulate for one month
11. No
12. No
13. N/AN
14. No
15. No

FLEMINGTON

Hunterdon County Historical Society, Hiram E. Deats Memorial Library
114 Main St, 08822
Tel: 201-782-1091

1. Th,Sa, 1-3; other times by appointment
2. Roxanne K. Carkhuff, Librarian
3. English, 500; German, 2
4. 50: family history papers, local history, slave manumissions (1804–30)
5. 500

6. Hunterdon County; abutting counties of Somerset, Mercer, Warren, Sussex, Morris
7. Tel: no; letter: yes, NC except for copies
8. Roxanne K. Carkhuff
9. No
10. No
11. No
12. Yes, $4
13. Index to MS collections in progress. Finding aids available for: Dr. Bowne Day Books; Case Tannery Account Books; miscellaneous genealogical file; death, marriage notices abstracted from *Hunterdon Gazette*, 1825–49; alphabetical tombstone inscription file from 50+ cemeteries; index to Bible Records collection
14. Yes
15. No

Hunterdon County Library
State Hwy 12, 08822
Tel: 201-788-1442

1. M-F, 8:30am-9pm; Sa, 9-5
2. Margot J. Siegel
3. 500
4. None
5. Hunterdon County *Democrat* (1870–); US Census, Hunterdon County
6. Jerseyana (Hunterdon County especially; NJ in general)
7. Tel & letter: yes, NC
8. No
9. No
10. Yes, duplicate copies only
11. No
12. *Jerseyana*, $1
13. N/AN
14. No
15. OCLC: HUN
Books & Sets: 1,19(2-v. set only)
Periodicals: 4 (5 years + current year)

GLASSBORO

Glassboro State College, Savita Library, Stewart Room, 08028
Tel: 609-863-6303

1. Semester hours: M,W, 8-4; Th, 8-9:30; F, 8-3
2. Clara M. Kirner
3. English, 350, including bound periodicals
4. 28 file drawers
5. None
6. NJ primarily; some Philadelphia (PA), other areas
7. Tel: no; letter: yes, time allowing, but will not do genealogical research
8. No
9. No
10. No
11. No
12. Yes, but needs updating; currently not available. No charge when available
13. Catalog to MSS not completely subject-indexed; name file, not complete
14. No
15. OCLC: yes
    RLIN: yes
Books & Sets: 5,7(v.2)
Periodicals: 1(v.1–12),5

HACKETTSTOWN

Hackettstown Free Public Library, 110 Church St, 07840
Tel: 201-852-4936

1. M-Th, 10-9; F, 10-5; Sa, 9-12
2. None
3. English, 450
4. None
5. 103
6. Northwestern NJ
7. Tel: no; letter: yes, NC
8. No
9. Yes, $30/yr per family to borrow material. LH material does not circulate
10. No
11. No
12. No
13. N/AN
14. No
15. No

HADDONFIELD

Haddonfield Public Library
Haddon Ave & Tanner St, 08033
Tel: 609-429-1304

1. M-F, 10-5, 7-9; Sa, 10-5; Su, 1-5
2. None
3. English, 1,000
4. None
5. 100 (mostly local newspapers)
6. Haddonfield and vicinity, southern NJ
7. Tel & letter: yes, NC
8. No
9. No
10. No
11. No
12. No
13. Local newspaper index, 1970–
14. No
15. No
Books & Sets: 3(3v.),7(v.2),10,11

HAMILTON

Hamilton Township Public Library, 1 Municipal Dr, 08619
Tel: 609-890-3460

1. M-Th, 9-8:30; F,Sa, 9-5
2. N/AP
3. English, LH, 30, G, 40
4. None
5. Local newspapers: *Trenton Times,* 1976–; *Trentonian,* 1978–
6. Mercer County, NJ
7. Tel: yes, NC, local patrons only; letter: no
8. No
9. No
10. No
11. No
12. No
13. N/AV
14. No
15. OCLC: HMT (partial)
Books & Sets: 1,3(no suppl)

IRVINGTON

Irvington Public Library
Civic Sq, 07111
Tel: 201-372-6400

1. M,T,Th, 9-9; W,F, 9-5:30; Sa (mid-Sept–mid-June), 9-5
2. Quentin Van Buren
3. English, 30
4. 5
5. 6: Irvington census, 1840–1900
6. Irvington/Newark, NJ state
7. Tel: yes, NC; letter: yes, $5–$20/hr plus 25¢/copy with $3 service charge
8. No
9. No
10. Yes
11. No
12. No
13. N/AN
14. No
15. No

JERSEY CITY

Jersey City Public Library, New Jersey Room
472 Jersey Ave, 07302
Tel: 201-547-4503

1. Sept-June: M-Sa, 9-5; June-Sept: M-F, 9-5
2. Joan Doherty
3. English, 2,000
4. None
5. None
6. Hudson County, NJ
7. Tel & letter: no
8. No
9. No
10. No
11. No
12. No
13. Index to local newspaper, 1910–54, 1968–; does not include obituaries
14. Yes
15. OCLC: JCPM (new acquisitions)
Books & Sets: 3,5(v.1,2),6
Periodicals: 9

LIVINGSTON

Free Public Library of Livingston, Robert H. Harp Dr, 07039
Tel: 201-992-4600

   1. M,W,Th, 10-9; T,F, 10-6; Sa, 10-5; Su, 1-5
   2. Doris Adamus, Local History
   3. English, 173 (Livingston, NJ)
   4. Videotaped, cassette-taped oral history interviews with local residents
   5. 66 reels: local newspaper, *West Essex Tribune*
   6. N/AN
   7. Tel & letter: yes, NC except 10¢/copy
   8. N/AN
   9. No
   10. No
   11. No
   12. No
   13. N/AN
   14. No
   15. N/AN
Periodicals: 4(1981–)

LONG BRANCH

Long Branch Public Library
328 Broadway, 07740
Tel: 201-222-3900

   1. M, noon-8; T,Th, 9-8; W,F,Sa, 9-5
   2. Muriel Scoles
   3. English, 400
   4. 4
   5. 200: local newspaper
   6. Monmouth and Ocean Counties
   7. Tel & letter: yes, NC
   8. No
   9. No
   10. No
   11. No
   12. No
   13. N/AN
   14. No
   15. No

MADISON

Madison Public Library
39 Keep St, 07940
Tel: 201-377-0722

   1. W,F, 9-6; M,T,Th, 9-9; Sa, 9-5; Su, 2-5
   2. Edna Ierley-Byrne
   3. English, 650; French, 1
   4. 10
   5. 73
   6. Madison, NJ
   7. Tel & letter: yes, NC
   8. No
   9. No
   10. Yes, through ILL
   11. No
   12. No
   13. None
   14. No
   15. No
Books & Sets: 19

MAPLEWOOD

Maplewood Memorial Library
51 Baker St, 07040
Tel: 201-762-1622

   1. M,W, 10-9; T,Th, 10-6; F, 10-5; Sa, 10-5 (closed Sa late June to Labor Day)
   2. N/AN
   3. LH: 4 file drawers, mostly clippings and pamphlets
   4. G: Local collection compiled by the Maplewood chapter of DAR; also, Mattingly family
   5. 4: Pierson diaries
   6. Mostly Maplewood, some NJ state
   7. Tel & letter: yes, NC
   8. No
   9. No
   10. Yes
   11. No
   12. No
   13. N/AN
   14. No
   15. N/AN
Books & Sets: 2(various v.)

MAYS LANDING

Atlantic County Library
2 S Farragut Ave, 08330
Tel: 609-625-2776, ext 24

   1. M-Th, 9-9; F,Sa, 9-5
   2. Louisa C. Mazetis
   3. English, 600
   4. 10
   5. 50
   6. Atlantic County, Burlington, Camden
   7. Tel & letter: yes, NC except for copies
   8. No
   9. No
   10. No
   11. No
   12. No
   13. Computer catalog
   14. No
   15. N/AN
Periodicals: 4(1986–)

MIDDLETOWN

Middletown Township Public Library, 55 New Monmouth Rd, 07748
Tel: 201-671-3700

   1. M-Th, 9-9; F, 9-5; Sa (closed July, Aug), 9-5
   2. Felicia Huang
   3. English, 200
   4. 5
   5. 200
   6. Middletown, Monmouth County, NJ state
   7. Tel & letter: no
   8. No
   9. No
   10. No
   11. No
   12. No
   13. N/AN
   14. Yes
   15. No
Books & Sets: 6,19

MORRISTOWN

Joint Free Public Library of Morristown and Morris Township, 1 Miller Rd, 07960
Tel: 201-538-6161

1. M-Th, 9:30-9; F, 9:30-6; Sa, 9:30-5; Su, 1-5. Call for summer hours
2. Diane M. Solomon
3. English, 22,000
4. 50–100
5. 2,000 reels of microfilm; 5,500 titles on microfiche
6. NJ, NY, PA, CT, MA, VT, NH, RI, VA, MD, OH
7. Tel & letter: yes, NC except 10¢/copy
8. No certified genealogist, but qualified librarians
9. No
10. Yes, fiche of duplicates only; otherwise photocopies
11. Yes, duplicates only; otherwise, photocopies
12. Barbara Hoskins, *The Genealogy and Local History Collections of the Joint Free Public Library of Morristown and Morris Township, New Jersey* (1978, rev 1983), no charge
13. Too numerous to list but include indexes or guides to local newspapers, MS collections, vital records, church records, special books collections, local histories
14. Yes
15. OCLC: NWM
Books & Sets: 1–5,7,10–15,17(on microfilm),18,19(no suppls),22,26
Periodicals: 1,4(1960–63,1969–78, 1981–),5,7,9

MOUNT HOLLY

Burlington County Library
Woodlane Rd, 08060
Tel: 609-267-9660

1. M-Th, 9-9; F,Sa, 9-5; Su, 1-5
2. Albert Addis
3. English, 2,000
4. 25

5. 25
6. Burlington County, southern NJ
7. Tel: no; letter: yes, NC
8. No
9. No
10. No
11. No
12. No
13. N/AN
14. Yes
15. No
Books & Sets: 1,3,4,7(v.2),10–14, 19
Periodicals: 4(1957–),8(1967–)

NEWARK

Newark Public Library, New Jersey Department
5 Washington St (mailing address: Box 630, 07101-0630)
Tel: 201-733-7776

1. M,T,Th,F, 9-5:30; W, 9-9; Sa, 9-5
2. Charles F. Cummings, Assistant Chief Librarian, New Jersey Dept
3. English, LH, 35,000. Genealogy at Library divided between general in Humanities Dept and NJ special in New Jersey Dept
4. N/AN
5. 2,500 (NJ state census, US census for NJ, newspapers, etc)
6. Newark, Essex County, NJ state
7. Tel: yes, NC, for brief queries; letter: yes, NC
8. No. Refer to New Jersey Historical Society
9. No
10. No; will make photocopies
11. Yes, duplicate newspapers on microfilm
12. N/AN
13. Approx 60 indexes, including NJ Illustration Index (50,000 entries to NJ portraits); index to *Star-Ledger*, 1970–; index to WOR-TV and WNET-TV evening news shows, 1984–; information files (biographies of inventors,

physicians, artists, et al.); Newark *Evening News* collection (800,000 photos, 2 million clippings)
14. Yes
15. OCLC: NPL
Books & Sets: 1,3,6,10–12,19,26

New Jersey Historical Society
230 Broadway, 07924
Tel: 201-483-3939, ext 41

1. T-Sa, 10-4
2. Sarah Collins, Library Director
3. English, all
4. N/AN
5. N/AN
6. NJ and surrounding areas
7. Tel: yes, NC; letter: yes, sliding scale
8. No
9. Yes, $1
10. No
11. No
12. *A Guide to Family History and Genealogical Resources*, free
13. N/AN
14. Yes
15. No
Books & Sets: 1–6,7(v.1,2,4–7), 10–14,26
Periodicals: 1,4,5,7–9

NUTLEY

Nutley Public Library
93 Booth Dr, 07110
Tel: 201-667-0405

1. N/AN
2. Eve Weinberg, Reference Librarian
3. N/AN
4. N/AN
5. Nutley *Sun*, 1915–
6. Nutley
7. Tel: yes, NC; letter: yes, NC except for copies with SASE
8. No
9. No
10. No
11. No
12. No
13. Subject headings for vertical file

14. No
15. No

PARAMUS

Paramus Public Library
E 116 Century Rd, 07652
Tel: 201-265-1800

1. M-Th, 9:30-9; F,Sa, 9:30-5;
Su, 1-5
2. Jean B. Moore
3. English, 50
4. 1
5. None
6. Bergen County, NJ state
7. Tel: no; letter: yes, NC
8. No
9. No
10. No
11. No
12. No
13. N/AN
14. No
15. No

PRINCETON

Princeton Public Library
65 Witherspoon St, 08542
Tel: 609-924-9529

1. M-Th, 9-9; F,Sa, 9-5:30
2. Eric Greenfeldt
3. English, 35; also, some
"how-to" titles
4. None
5. 15
6. Princeton, NJ
7. Tel: no; letter: yes, NC
8. No
9. No
10. Yes, circulating volumes,
2-week loan
11. No
12. No
13. N/AN
14. No
15. OCLC: PPR
Books & Sets: 10–14
Periodicals: 5

RAMSEY

Ramsey Free Public Library
30 Wyckoff Ave, 07446
Tel: 201-327-1445

1. M-Sa; closed Sa in summer
2. Leona F. Schauble
3. English, 2,150
4. 1: Ramsey Charter
5. 120
6. NJ state
7. Tel: no; letter: yes, NC
8. No
9. No
10. Yes, through ILL
11. No
12. No
13. N/AN
14. No
15. N/AN

RUTHERFORD

**Fairleigh Dickinson University,
Messler Library,** Montross Ave,
07070
Tel: 201-460-5074

1. M, 8:30am-9pm; T, 8:30am-
10pm; W,Th, 8:30-6; F, 8:30-5
2. Richard Goerner
3. English, 20,000
4. 1,200 (36 ft)
5. 381 reels; 263 microcards;
183 microfiche
6. Bergen County, NJ state
7. Tel & letter: yes, NC
8. No
9. No, except for copies
10. Yes
11. No
12. No
13. N/AN
14. No
15. OCLC: FDR
Books & Sets: 6,7,13,16

SOMERS POINT

**Atlantic County Historical
Society,** 907 Shore Rd,
PO Box 301, 08244
Tel: 609-927-5218

1. W-Sa, 10-4
2. Frederic M. Cramer
3. English, 1,160; German,
some bound 19th-century newspapers
4. 63
5. 31
6. Atlantic County, adjacent
counties of South Jersey
7. Tel & letter: yes, NC
8. Frederic M. Cramer
9. Yes, $1 for nonmembers
10. No
11. No
12. *Guide to the Library*, $3
plus $1 postage
13. N/AN
14. Yes
15. No
Books & Sets: 2,3,5
Periodicals: 9

SOUTH ORANGE

**Seton Hall University, University
Archives, McLaughlin Library**
Duffy Hall, South Orange Ave,
07079
Tel: 201-761-9476

1. M-F, 9:15-4:30, by appointment only
2. Barbara Geller, University
Archivist
3. English, none
4. 5
5. 275
6. Bergen, Essex, Hudson,
Union Counties; NJ state
7. Tel & letter: yes, NC
8. Barbara Geller
9. No
10. N/AN
11. No
12. No
13. N/AN
14. No
15. N/AN

SPARTA

Sparta Public Library
22 Woodport Rd, 07871
Tel: 201-729-3101

1. M,W,Th, 9-9; T, 9-6; F, 9-5; Sa, 9-2
2. None
3. LH: small collection, mostly newspaper clippings
4. None
5. None
6. Sparta, Sussex County
7. Tel & letter: yes, NC
8. No
9. No
10. No
11. No
12. No
13. None
14. No
15. No

SUCCASUNNA

Roxbury Public Library
Main St, 07876
Tel: 201-584-4222

1. M-F, 9:30-8; Sa, 9:30-1
2. N/AN
3. N/AN
4. N/AN
5. N/AN
6. NJ, especially Succasunna, Roxbury Township, Morris County, Newark
7. N/AN
8. No
9. N/AN
10. N/AN
11. N/AN
12. N/AN
13. C. Lane, "Holdings in Local History"
14. N/AN
15. N/AN

TOMS RIVER

Ocean County Library
101 Washington St, 08753
Tel: 201-349-6200

1. M,W, 1-8; T,Th, 10-5; Sa, 1-5
2. John Franklin
3. English, 2,250

4. None
5. 600
6. Southern NJ, NJ state
7. Tel & letter: yes, NC for brief queries
8. No
9. No
10. No
11. No
12. No
13. N/AN
14. No
15. OCLC: OCJ
Books & Sets: 3,5

TRENTON

Free Public Library of Trenton
120 Academy St, 08608
Tel: 609-392-7188

1. M,W,Th, 9-9; T,F,S, 9-5
2. Richard W. Reeves
3. English, 58
4. N/AN
5. N/AN
6. US
7. Tel: no; letter: yes, NC except 10¢/copy
8. No
9. No
10. No
11. No
12. No
13. N/AN
14. Yes
15. OCLC: TFP
Books & Sets: 3,7(v.2),12, 26(v.6,8)
Periodicals: 5,7

New Jersey State Library, Department of Education
Reference Services, 185 W State St, CN 520, 08625
Tel: 609-292-6274

1. M-Th, 8:30-8:30; F, 8:30-5; Sa, 9-5; Aug: M-F, 8:30-5, closed Sa
2. Robert Lupp, Supervising Librarian
3. English, more than 500 full

shelves; German, 1; French, 15
4. None
5. 1,020+
6. NJ state; Middle Atlantic, New England states
7. Tel & letter: yes, NC except for copies
8. No
9. No
10. Yes, duplicates only, after 1900
11. Yes, duplicates only
12. No
13. "Family name index" to genealogies in books and periodicals
14. Yes
15. OCLC: 848785445
Books & Sets: 1–7,10–14,17–19, 23,25,26
Periodicals: 1,3–5,7–9

VINELAND

Vineland Historical and Antiquarian Society
PO Box 35, 108 S Seventh St, 08360
Tel: 609-691-1111

1. T-Sa, 1-4; closed July
2. Joseph Sherry
   Rachel Lampe, Assistant
3. English, nearly all
4. Over 30
5. 18: Sheppard genealogy; 70: census records
6. Vineland, Cumberland County; Salem, Gloucester, Atlantic, Cape May Counties, NJ; PA, New England, other US
7. Tel: yes, NC for brief queries; letter: yes, small charge for research, copies, postage, and handling
8. No
9. Yes, $1 donation
10. No
11. No
12. Not complete
13. N/AN
14. No
15. N/AN

Books & Sets: 7
Periodicals: 4(incomplete),
7(missing v.1),9

VOORHEES

Camden County Library
Echelon Urban Center, Laurel Rd,
08043
Tel: 609-772-1636

1. M-F, 10-9; Sa, 10-6; Su,
1-5 (closed Su July, Aug)
2. N/AN
3. English, 200
4. N/AN
5. N/AN
6. Camden County, NJ;
southern NJ
7. Tel & letter: yes, NC
8. No
9. No
10. Yes, circulating books only
11. No
12. No
13. N/AN
14. No
15. OCLC: NCL
Books & Sets: 1,3,4,13,14
Periodicals: 4(v.31–34, 1977–80)

WESTFIELD

Westfield Memorial Library
425 E Broad St, 07090
Tel: 201-789-4090

1. M-F, 10-9; Sa (except July,
Aug), 10-5
2. Marlyn Harrison, Reference
Librarian
3. English, 1,365+
4. 12, plus 200 vertical file
folders of local family names
5. 100: local newspapers; 52:
census. Also, *Mayflower* Descendants, Pilgrim Notes and Queries
on microfiche
6. NJ, PA, VA, NY, New
England
7. Tel: no; letter: yes, NC but
$5 minimum donation suggested to
Genealogical Society of the West
Fields
8. No

9. No
10. No
11. No
12. No
13. "Checklist of Genealogical
Resources"
14. No
15. No
Books & Sets: 2(missing v. 2–5
and v. 1 index),3,5,7(v.2),26
Periodicals: 1(1966–),4(1965–),
5(1962–65,1968,1969,1974–85),
7,8(v.54–70,1966–82),9(1945–)

WHIPPANY

**The New Jersey Collection,
Morris County Free Library**
30 E Hanover Ave, 07981
Tel: 201-829-0360 or 201-829-
0505, ext 41

1. M-Th, 9-9; F,Sa, 9-5
2. Evelyn L. Klingler
3. English, 500
4. 300
5. 750
6. NJ state
7. Tel & letter: yes, NC
8. Evelyn L. Klingler
9. No
10. Yes, through ILL
11. No
12. No
13. Two in-house pamphlets:
*The New Jersey Collection, The
Morris County Free Library*
(contains titles and call numbers);
and *The New Jersey Collection,
Morris County Free Library* (describes the collection as a whole)
14. Yes
15. OCLC: NWM
Books & Sets: 1,3–6,7(v.2&3),
10–12,17,19(1950,1972 only),
22,23
Periodicals: 1(1981–),4(1976–),5,
7,8(1985–),9(1982–)

WILLINGBORO

Willingboro Public Library
Salem Rd, 08046
Tel: 609-877-6668

1. M-Th, 9-9; F,Sa, 9-5; Su
(closed in summer), 1-5
2. Florence M. Brems, Reference Librarian
3. English, 150 (includes
Willingboro and NJ census data).
Predominantly LH
4. 6: vertical file; Willingboro
Township minutes, etc., 1964–
5. 320: Burlington County
Times, 1954–; Mount Holly
Herald, 1954–58; Willingboro
newspapers, 1960–68; Willingboro
Township minutes, 1809–1973
6. Willingboro, Burlington
County, NJ
7. Tel & letter: yes, NC
8. No
9. No
10. Yes, NC to residents, annual
fee to nonresidents
11. No
12. No
13. Vertical file catalog
14. No
15. No
Books & Sets: 1

WOODBRIDGE

Woodbridge Public Library
George Frederick Plaza, 07095
Tel: 201-634-4450

1. Winter: M-Th, 9am-
9:30pm; F, 9-9; Sa, 9-5; Su, 1-5;
summer: M-Th, 9-9; F, 9-5; Sa, 9-5
2. N/AN
3. English, 200
4. None
5. None
6. Woodbridge area
7. Tel & letter: yes, NC
8. No
9. No
10. No
11. N/AP
12. No
13. None
14. No
15. OCLC: WRR
Books & Sets: 1,3(no suppl),19,26
Periodicals: 4(1973–84)

WOODBURY

Gloucester County Historical Society Library, 17 Hunter St, PO Box 409, 08096
Tel: 609-845-4771

1. M,Th, 1-4; F, 1-4, 7-9:30; last Su of month, 2-5
2. Edith Hoelle
3. English, 3,500
4. 80,000
5. 1,085, plus 1,275 microfiche
6. NJ, PA, NY, DE; some New England, MD, VA, NC
7. Tel: yes, NC; letter: yes, NC for brief queries
8. Suzanne Cain
9. No
10. No
11. No
12. No
13. "Guide to County Document Collection, 1686–1900"
14. Yes
15. No
Books & Sets: 3–5,7,10–12,26
Periodicals: 1(v.1–8,35–),4(v.35–), 7,8(v.21–)

NEW MEXICO

ALAMOGORDO

Alamogordo Public Library
920 Oregon Ave, 88310
Tel: 505-437-9058

1. M,T,Th, 9-8; W,F,Sa, 9-6
2. Josephine Anderson, Genealogy; June Harwell, Local History
3. English, G, 900, LH, 1,200
4. 12
5. 100: early Otero County newspapers
6. G: general; LH: Otero County and southwest NM
7. Tel: no; letter: yes, NC except 10¢/copy
8. Josephine Anderson
9. No
10. Yes, 2-week loan, through ILL
11. No
12. No
13. N/AN
14. No
15. OCLC: AMO
Books & Sets: 2,3,5,6,10–12,26
Periodicals: 4(last 5 years),5

ALBUQUERQUE

Albuquerque Public Library, Special Collections Branch
423 Central NE, 87102
Tel: 505-848-1376

1. T,Th, 12:30-8; W,F,Sa, 9-5:30
2. Laurel E. Drew
3. English, 22,000+; German, 3; Spanish, 12; French, 4; Portuguese, 1
4. 5–10 (not generally collected; nonbook items of small size are generally placed in vertical file)

5. Microfilm, 2,500+ reels; microfiche, 80+ titles
6. LH: NM state; G: US, with emphasis on NM, plus eastern (east of Mississippi) states
7. Tel & letter: yes, NC for brief queries except 10¢/copy
8. Laurel E. Drew
9. No
10. Yes, duplicate copies through ILL
11. No
12. No
13. General guide to collection available to visitors
14. Yes
15. OCLC: ABQ (partial)
Books & Sets: 2–5,7(partial), 10–12,18,19,22–26
Periodicals: 1,3–5,6(partial),7–9

DEMING

Deming Public Library
301 S Tin Ave, 88030
Tel: 505-546-9202

1. M,W,F, 9-6; T,Th, 9-9; Sa, 1-5
2. Vona Van Cleef, Reference Librarian
3. English, approx 325
4. 7
5. None
6. Deming, Luna County, NM state; other US, with most on original 13 states
7. Tel: no; letter: yes, NC
8. No
9. No
10. No, but will copy at 10¢/page
11. No
12. No
13. Card catalog
14. No
15. No

Books & Sets: 2(incomplete),7,26
Periodicals: 4,8

LAS CRUCES

Thomas Branigan Memorial Library, 200 East Picacho Ave, 88005
Tel: 505-526-1045

1. M-Th, 10-9; F,Sa, 10-6; Su (Sept.-May), 1-5
2. Marjorie F. Day, Genealogy; Miriam Levine, Reference
3. English, G, 600, LH, 3,000
4. G: 50; LH: 40
5. G: 42; LH: 183
6. Southwestern US
7. Tel & letter: yes, NC except for copies and postage
8. Marjorie F. Day
9. No
10. Yes, LH only, 2-week loan
11. No
12. No
13. List of genealogical holdings
14. Yes
15. OCLC: TBL
Books & Sets: 2(partial),5,26
Periodicals: 3(1959–60),4(1947–), 8(1977–84),9(1961–80,1985)

LOS ALAMOS

Mesa Public Library, Los Alamos County Library System
1742 Central Ave, 87544
Tel: 505-662-8253

1. M-Th, 10-9; F, 10-6; Sa, 9-5; Su, 11-5
2. N/AP
3. English, 85
4. None
5. Sutro Library card catalog on microfiche

6. NM (a few), US (general), British Isles (very few)

7. Tel & letter: no. General reference questions only

8. No

9. No

10. Yes, circulating titles only

11. No

12. No

13. Card catalog

14. No

15. OCLC: LAN

Books & Sets: 10,11(1972–76), 12–14

Periodicals: 4(1986–),8(1987–), 9(1987–)

PORTALES

Portales Public Library
218 S Ave B, 88130
Tel: 505-356-3940

1. M-W,F, 9-5:30; Th, 9-8; Sa, 10-2

2. Sandy White

3. English, all

4. N/AN

5. 30

6. NM; southern states, PA, NY

7. Tel & letter: yes, NC

8. No

9. No

10. No

11. No

12. No

13. N/AN

14. No

15. N/AN

Books & Sets: 2,7,26

Periodicals: 4(1977–)

SILVER CITY

Silver City Public Library
515 W College Ave, 88061
Tel: 505-538-3672

1. M,Th, 9-8; T,W, 9-6; F, 9-5; Sa, 9-1

2. N/AN

3. English, G, 143, LH, 337; German, 1

4. 4

5. 176

6. LH: southwestern NM including Grant, Catron, Hidalgo, and Luna Counties

7. Tel & letter: yes, NC for brief queries, $10/hr for research

8. No

9. No

10. No

11. No, but will make copies

12. No

13. N/AN

14. No

15. No

Books & Sets: 2,3

Periodicals: 4(v.19–39, 1965–85)

ALBANY

**Albany Public Library,
Pruyn Library**
161 Washington Ave, 12210
Tel: 518-449-3380

1. M-F, 9-9; Sa, 9-5; Su
(except summer), 1-5
2. James R. Hobin
3. English, 6,000
4. None
5. 25
6. Albany, NY (city and
county)
7. Tel & letter: yes, NC for
brief queries
8. No
9. No
10. No
11. No
12. No
13. None
14. Yes
15. No
Books & Sets: 3,10–12
Periodicals: 4(1985–)

**New York State Library,
Humanities/History**, 6th Floor,
Cultural Education Center, 12230
Tel: 518-474-5161

1. M-F, 9-5
2. Jean Hargrave
3. No count available
4. No count available
5. UMI Genealogy and Local
History (NY only) Collection on
microfiche; also, some genealogies, local histories on microfilm
or microfiche
6. NY state, New England
7. Tel: no; letter: Library's
information sheets are sent in
response to letters. Refer to Albany
County Records Management

Program, Albany County Clerk's
Office; send inquiries to Ms.
Barbara Ruch, Archivist, 250 S
Pearl St, Albany, NY 12202
8. No. Refer to Capital District
Genealogical Society, Empire
State Plaza Station, Box 2175,
Albany, NY, 12220
9. No
10. Yes, duplicates of local
history only
11. Yes, microfilms from
collection of NY county and
regional histories and atlases;
copies of local histories and
genealogies on microfiche
12. No
13. *Gateway to America: Genealogical Research in the New York
State Library*, $3
14. Yes
15. N/AN
Books & Sets: 1–7,9–19,22–24,26
Periodicals: 1(v.9–, 1932–),3–5,
6(v.12, 1956),7–9

AUBURN

**Cayuga Community College,
Norman F. Bourke Memorial
Library**, Franklin St, 13021
Tel: 315-255-1743

1. M-Th, 8-9:30; F, 8-5; Sa,
closed; Su, 3-9:30
2. Douglas O. Michael
3. English, 1,500
4. 1
5. 400
6. Auburn, Cayuga County,
central NY state
7. Tel: no; letter: yes, NC
8. No
9. No
10. No
11. No
12. No

13. Several subject bibliographies
14. No
15. OCLC: ZZY
Books & Sets: 6,26

BABYLON

Babylon Public Library
24 S Carll Ave, 11702
Tel: 516-669-1624

1. M-Th, 9:30-9; F,Sa, 9:30-5;
Su, 1-5; summer: M,W, 9:30-9;
T,Th,F, 9:30-5; Sa, 9:30-1
2. Carol Simpson
3. English, 200
4. 2
5. None
6. Village of Babylon; Suffolk
County, NY
7. Tel & letter: yes, NC except
for copies
8. No
9. No
10. No
11. No
12. No
13. None
14. No
15. No

BALDWINSVILLE

Baldwinsville Public Library
43 Oswego St, 13027
Tel: 315-635-5631

1. M-Th, 10-9; F, 10-5; Sa,
10-4
2. Margaret A. Van Patten
3. English, 350
4. 350
5. 109
6. Village of Baldwinsville;
towns of Lysander and Van Buren,
NY

7. Tel & letter: yes, NC
8. No
9. No
10. No
11. No
12. No
13. N/AN
14. No
15. No

BATAVIA

Richmond Memorial Library
19 Ross St, 14020
Tel: 716-343-9550

1. M,T,Th, 9-9; W, 9-6; F,Sa,
9-5; closed Sa (July-Aug)
2. Kathleen Facer
3. English, 2,000
4. 50
5. 600
6. Mainly western NY state;
some New England, rest of NY
state
7. Tel & letter: yes, NC except
for copies
8. No
9. No
10. Yes, 4-week loan
11. No
12. No
13. N/AN
14. Yes
15. No
Books & Sets: 2,3,5,7,10–14
Periodicals: 1(v.41–55),4(v.17–,
1963–),8(v.50–67, 1962–79),
9(v.51–66, v.104–28, 1897–
1912,1950–74)

BINGHAMTON

**Broome County Historical
Society Library,** 30 Front St,
13865
Tel: 607-772-0660

1. T-F, 10-5
2. Marjory B. Hinman
3. English, 170 (includes
biographies)
4. 200
5. None
6. Broome County and vicinity

7. Tel: N/AN; letter: yes, NC
8. No
9. No
10. No
11. N/AP
12. No
13. N/AN
14. Yes
15. N/AN

Broome County Public Library
78 Exchange St, 13901
Tel: 607-723-6457

1. M-Th, 9-9; F,Sa, 9-5
2. Mary J. Brigiotta, Head,
Information Services
3. G/LH integrated with
information/reference collection
4. N/AV
5. N/AV
6. NY state
7. Tel & letter: yes, NC for
brief queries
8. No
9. No
10. No
11. No
12. No
13. Selected bibliography
14. No
15. N/AN
Books & Sets: 2,3(1986 missing),
10–12,19,26(8 v.)
Periodicals: 9

**State University of New York at
Binghamton, Glenn G. Bartle
Library,** Vestal Pkwy E, 13901
Tel: 607-777-2345; 777-4844
(Special Collections)

1. M-Th, 8:30am-midnight;
F, 8:30am-9pm; Sa, 10-9; Su,
10am-midnight; Special Collections: M-F, 1-4:30; summer hours
vary
2. Marion Hanscom, Head,
Special Collections; Ed Shephard,
History/Genealogy Reference
3. N/AV
4. N/AV
5. N/AV
6. Broome County, NY, and
surrounding area

7. Tel & letter: yes, NC for
brief queries
8. No
9. No
10. Yes, by purchase of
courtesy card. Special Collections
materials do not circulate
11. Yes, on restricted basis
12. No
13. "History Resources in
Microform"
14. No
15. RLIN: NYBG
Books & Sets: 1(8 v., 1981–85
suppl),3(1984 suppl),6,10,13,14,
17,19,21,23,24,26
Periodicals: 5,7,9(v.1–19,21,
23–49,91–119,123–)

BRENTWOOD

Brentwood Public Library
Second Ave & Fourth St, 11717
Tel: 516-273-7883

1. M,T,Th,F, 9-9; W,Sa, 9-5;
Su (Sept-May), 12-4
2. Martha Stepsis
3. English, 30; large collection
of scrapbooks
4. N/AN
5. LH: 13
6. Brentwood; Islip Township;
Long Island
7. Tel: yes, NC for LH
inquiries only; letter: yes, NC
except for copies
8. No
9. No
10. Yes
11. No
12. No
13. Card catalog
14. No
15. No
Books & Sets: 3,19
Periodicals: 4(only keep for 2
years)

BRONX

**Bronx County Historical Society,
Theodore Kazimiroff Library**
3309 Bainbridge Ave, 10467
Tel: 212-881-8900

1. M-F, 9:30-4:30
2. N/AN
3. N/AN
4. Bronx business records
5. *The Bronx Home News*, 1907–48
6. N/AN
7. N/AN
8. N/AN
9. N/AN
10. N/AN
11. N/AN
12. Laura Tosi and J. Butler, *Genealogy in the Bronx: An Annotated Guide to Sources of Information* (1983)
13. N/AN
14. N/AN
15. N/AN

City University of New York, Herbert H. Lehman College
Bedford Park Blvd W, 10468
Tel: 212-960-8603 (Director); 960-8677 (messages)

1. M-F, 9-5 (appointment recommended)
2. Janet Butler Munch, Special Collections Librarian
3. English, 500
4. 75; also, 300 oral history interviews
5. 325 film and fiche
6. Bronx, Westchester, northern Manhattan
7. Tel & letter: yes, NC
8. Janet Butler Munch
9. No
10. No, but will photocopy
11. Yes, through ILL
12. No
13. Bronx Institute, "Oral History Subject Guide"; Lehman College Library, "Bronx Library Resources," "Bronx History: Sources of Information"
14. No
15. OCLC: VYL
    RLIN: partially
Books & Sets: 3,5,6,26

BROOKLYN

Brooklyn Public Library, Local History Collection
Grand Army Plaza, 11238
Tel: 718-780-7794

1. M-Th, 9-8; F,Sa, 10-6; Su (except summer), 1-5; closed most holidays
2. Elizabeth L. White, Local History
3. English, several thousand
4. A few
5. Several hundred, including Brooklyn city directories, 19th- to early 20th-century Brooklyn newspapers
6. Brooklyn, Kings County
7. Tel & letter: yes, NC for limited requests, except for copies
8. No
9. No
10. No
11. No
12. No
13. N/AN
14. Yes
15. N/AN

BUFFALO

Buffalo and Erie County Historical Society Research Library
25 Nottingham Court, 14216
Tel: 716-873-9644

1. W,Th,F, 10-5; Sa, 12-5
2. Mary F. Bell, Director of Library and Archives
3. N/AP (not a separate section)
4. N/AP
5. N/AP
6. Buffalo, some Erie County
7. Tel & letter: yes, NC, but only if readily available
8. No
9. Yes, $2.50/day, or $10/yr membership. Free to Society members
10. No

11. No
12. No
13. N/AN
14. Yes
15. N/AN
Books & Sets: 2,3(no suppls)
Periodicals: 9

Buffalo and Erie County Public Library, Lafayette Square, 14203
Tel: 716-846-7103

1. M-W,F,Sa, 8:30-6; Th, 8:30am-9pm.
2. Ruth Willett, Head, History Dept
3. English, 35,000–40,000
4. N/AN
5. N/AN
6. Western NY; New England history
7. Tel: yes, NC, but no research done; letter: yes, $1 service charge to non-Erie County residents, plus copies and postage
8. No
9. No
10. No
11. No
12. *Searching Family History at the Buffalo and Erie County Public Library*, in-house use only
13. Local history file (continued by Western NY Index after 1982, on computer)
14. Yes
15. No
Books & Sets: 1–3,6,7,10–12,18, 19,24,26
Periodicals: 1,3–7,8(v.23–),9

CANANDAIGUA

Ontario County Historical Society, 55 N Main St, 14424
Tel: 716-394-4975

1. T-Sa, 10-5
2. N/AP
3. English, 500
4. 10,000 pieces
5. 50

6. Present-day Ontario County
7. Tel: no; letter: yes, NC except for copies
8. Gloria Dancause
9. No
10. No
11. No
12. No
13. N/AN
14. Yes
15. No
Periodicals: 4

CANTON

St. Lawrence County Historical Association History Center
3 E Main St, PO Box 8, 13617
Tel: 315-386-8133

1. M-Sa, 1-5
2. Jon N. Austin, County Historian
3. English, approx 1,500
4. 45 cu ft of MSS; 56 cu ft vertical files; 40 cu ft of maps, prints, oversize photos; approx 40 linear ft of scrapbooks
5. 60
6. St. Lawrence County, St. Lawrence River Valley
7. Tel: yes, NC but prefer mail or personal visit; letter: yes, NC with SASE
8. No
9. No
10. No
11. No
12. No
13. In-house biographical card file
14. Yes
15. No
Books & Sets: 3(3 v., 1981)
Periodicals: 1(v.21–57),4(1960–81),8(v.59–63),9(v.92–122, incomplete)

CENTRAL ISLIP

Central Islip Public Library
33 Hawthorne Ave, 11722
Tel: 516-234-9333

1. M-F, 10-8:30; Sa, 10-5; Su,
1-5; closed Su,F eve in summer
2. N/AN
3. English, LH, 129. Also, 23 pamphlets; old photographs of Central Islip area
4. N/AN
5. N/AN
6. Central Islip, Nassau and Suffolk Counties, Long Island
7. Tel & letter: yes, NC for brief queries
8. No
9. No
10. No
11. N/AN
12. No
13. N/AN
14. No
15. No

CORTLAND

Cortland County Historical Society, Kellogg Memorial Reading Room, 25 Homer Ave, 13045
Tel: 607-756-6071

1. T-Sa, 1-5
2. Shirley G. Heppell
3. English, 2,118; German, 1
4. 620 cu ft
5. 230
6. Cortland County, NY
7. Tel: no; letter: yes, $5/hr plus 25¢/copy
8. Anita Wright
9. Yes, $1.25/hr to non-members
10. No
11. No
12. No
13. "Checklist of Some Sources in Cortland County"
14. N/AN
15. No
Books & Sets: 2,26(NY,PA, New England)
Periodicals: 9(1929–)

DELMAR

Bethlehem Public Library
451 Delaware Ave, 12054
Tel: 518-439-9314

1. Winter: M-F, 9-9; Sa, 10-5; Su, 1-5; summer, closed Su
2. Marie S. Carlso
3. English, 500
4. 10
5. 10
6. Local area; US; Europe
7. Tel & letter: yes, NC
8. No
9. No
10. Yes, "how-to" books only
11. No
12. No
13. *A Pathfinder to the Genealogy Collection in the Media Center, Bethlehem Public Library;* card catalog
14. No. Refer to local genealogical societies
15. N/AN
Books & Sets: 2,5
Periodicals: 4(1978–),9(scattered, 1931–)

EAST HAMPTON

East Hampton Library, Long Island Collection, 159 Main St, 11937
Tel: 516-324-0222

1. M,Th, 10-3:30; T,W,F,Sa, 1-4:30 (mornings by appointment in advance)
2. Dorothy T. King
3. See below
4. Long Island Collection: books, pamphlets, maps, atlases, MSS, clippings, genealogies, periodicals, newspapers, family records, and government documents relating to history and people of Long Island. Includes Thomas Moran Biographical Arts, Seversmith, and Jeannette Edwards Rattray collections
5. N/AN
6. Long Island; some New England, NJ for early Long Island connections
7. Tel: no; letter: yes, NC except for copies
8. N/AN
9. No

10. No
11. No
12. No
13. Typed sheet describing Long Island Collection
14. No
15. N/AN
Periodicals: 1(1933–),9

ELIZABETHTOWN

Essex County Historical Society, Brewster Memorial Library
Court St, 12932
Tel: 518-873-6466

1. T,Th, 9-3
2. Pat Casselman
   Gayle Meaker
3. English, 2,500
4. 100
5. N/AN
6. Essex County, NY
7. Tel: N/AN; letter: yes, $5–$20
8. N/AN
9. No, but donations welcome
10. No
11. No
12. No
13. N/AN
14. Yes
15. N/AN

FLORAL PARK

Floral Park Public Library
Tulip Ave & Caroline Pl, 11002
Tel: 516-326-6330

1. M,T,Th, 10-9; W,F, 10-6; Sa, 9-5
2. N/AN
3. English, 3
4. N/AN
5. N/AN
6. Floral Park
7. Tel & letter: yes, NC
8. No
9. No
10. No
11. N/AN
12. No
13. N/AN
14. No

15. No

FONDA

Montgomery County Department of History and Archives
Old Courthouse, Railroad St, 12068
Tel: 518-853-3431, ext 293

1. M-F, 9-5; July-Aug: M-F, 9-4
2. Violet D. Fallone
3. English, 6,000
4. 20
5. 100
6. Hudson and Mohawk Valley areas, NY state
7. Tel & letter: yes, $10/hr for extensive search
8. Violet D. Fallone
9. No
10. No
11. No
12. *Catalog of Historical and Genealogical Material*
13. In-house indexes
14. Yes
15. N/AN
Books & Sets: 2(incomplete),3,5, 26(incomplete)
Periodicals: 8,9

FREDONIA

State University of New York, College at Fredonia, Reed Library, 14063
Tel: 716-673-3183

1. Winter: M-F, 8:30-5; summer: M-F, 8-4
2. Jack T. Ericson, Archivist/ Curator, Local History Collection
3. English, 1,300
4. 40
5. 170; also, 113 titles on microfiche
6. Chautauqua and Cattaraugus Counties, NY
7. Tel: no; letter: yes, NC
8. No
9. No
10. No, only microfiche copies
11. No, only microfiche copies

12. No
13. N/AN
14. No
15. OCLC: XFM

FULTON

Fulton Public Library
160 S First St, 13069
Tel: 315-592-5159

1. M,F, 10-5; T,W,Th, 10-5, 7-9; Sa, 9-12
2. Joyce H. Cook, Library Director
3. English, 306
4. 1: Falley Seminary (private school), incorporated 1857
5. 171
6. Fulton, Oswego County, NY state
7. Tel & letter: yes, NC
8. Joyce H. Cook
9. No
10. No
11. No
12. No
13. Indexes to Oswego County censuses
14. No
15. No
Books & Sets: 2,10–12,26(NY, MA,CT)
Periodicals: 4(1981–)

GARDEN CITY

Garden City Public Library
60 Seventh St, 11530
Tel: 516-742-8405

1. Winter: M-Th, 9:30-9; F, 9:30-5:30; Sa, 9-5; summer: M,T,Th, 9:30-9; W,F, 9:30-5:30
2. Vincent F. Seyfried, Village Historian
3. English, LH, 1,500
4. LH: 5
5. None
6. LH: Long Island, Garden City
7. Tel & letter: yes, NC
8. No
9. No
10. Yes, duplicates only

11. N/AP
12. No
13. Index to 5 file cabinets of printed material and photos
14. No
15. No
Books & Sets: 3(no suppls),10,11
Periodicals: 4,7(1963–66)

GLEN COVE

Glen Cove Public Library
Glen Cove Ave, 11542
Tel: 516-676-2130

1. M-F, 9-9; Sa, 9-5
2. N/AN
3. English, 550
4. Uncataloged
5. N/AN
6. Long Island, NY
7. Tel & letter: yes, NC
8. No
9. No
10. No, but will provide copies
11. No, but will provide copies
12. No
13. Catalog
14. No
15. No

GLENS FALLS

Crandall Library
City Park, 12801
Tel: 518-792-6508

1. Winter: M-Th, 9-9; F,Sa, 9-5; Su, 1-5; summer: M-Th, 9-9; F, 9-5
2. William Crawshaw, Head, Reference
3. English, 3,000
4. Too numerous to list. Holden, Miller Collections
5. 1,093, including local newspaper, census records
6. NY state, particularly northeastern section; New England
7. Tel & letter: yes, NC for brief queries except 10¢/copy with $1 minimum. Refer to local genealogists

8. Bruce G. Cole
9. No
10. No
11. No
12. "Archival Collections of Crandall Library," brochure, $1 postage; *Guide to Local Historical Materials* (1977), a union list of holdings of public libraries in Saratoga, Warren, Washington, and Hamilton Counties, Saratoga Springs, NY; *Guide to Historical Resources in Warren County, New York, Repositories* (1982)
13. Card catalogs, some soon automated
14. Yes
15. OCLC: yes
Books & Sets: 1,2,3(3 v., 1981),7, 10(1972–76),11–14,19(2 v., 1972), 26(NH, NY)
Periodicals: 1(misc),4(misc),7, 8(misc),9(misc)

GREAT NECK

Great Neck Library
Bayview Ave, 11024
Tel: 516-466-8055

1. M,T,Th,F, 9-9; W, 10-9; Sa, 9-6
2. Leila Mattson
3. English, 200
4. None
5. 160
6. Great Neck; Nassau County
7. Tel & letter: yes, NC for brief queries except 25¢/copy plus postage
8. No
9. No
10. No
11. No
12. No
13. Nassau County telephone directories, 1913–; *Great Neck News*, 1926–; *North Hempstead Record*, 1918, 1925–35; *Great Neck Record*, 1935–
14. No
15. No
Books & Sets: 3,19

HAMBURG

Western New York Genealogical Society Library, Hamburg Historical Museum
5859 S Park Ave, 14075
Tel: None

1. Easter to Thanksgiving: M,T,Sa,Su, 1-4
2. Betty V. Walter, Library Committee Chairperson
3. English, 1,300
4. None
5. 165
6. NY counties: Allegany, Cattaraugus, Chautauqua, Erie, Genesee, Niagara, Orleans, Wyoming. Also some NY state; other US states; Ireland, Scotland, England, Germany, Poland, Asia, Canada
7. Tel & letter: no
8. Yes
9. No
10. No
11. No
12. No
13. Vital Index of Early Western New York Families: card file
14. No
15. No
Books & Sets: 1,3,5,7(v.3)
Periodicals: 1(v.52–58),4(v.2–38),5(v.18, 1979),8(v.52,53,64,74, 1964–5,1976,1986),9(v.104-37, 1950–83)

HEMPSTEAD

Hempstead Public Library
115 Nichols Ct, 11550
Tel: 516-481-6990

1. By appointment only
2. Susan J. Alessi, Head, Reference Dept
3. English, 500–1,000
4. 3 or 4
5. 14
6. Primarily Long Island; also NY state, some northeastern US
7. Tel: no; letter: yes, NC for brief queries except $1/page for microfilm

8. No
9. No
10. No
11. No
12. No
13. Card catalog
14. No
15. No
Books & Sets: 2(incomplete),19

HUNTINGTON

Huntington Historical Society Library, 209 Main St, 11743
Tel: 516-427-7045

1. T-Sa, 10-4
2. Irene Sniffin
3. English, 4,000
4. 50
5. 136
6. Huntington, other areas of Long Island
7. Tel & letter: no
8. Irene Sniffin
9. Yes, $1/day to nonmembers; free for members
10. No
11. No
12. No
13. Indexes to marriages, deaths in the *Long Islander,* 1839–81
14. No
15. No
Books & Sets: 26(NY,MA,CT, NH,VT)
Periodicals: 7(v.3),8(1937–58), 9(scattered 1952–82)

Huntington Public Library
338 Main St, 11743
Tel: 516-427-5165

1. M-F, 9-9; Sa, 9-5
2. Antoinette McGrath
3. English, 700
4. N/AN
5. 30
6. Nassau and Suffolk Counties, NY
7. Tel & letter: no
8. No
9. No
10. No
11. No

12. No
13. None
14. No
15. No
Books & Sets: 7,10–13,15, 16,19,26
Periodicals: 1,4,8,9

JAMESTOWN

Fenton Historical Center
67 Washington St, 14701
Tel: 716-483-7521

1. M-Sa, 10-4
2. Frances TeCulver
3. English, 4,000
4. 600
5. 35
6. Chautauqua County
7. Tel: yes, NC for brief queries; letter: yes, $7.50 plus copies
8. Yes, volunteers
9. Yes, $1/adults
10. No
11. No
12. No
13. Index to Jamestown *Journal,* 1800s
14. Yes
15. N/AN
Books & Sets: 2,26
Periodicals: 4,8,9

James Prendergast Library Association
509 Cherry St, 14701
Tel: 716-484-7135

1. M-F, 9-9; Sa, 9-5; Su (Nov-Apr), 1-4
2. Carol Milazzo
3. English, 200
4. None
5. 64
6. Chautauqua and Cattaraugus Counties, NY
7. Tel & letter: yes, NC for limited queries except 25¢/copy. Refer to Fenton Historical Society, 67 Washington Ave, Jamestown, NY 14701
8. No
9. No

10. Yes, duplicates only
11. No
12. No
13. None
14. Yes
15. OCLC: VXU (partial)
Books & Sets: 3,19(6v., 1903–26, 1967),26(NY only)

JERICHO

Jericho Public Library
1 Merry Lane, 11791
Tel: 516-935-6790

1. M-Th, 9-9; F,Sa, 9-5
2. Ruby M. Stern, Local History Librarian
3. English, 450
4. No estimate
5. 24 tape cassette interviews with older residents
6. Jericho, other areas of Long Island
7. Tel & letter: yes, NC
8. No
9. No
10. No
11. No, but will lend duplicate microfilm to residents
12. No
13. None
14. No
15. No
Books & Sets: 7

LOCUST VALLEY

Locust Valley Library
170 Buckram Rd, 11560
Tel: 516-671-1837

1. M-Th, 10-9; F,Sa, 10-5
2. Librarian on duty
3. English, 300; some pamphlet files
4. 5
5. 25
6. Locust Valley and vicinity
7. Tel & letter: yes, NC if time permits
8. No
9. No
10. No
11. No

12. No
13. N/AN
14. No
15. No

LOUDONVILLE

William K. Sanford Town Library, 629 Albany-Shaker Rd, 12211
Tel: 518-458-9274

1. M-F, 9-9; Sa, 9-5; Su (closed summer),1-5
2. Mary Bobear
3. English, 175
4. 12
5. 36: US Census, 1790–1910, mostly Albany County
6. Town of Colonie, cities of Albany, Troy, Schenectady, Watervliet; some NY state
7. Tel & letter: yes, NC
8. No
9. No
10. LH: yes
11. No
12. No
13. Index to clippings in LH file
14. Yes
15. No
Books & Sets: 3,26(NY,NC,PA,NY)
Periodicals: 4(1983–)

MERRICK

North Merrick Public Library
1691 Meadowbrook Rd, 11566
Tel: 516-378-7474

1. M,T,Th, 10-9; W, 1-9; F, 10-6; Sa, 10-5; Su, 1-4
2. D. Lutrin, Local History
3. English, 5
4. N/AN
5. 9 audio cassettes
6. North Merrick; Merrick
7. Tel: no; letter: yes, NC
8. No
9. No
10. Yes, some
11. Yes, audio cassettes

12. No
13. N/AN
14. No
15. N/AN

MOUNT VERNON

Mount Vernon Public Library
28 S First Ave, 10550
Tel: 914-668-1840, ext 315

1. M-F, 9-1, and by appointment
2. Robert Fucci, Curator; Maureen Shields, Librarian
3. English, 180
4. N/AN
5. Microfiche, 2,000+; microfilm, 3,700+ (2 newspapers)
6. Mount Vernon; old town of Eastchester; Wakefield section of the Bronx
7. Tel & letter: yes, NC
8. Robert Fucci
9. No
10. Yes, some LH, by permission of library director
11. Yes, some LH, by permission of library director
12. No
13. Card catalog; subject catalog to clipping file
14. No
15. No
Books & Sets: 1,2(partial),3,6,7,26

NEWBURGH

Newburgh Free Library
124 Grand St, 12550
Tel: 914-561-1836, ext 7

1. M-Th, 9-9; F,Sa, 9-5; Su, 1-4
2. Joan Chernoff, Librarian
3. English, 600–650
4. 21 vertical file drawers
5. Over 1,000
6. NY counties: Orange, Rockland, Ulster, Sullivan, Dutchess, Putnam. Also, histories of all NY state counties on microfilm
7. Tel & letter: yes, NC except for copies

8. No
9. No
10. No
11. Yes, some early newspapers in duplicate, through ILL
12. No
13. Ruttenber Collection; Orange County Settlements; Union List of City Directories; Union List of Newspapers (Orange, Sullivan, Ulster); Guide to Societies and Sources of Information. Each sold for $3–$5
14. Yes
15. No
Books & Sets: 2,3,5–7,10–16, 18,19,22,26
Periodicals: 1(1974–),4(v.16–, 1962–),5(1974–77),8(v.6–, 1980–), 9

NEW CITY

New City Library,
The Rockland Room
220 N Main St, 10956
Tel: 914-634-4997

1. M-F, 9-9; Sa, 9-5; Su, 12-8; summer: M-F, 9-9; Sa, 10-2; closed Su
2. Yvonne H. Yare
3. English, 1,900
4. 1: George H. Budke Collection on microfilm and photocopied bound vols (original in New York Public Library)
5. 233
6. Rockland County; New York City (Dutch period); NY state (history, geology); Bergen County, Orange County, NJ (history, genealogy)
7. Tel & letter: yes, NC for brief queries
8. No
9. No
10. No
11. No
12. No
13. Card catalog
14. Yes
15. No
Books & Sets: 1,3,5–7,10–14, 22,26(NY only)

Periodicals: 4(1985–; keep 2 years + current),5(1974–),7,8(index to v.1–50, 1912–62),9(v.117–, 1963–; index, 1897–1930)

NEW YORK

Holland Society of New York Library, 122 E 58th St, 10022
Tel: 212-758-1875

1. F, 11-4; closed Aug
2. Carol S. Day
3. English, 5,000; German, 25; Dutch, 50
4. Approx 35 linear ft of MS material in vertical files
5. None
6. US, especially New Netherland
7. Tel: no; letter: yes, NC for brief queries
8. Isabel Egan
9. Yes, $2 donation
10. No
11. N/AN
12. No
13. "Inventory and Digest of Early Church Records in the Library of the Holland Society of New York"; *Yearbook of the Holland Society of New York* (1912)
14. Yes
15. No
Books & Sets: 19,26(NY,PA)
Periodicals: 4(1986–),9(1983–)

New York Genealogical and Biographical Library
122 E 58th St, 10022-1939
Tel: 212-755-8532

1. Oct-May: M-Sa, 9:30-5; June, July, Sept: M-F, 9:30-5; closed Aug
2. Gunther E. Pohl, Librarian-Trustee; Betty Hall Payne, Associate Librarian
3. English, ca 50,000; German, very few; Dutch, French, very few
4. 300
5. 3,000
6. NY, Northeast, US; Canada; England
7. Tel: yes, NC for brief queries; letter: yes, NC for brief queries, with SASE
8. No, but library staff has research experience
9. Yes, minimum nonmember donation, $3; minimum annual membership, $50
10. No
11. No
12. Quarterly accession list published since 1870 in periodical, *The New York Genealogical & Biographical Record.* Full run of *Record* available on microfiche for purchase
13. Card catalog; various finding aids
14. Yes
15. RLIN: yes (partial)
Books & Sets: 1–7,8(North America, Great Britain, France), 10–19,22,23,24(both),26
Periodicals: 1–9

New-York Historical Society
170 Central Park West, 10024-5194
Tel: 212-873-3400

1. T-Sa, 10-5; Memorial Day-Labor Day: M-F, 10-5
2. Jean Ashton
3. English, 143,000; German, 100
4. 100
5. 30
6. New York City, NY state, US
7. Tel: yes, NC for brief queries; letter: yes, $5
8. No
9. Yes, $2 admission, $1 Library use. Free to members ($35/yr)
10. No
11. No, except occasionally to RLG libraries
12. *A Guide to the Manuscript Collections of the NYHS,* out of print (contact museum store for information on purchasing); *Collections of the NYHS, 1892–1908; Abstracts of Wills, 1665–1796*
13. *New York City Church and Cemetery Records Both Printed and Manuscript Available at the NYHS;* Gertrude A. Barber, *New York Evening Post Death and Marriage Notices, 1801–1890*
14. No
15. OCLC: NPU (newspapers) RLIN: NYHR
Books & Sets: 3,5(1983–85), 6,7(v.1–6 of 1936 ed),10–14,18,19 (suppls 1904–54), 22–24, 26
Periodicals: 1,3(v.1–27, 1937–64), 7–9

New York Public Library, The Research Libraries, US History, Local History and Genealogy Division, 5th Ave & 42nd St, 10018
Tel: 212-930-0828

1. M,W-Sa, 10-6; T, 10-9
2. John Miller, Chief
3. English, 105,000; German, no estimate
4. Separate Rare Books and Manuscripts Division
5. Separate Microforms Division
6. Worldwide in coverage
7. Tel & letter: yes, NC
8. Yes
9. No
10. No; reproductions supplied and some lending done for RLG institutions
11. No
12. G. K. Hall, *Dictionary Catalog of the Local History and Genealogy Division,* 18 vols (1974)
13. N/AN
14. Yes
15. RLIN: yes
Books & Sets: 1–8,10–17,19, 20–26
Periodicals: 1–9

NIAGARA FALLS

**Niagara Falls Public Library,
Local History Department**
1425 Main St, 14305-1574
Tel: 716-278-8228 (Local History)

1. Hours vary; patrons should call first
2. Donald E. Loker, Local History Specialist
3. English, 10,000
4. Unknown
5. 500
6. Niagara Falls; western end of Niagara County, NY
7. Tel & letter: yes, NC
8. No
9. No
10. No
11. No
12. No
13. Card catalog
14. No
15. No
Books & Sets: 26

NORTH TONAWANDA

North Tonawanda Public Library, 505 Meadow Dr, 14120
Tel: 716-693-4132

1. M,T,Th, 10-9; W, 1-9; F,Sa, 10-5
2. None
3. English, 100
4. None
5. Census, 18 reels
6. North Tonawanda, Niagara County
7. Tel: no; letter: yes, research fee varies. 15¢/microform copy, 10¢/photocopy
8. No
9. No
10. Yes, 28-day loan
11. No
12. No
13. N/AN
14. No
15. No

OGDENSBURG

Ogdensburg Public Library
312 Washington St, 13669
Tel: 315-393-4325

1. M-Th, 10-9; F, 10-6; Sa, 10-5
2. Persis Boyesen
3. English, 700; French, 14
4. N/AN
5. 115
6. NY; New England; Quebec; Ontario
7. Tel & letter: yes, NC for brief queries; otherwise, $12/hr
8. No
9. No
10. No
11. No
12. No
13. N/AN
14. No
15. No
Books & Sets: 2,3,5(v.1&2),7(v.3), 9–11,24,26(VT,NY,NH,CT,MA)
Periodicals: 4(1918–),5(v.14,15), 7,9(1965–)

ONEIDA

Madison County Historical Society Library
PO Box 415, 435 Main St, 13421
Tel: 315-363-4136

1. Winter: M-F, 9-5; summer: M,W-Sa, 10-5; Su, 1-5; T, closed
2. James DeMauro
3. English, 20–30
4. 25
5. 5
6. Madison County; upstate, central NY
7. Tel: no; letter: yes, $5/hr plus copies
8. No
9. Yes, $1
10. No
11. No
12. No
13. "List of Holdings"; "Guide to Holdings"

14. Yes
15. No
Books & Sets: 2,6–8,13,14,16,26
Periodicals: 4,9

ONEONTA

Huntington Memorial Library
62 Chestnut St, 13820
Tel: 607-432-1980

1. M-Th, 9-9; F,Sa, 9-5:30
2. Kay Benjamin
3. English, 500
4. 75
5. 382
6. Otsego and Delaware Counties
7. Tel & letter: yes, NC for brief queries
8. No
9. No
10. No
11. No
12. *Guide to Historical Resources in Otsego County, New York, Repositories* (1982), $11
13. N/AN
14. Yes
15. No
Books & Sets: 2,7(v.3)

PEEKSKILL

Field Library
4 Nelson Ave, 10566
Tel: 914-737-0010

1. W, 5-9; F, 1-3; alt M, 10-1
2. Barbara J. Zimmer
3. English, 3,000
4. 1: Couch file of over 100 local names
5. 6: US census, population schedules and censuses for Westchester and Kings Counties, 1810, 1830–50
6. Peekskill and environs
7. Tel: yes, NC; letter: yes, $1 for 1st copy, 25¢ thereafter
8. No
9. No
10. No

11. No
12. No
13. Card catalog, general file, obituary file
14. No
15. No
Books & Sets: 2,7(v.3 only), 26(NY,VA)
Periodicals: 3(v.3–7,10–17,19–23, 1940–49,1951–60),9(v.30,81–94 broken, 1876,1927–40)

PENFIELD

Penfield Public Library
1985 Baird Rd, 14526
Tel: 716-377-8650 (Library); 377-8654 (Local History Room)

1. Library: M-Th, 10-9; F,Sa, 10-5; Su (Sept-June), 2-5; Local History Room: M, 10-12; T, 1-5, 7-9; W, 10-12, 7-9; Th, 1-5; Su (Sept-June) 2-5
2. LH Room: Town Historian
3. English, 125
4. LH Room: no estimate
5. LH Room: census for 1800–50; Library: 29 reels of local newspapers, 1951–
6. Monroe, Wayne, and Ontario Counties, NY; other nearby counties
7. Tel: yes, NC for Library, no for LH Room; letter: yes, NC except for copies and postage
8. LH Room: Julie Steitz
9. No
10. LH Room: no; Library: yes
11. No
12. No
13. Card catalog
14. LH Room: yes
15. OCLC: yes
Books & Sets: LH Room: N/AN; Library: none

PLATTSBURGH

Clinton-Essex-Franklin Library System, 17 Oak St, 12901
Tel: 518-563-5190

1. Not open to the public

2. Elizabeth Rogers
3. English, 250
4. None
5. None
6. Adirondack Mountains, especially Clinton, Essex, and Franklin Counties; some Lake Champlain
7. Tel & letter: no
8. No
9. No
10. Yes, only to libraries, through ILL
11. N/AP
12. No
13. None
14. No
15. OCLC: VZC

PLEASANTVILLE

Mount Pleasant Public Library
350 Bedford Rd, 10570
Tel: 914-769-0548

1. Winter: M-Th, 9-9; F, 9-6; Sa, 9-4; Su, 1-4; summer: M-Th, 9-9; F, 9-6; Sa, 9-1
2. N/AN
3. English, 400
4. N/AN
5. N/AN
6. Town of Mount Pleasant; Westchester County; NY state
7. Tel & letter: yes, NC
8. No
9. No
10. No
11. No
12. No
13. N/AN
14. No
15. N/AN
Books & Sets: 3
Periodicals: 8(incomplete)

PORT CHESTER

Port Chester Public Library
1 Haseco Ave, 10573
Tel: 914-939-6710

1. Winter: M, 9-9; T,W, 9-8; Th,F, 9-5; summer: M, 9-9; T-Sa, 9-5

2. Carol M. Woodger, Reference Librarian
3. English, 70–75
4. 4 or 5
5. None
6. Westchester County, NY; parts of CT, Long Island
7. Tel & letter: yes, NC
8. No
9. No
10. No
11. No
12. No
13. Bibliography of holdings
14. No
15. N/AN
Books & Sets: 1,26(microfilm)

PORT WASHINGTON

Port Washington Public Library
245 Main St, 11050
Tel: 516-883-4400

1. Sept-June: M-F, 9-9; Sa, 9-5 (July-Aug) 9-1; Su (Oct-Apr), 1-5
2. Priscilla Ciccariello, Head of Information Services; Elly Shodell, Historian
3. English, 1,000
4. 10 collections; 4 NUCMC listings
5. 10
6. Port Washington; Cow Neck Peninsula, which includes villages of Manorhaven, Sands Point, Baxter Estates, Port Washington North
7. Tel & letter: yes, NC
8. No
9. No
10. No
11. No
12. No
13. Shelf lists; guides to Port Washington Play Troupe, Village Welfare Society, Ernie Simon Collection, Oral History Collection
14. No. Refer to Nassau Genealogy Workshop
15. No
Books & Sets: 2,3(1 v.),7(v.3),26
Periodicals: 4

RIVERHEAD

Suffolk County Historical Society Library, 300 W Main St, 11901
Tel: 516-727-2881

1. M-Sa, 12:30-4:30
2. Joanne J. Brooks, Librarian
3. English, 9,000
4. 160 documents and MSS
5. 200
6. Long Island, NY, particularly Suffolk County
7. Tel: yes, NC; letter: yes, $10/2 hrs for nonmembers
8. No
9. Yes, $2 for nonmembers
10. No
11. No
12. No
13. Vertical file index; index to members' ancestor charts
14. No
15. No
Books & Sets: 7(1940),26(CT, MA,NY)
Periodicals: 4,7,9

ROCHESTER

Gates Public Library
1605 Buffalo Rd, 14624
Tel: 716-247-6446

1. M-F, 10-9; Sa, 10-5
2. No individual so designated
3. English, 300–400
4. None
5. 50+: *Gates-Chili News,* 1962–80; *Gates-Chili Press,* 1947–58
6. Town of Gates; some western NY state
7. Tel & letter: yes, NC for brief queries
8. No
9. No
10. Yes, some; most books are reference
11. No. Refer to State Library, Albany, and Rochester Public Library
12. No

13. Indexes in progress to *Gates-Chili Press, Gates-Chili News*
14. No
15. N/AN

Rochester Public Library, Local History Division
115 South Avenue, 14604
Tel: 716-428-7338

1. M-Th, 9-9; F, 9-6; Sa, 10-5
2. Wayne K. Arnold, Head Librarian, Local History Division
3. N/AN
4. Some pamphlet material; no MS collections as such concerning genealogy
5. 1,500: chiefly US census
6. New England, NY, PA, NJ
7. Tel & letter: yes, NC for brief queries
8. No
9. No
10. No
11. No
12. No
13. N/AN
14. Yes
15. No
Books & Sets: 1,3–7,10–15,18, 19,26
Periodicals: 1,3–5,7–9

ROME

Jervis Public Library
613 N Washington St, 13340
Tel: 315-336-4570

1. M-Th, 9:30-9; F, 9:30-5:30; Sa, 9:30-5
2. Lori L. Esworthy
3. English, not counted
4. 3: John B. Jervis Papers; Huntington Collection; Bright Collection
5. 500: local newspapers; 80: census, other
6. Rome, NY; Oneida County, NY; NY state
7. Tel: no; letter: yes, $4–$6/hr
8. No
9. No
10. No

11. No
12. No
13. *Selected Genealogy/Local History Sources at Jervis Public Library; Rome Sentinel* (newspaper) *Index, 1900–1918; Sentinel* card index, 1964–
14. Yes
15. OCLC: ZVA (incomplete; also under Mid-York Library System code ZTM)
Books & Sets: 2(v.23–28,37–40, 44,47–48,128–37, 1898–99, 1917–18),3(1981 only),6(NY only), 7(v.3),10,11,13,19(1950,1972),26
Periodicals: 4(current 2 yrs only), 8(v.49–51, 1961–63),9(broken set to 1965)

SAINT JOHNSVILLE

Margaret Reaney Memorial Library, 19 Kingsbury Ave, 13452
Tel: 518-568-7822

1. M, 10-12, 1-5, 7-9; T,Th, 1-5; W, 10-12, 1-5; F, 1-5, 7-9; Sa (June-Sept), 1-3
2. Marta Zimmerman, Assistant Library Director
3. English, 350
4. 150
5. 50
6. Mohawk Valley, NY state
7. Tel: yes, NC; letter: yes, NC except for copies
8. No
9. No
10. No
11. No
12. No
13. Index to local newspaper, including marriages and obituaries
14. No
15. No
Books & Sets: 2

SCARSDALE

Scarsdale Public Library
Post & Olmsted Rds, 10583
Tel: 914-723-2005, 723-2006

1. Winter: M-Th, 10-9; F,Sa, 10-6; Su, 1-5; summer: M,W, 10-9; T,Th-F, 10-6; Sa, 10-1
2. Florence Sinsheimer
3. English, 120
4. None
5. Local newspaper from 1901
6. Scarsdale
7. Tel & letter: yes, NC
8. No
9. No
10. No
11. No
12. No
13. Loose-leaf index
14. No
15. No

SCHENECTADY

Schenectady County Historical Society, 32 Washington Ave, 12305
Tel: 518-374-0263

1. M-F, 1-5
2. Elsa Church
3. English, 2,500. Also, 109 vols bound local newspapers
4. 25–30
5. 500
6. Schenectady County
7. Tel & letter: yes, NC for brief queries, otherwise $10/hr
8. Yes, amateurs
9. Yes, $1/day for non-members
10. No
11. No
12. Brochure
13. Card index to older material has been microfilmed; copies could be made
14. No
15. No
Periodicals: 1,4(recent),7,9(incomplete)

Schenectady County Public Library, Liberty & Clinton Sts, 12305
Tel: 518-382-3500

1. M-Th, 9-9; F,Sa, 9-5; Su (closed Apr-Labor Day), 1-5

2. Margaret Leonhardt
3. English, 2,442
4. None
5. 18
6. Schenectady County
7. Tel: yes, NC; letter: yes, $3 minimum plus copy charge
8. No
9. No
10. No
11. No
12. No
13. N/AN
14. No
15. N/AN
Books & Sets: 1,10,11,19(1950 reprinted 1965, 2v.),26(NY only)
Periodicals: 4(v.30–)

SMITHTOWN

Smithtown Library, Richard H. Handley Long Island History Room, One North Country Rd, 11787
Tel: 516-265-2072, ext. 38

1. T, 1-5, 6-9; W-F, 10-1, 2-6; Sa, 9-1, 2-5
2. Vera Toman
3. English, 3,000
4. 20,000
5. 306: US Census, 1800–1910, Suffolk, Queens, Nassau Counties; newspapers (*Long Islander, Newsday, Smithtown Messenger*); Library holdings (Smithtown Long Island Room, East Hampton Free Library); British Colonial Office Records
6. Suffolk County; some Nassau, Queens, Brooklyn; to a lesser extent, Manhattan, New England
7. Tel & letter: yes, NC for brief queries
8. No
9. No
10. No
11. No
12. No. Library's holdings are included in R. B. Sealock, *Long Island Bibliography* (Baltimore, 1940), and in M. V. Doggett, *Long Island Printing, 1791–1830: A*

Checklist of Imprints (Long Island Historical Society, 1979)
13. N/AN
14. Yes
15. No
Books & Sets: 3,7(v.1,2,3, 1936),10–12,26(NY only)
Periodicals: 1(v.1–20,45–,1922–44,1969–),4(v.36–,1982–),7, 9(v.76–97,123–, 1922–43,1969–)

SOUTHAMPTON

Rogers Memorial Library
9 Job's Lane, 11968
Tel: 516-283-0774

1. M-Th, 10-9; F,Sa, 10-5
2. Sue Ann Berkebile
3. English, 400
4. None
5. None
6. Southampton, NY; Long Island
7. Tel & letter: yes, NC
8. No
9. No
10. No
11. No
12. No
13. None
14. No
15. No

SYOSSET

Syosset Public Library
225 S Oyster Bay Rd, 11791
Tel: 516-921-7161

1. Winter: M-F, 10-9; Sa, 9-5; Su, 12-5; summer: M-F, 10-9; Sa, 9-1
2. Isabel Goldenkoff
3. English, LH, 130
4. None
5. None
6. Syosset, Long Island
7. Tel & letter: yes, NC
8. No
9. No
10. No
11. No
12. No
13. Card catalog

14. No
15. No
Books & Sets: 3

SYRACUSE

Onondaga County Public Library, 335 Montgomery St, 13202
Tel: 315-473-2701

1. M-Sa, 8:30-4:30
2. Ann Devenish-Cassell Patricia Finley
3. English, 33,000; other, N/AV
4. N/AN
5. 6,100
6. Syracuse, Onondaga County, central NY, NY state; VT, CT, MA, PA, northeastern US
7. Tel & letter: yes, NC
8. No
9. No
10. No
11. No
12. No
13. Onondaga County Pioneer Index (prior to 1850); other indexes to specific works and collections
14. Yes
15. OCLC: YVO (in part)
Books & Sets: 1–3,5,7,10–15, 16(nosuppl),17–20,21(v.1,2),24, 25(3 v., 1957–64),26
Periodicals: 1(v.9–),3,4(v.22–),5, 7(1932,1948,1953),8,9

TARRYTOWN

Historical Society of the Tarrytowns
1 Grove St, 10591
Tel: 914-631-8374

1. T-Sa, 2-4
2. Ruth Neuendorffer, Librarian
3. English, 350
4. 50; vertical files on more than 125 families
5. 50: *Tarrytown Argus, Press Record,* 1875–1946

6. Tarrytown, North Tarrytown, Irvington, Westchester County
7. Tel & letter: yes, NC except for copies
8. No
9. No, but donations welcome
10. No, with exceptions
11. No
12. No
13. Brochure on holdings
14. Yes
15. No
Periodicals: 9(v.106–11, 1952–60)

Warner Library
121 N Broadway, 10591
Tel: 914-631-2189

1. M,Th, 1-9; T,W,F,Sa, 10-5
2. Dee Cerulli
3. English, 50
4. None
5. None
6. Tarrytown, North Tarrytown
7. Tel: no; letter: yes, NC
8. No
9. No
10. No
11. No
12. No
13. Card catalog
14. No
15. No
Books & Sets: 1,3,6

TONAWANDA

Historical Society of the Tonawandas
113 Main St, 14150
Tel: 716-694-7406

1. W-F, 10-5
2. Willard B. Dittmar, Executive Director
3. English, several thousand
4. 8 file cabinets, plus marriages, births, 30,000 obituaries
5. 62: US census, including Erie and Niagara Counties
6. Tonawanda, North Tonawanda

7. Tel & letter: yes, NC
8. No
9. No
10. No
11. No
12. No
13. N/AN
14. No
15. No

TROY

Troy Public Library
100 Second St, 12180
Tel: 518-274-7071

1. M,T,Th, 10-9; W, 10-6; F, 10-5; Sa, 9-5; summer hours often shorter
2. Kathryn B. Turner
3. English, 3,100
4. None
5. 250: newspapers, city directories, censuses
6. Troy, Rensselaer County; towns across Hudson River from Troy: Watervliet, Cohoes, Waterford; some Capital District, eastern NY, NY state, New England
7. Tel: no; letter: yes, NC except for copies
8. No
9. No
10. No
11. No
12. No
13. *A Selected Bibliography of Local History Sources at the Troy Public Library;* another being compiled on genealogy sources
14. Yes
15. No
Books & Sets: 3,5,6,7(v.3),10, 11,26
Periodicals: 4(1978–),9(1847–60, 1898–1909,1921–33,1945–46,1978–)

VALLEY STREAM

Henry Waldinger Memorial Library, 60 Verona Place, 11582-3011
Tel: 516-825-6422

1. M,T,Th,F, 10-9; W, 10-5:30; Sa, 10-4 (10-1 summer)
2. Mamie Eng
3. English, LH, 75–100
4. 1
5. 45: *The Maileader* (local newspaper)
6. Valley Stream, NY; Long Island, NY
7. Tel & letter: yes, NC (LH only)
8. No
9. No
10. Yes, duplicates only of LH
11. No
12. No
13. *Long Island and Local History: A Bibliography*, compiled by Joanne Lynn
14. No
15. No

WESTFIELD

Patterson Library
40 S Portage St, 14787
Tel: 716-326-2154

1. Winter: M-W, 9-8; Th-Sa, 9-5; summer: M,T, 9-8; W-F, 9-5; Sa, 9-1
2. Billie Dibble, Town Historian
3. N/AN
4. 5
5. 430
6. Chautauqua County, NY
7. Tel & letter: yes, NC except for copies
8. No
9. No
10. No
11. No
12. No
13. Newspaper index, obituary index (Westfield)
14. No
15. No
Books & Sets: 2,6,26

WEST ISLIP

West Islip Public Library
3 Higbie Lane, 11795
Tel: 516-661-7080

1. M-F, 9-9; Sa, 9-5; Su (Oct-May), 1-5
2. Mary Scanlon, Head of Reference
3. English, 100
4. None
5. None
6. Long Island, NY state
7. Tel, yes, NC for brief queries; letter: yes, NC
8. No
9. No
10. No
11. N/AP
12. No
13. None
14. No
15. No

North Carolina

ALBEMARLE

Stanly County Public Library
133 E Main St, 28001
Tel: 704-983-7329

1. M-Th, 9-8; F, 9-5; Sa, 9-1
2. Lu J. Koontz
3. English, 2,500
4. 200
5. 450
6. NC history; Stanly County, adjacent counties, history and genealogy
7. Tel: no; letter: yes, NC
8. Lu J. Koontz
9. No
10. No
11. No
12. No
13. Many of local interest only
14. Yes
15. No
Books & Sets: 2(v.54 only), 3(v.1–3, 1983 suppl only),7(v.1 only),12,26
Periodicals: 4(1976–),7,8(v.67, 73,74)

ASHEBORO

Randolph Public Library
201 Worth St, 27203
Tel: 919-629-2131, ext 2118

1. M,W,F, 9-6; T,Th, 9-8:30; Sa, 10-4
2. Carolyn N. Hager
3. English, 2,000+
4. N/AN
5. 235
6. Randolph County, surrounding counties, NC
7. Tel: yes, NC for LH, not G; letter: yes, NC except 50¢/copy
8. Carolyn N. Hager
9. No

10. No
11. No
12. No
13. *Randolph Room*, brochure
14. Yes
15. N/AN
Books & Sets: 7(v.1,3,7),10,11, 19(incomplete),26(NC only)
Periodicals: 4(1985–),8(1986–)

ASHEVILLE

Old Buncombe County Genealogical Society
2 Wall St, Suite 111, 28802
Tel: 704-253-1894

1. M-F, 9-5
2. Ethel M. Kirkpatrick, Genealogist; Evelyn Hess, Librarian
3. English, 1,000
4. 500 (some unpublished)
5. 25 (mostly census records)
6. Old Buncombe County, western NC, NC state; US; other countries
7. Tel & letter: yes, NC except 25¢/copy
8. Ethel M. Kirkpatrick
9. No
10. No
11. No
12. No
13. N/AN
14. Yes
15. N/AN
Periodicals: 4,5,7(v.1–3, reissued 1978),8,9

BARCO

Currituck County Library
Star Route Box 826, Hwy 158, 27917
Tel: 919-453-8345

1. M-T,Th-F, 8:30-5:30; W, 8:30-8; Sa, 9-1
2. Joan H. Dunton
3. English, 500
4. 18
5. 78
6. Albemarle area, NC; some Tidewater VA, MD
7. Tel: N/AN; letter: yes, NC for brief queries except for copies
8. Yes
9. No
10. Yes, with restrictions
11. No, only for use in regional libraries
12. No
13. N/AN
14. No
15. No
Books & Sets: 26(NC)
Periodicals: 4(1980–)

BURLINGTON

Central North Carolina Regional Library
342 S Spring St, 27215
Tel: 919-227-2096

1. M-W, 9-9; Th-Sa, 9-6; Su, 2-6
2. Melanie Maupin
3. English, 500
4. 2
5. 20
6. Alamance County, NC
7. Tel & letter: yes, NC
8. No
9. No
10. No
11. No
12. No
13. Card catalog; list of subject headings for clipping file
14. No
15. No

Books & Sets: 3,7(v.1)11
Periodicals: 4(1977–84),8(1978–85),9(1980–85)

CHAPEL HILL

University of North Carolina at Chapel Hill, Southern Historical Collection and Manuscripts Department, Wilson Library
024-A, 27514
Tel: 919-962-1301

   1. Manuscripts Dept: M-F, 8-5
   2. N/AN
   3. N/AN
   4. No estimate. Southern Historical Collection: private papers of North Carolinians and other southerners—individuals, families, institutions; also, unpublished records of the University
   5. N/AN
   6. NC; other southern states
   7. Tel: yes, NC for brief queries; letter: yes, NC for brief queries except for copies
   8. No
   9. No
  10. N/AP
  11. N/AP
  12. Wallace R. Draughon and William Perry Johnson, *North Carolina Genealogical Reference* (1966)
  13. N/AN
  14. Yes
  15. N/AN

CHARLOTTE

Public Library of Charlotte and Mecklenburg County
210 N Tryon St, 28202
Tel: 704-336-2980

   1. M-F, 9-9; Sa, 9-6; Su (Sept-May), 2-6
   2. Patricia Ryckman
   3. English, 15,000
   4. 6
   5. 10,800
   6. Charlotte, Mecklenburg County, NC; SC, Southeast in general; major migration routes

into and out of area
   7. Tel: yes, NC for brief queries; letter: yes, $5 minimum if copies involved
   8. No
   9. No
  10. No
  11. No
  12. No
  13. N/AN
  14. Yes
  15. N/AN
Books & Sets: 2–5,7,10–14,19, 23,26
Periodicals: 1(incomplete), 4(v.10–),7,8(v.16–),9(v.105–)

CONCORD

Charles A. Cannon Memorial Library
27 Union St N, 28025
Tel: 704-788-3167

   1. T, 11-12, 1-5; Th, 9-12, 1-5
   2. Kathryn L. Bridges
   3. English, 600
   4. 1: Lore Files
   5. 203
   6. Cabarrus County, NC
   7. Tel: yes, NC; letter: yes, charge varies
   8. No
   9. No
  10. No
  11. No
  12. No
  13. None
  14. No
  15. OCLC: NQCOdc, NQCCdc
Books & Sets: 3,7(NC),26(NC)
Periodicals: 4(1977–)

DURHAM

Durham County Library
300 N Roxboro, 27701
Tel: 919-683-2626
   1. M-Th, 9-9; F,Sa, 9-6; Su (except Memorial Day-Labor Day), 2-6
   2. Anne Berkley
   3. English, 10,000
   4. 20
   5. 1,960; also, microfiche of

Durham Morning Herald clipping file (2 drawers, 11,250 fiche)
   6. NC, especially Durham, Orange, Wake, neighboring counties
   7. Tel & letter: yes, NC for brief queries except for copies
   8. Anne Berkley
   9. No
  10. No
  11. No; will lend local newspapers on microfilm (but not clipping file fiche)
  12. No
  13. N/AN
  14. Yes
  15. N/AN
Books & Sets: 3,7(NC),10–12, 26(NC,VA)
Periodicals: 4(keep for 3 yrs)

ELIZABETHTOWN

Bladen County Public Library
S Cypress & Queen Sts, 28337
Tel: 919-862-8171

   1. M,W,F, 8:30-6; T,Th, 8:30-8:30; Sa, 8:30-4; Su, 2-5
   2. N/AN
   3. English, 500
   4. 150
   5. 100
   6. Bladen County, NC, and contiguous counties
   7. Tel & letter: yes, NC
   8. No
   9. No
  10. Yes
  11. No
  12. No
  13. N/AN
  14. No
  15. No

FAYETTEVILLE

Cumberland County Public Library
300 Maiden Lane, 28301
Tel: 919-483-3745

   1. M-Th, 9-9; F,Sa, 9-12; Su (Sept-May), 2-6
   2. Walter W. Mitchell

3. English, 3,000
4. 5
5. 300
6. NC state; some VA, SC, TN, MD
7. Tel: yes, NC; letter: yes, NC except for copies
8. Walter W. Mitchell
9. No
10. No
11. No
12. No
13. Magazine index; Fayetteville newspapers, 1979–
14. Yes
15. OCLC (soon)
Books & Sets: 3,10–14
Periodicals: 4(v.28, 1974–)

GASTONIA

Gaston County Public Library
1555 E Garrison Blvd, 28054
Tel: 704-868-2110

1. M-Th, 9-8:45; F,Sa, 9-5:45
2. None
3. N/AN
4. None
5. 275–300
6. Mainly eastern US
7. Tel: yes, NC; letter: yes, NC except for copies
8. No
9. No
10. No
11. No
12. No
13. N/AN
14. No
15. No
Books & Sets: 1–3,6–11,18,23,26
Periodicals: 1,4

GOLDSBORO

Wayne County Public Library
PO Box 2046, 1001 E Ash St, 27530
Tel: 919-735-1824

1. M-Th, 10-9; F,Sa, 10-5; Su, 1-5
2. Carolyn Griffin
3. English, 1,000

4. 1
5. 45
6. Eastern NC, NC state, southern VA
7. Tel & letter: yes, NC except for copies plus postage
8. Carolyn Griffin
9. No
10. No
11. No
12. No
13. Card catalog
14. Yes
15. No
Books & Sets: 7(v.1,6),10, 11(1972–76),26
Periodicals: 4(1974–),8(1978–80)

HICKORY

Elbert Ivey Memorial Library
420 Third Ave NW, 28601
Tel: 704-322-2905

1. M-Th, 9-9; F,Sa, 9-5; Su (Sept-May), 2-5
2. Lynne Bolick
3. English, 820
4. 2
5. 112: records; 672: newspapers
6. Catawba County, NC state
7. Tel & letter: yes, NC except 10¢/copy
8. No
9. No
10. No
11. No
12. No
13. *Local History and Genealogy Records on Microfilm*
14. No
15. No
Periodicals: 4(v.31–),8(1987–)

HIGH POINT

High Point Public Library
411 S Main St, 27261
Tel: 919-887-3006

1. M-Th, 8am-9pm; F,Sa, 8-6; Su (Sept-May), 2-6
2. Kem Ellis
3. English, 800

4. N/AN
5. 50
6. Mainly NC, with concentration on Guilford County
7. Tel: no; letter: yes, NC except for copies
8. No
9. No
10. Yes, 3-week loan
11. No
12. No
13. In-house card file
14. Yes
15. No
Books & Sets: 1,7
Periodicals: 4

JACKSONVILLE

Onslow County Public Library
58 Doris Ave E, 28540
Tel: 919-455-7350

1. M-Th, 9-9; F-Su, 1-6
2. Joan Dillemuth
3. English, 500
4. N/AP
5. 60
6. NC; some states
7. Tel & letter: yes, NC
8. No
9. No
10. No
11. No
12. No
13. N/AN
14. No
15. N/AP
Books & Sets: 3
Periodicals: 4

KINGS MOUNTAIN

Mauney Memorial Library
100 S Piedmont, 28086
Tel: 704-739-2371

1. M, 12-8; T-Sa, 10-6
2. N/AN
3. English, 100
4. N/AN
5. None
6. Kings Mountain
7. Tel & letter: no
8. No

9. No
10. No
11. No
12. No
13. N/AN
14. No
15. No

LAURINBURG

**Scotland County
Memorial Library**
312 W Church St, 28352
Tel: 919-276-0563

1. M,W,F, 10-6; T,Th, 10-8;
Sa, 9-5; Su (closed summer), 2-6
2. No specialized staff
3. English, 600
4. N/AN
5. 100
6. NC; some SC, southern US;
Scottish immigrants
7. Tel: no; letter: yes, NC for
brief query except 10¢/copy
8. No
9. No
10. No
11. No
12. No
13. *Scotland County Memorial
Library North Carolina Collection*
(1986), compiled by William Reid
Thomas
14. No
15. No
Periodicals: 4(1979–81)

LENOIR

Caldwell County Public Library
606 College Ave SW, 28645
Tel: 704-758-8451, ext 273

1. M,W,F, 8:30-5:30; T,Th,
8:30-8; Sa, 8:30-5
2. N/AN
3. English, 906
4. 500 folders
5. 36
6. NC state
7. Tel & letter: yes, NC except
for copies plus postage
8. N/AN
9. No

10. No
11. No
12. No
13. N/AN
14. Yes
15. No
Books & Sets: 26

LEXINGTON

**Davidson County
Public Library**
602 S Main St, 27292
Tel: 704-246-2520

1. M-Th, 9-9; F,Sa, 9-5:30
2. N/AN
3. English, 1,200; French, 1
4. 2: Genealogical Society of
Davidson County, Henry Reeves
Collection
5. 500
6. US; England
7. Tel: yes, NC; letter: yes, NC
except for copies
8. Jeanette Wilson
9. No
10. No
11. No
12. No
13. Card catalog
14. No
15. No
Books & Sets: 2,3,7,10–12,
26(2 v. only)
Periodicals: 4

LUMBERTON

Robeson County Public Library
101 N Chestnut St, 28358
Tel: 919-738-4859

1. M,W,F,Sa, 9-6; T,Th, 9-9
2. Michael I. Shoop
3. English, 2,500
4. 3
5. 300–400
6. Robeson County; NC, VA,
SC
7. Tel & letter: yes, NC except
15¢/photocopy, 10¢/microfilm
copy
8. No
9. No

10. No
11. No
12. No
13. Index to Kate Britt Biggs
Collection; computer lists for book
holdings, Henry Hodgin Collection; vertical file
14. Yes
15. No
Books & Sets: 2(scattered),3,10
Periodicals: 4

MADISON

Madison Public Library
140 E Murphy St, 27025
Tel: 919-548-6553

1. M,W,F, 9-6; T,Th, 12-9;
Sa, 9-4
2. Sarah Pell, Branch Librarian
3. English, 920
4. 50
5. 200
6. Mainly Rockingham,
Stokes, Guilford, and Forsyth
Counties; border counties of
southern VA; some US
7. Tel & letter: yes, NC
8. No
9. No
10. No
11. No
12. *A Bibliography of Genealogical Materials in the Madison
Public Library,* $2.50
13. N/AN
14. No
15. No
Books & Sets: 3
Periodicals: 4

MARION

**McDowell County
Public Library**
100 W Court St, 28752
Tel: 704-652-3858

1. M,W,F,Sa, 9-5:30; T,Th,
9-8:30
2. N/AN
3. English, 300
4. N/AN
5. 364

6. Western NC
7. Tel & letter: yes, NC for brief queries
8. No
9. No
10. No
11. No
12. No
13. N/AN
14. Yes
15. OCLC: yes
Books & Sets: 3,7

MONROE

Union County Public Library
316 E Windsor St, 28110
Tel: 704-283-8184

1. M,W,F, 9-6; T,Th, 9-8; Sa, 9-5; Su (school months), 2-5
2. Reference Dept staff
3. English, 350
4. None
5. 30
6. Mostly NC; some SC, VA
7. Tel: yes, NC; letter: yes, NC except 15¢/copy
8. No
9. No
10. Yes, through ILL
11. No
12. No
13. N/AN
14. No
15. No
Books & Sets: 3,26

MORGANTOWN

Burke County Public Library
204 S King St, 28655
Tel: 704-437-5638

1. M-Sa, 9-12, 1-5:30
2. Katie K. Snyder
3. English, 450
4. 250
5. 40
6. Burke, Caldwell, and McDowell Counties
7. Tel & letter: yes, NC
8. Katie K. Snyder
9. No
10. No

11. No
12. No
13. Index to early land grants
14. Yes
15. No
Books & Sets: 7(v.1),26
Periodicals: 4

NEW BERN

New Bern-Craven County Public Library
400 Johnson St, 28560
Tel: 919-638-2127 (Ref)

1. M-F, 10-9; Sa, 10-6
2. Emily Miles
3. English, 750
4. None
5. 400
6. NC (eastern counties); VA, MD, some New England
7. Tel & letter: yes, NC except for copies
8. No
9. No
10. No
11. No
12. No
13. N/AN
14. Yes
15. No
Books & Sets: 2,3,7,26
Periodicals: 5,7,8

NEWTON

Catawba County Library
115 W "C" St, 28658
Tel: 704-464-2421

1. M-Th, 8:30-8:30; F,Sa, 8:30-5
2. Evelyn D. Rhodes
3. English, 2,060
4. 15
5. 537
6. NC, SC, TN, KY, MO, VA, MD, GA, PA
7. Tel & letter: yes, NC except for copies
8. Evelyn D. Rhodes
9. No
10. No
11. No

12. No
13. Family History Index
14. Yes
15. No
Books & Sets: 1,3,4,5,7(NC)
Periodicals: 4

OXFORD

Richard H. Thornton Library
Main at Spring St, 27565
Tel: 919-693-1121

1. M,W,F,Sa, 9-5; T,Th, 9-8:30; Su (closed summer), 2:30-4:30
2. Violet B. Coats
3. English, 3,000
4. 300
5. 200
6. Granville County, NC; surrounding area
7. Tel & letter: no
8. Yes
9. No
10. No
11. No
12. No
13. N/AN
14. No
15. No
Periodicals: 4

RALEIGH

North Carolina Department of Cultural Resources, Division of State Library, Genealogical Services Branch
109 E Jones St, 27611
Tel: 919-733-7222

1. M-F, 8-5:30; Sa, 9-5
2. Lee Albright, Head, Genealogical Services Branch
3. English, 12,500; German, 5
4. None
5. 11,000
6. NC; southeastern states from and to which North Carolinians migrated
7. Tel & letter: yes, NC for brief queries except for copies
8. Yes
9. No

10. No
11. Yes, NC census and county records (to 1868) to NC libraries only
12. No
13. N/AN
14. Yes
15. OCLC: NCS
Books & Sets: 2–6,10–14,17–19, 24(v.1),26
Periodicals: 1,4(latest 2 yrs only), 5,7–9

ROBERSONVILLE

Robersonville Public Library
PO Box 1060, S Main St, 27871
Tel: 919-795-3591

1. M-F, 10-6
2. N/AN
3. English, 138
4. N/AN
5. N/AN
6. NC, VA, SC
7. Tel: no; letter: yes, NC
8. No
9. No
10. No
11. N/AN
12. No
13. N/AN
14. No
15. N/AN

ROCKY MOUNT

Thomas Hackney Braswell Memorial Library
344 Falls Rd, 27804
Tel: 919-442-1951

1. M-Th, 10-9; F,Sa, 10-6
2. N/AP
3. English, 331
4. G: 331
5. 90: census
6. Rocky Mount; Nash and Edgecombe Counties
7. Tel & letter: no
8. No
9. No
10. No
11. No
12. No

13. Card catalog; list of microfilm
14. Yes
15. No
Books & Sets: 7

ROXBORO

Person County Public Library
307 S Main St, 27573
Tel: 919-599-7615

1. M-Th, 10-8; F, 10-5; Sa, 10-2
2. Cindi C. McLendon
3. English, 1,200
4. 10
5. None
6. N/AN
7. Tel & letter: yes, NC
8. No
9. No
10. Yes, 3-week loan, renewable
11. No
12. No
13. N/AN
14. Yes
15. N/AN

SALISBURY

Rowan Public Library, Edith M. Clark History Room
PO Box 4039, 201 W Fisher St, 28144
Tel: 704-633-5578

1. M-F, 9-9; Sa, 9-5; Su (Sept-May), 1-5. History Room: M-Sa, 9-5
2. Kay Terrell, History Room Supervisor; Shirley Hoffman, History Room Attendant
3. N/AN
4. Several. McCubbins Collection contains approx 150,000 documents
5. 882
6. Piedmont area, NC; VA, MD, PA, SC; also some IL, KY, TN, IN, MO
7. Tel & letter: yes, NC except 20¢/copy. Refer to local

researchers and certified genealogists for extensive work
8. No
9. No
10. No
11. No
12. No
13. *Edith M. Clark History Room*, brochure
14. Yes
15. No
Books & Sets: 3(1982–84 suppl), 5,7,10–12,20,26(NC,MD,VA, KY,SC)
Periodicals: 4(1979–),5(1969, 1974–85),7–9

SHELBY

Cleveland County Memorial Library
104 Howie Dr, 28150
Tel: 704-487-9069

1. M-Th, 9-9; F,Sa, 9-5
2. James W. Holland
3. English, 2,000
4. N/AN
5. 500
6. Cleveland and Rutherford Counties; some Lincoln County
7. Tel: no; letter: yes, NC except 15¢/copy
8. No
9. No
10. No
11. No
12. No
13. N/AN
14. No
15. No
Books & Sets: 2,19,20,26

STATESVILLE

Iredell County Library
PO Box 1810, 135 E Water St, 28677
Tel: 704-878-3093

1. M-Th, 9-9; F,Sa, 9-6
2. David A. Bunch, M-Sa, 9-3 (volunteer)
3. English, 1,200
4. 920

5. 480
6. Statesville; Iredell County; NC state
7. Tel & letter: yes, NC except 10¢/copy
8. No. Refer to professional genealogists
9. No
10. Rarely
11. Rarely
12. No
13. Collection catalog; inventory of cemeteries, 1759–1976
14. Yes
15. No
Books & Sets: 2,3,5,7,19,26
Periodicals: 4,7

TARBORO

Edgecombe County Memorial Library, 909 Main St, 27886
Tel: 919-823-1141

1. M-Th, 9-9; F, 9-6; Sa, 9:30-5
2. Maurice C. York
3. English, 1,250
4. 20
5. 200
6. Edgecombe County, NC; some NC state history, genealogy holdings
7. Tel & letter: yes, NC
8. No
9. No
10. No
11. No
12. No
13. N/AN
14. No
15. No

WILMINGTON

New Hanover County Public Library, North Carolina Room
201 Chestnut St, 28401
Tel: 919-763-7187

1. M-F, 9-9; Sa, 9-5; Su, 1-5
2. Beverly Tetterton
3. English, 4,000
4. 30

5. 2,000
6. LH: Wilmington and New Hanover County; G: NC state, with emphasis on southeastern NC
7. Tel: no; letter: yes, NC except 10¢/copy with $2 minimum
8. No
9. No
10. No
11. No
12. No
13. Indexes and finding aids
14. No
15. N/AN
Books & Sets: 1–3,5,7,10–14,26
Periodicals: 4,8

WILSON

Wilson County Public Library
PO Box 400, 27893
Tel: 919-237-5355

1. M-Th, 9-9; F,Sa, 9-6
2. Deborah Webb
3. English, 479
4. N/AN
5. N/AN
6. Wilson County, surrounding counties
7. Tel & letter: yes, NC for simple requests
8. No
9. No
10. No
11. No
12. No
13. N/AN
14. Yes
15. No
Books & Sets: 2,7
Periodicals: 8

WINDSOR

Lawrence Memorial Public Library, 204 E Dundee St, 27983
Tel: 919-794-4898

1. M-T,Th-F, 10-6; W, 2-6; Sa, 9-12
2. Nancy B. Hughes
3. English, all
4. None

5. 79
6. Bertie County and eastern NC
7. Tel & letter: yes, NC
8. No
9. No
10. No
11. No
12. No
13. None
14. No
15. N/AN

WINSTON-SALEM

Forsyth County Public Library, North Carolina Room
660 W Fifth St, 27101
Tel: 919-727-2152

1. M-F, 9-9; Sa, 9-5; Su (Sept-May), 1-5
2. Jerry R. Carroll
3. English, 20,000 (NC Room)
4. None
5. 2,000
6. Winston-Salem; NC counties: Surry, Stokes, Forsyth, Rowan; NC state; VA, MD, TN, GA, SC; some IN, PA, KY, AL
7. Tel & letter: yes, NC
8. No
9. No
10. No
11. No
12. No
13. N/AN
14. Yes
15. No
Books & Sets: 1,2(v.43–123), 3(1982–84 suppl),4,7,10–13,19,26
Periodicals: 4(1970,1972–),5, 7,8(1951–53,1958–79,1985–)

WINTON

Hertford County Library
Tryon St, 27986
Tel: 919-358-7855

1. M,W-F, 10-6; T, 12-8; Sa, 9-12
2. Beth Ward
3. English, 450

4. 15

5. 283 reels; NC Bride &
Groom Index on microfiche

6. Hertford, Gates, Northampton, and Bertie Counties in NC;
some southeastern VA counties

7. Tel: no; letter: yes, NC

8. No

9. No

10. No

11. No

12. No

13. N/AN

14. No

15. No

Books & Sets: 7,26

NORTH DAKOTA

BISMARCK

Germans from Russia Heritage Society
1008 E Central Ave, 58501
Tel: 701-223-6167

1. M-F, 10-4
2. None
3. English, 1,000; German, 500
4. N/AN
5. None
6. Germany, Russia; Canada; US
7. Tel: yes, NC; letter: yes
8. Yes
9. No
10. No
11. No
12. Michael Miller, *Researching the Germans from Russia*
13. None
14. No
15. No
Periodicals: 4(some)

State Archives and Historical Research Library, State Historical Society of North Dakota
Heritage Center, 58505
Tel: 701-224-2668

1. M-F, 8-5
2. Gerald Newborg, Division Director/State Archivist
3. English, LH, 1,000
4. 500 cu ft: naturalization records
5. 7,700: primarily newspapers, but also census records, land office tract books, and a few MS collections
6. ND state
7. Tel & letter: yes, charge for census searches ($1) and copies: 10¢/photocopy, 25¢/microprint

8. N/AN
9. No
10. No
11. Yes, newspaper microfilms for 2-week loan, limit of 5 rolls/request
12. David Gray, *Guide to North Dakota State Archives;* David Gray, *Guide to Manuscripts*
13. N/AN
14. Yes
15. OCLC: HND
Books & Sets: 2,3,26
Periodicals: 9

CROSBY

Divide County Public Library
Box 90, 204 1st St NE, 58730
Tel: 701-965-6305

1. M-F, 9-5
2. Ruth Ralph
3. N/AN
4. N/AN
5. 2: census records, 1910–25
6. Northwestern ND
7. Tel & letter: yes, NC
8. No
9. No
10. Yes, 3-week loan
11. No
12. No
13. Index to farm owners in 1915
14. No
15. No

FARGO

Fargo Public Library
102 N 3rd St, 58102
Tel: 701-241-1492

1. M-Th, 9-9; F,Sa, 9-6; Su, 1-5; June-Aug: M-Th, 9-8; F,Sa, 9-6
2. Linda Clement-Sherman

3. English, 150
4. None
5. 600 (*Fargo Forum* on microfilm: 1880–)
6. Fargo and Cass County, ND
7. Tel: no; letter: yes, NC except 20¢/copy
8. N/AN
9. N/AN
10. Yes, 2-week loan
11. No
12. *Guide* (1979)
13. N/AN
14. No
15. No
Books & Sets: 2(v.1–14,45–150)
Periodicals: 4(v.28–, 1974–)

North Dakota State University Library, North Dakota Institute for Regional Studies, SU Station, PO Box 5599, 58105-5599
Tel: 701-237-8914

1. M-F, 8-5
2. John E. Bye, Archivist
3. English, 4,000; German, 250; Norwegian, 20
4. 1,000
5. 75
6. ND state
7. Tel & letter: yes, NC
8. No
9. No
10. Yes, from Germans from Russia Heritage Collection only
11. No
12. *Guide to Manuscripts and Archives* (1985), $10; *Researching the Germans from Russia* (1987), $20
13. Indexes to extensive ND biographies
14. Yes
15. OCLC: TRN
Books & Sets: 1,6

GRAFTON

Carnegie Regional Library
7th & Griggs, 58237
Tel: 701-352-2754

1. M-Sa, 10-5; Su, 1-5
2. None
3. English, 50
4. 100
5. 36
6. Walsh County, ND
7. Tel: N/AN; letter: yes, NC
8. No
9. No
10. Yes
11. Yes
12. No
13. N/AN
14. No
15. N/AN

MINOT

Minot Public Library
516 2nd Ave SW, 58701
Tel: 701-852-1045

1. M-F, 9-9; Sa, 9-5; Su (Sept-May), 1-5
2. Marilyn Lawler, Reference Librarian
3. English, 850
4. None
5. 63
6. North central ND
7. Tel & letter: yes, 1/2 hr free; each additional 1/2 hr, $5
8. No
9. No
10. Yes
11. No
12. No
13. None
14. Yes
15. OCLC: yes

Books & Sets: 3,5(v.4)
Periodicals: 1(v.59–, 1983–), 4(v.30–, 1977–),5(v.13,14,17),7, 8(1983–),9(v.129–, 1979–)

WEST FARGO

Red River Valley Genealogy Society, 626 22d St E, 58078
Tel: 701-282-8445

1. M-Su: by appointment only
2. Shirley Simmons
3. English, 2,050; German, 23; Scandinavian, 100
4. 20 typed family histories
5. None
6. Entire US; Canada; many foreign countries
7. Tel: yes, NC; letter: yes, charge for mileage plus copies
8. Yes
9. No
10. Yes, to local members only
11. N/AP
12. Partial guide; not for sale
13. None
14. Yes
15. No

Books & Sets: 2(plus all suppls), 5,7,10–14,16,17,24(v.1),26
Periodicals: 1(1932–38),2(few), 3(5 years),4,5(2 years),6(few),7, 8(1969–75), 9(1900s)

ALLIANCE

Rodman Public Library
215 E Broadway St, 44601
Tel: 216-821-2665

1. M-Th, 9-9; F,Sa, 9-5:30
2. Leah Agnoni
3. English, moderate number
4. None
5. 529: local newspapers; 22: census
6. Alliance; Stark County
7. Tel & letter: yes, NC
8. No
9. No
10. Yes, through ILL
11. Yes, through ILL
12. No
13. *Ohio Genealogical and Biographical Resources Available at Rodman Public Library*, prepared by Michelle Dillon. This bibliography can be borrowed through ILL
14. No
15. No
Books & Sets: 2,3,10–12

ATHENS

Ohio University, Alden Library
Park Pl, 45701-2978
Tel: 614-593-2710

1. M-F, 8-5. Microforms Dept open evenings, weekends when university is in session
2. George W. Bain, Head, Archives and Special Collections
3. English, 1,200
4. 25
5. 2,800
6. Primarily 18 counties in southeastern OH. Also, published

books ca 1780–1820 for many East Coast states, KY, TN
7. Tel: yes, NC for brief queries; letter: yes, $3/search plus copies
8. George W. Bain
9. No
10. No
11. Yes, on a limited basis
12. *Guide to Local Government Records at the Ohio University Library* (1986 ed), $5
13. *Genealogical Resources in the Ohio University Library*, free handout; *United States Newspapers in the Microform Collection of Ohio University Library*, free handout. Other inventories for archives and MS materials
14. No
15. OCLC: OUN
Books & Sets: 1,3,6,7(v.4,5), 10–13,26
Periodicals: 4(1972–),5(1962–65, 1974–83),7,8(1978–),9

BARBERTON

Barberton Public Library
602 W Park Ave, 44203
Tel: 216-745-1194

1. Winter: M-F, 10-9; Sa, 10-6; summer: M-Th, 10-9; F, Sa, 10-6
2. Phyllis Taylor
3. English, 1,500
4. None
5. 68: local newspapers; 12: census records
6. Barberton history; Summit County; some Medina, Stark, Portage Counties, OH
7. Tel & letter: yes, NC except for 10¢/copy plus postage
8. No
9. No

10. Yes, through ILL
11. Yes, microfilm of *Barberton Herald*
12. No
13. *Key to Genealogy, Barberton Public Library*, handout for in-house use
14. No
15. N/AN
Periodicals: 4(1978)

BELLEFONTAINE

Logan County District Library
Main & Sandusky Sts, 43311
Tel: 513-599-4189

1. M-F, 9-8:30; Sa, 9-5:30
2. Betsy Forsythe Shoffstall
3. English, 304
4. None
5. 272
6. Logan County; some nearby counties; Miami Valley area
7. Tel: no; letter: yes, NC except 10¢/copy, 25¢/microfilm print
8. No
9. No
10. No
11. No
12. No
13. In-house shelf list
14. No
15. No
Periodicals: 4(1985–)

Logan County Genealogical Society Library, Chillicothe & Seymour Sts, PO Box 36, 43311
Tel: 513-592-6191, phone of president of Society. No phone on premises

1. May-Oct: W,F, 1-5; Su, 2-5
2. Edith Eads

3. English, 500
4. 75
5. 150
6. Logan County, OH; some histories of surrounding counties
7. Tel: no; letter: yes, $7/hr
8. No
9. No
10. No
11. No
12. No
13. N/AN
14. No
15. No
Periodicals: 4(1980–)

BELLEVUE

Bellevue Public Library
224 E Main St, 44811
Tel: 419-483-4762

1. M-Th, 10-8:30; F,Sa, 10-5
2. Theodore R. Allison
3. English, 300–400
4. 10
5. 250: local newspapers
6. Ohio counties of Huron, Erie, Seneca,Sandusky; OH state; some US
7. Tel & letter: yes, NC except for copies
8. Theodore R. Allison
9. No
10. No
11. Yes, 3-day loan, to registered borrowers only
12. No
13. Currently developing lists
14. No
15. No
Books & Sets: 3
Periodicals: 1,4,8

BOWLING GREEN

Bowling Green State University, Center for Archival Collections
5th Floor, Jerome Library, 43403
Tel: 419-372-2411

1. M, 8:30-8; T-F, 8:30-4:30; Su, 4-8
2. Paul Yon, Director

3. English, 3,500
4. 494
5. 10,000
6. Allen, Crawford, Defiance, Erie, Fulton, Hancock, Hardin, Henry, Huron, Lucas, Ottawa, Paulding, Putnam, Sandusky, Seneca, Van Wert, Williams, Wood, and Wyandot Counties in northwestern OH
7. Tel: N/AN; letter: yes, $2.50/half hr for 1st 2 half hrs, then $10/hr
8. No
9. No
10. No
11. No
12. No
13. Guides to newspapers, local records, Wood County church records
14. No
15. OCLC: BGSU

Wood County Public Library
251 N Main St, 43402
Tel: 419-352-5104

1. M-Th, 10-8:30; F,Sa, 10-5
2. Marian Shemberg
3. English, 600
4. 100
5. 150
6. Bowling Green; Wood County, northwestern OH, OH state
7. Tel & letter: yes, charge based on research time, copies made
8. No
9. No
10. Yes
11. Yes
12. No
13. N/AN
14. No
15. OCLC: OWCH
Periodicals: 4(1965–85, Index, 1971–81),8(1976–79),9(1976–81)

BRYAN

Bryan Public Library
107 E High St, 43506
Tel: 419-636-6734

1. M-F, 10-8:30; Sa, 10-5
2. Joyce E. Yoder, Reference Librarian
3. English, 550; German, 2
4. 50
5. 290: local newspapers; 69: other genealogy
6. Williams County; OH state; some surrounding states
7. Tel & letter: yes, nominal charge for search and copies
8. No
9. No
10. No
11. No
12. In process; free
13. Obituary index to county newspapers
14. Yes
15. No
Books & Sets: 3,5,8,26
Periodicals: 4

BURTON

Burton Public Library
14588 West Park, 44021
Tel: 216-834-4466

1. M-F, 9-9; Sa, 9-6
2. N/AN
3. English, 300
4. N/AN
5. 175
6. Burton, Geauga County, OH state
7. Tel & letter: no
8. No
9. No
10. Yes, to county library card holders, 2–3-week loan
11. No
12. No
13. N/AN
14. No
15. OCLC: yes

CAMBRIDGE

Guernsey County District Public Library, 800 Steubenville Ave, 43725-2385
Tel: 614-432-5946

1. Sept-June: M-Th, 1-5:30; F, 11:30-8; Sa, 9-5; June-Sept: M-Th, 1-5:30; F, 9-5:30; closed Sa
2. Lois M. Bell
3. English, 2,600
4. None
5. 688
6. OH, parts of other states
7. Tel: yes, NC; letter: yes, NC except 25¢/copy
8. Lois M. Bell
9. No
10. No
11. No
12. No
13. N/AN
14. Yes
15. No

Books & Sets: 3,4,7,18(v.1–30), 26(MA,PA,VA,MD,RI)
Periodicals: 1(1975–86),4(1972–), 8(1960–77)

CAMDEN

Preble County District Library, Camden Branch
104 S Main, 45311
Tel: 513-452-3142

1. M,W, 2-7; F, 10-4
2. Ruth Neff
3. English, 8 family histories
4. N/AN
5. N/AN
6. N/AN
7. Tel & letter: yes, NC
8. No
9. No
10. No
11. No
12. No
13. N/AN
14. No
15. N/AN

CANAL FULTON

Canal Fulton Public Library
44614
Tel: 216-854-4148

1. M-Sa, 9-9
2. Tom Brownfield
3. English, 300
4. None
5. None
6. Canal Fulton; Lawrence Township; Clinton County; OH state
7. Tel & letter: yes, NC
8. No
9. No
10. Yes
11. N/AP
12. No
13. N/AN
14. No
15. No

CANTON

Stark County District Library
715 Market Ave North, 44702-1080
Tel: 216-452-0665, ext 225

1. M-Th, 9-9; F,Sa, 9-5
2. Barbara Grant Fox
3. English, 3,600
4. 100
5. 2,000
6. MA, NJ, CT, PA, OH, VA, WV, MD, KY
7. Tel: yes, NC, if brief query; letter: yes, NC except for copies plus postage
8. Barbara Grant Fox
9. No
10. No
11. No
12. *Genealogy, Bibliography, and Related Information from Stark County District Library Reference Department*
13. N/AN
14. No. Refer to Stark County Chapter of Ohio Genealogical Society
15. OCLC: SDL

Books & Sets: 1–3,5(5 v.),7, 8(US,Canada),10–14,17,26
Periodicals: 1(v.1–59, 1922–83), 4,5,7–9

CHILLICOTHE

Chillicothe and Ross County Public Library
140-146 S Paint St, 45601
Tel: 614-773-4145

1. M-Th, 9-9; F,Sa, 9-5:30
2. Susan Johnson
3. English, 800
4. N/AN
5. 646: Ross County Probate; 50: census records; 476: local papers; 10: miscellaneous
6. Ross County; some OH, surrounding states
7. Tel: no; letter: yes, NC except for copies, $1 minimum plus 30¢/microfilm, 10¢/copy
8. No
9. No
10. No
11. No
12. No
13. In-house brochure
14. Yes
15. OCLC: OCH (most of collection)

Books & Sets: 2(v.1–16,19–29, 43–53),7(v.4,5),26
Periodicals: 4(1973–)

Ross County Genealogical Society, 38 Rear S Paint St, 45601
Tel: 614-773-2715

1. M,W,F, 1-4
2. Luvada Kuhn
3. English, 1,403; German, 3
4. 120
5. 142 plus microfiche index of LDS collection US and Europe
6. OH state; PA, VA, KY, IN, MD, WV; some other states, mostly east of Mississippi River
7. Tel: yes, NC; letter: yes, $5/hr
8. No
9. No
10. No
11. No

12. No
13. N/AN
14. Yes
15. No
Books & Sets: 3,5(v.1–5),26(CT,
ME,MD,MA,NY,NC,PA,
SC,VT,VA)
Periodicals: 4(1954–),8(1973–)

CINCINNATI

Cincinnati Historical Society
Eden Park, 45202
Tel: 513-241-4622

1. T-Sa, 9-4:30
2. Laura L. Chace
3. English, 16,000
4. 400
5. 1,425
6. Metropolitan Cincinnati,
OH state; Old Northwest Territory
7. Tel: no; letter: yes, NC,
holdings only
8. No
9. No
10. No
11. No
12. No
13. Catalogs to books and
periodicals, small MS collections;
inventories of large collections
14. Yes
15. OCLC: CHT
Books & Sets: 2(v.1,8,11–16,
35–37,39,43–166),3,5–7,10–14,
17,18,26
Periodicals: 1(v.9–, 1932–),3,5,7–9

**Public Library of Cincinnati and
Hamilton County**, 800 Vine St,
Library Sq, 45202-2071
Tel: 513-369-6905, 6906, 6907
(Reference); 6909 (Maps); 6910
(Newspapers)

1. M-F, 9-9; Sa, 9-6
2. J. Richard Abell, Head,
History Dept; Susan J. Kober, First
Assistant, History Dept
3. English, 80,000; German,
500; other, 250
4. 90 MS boxes (housed in
Dept of Rare Books and Special
Collections)

5. 25,000 microfilm reels
(includes extensive US Census
collection); 17,000 microfiche
pieces
6. East of Mississippi River,
TX, LA, MO; US; British Isles
7. Tel & letter: yes, NC except
20¢/copy plus postage ($1 mini-
mum)
8. Yes, experienced librarians
9. No
10. No, with exceptions: "how-
to" books, few others
12. No
13. Surname Index (family
names in printed family histories);
Local History Index; Newspaper
Index; Geographic List of Periodicals on Genealogy and Local
History
14. No. Refer patrons to local
genealogical society
15. OCLC: OCP
Books & Sets: 1–14,16–24,26
Periodicals: 1–5,6(17–,1975–),7–9

**University of Cincinnati,
German-Americana Collection**
Langsam Library ML 33, 45221
Tel: 513-475-6459

1. M,W, 8-noon; F, 8-5
2. Don Heinrich Tolzmann
3. German, 1,500
4. 5
5. N/AN
6. German-American settlement region
7. Tel & letter: yes, NC
8. No
9. No
10. No
11. N/AN
12. K. G. Saur, *Catalog of the
German-Americana Collection*
(1987), $150
13. Card catalog
14. No
15. OCLC: CIN (part)
Books & Sets: 1

CLEVELAND

Cleveland Public Library
325 Superior Ave, 44114-1271
Tel: 216-623-2864

1. M-Sa, 9-6
2. Jo Ann Petrello, Head of
History and Geography Dept
3. English, 3,500; German,
300; other, 100
4. None
5. 550
6. G: basically British, also
German, French; LH: OH, Cuyahoga County, Western Reserve,
Cleveland
7. Tel & letter: N/AN
8. No
9. No
10. No
11. No
12. No
13. *Index to British Parish
Registers Collection*; *Index to
Coats-of-Arms in Heraldry Collection*; Index to books and periodical articles on local history
14. No
15. N/AN
Books & Sets: 1–7,10–12,14,
17–24,26
Periodicals: 1,5–9

**Western Reserve Historical
Society Library**
10825 East Blvd, 44106
Tel: 216-721-5722

1. T-Sa, 9-5
2. Ann K. Sindelar, Reference
Supervisor
3. English, 100,000+; German,
100; other: Czech, Slovenian,
French
4. 1,000
5. 30,000
6. US, especially states east of
Mississippi River
7. Tel: no; letter: yes, $20/hr
8. No
9. Yes, $3/day for non-
members
10. No
11. No
12. *Ohio Genealogical Records*
(1976), out of print; *Guide to
Manuscripts and Archives* (1972),
$10; guides to Shaker (1974) and
Jewish (1983) sources, $7.50 and
$5, respectively

13. "Profile of Genealogical Collections"; in-house indexes, guides, and card catalogs
14. Yes
15. No
Books & Sets: 2–8,10–14,18, 22–24,26
Periodicals: 1,2(v. 3,4),3(v.1–47), 4–9

COLUMBUS

Clements Memorial Library, Franklin County Historical Society, 280 E Broad St, 43215
Tel: 614-228-6362

1. M-Sa, 10-5; Su, 1-5:30
2. Ted Kessel, Curator
3. (Library is undergoing overhaul and looking for new location; reference material currently not available)
4. See #3
5. See #3
6. Columbus, Franklin County; OH state
7. Tel & letter: yes, NC
8. No
9. No
10. No
11. No
12. No
13. N/AN
14. Yes
15. N/AN

Grandview Heights Public Library, 1685 W First Ave, 43212
Tel: 614-486-2951

1. M-F, 9-9; Sa, 9-5; summer: M-F, 9-9; Sa, 9-3
2. Reference Department
3. English, 60
4. N/AN
5. N/AN
6. Village of Marble Cliff, Grandview Heights, Franklin County, OH
7. Tel & letter: yes, NC
8. No
9. No
10. No
11. No

12. No
13. N/AN
14. No
15. No
Periodicals: 4(v.39–, 1985–)

Ohio Historical Society, Archives-Library Division
1985 Velma Ave, 43211
Tel: 614-297-2510

1. T-Sa, 9-5
2. Gary J. Arnold, Head of Reference Services
3. English, 50,000; German, 1,250
4. 500
5. 40,000
6. Primarily OH state
7. Tel: yes, NC for brief queries; letter: yes, $8/letter for nonmembers and nonresidents
8. Bonnie Linck
9. No
10. No
11. Yes, through ILL
12. *Guide to Ohio Newspapers, 1793–1973*, $10 plus shipping; *Guide to Manuscripts at the Ohio Historical Society*, $10 plus shipping
13. Card catalogs; inventories to MS collections, audiovisual materials, government records
14. Yes
15. OCLC: OHT (since 1979)
Books & Sets: 2–8,10–14,17–19, 24,26
Periodicals: 1,3,4(1950–), 5(1962–65,1969,1974–75, 1977–85),7,8,9(incomplete)

Public Library of Columbus and Franklin County, Biography, History, Travel Division, 96 S Grant Ave, 43213 (mailing address: 28 S Hamilton Rd, 43213)
Tel: 614-222-7154

1. M-Th, 9-9; F,Sa, 9-6
2. Sam Roshon, Subject Specialist
3. English, 6,700
4. None
5. 50

6. All OH counties (represented by at least one history or atlas), OH state
7. Tel: yes, NC for brief queries; letter: yes, NC except 10¢/copy
8. No
9. Yes, nonresident's fee to check out books
10. No
11. No
12. No
13. Computer catalog (VTLS)
14. No. Refer to Franklin County Genealogical Society
15. OCLC: OCO

State Library of Ohio
65 S Front St, 43266-0334
Tel: 614-462-6966

1. M-Th, 8-5; F, 9-5
2. Petta Khouw
3. English, 9,000
4. N/AP
5. 4,600
6. OH, New England states, VA, KY, WV, PA, NY
7. Tel: yes, NC for brief queries; letter: yes, NC except 20¢/copy ($1 minimum)
8. No
9. No
10. No
11. No
12. *County by County in Ohio Genealogy* (1978), $5
13. N/AN
14. Yes
15. OCLC: OHI
Books & Sets: 1–7,10–12, 17–19,26
Periodicals: 1(v.10–),3(v.1–10, 27–28),4(v.11–, 1957–), 5(1974–84),7–9

CUYAHOGA FALLS

Taylor Memorial Public Library, 2015 Third St, 44221
Tel: 216-928-2117

1. M-Th, 10-9; F, 10-6; Sa, 10-5; Su (Oct-May), 1-5

2. Kathleen Fenning, Head, Reference Dept; Virginia Bloetscher
3. English, 660
4. 24
5. 55: local paper, 1888–1983
6. Cuyahoga Falls, OH state, some neighboring states
7. Tel & letter: yes, NC
8. No
9. No
10. Yes, duplicate copies only
11. No
12. No
13. Local History Room card catalog
14. No
15. No
Books & Sets: 26
Periodicals: 4(v.22–41)

DAYTON

Dayton and Montgomery County Public Library, 215 E Third St, 45402-2103
Tel: 513-227-9500, ext 211

1. M-F, 9-9; Sa, 9-6
2. Stanley Clarke Wyllie
3. English, 3,200
4. N/AN
5. 340
6. OH, especially Miami Valley; some PA, KY, the South
7. Tel: yes, NC for brief queries; letter: yes, $1/service charge plus 25¢/copy
8. Stanley Clarke Wyllie
9. No
10. No
11. No
12. *Guide to Genealogical Materials in the Dayton & Montgomery County Public Library,* $5 plus postage
13. Indexes to Montgomery County, Miami Valley
14. Yes
15. OCLC: yes
Books & Sets: 1–7,10–14,16, 18,19,26

Periodicals: 1(v.56–, 1980–),4, 5(v.1–3,8,13–),7,8(v.26–, 1938–), 9(1936–)

Wright Memorial Public Library, 1776 Far Hills Ave, 45419
Tel: 513-294-7171

1. M-F, 9-9; Sa, 9-5; Su, 1-5
2. N/AN
3. English, 1,200
4. N/AP
5. N/AP
6. Dayton area
7. Tel & letter: yes, NC for brief queries
8. No
9. No
10. No
11. No
12. No
13. N/AN
14. No
15. N/AN
Books & Sets: 5,26
Periodicals: 4(1987–)

DEFIANCE

Defiance Public Library
320 Fort St, 43512
Tel: 419-782-1456

1. M-Th, 9-8; F,Sa, 9-5:30; summer Sa, 9-12
2. Jane Small
   Pat Little
3. English, 1,000
4. None
5. 400
6. Northwestern OH
7. Tel & letter: yes, NC for brief queries
8. Jane Lewis
9. No
10. No
11. No
12. No
13. In process
14. Yes
15. OCLC: yes
Books & Sets: 26(OH)

Periodicals: 4,8(v.73–),9(some later vols)

DELAWARE

Delaware County Historical Society, PO Box 317, 157 E William St, 43015
Tel: 614-369-3831

1. Mar-Dec: W,Su, 2-4:30; other by appointment
2. Marilyn M. Cryder
3. English, 400
4. 250
5. 50
6. Delaware, Union, and Morrow Counties, OH; some Franklin, Marion Counties
7. Tel & letter: yes, donation to Society
8. Marilyn M. Cryder
9. No
10. No
11. No
12. In process
13. Index to 200 items compiled by Margaret Bouic; guide to cemeteries of Delaware County
14. Yes
15. No
Periodicals: 4(various),8(various),9(various)

EATON

Preble County District Library, Eaton Branch, 301 N Barron St, 45320
Tel: 513-456-4331

1. M-W,F, noon-8; Th, 9-8; Sa, 9-5
2. Susan H. Kendall
3. English, 720
4. None
5. 260
6. Preble, Darke, Montgomery, and Butler Counties, OH; Wayne County, IN; KY, VA, TN, NC, NJ, MD, PA
7. Tel: yes, NC; letter: yes, NC except for copies and postage

8. Susan H. Kendall
9. No
10. No
11. No
12. No
13. Preble County Genealogical Society, "Guide to Researching in Preble County, Ohio"
14. No
15. No
Books & Sets: 3,4,7(v.5), 26(3 v. only)
Periodicals: 4(1950–)

ELMORE

Harris-Elmore Public Library
Box 84, 300 Toledo St, 43416
Tel: 419-862-2482

1. M-Th, 2-8:30; F, 12-5:30; Sa, 9-5:30
2. Grace Luebke
3. English, 300
4. 1,500
5. 165
6. Ottawa, Wood, Sandusky, and Seneca Counties,OH
7. Tel: no; letter: yes, $5 minimum per request
8. Grace Luebke
9. No
10. No
11. No
12. No
13. Every-name indexes to census, church records, newspapers, county histories, atlases, probate, and infirmary records
14. Yes
15. No
Books & Sets: 3,4
Periodicals: 4,9

EUCLID

Euclid Public Library
631 E 222 St, 44123
Tel: 216-261-5300

1. M-Th, 9-9; F,Sa, 9-5; Su (Sept-May), 1-5

2. None
3. English, 100
4. None
5. 21 cassette tapes
6. OH, PA
7. Tel & letter: yes, NC
8. No
9. No
10. Yes, to other libraries for in-house use
11. Yes, loan cassettes for 3 weeks
12. No
13. None
14. No
15. OCLC: ECU
Books & Sets: 3(incomplete)
Periodicals: 4(1978–)

FAIRVIEW PARK

Cuyahoga County Public Library, Fairview Park Regional Branch, 4449 W 213 St, 44126
Tel: 216-333-4700

1. M-Th, 9-9; F,Sa, 9-5:30; Su (Sept-May), 1-5
2. Barbara A. Musselman
3. English, 5,500; German, 10; French, 10
4. None
5. 1,350
6. Cuyahoga County, OH state; states east of Mississippi River; Canada
7. Tel: yes, NC; letter: yes, NC for brief queries
8. Yes
9. No
10. Yes
11. No
12. "Genealogy," free brochure
13. G/LH source file (card file)
14. Yes
15. OCLC: CXP
Books & Sets: 1,3–7,9–14, 17,19,22–24,26
Periodicals: 1(v.53–, 1977–), 3(v.40–, 1976–),4(1950–),5,7(rev ed 1983),8,9(v.131–, 1977–)

FINDLAY

Findlay-Hancock County Public Library, 206 Broadway, 45840
Tel: 419-422-1712

1. Winter: M-Th, 9:30-8:30; F,Sa, 9:30-5; summer: M,W, 9:30-8:30; T,Th, F,Sa, 9:30-5
2. Jeanette M. Lust
3. English, 2,000
4. None
5. 500
6. Hancock County, other OH counties; some surrounding states
7. Tel: yes, NC; letter: yes, NC except 10¢/copy
8. Jeanette M. Lust
9. No
10. No
11. No
12. No
13. N/AN
14. Yes
15. No
Books & Sets: 1–5,7,10–14,26
Periodicals: 4(1977–),5(all but 3 v.),7(v.1)

FREMONT

Rutherford B. Hayes Presidential Center Library, 1337 Hayes Ave, Spiegel Grove, 43420-2796
Tel: 419-332-2081

1. M, 1:30-5; T-Sa, 9-5
2. Rebecca Hill
   Barbara Paff
3. English, 10,000
4. 300
5. 4,000
6. OH, especially Sandusky County; New England, NY, PA, MI, IN, IL, WI
7. Tel: yes, NC; letter: yes, $10/hr
8. Rebecca Hill
9. No
10. No
11. Yes, 1-month loan, duplicates only

12. Andrea D. Lentz, *Guide to Manuscripts at the Ohio Historical Society* (1973), out of print
13. N/AN
14. Yes
15. No
Books & Sets: 2,3,6,10–12,26
Periodicals: 4(1981–),9(v.1–14, 48–55,81–95)

GIRARD

Girard Free Library
105 E Prospect St, 44420
Tel: 216-545-2508

1. M-Th, 10-8; F,Sa, 10-5
2. Sondra K. Fisher
3. English, 63
4. One magazine from 1973, vertical file
5. 60
6. Trumbull, Mahoning Counties; Western Reserve
7. Tel & letter: yes, NC
8. No
9. No
10. No
11. No
12. No
13. None
14. No
15. No

GREENVILLE

Greenville Public Library
520 Sycamore St, 45331
Tel: 513-548-3915

1. M-F, 9-8; Sa, 9-5
2. Polly Ann Weaver, Library Assistant
3. English, 765
4. 200
5. 315: local newspapers, 1851– (some early years missing)
6. Greenville, Darke County, OH state; some US
7. Tel: N/AN; letter: yes, NC except 25¢/copy, 75¢/microprints
8. No
9. No
10. No

11. No
12. Guide in progress
13. N/AN
14. No
15. No
Books & Sets: 2(1958),3

HUDSON

Hudson Library and Historical Society, 22 Aurora St, 44236
Tel: 216-653-6658

1. M,T, 10-4:30,6-9; Th, 10-6; F, 10-4:30; Sa, 10-4; closed W,Su
2. James F. Caccamo
3. English, 2,400
4. 40
5. 355
6. OH, with emphasis on Western Reserve; some eastern US, primarily New England; some Midwest
7. Tel & letter: yes, NC
8. No
9. No
10. No
11. No
12. No
13. Inventory of MS holdings. Non-MS holdings in Cleveland Public Library's CLEVNET automated data base
14. Yes
15. N/AN
Books & Sets: 2(v.1–25),3(v.1–3, 1982–83 suppl),5,22,23,26
Periodicals: 4(1985–),8(v.70–), 9(v.1–17,136–)

JACKSON

Jackson City Library
21 Broadway St, 45640
Tel: 614-286-2609

1. M,T,W, 10-8; Th,F, 10-5; Sa, 9-5
2. None
3. English, all
4. 100
5. 16
6. Jackson County and surrounding counties

7. Tel: yes, NC; letter: yes, charge
8. No
9. No
10. No
11. No
12. No
13. N/AN
14. Yes
15. No

KENT

Kent Free Library
312 W Main St, 44240
Tel: 216-673-4414

1. M-F, 9-9; Sa, 10-6; Su (seasonally), 1-5
2. None
3. English, 150
4. N/AP
5. N/AP
6. Kent; Portage, Summit Counties; OH state
7. Tel & letter: yes, NC
8. No
9. No
10. Yes
11. No
12. No
13. None
14. No
15. No
Periodicals: 4

KENTON

Mary Lou Johnson-Hardin County District Library
325 E Columbus St, 43326
Tel: 419-673-2278

1. M-Th, 9-8; F,Sa, 9-5
2. N/AN
3. English, 250
4. N/AN
5. 365
6. OH state
7. Tel: yes, NC; letter: yes, NC except for copies
8. No
9. No
10. No

11. No
12. No
13. Card catalog
14. No
15. No
Books & Sets: 2(v.1–84), 2(1 v., 1980)
Periodicals: 4(1983–)

LAKEWOOD

Lakewood Public Library
15425 Detroit Ave, 44102
Tel: 216-226-8275

1. M-F, 9-9; Sa, 9-6; Su (winter), 1-5
2. None
3. English, 600
4. None
5. 53
6. OH, especially Cleveland and northern OH
7. Tel & letter: yes, NC
8. No
9. No
10. Yes
11. No
12. No
13. None
14. No
15. OCLC: LAP
Books & Sets: 1,3,11(1972–76)
Periodicals: 4(1963–),7

LANCASTER

Fairfield County District Library, 219 N Broad St, 43130
Tel: 614-653-2745

1. M-Th, 9-9; F,Sa, 9-5; Su (winter), 1-5
2. Joyce Harvey
3. English, 1,433
4. N/AN
5. 125
6. Fairfield County, OH, and surrounding counties
7. Tel & letter: yes, NC for brief queries, otherwise $7/hr

8. No. Refer to Fairfield County Chapter, OGS
9. No
10. No
11. No
12. *Genealogies in the Historical Collection of the Fairfield County District Library*, $2 plus $1.50 postage
13. N/AN
14. Yes
15. OCLC: OFA (partial)
Books & Sets: 2–5,7,26
Periodicals: 4

LIMA

Lima Public Library
650 W Market St, 45801
Tel: 419-228-5113

1. M-Th, 9-8:30; F,Sa, 9-5; (Sa, 9-12 summer)
2. Robert Bertrand, Reference Head
3. English, 800
4. None
5. 720: local newspapers, US Census for Allen County
6. Allen County primarily; some material on neighboring counties; west-central OH; OH state
7. Tel & letter: yes, NC for OH residents. For out-of-state residents, $5/hr for research and 10¢/copy
8. No
9. No
10. No
11. No
12. No
13. Index to obituaries in *Lima News*
14. No
15. OCLC: LIM
Books & Sets: 2,26
Periodicals: 4(1980–83,1985–)

LORAIN

Lorain Public Library
351 Sixth St, 44052
Tel: 216-244-1192

1. M-Th, 9-8:30; F,Sa, 9-6
2. Joe Jeffries
3. English, 3,200
4. N/AN
5. 132: census; 7: court records
6. Lorain; Lorain County; OH, PA, New England
7. Tel: yes, NC; letter: yes, NC except 15¢ or 25¢/copy
8. No
9. No
10. No
11. No
12. No
13. *Adventures in Ancestry: A Research Guide to Special Collections and Public Records*
14. No
15. OCLC: LXP
Books & Sets: 1,2(v.1–141),3, 4,5(v.1–3),6,7,10–14,23,26
Periodicals: 1(1974–),3(1973–), 4(1956–59,1974–),5,7, 8(1957–59,1963–71,1973–),9

LOUDONVILLE

Loudonville Public Library
122 E Main St, 44842
Tel: 419-994-5531

1. M,T,Th,F, 9-8; W,Sa, 9-5; Su (through May), 1-4
2. Brenda C. Spier
3. English, 50
4. 25
5. 60
6. OH counties of Ashland, Richland, Wayne, Holmes, Knox
7. Tel & letter: yes, NC
8. No
9. No
10. No
11. No
12. No
13. *Loudonville Times* Death Notices, 1922–54, 1973–86; Death Index, *Loudonville Times, Loudonville Advocate*, 1903–20
14. No
15. N/AN
Periodicals: 4

MADISON

MacKenzie Memorial Public Library, 6111 Middle Ridge Rd, 44057
Tel: 216-428-2189

1. M-Th, 10-8:30; F,Sa, 10-5
2. R. E. Johnson, Library Director; Carol Vincent, Genealogy Clerk
3. English, 430
4. None
5. 99
6. Northeastern OH; counties of Lake, Ashtabula, Cuyahoga, Geauga
7. Tel: no; letter: yes, NC
8. No
9. No
10. No
11. No
12. No
13. Separate genealogy catalog
14. No
15. No
Books & Sets: 3,26(8 v.)
Periodicals: 4(1978–)

MANSFIELD

Mansfield-Richland County Public Library, Sherman Room, 43 W Third St, 44902
Tel: 419-524-1041, ext 24

1. Sherman Room: winter: T,Th,F,Sa, 9-5:30; W, 12:30-9; summer: M,T,Th,F, 9-5:30; W, 12:30-9
2. Mary Lou Altvater, Head Reference Librarian; Karen Furlong, Sherman Room (G/LH Collection)
3. English, 1,000
4. None
5. 1,175
6. Primarily OH; some PA, other
7. Tel & letter: yes, NC for brief queries except 15¢/copy and 25¢/microfilm ($1 minimum)
8. Karen Furlong
9. No
10. No

11. No
12. No
13. *North Central Library Cooperative Resource Guide to the Holdings of Twenty-Three Member Libraries*
14. No
15. No
Books & Sets: 2(missing v.13–19, 31–42),3,4,6,13,14
Periodicals: 4. (Periodicals before 1987 are packed and will be stored for 2 years while Library moves to temporary quarters)

Ohio Genealogical Society Library, 419 W Third St, PO Box 2625, 44906
Tel: 419-522-9077

1. T-Sa, 9-5
2. Thomas Stephen Neel, Manager; Florence Main, Librarian
3. English, 10,000; German, 10; Welsh, French, 5
4. 45 boxes
5. 800
6. OH, PA; some on other states, countries
7. Tel & letter: yes, NC for brief queries except 15¢/copy, 50¢/microcopy; plus postage
8. Yes, have able people
9. No
10. No
11. No
12. No
13. None
14. Yes
15. No
Books & Sets: 3,5,8(US,Canada), 26
Periodicals: 4,5,8,9

MARIETTA

Washington County Public Library, 615 Fifth St, 45750
Tel: 614-373-1057

1. M-Th, 9-8:30; F,Sa, 9-5
2. Louise Zimmer
3. English, 1,600; 94 scrapbooks, numerous family genealogies

4. N/AN
5. 450 (probate records for Washington County, census records, local newspapers)
6. Washington County, southeastern OH
7. Tel & letter: yes, NC except for copies
8. Louise Zimmer, CGL
9. No
10. No
11. No
12. No
13. N/AN
14. Yes
15. N/AN
Books & Sets: 26
Periodicals: 4(1983–),7, 9(1895,1982–)

MARION

Marion Public Library
445 E Church St, 43302
Tel: 614-387-0992

1. M-F, 9-9; Sa, 9-5:30
2. Lynda Williams
3. English, 1,500
4. None
5. 750
6. Primarily OH state
7. Tel & letter: yes, $1 minimum plus copies
8. No
9. No
10. No
11. No
12. No
13. N/AN
14. Yes
15. OCLC: OMP
Books & Sets: 2(incomplete), 3(3 v., 1981),4,8,12,26
Periodicals: 4(1973–)

MARYSVILLE

Marysville Public Library
231 S Court St, 43040-1596
Tel: 513-642-1876

1. M-F, 10-8; Sa, 10-5; 1st Su of month (Sept-May), 1-5
2. None

3. English, all
4. 50
5. 300
6. Union County and surrounding counties; some PA, KY, CT, MD, VA
7. Tel & letter: yes, NC
8. No
9. No
10. No
11. No
12. No
13. N/AN
14. No
15. No

McCOMB

McComb Public Library
213 S Todd St, 45858
Tel: 419-293-2425

1. M-Th, 10-8; F,Sa, 10-5; shorter hours in summer
2. N/AN
3. English, 79, plus 26 booklets
4. 16
5. 40
6. Hancock County and surrounding counties
7. Tel & letter: yes, NC for brief queries except for copies
8. No
9. No
10. No
11. No
12. No
13. N/AN
14. No
15. No

MIDDLETOWN

Middletown Public Library
125 S Broad St, 45044
Tel: 513-424-1251

1. M-F, 9-8:30; Sa, 9-4
2. Patricia Brewer, Reference Librarian
3. English, 2,000
4. 50 individual works

5. 1,000: primarily local newspapers, Butler County census records
6. OH state; KY, WV, New England states, NJ, PA, MD, DE, VA
7. Tel & letter: yes, NC for brief queries except 50¢/copy with $2 minimum
8. No
9. No
10. No
11. No
12. No
13. "Selected Sources for Genealogical Research: A Brief Tour of the Genealogy and Ohio History Room–Middletown Public Library," brochure
14. Yes
15. OCLC: OMI
Books & Sets: 1–4,7,10–14,26
Periodicals: 4(last 5 yrs),7,8(v.26–, 1938–),9(v.1–106, 1847–1952)

MOUNT VERNON

Public Library of Mount Vernon and Knox County
201 N Mulberry St, 43050
Tel: 614-392-8671

1. M-F, 10-9; Sa, 10-6
2. Included in Reference Dept
3. English, 200
4. None
5. 300
6. Knox County, OH state
7. Tel & letter: yes, NC for brief queries except 15¢/copy
8. No
9. No
10. No
11. No
12. No
13. N/AN
14. Yes
15. No

NEWARK

Licking County Genealogical Society Library, 743 E Main St, 43055
Tel: 614-345-3571

1. T-Th, Sa, 1-4
2. Betty Rose, Librarian
3. English, 3,000; German, 2; French, 3
4. 200
5. 300
6. OH counties of Licking, Perry, Muskingum, Delaware, Knox, Franklin, Coshocton, Fairfield; all other OH counties
7. Tel: no; letter: yes, $10 donation
8. Ronna Eagle
   Polly Barcus
   Betty Rose
   Dilcie Pound
   Nancy Ciroli
   Vera Close
9. No
10. No
11. No
12. No
13. N/AN
14. Yes
15. N/AN
Books & Sets: 2(partial),3,5
Periodicals: 4(partial),5,8(partial)

NEW LONDON

New London Public Library
67 S Main St, 44851
Tel: 419-929-3981

1. M, 9-5; T,Th, 9-5, 7-8:30; W,F, 9-5; Sa, 10-5
2. Melissa Karnosh
3. English, 200
4. None
5. 55
6. City of New London, New London and Fitchville Townships; Huron, Lorain, and Ashland Counties
7. Tel & letter: yes, $2 for up to 10 copies
8. No
9. No
10. No
11. No
12. No
13. Index to *New London Record*, 1873–
14. No
15. No

NILES

McKinley Memorial Library
40 N Main St, 44446
Tel: 216-652-1704

1. M-Th, 9-8; F, 9-5:30; Sa, 9-4; special summer hours
2. None
3. English, 150
4. None
5. None
6. Niles, with Trumbull and Mahoning Counties; Western Reserve
7. Tel & letter: yes, NC
8. No
9. No
10. Yes, 2-week loan
11. No
12. No
13. Card catalog
14. No
15. OCLC: MML

NORWALK

Firelands Historical Society
4 Case Ave, 44857
Tel: 419-668-6038

1. Daily 9-6 (varies seasonally); closed Dec-Mar except by appointment
2. Henry R. Timman
3. English, 2,000
4. 4 ft
5. 50
6. Firelands area: Huron, Erie Counties, OH; OH state; MA, CT, NH, VT, NY, NJ, PA, MD, VA, KY
7. Tel: no; letter: yes, NC except 25¢/copy. Refer to local genealogist
8. No
9. Yes, $1/day
10. No
11. No
12. No
13. Out of print
14. Yes
15. No

OTTAWA

Putnam County District Library
525 N Thomas St, 45875
Tel: 419-523-3747

1. M-Th, 9-8; F,Sa, 9-5
2. Marguerite Calvin
3. English, 450
4. 12
5. 180
6. Putnam County, northwestern OH; PA
7. Tel & letter: yes, NC for index search
8. No
9. No
10. No
11. No
12. In progress
13. Indexes to Putnam County first families, doctors
14. Yes
15. No
Books & Sets: 2(OH, 3 v.),7(PA, OH, 2 v.)
Periodicals: 4(1972–)

OXFORD

Smith Library of Regional History, Lane Public Library
15 S College Ave, 45056
Tel: 513-523-3035

1. M-F, 10-12, 2-5
2. Irene M. Lindsey
3. English, 1,000
4. N/AP
5. 159
6. Southwestern OH; southeastern IN
7. Tel: yes, NC; letter: yes, NC except for copies plus postage
8. No
9. No
10. No
11. No
12. No
13. *List of Resources for Butler County, Ohio, and Surrounding Counties*
14. Yes
15. No

Books & Sets: 3(3 v. 1981, 1982–85 suppls),13,14,26(11 v.)

PAINESVILLE

Morley Library
184 Phelps St, 44077
Tel: 216-352-3383, ext 04

1. M-Th, 9-9; F, 9-6; Sa, 9-5
2. Sara Payne
3. English, 2,200; other, 10
4. 20
5. 265: includes Painesville *Telegraph*
6. Lake and Geauga Counties, OH; OH state
7. Tel: yes, NC for brief queries; letter: yes, NC except for copies
8. No
9. No
10. No
11. No
12. No
13. Index to obituaries in Painesville *Telegraph*, 1822–1986
14. Yes
15. OCLC: MRP (partial)
Books & Sets: 2,3,5,19,26
Periodicals: 4(v.30–, 1974–), 5(1976– 85),7,8(1942–84), 9(1955,1971–83)

PEMBERVILLE

Pemberville Public Library
375 E Front St, 43450
Tel: 419-287-4012

1. M,T, 9-8; W, 9-5; Th, 12-8; F, 12-5
2. Laura Zepernick King
3. English, 200
4. 220, includes periodicals, newspapers
5. 44
6. Wood County, other scattered OH counties; OH state
7. Tel & letter: yes, NC except for copies
8. Laura Zepernick King, CGRS, CGL
9. No

10. Yes, some nonreference books on 3-day loan
11. No
12. No
13. N/AN
14. Yes
15. No
Periodicals: 4(1977–)

PERRYSBURG

Willard V. Way Public Library
101 E Indiana, 43551
Tel: 419-874-3135

1. M-Th, 9-8:30; F,Sa, 9-5:30
2. Barbara K. Roberson
3. English, under 1,000
4. Indeterminate
5. 50
6. Perrysburg area of northwestern OH
7. Tel & letter: yes, $10/hr and 15¢/copy plus postage
8. No
9. No
10. No
11. No
12. *Genealogical Resources Guide, Northwest Ohio Libraries* (1983), compiled by Northwest Library District (NORWELD), Bowling Green, OH
13. N/AN
14. No
15. No

PIQUA

Flesh Public Library
124 W Greene St, 45356
Tel: 513-773-6753

1. M-Th, 9-8:30; F,Sa, 9-5:30
2. James C. Oda
3. English, 3,500
4. 20
5. 300
6. OH, PA, NY, VA
7. Tel & letter: yes, NC
8. N/AN
9. No
10. No
11. No

12. No
13. Card catalog; typed MS collection inventories
14. No
15. No
Books & Sets: 2,7

PORT CLINTON

Ida Rupp Public Library
310 Madison St, 43452
Tel: 419-732-3212

1. M-Th, 10-8:30; F,Sa, 10-5:30; summer: Sa closes at 1:30
2. N/AP
3. English, 292
4. 15
5. Ottawa County Census, 1850–1910; 67 reels of local newspapers
6. OH (Ottawa, Sandusky, Erie Counties)
7. Tel: no; letter: yes, NC for brief queries
8. No
9. No
10. No
11. No
12. No
13. None
14. No
15. No

RAVENNA

Reed Memorial Library
167 E Main St, 44266
Tel: 216-296-2827

1. M-F, 10-9; Sa, 10-6
2. None
3. English, 200
4. 1
5. None
6. Primarily Portage County
7. Tel & letter: yes, NC except 10¢/copy
8. No
9. No
10. No
11. N/AP
12. Update in progress

13. N/AN
14. Yes
15. No
Books & Sets: 2

SALEM

Salem Public Library
821 E State St, 44460
Tel: 216-332-0042

1. M-Th, 10-9; F,Sa, 10-6
2. None
3. English, LH, 50
4. LH: 50
5. LH: 400. Local newspapers on microfilm
6. Salem; Columbiana County
7. Tel: no; letter: yes, postage, for brief queries
8. No
9. No
10. No
11. No
12. No
13. None
14. No
15. No
Books & Sets: 7

SANDUSKY

Sandusky Library
114 W Adams St, 44870
Tel: 419-625-3834

1. M-Th, 9-8:30; F,Sa, 9-5; Su (Oct-Apr), 12-5
2. Molly Carver, Head of Media and Special Services
3. English, 1,500
4. None
5. N/AN
6. OH state; PA, NY, New England, KY, TN, VA, MD; Germany, England
7. Tel: yes, NC; letter: yes, NC except for copies
8. No
9. No
10. No
11. No
12. No
13. N/AN

14. Yes
15. N/AN
Books & Sets: 2,3,5,7(v.4,5),10,11,
26(CT,MD,ME,NY,MA,NC,PA)
Periodicals: 4(1977–),5(1978),
8(1967–70,1983–),9

SIDNEY

Amos Memorial Public Library
230 E North St, 45365
Tel: 513-492-8354

1. Winter: M-Th, 10-9; F,Sa,
10-6; summer: M-Th, 10-9; F, 10-6
2. Bonnie Banks
3. English, 2,670; German, 4
4. 140
5. 1,280
6. Extensive Shelby County,
OH, and bordering southern states;
VA, WV
7. Tel & letter: yes, NC for
brief queries except for copies
8. No
9. No
10. No
11. No
12. No
13. "Amos Memorial Public
Library - Genealogy Collection,"
pamphlet
14. No. Refer to Shelby County
Genealogy Society
15. OCLC: SIDG (since 1983)
Books & Sets: 2–5,7,10
Periodicals: 4

SPRINGFIELD

Warder Libraries
137 E High St, PO Box 1080,
45501-1080
Tel: 513-323-8616

1. M-F, 9-9; Sa, 9-6; Su, 1-5
2. Carol Maiorano, Reference
Supervisor
3. English, 186 linear ft
4. N/AN
5. 45
6. Clark County, OH
7. Tel & letter: yes, NC for
brief queries

8. No
9. No
10. No
11. No
12. No
13. Springfield Index
14. Yes
15. No
Books & Sets: 1(1st ed),2(incomplete),3,7(v.4,5),18,19,26
Periodicals: 4,5,7

STEUBENVILLE

**Public Library of Steubenville
and Jefferson County, Schiappa
Memorial Branch Library**
4141 Mall Dr, 43952
Tel: 614-264-6166

1. M-F, 9-9; Sa, 9-5; Su, 1-5
2. Judy Dobzynski
3. English, 800
4. None
5. 700
6. Jefferson County, OH
7. Tel: no; letter: yes, NC
except 10¢/copy
8. No. Refer to Jefferson
County Genealogical Society
9. No
10. No
11. Yes, to other libraries for
in-house use
12. No
13. N/AN
14. No
15. No
Books & Sets: 26

TIFFIN

Tiffin-Seneca Public Library
77 Jefferson St, 44883
Tel: 419-447-3751

1. M-Th, 10-9; F,Sa, 10-5:30
2. Jane B. Wickham
3. English, 700
4. Included in #3
5. 15
6. Seneca County, OH; some
Fairfield, Stark, other OH counties;
some PA, NY

7. Tel: yes, NC except 15¢/
copy, 20¢/microfilm print; letter:
yes, $6/hr plus copy charges
8. No
9. No
10. No, except for some county
histories; 2-week loan through ILL
11. No
12. No
13. *The Genealogy and Local
History Collection, Discover Your
Roots,* brochure
14. Yes
15. N/AN
Books & Sets: 2(few)
Periodicals: 4,5(1976,1978),
8,9(1975–80)

TOLEDO

**Toledo-Lucas County Public
Library, Local History and
Genealogy Department**
325 Michigan St, 43624-1614
Tel: 419-255-7055, ext 233

1. M-Th, 9-9; F,Sa, 9-5:30
2. James C. Marshall
3. English, 12,000+
4. 100+
5. 11,500+
6. OH; neighboring states;
original 13 states; Ontario, Canada
7. Tel & letter: yes, NC for
Lucas County residents only. Out-
of-county residents charged $10/hr
plus 15¢/copy
8. No
9. No
10. No
11. No
12. N/AN
13. N/AN
14. Yes
15. OCLC: TLM
Books & Sets: 2–5,7,10–12,
17,19,24,25
Periodicals: 1,3,4,7–9

TROY

**Troy Historical Society, Local
History and Genealogy Library**
301 W Main St, 45373
Tel: 513-339-0457

1. T,W, 10-4, 7-9; Th-Sa, 10-4; Su, 1-4
2. Genia Fraula
3. English, 3,094
4. 1,458
5. 356
6. Miami County; eastern US; PA, VA, NJ
7. Tel: yes, NC; letter: yes, NC (donation accepted)
8. Virginia Boese
9. No
10. No
11. No
12. No
13. N/AN
14. Yes
15. No
Books & Sets: 3,5,7,17

WARREN

Warren-Trumbull County Public Library, Ohioana Room
444 Mahoning Ave NW, 44483
Tel: 216-399-8807

1. W, 9-9; Th, 1-5
2. Pamela R. Daubenspeck
3. English, 2,500
4. None
5. 25: census; 800: local newspapers; 60: court records
6. Warren, OH; Trumbull County, OH; Western Reserve
7. Tel & letter: yes, NC for brief queries
8. No
9. No
10. No
11. No
12. No
13. *Ohioana Room (Guide to Resources)*
14. Yes
15. OCLC: WPL (partially)
Books & Sets: 3,7(v.4-5; OH only),10,11(1972–76),12,26
Periodicals: 4(v.3–38, 1949–84), 7,8(v.19–72, 1925–84; broken set)

WEST ALEXANDRIA

West Alexandria Archive
6 N Main St, 45381
Tel: None

1. M,W, 2-4; and by appointment
2. Audrey Gilbert
3. English, all
4. All
5. 50
6. Primarily Preble County; some Darke, Montgomery, and Butler Counties
7. Tel: no; letter: yes, donations accepted, charge for copies and postage
8. Audrey Gilbert
9. No
10. No
11. No
12. No
13. N/AN
14. No
15. No

WESTLAKE

Porter Public Library
27333 Center Ridge Rd, 44145
Tel: 216-871-2600

1. M-Th, 9-9; F,Sa, 9-5
2. Deborah Root
3. English, 63
4. 20
5. N/AN
6. Westlake (Dover, Dover Township); Cuyahoga County; Cleveland
7. Tel & letter: yes, NC, except for copies
8. Deborah Root
9. No
10. Yes, books designated as circulating
11. No
12. No
13. Bibliography of genealogical materials available
14. Yes

15. OCLC: yes
Books & Sets: 3
Periodicals: 4,9

WILLARD

Willard Memorial Library
6 W Emerald St, 44890
Tel: 419-933-8564

1. M-Th, 10-8:30; F,Sa, 10-5
2. N/AN
3. English, LH, 50
4. LH: 15
5. Local newspaper, 1883–1981
6. Huron County
7. Tel: no; letter: yes, NC except 15¢/copy and postage
8. No
9. No
10. No
11. No
12. No
13. N/AV
14. No
15. No
Books & Sets: 3(3 v., 1981)

WILMINGTON

Wilmington Public Library of Clinton County
268 N South St, 45177
Tel: 513-382-2417

1. M-Th, 12-8; F,Sa, 10-5
2. N/AP
3. English, 540
4. N/AN
5. 292
6. OH, especially Clinton, Highland, and Brown Counties, and city of Wilmington
7. Tel & letter: yes, NC for brief queries. For research, refer to Clinton County Historical Society
8. No
9. No
10. Yes, 2-week loan
11. No
12. No

13. Indexes to US Census, Clinton County, for 1870, 1880, 1900, 1910
14. Yes
15. No

WOOSTER

Wayne County Public Library
304 N Market St, 44691
Tel: 216-262-0916

1. M-F, 9-9; Sa, 9-6; Su, 1-5 during school year with Genealogy Dept closed
2. Alice Finley, Head, Adult Services
3. English, 1,025; other, 300
4. Approx 300 family histories; vertical files; approx 76 loose-leaf notebooks containing newspaper clippings on township histories
5. 317
6. OH, PA; some CT, MD, NJ, NY, VA, NC, SC, DE
7. Tel: yes, NC; letter: yes, NC except 20¢/photocopy, 25¢/microfilm photocopy
8. Bonnie S. Wipert
9. No
10. Rarely
11. No
12. No
13. N/AN
14. N/AN
15. OCLC: WCP (partly; post-1981 acquisitions)
Books & Sets: 2,3,7(v.2)
Periodicals: 4(1980–),8

WORTHINGTON

Worthington Historical Society Library
50 W New England Ave, 43085
Tel: 614-885-1247

1. W, 10-3, or by appointment
2. Lillian Skeele, Librarian
3. English, 225
4. 4-drawer file of clippings

5. None
6. Worthington, Franklin County, some surrounding counties; New England areas of migration to OH
7. Tel: yes, NC; letter: yes, NC except for copies
8. Yes
9. No
10. N/AP
11. No
12. No
13. N/AN
14. Yes
15. No

XENIA

Greene County District Library, Greene County Room
76 E Market St, 45385
Tel: 513-376-4952

1. M-Th, 9-9; F,Sa, 9-5
2. Julie M. Overton
3. English, 2,500; German, 5; French, 2
4. 15
5. 1,500
6. Greene County, OH; southwestern OH; OH state; basic out-of-state and European information (indexes, gazetteers), immigration materials
7. Tel & letter: yes, NC for brief queries
8. Julie M. Overton
9. No
10. No
11. No
12. No
13. Handouts: *Welcome, Greene County District Library; Tips for New Patrons; Dating a Structure; Black History Resources; Draper Manuscripts*
14. Yes
15. OCLC: GRC
Books & Sets: 2(v.1–52),3–5, 7,8(US, Canada),10–12,22,23,26
Periodicals: 4(1952–),8,9(1972–)

YOUNGSTOWN

Public Library of Youngstown and Mahoning County
Reference Department,
305 Wick Ave, 44503
Tel: 216-744-8636, ext 51

1. M,T, 9-8; W-Sa, 9-5:30; closed Sa in summer
2. Diane Vicarel, Regional Supervisor
3. English, 4,500
4. Collection temporarily inaccessible
5. Collection temporarily inaccessible
6. OH, with emphasis on northeast OH; PA, western MD, New England
7. Tel: no; letter: yes, NC for brief queries
8. No
9. No
10. No
11. No
12. No
13. Henry R. Baldwin Notebooks: 8-vol annotated index
14. Yes
15. OCLC: YMM
Books & Sets: 2–7,10–14,18, 19,23,26
Periodicals: 1(v.21–27, 1945–51), 3(v.2–14 [incomplete], 1939–50), 4(v.9–15,27–32,35–, 1955–61, 1973–78,1981–),5(v.13–, 1974–), 7,8(v.32–, 1944–),9

ZANESVILLE

John McIntire Public Library
220 N Fifth St, 43701
Tel: 614-453-0391

1. M-Th, 9-8; F,Sa, 9-5:30; Su (winter), 1-5
2. Head of Reference
3. English, 1,000
4. N/AN
5. 250, plus local newspapers, 1964–

6. Muskingum County, OH; also Perry, Guernsey, Morgan, and Washington Counties

7. Tel: yes, NC; letter: yes, NC except 10¢/copy with $1 minimum

8. No

9. No

10. No

11. No

12. No

13. Cemeteries listed by township

14. Yes

15. N/AN

Books & Sets: 18,26(OH)

Periodicals: 1(1983–),4(1983–)

Muskingum County Genealogical Library, Herrold Hall, Zanesville Campus Library, Ohio University, 1425 Newark Rd, 43701

Tel: 614-453-0762, ext 45

1. M-Th, 9-9; F, 9-5; Sa, 11-5

2. Ione B. Supplee

3. English, 2,000; German, 3; French, some

4. 500

5. 400

6. Muskingum County and other OH counties; some PA, VA, other US; some Canada, England, Ireland, Scotland

7. Tel: yes, NC; letter: yes, $6 to check 3 resources per surname

8. No

9. No

10. No

11. No

12. Yes

13. N/AN

14. Yes

15. N/AN

Books & Sets: 2–5,7(v.5),8

Periodicals: 4(1987),8(some)

OKLAHOMA

ALVA

Alva Public Library
504 Seventh St, 73717
Tel: 405-327-1833

1. M, 10-9; T-Sa, 10-5
2. Larry R. Thorne, Librarian
3. English, 600
4. 10
5. 243
6. General areas
7. Tel & letter: yes, NC except $3 fee for photocopying
8. No
9. No
10. No
11. No
12. Update in progress
13. None
14. Yes
15. No
Books & Sets: 7(v.3,5)
Periodicals: 4(1984–),8(1962–), 9(1986–)

BARTLESVILLE

Bartlesville Public Library, Bartlesville Area History Museum and Archives, Genealogy Room
6th & Johnstone, 74003
Tel: 918-337-5217 (History Museum); 337-5211 (Genealogy Room)

1. History Museum: winter: M-Th, 9-6; F, 9-5; Sa, 9-4; summer: M-F, 9-6; Genealogy Room: M-Th, 9-9; F, 9-6; Sa, 9-4
2. HM: Susan C. Box, Curator. GR: N/AN
3. HM: English, 2,200. GR: English, 1,000+
4. HM: 4 (Griggs, Sark, Weslager, Farrar). GR: N/AN
5. HM: 1,200 reels of local newspapers, funeral home records, city directories; 1900, 1910 census for IN, TN, OK; Cherokee Indians. GR: 53
6. HM: Bartlesville, Washington County, OK state; Delaware and Cherokee Indian research materials. GR: all states
7. HM: tel & letter: yes, NC except 10¢/Xerox and 50¢/ microfilm. GR: tel & letter: no
8. No
9. No
10. No
11. No
12. No
13. HM: obituary index (60,000+ names); genealogies of local pioneers, Delaware and Cherokee Indians; biography files; vertical files of area and state; Griggs Collection of photos of area. GR: card catalog
14. No
15. No
Books & Sets: 3,5,7(v.1,3,4), 26(also complete 1850 index)
Periodicals: 4,8(v.52–74, 1964– 86),9(incomplete)

CHEROKEE

Cherokee City-County Library
602 S Grand Ave, 73728
Tel: 405-596-2366

1. M-F, 1-6; Sa, 9-12
2. Mary Berry
3. English, G, 250
4. LH: 2
5. None
6. Alfalfa County
7. Tel & letter: yes, NC
8. No
9. No
10. No
11. N/AP
12. No
13. N/AN
14. No
15. N/AN

ENID

Public Library of Enid and Garfield County, 120 W Maine, PO Box 8002, 73702-8002
Tel: 405-234-6313

1. M-Th, 9-9; F,Sa, 9-6
2. Betty Irene Smith
3. N/AN
4. Marquis James Collection
5. 166
6. Enid, Garfield County, OK state, US
7. Tel: yes, NC; letter: yes, NC except 10¢/copy plus postage over $1
8. No. Refer to Genealogy Society
9. No
10. No
11. No
12. No
13. *Books in the Enid Public Library as of December 1, 1982*
14. No
15. OCLC: some
Books & Sets: 1,2(v.34–56), 7(v.1),10,11
Periodicals: 4(v.15–35, 1961–85), 5(v.15, 1976)

McALESTER

McAlester Public Library
401 N Second St, 74501
Tel: 918-426-0930

1. M,T,Th, 9-8; W,F, 9-5; Sa, 9-1
2. N/AP

3. English, 400
4. 15
5. 250
6. Pittsburg County, OK
7. Tel: no; letter: yes, NC except 25¢/copy
8. N/AN
9. No
10. No
11. Yes, through ILL, 1-month loan
12. No
13. Card catalog
14. No
15. N/AN
Books & Sets: 1,3,8,16
Periodicals: 4

MUSKOGEE

Muskogee Public Library
801 W Okmulgee, 74401
Tel: 918-682-6657

1. M-Th, 9-9; F, 9-6; Sa, 9-4
2. Karen Thomas
3. English, 2,800; Cherokee, few
4. 75
5. 255
6. OK; scattered holdings from other states
7. Tel: yes, NC; letter: yes, NC except for copies and handling
8. No
9. No
10. No
11. No
12. No
13. Typed list
14. Yes; volunteers
15. OCLC: OEA (partially)
Books & Sets: 2,3,10–12,26
Periodicals: 4(1979–),5(v.16–24), 7(rev ed),8(1968, 1971, 1980–84), 9(1970–72)

OKLAHOMA CITY

Metropolitan Library System, Downtown Branch
131 Dean A. McGee Ave, 73102
Tel: 405-235-0571

1. M,W,Th, 9-6; T, 9-9; F, Sa, 9-5
2. Saundra Shuler
3. English, 10,000; German, 5
4. 100
5. 200 microcards
6. OK state; northeastern US
7. Tel & letter: yes, NC for brief queries except for copies, plus $1 service charge
8. Yes
9. No
10. G: yes, 30-day loan, through ILL; LH: no, not Oklahoma Collection
11. No
12. No
13. Card catalog
14. Yes
15. OCLC: OKE
Books & Sets: 1–3,6,10,11, 18,19,26
Periodicals: 4(1962–),9(1847–1974)

Oklahoma Historical Society
Library Resources Division,
2100 N Lincoln Blvd, 73105
Tel: 405-521-2491

1. M, 8-8; T-Sa, 8-5
2. Carolyn Grangaard Smith, Library Director
3. English, 48,000+ total. Entire collection is historical
4. 35
5. 15,000
6. OK, trans-Mississippi West primarily; some Old Northwest, immigration routes into OK (AR, KY, TN, VA, NC, SC)
7. Tel & letter: yes, NC for brief queries except 10¢/photocopy, 25¢/sheet microfilm copy plus $1.50 postage
8. No
9. No
10. No
11. No
12. No
13. Biographical Index File; Selected Bibliographies; OK Cemetery Index
14. Yes

15. OCLC: OUY (post-1985)
Books & Sets: 2,3(no suppl),5–7, 10,16(microfilm),17,18,26
Periodicals: 1(v.41–56),3(v.4–, 1941–),4(v.5–),5,7–9

PONCA CITY

Ponca City Library, Genealogy Department
515 E Grand Ave, 74601
Tel: 405-762-6311

1. M-Th, 9-9; F,Sa, 9-5
2. Roseanna Ratliff
3. English, 1,600; German, 4
4. 200
5. 175, plus 94 years of local newspapers; also, newspapers ca. 1900–20 of nearby communities
6. Great Britain (Doomsday Books); Ireland; Germany
7. Tel & letter: yes, NC for brief queries
8. Roseanna Ratliff
9. No
10. No
11. No
12. Brochure, no charge
13. Forthcoming
14. Yes
15. OCLC: PCL
Books & Sets: 2,3,7,26
Periodicals: 4,8(1970–), 9(1964–83)

STILLWATER

Stillwater Public Library
206 W Sixth Ave, 74074
Tel: 405-372-3633

1. M-Th, 9-9; F,Sa, 9-6; Su, 1-5
2. N/AN
3. English, 715
4. N/AN
5. 317
6. Primarily US, with emphasis on southern region
7. Tel: no; letter: yes, refer to local genealogical society
8. No
9. No

10. No
11. No
12. No
13. N/AN
14. Yes
15. OCLC: STW
Books & Sets: 3(3 v., 1981),5(v.1–4),7(v.1,3,6),9–14,26
Periodicals: 4(1971–82 incomplete, 1983–)

TULSA

Tulsa City-County Library System, Rudisill North Regional Library
1520 N Hartford, 74106
Tel: 918-462-7624

1. M-Th, 9-9; F,Sa, 9-5; Su (Oct-Apr), 1-5
2. Marion Edwards
3. English, 3,000
4. None
5. 700
6. OK state; US, especially southern states
7. Tel: no; letter: yes, NC except 10¢/copy
8. Marion Edwards
9. No
10. No
11. No

12. No
13. Genealogy collection card catalog
14. Yes
15. OCLC: TUL
Books & Sets: 2–5,7,10,11,19,23,26
Periodicals: 1(v.9–14,42–46),4(v.1–6,9–),5(1977–),7,8(v.16–25,36,39–55,59–61,70–),9(v.73–75,77,79,82,92–126,133–35)

OREGON

ALBANY

Albany Public Library
1390 Waverly Dr SE, 97321
Tel: 503-967-4304

1. M-F, 12-9; Sa, 10-5
2. Edward House
3. English, 400
4. None
5. 44: census; 18: death records; 350: Linn County and Albany newspapers, 1859–
6. OR, especially Linn County; state censuses and genealogies for VA, other US
7. Tel & letter: no
8. No
9. No
10. No
11. No
12. No
13. N/AN
14. Yes
15. OCLC: ABY
Books & Sets: 2(partial)
Periodicals: 4

CORVALLIS

Corvallis Public Library
645 NW Monroe Ave, 97330
Tel: 503-757-6928

1. M-W, 10-9; Th-Sa, 10-5:30
2. None
3. English, 150+
4. 15
5. None
6. Benton County
7. Tel & letter: no
8. No
9. No
10. No
11. No
12. No

13. N/AN
14. No
15. No

COTTAGE GROVE

Cottage Grove Genealogical Society Library
PO Box 388, 207 N H St, 97424
Tel: None

1. W-Sa, 1-4
2. Gene Savage
3. English, 2,000; German, 2
4. 50
5. 48
6. US; Canada; Europe
7. Tel: N/AN; letter: yes, $5/hr
8. Frances Quinn
9. No
10. Yes, to local members only
11. No
12. No
13. N/AN
14. No
15. N/AN
Periodicals: 4,8

KLAMATH FALLS

Klamath County Library
126 S Third St, 97601
Tel: 503-882-8894

1. M, 11:30-8; T-Sa, 9:30-6 (closed Sa summers)
2. N/AP
3. English, LH, 70, G, 700
4. Minimal. Klamath County Museum Library holds some MSS
5. 520, including 430 of local newspaper
6. Klamath County; US, with emphasis on indexes, particularly for original 13 colonies
7. Tel: no; letter: yes, $3

minimum/search fee plus $1 minimum/copies, thereafter, 10¢/copy
8. No
9. No
10. Yes, sources are loaned, with discretion, to OR libraries; no renewal and in-library use only
11. Yes, within OR
12. No
13. Alan Clark Miller, *Local History for Genealogists: A Selected Bibliography of Materials in the Oregon Collection of the Klamath County Library*
14. Yes
15. OCLC: KCL
Books & Sets: 3(1982–84 suppls; 1982–85 cumulative suppls),7, 10–14,26
Periodicals: 4(partial),5(v.8, 1969), 7,9(partial)

LA GRANDE

Eastern Oregon State College, Walter M. Pierce Library
8th & K, 97850
Tel: 503-963-1540

1. M-Th, 7:30am-11pm; F, 7:30-5; Sa, 1-5; Su, 5pm-11pm; vacation periods, M-F, 7:30-5
2. Douglas Oleson, Director
3. Genealogy, 1,000; Northwest history, includes local, 3,000
4. 5
5. 4,800
6. Local; northeastern and eastern OR, OR state; Pacific Northwest; some census material for entire US (1790–1800), Midwest (1850)
7. Tel & letter: yes, usually $1–$5
8. John W. Evans
9. No

10. Yes, some titles circulate, through ILL only
11. No, not usually; if so, through ILL only
12. Yes
13. Card catalog
14. Yes
15. OCLC: EOS-OR
Books & Sets: 1,3,4–7,10–14, 19,26
Periodicals: 4(scattered)

LEBANON

Lebanon Public Library
626 Second St, 97355
Tel: 503-451-7461

1. M,F,Sa, 10-5; T-Th, 10-8
2. Roy Wilson, Volunteer
3. English, 1,000+
4. 1,000+
5. 19
6. Entire US
7. Tel & letter: yes, NC
8. No
9. No
10. No
11. No
12. No
13. None
14. Yes
15. No
Periodicals: 3(broken set),4(1961–),8(later vols)

OREGON CITY

Oregon City Public Library
606 John Adams, 97045
Tel: 503-657-8269

1. M-Th, 10-8; F,Sa, 10-5; Su (Oct-May), 1-5
2. Judy Bieber
3. English, 500
4. None
5. 218 newspaper reels; federal census for Oregon, 1850–1910; 12 death reels
6. Primarily Clackamas County, OR
7. Tel & letter: yes, $7.50/hr plus copies and postage
8. Judy Bieber

9. No
10. No
11. Yes, microfilmed newspapers only; 3-week loan
12. *A Guide to Genealogical Materials in the Oregon City Public Library* (1986), $1
13. N/AN
14. No
15. No
Books & Sets: 2(v.45–54),3(3v., 1981, 1982–84),11
Periodicals: 4(1980–)

PORTLAND

Genealogical Forum of Oregon
1410 SW Morrison St, 97080
Tel: 503-227-2398

1. M-W,F,Sa, 9:30-3; Th, 9:30-8
2. Mary Lou Stroup, Librarian
3. English, 10,000; German, 40; other, 3 or 4
4. No estimate
5. 126: census; 6: genealogies
6. Entire US, with emphasis on OR; some England, Scotland, Ireland
7. Tel: yes, NC (minimal); letter: yes, charge for search
8. Yes
9. Yes, $1/visit
10. Yes, but only to members
11. No
12. "Library Shelf List of the Genealogical Forum of Portland," $22; "A Guide to Genealogical Material in the Multnomah County Library, Portland," $8.25
13. Card file to lineage charts of members
14. Yes
15. N/AN
Books & Sets: 2–5,7,9,12, 22–24,26
Periodicals: 1(1971–),3(1968–),4, 5(1968–75,1979–81),8(1971–), 9(1910–39,1942–)

Multnomah County Library (Library Association of Portland), 801 SW 10th Ave, 97205
Tel: 503-223-7201

1. M-Th, 10-9; F,Sa, 10-5:30; Su, 1-5
2. Barbara Kahl
3. English, N/AP
4. N/AP
5. 375
6. All areas, with emphasis on OR
7. Tel: no; letter: yes, NC for brief queries
8. No
9. No
10. Circulating books are routinely loaned; reference occasionally, through ILL
11. No
12. *Guide to Genealogical Material in the Multnomah County Library*, $8.25; available from the Genealogical Forum of Oregon
13. *Genealogy in the Multnomah County Library*, free brochure
14. No
15. No
Books & Sets: 1,3–6,8,10-14,17, 19,23,26
Periodicals: 1(v.23–, 1946–), 3(v.14–, 1950–),4(v.1–, 1947–), 5(v.1–6,8,13–, 1962–67,1969, 1974–),6(v.11–16, 1951–70),7, 8(v.30–, 1942–),9

Oregon Historical Society
1230 SW Park Ave, 97068
Tel: 503-222-1741

1. M-Sa, 10-4:45
2. Gordon Manning
3. English, 1,650
4. Over 1,000,000 pieces in MS Dept. Included are thousands relating to LH and biography on such topics as early exploration, fur trade, missionaries, overland migration, ethnic groups. Vertical file of newspaper clippings includes many state/LH subjects and 1,500 biographies and genealogies of prominent Oregonians
5. 10,000: mostly newspaper
6. Pacific Northwest
7. Tel: yes, NC for ready reference questions; letter: yes, $4/15 minutes

8. No
9. No
10. No
11. No
12. No
13. *Oregon Historical Society,* brochure; *Information from the Oregon Historical Society,* 3-page handout
14. Yes
15. OCLC: OHY (since 1984)
Books & Sets: 6,12,13
Periodicals: 4,8

SALEM

Oregon State Library
Court & Summer Sts, NE, 97310
Tel: 503-378-4276

1. M-F, 8-5
2. Craig Smith, Reference Supervisor
3. English, 6,000
4. N/AP
5. 1,250
6. OR, Pacific Northwest
7. Tel & letter: no
8. Addie Dyal (part-time)
9. No
10. Yes, through ILL
11. Yes, through ILL
12. Oregon State Library catalog on microfiche, $55. Lists

all monograph holdings acquired from 1966 to present
13. N/AN
14. Yes
15. OCLC: OSO
Books & Sets: 1,2(v.43–54),3–7, 10–14,18,19,22–24,26
Periodicals: 1(v.33–61),4(v.4–), 5,7,8,9(v.1–69, microfilm)

SPRINGFIELD

Springfield Public Library
225 N 5th St, 97477
Tel: 503-726-3766

1. M-Th, 10-8; F,Sa, 10-5
2. Jenny Peterson, Reference Librarian
3. English, 100–150
4. None
5. None
6. OR, Northwest; general US; some foreign
7. Tel & letter: yes, for brief queries only
8. No
9. No
10. Circulating books, 28-day loan; no renewals
11. N/AP
12. No
13. None

14. No
15. OCLC: OXY (in process of converting)
Books & Sets: 3
Periodicals: 4(v.22–, 1968–)

TILLAMOOK

Tillamook County Pioneer Museum, Research Library
2106 2nd St, 97141
Tel: N/AN

1. M-Sa, 8:30-5; closed M Oct-May
2. N/AN
3. English, 250
4. Number unknown
5. 18: Tillamook County newspapers, 1895–1933
6. Cemetery records and family histories for Tillamook County
7. Tel: yes, NC; letter: yes, NC except for copies
8. N/AN
9. No
10. No
11. No
12. No
13. N/AN
14. No
15. N/AN

PENNSYLVANIA

ALTOONA

Altoona Area Public Library
1600 Fifth Ave, 16602
Tel: 814-946-0417

1. Winter: M,T,Th, 8:30am-
9pm; W,F, 8:30-5; Sa, 9-5; Su,
11-4; summer hours vary
2. Alberta Y. Haught, Reference Librarian
3. English, no count available
4. None
5. 20: PA census; 2: PA
county histories
6. Mainly Blair County, some
PA state
7. Tel & letter: yes, NC for
brief queries except $1/copy
8. No
9. No
10. No
11. No
12. No
13. N/AN
14. Yes
15. OCLC: AOP
Books & Sets: 2(v.46–54),10,26

BEAVER FALLS

**Carnegie Free Library, Resource
and Research Center for Beaver
County and Local History**
1301 Seventh Ave, 15010
Tel: 412-846-4340, ext 5

1. M, 5-8 pm; T-Th, 11-5; F,
11-4
2. Vivian C. McLaughlin,
Director
3. English, 2,500
4. N/AN
5. 200
6. Beaver County and sur-
rounding counties; PA state

7. Tel: yes, NC; letter: yes, NC
except for copies and postage
8. Vivian C. McLaughlin
Mark Welchley
9. No
10. No
11. No
12. No
13. N/AN
14. No
15. OCLC: yes
Books & Sets: 2,3,6

BELLEFONTE

**Centre County Library
and Historical Museum**
203 N Allegheny St, 16823
Tel: 814-355-1516

1. M-F, 9-5; Sa, 9-12
2. Gladys C. Murray
3. English, 2,850
4. 800
5. 75
6. PA; some New England, NJ,
MD
7. Tel & letter: yes, NC for
brief queries
8. Gladys C. Murray
9. No
10. Yes, will lend books that
can be replaced, to registered
library patrons
11. Yes, to registered library
patrons
12. No
13. *A Brief List of Published
and Unpublished Genealogical
Source Materials,* handout
14. No
15. OCLC: PCB
Books & Sets: 2,3,5,7(v.2–3),
10–12,19(Rietstap, 2v.),26
Periodicals: 4,7

BROOMALL

**Philadelphia Pennsylvania Stake
Branch Genealogical Library**
721 Paxon Hollow Rd, Box 284,
19008
Tel: 215-356-8507

1. T, 11-4; W,Th, 9:30-2:30,
7–10pm; Sa, 9:30-2:30
2. Pierre J. Koucurat
3. English, 620+
4. None
5. 300
6. International; library is a
branch of the Genealogical Library
of the Church of Jesus Christ of
Latter-day Saints in Salt Lake
City, UT
7. Tel & letter: yes, NC
8. Patricia Dorny
9. No
10. No
11. No
12. No
13. Patron Help Shelf
14. Yes
15. No
Books & Sets: 2,8,26
Periodicals: 1,4

CAMP HILL

West Shore Public Library
30 N 31st St, 17011
Tel: 717-761-3900

1. M-F, 9-9; Sa, 9-5; Su, 1-5
2. N/AN
3. N/AN
4. N/AN
5. N/AN
6. LH: Camp Hill, Cumberland
County, PA state
7. Tel & letter: N/AN

8. No
9. No
10. Yes, duplicates only
11. N/AN
12. N/AN
13. N/AN
14. N/AN
15. N/AN

CHAMBERSBURG

Coyle Free Library
102 N Main St, 17201
Tel: 717-263-1054

1. M-F, 9-8:30; Sa, 9-5
2. Eleanor B. Giltinan, Reference Librarian
3. English, 250
4. 50
5. 20
6. PA counties: Franklin, Fulton, Cumberland
7. Tel & letter: yes, NC
8. No
9. No
10. Yes, only duplicate, circulating copies
11. No
12. No
13. Card catalog, shelf list
14. Yes
15. OCLC: PCO
Books & Sets: 26 (PA)

Kittochtinny Historical Society
"Old Jail," 175 E King St, 17201
Tel: 717-264-1667

1. Winter (Dec-Apr): T, 12-8; W,Th, 12-4; summer (May-Aug): T, 5-8pm; W-Sa, 9:30-4; fall (Sept-Nov): T, 5–8pm; Th-Sa, 9:30-4
2. N/AN
3. English, 5,000; German, several Bibles
4. N/AN
5. 1,500
6. Franklin County, PA, and Cumberland Valley
7. Tel: no; letter: yes, NC
8. No
9. No
10. No

11. No
12. No
13. Kittochtinny Historical Society's 18 volumes
14. No
15. No
Books & Sets: 26

CHESTER

Delaware County Historical Society, 15th & Walnut Sts, 19013
Tel: 215-874-6444

1. M-F, 10-3; 1st Su, 1-5
2. Julia Colflesh
3. English, 6,000
4. 375
5. 550
6. Delaware County, PA
7. Tel & letter: yes, NC for brief queries
8. Julia Colflesh
9. Yes, $1
10. No
11. No
12. No
13. None
14. No
15. N/AN

DOYLESTOWN

Spruance Library, Bucks County Historical Society
Pine St, 18901
Tel: 215-345-0210

1. T, 1-9; W-Sa, 10-5
2. Terry A. McNealy, Librarian
3. English, 10,000
4. 350
5. 1,500
6. Bucks County, PA, and neighboring areas
7. Tel: no; letter: yes, NC, limited to 20-minute search
8. Terry A. McNealy
Frances W. Waite
9. Yes, $3 ($2.50, senior citizens; $1.50, students)
10. No

11. No
12. *Guide to the Manuscript Collections of Five Historical Organizations in Bucks County*, $15
13. Numerous indexes
14. Yes
15. No
Books & Sets: 2–4,6,7,26
Periodicals: 4(1948–, incomplete), 5(1962–65,1976–85),6(1969–),7, 8(1974–),9(1931–46,1970–)

EASTON

Easton Area Public Library
6th & Church Sts, 18042
Tel: 215-258-2917

1. History Room: Sept-June: M-F, 1-5; Sa, 9-12, 1-5
2. Barbara Bailey Bauer
3. English, 10,000; German, 10%
4. Not known
5. 1,325
6. Northampton County, northeastern PA; contiguous NJ counties; some western PA, OH
7. Tel & letter: yes, NC except for copies
8. No
9. No
10. No
11. No
12. In progress
13. Indexes to church, newspaper records
14. Yes
15. No
Books & Sets: 2,7,18,26
Periodicals: 1,4,9

Northampton County Historical and Genealogical Society, Mary Illick Memorial Library
101 S 4th St, 18042
Tel: 215-253-1222

1. Th,F, 9-4
2. Jane S. Moyer, Librarian
3. English, no estimate; German, 150+
4. G: 2,500 folders

5. None
6. Northampton, Lehigh, and Monroe Counties, PA; Warren County, NJ
7. Tel & letter: yes, $10/hr
8. Yes
9. Yes, $2/day to nonmembers and nonresidents
10. No
11. No
12. No
13. Vertical file; genealogical file
14. Yes
15. No
Books & Sets: 2,7,26
Periodicals: 1,4,9

EPHRATA

Historical Society of the Cocalico Valley, 249 W Main St, PO Box 193, 17522
Tel: 717-733-1616

1. T,W,F, 9-5; F (Apr 1-Oct 1), 9-5, 6:30-9
2. Cynthia Marquet, Librarian
3. English, 780; German, 45
4. 3,060; 6,000 photographs
5. 118
6. Lancaster County, PA: East and West Cocalico Townships; Ephrata and Clay Townships; West Earl and Earl Townships
7. Tel: yes, NC; letter: yes, donation suggested
8. Linda Spang (volunteer)
9. No
10. No
11. No
12. No
13. N/AN
14. No
15. No
Books & Sets: 3,26

ERIE

Erie County Library System
3 S Perry Square, 16501
Tel: 814-452-2333

1. M,T, 9-9; W,Th,F, 9-8; Sa, 9-5

2. Cindy Kerchoff
3. English, 4,233
4. None
5. 79
6. Erie County, PA; north-western PA; PA state
7. Tel: yes, NC; letter: yes, $1/copy with SASE
8. No
9. No
10. Yes, limited lending through ILL
11. Yes, limited lending through ILL
12. No
13. N/AN
14. No
15. OCLC: EPL
Books & Sets: 2,3,7(v.2, PA,NJ), 10,26
Periodicals: 1,3(1955–77), 8(1921–),9(1985–)

FRANKLIN

Franklin Public Library
421 12th St, 16323
Tel: 814-432-5062

1. M,T, 10-5
2. Helen Ray
3. English, 415
4. G: 62
5. 498
6. Venango County, PA state
7. Tel: yes, NC; letter: yes, donation
8. Helen Ray
9. Yes, donation
10. No
11. No
12. No
13. None
14. Yes
15. N/AN

HARRISBURG

State Library of Pennsylvania
Corner of Commonwealth Ave & Walnut St, Box 1601, 17105
Tel: 717-783-5991

1. M,W-F, 8:30-5; T, 8:30-8:30

2. Janice B. Newman
3. English, 10,000
4. N/AN
5. 6,000 microform (film & fiche)
6. Emphasis on PA
7. Tel & letter: yes, NC except for copies ($1 minimum)
8. No
9. No
10. No
11. Yes, some titles through ILL
12. No
13. *A Guide to the Genealogy/ Local History Section of the State Library of Pennsylvania*
14. Yes
15. OCLC: PHA
Books & Sets: 2–7,10–14,16–20, 22–24,26
Periodicals: 1(missing v.42, 1966), 3(v.2–4,13-28,30–),4(v.24–, 1970–),5,6(v.16–, 1970–),7–9

HAVERFORD

Haverford College Library, Quaker Collection, 19041-1392
Tel: 215-896-1161

1. Weekdays, 9-12:30, 1:30-4:30
2. Edwin B. Bronner, Curator
3. English, 325. Reference books, histories of monthly meetings
4. 500: Philadelphia Yearly Meetings; 1,500: Quaker Collection
5. 400
6. PA, NJ, DE, MD, VA
7. Tel: yes, NC for brief queries; letter: yes, NC, 30-minute limit
8. Eva Walker Myer
9. No
10. No
11. No
12. No
13. Typescript indexes to MS collections
14. Yes
15. OCLC: HVC (partial)

Books & Sets: 7,10,11,26
Periodicals: 8(v.74–)

JOHNSTOWN

**Cambria County Library
System,** 248 Main St, 15901
Tel: 814-536-5131

1. Winter: M-Th, 9-9; F,Sa, 9-5; Su, 2-5; summer: closed Sa,Su
2. Cathy Fitzpatrick
3. English, 300; German, 1
4. None
5. 140+
6. PA counties: Cambria, Blair, Somerset, Fulton, Westmoreland
7. Tel: no; letter: yes
8. Yes
9. No
10. No
11. No
12. *Cambria County Library Genealogy Holdings*, reference desk copy
13. N/AN
14. Yes
15. OCLC: JOC (partial)
Books & Sets: 3(no suppls)

LANCASTER

**Lancaster County Historical
Society,** 230 N President Ave, 17603
Tel: 717-392-4633

1. M-W,F,Sa, 9:30-4:30; Th, 9:30-9:30
2. Salinda Matt, Librarian
3. English, unknown; German, unknown
4. Unknown
5. 700 reels, 780 newspapers
6. Lancaster, surrounding counties
7. Tel: no; letter: yes, $2.50/ specific document requested
8. Debra Smith, Director
9. Yes, $3/day
10. No
11. No
12. No

13. N/AN
14. Yes
15. N/AN
Books & Sets: 2(few),3,5,7,26
Periodicals: 8

Lancaster County Library
125 N Duke St, 17602
Tel: 717-394-2651
1. M-Th, 9-9; F,Sa, 9-5:30
2. Gerald Bruce, Reference Librarian
3. English, 1,150; German, 1
4. N/AN
5. 3,000
6. Lancaster County, PA
7. Tel & letter: yes, NC
8. No
9. No
10. No
11. No
12. No
13. N/AN
14. Yes
15. OCLC: LKC
Books & Sets: 10,12,26
Periodicals: 4(v.36–, 1982–)

**Lancaster Mennonite Historical
Society,** 2215 Millstream Rd, 17602-1499
Tel: 717-393-9745

1. T-Sa, 8:30-4:30
2. Lloyd Zeager, Librarian
3. English, 3,640; German, less than 50
4. 25
5. 270 (mostly US federal census)
6. Lancaster County, other PA counties where Mennonites have lived, plus other areas in US and Canada where PA Mennonites migrated
7. Tel: yes, NC for brief queries; letter: yes, $10/hr for members, $15/hr for nonmembers
8. David J. R. Smucker
9. Yes, $2/day, nonmembers; no charge for members
10. No
11. No
12. No

13. *Genealogical Resources at the Lancaster Mennonite Historical Society*, handout
14. Yes
15. No
Books & Sets: 3,4,10–12, 26(PA,VA,MD)
Periodicals: 4(v.29–, 1975–), 5(v.15–, 1976–),8(v.1–65,69–, 1912–77, 1981–)

LEBANON

Lebanon Community Library
125 N 7th St, 17003
Tel: 717-273-7624

1. M-Th, 9-8; F,Sa, 9-5
2. Curtis Moore, Director
3. English, 150
4. N/AN
5. N/AN
6. Lebanon County
7. Tel & letter: yes, NC
8. No
9. No
10. Yes, 2 weeks to county patrons
11. N/AN
12. N/AN
13. In-house catalog, pamphlet file index
14. No
15. N/AN

**Lebanon County Historical
Society, Hauck Memorial
Library,** 924 Cumberland St, 17042
Tel: 717-272-1473

1. M,W,F,Su, 1-4:30
2. Christine L. Mason, Assistant Coordinator
3. English, 10,000; German, 200
4. 82
5. 1,500
6. Lebanon County; some Berks, Lancaster, and Dauphin Counties
7. Tel: no; letter: yes, $8/hr for members, $10/hr for nonmembers
8. No

9. Yes, $2/hr for nonmembers
10. No
11. No
12. *Guide to Genealogical Materials of the Hauck Memorial Library Housed in the Lebanon County Historical Society*, $5
13. Catalog file of Society publications; surname and vertical file catalog files
14. No
15. No
Books & Sets: 2,3,5,19,26
Periodicals: 4,6,9

LENHARTSVILLE

Pennsylvania Dutch Folk Culture Society, Baver Memorial Library, Main & Willow Sts, 19534
Tel: 215-562-4803

1. M-Sa, 10-5; Su, 1-5
2. Florence Baver
3. English, 2,000; German, 25
4. 200
5. 25: Berks County census, other
6. Berks County and neighboring counties; some PA state
7. Tel: N/AN; letter: yes, $5/hr
8. Yes
9. Yes, $2 to nonmembers
10. No
11. No
12. No
13. N/AN
14. No
15. N/AN

LOCK HAVEN

Annie Halenbake Ross Library
232 W Main St, 17745
Tel: 717-748-3321

1. M,T,Th, 9-9; W,F,Sa, 9-5
2. Audrey Miller-Bongar
3. English, 1,250
4. 150
5. 670
6. Clinton County, some Centre and Lycoming Counties; New England, NY, NJ

7. Tel: yes, for brief queries; letter: yes, $5/hr plus copies
8. Audrey Miller-Bongar
9. N/AN
10. Yes
11. No
12. No
13. N/AN
14. No
15. N/AN
Books & Sets: 2,26
Periodicals: 4

MONTROSE

Susquehanna County Historical Society and Free Library Association, Monument Sq, 18801
Tel: 717-278-1881

1. Historical Society: M-F, 9-12, 1-5; Library: M-F, 9-9; Sa, 9-3
2. Elizabeth A. Smith, Curator
3. English, 1,100
4. No estimate
5. 332, including US census for Luzerne, Lackawanna, Wayne, Wyoming, and Bradford Counties, PA, and Broome County, NY
6. Susquehanna County, PA
7. Historical Society: tel: yes, NC; letter: yes, $10 per family surname
8. No, but experienced staff
9. Yes, $1/day to $4
10. No
11. No
12. No
13. N/AN
14. No
15. No
Books & Sets: 2(some),5,26(PA, CT,NY)
Periodicals: 4(some),9

MYERSTOWN

Whitmoyer Community Library
199 N College St, 17067
Tel: 717-866-2800

1. M,W,Th, 12-8; T,F, 12-6; Sa, 9:30-noon
2. Linda Manwiller, Librarian
3. English, 2,000

4. N/AP
5. None
6. Lebanon, Berks, and Lancaster Counties; some southeastern PA
7. Tel & letter: yes, NC for brief queries
8. Viola Kohl Mohn
9. Yes, for nonresidents
10. No
11. N/AP
12. No
13. Card catalog
14. N/AN
15. No

NEW CASTLE

New Castle Public Library
207 E North St, 16101
Tel: 412-658-6659

1. Winter: M-Th, 8:30-9; F,Sa, 8:30-5:30
2. Dolores G. Grossman
3. English, 4,500
4. N/AN
5. 2,000
6. All PA counties; some eastern OH, VA, NY
7. Tel & letter: yes, NC for brief queries; charge for time spent on extensive research
8. Margaret Sica (volunteer)
9. No
10. Yes, only duplicates
11. No
12. No
13. N/AN
14. Yes
15. OCLC: QNC (partial)
Books & Sets: 1–3,6,7,10–14, 19,26
Periodicals: 4,5,7–9

NORRISTOWN

Montgomery County-Norristown Public Library
Swede & Elm Sts, 19401
Tel: 215-277-3355

1. M-Th, 9-9; F, 9-6; Sa, 9-5
2. Loretta Righter, Head, Reference Dept

3. English, 9,500; PA German, 5
4. None
5. 4
6. PA state
7. Tel & letter: yes, NC for brief queries
8. Dorothy A. Griffith
9. No
10. Yes, only duplicates
11. No
12. No
13. N/AN
14. Yes
15. OCLC: MNL
Books & Sets: 19(2v., 1950), 26(PA)
Periodicals: 4

PHILADELPHIA

Free Library of Philadelphia, Social Science and History Department, Logan Square, 19103
Tel: 215-686-5396

1. M-W, 9-9; Th,F, 9-6; Sa, 9-5; Su (closed in summer), 1-5
2. William Handley
3. English, 5,400
4. None
5. 130 (25 county histories, 45 periodicals on micro, 60 Philadelphia census)
6. PA; few specific family histories
7. Tel: no; letter: yes, NC except 10¢/copy for more than 10 copies
8. No
9. No
10. No
11. No
12. No
13. N/AN
14. Yes
15. OCLC: PLF
Books & Sets: 1–4,6,7,10,12,13, 16,18,19,24,26
Periodicals: 1,4

Genealogical Society of Pennsylvania, 1300 Locust St, 19107
Tel: 215-545-0391

1. T,Th,F, 9-5; W, 1-9
2. Antoinette J. Segraves, Executive Director
3. 205,500+ combined with Historical Society of Pennsylvania
4. 25,000+, plus MS collections in Historical Society of Pennsylvania
5. 35,000+
6. 13 original states and those immediately adjoining
7. Tel & letter: yes, $15/hr
8. Antoinette J. Segraves
9. Yes, $5/day to nonmembers
10. No
11. No
12. Holdings appear in Society's *Journal*
13. Card catalog
14. Yes
15. No
Books & Sets: 2–8,10–14, 17–19,21–26
Periodicals: 1,3–9

PITTSBURGH

Carnegie Library of Pittsburgh, Pennsylvania Department
4400 Forbes Ave, 15213
Tel: 412-622-3154

1. M-F, 9-9; Sa, 9-5:30; Su (Sept-May), 1-5
2. Maria Zini
3. English, 30,000
4. 20,500 items
5. 14,000, including local newspapers
6. Western PA; PA state; eastern, mid-Atlantic states; British, some European materials
7. Tel & letter: yes, NC for limited research. $3/minimum photocopy fee plus postage
8. No
9. No
10. No
11. No
12. No
13. *Index to Marriage Notices from Pittsburgh Gazette, 1786–1911* (microfilm); *Index to Death Notices from Pittsburgh Gazette, 1786–1913, 1968–* (microfilm); in-house guides, biography index
14. Yes
15. OCLC: CLP (partial)
Books & Sets: 1–7,10–12,17,19,26
Periodicals: 4(v.38–, 1984–),5,7,8(v.16–, 1928–),9

Historical Society of Western Pennsylvania, 4338 Bigelow Blvd, 15213-2695
Tel: 412-681-5533

1. T-Sa, 9:30-4:30
2. Donald L. Haggerty, Director, Archives and Library
3. English, 3,250; German, 10; other, 10
4. 425 ft: 725 bound vols
5. 270
6. Western PA counties: Allegheny, Armstrong, Beaver, Bedford, Blair, Butler, Cambria, Cameron, Clarion, Clearfield, Crawford, Elk, Erie, Fayette, Forest, Greene, Indiana, Jefferson, Lawrence, McKean, Mercer, Somerset, Venango, Warren, Washington, Westmoreland; Western Reserve, Northwest Territories
7. Tel: yes, NC; letter: yes, $1 for quick answer, $3/hr for more extensive research
8. Helen M. Wilson, Librarian
9. Yes, $1 donation
10. Yes, history books through ILL
11. Yes, through ILL
12. Guide to the Archives in *Western Pennsylvania Historical Magazine*, v. 49–55, 1966–72; genealogical collection in *Western Pennsylvania Genealogical Society Quarterly*, v.1,4,5,6, additions reviewed quarterly
13. N/AN
14. Yes
15. No
Books & Sets: 2–6,26 (PA, MD, VA)
Periodicals: 4(1969–),7(v.1), 8(v.62–),9(v.30–)

POTTSVILLE

Pottsville Free Public Library
Third & W Market Sts, 17901
Tel: 717-622-8880

1. Winter: M-Th, 8:30-8:30;
F-Sa, 8:30-5; summer: M,Th, 8:30-
8:30; T,W,F, 8:30-5; Sa, 8:30-12
2. Jonelle Miller, Head Reference Librarian
3. English, 1,000
4. 12
5. 50
6. Schuylkill County, PA, with
emphasis on Pottsville, the county
seat
7. Tel & letter: yes, NC
8. No
9. No
10. Yes
11. No
12. No
13. N/AN
14. No
15. OCLC: POT

READING

**Berks County Genealogical
Society Library,** PO Box 777,
13th & Exeter Sts, 19604
Tel: 215-929-0927

1. Open to members only
2. Mary Ellen G. Heckman
3. English, 475; German, 3
4. N/AN
5. 50
6. Berks County, PA state
7. Tel & letter: yes, NC
8. Mary Ellen G. Heckman
9. Open to members only
10. No
11. Yes, 1-month loan to
members, with $15 refundable
security deposit and $2.50 fee
12. Library List, published
annually, free with 2-stamp SASE
13. N/AN
14. Yes
15. No
Books & Sets: 26
Periodicals: 4(1986–)

Reading Public Library
Fifth & Franklin Sts, 19602
Tel: 215-374-4548

1. M,T,W, 8:15am-9pm; Th, F,
8:15-5:30; Sa (closed in summer),
8:45-5
2. Patricia Weiherer
3. English, 5,000; German,
1,000
4. 3 or 4
5. 100
6. Berks County; some PA
state
7. Tel & letter: yes, NC except
$1.20/copy
8. Patricia Weiherer
9. No
10. No
11. No
12. No
13. N/AN
14. No. Refer to Berks County
Genealogical Society
15. OCLC: PR
Books & Sets: 1,3,6,7,10–14,19,26

RICHFIELD

Historical Center
HCR 63, 17086
Tel: 717-694-3211; if no answer,
694-3543

1. T, 7-9pm; Sa, 9-4:30
2. Noah L. Zimmerman
   J. Lloyd Gingrich
3. English, 200–300
4. 3 file cabinets
5. None
6. PA counties: Juniata,
Snyder, Union, Perry, Mifflin, and
surrounding counties
7. Tel & letter: yes, NC
8. Noah L. Zimmerman
9. No
10. No
11. N/AP
12. No
13. Card file
14. No
15. N/AN
Books & Sets: 26(PA)

SEWICKLEY

Sewickley Public Library
Thorn & Broad Sts, 15143
Tel: 412-741-6920

1. Winter: M-Th, 10-9; F,Sa,
10-5; summer: M-Th, 10-8; F,Sa,
10-5
2. Marie Rossi
3. English, 3,000
4. N/AN
5. Sewickley *Herald*, 1903–
6. Sewickley Valley; some OH
Valley, western PA
7. Tel: yes, NC; letter: yes, NC
except 25¢/copy
8. No
9. No
10. No
11. No
12. *An Annotated Catalog of the
Alexander C. Robinson Collection
of Western Pennsylvania,* out of
print
13. N/AN
14. Yes
15. No

SHARON

Buhl-Henderson Library
11 N Sharpsville Ave, 16146
Tel: 412-981-4360

1. M,W,F, 9-5; T,Th, 9-9;
Sa, 9-12
2. Ruth Mizick
3. English, 350
4. 200: family histories,
vertical file on LH
5. 793
6. Primarily Mercer County,
PA; Lawrence and Crawford
Counties, PA; Trumbull County,
OH
7. Tel: no; letter: yes, $5/name
8. No
9. No
10. No
11. No
12. No
13. Acquisitions list

14. No. Refer to Genealogy
Society
15. No
Books & Sets: 2,10
Periodicals: 4

STROUDSBURG

**Monroe County Historical
Society,** PO Box 488,
900 Main St, 18360
Tel: 717-421-7703

1. T,W,Th, 10-12, 1-4; 1st, 3d
Su, 1-4
2. Vertie Knapp
3. English, 2,400; German, 10
4. 40, including collections of
wills or papers, 5 genealogical
collections; over 600 files on local
families
5. 271, including Monroe
County census to 1910 and county
newspapers, 1840–1953
6. Primarily Monroe County,
PA, with surrounding Northampton, Pike, Wayne, and Luzerne
Counties
7. Tel: yes, NC; letter: yes,
NC for brief queries, otherwise
$7.50/hr
8. Vertie Knapp
9. No
10. No
11. No
12. Not current
13. Card index to genealogies,
genealogical files and news items;
finding aids to Stroud and other
collections
14. No
15. No
Books & Sets: 26(PA)
Periodicals: 1(v.51–, 1975–),
4(v.35–, 1981–),7,8(v.69–, 1981–),
9(scattered 1937–62)

Monroe County Public Library
913 Main St, 18360
Tel: 717-421-0800

1. M-Th, 9-8; F, 9-6; Sa, 9-5
2. Ann Kane, Reference
3. English, 30-50
4. Local cemetery records

5. 8–10 census tapes for
Monroe County
6. Monroe County, PA;
northeastern PA; some NY
7. Tel: yes, NC; letter: yes, NC
except for copies and postage
8. No
9. No
10. No
11. No
12. No
13. N/AN
14. No
15. No

SWARTHMORE

**Friends Historical Library of
Swarthmore College**
Swarthmore College, 19081
Tel: 215-328-8496

1. M-F, 8:30-4:30; Sa, 9-12
(closed during Aug, college
vacations)
2. N/AN
3. English, 1,000
4. 70
5. 2,000
6. Principally Quaker meetings
and Quaker families in US,
Canada, Great Britain
7. Tel & letter: no
8. No
9. No
10. No
11. No
12. *Catalog of the Book and
Serials Collections of the Friends
Historical Library,* 6 vols (1982),
$655; *Guide to the Manuscript
Collections of the Friends Historical Library* (1982), $4
13. William Wade Hinshaw
Index to Quaker Meeting Records
14. Yes
15. OCLC: PSH
Books & Sets: 7,26

UPPER DARBY

**Upper Darby Township and
Sellers Memorial Free Public
Library,** 76 S State Rd, 19082
Tel: 215-789-4440

1. Special Collections-Local
History Section: M,T, 2-4
2. Thomas R. Smith, Sellers
Archivist
3. English, 50
4. 1 cu ft Lukens family; 1 cu
ft Sellers family
5. None
6. Lower Darby Creek Valley
and Upper Darby Township in
southeastern Delaware County
7. Tel: no; letter: yes, NC
except 10¢/copy and postage
8. No
9. No
10. No
11. No
12. No
13. Indexes to LH files
14. No
15. No

WAYNE

**Memorial Library of Radnor
Township,** 114 W Wayne Ave,
19087
Tel: 215-687-1124

1. Winter: M-F, 9-9; Sa, 9-5;
Su, 2-5; summer: M-F, 9-9
2. N/AN
3. English, all
4. None
5. None
6. PA, especially southeastern
corner
7. Tel: no; letter: yes, NC
8. No
9. No
10. No
11. No
12. No
13. Guide to LH audio tapes
14. No
15. OCLC: yes

WEST CHESTER

**Chester County Historical
Society,** 225 N High St, 19380
Tel: 215-692-4800

1. T,Th,F,Sa, 10-4; W, 1-8
2. None

3. English, 20,000; German, a few; other, a few
4. No estimate available
5. 3,000
6. Southeastern PA; NJ, DE, MD
7. Tel: no, except for ready-reference questions; letter: yes, $15/query
8. No
9. Yes, $2/day nonmembers; $1/day senior citizens
10. No
11. No
12. No
13. N/AN
14. No
15. N/AN

Books & Sets: 2,3,6,7,10–14, 26(PA,MD,NC)
Periodicals: 1,4(partial),7–9

WILKES-BARRE

Osterhout Free Library
71 S Franklin St, 18701
Tel: 717-823-0156, ext 11

1. Sept-June: M-Th, 9-9; F, 9-6; Sa, 9-5; June-Sept: M,Th, 9-9; T,W, 9-6; F, 9-5
2. Dianne Suffren
3. English, 200
4. None
5. None
6. Cities and boroughs in Luzerne County, PA
7. Tel & letter: yes, NC except 10¢/copy
8. No
9. No
10. No
11. No
12. No
13. None
14. No
15. OCLC: OST

WILLIAMSPORT

James V. Brown Library
19 E Fourth St, 17701
Tel: 717-326-0536, ext 24 or 13

1. M-Th, 9-9; F, 9-6; Sa, 9-5

2. Rhonda Fisher, Reference Librarian
3. English, 2,000; German, 3
4. 40–50
5. 800, includes census microfilm of PA up to 1860; after that, Lycoming County, nearby counties
6. Lycoming County, PA
7. Tel: no; letter: yes, NC except for copies
8. No
9. No
10. No
11. No
12. No
13. *Tracing Family Roots: A Guide to Local Sources* (1978), flyer
14. Yes
15. OCLC: JVB

Books & Sets: 2(incomplete),3 (incomplete),7(incomplete),10,19(incomplete),26(incomplete)
Periodicals: 4(1975–)

RHODE ISLAND

NEWPORT

Newport Historical Society
Library, 82 Touro St, 02840
Tel: 401-846-0813

1. T-F, 9:30-4:30; Sa, 9:30-noon
2. Bertram Lippincott III
3. English, 8,000
4. Unknown
5. 250
6. Newport, RI state; southeastern New England (Plymouth, Salem, Boston)
7. Tel: N/AN; letter: yes, $20/hr
8. Bertram Lippincott III
9. No
10. Yes, to libraries through ILL
11. No
12. No
13. 2 library card catalogs; 1 MSS collection index card catalog
14. Yes
15. OCLC: in process
    RLIN: in process
Books & Sets: 3(3 v., 1981),5(2 v.)
Periodicals: 1(v.9–, incomplete), 7,9

PROVIDENCE

Providence Public Library
150 Empire St, 02903
Tel: 401-521-7722

1. M,T,Th, 9:30-9; closed W; F,Sa, 9:30-5:30; open Sa after July
2. N/AN
3. English, LH, 10,000
4. LH: none
5. LH: Providence city directories on film
6. RI, with emphasis on Providence
7. Tel & letter: yes, NC
8. No

9. No
10. No
11. No
12. No
13. Rhode Island Index: subject guide to books, maps, photos; index to Providence *Journal, Evening Bulletin*
14. No
15. No
Books & Sets: 19
Periodicals: 9

Rhode Island State Archives
Room 43, State House, 02903
Tel: 401-277-2353

1. M-F, 8:30-4:30
2. Phyllis Silva, Archivist
3. No estimate
4. 12,000
5. None
6. RI state
7. Tel & letter: yes, NC except 50¢/copy
8. Phyllis Silva
9. No
10. No
11. No
12. No
13. Card catalog
14. No
15. No

WARWICK

Warwick Public Library
600 Sandy Lane, 02886
Tel: 401-739-5440

1. M-Th, 9-9; F,Sa, 9-5; Su (Sept-May), 1-5
2. N/AN
3. English, 450
4. None
5. None
6. RI state
7. Tel: yes, NC; letter: yes,

NC except for copies
8. No
9. No
10. No
11. No
12. No
13. Card index for *Old Stone Bank History of Rhode Island, Rhode Island Yearbook*
14. Yes
15. No
Books & Sets: 19,26

WESTERLY

Westerly Public Library
Box 356, Broad St, 02891
Tel: 596-2878/2877

1. M-W, 8am-9pm; Th,F, 8-5; Sa (except summer), 8-3
2. Margaret Victoria, Head of Reference
3. English, 5,500; Italian, some
4. 250
5. 500: local newspapers, 1858–; 14: federal census, Washington County, RI, 1800–1910, and New London County, CT, 1910
6. RI, with concentration on Washington County and Stonington (New London County), CT; some NY, MA, CT, other New England states
7. Tel: yes, NC; letter: yes, $5/item
8. No
9. No
10. No
11. No
12. No
13. Index for local newspapers (1850–) on microfilm
14. No
15. No
Books & Sets: 2,3,7,10–14,26
Periodicals: 1(v.43–, 1967–), 4(1980–),5(1962–69),7–9

SOUTH CAROLINA

CAMDEN

Kershaw County Library
1304 Broad St, 29020
Tel: 803-425-1508

1. M-Th, 9-9; F, 9-6; Sa, 9-1; Su, 2-5
2. None
3. English, 150
4. None
5. None
6. Southern states
7. Tel & letter: yes, NC
8. No
9. No
10. No
11. N/AN
12. No
13. None
14. No
15. No

CHARLESTON

Charleston County Library
404 King St, 29403
Tel: 703-723-1645

1. M-Th, 9:30-9; F,Sa, 9:30-6; Su, 2-6
2. Elizabeth W. Carter
3. English, 3,000+
4. None
5. 100
6. SC, especially Charleston
7. Tel & letter: no
8. No
9. No
10. No
11. No
12. No
13. "Information for Genealogists Searching in Charleston"
14. Yes
15. OCLC: SXC

Books & Sets: 1,3,4,6,10–12,17,19
Periodicals: 4(1986–)

South Carolina Historical Society, 100 Meeting St, 29401
Tel: 803-723-3225

1. M-F, 9-4; Sa, 9-2; closed week between Christmas and New Year's
2. Connee Parks
3. English, 5,000
4. 500
5. 200
6. Primarily SC; some East Coast states
7. Tel: no; letter: yes, $10/hr ($35 minimum) plus copies
8. No
9. Yes, $5/day for non-members
10. No
11. No
12. *South Carolina Historical Society Manuscript Guide*, $5
13. N/AN
14. No
15. No

Books & Sets: 3,26(SC)
Periodicals: 9

COLUMBIA

University of South Carolina, South Caroliniana Library
29208
Tel: 803-777-3132 (books); 777-5183 (manuscripts)

1. M,W,F, 8:30-5; T,Th, 8:30-8; Sa, 9-5; schedule varies during intersession periods
2. Herbert J. Hartsook, Curator of Manuscripts; Eleanor Richardson, Reference Librarian
3. English, 6,000; German, less than 10

4. No estimate
5. 11,000: mostly newspapers
6. SC state; some New England, Middle Atlantic, Southeast; some British Isles, northern Europe
7. N/AN
8. N/AN
9. N/AN
10. N/AN
11. N/AN
12. N/AN
13. N/AN
14. N/AN
15. N/AN

Books & Sets: 3–5,7,10,17–19,26
Periodicals: 4,5,7–9

CONWAY

Horry County Memorial Library, 1008 Fifth Ave, 29526
Tel: 803-248-4898

1. M-Th, 8-8; F,Sa, 8-5
2. N/AN
3. English, 300
4. 100
5. 100
6. Horry County, SC, and adjacent areas
7. Tel: no; letter: yes, $1/copy
8. No
9. No
10. No
11. No
12. No
13. N/AN
14. No
15. OCLC: SHM

Books & Sets: 3,26(SC only)

DARLINGTON

Darlington County Library
127 N Main St, 29532
Tel: 803-393-5864

1. M,W, 9-9; T,Th,F, 9-6; Sa, 12-5; Su, 2-5
2. N/AP
3. English, 1,500
4. N/AP
5. N/AP
6. Darlington County, SC state
7. Tel & letter: yes, NC
8. No
9. No
10. Yes
11. N/AP
12. No
13. N/AN
14. Yes
15. OCLC: SCD (partial)
Books & Sets: 1(partial)

EASLEY

Pickens County Library
110 W First Ave, 29640
Tel: 803-859-9679

1. M, 9-9; T-F, 9-6; Sa, 9-4; Su, 2:30-5:30
2. Vacant
3. English, 1,000
4. 25
5. 100; also, quite a lot of microfiche
6. Southeast, with emphasis on South Caroliniana
7. Tel: no; letter: yes, NC
8. Penny Forrester
9. No
10. No
11. No
12. No
13. N/AN
14. No
15. No

GAFFNEY

Cherokee County Public Library, 300 E Rutledge Ave, 29340
Tel: 803-489-4381

1. M,T, 10-8; W-F, 10-6; Sa, 10-4
2. D. Eden
3. English, 10,000
4. 2

5. 1,000
6. Cherokee County, SC; upstate SC; some western NC
7. Tel & letter: yes, NC except 15¢/copy
8. No
9. No
10. No
11. No
12. No
13. *Cherokee County Heritage Room Guide*
14. Yes
15. No
Books & Sets: 2(partial),26
Periodicals: 4

GREENVILLE

Church of Jesus Christ of Latter-day Saints, Greenville SC Branch Genealogical Library
Boiling Springs Rd off Pelham (mailing address: Rt 3, Box 52, Seneca, 29678)
Tel: 803-234-5862

1. T,Th, 9:30-2:30, 7-9pm
2. Mary Ann Montgomery, Librarian
3. English, 100; German, 2
4. Developing Leonardo Andrea Collection of Family Files, on indefinite loan
5. 525
6. Southern states; some US
7. Tel & letter: yes, NC
8. Mary Ann Montgomery
9. No
10. No
11. No
12. No
13. N/AN
14. Yes
15. No
Books & Sets: 8,9
Periodicals: 4,8

Greenville County Library, Charles Stow South Carolina History Collection
300 College St, 29601
Tel: 803-242-5000, ext 60

1. M-F, 9-9; Sa, 9-6; Su, 2-6

2. Dianne Tyler Glymph, Acting Head
3. English, 8,000
4. 30 ledgers of county records
5. 3,900
6. South Caroliniana; southern states; 13 colonies
7. Tel: no; letter: no. Refer to professional genealogists
8. No
9. No
10. No
11. No
12. No
13. *Basic Guide to Genealogical Research*, free
14. Yes
15. OCLC: SGR (partial)
Books & Sets: 1–4,7,10–17,19, 26 (VA,MD,ME,NH,MA,NY,RI,NC,SC)
Periodicals: 4(v.13–, 1959–), 5(v.8),7(Boyer, rev ed, 1983), 9(v.134–38, 1980–84)

LANCASTER

Lancaster County Library
313 S White St, 29720
Tel: 803-285-1502

1. M-Th, 9-8; F, 9-5:30; Sa, 9-5
2. Richard A. Band, Library Director
3. English, 3,800
4. 2
5. 350
6. Lancaster, and SC in general
7. Tel: no; letter: yes, NC except 15¢/copy
8. No
9. No
10. Yes, through ILL, in-house use only
11. No
12. *Guide to Perry Belle Hough Collection in the Lancaster County Library*, $7.50
13. Guide to Viola C. Floyd Collection
14. No
15. No
Books & Sets: 3

LAURENS

Laurens County Library
321 S Harper St, 29360
Tel: 803-984-0596

1. M,Th, 9-9; T,W, 9-6; F, 9-5; Sa, 9-1
2. Elaine Martin
3. English, 1,750
4. 1,740
5. 462
6. Laurens County, SC; SC, NC, VA
7. Tel: yes, NC; letter: yes, $2 minimum plus copies
8. Elaine Martin
9. No
10. No
11. No
12. Richard N. Cote, *Local and Family History in South Carolina: A Bibliography* (1981), $15
13. N/AN
14. Yes
15. No
Books & Sets: 2,7(v.1,2), 26(SC,VA,MD,PA)
Periodicals: 4(1986–)

MARION

Marion County Library
101 E Court St, 29571
Tel: 803-423-2244

1. M,W, 9:30-8:30; T,Th,F, 9:30-6; Sa, 9:30-1
2. N/AP
3. English, 814; other, 1
4. N/AP
5. 97
6. Marion County, Pee Dee River area, southeast SC
7. Tel: no; letter: yes, NC except for copies
8. No
9. No
10. No
11. No
12. R. Cote, *Local and Family History in South Carolina: A Bibliography* (1981)

13. "Books of Genealogical Interest"
14. No
15. No
Books & Sets: 2
Periodicals: 4

NEWBERRY

Newberry-Saluda Regional Library, 1300 Friend St, 29108
Tel: 803-276-0854

1. M-F, 9-5:30; Sa, 9-4
2. None
3. English, 4,000
4. 1: 115 packets of original correspondence re local families
5. 60
6. Newberry County, Saluda County, SC
7. Tel & letter: yes, NC if brief query
8. No
9. No
10. Yes, some
11. No
12. R. Cote, *Local and Family History in South Carolina: A Bibliography* (1981)
13. N/AN
14. No
15. No
Books & Sets: 7(v.1),26(NC,SC)

ORANGEBURG

Orangeburg County Library
510 Louis St NE, 29115
Tel: 803-531-4636

1. M,T, 10-9; W-F, 10-6; Sa, 9-5
2. Capers B. Bull, Jr.
3. English, 141
4. 75
5. 362
6. Orangeburg County
7. Tel: no; letter: yes, $1.50/ transaction plus 10¢/copy
8. No
9. No
10. No

11. No
12. R. Cote, *Local and Family History in South Carolina: A Bibliography* (1981)
13. N/AN
14. No
15. No
Books & Sets: 1,2(v.34-51)

ROCK HILL

York County Library
PO Box 10032, 138 E Black St, 29731
Tel: 803-324-3055

1. M-Th, 9-9; F,Sa, 9-6
2. Mary Mallaney
3. English, 4,000
4. 4,000 vols, including MSS, area family genealogies, Catawba Indian resources
5. 1,089 microforms
6. Rock Hill, York County, SC; some NC. Special collection on Catawba Indians
7. Tel: no; letter: yes, $10/first hr, $5/each additional hr, plus copies
8. No
9. No
10. No
11. No
12. No
13. Marriage and death notices from Yorkville (SC) *Enquirer*, 1823–89, and Rock Hill (SC) *Herald*, 1880–1918; tombstone index of area cemeteries; index to local newspaper
14. No
15. No
Books & Sets: 2(v.21,27,29–32, 34–51,64),3(1983),6,26(10 v.)
Periodicals: 4(1967–)

WALHALLA

Oconee County Library
501 W South Broad St, 29691
Tel: 803-638-5837

1. M,T, 9-9; W-F, 9-6; Sa, 9-1

2. N/AP
3. English, 1,035
4. None
5. 85
6. SC, particularly Oconee County

7. Tel & letter: yes, NC for brief queries
8. No
9. No
10. No

11. No
12. No
13. N/AN
14. Yes
15. N/AN

SOUTH DAKOTA

ABERDEEN

Alexander Mitchell Public Library, 519 S Kline St, 57401
Tel: 605-225-4186

1. M-F, 9-6
2. Delores B. Campton
3. English, 4,500; German, 30; Sioux, 9; French, 1
4. N/AN
5. 620
6. Aberdeen, SD; Brown County, SD; SD state; northern Great Plains: ND, MT, NE, MN; some Canada
7. Tel: yes, NC; letter: no
8. No
9. No
10. Yes, through ILL only, 2-week loan. Photocopying charges: 10¢/copy after first 10 pages
11. No
12. No
13. *AFRA (American Family Records Association) Collection Genealogical Resources in the Alexander Mitchell Library*
14. No
15. OCLC: AML
Books & Sets: 2–4
Periodicals: 1(1981–82,1984), 3(1978–83),4(1975–),5(v.17, 1978),7,8, (1978–),9(1928–42, 1975–85)

BELLE FOURCHE

Belle Fourche Public Library
905 5th Ave, 57717
Tel: 605-892-4407

1. M-Th, 10-7; F,Sa, 10-5
2. Pat Engebretson, Librarian
3. English, 500
4. N/AN

5. 86: local newspaper from 1896–; SD census for 1870, 1880
6. Black Hills, Butte County, SD state
7. Tel: yes, NC; letter: yes, NC except 15¢/copy
8. No
9. No
10. No
11. Yes, through ILL for in-house use
12. No
13. N/AN
14. No. Refer to local society
15. OCLC: yes
    RLIN: yes
Books & Sets: 3–5
Periodicals: 1(1973–85),4(1966–), 8(1979–),9(1978–)

BROOKINGS

Brookings Public Library
515 Third St, 57006
Tel: 605-692-9407

1. M-Th, 10-9; F, 10-5; Sa, 9-5; Su (except Aug), 2-5
2. None
3. English, 300
4. 10
5. 150
6. Mainly Brookings County, other SD state
7. Tel & letter: yes, NC
8. No
9. No
10. No
11. No
12. No
13. "Bibliography of Genealogical Materials at the Brookings Public Library" (1986)
14. No
15. OCLC: SBR
Books & Sets: 5(v.1–4)
Periodicals: 4,5

MITCHELL

Mitchell Public Library
221 N Duff, 57301-2596
Tel: 605-996-6693

1. Winter: M-Th, 10-8; F,Sa, 10-6; Su, 2-5; summer: M-Sa, 10-6
2. Linda Bollinger
3. English, 185
4. None
5. 2: census; 6: local newspapers, 1883–
6. SD state
7. Tel & letter: yes, NC except 15¢/copy
8. No
9. No
10. No
11. No
12. No
13. Card catalog
14. Yes
15. OCLC: yes, for newest books only
Books & Sets: 2(v.1–5)
Periodicals: 4

PIERRE

South Dakota State Archives
Memorial Building Branch, 800 Governors Dr, 57501-2294
Tel: 605-773-3615; 773-4369

1. M-F, 8-5
2. Dayton Canaday, History; Laura Glum, Genealogy
3. Unknown
4. Not broken down
5. 10,000
6. Mainly SD; original 13 states; other US
7. Tel & letter: yes, charge for search and copies
8. Laura Glum
9. No

10. Yes, 1-month loan
11. Yes, 1-month loan, 4 reels
12. In process
13. None
14. Yes
15. OCLC: yes
Books & Sets: 2,6,17
Periodicals: 1(v.9–21, 1932–45), 4(1967–74),9(v.132, 1978)

South Dakota State Historical Society Library, Memorial Bldg, 500 E Capitol, 57501-5053
Tel: 605-773-3615

1. M-F, 8-5
2. Laura Glum, Genealogy; D. W. Canaday, History
3. English, 30,000
4. 3,000
5. 10,000
6. SD; West
7. Tel: N/AN; letter: yes, NC except 20¢/copy
8. Laura Glum
9. No
10. Yes, through ILL on limited basis
11. Yes, through ILL
12. No
13. *South Dakota Periodicals Holdings*
14. Yes
15. OCLC: yes
Books & Sets: 2,6,17
Periodicals: 4,9

RAPID CITY

Rapid City Public Library
610 Quincy St, 57701
Tel: 605-394-4171

1. M-Th, 9-9; F,Sa, 9-5:30
2. Eka M. Parkison
3. English, most; German, several
4. 48 local histories
5. Local newspapers on film from 1878
6. Each geographic area
7. Tel: no; letter: yes, NC except for copies
8. Eka M. Parkison
9. No
10. No
11. No
12. No
13. Genealogy bibliography; index to area county histories
14. Yes
15. OCLC: RCP (partial)
Books & Sets: 5(v.1),6,7,10, 11(1972–76),24(v.1–5),26
Periodicals: 4

SIOUX FALLS

Sioux Falls Public Library
201 N Main Ave, 57102
Tel: 605-339-7082

1. M-Th, 9:30-9; F, 9:30-6; Sa, 9:30-5; Su, 1-4
2. N/AN
3. English, 900
4. None
5. 66, including census for KY, IL, VA
6. Dakota Territory; New England (local DAR genealogy collection)

7. Tel: no; letter: yes, NC for local history
8. No
9. Yes, charge to nonmembers
10. No
11. No
12. No
13. N/AN
14. No
15. OCLC: Sd SIF
Books & Sets: 2,3,24(v.1),26
Periodicals: 4,9

VERMILLION

Vermillion Public Library
18 Church St, 57069
Tel: 605-624-2741

1. M-Th, 10-9; F, 10-6; Sa, 10-5; Su (except summer), 1-5
2. Jane Larson
3. English, 1,500
4. N/AN
5. None
6. SD state
7. Tel & letter: yes, NC
8. N/AN
9. No
10. Yes, through ILL
11. N/AN
12. *South Dakota: Changing, Changeless, 1889–1989*
13. N/AN
14. No
15. No
Books & Sets: 3,26
Periodicals: 4(last 5 years)

TENNESSEE

BLOUNTVILLE

Sullivan County Library
205 Main St, PO Box 510, 37617
Tel: 615-323-5301

1. M-Sa, 9-5
2. Roberta J. Slagle, Librarian
3. English, 250
4. 115
5. 137
6. Sullivan County, TN state
7. Tel & letter: no
8. No
9. No
10. Yes, through ILL
11. No
12. No
13. N/AN
14. No
15. No

CHATTANOOGA

**Chattanooga-Hamilton County
Bicentennial Library**
1001 Broad St, 37402
Tel: 615-757-5317

1. M,T, 9-9; W-Sa, 9-6
2. Clara W. Swann
3. English, 25,100
4. 277
5. 15,172 (includes microfilm
and microfiche)
6. Southeastern US
7. Tel: yes, NC; letter: $3
in-state, $5 out-of-state
8. James D. Tingen
   Clara W. Swann
9. No
10. No
11. No
12. No

13. Index to obituaries from
Chattanooga newspapers, 1897–
1957, 1969–
14. Yes
15. OCLC: TCH
Books & Sets: 1–5,7,10–14,
18,19,23,26
Periodicals: 4(v.17–, 1963–),5,
7,8(v.30–, 1942–),9

JACKSON

**Jackson-Madison County
Library,** 433 E Lafayette, 38301
Tel: 901-423-0225

1. M-Th, 9:30-9; F,Sa, 9:30-
5:30
2. Jack D. Wood, Tennessee
Room
3. English, 4,500
4. Tennessee Room has
vertical file containing clippings,
letters, notes, pamphlets pertaining
to state, local history
5. 1,700
6. TN, NC, SC, GA, VA
7. Tel & letter: yes, NC for
brief queries except for copies,
with SASE
8. No
9. No
10. No
11. No
12. No
13. "Hidden Families" index by
surnames; map index; business
history index for Jackson; Tennessee Room card file
14. No
15. No
Books & Sets: 2,3(3v., 1981),4,
5(v.1–4 only),7,10–12,26
Periodicals: 4(partial to 1987),
8(1955–)

JONESBOROUGH

**Washington County-
Jonesborough Library**
200 Sabine Dr, 37659
Tel: 615-753-5000

1. M,Th, 9-8; T,W,F, 9-6;
Sa, 9-2
2. Suzanne S. Tuggle, Director
3. English, 150–200
4. N/AN
5. 150
6. Washington County, upper
eastern TN
7. Tel & letter: no
8. No
9. No
10. No
11. No
12. No
13. N/AN
14. Yes
15. No

KINGSPORT

Kingsport Public Library
Broad & New Sts, 37660
Tel: 615-229-9400, ext 565

1. M,T,Th, 9-6; W, 9-5; F, 9-
5:15; Sa, 9-12
2. Cynthia Berry
3. English, 2,000
4. 140
5. 30
6. Upper eastern TN; southwestern VA; NC
7. Tel & letter: yes, NC for
simple queries
8. Cynthia Berry
9. No
10. No
11. No
12. No
13. N/AN

14. No
15. N/AN
Books & Sets: 3,5,7(v.1),10–14,26
Periodicals: 4(1975–),8(1973–)

KNOXVILLE

**Knox County Public Library
System, Calvin M. McClung
Historical Collection,** 314 W
Clinch Ave, 37902-2203 (mailing
address: 500 W Church Ave,
37902-2505)
Tel: 615-523-0781

1. M,T, 9-8:30; W-F, 9-5:30
2. Steve Cotham
3. English, 27,633; Welsh,
German, French, less than 10 titles
total
4. 900
5. 6,065
6. Eastern TN; southeastern
US
7. Tel & letter: yes, NC except
for copies
8. Steve Cotham
9. No
10. No
11. No
12. No
13. *Calvin M. McClung Historical Collection* (1921); Linda L.
Posey, *A Guide to the Manuscript
Collections of the Calvin M.
McClung Historical Collection*
(1974); card indexes
14. Yes
15. OCLC: TKL
Books & Sets: 1–5,7,10–19,
22,23,26
Periodicals: 1,4–9

MARYVILLE

Blount County Public Library
301 McGhee St, 37801
Tel: 615-982-0981

1. M-Th, 9-8; F,Sa, 9-5:30
2. Lorene B. Smith
3. English, 600
4. 600
5. 1,000
6. Blount County, eastern TN;
some NC

7. Tel: N/AN; letter: yes, small
fee plus copies
8. No
9. No
10. No
11. No
12. No
13. N/AN
14. N/AN
15. N/AN
Books & Sets: 7(NC),26(8 v.)
Periodicals: 4(recent years)

McKENZIE

**McKenzie Memorial Library,
Gordon Browning Room**
141 N Broadway, 38201
Tel: 901-352-5741

1. M,T,Th,F, 9-4:30; Sa, 12-3
2. Mary Ruth Devault
3. English, 1,625
4. 25
5. 112
6. Carroll County and surrounding counties, western TN,
middle TN; NC, SC, VA
7. Tel: yes, NC for brief
queries; letter: yes, donations
appreciated
8. Mary Ruth Devault
9. No
10. No
11. No
12. No
13. Accessions list
14. No
15. N/AN
Books & Sets: 26
Periodicals: 4(few),5(few)

McMINNVILLE

Magness Memorial Library
118 W Main St, 37110
Tel: 615-473-2428

1. M-W,F,Sa, 10-4:30; M,
7-9pm
2. N/AN
3. English, 228
4. 14
5. 227
6. N/AN

7. Tel: N/AN; letter: yes,
$5/hr plus copies
8. No
9. No
10. Yes
11. No
12. No
13. N/AN
14. No
15. No
Books & Sets: 1,3,4,26(NC,VA,
MA,CT,SC,MD,PA)

MEMPHIS

**Memphis and Shelby County
Public Library and Information
Center,** 1850 Peabody Ave, 38104
Tel: 901-725-8820

1. M-Th, 9-9; F,Sa, 9-6;
Su, 1-5
2. James R. Johnson
3. English, 12,500
4. 30
5. 9,000
6. Strongest in 17th- and 18th-
century America and southern
states, especially TN, NC, VA
7. Tel: no; letter: yes, charge
for research
8. N/AN
9. No
10. N/AN
11. No
12. No
13. "Guide to the Genealogy
Collection," flyer; typescript lists
of county, family, church, Indian,
census, and military records and
newspapers, all on microfilm;
M. L. Mazor, "Genealogical
Sources Available for Shelby
County in Memphis, Tennessee,"
typescript
14. Yes
15. OCLC: TMN
Books & Sets: 1–7,10–19,22,23,26
Periodicals: 1,4,5,7–9

**Tennessee Genealogical Society
Library,** 3340 Poplar Ave, Suite
327, PO Box 12124, 38182-0124
Tel: 901-327-3273

1. Th, 10-2; other times irregular
2. Amelia P. Eddlemon, Librarian
3. English, 5,900 (emphasis on genealogy)
4. Developing collection of TN family histories in TN Ancestry Program
5. Small collection, for staff use only
6. Emphasis on TN, the South, mid-South; entire US
7. Tel & letter: yes, NC for brief queries. No research
8. Yes
9. For members only; current membership is $15/yr
10. No
11. No
12. No
13. Master surname index, vertical file, TN Ancestry Program
14. Yes
15. No
Books & Sets: 1,2(partial),3, 5,26(some)
Periodicals: 1(some),4(most), 5(some),8(some),9(index only)

NASHVILLE

Public Library of Nashville and Davidson County, Nashville Room, 8th Ave N & Union, 37203
Tel: 615-244-4700, ext 68

1. M-F, 9-8; Sa, 9-5; Su (Oct-May), 2-5
2. Mary Glenn Hearne
3. English, 8,000
4. 100
5. 200
6. Middle TN
7. Tel: yes, NC for brief queries; letter: yes, $3.50/in state, $5/out of state

8. Mary Glenn Hearne
9. No
10. No
11. No
12. No
13. In-house indexes to specific collections; brochure guide
14. Yes
15. OCLC: TNN
Books & Sets: 2(v.1–98),3, 4,12,19(2 v., 1950,1972),26
Periodicals: 4,8(v.38–, 1950–)

Tennessee State Library and Archives, 403 7th Ave N, 37219
Tel: 615-741-2764

1. M-Sa, 8-8; Su, 12:30-9
2. John McGlone, Director, Public Services
3. English, unknown
4. 900
5. 75,000
6. Southeastern US
7. Tel & letter: yes, NC
8. No
9. No
10. Yes, duplicates only
11. Yes
12. *Guide to the Microfilmed Holdings of the Tennessee State Library and Archives*; *Writings on Tennessee Counties*; *Tennessee Newspapers*
13. Surname file; family and LH file; vertical files
14. Yes
15. OCLC: TNS
Books & Sets: 2–7,10–15,17,18,26
Periodicals: 1,4,5,7–9

OAK RIDGE

Oak Ridge Public Library
Civic Center, 37830
Tel: 615-482-8455

1. M-Th, 10-9; F, 10-6; Sa, 9-6; Su, 2-6
2. Kathy E. McNeilly, Head of Reference
3. English, 150–200
4. 150
5. Local papers on microfilm
6. Oak Ridge; Anderson County; eastern TN; TN state
7. Tel & letter: yes, NC with SASE
8. No
9. No
10. No
11. No
12. No
13. None
14. No
15. No
Books & Sets: 3

ROGERSVILLE

H. B. Stamps Memorial Library
407 E Main St, 37857
Tel: 615-272-8710

1. M,W-F, 9:30-5; T, 9:30-8; Sa (Oct-Mar), 9:30-5
2. Kathy Moore
3. English, 500
4. 120
5. 318
6. Hawkins County
7. Tel & letter: no
8. No
9. No
10. No
11. No
12. No
13. None
14. No
15. No
Periodicals: 4(incomplete)

TEXAS

ABILENE

Abilene Public Library
202 Cedar St, 79601
Tel: 915-677-2474, ext 37

1. M,T,Th, 9-9; W,F,Sa, 9-6
2. Mildred Shirley
3. English, 300
4. N/AN
5. 1,500
6. US; some foreign
7. Tel & letter: yes, NC for brief queries
8. Mildred Shirley
9. No
10. No
11. No
12. No
13. Cemetery records for some TX counties
14. No
15. N/AN
Books & Sets: 2(partial),3–5, 10–14,26
Periodicals: 4

AMARILLO

Amarillo Public Library
413 E Fourth St, 79189-2171
Tel: 806-378-3054

1. M-Th, 9-9; F,Sa, 9-6; Su, 2-6
2. Mary Kay Snell
3. No estimate
4. No estimate
5. 2,026
6. TX Panhandle and surrounding areas of OK, NM; some KS, CO, AR
7. Tel: yes, NC; letter: N/AN
8. Mary Kay Snell
9. No
10. No
11. No

12. No
13. Genealogy bibliography
14. Yes
15. OCLC: TAP
Books & Sets: 1–5,7,10–14, 17–19,22,26
Periodicals: 1,3–5,7–9

ANAHUAC

Chambers County Library
PO Box 520, 202 Cummings St, 77514
Tel: 409-267-3372

1. M,T, Th,F, 8-6; W, 1-5; Sa, 9-1
2. Ann Weaver
3. English, 1,000
4. 5
5. 15
6. Chambers County, TX state; other states
7. Tel: no; letter: yes, NC except for copies
8. No
9. No
10. No
11. No, but will copy short requests for 10¢/page
12. No
13. N/AN
14. No
15. No
Books & Sets: 2

AUSTIN

Texas State Library, Archives Division, 1201 Brazos, PO Box 12927, 78711
Tel: 512-463-5480

1. M-F, 8-5
2. N/AN
3. N/AN
4. Indeterminate

5. Indeterminate
6. TX state
7. Tel & letter: yes, NC except for copies and postage
8. Yes
9. No
10. No
11. No
12. *Guide to Genealogical Resources in the Texas State Archives,* $2.24, plus tax, postage, and handling
13. Unpublished in-house finding aids
14. Yes
15. OCLC: yes, for newspapers only

Texas State Library, Information Services Division, Genealogy Collection, 1201 Brazos, PO Box 12927, 78701
Tel: 512-463-5463

1. M-Sa, 8-5
2. Jan Carter, Supervisor, Genealogy Collection
3. English, 20,500; German, 25; French, Spanish, 10–20
4. None
5. 25,000
6. All 50 states; emphasis on TX, southern states; some foreign countries
7. Tel & letter: yes, NC except for copies ($1 minimum)
8. Jan Carter
   Colleen Munds
   David Baskin
   Ann Graves
9. No
10. Yes, duplicates only. Requests are by ALA or OCLC
11. Yes, tax rolls for TX counties only; ALA request
12. No

13. *Genealogical Resources at the Texas State Library*, free brochure
14. Yes
15. OCLC: IKM
Books & Sets: 2–7,10–14,17–19, 23–26
Periodicals: 1(v.42–52,54–61),4 (v.5–),5,6(v.15–19),7,8(v.40–41,43–),9

Texas State Library, Local Records Division–Network of Statewide Depositories (RHRD) 1201 Brazos, PO Box 12927, 78701
Tel: 512-463-5463

1. Varies; generally M-F, 8-5
2. Marilyn von Kohl, Local Records Division
3. English, 2,000
4. 300
5. 1,100
6. TX state
7. Tel & letter: yes, NC
8. No
9. No
10. No
11. Yes, through ILL and to RHRD depositories
12. *Guide to Microfilm Records of County and District Clerks*, out of print (to be revised 1988)
13. N/AN
14. No
15. No

University of Texas at Austin, Eugene C. Barker Texas History Center, General Libraries Sid Richardson Hall 2.101, 78713
Tel: 512-471-5961

1. M-Sa, 8-5
2. Dr. Don E. Carleton, Director; Ralph Elder, Head, Public Services Unit
3. English, 130,000; French, Swedish, Czech, Spanish, German, minor amounts
4. 3,000
5. No estimate
6. TX state; some southern, southwestern, western states

7. Tel & letter: yes, NC for brief queries
8. No. Library maintains list of proxy researchers
9. No
10. Yes, some duplicates only, through ILL
11. Yes, some duplicates only, through ILL
12. Chester Kielman, *The University of Texas Archives, Vol I* (1967). Second volume being prepared
13. Inventories to every MS and archival collection processed; catalog access to books, serials; in-house card files to genealogical vertical files, biographical files, OCLC catalog to newspapers
14. Yes
15. OCLC: IXA

BAYTOWN

Sterling Municipal Library Mary Elizabeth Wilbanks Ave, 77520
Tel: 713-427-7331

1. M-Th, 9-9; F,Sa, 9-6
2. Victoria L. Klehn
3. English, 1,006; French, 9
4. None
5. 1,139
6. Primarily TX, but includes all US
7. Tel & letter: no
8. No
9. No
10. Yes, through ILL only (for in-library use)
11. Yes, through ILL only (for in-library use). Do not lend federal census
12. *Genealogical Materials in the Sterling Municipal Library*, approx 86 pp. Photocopy available, 10¢/page
13. Index to Baytown *Sun* (newspaper)
14. Yes
15. No

Books & Sets: 3(1981, 1983 suppl only),7(v.1),24(v.1),26
Periodicals: 4(v.15–, 1960–), 5(1962), 7,8(v.54–, 1966–)

BEAUMONT

Tyrrell Historical Library, Beaumont Public Library System, PO Box 3827, 695 Pearl St, 77704
Tel: 409-838-0780

1. T-Th,Sa, 9-6
2. Vacant; Maurine Gray, Director of Libraries
3. English, 10,000
4. None
5. 700
6. LH: TX, particularly southwestern TX; G: TX, LA, worldwide
7. Tel: no; letter: yes, NC except 15¢/copy
8. No
9. No
10. No
11. No
12. Yes, out of print
13. N/AN
14. Yes
15. No
Books & Sets: 2,3,5,7(v.1–6), 24(microfiche),25(microfiche),26
Periodicals: 1,3–6,8,9

BELTON

Belton City Library 301 E 1st, 76513
Tel: 817-939-1161

1. M-F, 12-5; Sa, 9-1
2. Lena Armstrong, Director
3. English, 2,426; German, 3; French, 1
4. None
5. 62
6. TX, specifically Bell County; southern states; some Scottish and Irish books and Scottish cemetery records
7. Tel: no; letter: yes, NC with SASE

8. No
9. No
10. No
11. No
12. No
13. N/AN
14. Yes
15. No
Books & Sets: 2(v.2–5,11,12,
40,119 missing),3–5,10–12,26
Periodicals: 4(1970–),8(v.53–68),
9(v.116–36)

BROWNSVILLE

**Arnulfo Oliveira Memorial
Library,** 1825 May St, 78520
Tel: 512-544-8221

1. M-Th, 7:30am-10pm; F,
7:30-5; Sa, 10:30-4; Su, 2-9
2. Yolanda Gonzalez
3. English, 3,165; Spanish, 121
4. 24
5. 125
6. Southern TX, from Nueces
River south to the Rio Grande;
northern Mexico (Tamaulipas,
Nuevo Leon, Coahuila)
7. Tel & letter: yes, NC for
brief queries. Research: $5–$8/hr
8. Yolanda Gonzalez
9. No
10. Yes, duplicates only
11. No
12. No
13. City cemetery index project
in progress
14. Refer to Fort Brown
Genealogical Society
15. OCLC: TBS
Books & Sets: 7(v.2,3),10,11,13,14
Periodicals: 4(v.28–33,34–,
1974–79,1981–),7,8(v.63–65,
1975–77)

BRYAN

Bryan Public Library
201 E 26th St, 77802
Tel: 409-779-1736 (Reference)

1. M,T,Th, 9-9; W,F,Sa, 9-5
2. No designated head

3. English, 3,500
4. No estimate
5. 420, including 340 reels of
local newspaper; not indexed
6. TX, AL, NC, SC, VA, MD,
LA, MS, KY, TN
7. Tel: no; letter: yes, NC for
brief queries except 15¢/copy,
25¢/microfilm copy
8. No
9. No
10. No
11. No
12. No
13. Card catalog; *Texas County
Histories, Records, etc., in the
Bryan Public Library*, notebook
for in-house use
14. No
15. No
Books & Sets: 3–6,26(partial)
Periodicals: 4(1981–),5(1976–80)

BURKBURNETT

Burkburnett Library
215 E 4th St, 76354-3446
Tel: 817-569-2991

1. T-F, 11:30-6; Sa, 10-2
2. G. Thomas Fairclough,
Librarian
3. English, 35
4. None
5. 43
6. N/AN
7. Tel & letter: yes, NC
8. No
9. No
10. Yes, 2-week loan, with one
2-week renewal
11. Yes, 2-week loan, no
renewal
12. No
13. Index to obituaries in
Burkburnett newspapers, 1967–
(in preparation); surname index to
transcription of 1900 census for
Burkburnett area
14. No
15. No
Books & Sets: 26
Periodicals: 4(v.28–32,35–,
1974–78, 1981–)

BURNET

**Herman Brown Free Library,
Burnet County Library System**
100 E Washington, 78611
Tel: 512-756-2328

1. T-F, 9-6; M, 1-6; 1st & 3d
Sa, 9-1
2. Cookie Wallace, Director
3. English, 1,500
4. 50
5. 200
6. Mostly TX; some northeastern, southern states
7. Tel: no; letter: yes, NC
except for copies
8. Elizabeth Breeding
9. No
10. Yes, through ILL, for
in-house use only
11. Yes, through ILL, for
in-house use only
12. No
13. "Genealogy Holdings in the
J. Frank Dobie Room at the
Herman Brown Free Library"
14. No
15. No
Periodicals: 4(1971–),8(1980–82),
9(1965–76)

CAMERON

Cameron Public Library
304 E Third St, 76520
Tel: 817-697-2401

1. M-Th, 10-5:30; F,Sa, 10-4
2. Kay King, Director
3. English, 364
4. 364 [*sic*]
5. 86
6. Local area, TX state; AL,
GA, NC, SC, VA
7. Tel & letter: yes, NC
8. No
9. No
10. No
11. No
12. No
13. N/AN
14. No
15. No
Books & Sets: 2(incomplete)

CONROE

Montgomery County Library
San Jacinto at Phillips, 77301
Tel: 409-756-4484

1. M,F, 10-5; T-Th, 10-8;
Sa, 9-5
2. Imogene Kinard Kennedy
3. English, 7,000
4. 10
5. 3,705
6. US, specializing in the
South; Europe, Great Britain
7. Tel & letter: no
8. Imogene Kinard Kennedy
9. No
10. Yes, duplicates only, to
county residents
11. No
12. No
13. Index to all periodicals held,
by topic and surname
14. Yes
15. N/AN
Books & Sets: 3,5–7,10,11,26
Periodicals: 3–9

CORPUS CHRISTI

Corpus Christi Public Library
Local History/Genealogy Depart-
ment, 805 Comanche, 78401
Tel: 512-880-7030

1. M-Th, 9-9; F,Sa, 9-6
2. Margaret Rose, Librarian
3. English, 7,500; Spanish, 150
4. 7,500: includes 3,500 G,
1,500 Nueces County LH, 2,500
TX LH
5. 3,000
6. LH: Nueces County; TX
history: TX state, especially
southern TX, northern Mexico;
genealogical collection: emphasis
on TX, southern US, some Mexico
7. Tel & letter: yes, NC for
brief queries except 15¢/copy
8. Margaret Rose
9. No
10. No
11. No
12. No

13. In-house bibliographies,
finding aids
14. Yes
15. OCLC: CCA, partial
Books & Sets: 1(on Dialog),2–14,
19,26
Periodicals: 3(1985–),4(v.16–),5,7,
8(v.37–),9(v.1–50)

**Corpus Christi State University,
University Library**
6300 Ocean Dr, 78412
Tel: 512-991-6810

1. M-F, 8-5
2. Paul Medley
3. English, LH, 10,000;
Spanish, 300
4. LH: 5
5. LH: Vera Cruz archives
6. Southern TX and northern
Mexico
7. Tel & letter: no
8. No
9. No
10. No
11. No
12. No
13. N/AN
14. No
15. OCLC: TXF
Books & Sets: 6,10,11,13,14,19

CROCKETT

**John H. Wootters Crockett
Public Library**, 708 E Goliad,
PO Box 1226, 75835
Tel: 409-544-3089

1. M-F, 9-5; Sa, 10-1
2. None
3. English, 1,472
4. 225
5. 275
6. National and limited
international
7. Tel: no; letter: yes, NC
8. No
9. No
10. No
11. No
12. No
13. Card catalog
14. No

15. No
Books & Sets: 1–3,5
Periodicals: 4

DALLAS

**Dallas Public Library,
Genealogy Section**
1515 Young St, 75201
Tel: 214-670-1433

1. M-Th, 9-9; F,Sa, 9-5;
Su, 1-5
2. Lloyd DeWitt Bockstruck,
Supervisor, Genealogy Section
3. 47,200 (no statistics for
languages)
4. N/AN
5. 45,000 microforms
6. US, Canada; Europe
7. Tel & letter: yes, NC
8. Lloyd DeWitt Bockstruck
9. No
10. No
11. No
12. No
13. N/AN
14. Yes
15. OCLC: IGA
Books & Sets: 1–26
Periodicals: 1–9

DEER PARK

Deer Park Public Library
3009 Center St, 77536
Tel: 713-479-5276

1. M,W, 9-6; T,Th, 9-9; F,Sa,
9-5
2. None
3. English, 70
4. None
5. 7
6. TX, US, Europe
7. Tel: no; letter: yes, NC
8. No
9. No
10. No
11. No
12. *Genealogy*, free
13. N/AN
14. No
15. No

Books & Sets: 1,3,4,22,26
Periodicals: 4(1985–)

DENTON

Denton Public Library
502 Oakland, 76201
Tel: 817-566-8478

1. Oct-May: T, 9-9; W-S, 9-6;
June-Sept: M,W-F, 9-6; T, 9-9
2. Linda Touraine
3. English, 2,055
4. 162
5. 243
6. US, with heaviest coverage
on TX, southern states
7. Tel: yes, NC for brief
queries; letter: yes, NC except for
copies
8. No
9. No
10. Yes, through ILL for
in-house use only
11. Yes, only newspapers,
through ILL
12. No
13. N/AN
14. No. Refer to Denton County
Genealogical Society
15. No
Books & Sets: 1,2(v.1,81,95,111,
125,126),3(1982–85),26
Periodicals: 4(v.13–, 1959–),
8(few),9(broken set)

EL PASO

El Paso Public Library
501 N Oregon, 79901
Tel: 915-541-4873 (Genealogy),
541-4869 (Southwest Collection)

1. M-Th, 8:30am-9pm; F,Sa,
8:30-5:30
2. Jane Bartlett, Genealogy;
Mary Sarber, Southwest Collection
3. English: 5,000, Genealogy;
2,000, Southwest Collection
4. 1, Genealogy; 4, Southwest
Collection

5. 300, Genealogy; 300,
Southwest Collection
6. Genealogy: US, with
emphasis on TX, NM; Southwest
Collection: Southwest, El Paso
area
7. Tel: yes, NC; letter: yes, NC
except for copies
8. No
9. No
10. Yes, selected items through
ILL, for in-house use
11. No
12. No
13. N/AN
14. No
15. OCLC: TXPF
Books & Sets: 1,2(v.1–143,151,
155,160,162-65),3–7,10–19,24,26
Periodicals: 1(v.44–, 1968–),
3(1987–),4(v.21–, 1967–),5,
6(v.17–, 1972–),7,8(v.50–, 1962–),
9(v.102–14,120–, 1948–60, 1966–)

FORT WORTH

**Fort Worth Public Library,
Genealogy and Local History
Section,** 300 Taylor St, 76102
Tel: 817-870-7740

1. M-Th, 9-9; F,Sa, 10-6
2. Patricia Chadwell Jackson
3. English, 35,000; French, 20
4. 30
5. 12,000
6. US, with emphasis on
southern states
7. Tel & letter: yes, NC
8. Patricia Chadwell Jackson
   Paul Campbell
9. No
10. No
11. No
12. No
13. Analytical Index (card file);
computerized catalog
14. Yes
15. OCLC: IFA
Books & Sets: 1–7,10–14,17–19,
22–26

Periodicals: 1,4,5,7–9

GALVESTON

Rosenberg Library
2310 Sealy, 77550
Tel: 409-763-8854

1. T-Sa, 10-5
2. Jane A. Kenamore
3. English, 10,000; German,
under 200
4. Approx 2,000 linear ft of
MSS
5. 200
6. Galveston; Galveston
County; Galveston Island; TX state
7. Tel: yes, NC; letter: yes, $5
fee for extensive research
8. No
9. No
10. No
11. Yes, First Baptist Church
and First Lutheran Church records,
through ILL
12. Jane A. Kenamore &
Michael E. Wilson, *Manuscript
Sources in the Rosenberg Library:
A Selective Guide* (1983)
13. Inventories, thesaurus
14. Yes
15. No

GARLAND

Nicholson Memorial Library
625 Austin, 75040
Tel: 214-272-3216

1. M-Th, 9:30-9; F,Sa, 9:30-6
2. Barbara A. Radke
3. English, ca 500
4. N/AN
5. 43
6. Mainly TX, with indexes for
some other states
7. Tel & letter: no
8. No
9. No
10. No
11. No

12. *Guide to Genealogy Collections* (1985), $10
13. None
14. No
15. No
Periodicals: 4

GRAPEVINE

Grapevine Public Library
1201 S. Main, 76051
Tel: 817-481-0336

1. M,T,Th, 10-8; W,F, 10-6; Sa, 10-5
2. Jerre Williams, Reference Librarian
3. English, 1,000
4. 27 oral history tapes with transcriptions; 16 miscellaneous items
5. 3,276
6. US, with emphasis on South, Southwest
7. Tel: no; letter: yes, NC with SASE
8. No
9. No
10. No
11. No
12. *Guide to Genealogy Collections* (1985), $10
13. N/AN
14. No
15. No
Books & Sets: 3,5
Periodicals: 4(1956–69,1971–76, 1979–85)

GREENVILLE

W. Walworth Harrison Library
3716 Lee St, 75401
Tel: 214-455-2205

1. M, 10-4:30; T-F, 9-4:30
2. Gail Slater
3. English, 312
4. 450
5. 325: local newspapers
6. Local migration pattern, generally from PA, VA, southern states
7. Tel & letter: yes, NC for brief queries

8. No
9. No
10. No
11. No
12. No
13. None
14. Yes
15. No
Books & Sets: 2(v.16,17,44–166)

HOUSTON

Genealogy Books and Consultation Library
1217 Oakdale, 77004
Tel: 713-522-7444

1. M,T,F,Sa, 10-5; W, 11-5
2. Norma Chudleigh
3. English, 500 (many family histories)
4. N/AN
5. N/AN
6. Southern states
7. Tel & letter: yes, $12/hr
8. Norma Chudleigh
9. Yes, $1.75/hr
10. Yes, rent by week
11. Yes, rent by the film
12. Yes, $3
13. N/AN
14. No
15. No
Books & Sets: 8

Houston Public Library, Clayton Library, Center for Genealogical Research, 5300 Caroline, 77004
Tel: 713-524-0101

1. M,T,Th-Sa, 9-5; W, 12-9
2. Maxine Alcorn
3. English, 35,000; German, 50; French, several
4. 25 filing cabinets of vertical file materials
5. 25,000 reels; 3,000 microcards; 15,000 microfiche
6. US, Canada, Mexico; Europe, Great Britain
7. Tel & letter: no, except for limited requests
8. Maxine Alcorn
   Vivian Jordan
9. No

10. No
11. No
12. No, but many booklets on various states and subjects
13. Microprint catalog; surnames in vertical file
14. Yes
15. OCLC: yes
Books & Sets: 2–26
Periodicals: 1,2(v.7–, 1985–), 3,4(v.4–, 1950–),5–9

LAREDO

Laredo Public Library
Bruni Plaza, 78040
Tel: 512-722-2435

1. T-Th, 9-9; F,Sa, 9-6
2. None
3. N/AN
4. None
5. N/AN
6. N/AN
7. Tel & letter: yes, NC
8. No
9. No
10. Yes, 2-week loan
11. No
12. No
13. N/AN
14. No
15. No
Periodicals: 4,8

LONGVIEW

Longview Public Library
222 W Cotton, 75601
Tel: 214-237-1350

1. M,W,Th,F, 9-12, 1-6
2. Pauline Cox
3. English, 2,200
4. N/AN
5. 4,200
6. Southern states
7. Tel: no; letter: yes, NC except for copies
8. No
9. No
10. No
11. No
12. No
13. N/AN

14. No
15. No
Books & Sets: 2–5,7
Periodicals: 4,7,8(1986–)

LUFKIN

Kurth Memorial Library,
Ora McMullen Room
101 Calder Sq, 75901
Tel: 409-634-7617, ext 76

1. M-W, 10-6; Th, 10-8; F, 10-5:30; Sa, 10-2
2. John W. Wilkins
3. English, 3,045
4. N/AN
5. 1,000
6. TX, LA, AR, TN, MS, AL, GA, NC, SC, KY, MO, VA, WV, MD, PA, New England; England
7. Tel & letter: yes, NC
8. John W. Wilkins
9. No
10. No
11. No
12. No
13. N/AN
14. No
15. N/AN
Books & Sets: 26
Periodicals: 4

McALLEN

McAllen Memorial Library
601 N Main, 78501
Tel: 512-682-4531

1. M-F, 9-5:30; S,Su, 1-5
2. Janette Josserand, Librarian, McAllen Genealogical Society
3. English, ca 1,600
4. None
5. 20
6. New England; Central South; Midwest; TX state
7. Tel & letter: yes, NC
8. Volunteers only
9. No
10. No
11. No
12. No
13. N/AN
14. No

15. OCLC: yes
Books & Sets: 2–5,7(v.2),10–14,26
Periodicals: 1(1983–),4(1981–), 5(1984),8,9(1916–49,1955–58, 1971–74,1978–)

MESQUITE

Mesquite Public Library
300 Grubb Drive, 75149
Tel: 214-216-6229

1. M-Th, 9-9; F,Sa, 9-6
2. Marjorie Bays
3. English, 3,000+
4. 250+
5. 500+
6. All states but AK, HI; emphasis on TX, southern states
7. Tel & letter: yes, NC
8. Marjorie Bays
9. No
10. No
11. No
12. *Bibliography of Genealogical Material in PLANT*
13. N/AN
14. Yes
15. No
Books & Sets: 2,3,5,7(v.1),26
Periodicals: 4,5(1967–68,1974),7, 8(1970–),9(1972–80)

MIDLAND

Midland County Public Library,
The John and Rosalind Redfern
Genealogical Research Center
301 W Missouri, 79701
Tel: 915-683-2708

1. Sept-May: M-Th, 9-9; F,Sa, 9-6; June-Aug: M, 9-9; T-Sa, 9-6
2. Sandra De Fore Wegner, Assistant County Librarian
3. English, 10,000
4. 1
5. 1,200
6. Entire US, with emphasis on the South
7. Tel & letter: yes, NC for limited queries
8. No
9. No
10. Yes, but very few

11. No
12. No
13. N/AN
14. No
15. OCLC: MCY since 1983
Books & Sets: 1,2(incomplete), 3–5,7,8(US),10–14,19,22,23,26
Periodicals: 1,2,3(v.1–30),4(v.21–, 1967–),5(v.8,13–24),6(v.17–),7, 8(v.42–),9

NACOGDOCHES

Stephen F. Austin State
University, Steen Library, Special
Collections Department, 75962
Tel: 409-568-4100

1. M-F, 8-5; Sa, 10-6
2. Linda Cheves Nicklas
3. English, 4,000
4. 50
5. 2,000
6. Eastern TX; some TX state; very limited for other US
7. Tel & letter: yes, NC for brief queries
8. No
9. No
10. No
11. No, except for Regional Historical Resource Document Program MF
12. Yes, out of date
13. Card index to R. B. Blake Research Collection; inventories, other finding guides to MS collections
14. Yes
15. OCLC: TXK (partially)
Books & Sets: 1(1981–83),3(3v., 1981),6,7,11(1977),13(1973), 19(1972),26
Periodicals: 4(v.12–, 1958–, some issues missing),5(scattered), 7,8(v.47–, 1959–),9(v.1–20, 1847–66)

ODESSA

Ector County Library
321 W 5th St, 79761
Tel: 915-332-0634

1. M-Th, 8:30-8:30; F,Sa, 9-6

2. Betty Theda
3. English, 3,500
4. N/AN
5. 3,200 rolls microfilm; 8,000 microfiche
6. US (fewer books on northern states); international, excluding Australia, Austria (except IGI index)
7. Tel & letter: yes, NC except 20¢/copies, 25¢/photocopies
8. Betty Theda
   Kathryn Boone
9. No
10. Yes, circulating copies only
11. No
12. No
13. N/AN
14. No
15. OCLC: ECT (partial)
Books & Sets: 2(mostly complete), 3,4,7,8,10–12,15,16,26
Periodicals: 3(v.29–36, 1965–73), 4(1956–),7,8(1915–77),9(1956–73)

PLANO

Gladys Harrington Public Library, 1501 18th St, 75074
Tel: 214-578-7175

1. M-Th, 10-9; F,Sa, 10-6; Su, 1-5
2. Carole C. Deily, Reference
3. English, 500
4. None
5. 150
6. TX, VA, TN, PA, NC, SC, GA, KY; other southern, midwestern states
7. Tel & letter: yes, NC for brief questions
8. No
9. No
10. No
11. No
12. No
13. N/AN
14. No
15. N/AN
Books & Sets: 3
Periodicals: 1(v.56–57, 1980–81), 4(1967–84, incomplete),8(v.68–74, incomplete)

PORT ARTHUR

Port Arthur Public Library
3601 Cultural Center Drive, 77642
Tel: 409-985-8838

1. M-F, 9-9; Sa, 9-5; Su, 2-5 (except summer)
2. Mike Babin, Head, Reference Division
3. English, 300
4. None
5. 50: US Census
6. General, some emphasis on Acadia (LA French)
7. Tel: no; letter: yes, NC for brief queries
8. No
9. No
10. No
11. No
12. No
13. No
14. No
15. No
Books & Sets: 2(partial),3

RICHMOND

George Memorial Library of Fort Bend County
1001 Golfview Dr, 77469
Tel: 713-342-4455, ext 346, 347, 348

1. M-W, 9-7; T,Th, 9-9; F,Sa, 9-5; Su, 1-5
2. Mary L. Bennett
3. English, ca 4,000; German, 6; Czech, 6; Spanish, 4
4. 10 volumes
5. 2,000 rolls; 1,000 microfiche
6. Fort Bend County, TX; southern states
7. Tel & letter: yes, NC except 10¢/copy, 25¢/microfiche/film copy
8. Mary L. Bennett
9. No
10. No
11. No
12. N/AN
13. N/AN

14. No
15. N/AN
Books & Sets: 1,3–5,7,26
Periodicals: 4(1972–),5(1983), 6(1986–),8(1986–)

ROCKDALE

Lucy Hill Patterson Memorial Library, 201 Ackerman St, 76567
Tel: 512-446-3410

1. M,W,F, 1-5; T, 9-5; Th, 1-7; Sa, 9-1
2. N/AP
3. English, 70
4. Some church histories
5. None
6. Rockdale, Milam County, other TX; other southern states
7. Tel: no; letter: yes, NC
8. No
9. No
10. No
11. N/AP
12. No
13. N/AN
14. No
15. No

SAN ANTONIO

Daughters of the Republic of Texas Library, PO Box 1401, 78295-1401
Tel: 512-225-1071/8155

1. M-Sa, 9-5
2. N/AN
3. N/AN
4. N/AN
5. N/AN
6. San Antonio, the Alamo, TX; Republic period of TX history
7. Tel: yes, NC; letter: yes, NC for first half hour, thereafter $10/hr
8. No
9. No
10. No
11. No
12. *A Guide to the Texana Holdings of the Texas History Library of the Daughters of the Republic of Texas* (1978), $10 plus postage

13. N/AN
14. No
15. No

San Antonio Public Library, History and General Reference Department, 203 S St. Mary's St, 78205
Tel: 512-299-7813

1. M-F, 9-9; Sa, 9-6
2. Marie B. Berry
3. English, 14,700; German, 10; Spanish, some
4. N/AN
5. 40,500
6. San Antonio; TX state; South, Southwest, Midwest, East
7. Tel: yes, NC, limited to catalog search; letter: yes, NC, no searches
8. No
9. No
10. No
11. No
12. No
13. General catalog of library system
14. No
15. OCLC: SAP
Books & Sets: 1(incomplete),2, 3(incomplete),5–7,10–14,19,26
Periodicals: 4,5,7,8(incomplete)

SHERMAN

Sherman Public Library
421 N Travis St, 75090
Tel: 214-892-7239

1. M,W,F, 9-6; T,Th, 9-9; Sa, 9-5
2. Jacqueline Banfield
3. English, 2,000
4. 168 vertical file; name file
5. 837
6. Grayson County; TX, TN, KY, AR, VA, WV, MO
7. Tel & letter: yes, $1 minimum copying charge: 15¢/photocopy, 25¢/film copy
8. Jacqueline Banfield
9. No
10. Yes, duplicates only on Grayson County, through ILL

11. Yes, of Texas State Library county record project; 3-week loan through ILL
12. No
13. None
14. No
15. No
Books & Sets: 1(incomplete), 2(incomplete),3–5,7(v.1),10–14,26
Periodicals: 3(partial),4(2–, 1948–),8(partial, through v. 74, 1986),9(partial through v.136–, 1982–)

TEMPLE

Temple Public Library
101 N Main, 76501
Tel: 817-778-5556

1. M,W-F, 10-6; T, 10-9; Sa, 10-5
2. Ming-Ming Time, Reference Librarian
3. English, 1,500
4. N/AN
5. 750
6. TX state; AR, NC, SC, GA, following immigration line
7. Tel & letter: yes, NC for brief queries except 10¢/copy, 50¢/microform ($1 minimum)
8. No
9. No
10. Yes
11. No
12. No
13. N/AN
14. Yes
15. No
Books & Sets: 2,3,7,10–12,26
Periodicals: 4(1978–),7,8(1965–),9

TEXARKANA

Texarkana Public Library
600 W Third, 75501
Tel: 214-794-2149

1. M-W, 9-9; Th-Sa, 9-6
2. None
3. English, 2,800
4. None
5. 859

6. Southwestern AR, northeastern TX, southern states
7. Tel: no; letter: yes, NC except for copies
8. No
9. No
10. No
11. No
12. No
13. None
14. No
15. No
Books & Sets: 2,7(v.1)
Periodicals: 4(v.29–, 1975–), 8(v.31–47, 1943–59),9(v.105–12, 120–31, 1951–58,1975–77)

TEXAS CITY

Moore Memorial Public Library
1701 9th Ave N, 77590
Tel: 409-948-3111, ext 160

1. M-W, 9-9; Th,F, 9-6; Sa, 10-4
2. Berylyn Bazzoon
3. English, 1,200
4. 5
5. 400
6. TX, OK, southeastern US
7. Tel: no; letter: yes, NC
8. No
9. No
10. No
11. No
12. *Bibliography of Genealogy Collection,* $3
13. N/AN
14. Yes
15. No
Books & Sets: 3,4,6,7(microfilm), 10–14,26
Periodicals: 4(1970–)

TYLER

Tyler Public Library
201 S College Ave, 75702
Tel: 214-593-7323, ext 10

1. M-W, 10-8; Th-Sa, 10-5; Su, 1-5
2. Sarah H. Harper
3. English, 4,465

4. LH: 1
5. 3,384
6. Tyler, Smith County, TX; northeastern TX; southern states
7. Tel & letter: yes, NC for brief queries
8. No
9. No
10. No
11. No
12. Sarah H. Harper, "Bibliography of Smith County," in *Chronicles of Smith County* (1977), not for sale
13. N/AN
14. No
15. No
Books & Sets: 1,2(v.42–166),3–5, 8,10–14,26
Periodicals: 4,5,7,8(1965–)

WACO

Waco-McLennan County Library, 1717 Austin Ave, 76701
Tel: 817-754-0189

1. M-Th, 9-8:30; F,Sa, 9-5:30; Su, 1-5
2. S. Kethley, Librarian
3. English, ca 13,000
4. None
5. 47 book titles on 336 rolls; 2,500 rolls, census
6. Southern states; basic New England; Midwest
7. Tel & letter: yes, NC for brief queries except 10¢/copy, 75¢/microcopy plus postage with SASE
8. S. Kethley
9. No
10. No
11. No
12. No
13. N/AN
14. Yes
15. OCLC: yes, since July 1987
Books & Sets: 2(v.1–41,43–64, 67,69–99,101–21,124–26,145), 7(v.71),10–12,18, 22–24,26
Periodicals: 1(v.44–),3(v.30–48), 4(v.6–11,14–),5(v.1–8,13–23), 7,8(v.48–),9(v.90–91, 101,104, 110–11,115–16,122–)

WHITESBORO

Whitesboro Public Library
308 W Main St, 76273
Tel: 214-564-5432

1. M-F, 9-5:30
2. Priscella Thetford, Library Director
3. English, 150
4. 50
5. 25
6. Grayson and Cooke Counties
7. Tel: yes, NC; letter: yes, NC except SASE
8. No
9. No
10. No
11. No
12. No
13. Histories of local families
14. No
15. N/AN

UTAH

CEDAR CITY

**Southern Utah State College
Library, Special Collections**
351 West Center, 87420
Tel: 801-586-7945

1. M-F, 8-5 (subject to change)
2. Jackie F. Robinson
3. English, 3,250; German, 25; other, 25
4. 800
5. 200
6. Southwestern UT
7. Tel & letter: yes, NC
8. Jackie F. Robinson
9. No
10. Yes, restricted
11. No
12. No
13. Document Collection General Filing System
14. No
15. OCLC: M300

LOGAN

Logan Library
255 N Main, 84321
Tel: 801-752-2365

1. M-Th, 10-9; F,Sa, 10-6
2. Ronald Jenkins
3. English, 100
4. None
5. None
6. Cache County, UT state
7. Tel: no; letter: yes, NC
8. No
9. No
10. No
11. No
12. No
13. N/AN
14. No
15 OCLC: UUD

OGDEN

Ogden Utah Branch Genealogical Library, 539 24th St, 84401
Tel: 801-393-5248

1. M,W,Th,Sa, 9-5; T,F, 9-9
2. N/AN
3. All areas: 7,000
4. Few
5. 20,000
6. US; some foreign
7. Tel: no; letter: yes, charge
8. No
9. No
10. No
11. No
12. No
13. N/AN
14. No. Refer to Genealogical Library, Salt Lake City
15. No
Books & Sets: 2,3,8,26
Periodicals: 4,5,8,9

**Weber County Library,
Special Collection Room**
2464 Jefferson, 84401
Tel: 801-627-6921

1. M-Th, 10-9; F,Sa, 10-6
2. Mary Petterson, Nonfiction Dept
3. English, 600
4. None
5. 1,275 reels of Ogden newspapers, 1870–
6. UT state; western Americana
7. Tel & letter: yes, NC for brief queries except $1/copy
8. Fran Zedney (hobbyist)
9. No
10. Yes, duplicates only, through ILL
11. No
12. No

13. N/AN
14. No
15. OCLC: UTW (partial)

PROVO

**Brigham Young University,
Harold B. Lee Library,** 84602
Tel: 801-378-4995

1. M-F, 7am-11pm; Sa, 8am-11pm
2. Susan L. Fales
3. English, approx 19,150; 3,200 in various languages
4. N/AP
5. 180,535
6. US, especially New England, NY, IL, OH, UT; Great Britain; Scandinavia
7. Tel & letter: yes, NC for brief queries
8. Yes
9. No
10. Yes, through ILL
11. No
12. No
13. *Lee Library Genealogy Serials,* 135 pp; *US County & Township Histories at the Lee Library,* 3 vols, looseleaf
14. Yes
15. RLIN: UTBG (partial)
Books & Sets: 1,2(v.1–128), 3–18,19(orig 2v.),22–26
Periodicals: 1(v.10–13,52–), 3(v.2–),4–9

Provo Public Library
13 N 100 E, 84057
Tel: 801-373-1494

1. Winter: M-Th, 9:30-9; F,Sa, 9:30-6; summer: M, 9:30-9; T-Sa, 9:30-6
2. N/AN
3. N/AN

4. LH: approx 650 titles
5. *Daily Herald* newspaper, 1873–
6. Utah County, UT state
7. Tel & letter: yes, NC
8. No
9. Yes, $25/year for out-of-city residents
10. No
11. Yes, 3-week loan
12. No
13. Index to *Daily Herald*, 1982–
14. No
15. No
Periodicals: 4(current year)

SALT LAKE CITY

Genealogical Library of the Church of Jesus Christ of Latter-day Saints
35 N West Temple, 84150
Tel: 801-531-2331

1. M, 7:30-6; T-F, 7:30am-10pm; Sa, 7:30-5
2. Raymond S. Wright III, Manager, Main Library Operations
3. English, 165,000; other foreign languages, 20,000
4. 98% of collection is MS on microfilm
5. 1.4 million
6. Approx 200 countries worldwide
7. Tel & letter: yes, NC
8. Yes, more than 100
9. No
10. No
11. Yes, but microforms must be used on premises of either the main library or any of over 700 branch genealogical libraries
12. *General Overview Guide*
13. Genealogical Library Catalog (GLC), an automated index available at the main library, all branch libraries, and selected public and private libraries
14. Yes
15. No
Books & Sets: 1–26
Periodicals: 1–9

Salt Lake City Public Library
209 E 500 South St, 84111
Tel: 801-363-5733

1. M-Th, 9-9; F,Sa, 9-6
2. Billie J. Jones, Head, Special/Periodicals
3. English, 7,500
4. None
5. 3,000: local newspapers, Salt Lake City
6. UT state
7. Tel & letter: no. Refer to Genealogical Library
8. No
9. No
10. Yes, 7/14/28-day loan
11. No
12. No
13. Obituary index on microfilm
14. No
15. N/AN
Books & Sets: 2(v.1),19,26
Periodicals: 4,7

Utah State Historical Society Library, 300 Rio Grande, 84101
Tel: 801-533-5808

1. M-F, 9-5
2. Jay M. Haymond
3. English, 23,000
4. 3,000
5. 7,000
6. UT; the West
7. Tel & letter: yes, NC except for copies
8. No
9. No
10. No
11. No
12. No
13. *Guide to the Women's History Holdings at the Utah State Historical Society*
14. No
15. No

Utah State Library
2150 S 300 West, 84115
Tel: 801-466-5888

1. M-F, 8-5
2. None
3. English, 200
4. None
5. None
6. UT cities and counties
7. Tel & letter: yes, NC
8. No
9. No
10. Yes, via OCLC or ALA form
11. No
12. No
13. None
14. No
15. OCLC: ULC
Books & Sets: 3

WOODS CROSS

Genealogical Institute
934 W 1500 South, 84087
(mailing address: PO Box 22045, Salt Lake City, 84122)
Tel: 801-532-3327

1. By appointment
2. Arlene H. Eakle
3. English, 7,000+; German, 25; a few French, Spanish. Periodicals, 50 titles
4. Every-name computer index to research files commissioned by clients; Woods Cross city archives collected in 1975–76; Pingree and Ellison family archives, collected 1979–84; Smith family data, mostly NY and some OH and MI, 12,000 items, several vols; "A Little Bit of Indian . . .," 6,000 items, 200 vols, Indian-white genealogies comprising 2,000+ lineages
5. Few reels, few fiche
6. US, with focus on PA, NJ, and the South; some OH, IL, IN, NY, New England; England, Scotland
7. Tel: yes, NC; letter: yes, charge depending on research
8. Arlene H. Eakle
   Donald J. Martin

9. Yes, $3/day; $25/yr for membership fee
10. No
11. No

12. No
13. Card catalog; converting to computer printout
14. Yes

15. No
Books & Sets: 1,3–6,22,23,26
Periodicals: 4,5,7; some issues of 1–3,6,8,9

VERMONT

ARLINGTON

**Martha Canfield Library,
Russell Vermontiana Collection**
Main St, 05250
Tel: 802-375-6307

1. T, 8:30-11:30, 2-5; and by appointment
2. David and Mary Lou Thomas, Directors
3. English, 8,000
4. 12 linear ft of vertical files; 20 document boxes of archival material
5. N/AN
6. VT state, particularly Arlington, Sandgate, Sunderland
7. Tel & letter: yes, NC
8. Mary Lou Thomas
9. No
10. No
11. No
12. No
13. N/AN
14. No
15. OCLC: VSNA (in process)
Books & Sets: 6(VT only),26(VT only)

BELLOWS FALLS

Rockingham Free Public Library, 65 Westminster, 05101
Tel: 802-463-4270

1. T,F, 9-11, 1-8; M,W,Th, 1-8; Sa, 1-5; closed W June 15-Labor Day
2. Betty Ann Fish, Library Director
3. English, 400
4. L. S. Hayes files: 20 boxes of clippings, letters used in compilation of Rockingham History, 1907

5. *Bellows Falls Intelligencer*, subsequent newspapers, 1817–
6. VT, NH, MA
7. Tel & letter: yes, NC for brief queries
8. Yes
9. Yes, lending charge for nonresidents
10. No
11. No
12. No
13. N/AN
14. Yes
15. No
Periodicals: 9

BENNINGTON

Bennington Museum, Genealogy Library, West Main St, 05201
Tel: 802-447-1571

1. By appointment, Nov 1–May 30; limited hours posted, June 1–Oct 31
2. Anita M. Gauthier, Assistant Director
3. English, ca 3,800
4. Indeterminate number. Eleven 4-drawer file cabinets contain vertical file, MS collections
5. Negligible
6. Bennington, Bennington County towns, VT state; adjacent Washington County, NY; New England
7. Tel: no; letter: $10/hr plus copies and postage
8. Anita M. Gauthier
9. Yes, $4 for walk-in researchers
10. No
11. No
12. No
13. N/AP

14. No
15. No
Books & Sets: 2,3,18–20
Periodicals: 9

BRATTLEBORO

Brooks Memorial Library
224 Main St, 05301
Tel: 802-254-5290

1. M-Th, 9-9; F, 9-6; Sa, 9-12
2. George R. Lindsey
3. English, 1,000
4. N/AP
5. 360
6. VT; some New England
7. Tel & letter: yes, NC for brief queries
8. George R. Lindsey
9. No
10. No
11. No
12. No
13. N/AN
14. No
15. N/AN
Books & Sets: 2–5,10–14, 26(New England)
Periodicals: 9

MONTPELIER

Vermont Department of Libraries, 111 State St, c/o State Office Bldg PO, 05602
Tel: 802-828-3268

1. M-F, 7:45-4:30
2. N/AP
3. English, 500
4. None
5. 60: US Census
6. VT state
7. Tel: no; letter: yes, NC except for copies; free for 5 pages,

8¢/page thereafter, 12¢/microprint page
8. No
9. No
10. No
11. Yes, 4 reels at a time, through ILL
12. No
13. None
14. No
15. No
Books & Sets: 6

Vermont State Archives, Office of the Secretary of State
26 Terrace St, Redstone Bldg, 05602-2710
Tel: 802-828-2363

1. M-F, 7:45-4:30
2. No special section
3. English, 200
4. Several, totaling 150 ft
5. None
6. VT, New England, Canada
7. Tel & letter: yes, NC
8. No
9. No
10. No
11. No
12. *State Papers of Vermont Series*, I-XIX (1986); *Guide to Vermont's Repositories* (1987); a guide to the Library's collection is in progress
13. Descriptions, indexes, or guides to nearly all collections
14. Yes
15. No
Books & Sets: 26

ORLEANS

Orleans County Historical Society/Old Stone House Museum, Brownington Village, 05860
Tel: 802-754-2022

1. By appointment only

2. Reed Cherington
3. English, 1,000
4. 1,000
5. None
6. Orleans County, VT
7. Tel & letter: yes, NC
8. No
9. No
10. No
11. No
12. No
13. N/AN
14. No
15. N/AN

RUTLAND

Rutland Free Library
Center & Court Sts, 05701
Tel: 802-773-1860; 773-1861

1. M-Th, 9-9; F, 9-5:30; Sa, 9-5
2. None
3. English, 3,000
4. None
5. 700: Rutland *Herald*, 1794– (625); census microfilm, others (75)
6. VT, New England, NY (adjacent eastern), OH; vital records in other US
7. Tel: no; letter: no, refer queries to local genealogist
8. No
9. No
10. No
11. No
12. No
13. N/AN
14. Yes
15. No
Books & Sets: 2,3(v.1–3),26(VT, NH,MA,ME, CT,NY)
Periodicals: 9

SPRINGFIELD

Springfield Town Library
43 Main St, 05156
Tel: 802-885-3108

1. T-Th, 10-8; F, 10-5; Sa, 10-3
2. Russell Moore
3. N/AN
4. N/AN
5. N/AN
6. Springfield, Windsor County, VT; New England
7. Tel: yes, NC for brief queries; letter: yes, NC
8. No
9. No
10. Yes, duplicates only
11. No, but will make prints from microfilm records
12. Card catalog
13. N/AN
14. Yes
15. No
Books & Sets: 26(CT,MA,NH,VT)

WOODSTOCK

Norman Williams Public Library, 10 S Park St, 05091
Tel: 802-457-1710

1. M,T,Th,F, 10-5; W, 10-5, 7-9; Sa, 10-4
2. None
3. English, 200
4. 40
5. Local weekly paper, 1853–
6. Windsor County, other areas of VT
7. Tel & letter: yes, NC
8. No
9. No
10. No
11. No
12. No
13. N/AN
14. Yes
15. No
Periodicals: 9

VIRGINIA

ABINGDON

Historic Society of Washington County, Main St, 24210
Tel: None

1. M-F, 10-4
2. L. C. Angle, Jr., President
3. English, 5,000
4. 150
5. 200
6. Southwestern VA; eastern TN
7. Tel: no; letter, yes, charge for time
8. Junior Allen
9. No, but contributions encouraged
10. No
11. No
12. No
13. N/AN
14. Yes
15. N/AN
Books & Sets: 26
Periodicals: 4,8

Washington County Public Library, Oak Hill & Valley Sts, 24210
Tel: 703-628-2971

1. M,W,F,S, 9-5; T,Th, 9-9
2. Charlotte Lewis, Reference Librarian
3. English, 150
4. None
5. None
6. Southwestern VA
7. Tel: no; letter: yes, NC
8. No
9. No
10. No
11. No
12. No
13. None
14. Yes
15. No

ALEXANDRIA

Alexandria Public Library, Lloyd House Branch
220 N Washington St, 22314
Tel: 703-838-4577

1. M-Sa, 9-6; Sa, 9-1 (July-Aug)
2. Lloyd House Librarian
3. English, 25,000
4. 125
5. 300
6. Alexandria; VA state; nearby states
7. Tel & letter: yes, NC
8. No
9. No
10. No
11. No
12. No
13. *Miller's Guide on Source Material in Lloyd House Files*
14. Yes
15. OCLC: yes
Books & Sets: 3,5(v.1,2,5),7, 10–12,26
Periodicals: 4(1959–79),8(1952–60,1971–)

ARLINGTON

National Genealogical Society Library, 4527 N 17th St, 22207-2363
Tel: 703-525-0050

1. M,W, 10-9; F,Sa, 10-4
2. Marion R. Beasley, Librarian
3. English, 17,000; German, 40
4. 80
5. Several
6. US primarily
7. Tel & letter: yes, NC to members

8. N/AN
9. Yes, $5/day to nonmembers
10. Yes, to members only through ILL
11. No
12. *National Genealogical Society Library Booklist and Supplement,* $15
13. Titles not added since 1983
14. No
15. No
Books & Sets: 1,3–5,7,8,10–12,14, 19,22,23,26
Periodicals: 1,3–9

BRIDGEWATER

Bridgewater College, Alexander Mack Memorial Library
E College St, 22812
Tel: 703-828-2501, ext 510

1. M-Th, 8am-11pm; F, 8-5; Sa, 9-5; Su, 3-11
2. Ruth Greenawalt
3. English, 2,100
4. N/AN
5. 397
6. VA, WV, some PA
7. Tel: no; letter: yes, NC
8. No
9. No
10. Yes, through ILL
11. No
12. No
13. N/AN
14 No
15. OCLC: VBC
Books & Sets: 10–12,19,26

BRISTOL

Bristol Public Library
701 Goode St, 24201
Tel: 703-669-9444

1. M-Th, 9-9; F,Sa, 9-5; Su, 1-5
2. N/AN
3. English, 1,500
4. 200
5. 144
6. Emphasis on TN, VA
7. Tel & letter: yes, NC
8. No
9. No
10. No
11. No
12. No
13. N/AN
14. No
15. No
Books & Sets: 3,26
Periodicals: 4(1974–),5(1978), 8(1960–61)

CHARLOTTESVILLE

Albemarle County Historical Society Library
201 E Market St, 22901
(mailing address: 220 Court Sq)
Tel: 804-296-7294

1. M-F, 10-4; Sa, 10-12
2. A. Robert Kuhlthan
3. English, 1,500
4. 120
5. 5
6. Charlottesville, Albemarle County, adjacent counties, VA state; some states to which local residents emigrated
7. Tel & letter: yes, NC
8. No
9. No
10. No
11. No
12. No
13. N/AN
14. Yes
15. No
Periodicals: 4(1961–),8(v.46–70)

University of Virginia, Alderman Library, 22903
Tel: 804-924-3021 (Reference Department)

1. Varies; call 804-924-7911 for hours
2. No separate section
3. N/AV
4. N/AV
5. N/AV
6. VA state; southeastern US; other US
7. Tel & letter: no (we do not search but will help patrons who visit)
8. No
9. No
10. Yes, to VA residents
11. Yes, through ILL
12. *Virginia Genealogy* (1983), $4.95
13. Addendum to *Virginia Genealogy* in progress
14. No. Refer to Virginia State Library, Richmond
15. OCLC: VAa
Books & Sets: 1,2(incomplete),3,5, 6,7(v.6),10–14,17–19,22,23,26
Periodicals: 1,3(v.4–),4(v.1–33, 41–),5(v.1–8,12–),7,8(v.28–39),9

CHESAPEAKE

Chesapeake Public Library, Wallace Memorial Room
300 Cedar Rd, 23320
Tel: 804-547-6591

1. M-Th, 9-9; F,Sa, 9-5; Su, 1-5
2. Kevin Clark
3. English, 3,000
4. None
5. 100
6. Chesapeake, Norfolk County, VA
7. Tel & letter: yes, NC
8. No
9. No
10. No
11. No
12. No
13. Card catalog
14. Yes
15. OCLC: TWA
Books & Sets: 1,3,10–12,26
Periodicals: 4(v.31, 1977–)

CHESTERFIELD

Chesterfield County Library
9501 Lori Rd, PO Box 29, 23832
Tel: 804-784-1603

1. M,T,Th, 9-9; W,F,Sa, 9-5:30
2. Ann R. White
3. English, 325
4. None
5. 200
6. Primarily Chesterfield County; Henrico County to 1749
7. Tel: yes, NC; letter: yes, NC except for copies over 10 pages
8. No
9. No
10. No
11. No
12. No
13. Chesterfield County Records Bibliography (will photocopy, 10¢/page)
14. No
15. No
Books & Sets: 1,26(VA only)
Periodicals: 4(1984–),5(1962–65, 1974–),7

CHRISTIANSBURG

Montgomery-Floyd Regional Library, 125 Sheltman St, 24073
Tel: 702-382-6966

1. M-Th, 10:30-8:30; F, closed; Sa, 10:30-5:30; Su, 2-5:30
2. None
3. English, 155
4. None
5. None
6. Montgomery and Floyd Counties
7. Tel & letter: yes, NC
8. No
9. No
10. No, only to libraries within system
11. No
12. No
13. N/AV
14. Yes

15. No
Periodicals: 8

COURTLAND

Walter Cecil Rawls Library and Museum, Main St, 23837
Tel: 804-653-2821

1. M,W,Th, 9-8:30; T,F, 9-5; Sa, 9-3
2. None
3. English, 300–350
4. Approx 15 individual MSS
5. 50 (mostly census records)
6. Southeastern VA (Southampton, Isle of Wight, Sussex, Surry Counties); VA state; northeastern NC
7. Tel: yes, NC; letter: yes, NC except 15¢/copy over 10 pages
8. No
9. No
10. Yes, to registered borrowers and through ILL. Reference books do not circulate
11. No
12. No
13. None
14. Yes
15. No
Books & Sets: 1,3,7(v.1,6), 26(VA,NC)
Periodicals: 4(1975–78,1983–)

DANVILLE

Danville Public Library
511 Patton St, 24541
Tel: 804-799-5196

1. M-Th, 9-9; F, 9-5; Sa, 9-1
2. Charlotte Lowther
3. English, 6,000
4. Unknown
5. 1,000
6. VA state; some WV, NC
7. Tel: no; letter: yes, NC except 15¢/copy with $2 minimum
8. No
9. No
10. No
11. No
12. No
13. Local history bibliography

14. No
15. No
Books & Sets: 2,3(suppls only), 5,7(v.6),10,11,18,26
Periodicals: 4(1976–)

EDINBURG

Shenandoah County Library, Shenandoah Room, Rt 1, Box 1-B, Stoney Creek Blvd, 22824
Tel: 703-984-8200

1. T, 10-9; W-F, 10-6; Sa, 11-5
2. David L. Steinberg, Director
3. English, 1,200
4. None. Correspondence files, family group sheet file
5. 75: census, marriage records
6. Shenandoah County and Valley, VA state; WV, mid-Atlantic states, other US
7. Tel: no; letter: yes, $10/surname
8. David L. Steinberg
9. No
10. No
11. No
12. No
13. Copies of queries received; family group sheet file
14. Yes
15. No
Books & Sets: 3,4,26
Periodicals: 4

FAIRFAX

Fairfax County Public Library, Fairfax City Regional Library, Virginia Room, 3915 Chain Bridge Rd, 22030
Tel: 703-691-2123

1. M-Th, 9-9; F, 9-6; Sa, 9-5; Su, 12-8
2. Suzanne Levy, Virginia Room Librarian
3. English, 20,000; other, French, Spanish
4. 145 boxes
5. 1,500 reels; 9,000 fiche
6. VA, WV; states Virginians came directly from or went directly to

7. Tel & letter: yes, NC
8. No
9. No
10. Yes
11. No
12. "The Virginia Room," free flyer
13. Fairfax County history index; cemetery index
14. Yes
15. No
Books & Sets: 1,3,5–7,10–14, 19,22,24,26(plus microfiche)
Periodicals: 1(incomplete),4(v.8–, 1954–),5,7,8,9(v.92–135)

FISHERSVILLE

Augusta County Library
PO Box 600-C, 22939
Tel: 703-949-6354 or 885-3961

1. M-Th, 9-9; F,Sa, 9-5
2. Barbara Olsen, Reference Librarian
3. English, 750
4. None
5. 100
6. Augusta County, Shenandoah Valley; other VA
7. Tel & letter: yes, NC
8. No
9. No
10. Yes
11. No
12. No
13. N/AN
14. No
15. No
Books & Sets: 10,11
Periodicals: 1(1985–),4(1980–), 8(1985–)

FREDERICKSBURG

Central Rappahannock Regional Library, 1201 Caroline St, 22401
Tel: 703-371-3311

1. M-Th, 9-9; F,Sa, 9-5:30
2. Barbara P. Willis
3. English, 2,859
4. 3
5. 523
6. Fredericksburg; Stafford,

Spotsylvania, King George, and Caroline Counties
   7. Tel & letter: yes, NC
   8. No
   9. No
   10. No
   11. No
   12. No
   13. Local newspapers, 1788–1900; obituaries, 1788–1985
   14. Yes
   15. OCLC: VCR
Books & Sets: 3,6
Periodicals: 4,7

FRONT ROYAL

Samuels Public Library
538 Villa Ave, 22630
Tel: 703-635-3153

   1. M-Th, 10-9; F-Su, 10-5
   2. N/AP
   3. English, 300
   4. 2
   5. 1
   6. Warren County, VA
   7. Tel & letter: no
   8. No
   9. No
   10. No
   11. No
   12. No
   13. N/AV
   14. Yes
   15. No

GRUNDY

Buchanan County Public Library, Rt 5, Box 216, 24614
Tel: 703-935-2959

   1. M, 1-8; T,W,F,Sa, 8:30-5; Th, 8:30-8
   2. Pat Hatfield
   3. English, 800+. Also, privately printed family histories
   4. 100+
   5. 30
   6. Southwestern VA; eastern KY
   7. Tel: yes, NC; letter: yes, NC except for copies
   8. No
   9. No

   10. No
   11. No
   12. No
   13. N/AN
   14. No
   15. N/AN
Books & Sets: 3,7(1 v.)
Periodicals: 4

HAMPTON

Hampton Public Library
4207 Victoria Blvd, 23669
Tel: 804-727-6234, ext 124

   1. M-Th, 9-9; F,Sa, 9-5; Su, 1-5
   2. Cheryl E. Yielding, Senior Library Assistant
   3. English, 3,000
   4. None
   5. 500
   6. VA; some NC, SC, GA, KY, TN, MD, PA, OH; some New England
   7. Tel: yes, NC; letter: yes, NC for brief queries
   8. No
   9. No
   10. No
   11. No
   12. No
   13. None
   14. Yes
   15. No
Books & Sets: 1,3,7(v.1,6), 10–12,26
Periodicals: 4(1969–),5(1967, 1974–78),7,8(1981–)

HANOVER

Pamunkey Regional Library
PO Box 119, 23069
Tel: 804-537-6211

   1. M, 9-8; T-F, 9-5; Sa, 9-1
   2. N/AN
   3. English, 60
   4. 10
   5. None
   6. Hanover, King William, Goochland Counties
   7. Tel: no; letter: yes, NC
   8. No

   9. No
   10. No
   11. No
   12. No
   13. N/AN
   14. No
   15. N/AN
Books & Sets: 2,3

HARRISONBURG

Eastern Mennonite College, Menno Simons Historical Library Archives
1200 Park Rd, 22801
Tel: 703-433-2771, ext 178

   1. M-F, 8-12, 1-5; Sa (Sept-May), 10-1. Hours vary during college vacations, summers
   2. Grace I. Showalter
   3. English, 2,500; German, 300; Dutch, several
   4. 100, including Lutheran and Reformed church records. Strong in Germanic genealogy
   5. 100, including 90 US Census, PA Direct Tax of 1798
   6. Rockingham County, Shenandoah Valley, VA, PA, MD, WV, OH
   7. Tel & letter: yes, NC but donations appreciated
   8. Grace I. Showalter
   9. No
   10. Very rarely
   11. No
   12. No
   13. None
   14. Yes
   15. OCLC: VEM
Books & Sets: 3(3 v., 1981), 26(VA,PA,MD,NC)
Periodicals: 4(v.25–, 1971–), 5,8(incomplete)

Rockingham Public Library
45 Newman Ave, 22801
Tel: 703-434-4475

   1. M,W, 9-6; T,Th,F, 9-9; Sa, 9-5
   2. Joyce Moyers, Library Director
   3. English, 2,500; German, 50

4. 1

5. 80, mostly US Census schedules

6. Rockingham and adjoining counties (Augusta, Page, Shenandoah Counties, VA; Pendleton, Hardy Counties, WV)

7. Tel: yes, NC; letter: yes, NC except 10¢/copy plus postage

8. No

9. No

10. Yes, through ILL

11. No

12. No

13. N/AN

14. Yes. Refer to local historical society

15. No

Books & Sets: 2(v.1–3),3(3 v., 1982 suppl),7(reprint v.6,VA), 10–14,19,26(MD,PA,SC,VA)
Periodicals: 4(v.18–33, 1964–69),8(v.51–60, 1963–72)

LANCASTER

Mary Ball Washington Museum and Library, PO Box 97, Rt 3, 22503
Tel: 804-462-7892

1. M-Sa, 9-5

2. Margaret L. Hill

3. English, 1,000

4. 500

5. 100

6. VA, concentrating on Lancaster, Northumberland, Richmond, and Westmoreland Counties; some other states, mostly bordering VA

7. Tel: yes, NC for brief queries; letter: yes, $4/hr

8. Margaret L. Hill

9. No

10. No

11. No

12. No

13. Lancaster County, VA, indexes to: individual tithables, 1653–1720; marriages; cemeteries; deed book; order books, 1656–86; Revolutionary War veterans

14. Yes

15. No
Books & Sets: 26(MD,NC,RI,VA)
Periodicals: 4(v.37–40, 1983–86), 8(v.45–71, 1957–83)

LEESBURG

Thomas Balch Library of the Loudoun County Public Library
208 W Market St, 22075
Tel: 703-777-0323

1. M,F, 10-6; T-Th, 10-9; Sa, 10-5

2. Ellen Henry, Branch Head

3. English, 500

4. None

5. 100

6. Loudoun County, VA state

7. Tel: yes, NC; letter: yes, NC for brief queries

8. No

9. No

10. Yes, at the discretion of the branch head. Some material through ILL

11. No

12. No

13. Typed list of selected holdings

14. Yes

15. No

LEXINGTON

George C. Marshall Research Library, PO Box 1600, VMI Parade, 24450
Tel: 703-463-7103

1. M-F, 8:30-4:30 except holidays

2. None

3. N/AN

4. 5

5. N/AN

6. Shenandoah Valley of VA

7. Tel & letter: yes, NC

8. No

9. No

10. N/AN

11. No

12. *Manuscript Collections of the George C. Marshall Library: A Guide*

13. Registers to Smith-Crum Papers, Donald Wilson Papers, Kathleen B. Carter Collection

14. No

15. No

MANASSAS

Prince William Public Library, Virginiana Collection
8601 Mathis Ave, 22111
Tel: 703-361-8211

1. M-Th, 10-9; F,Sa, 10-5; Su (Sept-May), 12-5

2. Donald L. Wilson, Virginiana Librarian

3. English, 5,000

4. 10

5. 500; some material on microfiche

6. VA (primarily Prince William County, surrounding areas)

7. Tel & letter: yes, NC

8. Virginiana Librarian can assist with research

9. No

10. No

11. No

12. No

13. *Prince William County: A Guide to Sources*, leaflet

14. No. Refer to Prince William County Genealogical Society

15. OCLC: VPW
Books & Sets: 1,3,6,7(v.6), 10–14,26(6v.)
Periodicals: 4(1950–),5(1974–), 7,8(1985–)

NEWPORT NEWS

Newport News Public Library System, West Avenue Branch
30th St & West Ave, 23607
(Administrative Office: 2400 Washington Ave, 23607)
Tel: 804-247-8505

1. M,T,Th,F, 9-6; W, 11:30-8:30

2. None

3. English, 5,000+

4. 1: Old Dominion Land Company papers
5. 2,038
6. VA Tidewater Peninsula area
7. Tel & letter: yes, NC
8. No
9. No
10. No
11. No
12. No
13. Virginiana Room listing on public access catalog terminals; finding aid for Old Dominion Land Company papers
14. No
15. No
Books & Sets: 2,7,10,12
Periodicals: 4(1974–),8(1921–54, 1984–),9

NORFOLK

Kirn Memorial Library, Sargeant Memorial Room, Norfolk Public Library
301 E City Hall Ave, 23510
Tel: 804-441-2503

1. M,T,Th-Sa, 9-5; W, 9-9
2. Anne Richardson
3. English, 14,000
4. 100
5. 3,300
6. VA counties and cities; contiguous out-of-state counties (Currituck, Gates Counties, NC, and Somerset, Worcester Counties, MD)
7. Tel: yes, NC; letter: yes, NC except 15¢/copy plus postage
8. No
9. No
10. No
11. No
12. No
13. *Journey into the Past: Family & Local History at the Sargeant Memorial Room*, leaflet
14. Yes
15. No
Books & Sets: 2(v.1–155, incomplete),3,4,7,10–14,19,26
Periodicals: 4(v.22–, 1968–), 5(1976–),8(v.60–, 1972–),9

PEARISBURG

Pearisburg Public Library
112 Tazewell St, 24134
Tel: 703-921-2556

1. M, 12-8; T, 12-5; W,F, 9-5; Th, 9-8; Sa, 9-1
2. N/AN
3. N/AN
4. N/AN
5. N/AN
6. Giles County, VA, and surrounding areas
7. Tel: yes, NC; letter: yes, NC except 15¢/copy
8. No
9. No
10. Yes, through ILL
11. N/AN
12. No
13. N/AN
14. No
15. N/AN

PETERSBURG

Petersburg Public Library
William R. McKenney Building, Reference Department, 137 S Sycamore St, 23803
Tel: 804-733-2387

1. M,W, 9-9; T,Th-Sa, 9-5
2. Michael C. Walker, Public Services Librarian
3. English, 3,000
4. None
5. Petersburg newspapers only on microfilm
6. Petersburg and surrounding area; VA county histories
7. Tel & letter: yes, NC
8. No
9. No
10. No
11. No
12. No
13. Virginia State Library Microfiche listing of holdings - CAVALIR
14. Yes
15. No

PORTSMOUTH

Portsmouth Public Library
601 Court St, 23704
Tel: 804-393-8501

1. M-F, 9-9; Sa, 9-5
2. Susan H. Burton
3. English, 7,000
4. 50
5. 10
6. Portsmouth, Norfolk County (pre-1960), VA
7. Tel & letter: yes, NC
8. No
9. No
10. No
11. No
12. No
13. CAVALIR
14. Yes
15. No
Books & Sets: 1,3,7(v.1,6),19(6 v., 1903–26,1967),26(VA only)
Periodicals: 4

RADFORD

Radford Public Library
30 First St, 24141
Tel: 703-731-3621

1. M-W, 10-8:30; Th,F, 10-5:30; Sa, 10-4:30; Su (winter), 2-5
2. Sue Barton
3. English, 400+
4. None
5. None
6. Southwestern, central, eastern VA; WV
7. Tel: yes, NC; letter: yes, NC except 10¢/copy
8. No
9. No
10. No
11. N/AP
12. No
13. Typed index with book titles
14. No
15. No

RICHMOND

Richmond Public Library
101 E Main St, 23219
Tel: 804-780-4672

1. Sept-May: M-F, 9-9; Sa,
9-5; Su, 2-6; June-Aug: M-F, 9-9;
Sa, 9-1
2. William S. Simpson, Jr.
3. English, LH, 1,200
4. None
5. 2,500: Richmond news-
papers, 1852–
6. Richmond; VA state
7. Tel: yes, NC; letter: yes, NC
except 10¢/copy
8. No
9. No
10. Yes, through ILL
11. No
12. No
13. Local newspaper clipping
file, local biography index, local
periodical index
14. No
15. OCLC: VRP
Books & Sets: 6

Virginia Historical Society
428 N Boulevard, 23220
Tel: 804-358-4901

1. M-Sa, 9-4:45
2. Frances Fugate
3. English, 13,975
4. 1,500
5. 787
6. Primarily VA; some
southern states
7. Tel & letter: yes, NC
8. No
9. No
10. No
11. No
12. *Guide to the Manuscript
Collections of the Virginia
Historical Society*, $10
13. N/AN
14. Yes
15. No

Books & Sets: 2(v.1–15),3(1982
suppl),7,10–12,13(South,VA,
WV), 14,26
Periodicals: 6(v.1–20),8(v.1–74),
9(v.102–41)

**Virginia State Library and
Archives**, 11th St at Capitol Sq,
23219-3491
Tel: 804-786-8929 (Local His-
tory); 786-2306 (Genealogy and
Archives)

1. M-Sa, 8:15-5
2. Phyllis Young (Local
History); Conley L. Edwards
(Genealogy and Archives)
3. 1,100,000 in English,
French, German, other languages
4. 49,000 cu ft of VA state,
local, genealogical records
5. 13,000
6. VA; areas formerly part of
VA; surrounding states
7. Tel: no; letter: yes, NC
8. Yes
9. No
10. Yes, to VA residents and
libraries only
11. Yes, through ALA, 2-week
loan
12. Guides found in current list
of publications available for
purchase from Virginia State
Library and Archives
13. Numerous unpublished
guides and catalogs
14. Yes
15. OCLC: VIC
Books & Sets: 1–7,10–20,26
Periodicals: 1,4,5,7–9

ROANOKE

**Roanoke City Public Library,
Virginia Room**
706 S Jefferson St, 24016
Tel: 703-981-2073

1. M-Sa, 9-5
2. Alice Carol Tuckwiller
3. English, 13,500+

4. No estimate
5. 1,615
6. Roanoke Valley; VA state;
WV, PA, MD, NC, TN, KY; some
DE, SC, GA
7. Tel & letter: yes, NC except
10¢/photocopy, 50¢/microfilm
8. No
9. No
10. No
11. No
12. No
13. None
14. Yes
15. No
Books & Sets: 2,3,5,7,10–14,
16,18(v.22–),19,26
Periodicals: 1(v.44–, 1968–),
4(v.13–, 1959–),5,8(v.1–26,
45–),9(incomplete)

ROCKY MOUNT

Franklin County Public Library
E Court St, 24151
Tel: 703-483-3098

1. M,T,W,F, 8:30-5; Th,
8:30am-9pm; Sa, 9am-12 noon
2. Dorothy Comer
3. English, 250
4. 25
5. 50
6. VA counties of Franklin,
Patrick, Henry, Pittsylvania,
Montgomery; TN counties of
Davidson, others
7. Tel & letter: yes, NC for
brief queries. Refer to local
genealogist
8. Dorothy Comer
9. No
10. No
11. No
12. No
13. N/AN
14. Yes
15. No
Books & Sets: 26 (VA only)
Periodicals: 4(incomplete),
8(incomplete)

RUSTBURG

Campbell County Public Library, Main St, 24588
Tel: 804-332-5161, ext 127

1. M,W,F,Sa, 9-5:30; T, Th, 9-9
2. N/AN
3. English, 500
4. 10
5. 11
6. Rustburg area
7. Tel & letter: yes, NC for brief queries
8. No
9. No
10. Yes
11. Yes
12. No
13. N/AN
14. No
15. No
Books & Sets: 7,10,26(VA)

STAUNTON

Staunton Public Library
19 S Market St, 24401
Tel: 703-885-8073

1. Sept-May: M-Th, 9-9; F,Sa, 9-5; June-Aug: M-Th, 9-9; F, 9-5; Sa, 9-1
2. Barbara M. Jenner
3. English, 1,000
4. None
5. 22
6. VA, especially Shenandoah Valley, Augusta County; some PA, WV
7. Tel & letter: yes, NC except 10¢/copy plus postage
8. No
9. No
10. Yes, through ILL, 3-book maximum for 1-month loan
11. No
12. *Bibliography of the Genealogy and Local History Collection of the Fannie Bayly King Public Library, Staunton, VA*, $3
13. None

14. Yes
15. No
Books & Sets: 2(through v.115),26
Periodicals: 4

TAZEWELL

Tazewell County Public Library
PO Box 929, 310 E Main St, 24651
Tel: 703-988-2541

1. M-W, F,Sa, 9-5:30; Th, 9-8:30; Su, 2-6
2. Michael Gilley, Reference Librarian
3. English, 746
4. 8 drawers of vertical file material: pamphlets, newsclippings, lineages
5. 59
6. Southwestern VA, surrounding VA area; WV, KY, NC
7. Tel & letter: yes, NC except for copies and postage
8. No
9. No
10. Yes, duplicates only, through ILL
11. No
12. No
13. *Genealogy/Local History: Selected Resources for Genealogical Research*
14. Yes
15. No
Books & Sets: 3,7(v.1),26(VA,NC)
Periodicals: 4(v.35–, 1981–), 8(v.1–62, 1912–74 incomplete; v.67–, 1979–)

WAYNESBORO

Waynesboro Public Library
600 S Wayne Ave, 22980
Tel: 703-949-6173

1. M-F, 9-9; Sa, 9-5
2. Dorothy Anne Reinbold, Library Director
3. English, 3,000+
4. 50 folders on local families
5. VA, PA census; 75 other assorted reels

6. VA, especially Shenandoah Valley, Augusta County; some PA, WV, MD; some Civil War material
7. Tel & letter: yes, NC for brief queries
8. Anne Covington Kidd
   Margaret Crizer Reese
9. No
10. Yes
11. No
12. No
13. N/AN
14. Yes
15. No
Books & Sets: 1,3,4,26
Periodicals: 1(v.46–, 1970–), 4(1960–),5,7,8(1970–)

WILLIAMSBURG

Colonial Williamsburg Foundation, Central Library
415 N Boundary St, PO Box C, 23187
Tel: 804-220-7423 (Reference Desk)

1. M-F, 8-5; Sa, 9-1
2. Susan S. Berg, Reader Services Librarian
3. English, 51,000
4. 90 collections, plus single items
5. 4,000
6. Williamsburg, VA, and surrounding counties. Primarily 17th- & 18th-century information; some 19th century
7. Tel & letter: yes, NC except for copies
8. No
9. No
10. Yes, through ILL
11. Yes, through ILL
12. Marylee G. McGregor, *Guide to the Manuscript Collections of Colonial Williamsburg*, 2nd ed (1969), free
13. Variety of in-house indexes
14. No
15. OCLC: VCWW
Books & Sets: 3,7,10–13,26
Periodicals: 8(incomplete), 9(incomplete)

WINCHESTER

Handley Library, Corner of
Braddock & Piccadilly Sts, 22601
Tel: 703-662-9041

1. Archives Dept: winter: M-W, 1-9; Th,F, 1-5; Sa, 9-5; summer: M-W, 1-7:30; Th,F, 1-5; Sa, 9-4
2. Archives Librarian
3. English, 4,000
4. 700
5. 500
6. Shenandoah Valley of VA, with emphasis on Frederick County and Winchester
7. Tel: yes, NC for brief queries; letter: NC for brief queries, otherwise refer to Winchester-Frederick County Historical Society
8. No
9. No
10. No
11. No
12. No
13. Register guides and inventories for collections; pathfinders for major topics
14. Yes
15. No
Books & Sets: 1,3,4,7,10–14
Periodicals: 4(1962–72,1979–), 5(v.4, 13–24)

YORKTOWN

York County Public Library
8500 George Washington
Memorial Hwy, 23692
Tel: 804-898-0077

1. M-Th, 10-9; F, 10-6; Sa, 10-5; Su, 1-5
2. None
3. English, 570; German, 2
4. 32 separate MSS
5. None
6. Eastern VA, with emphasis on York County and adjacent areas
7. Tel & letter: yes, NC
8. No
9. No
10. Yes, 4-week loan
11. No
12. No
13. N/AN
14. Yes
15. N/AN
Books & Sets: 26(VA)
Periodicals: 4(1982–85), 8(v.69–71)

WASHINGTON

DES MOINES

Highline Community College
Box 98000, 98198
Tel: 206-878-3710, ext 230

1. M-Th, 7:45am-9:30pm; F, 7:45am-4:45; Sa, 12-4 (fall, winter, spring quarters)
2. Nancy Lennstrom, Librarian
3. English, 500
4. Extensive vertical files
5. None
6. Miscellaneous
7. Tel & letter: no
8. No
9. No
10. No
11. No
12. No
13. Mimeo guide
14. No
15. No
Books & Sets: 2,5(v.6)
Periodicals: 4(1971–83)

OLYMPIA

Olympia Timberland Library
8th & Franklin Sts, 98501
Tel: 206-352-0595

1. M-Th, 10-9; F,Sa, 10-5; Su (Oct-May), 1-5
2. Alma Greenwood, Head, Reference Dept
3. English, 5,000; German, 6
4. None
5. 100
6. Thurston County, WA; WA state; US; some foreign
7. Tel: yes, NC for brief queries; letter: refer to local genealogical society
8. Alma Greenwood
   Jean Laws

9. No
10. Yes, family and county histories, but not records; will photocopy on ILL
11. No
12. No
13. Materials included in Library catalog and Western Library Network
14. Yes. Refer to local genealogical society
15. OCLC: WLN-WaO (NUC code)
Books & Sets: 1,3,6,7,10–14, 16,19,26
Periodicals: 1,4,5,7–9

Washington State Library
Capitol Campus, 98504
Tel: 206-753-4024

1. M-F, 8-5
2. Jeanne Engerman
3. English, 3,000
4. 300
5. 40,000: mostly WA state newspapers
6. LH: Pacific Northwest; G: WA state
7. Tel & letter: yes, NC for brief queries
8. No
9. No
10. Yes, through ILL
11. Yes, through ILL
12. *Historical Records of Washington State: Records and Papers Held at Repositories* (1981); 2-fiche guide to newspapers on microfilm
13. N/AN
14. No. Refer to Olympia Genealogy Society
15. No

ORTING

Heritage Quest Research Library, 220 W Bridge St, 98360
Tel: 206-893-2029

1. M-Th, 8:30-5:30; F, 8:30-4:30
2. Leland K. Meitzler
3. English, 3,500; German, 200; other, 50
4. 200
5. 4,000
6. US; Germany
7. Tel & letter: no
8. Leland K. Meitzler
9. No
10. No
11. No
12. No
13. N/AN
14. No
15. No
Books & Sets: 5
Periodicals: 4(almost complete),7

PORT ANGELES

Clallam County Genealogical Society, The Museum, 223 E 4th St, 98362
Tel: 206-452-7831, ext 384

1. M-F, 10-4
2. Kathleen Barrett, Society President
3. English, 500
4. N/AN
5. 30 film; 5,000 fiche
6. Clallam County, WA; US; foreign
7. Tel & letter: yes, $3/hr, plus copies
8. Kathleen Barrett
9. No

10. No
11. No
12. No
13. N/AN
14. Yes
15. N/AN
Books & Sets: 3,26
Periodicals: 4(1966–),8(1981–), 9(1985–)

RICHLAND

Richland Public Library
955 Northgate, 99352
Tel: 509-943-9117

1. M-Th, 10:30-9; F,Sa, 10:30-5:30
2. None
3. English, 300
4. 10 file drawers of LH, newspaper clippings, other ephemera
5. 45 old census films; 500 reels of local newspapers
6. Benton, Franklin Counties
7. Tel & letter: yes, NC for brief queries
8. No
9. No
10. No
11. No
12. No
13. None
14. No
15. No
Books & Sets: 2,6

SEATTLE

Seattle Public Library
1000 4th Ave, 98104
Tel: 206-625-4895 (Genealogy Reference Desk)

1. M-Th, 9-9; F,Sa, 9-6
2. Darlene E. Hamilton, Genealogy Librarian, History Dept
3. English, 14,000; French, Scandinavian languages, est 50 vols each
4. Not estimated
5. 2,000
6. Genealogy collection contains material from all parts of

US; WA, OR material included in separate Northwest History Collection; limited foreign
7. Tel: yes, NC for brief queries; letter: yes, NC except 25¢/copy
8. Darlene E. Hamilton
9. No
10. Yes, selected titles through ILL
11. Yes, selected microforms
12. No
13. None
14. Yes
15. No
Books & Sets: 1–7,10–14, 16–19,23–26
Periodicals: 1,3–5,6(v.11–12, 19–20),7–9

University of Washington, Suzzallo Library, Special Collections Division, 98195
Tel: 206-543-1929

1. M-F, 10-5; Sa, 9-5
2. Carla Rickerson
3. LH: English, 30,000+; some materials in French, Spanish, Russian, Japanese
4. LH: 3,500+
5. N/AN
6. WA, OR, British Columbia, AK, Yukon, western Alberta, western ID, western MT
7. Tel: yes, NC for brief queries; letter: $7 minimum for in-state requests of less than 20 photocopies
8. No
9. No
10. No
11. No
12. *Dictionary Catalog of the Pacific Northwest Collection* (out of print); *Pacific Northwest Newspapers on Microfilm at the University of Washington Libraries*, $5; *Explorers' and Travellers' Journals Documenting Early Contacts with Native Americans in the Pacific Northwest*, $5
13. N/AN
14. No
15. OCLC: WaU

Books & Sets: 1,2,6,11,13, 15–17,19,26
Periodicals: 5

SPOKANE

Spokane Public Library
W 906 Main Ave, 99201
Tel: 509-838-4226

1. M,T,Th,F, 9-9; W, 1-6; Sa (except late June-Sept), 9-6
2. None
3. English, 6,500
4. N/AN
5. 765
6. US; some foreign
7. Tel: no; letter: yes, $5/hr
8. No
9. No
10. Yes
11. No
12. *Genealogical Holdings of the Spokane Public Library*, $10 plus $1.50 postage; supplement, $5 plus $1 postage
13. N/AN
14. Yes
15. No
Books & Sets: 2–7,10,11,13,17, 19,24(1 v.),26
Periodicals: 4–9

TACOMA

Tacoma Public Library, Special Collections
1102 Tacoma Ave S, 98402
Tel: 206-591-5622

1. M-Th, 9-9; F,Sa, 9-6
2. Gary Fuller Reese, Managing Librarian
3. English, 5,000 (genealogy only); German, 5. Pacific Northwest Americana, 20,000
4. 50
5. 4,500
6. Pacific Northwest; genealogy mostly Midwest, South, New England
7. Tel & letter: yes, NC
8 No
9. No
10. Yes, through ILL

11. Yes
12. No
13. Biographical file, Northwest note file, local obituary file, local buildings file
14. No
15. OCLC: TAW
Books & Sets: 1–7,10–14,18, 19,22,23,26
Periodicals: 4,5,7,8(1957–), 9(1943–)

Washington State Historical Society, Hewitt Library
315 N Stadium Way, 98403
Tel: 206-593-2830

1. T-Sa, 9:30-5
2. Frank L. Green
3. English, 10,000
4. 5000 cu ft
5. 1,000
6. Pacific Northwest
7. Tel: no; letter: yes, $10/hr
8. No
9. No
10. No
11. No
12. Request publications list of the Washington State Historical Society. Library recommends *Genealogical Resources in Washington State*, available from Washington State Archives, PO Box 9000, Olympia, 98504
13. See #12. For an index to Library's family histories, contact Tacoma-Pierce County Genealogical Society, PO Box 1952, Tacoma, 98401

14. No. Refer to Tacoma-Pierce County Genealogical Society
15. N/AN
Books & Sets: 3,13
Periodicals: 9(incomplete)

WALLA WALLA

Walla Walla Public Library
238 E Alder, 99362
Tel: 509-527-4550

1. M-Th, 10-9; F,Sa, 10-5
2. Stephen C. Towery
3. English, 500
4. None
5. 20
6. Pacific Northwest, specifically WA state
7. Tel & letter: yes, NC for brief queries
8. No. Refer to local Genealogical Society
9. No
10. No
11. No
12. No
13. N/AN
14. No
15. N/AN
Books & Sets: 2(v.1–9,43–86), 3,10,11
Periodicals: 4

YAKIMA

Yakima Valley Genealogical Society Library, 221 East B St, PO Box 445-98907, 98901
Tel: 509-248-1328

1. M-W,F, 10-4, Th, 10-9; July, Aug: M-F, 10-4. Weekends by appointment
2. Ellen Brzoska, Librarian
3. English, 5,000; German, 2 or 3
4. 600 (vertical file)
5. 200
6. Yakima, Klickitat, Kittitas Counties; WA state; census indexes for entire US; approx 160 exchange periodicals from US, Canada; some England, Germany, Ireland
7. Tel: yes, NC; letter: yes, donation requested
8. Ellen Brzoska
   Wilbur Helm
9. Yes, $1/first day for nonmembers; thereafter, free
10. No
11. No
12. *Bibliography of Yakima Valley Genealogical Society Library* (1986), $12.50
13. Recent acquisitions published in each issue of *Yakima Valley Genealogical Society Quarterly*
14. Yes
15. No
Books & Sets: 3–5,7,10–14,17, 22–24,26
Periodicals: 1(v.1–13, 54–), 3(v.32–33, 1968–70),4(v.5–12 incomplete; v.13–, 1960–),5,7, 8(v.1–49 incomplete; v.50–, 1962–),9(v.1–131 on microfilm)

West Virginia

CHARLESTON

Kanawha County Public Library, 123 Capitol St, 25301
Tel: 304-343-4646

1. M-F, 9-9; Sa, 9-5; Su (Sept-Apr), 1-5
2. Susan H. Harper
3. N/AN
4. N/AN
5. N/AN
6. Charleston and Kanawha County, WV
7. Tel & letter: yes, NC for LH queries only
8. No
9. No
10. No
11. No
12. No
13. N/AN
14. Yes
15. OCLC: WVK

West Virginia Department of Culture and History, Archives and History Division, Cultural Center, Capitol Complex, 25304
Tel: 304-348-0230

1. M-Th, 9-9; F, 9-5; Sa, 1-5
2. N/AN
3. English, 5,500
4. 80
5. 24,000, including 20,000 rolls of local newspapers
6. WV, VA, surrounding states
7. Tel & letter: yes, NC except for copies
8. Yes
9. No
10. No
11. No
12. No
13. Unpublished guides to MS and archives collections

14. Yes
15. No
Books & Sets: 2–5,7,10–14,19,26
Periodicals: 4,7–9

CHARLES TOWN

Old Charles Town Library
200 E Washington St, 25414
Tel: 304-725-2208

1. M-Sa, 9:30-5
2. None
3. English, 1,500
4. None
5. None
6. WV state; MD, VA
7. Tel: no; letter: yes, NC
8. No
9. No
10. No
11. N/AP
12. No
13. Card catalog
14. No
15. No
Books & Sets: 5,26(VA)
Periodicals: 4(few)

CLARKSBURG

Clarksburg-Harrison Public Library, West Virginia Collection, 404 W Pike St, 26301
Tel: 304-624-6512, ext 21

1. M,W, 1-8; T,Th, 9-3; F, 9-5; Sa, 9-1
2. Lloyd J. Leggett, Historian/Curator
3. English, 3,000; German, 2
4. 100 linear ft
5. 50
6. North central WV (Harrison, Marion, Doddridge, Ritchie, Lewis, Taylor, Upshur, and Gilmer Counties)

7. Tel & letter: yes, NC for brief queries
8. Lloyd J. Leggett
9. No
10. Yes, 3-week loan, 1 renewal
11. No
12. No
13. N/AV
14. Yes
15. No
Books & Sets: 1–4,8,15–18
Periodicals: 4,8

HUNTINGTON

Cabell County Public Library
455 9th St Plaza, 25701
Tel: 304-523-9451

1. M-Th, 9-9; F,Sa, 9-5
2. Matt Onion, Head, Reference Dept
3. English, 3,000
4. None
5. 200
6. WV, VA, KY, OH
7. Tel: no; letter: yes, NC
8. No
9. No
10. No
11. No
12. No
13. N/AN
14. No
15. No
Books & Sets: 2
Periodicals: 4(1954–),9(incomplete)

Marshall University, James E. Morrow Library, Special Collections Department, 25705
Tel: 304-696-2343

1. University sessions: M-F, 8am-10pm; F, 8-4:30; Sa, 9-5; Su, 1-10

2. Lisle G. Brown
3. English, 1,000
4. 200
5. 130
6. WV state; OH, KY, VA, PA
7. Tel: no; letter: yes, NC
8. No
9. No
10. No
11. No
12. No
13. In-house guide to LH materials; will copy for patrons
14. No
15. OCLC: WVH
Books & Sets: 3,7,10–14,19,26

MARTINSBURG

Martinsburg-Berkeley County Public Library, 101 W King St, Public Square, 25401
Tel: 304-267-8933

1. M-F, 9-9; Sa, 9-5; Su, 1-5
2. Keith E. Hammersla
   Lois A. Brady
3. English, 900–1,000
4. 1–5
5. 500
6. Berkeley, Morgan, Jefferson Counties of WV; WV state; · Shenandoah Valley counties of VA; some VA, MD, PA, OH
7. Tel & letter: yes, NC for brief queries except 10¢/copy
8. Keith E. Hammersla
9. No
10. No
11. No
12. No
13. K. E. Hammersla, *Genealogy at the Martinsburg-Berkeley County Public Library: A Guide to Selected Genealogical Resources of Berkeley, Jefferson, and Morgan Counties of West Virginia*
14. Yes
15. No

Books & Sets: 3(v.1–3),10, 26(VA,MD,PA)
Periodicals: 4(v.33–37,41–, 1979–83,1987–)

PARKERSBURG

Parkersburg and Wood County Public Library, 3100 Emerson Ave, 26101
Tel: 304-485-6564

1. M-Th, 9-9; Sa, closed; Su, 1-5
2. Ann R. Lorentz, Reference Librarian
3. English, 1,500–2,000
4. None
5. 1,500 microfilm; 4,000 microfiche
6. WV state; some OH, KY, VA, PA
7. Tel & letter: yes, NC except 10¢/copy
8. No
9. No
10. Yes
11. No
12. No
13. N/AN
14. No
15. No

RIPLEY

Jackson County Library
208 N Church St, 25271
Tel: 304-372-5343; ask for Reference Department

1. M-Th, 10-8; F, 10-5; Sa, 10-3
2. E. DeWitt Williams
3. English, 1,600
4. Less than 100
5. Less than 100: mainly newspapers, census
6. Jackson County, WV, and adjoining counties in WV, OH; regions (VA, southern PA, MD)

from which settlers to this area came

7. Tel: no; letter: yes, NC for brief queries, otherwise $5/hr
8. E. DeWitt Williams
9. No
10. Yes, through ILL, 1-week loan
11. Yes, duplicates only, through ILL
12. No
13. Card catalog
14. No. Refer to Historical Society
15. No
Books & Sets: 3,26
Periodicals: 4(1984–)

WEIRTON

Mary H. Weir Public Library
3442 Main St, 26062-4590
Tel: 304-797-8510

1. Winter: M-Th, 12-8; F,Sa, 10-5; summer: M-F, 10-6; Sa, 10-5
2. Lois Aleta Fundis, Reference Librarian
3. English, 50
4. None
5. 700: US Census, local newspapers
6. City of Weirton and surrounding counties of Hancock and Brooke, WV
7. Tel & letter: yes, NC except 25¢/copy
8. No
9. No
10. Yes, through ILL
11. Yes, through ILL, to other libraries
12. No
13. "Index to the Archives of the Mary H. Weir Public Library"
14. Yes
15. No
Books & Sets: 3,14
Periodicals: 4

WISCONSIN

APPLETON

Appleton Public Library
1132 W Oklahoma St, 54911
Tel: 414-735-6178

1. M-Th, 9-9; F, 9-6; Sa, 9-5; Su, 1-5
2. Cecilia Wiltzius
3. English, 2,500
4. None
5. 250
6. WI state, with emphasis on Fox River Valley
7. Tel & letter: yes, NC
8. Susan Zolkowski
9. No
10. No
11. No
12. *Genealogical Resources*
13. N/AN
14. No
15. OCLC: WIQ
Books & Sets: 3,10,11,17
Periodicals: 4(1981–),7

BELOIT

Beloit Public Library
409 Pleasant St, 53511
Tel: 608-364-6715

1. M-Th, 9:30-8:45; F,Sa, 9:30-5:15
2. None
3. English, 1,200
4. 200 maps; 1,144 pamphlets
5. 1,000, including local newspapers
6. Rock County
7. Tel & letter: no
8. No
9. No
10. No
11. No

12. No
13. N/AN
14. No. Refer to local Genealogy Society
15. OCLC: yes (recent)
Books & Sets: 1(1st ed),2,3(suppls lacking),26(incomplete)
Periodicals: 4(broken run since 1970),9(1971–)

BLACK RIVER FALLS

Monroe, Juneau, Jackson County Genealogy Workshop Library, Rt 3, Box 253, 54615
Tel: 608-378-4388

1. By appointment only
2. Carolyn Habelman, President
3. English, 600; German, 5; Norwegian, 1
4. 1,500
5. 30
6. Monroe, Juneau, Jackson Counties, WI; New England; NY, VA, NC, OH, PA, MI; Germany, England
7. Tel: yes, NC; letter: yes, NC except for copies and donation
8. Joy Reisinger, CGRS; Carolyn Habelman, volunteer
9. No
10. Yes, 1-month loan; available at meetings for members
11. No
12. No
13. German Lutheran/Catholic church records of eastern Monroe County; county tombstone name index
14. Yes
15. N/AN
Books & Sets: 4,5
Periodicals: 3,4,8,9

CHIPPEWA FALLS

Chippewa Falls Public Library
105 W Central St, 54729
Tel: 715-723-1146

1. Winter: M-Th, 9-9; F, 9-6; Sa, 9-5; Su, 1-5; summer: M,Th, 9-9; T,W,F, 9-6
2. Rosemary Kilbridge
3. English, 300
4. None
5. 20
6. Chippewa Falls, Chippewa County, north central WI, WI state
7. Tel & letter: yes, NC for brief queries except for copies, with SASE
8. No
9. No
10. Yes, through ILL
11. Yes, through ILL
12. No
13. N/AN
14. Yes
15. No
Periodicals: 4(current ed only)

EAU CLAIRE

University of Wisconsin-Eau Claire, McIntyre Library
Special Collections, 54701
Tel: 715-836-2739

1. Sept-May: M,W,F, 8-5; T,W, 8-5, 7-9; Sa, 1-5; summer: M-F, 8-5
2. Richard L. Pifer
3. N/AN
4. 87 MSS and 25 public records
5. 100: MSS;100: public records
6. Primarily Chippewa Valley

in northwestern WI, other WI state

7. Tel: yes, NC; letter: yes, $7 for research beyond 2 hrs

8. Richard L. Pifer
   Rita Sorkness

9. No

10. Yes, through ILL

11. Yes, through ILL

12. Revision in progress

13. N/AN

14. Yes

15. OCLC: currently being cataloged

Books & Sets: 1,3,6,19,23

Periodicals: 9

FOND DU LAC

Fond du Lac Public Library
32 Sheboygan St, 54935
Tel: 414-921-0066

1. Winter: M-F, 9-9; Sa, 9-5; summer: M,W,F, 9-9; T,Th, 9-6

2. Kay Conrad

3. English, 800; French, 2

4. None

5. 750

6. Fond du Lac City and County; WI state

7. Tel & letter: yes, with charge for time and copies

8. Yes

9. No

10. No

11. No

12. No

13. *Fond du Lac County Genealogical and Local History Materials*, compiled by Reference Dept (1986)

14. Yes

15. OCLC: WIF

Books & Sets: 2(v.1–116),3

Periodicals: 4(1968–75,1977–)

GREEN BAY

Brown County Library
Local History and Genealogy,
515 Pine St, 54301
Tel: 414-497-3471

1. Winter: M,T,Th-Sa, 1-5; W, 1-5, 6-9; summer: M,T,Th,F, 1-5; W, 1-5, 6-8; Sa, 9-1 by appointment

2. Mary Jane Herber

3. English, 4,000; German, 30; French, 200–300

4. Less than 50

5. 1,325: local newspapers; 271: census index; 230: federal census; 76: WI census; 54: county histories, etc.

6. WI, French-Canadian marriage repertoires; other US

7. Tel & letter: yes, NC except 25¢/copy with $2 minimum

8. Mary Jane Herber

9. No

10. Yes, through ILL

11. Yes, but no census films beyond library system

12. In progress

13. Booklet annually through Genealogy Workshop

14. Yes

15. OCLC: GZG

Books & Sets: 2(v.1–126),3–5, 7(v.1),9–14,17,19,22–26

Periodicals: 2,3(v.40–, 1976–),4, 5(1980),7,8(v.62–, 1974–),9

University of Wisconsin-Green Bay, Library Learning Center, Special Collections/Area Research Center
2420 Nicolet Dr, 54301
Tel: 414-465-2539

1. M-F, 8:30-5; W, 5-9pm during academic year

2. Thomas Reitz

3. 5,000: French, German, Dutch, English

4. 100 MSS; 500 county archives series

5. 400

6. Northeastern WI

7. Tel: yes, NC, but prefer letter; letter: yes, $2 postage/handling, 15¢/photocopy, 25¢/microcopy

8. Yes

9. No

10. No

11. Yes, through ILL; limited lending policy

12. *Guide to Archives and Manuscripts in the University of Wisconsin-Green Bay Area Research Center*

13. N/AN

14. Yes

15. OCLC: GZW

Books & Sets: 3(3v., suppls to 1982)

Periodicals: 4

JANESVILLE

Janesville Public Library
316 S Main St, 53545
Tel: 608-755-2866

1. M-F, 9-9; Sa, 9-5:30; Su (Oct-May), 1-4

2. Richard Thayer

3. English, 1,100–1,200

4. One (14-tape set of Janesville Labor Movement oral history for GM and UAW)

5. 824

6. Janesville, Rock County, WI state

7. Tel & letter: yes, NC except 15¢/copy

8. Karen Helwig

9. No

10. Yes, only books in circulating collection

11. No

12. No

13. *Janesville Gazette Obituary Index, 1849–1894*; *Rock County History*, pamphlet; *Genealogy*, pamphlet

14. Yes

15. OCLC: WIJ

Books & Sets: 3,4,10–14,26

Periodicals: 4(v.14–, 1960–), 5(v.16–, 1977–),9(v.134–, 1980–)

Rock County Historical Society
10 S High St, PO Box 896, 53547
Tel: 608-756-4509

1. T-Sa, 1-4:30 by appointment

2. Maurice J. Montgomery, Archivist
3. English, 25,000
4. 500
5. N/AN
6. Rock County, WI
7. Tel: yes, but prefer visit or letter; letter: yes, $10 plus copies
8. No
9. Yes, $10/nonmembers
10. No
11. No
12. No
13. Card catalog
14. Yes
15. N/AN

KENOSHA

Kenosha County Historical Museum Library, 6300 3rd Ave, 53140
Tel: 414-654-5770

1. T,W,Th, 2-4:30 or by appointment
2. Lois Roepke Stein
3. English, most; German, few Bibles, cook books
4. No estimate: city directories, census records, newspapers (1845–1945), school records, atlases
5. None
6. Kenosha; some WI state
7. Tel & letter: yes, NC but donations accepted
8. Lois Roepke Stein
9. Yes, donation
10. No
11. N/AP
12. Yes
13. None
14. No
15. No

Kenosha Public Library, Gilbert M. Simmons Library
711 59th Place, 53140
Tel: 414-656-8035

1. M-Th, 9-8; F,Sa, 9-5
2. Linda Sytkowski

3. English, 2,932
4. None
5. 22: census; 684: local newspapers
6. Kenosha and Kenosha County
7. Tel: yes, NC; letter: yes, NC except for copies
8. No
9. No
10. No
11. No
12. "Genealogy - Resources & Services," $3
13. N/AN
14. No
15. OCLC: WIK
Books & Sets: 2,26
Periodicals: 4(1977–)

LA CROSSE

La Crosse Public Library
800 Main St, 54601
Tel: 608-784-8623

1. M-Th, 12-9; F,Sa, 10-5; Su (except July, Aug), 1-5
2. Amy Groskopf
3. English, 1,000; Norwegian, 5
4. 30
5. N/AN
6. La Crosse County, surrounding communities
7. Tel & letter: yes, NC for first half-hour research except for copies
8. No
9. No
10. Yes, through ILL
11. No
12. No
13. Limited biographical and obituary indexes
14. No
15. N/AN
Books & Sets: 1,2(v.20–44),3, 4,10–14,24,25
Periodicals: 1(1982–),4(1972–),5, 7,8(1985–),9(1937–47, 1981–)

MADISON

Madison Public Library
201 W Mifflin St, 53703
Tel: 608-266-6350

1. M,T,W, 8:30-9; Th,F, 8:30-5:30; Sa, 9-5:30
2. N/AN
3. English, 1,000
4. None
5. 44; also, local newspapers on film
6. WI state, with emphasis on Dane County
7. Tel & letter: yes, NC
8. No
9. No
10. No
11. No
12. *Guide to Genealogy Resources at the Madison Public Library*
13. Index to *Wisconsin State Journal*, 1972–
14. No
15. OCLC: WIM
Books & Sets: 1(8 v. & 1983 suppl),3,6,19(2 v., 1950)

State Historical Society of Wisconsin, 816 State St, 53706
Tel: 608-262-9590

1. Winter: M-Th, 8am-9pm; F,Sa, 8-5; summer: M-Sa, 8-5
2. James L. Hansen
3. No estimate
4. No estimate
5. No estimate
6. All US; Canada
7. Tel & letter: yes, NC
8. Yes
9. No
10. Yes, some LH
11. Yes
12. *Genealogical Research: A Guide to the Resources of the State Historical Society of Wisconsin*, $5.95 plus postage and handling
13. Too numerous to list
14. Yes

15. OCLC: WIH
Books & Sets: 2–7,9–18,22–26
Periodicals: 1,2(v.1,2, 1979–80),
3,4(v.6–, 1952–),5,7–9

Vesterheim Genealogical Center
4909 Sherwood Rd, 53711
Tel: 608-271-8826

1. By appointment
2. Gerhard B. Naeseth
3. English, 700; Norwegian,
365
4. None
5. 800
6. Norway; Norwegian
America
7. Tel: yes, NC; letter: yes,
$12/hr nonmembers, $8/hr
members
8. Gerhard B. Naeseth
9. No
10. Yes, $5/month
11. Yes, $5/month
12. No
13. N/AN
14. Yes
15. No

MANITOWOC

Manitowoc Public Library
808 Hamilton St, 54220
Tel: 414-683-4863

1. M-Th, 8:30am-9pm; F,Sa,
8:30-5:30
2. Rosemary Singh
3. English, 3,000
4. 3
5. 625
6. Manitowoc, Calumet
Counties, WI; northeastern WI
7. Tel: no; letter: yes, $10/hr
8. No
9. No
10. Yes, duplicates only,
through ILL
11. No
12. No
13. Proper name card index to
several local history sources
14. Yes

15. OCLC: WIA
Books & Sets: 3(3v., suppls 1982–
85),4,5(v.1–5),6,10–14,19,23,26
Periodicals: 7

MENOMONEE FALLS

Maude Shunk Public Library
W156 N8446 Pilgrim Rd, 53051
Tel: 414-255-8383

1. M-F, 10-9; Sa, 10-5
2. Anne Reid, Adult Services
Librarian
3. English, 50
4. 3–5
5. 75
6. Menomonee Falls, WI
7. Tel & letter: yes, NC
8. No
9. No
10. No
11. No
12. No
13. N/AN
14. No
15. OCLC: WMF
Books & Sets: 3
Periodicals: 4(current year plus 3)

MILWAUKEE

**Milwaukee County Historical
Society,** 910 N Third St, 53203
Tel: 414-273-8288

1. M-F, 9:30-12, 1-4:30
2. Charles W. Cooney, Jr.
3. No estimate given. Milwaukee city directories, 1847–1980;
early published histories of Milwaukee; school census records,
1913–54
4. No estimate given. Incorpo-
ration records, 1872–1960; Civil
War records of Wisconsin veterans; church records; National
Defense Program registration cards
(post-WWII)
5. No estimate given. Microfilmed obituaries and biographical
newsclippings

6. Milwaukee County only
7. Tel: yes, NC; letter: yes, $4
fee for genealogical research, $10
fee for census searches
8. Charles W. Cooney, Jr.
9. Yes, $1/day library use fee
10. No
11. No
12. No
13. Indexes to: naturalization
papers, 1836–1941; Old Settlers
Club obituaries; territorial and
federal census records, 1840s–
1910; court records, 1837–1931;
probate files, 1835–89; coroners'
inquests, 1873–1935; biographical
sketches. *Genealogical Resources
of the Milwaukee County Historical Society*, 2-page handout
14. No
15. No

Milwaukee Public Library
814 W Wisconsin Ave, 53233
Tel: 414-278-3000

1. M-Th, 8:30am-9pm; F,Sa,
8:30-5:30; Su (Oct-May), 1-5
2. Virginia Schwartz, Coordinator of Humanities
3. English, 30,000; German,
100; French, 50
4. 100
5. 1,300
6. Milwaukee, WI state; Midwest, Northeast, Middle Atlantic
7. Tel & letter: yes, NC for
brief queries
8. No
9. No
10. Yes, duplicates only,
through ILL
11. Yes, but not census rolls
12. No
13. *A Guide to Genealogical
Resources*, free pamphlet; monthly
acquisitions list
14. Yes
15. OCLC: GZO
Books & Sets: 1–14,16–26
Periodicals: 1–9

NEENAH

Neenah Public Library
240 E Wisconsin Ave, 54956
Tel: 414-729-4728

1. M-Th, 9-9; F, 9-6; Sa, 9-5
2. N/AN
3. English, 350
4. None
5. None
6. Fox River Valley, WI state
7. Tel: no; letter: yes, NC
8. Jane Laswell
9. No
10. No
11. No
12. No
13. N/AN
14. No
15. No

OSHKOSH

Oshkosh Public Library
106 Washington Ave, 54901-4985
Tel: 414-236-5226

1. Sept-May: T-F, 1-5; Sa, 9-5;
June-Aug: M-F, 1-5
2. Mara B. Munroe
3. English, 1,400
4. N/AN
5. 2,000, primarily census and
newspapers
6. WI state; northeastern US;
northern Europe
7. Tel & letter: yes, NC except
for copies
8. Mara B. Munroe
9. No
10. No
11. No
12. No
13. N/AN
14. Yes
15. OCLC: GZK
Books & Sets: 1–5,7,9–14,
17,19,22,26
Periodicals: 1,3(v.47–, 1983–),
4(1961–),7,8(v.51–, 1963–),9

RACINE

**Racine County Historical Society
and Museum, Local History and
Genealogical Library**
701 S Main St, 53403
Tel: 414-637-8585

1. Library: T,Sa, 1-4
2. Elvera V. Belden, Volunteer
3. English, 1,000; Bohemian,
several
4. 12 4-drawer vertical files;
about 10,000 pictures
5. None
6. Racine and Racine County,
southeastern WI; some WI state
7. Tel & letter: yes, NC for
brief queries except 25¢/copy, with
$3 minimum
8. Elvera V. Belden
   Gloria Bicha
   Hazel Franseen
9. No
10. No
11. No
12. No
13. Card indexes covering surnames, naturalization papers for
1837–1906, early county census,
WW II, Korean War
14. Yes
15. No
Books & Sets: 2,26
Periodicals: 3(1 v.),4(several),9

Racine Public Library
75 Seventh St, 53403
Tel: 414-636-9241

1. M-Th, 9-9; F,Sa, 9-5:30; Su
(Oct-May), 2-5
2. Ellen Snyder
3. English, LH, 2,000
4. G: 10
5. 1,428: newspapers
6. Racine City and County
7. Tel: no; letter: yes, $4/15
minutes or $16/hr plus 10¢/copy
8. No
9. No
10. Yes, through ILL

11. Yes, through ILL
12. In process
13. Z (Wisconsin and Racine
County) and Zr (Racine city) card
files, not for public use
14. No
15. OCLC: WIR

RIVER FALLS

**University of Wisconsin-River
Falls, Area Research Center-
Chalmer Davee Library**
4th & Cascade Ave, 54022
Tel: 715-425-3567

1. M-F, 8-4:30; Sa, 1-4;
Su, 7-9pm; summer and university holidays: M-F, 8-4:30
2. Susan Steinwall, Director
3. English, 500
4. Not estimated. All MS
collections relate to LH/G
5. 2,000
6. WI counties of Burnett,
Pierce, Polk, St. Croix, Washburn
7. Tel & letter: yes, NC except
for copies
8. N/AN
9. No
10. No
11. Yes, through ILL
12. No
13. Newspaper index
14. Yes
15. No
Books & Sets: 3,5(v.1,2,3),22,23
Periodicals: 4(v.37–, 1983–)

SHEBOYGAN

Mead Public Library, Information Services, 710 Plaza 8, 53081
Tel: 414-459-3400

1. M-F, 9-9; Sa, 9-5, Su, 1-4;
summer: M,W,F, 9-9; T,Th, 9-5;
Sa, 9-1
2. Susan Mathews, Coordinator of Information Services
3. N/AN
4. None

5. N/AN
6. Sheboygan County, WI
7. Tel: no; letter: yes, $12/hr for research after first hour, plus 15¢/copy
8. No
9. No
10. No
11. No
12. *A Guide to the Sheboygan Collection*, 2nd ed, no charge; *Tracing Your Roots: Genealogical Resources*, no charge
13. Personal name indexes for several significant biographical sources
14. Yes
15. No
Books & Sets: 1,2(incomplete),3, 6,10–14,17,19,22,23,26
Periodicals: 4

SPARTA

Monroe County Local History Room and Research Library
Rt 2, Box 21, 54656
Tel: 608-269-8680

1. M-F, 8-4:30
2. Audrey Johnson, County Historian
3. English, 1,000
4. 2,000
5. 100
6. Monroe County, WI
7. Tel: yes, NC; letter: yes, with donation and SASE requested, copy fee
8. Yes
9. No
10. No
11. No
12. No
13. Name index to all tombstones in county
14. Yes
15. N/AN
Books & Sets: 3
Periodicals: 4

STURGEON BAY

Door County Library
107 S Fourth Ave, 54235
Tel: 414-743-6578

1. M-Th, 9-9; F, 9-6; Sa, 9-5
2. Mary Tragesser
3. English, 1,000
4. N/AN
5. N/AN
6. Door County
7. Tel: yes, NC; letter: no
8. Mary Tragesser
9. No
10. No
11. No
12. No
13. N/AN
14. Yes
15. No

SUPERIOR

Superior Public Library
1204 Hammond Ave, 54880
Tel: 715-394-0535

1. M-Th, 9-9; F, 9-6; Sa, 9-5; Su, 2-5; closed Sa,Su (June-Aug)
2. David H. Lull
3. English, 800; German, 3; French, 25
4. 24 archival boxes, 12 vertical file drawers
5. 165 reels, plus 704 reels of local newspapers, 1855–
6. WI and other Old Northwest states; some New England
7. Tel: no; letter: yes, NC except for 10¢/copy, 25¢ microform print ($1 minimum)
8. Paul H. Gaboriault
9. No
10. No
11. Yes, through ILL
12. No
13. Card catalog of prominent birth/marriage/death statistics, biographies, businesses, historical articles, buildings, monuments, newspaper articles; card catalog of genealogical and heraldic works, including newspaper holdings in hard copy and microfilm; card catalog of birth/marriage/death statistics, 1975–
14. Yes
15. OCLC: WNW
Books & Sets: 2,3,10–12,17, 19,24,26
Periodicals: 1(incomplete), 9(v.1–75, 76–)

University of Wisconsin at Superior, Jim Dan Hill Library
19th St & Clough, 54880
Tel: 715-394-8341

1. M-F, 8-4:30 by request
2. Denise J. Johnson
3. English, 500
4. 50
5. 10
6. Douglas County, WI
7. Tel: yes, NC; letter: yes, NC except $1 minimum for copies
8. No
9. No
10. Yes, to other research centers in WI network
11. Yes, to other research centers in WI network
12. No
13. Refer to Wisconsin State Historical Society, Madison
14. No
15. No
Books & Sets: 1(1980)

WATERLOO

Waterloo Public Memorial Library, 117 E Madison St, 53594
Tel: 414-478-3344

1. Hours not given
2. Joel Zibell, Librarian
3. English, 100
4. 5
5. 70
6. Jefferson, Dane, Dodge, Green, and Juneau Counties

7. Tel & letter: yes, donations accepted, plus 15¢/copy

8. No

9. Yes, donations accepted

10. Yes, through ILL

11. Yes, through ILL; may be sent to another library in system for copying

12. No

13. Staff compilation of genealogical sources; index for Waterloo *Democrat*, 1873–1930, and Waterloo *Courier*, 1930–50

14. Yes

15. No

Periodicals: 4

WAUKESHA

Waukesha County Museum, Research Center
101 W Main St, 53186
Tel: 414-548-7186

1. M-F, 9-4:30

2. Jean Penn Loerke, County Historian

3. English, 2,700

4. No estimate

5. 13

6. Waukesha County, other WI state

7. Tel & letter: yes, NC except 10¢/copy

8. Terry Becker

9. No

10. No

11. No

12. "Family History Research in Waukesha County," 50¢ by mail

13. List of other research guides available at Museum

14. Yes

15. No

Periodicals: 4(v.32–37),7

Waukesha Public Library
321 Wisconsin Ave, 53186
Tel: 414-549-8162

1. M-F, 9-9; Sa, 9-6

2. Patricia Rediess

3. English, 688

4. None

5. 546

6. Waukesha County, WI state

7. Tel: yes, NC for brief queries; letter: yes, research fee

8. No

9. No

10. No

11. No

12. No

13. *Tracing Your Roots: Genealogical Aids at Waukesha Public Library* (1980; Addenda, 1983)

14. No

15. OCLC: yes (partial)

Books & Sets: 2(v.1–4, Index), 3(3v., 1981; 1982,1983,1984 suppls),6,10,11,13(1975), 19(2v.,1972)

Periodicals: 4(1975–)

WYOMING

CHEYENNE

**Laramie County Library
System, Genealogy Collection**
2800 Central Ave, 82009
Tel: 307-634-3561

1. M-Th, 9-9; F, 9-6; Sa, 10-6;
Su (Sept-May), 1-5
2. Venice N. Brown Beske
3. English, 15,000
4. None
5. None
6. US
7. Tel & letter: no
8. No
9. No
10. Yes, free to WY libraries;
out of state, $18/vol
11. Yes
12. No
13. Shelf list with updates
14. Yes
15. OCLC: WYLE
Books & Sets: 1–5,7,8,10,11,18,
19,26
Periodicals: 1,4,5(v.1–8),7,8(v.40–
46,54–69),9

CODY

Park County Library
1057 Sheridan Ave, 82414
Tel: 307-587-6205

1. M, 9-5:30, 7-9; T-F, 9-5:30;
Sa, 10-4
2. Altamae Markham
3. English, 100
4. None
5. 5
6. Some New England; some
southern US
7. Tel: yes, NC; letter: yes, NC
except 10¢/copy
8. N/AN
9. No
10. No
11. No
12. No
13. N/AN
14. No
15. N/AN
Periodicals: 4(1982–)

EVANSTON

Uinta County Library
701 Main, 82930
Tel: 307-789-1328

1. M-Th, 9-8; F, 9-6; Sa, 10-6
2. Leslie Bailey
3. English, 15
4. 100 oral histories
5. 2
6. Uinta County, WY
7. Tel: no; letter: yes, NC
8. No
9. No
10. No
11. No
12. No
13. N/AN
14. No
15. No

CANADA

**A Sample Questionnaire is located
on the inside back cover of this volume.**

ALBERTA

BOW ISLAND

Bow Island Municipal Library
510 Centre St, T0K 0G0
Tel: 403-545-2828

1. T-Sa, 10-5
2. Susan Andersen
3. English, 20
4. None
5. None
6. Southern Alberta
7. Tel & letter: yes, NC
8. No
9. No
10. Yes, 3-week loan
11. No
12. No
13. N/AN
14. No
15. No

CALGARY

**Calgary Public Library,
W. R. Castell Central Library**
616 Macleod Trail SE, T2G 2M2
Tel: 403-260-2785

1. M-Th, 9-9; F,Sa, 9-5; Su (Sept-June), 1:30-5
2. Barbara Nicholson, Head of Humanities (Genealogy located in Humanities Dept)
3. G: English, 1,000; German, 1; French, 30. LH: 15,000, including books, pamphlets, microfilm
4. None
5. G: 907
6. Calgary, Alberta, Canada; Great Britain; US
7. Tel & letter: yes, NC except for copies; $3 minimum charge for first 10 pages, 30¢/page thereafter
8. No
9. No
10. Yes, circulating books only

11. No
12. No
13. N/AN
14. No
15. No
Books & Sets: 1,3–5,9–14, 19,22,24,25
Periodicals: 2,4(v.28–, 1974–), 5(1976–),6(v.20–, 1981–),7(rev ed 1983)

**Glenbow Museum Library
and Archives,** 130 9th Ave SE, T2G 0P3
Tel: 403-264-8300

1. M-F, 8:30-5
2. None
3. English, LH, 2,250
4. 7,700
5. 100
6. Western Canada
7. Tel & letter: yes, NC
8. No
9. No
10. No
11. No
12. *Glenbow-Alberta Institute Library,* 4 vols
13. *Genealogical Sources at the Glenbow Library and Archives–An Outline* (1986), 5-page handout; *Glenbow Library & Archives,* brochure
14. Yes
15. No
Periodicals: 2

GRANDE PRAIRIE

Grande Prairie Public Library
8501-100 A St, T8V 3C4
Tel: 403-532-3580

1. M-F, 10-9; Sa, 10-6; Su, 2-5
2. None
3. English, 400
4. None

5. Local newspaper, 1913–
6. Grande Prairie and surrounding area (Peace River region of Alberta)
7. Tel & letter: yes, NC
8. No
9. Yes, $4/adult, $8/family
10. Yes, through ILL
11. No
12. No
13. Index to local newspapers, 1913–63
14. No
15. No
Books & Sets: 1,3,24

HIGH RIVER

High River Centennial Library
909 1st St W, T0L 1B0
Tel: 403-652-2917

1. N/AN
2. Lucille Dougherty
3. N/AN
4. N/AP
5. N/AP; library has loan of *High River Times,* 1907–71
6. Local histories of southern Alberta
7. Tel & letter: yes, NC
8. No
9. No
10. Yes, to card-holding members
11. No
12. No
13. N/AN
14. No
15. No

LACOMBE

Parkland Regional Library
Box 1000, T0C 1S0
Tel: 403-782-3850

1. Not open to the public

2. Rudi E. Denham, Reference Librarian
3. English, 150 (some duplicate titles)
4. None
5. None
6. Central Alberta
7. Tel & letter: yes, NC
8. No
9. No
10. Yes
11. No
12. No
13. No
14. No
15. No

LETHBRIDGE

Lethbridge Public Library
810-5 Avenue S, T1J 4C4
Tel: 403-329-3233

1. M-F, 9:30-9; Sa, 9:30-5:30; Su, 1:30-9
2. N/AN
3. N/AN
4. N/AN
5. N/AN
6. Southern Alberta
7. Tel: no; letter: yes, NC except for copies
8. No
9. No
10. No
11. No
12. No
13. N/AN
14. No
15. N/AN
Books & Sets: 3
Periodicals: 4

South Western Alberta Genealogical Library
Room 1:28, 909 3rd Ave N
(mailing address: Box 1001, T1J 4A2)
Tel: N/AN

1. T-Th, 1:30-4:30; July-Aug, by appointment only
2. None
3. English, LH, 50, G, 12
4. N/AN

5. N/AN
6. Southern Alberta, Canada; US, Britain, Europe, some Scandinavia
7. Tel: no; letter: N/AN
8. No
9. No
10. No
11. No
12. Guide in progress
13. Computer and card catalogs
14. No
15. N/AN
Periodicals: 2(v.4,6),4(1980–85)

PLAMONDON

Plamondon Municipal Library
PO Box 90, T0A 2T0
Tel: 403-798-3840

1. M-F, 9-4
2. Arthur J. Girard
3. English, 45; French, 7
4. 19
5. N/AP
6. Primarily Alberta, Canada
7. Tel: no; letter: yes, NC
8. Arthur J. Girard
9. No
10. No
11. N/AP
12. No
13. N/AN
14. No
15. No
Books & Sets: 24,25

SHERWOOD PARK

County of Strathcona Municipal Library
2001 Sherwood Dr, T8A 3J4
Tel: 403-464-8263

1. Call 464-8261 for recorded message
2. N/AN
3. English, LH, 155
4. N/AP
5. 52: local newspaper, *Sherwood Park News*
6. Strathcona County, including Sherwood Park
7. Tel & letter: yes, NC
8. No

9. Yes, $2/resident, $25/non-resident
10. No
11. No
12. No
13. None
14. No
15. No

SPRUCE GROVE

Spruce Grove Public Library
410 King St, T7X 2Z1
Tel: 403-962-4423

1. M-F, 10-8; Sa, 10-5
2. N/AP
3. English, 250
4. N/AP
5. N/AP
6. Alberta
7. Tel: no; letter: yes, NC
8. No
9. No
10. Yes, 3-week loan through ILL
11. No
12. No
13. N/AP
14. No
15. No
Books & Sets: 3

WETASKIWIN

Wetaskiwin Public Library
5002 51 Ave, T9A 0V1
Tel: 403-352-4055

1. M,W,F,Sa, 10-5; T,Th, 10-9
2. Charles Ottosen
3. English, 20
4. None
5. 35
6. City of Wetaskiwin and district
7. Tel & letter: yes, NC
8. Charles Ottosen
9. No
10. Yes, 3-week loan
11. Yes
12. No
13. N/AN
14. No
15. No

BRITISH COLUMBIA

ABBOTSFORD

Fraser Valley College, Learning Resources Centre, 33844 King Rd, RR#2, V2S 4N2
Tel: 604-853-7441

1. During terms: M-F, 8:30am-9pm; between terms: 8:30-4:30
2. Anne Knowlan, Public Services Coordinator
3. English, LH, 500
4. LH: none
5. LH: 25
6. Fraser Valley; British Columbia; Canada
7. Tel & letter: yes, NC
8. No
9. No
10. No
11. No
12. *The Fraser Valley– A Bibliography*
13. N/AN
14. No
15. No

Fraser Valley Regional Library
34589 Delair Rd, V2S 5Y1
Tel: 604-859-7141

1. T-Th, 10-9; F,Sa, 10-5
2. Goldie Carr, Coordinator of Reference Services
3. Not set up as such; all found in branches
4. None
5. None
6. Fraser Valley
7. Tel & letter: yes, NC
8. No
9. No
10. Yes
11. N/AP
12. No
13. None
14. No
15. No

COQUITLAM

Coquitlam Public Library
1063 Ridgeway Ave, V3J 1S6
Tel: 604-937-7121

1. T-F, 10-9; Sa, 10-5
2. Mrs. G. Campbell
3. English, 60
4. None
5. None
6. Coquitlam, Greater Vancouver, other world areas for genealogy
7. Tel & letter: yes, NC
8. No
9. No
10. Yes, 3-week maximum
11. No
12. No
13. Microfiche catalog
14. No
15. No

DAWSON CREEK

Dawson Creek Municipal Library, 1001 McKeller Ave, V1G 2S2
Tel: 604-782-4661

1. T,W,Th, 10-9; F,Sa, 10-5:30; Su (Sept-June), 2-5:30
2. Paola Durando
3. English, 200
4. 100
5. None
6. Peace River; northeastern British Columbia
7. Tel & letter: yes, NC
8. No
9. No
10. No
11. No
12. No
13. N/AN
14. No
15. No

FORT SAINT JOHN

Fort St. John Public Library Association
10349 100 St, V1J 3Z2
Tel: 604-785-3731

1. 7 days, 50 hours
2. Romi Haseo, Supervising Librarian
3. English, 473
4. N/AN
5. N/AN
6. N/AN
7. Tel & letter: yes, NC
8. No
9. No
10. No
11. No
12. No
13. N/AN
14. No
15. No

NANAIMO

Vancouver Island Regional Library, 6250 Hammond Bay Rd, V9R 5N3
Tel: 604-758-4697

1. Daily, 8:30-4:30
2. None
3. English, 3,468
4. N/AN
5. N/AN
6. British Columbia; Vancouver Island local history
7. Tel & letter: no
8. No
9. No
10. Yes, duplicates only, to Library's branches
11. No
12. *British Columbia and Northwest Collection* (1987), catalog
13. N/AN

14. No
15. No
Books & Sets: 3,10–12,24
Periodicals: 4

POWELL RIVER

Powell River District Public Library Association, 4411 Michigan Ave, V8A 2S3
Tel: 604-485-4796

1. M, 10-5; T,W,F, 10-9; Sa, 10-5
2. Betty Thornton, Powell River Genealogy Group
3. English, 152
4. None
5. Microfiche: 132 IGI sheets
6. N/AN
7. Tel: yes, NC; letter: yes, NC except 10¢/copy and postage
8. No
9. No
10. No, could arrange ILL
11. No
12. No
13. N/AN
14. No
15. No
Periodicals: 2(1983–),4(1982–)

SPARWOOD

Sparwood Public Library
139 Centennale Square, V0B 2G0
Tel: 604-425-2299

1. T-Sa, 10-2, 1-4:30
2. N/AN
3. N/AN
4. N/AN
5. N/AN
6. Michel, Natal, Crows Nest Pass, British Columbia
7. Tel & letter: yes, NC
8. No
9. No
10. No
11. N/AP
12. No
13. N/AN

14. No
15. N/AP

SURREY

Surrey Public Library
Surrey Centennial Branch, 15105 105 Ave, V3R 7G8
Tel: 604-588-4433

1. M-F, 10-9; Sa, 10-5
2. Paul Gutteridge, Manager, Collection Development; Edna Crane, Head of Adult Services
3. English, 800; French, 100
4. N/AN
5. 2,000
6. Canada; Europe
7. Tel & letter: yes, NC for brief queries
8. Paul Gutteridge
   Edna Crane
9. No
10. No
11. No
12. *Canadian Genealogical Resources: A Guide to the Material in Surrey Centennial Library*, $5
13. N/AN
14. No
15. No

TERRACE

Terrace Public Library
4610 Park Ave, V8G 1V6
Tel: 604-638-8177

1. T-F, 10-9; Sa, 10-5; Su, 1-5
2. N/AN
3. English, 800
4. None
5. 15: newspaper
6. Terrace and area
7. Tel & letter: yes, NC
8. No
9. No
10. No
11. No
12. No
13. N/AN
14. No
15. N/AN

VANCOUVER

British Columbia Genealogical Society Library, Aberthau, 4397 W 2nd Ave (mailing address: PO Box 94371, Richmond, V6Y 2A8)
Tel: 604-435-9806

1. By appointment only
2. Valerie Melanson, Librarian
3. English, 2,000; 100 total in French, German, Finnish, Dutch, Norwegian, Swedish, Flemish (mostly journals)
4. None
5. 200+ films, 2,000+ microfiche
6. Canada, with emphasis on British Columbia, Ontario; United Kingdom, Ireland; Europe; Australasia; US
7. Tel & letter: yes, NC for brief queries. $5 fee to nonmembers to consult British Columbia genealogical research materials
8. No, all amateur
9. No, public use at discretion of librarian
10. Yes, through ILL to public libraries
11. No
12. No
13. Catalogs for: microform holdings, serials, books; serials contents index; British Columbia Research Master Index
14. Yes
15. No
Books & Sets: 3(no suppls), 26(Index only)
Periodicals: 2,4(1966–),6(1969–), 9(v.133–)

Vancouver Public Library
750 Burrard St, V6K 1G2
Tel: 604-665-3566

1. M-Th, 9:30-9:30; F,Sa, 9:30-6; Su (winter only), 1-5
2. Rex DesBrisay
3. English, 6,000 in Northwest History Collection
4. N/AN

5. N/AN

6. British Columbia; Washington & Oregon Territories to 1849; Alaska to 1867; Yukon Territory to 1898

7. Tel & letter: yes, NC for brief queries

8. No

9. No

10. Yes, circulating collection through ILL; no, Northwest History Collection

11. No

12. No

13. Northwest History Collection has 52-drawer index catalog

14. No

15. No

Books & Sets: 1,3(no suppls),6, 10–12,19(no suppls),24

Periodicals: 2,5(1975–),6(v.17, 1972–)

VICTORIA

Greater Victoria Public Library

735 Broughton St, V8W 3H2

Tel: 604-382-7241

1. N/AN

2. N/AN

3. English, 1,040

4. None

5. None

6. LH: Victoria, British Columbia; G: Canada, North America

7. Tel & letter: yes, NC

8. No

9. No

10. No

11. No

12. *Guide to Greater Victoria Public Library Genealogy Collection*, $5

13. Microfiche and on-line catalogs

14. No

15. No

Books & Sets: 1,3,6,9,19

Periodicals: 2

MANITOBA

WINNIPEG

Legislative Library of Manitoba
200 Vaughan St, Main Floor East,
R3C 1T5
Tel: 204-945-4330

    1. M-F, 10-5; Legislative
Reading Room open to 6pm during
legislative session (M-Th)
    2. F. B. (Rick) MacLowick,
Head of Information Services
    3. English, 450; German, 30;
French, 70; some Ukrainian,
Icelandic, other European
languages
    4. None
    5. 4,100: local newspapers,
directories, theses
    6. Manitoba, western Canada
    7. Tel & letter: yes, NC except
10¢/copy, 50¢/microprint
    8. No
    9. No
    10. Yes, circulating books only
    11. Yes, duplicate microfilm
only
    12. No
    13. N/AN
    14. No
    15. N/AN
Books & Sets: 3(3v., 1981),
24(7v., 1871–90)
Periodicals: 2

**Manitoba Genealogical
Society Library**
420-167 Lombard Ave, R3B 0T6
Tel: 204-944-1153

    1. M-F, 9-4:30; first Sa each
month, 10-1
    2. Louisa J. Shermerhorn,
Library Committee Chair
    3. English, 1,300; French,
several
    4. None
    5. 22

    6. Manitoba, Ontario, Quebec,
Maritimes; British Isles; some
Europe, US
    7. Tel: yes, NC; letter: yes, NC
for members; $3/surname, non-
members
    8. No
    9. No
    10. Yes, to members only
    11. No
    12. *Library Holdings of the
Manitoba Genealogical Society*
(1984); *Supplement* (1985); *Sup-
plement* (1986)
    13. Card index to Manitoba
cemetery transcriptions; *Reference
Sources for Searching Family
History in Manitoba*, 4-page
handout
    14. Yes
    15. No
Books & Sets: 8,24(v.1)
Periodicals: 2,4,6,9

**United Church Archives,
Affiliated with the University
of Winnipeg Library**
515 Portage Ave, R3B 2E9
Tel: 204-783-0708

    1. M-F, 9-5
    2. John Baillie
    3. English, G, none
    4. G: 1,500
    5. G: None
    6. Manitoba, northwestern
Ontario
    7. Tel & letter: yes, NC
    8. No
    9. No
    10. No
    11. No
    12. No
    13. Pastoral Charge Inventory
Index; Vital Statistics Index
    14. Yes
    15. No

**University of Manitoba,
Elizabeth Dafoe Library**
R3T 2N2
Tel: 204-474-9844

    1. Regular term: M-Th,
8:30am-10pm; F, 8:30-5; Sa,
10-5; Su, 1-9; summer hours vary
    2. Carol Budnick, Bibli-
ographer
    3. English, not estimated;
some German, French, Slavic,
Icelandic
    4. 150
    5. N/AP; census of Canada,
local newspapers
    6. Manitoba, Canada
    7. Tel & letter: yes, NC; refer
research questions to appropriate
sources
    8. No
    9. No
    10. Yes
    11. No
    12. No
    13. None
    14. No
    15. No
Books & Sets: 1(suppls 1981–83),
3(3v., 1981,1982 suppl),5,9,22,24
Periodicals: 9(v.1–59)

University of Winnipeg Library
515 Portage Ave, R3B 2E9
Tel: 204-786-9802

    1. M-F, 8-4:45; hours change
with academic sessions
    2. N/AN
    3. English, 281
    4. N/AN
    5. 100
    6. Manitoba
    7. Tel & letter: yes, NC
    8. No
    9. N/AN
    10. No

11. No
12. No
13. N/AN
14. No. Refer to Rupert's Land Research Centre at the University of Winnipeg
15. N/AN
Books & Sets: 1(8v., 1980),6, 13,14

Winnipeg Public Library, Centennial Library (Main Branch)
251 Donald St, R3C 3P5
Tel: 204-985-6450

1. M-Th, 10-9; F,Sa, 10-6; Su (winter), 1-5
2. Edith Wiebe, Head of Adult Services
3. English, 200–300; some French at Library's St. Boniface Branch
4. N/AN
5. 3,000
6. Winnipeg, Manitoba; some Canada in general; some US, European guidebooks
7. Tel & letter: yes, NC except 10¢/copy
8. Yes
9. No
10. Yes
11. No
12. No
13. *Tracing Your Family Tree, An Annotated Booklist*, handout
14. No
15. No
Books & Sets: 1
Periodicals: 2

NEW BRUNSWICK

CAMPBELLTON

Campbellton Centennial Library, PO Box 607, E3N 3H1
Tel: 506-753-5253

1. T-Th, 10-8:15; F, 10-5:45; Sa, 9-5
2. James Katan, Librarian
3. English, 25; French, 12
4. 20
5. 97: local newspapers
6. Campbellton; some Resti-gouche County
7. Tel & letter: yes, NC except 25¢/copy
8. No
9. No
10. No
11. Yes, only to other libraries within New Brunswick
12. No
13. N/AN
14. No
15. No

FREDERICTON

Provincial Archives of New Brunswick, PO Box 6000, Bonar Law Bldg, University of New Brunswick Campus, E3B 5H1
Tel: 506-453-2122

1. M-Sa, 8:30-5
2. Fred Farrell
3. English, 1,500; French, 100
4. 2,000
5. 9,000
6. Province of New Brunswick
7. Tel: no; letter: yes, NC
8. No
9. No
10. No
11. Yes, through ILL
12. No
13. N/AP
14. No
15. No
Books & Sets: 10–12,25
Periodicals: 2

NEWCASTLE

The Old Manse Library
225 Mary St, E1V 1Z3
Tel: 506-622-0453

1. M-F, 1-8; Sa, 1-5
2. Catherine Bryan
3. English, 350; French, 3
4. 200+
5. None
6. Miramichi River region
7. Tel & letter: yes, NC
8. No
9. No
10. Yes
11. No
12. No
13. None
14. No
15. No

NEWFOUNDLAND

SAINT JOHN'S

Provincial Reference and Resource Library, Arts and Culture Centre, Allandale Rd, A1B 3A3
Tel: 709-737-3954/55

1. M-Th, 10-9:30; F,Sa, 10-5:30; mid-June–mid-Sept: M-Th, 10-8:30; F, 10-5:30
2. Lynne Cuthbert, Local History; Charles Cameron, Genealogy
3. English, 25,000
4. 35
5. 3,000
6. Newfoundland
7. Tel & letter: yes, NC
8. No
9. No
10. Yes, only to other institutions
11. No
12. No
13. *Genealogy in the General Reference Section*, 8-page bibliography
14. Yes
15. No
Books & Sets: 1,3(3 v., 1981)
Periodicals: 2(v.8–, 1986–)

NOVA SCOTIA

AMHERST

Cumberland Regional Library
PO Box 220, Ratchford St,
B4H 3Z2
Tel: 902-667-2135

1. M,Th, 12-9; T,F, 9-9; W,
11-5; Sa, 10-5
2. None
3. English, 150–200
4. 20–30
5. None
6. Cumberland County, Nova
Scotia
7. Tel & letter: yes, NC
8. No
9. No
10. Yes, 3-week loan. Reference material may be borrowed through ILL and used within borrowing library
11. No
12. No
13. *Trace Your Family Tree: Books on Genealogy* (1986), free
14. No
15. No

ANNAPOLIS ROYAL

Annapolis Valley Regional Library, Grange St, B0S 1A0
Tel: 902-532-2260

1. N/AN
2. David Witherly
3. English, 300
4. None
5. None
6. Nova Scotia: Annapolis, Kings, West Hants Counties
7. Tel & letter: yes, NC
8. No
9. No
10. Yes
11. N/AP
12. No

13. *Cemeteries of Annapolis County, Nova Scotia*
14. N/AN
15. No

BRIDGEWATER

South Shore Regional Library, Bridgewater Branch
547 King St, B4V 2W6
Tel: 902-543-9222

1. T,W,F, 12-5; Th, 9-9;
Sa, 10-5
2. Wanda Kushner, Library Assistant
3. N/AN
4. None
5. None
6. Nova Scotia: Lunenburg, Queens Counties
7. Tel & letter: yes, NC
8. No
9. No
10. No
11. N/AP
12. No
13. Microfiche list
14. No
15. N/AN

DARTMOUTH

Dartmouth Regional Library
100 Wyse Rd, B3A 1M1
Tel: 902-464-2315

1. M-F, 9:30-9; Sa, 9:30-5;
Su (winter only), 1-5
2. Barbara Prince
3. English, 275; French, 2
4. 275
5. 20: history only (newspapers, council minutes, etc.)
6. Nova Scotia
7. Tel: yes, NC; letter: no
8. No
9. No

10. Yes
11. No
12. No
13. N/AP
14. Yes
15. No
Books & Sets: 3
Periodicals: 4(1982–)

HALIFAX

Halifax City Regional Library
5381 Spring Garden Rd, B3J 1E9
Tel: 902-421-6985

1. T-F, 10-9; Sa, 10-6; Su
(winter), 2-5
2. L. Jantek
3. English, N/AP
4. None
5. N/AP
6. Nova Scotia; Halifax
7. Tel & letter: yes, NC
8. No
9. No
10. Yes, duplicates only
11. No
12. No
13. N/AN
14. No
15. No
Books & Sets: 19
Periodicals: 2

Nova Scotia Legislative Library
PO Box 396, Province House,
Hollis & Granville Sts, B2V 1X1
Tel: 902-424-5932

1. M-F, 8:30-4:30
2. N/AN
3. English, 700
4. None
5. None
6. Nova Scotia
7. Tel & letter: yes, NC
8. No
9. No

10. Yes, through ILL
11. Yes, through ILL
12. No
13. Index of photographs in the Novascotiana Collection
14. No
15. No

Public Archives of Nova Scotia
6016 University Ave, B3H 1W4
Tel: 902-423-9115

1. M-F, 8:30am-10pm; Sa, 9-6; Su, 1-10
2. Julie Morris, Genealogical Archivist
3. English, 500; German, very few; French, 75
4. 41.4m
5. 10,000: genealogy; 2,000: newspapers
6. Nova Scotia, 1624–; Prince Edward Island, pre-1770s; New Brunswick, pre-1784
7. Tel: yes, NC, but prefer letter; letter: yes, $5
8. No
9. No
10. No
11. No
12. *Tracing Your Ancestors in Nova Scotia*, $3
13. *Public Archives of Nova Scotia*, brochure
14. Yes
15. No
Books & Sets: 1,3,12,24,25
Periodicals: 2,4,9

MULGRAVE

Eastern Counties Regional Library, PO Box 250, B0E 2G0
Tel: 902-747-2597

1. M-F, 8:30-12, 1:30-5
2. David Cumby
3. English, 230; French, 12
4. None
5. 26; will be expanded considerably in 1988
6. Primarily Nova Scotia, but also Atlantic Provinces, Great Britain, US
7. Tel & letter: yes, NC
8. No

9. No
10. Yes
11. Yes
12. No
13. David Cumby, "Genealogical and Local History Materials in the Collection of Eastern Counties Regional Library"
14. No
15. N/AN

NEW GLASGOW

New Glasgow Library
182 Dalhousie St, B2H 5E3
Tel: 902-752-0022

1. T-F, 10-9; Sa, 10-5; Su, 1-5
2. None
3. English, 200
4. 65 vols of cemetery records
5. None
6. Pictou County, Nova Scotia
7. Tel: no; letter: yes, NC except for copies
8. No
9. No
10. No
11. N/AN
12. No
13. N/AN
14. No
15. No

SYDNEY

Cape Breton Regional Library
110 Townsend St, B1P 5E1
Tel: 902-562-3279

1. T-Th, 10-5:30, 7-9pm; F, 10-9:30; Sa, 10-5:30
2. Ian R. MacIntosh
3. English, 4,000
4. 300
5. 660
6. Nova Scotia
7. Tel & letter: yes, NC
8. No
9. No
10. No
11. No
12. No
13. Index to holdings on Fortress Louisbourg
14. Yes

15. No

YARMOUTH

Western Counties Regional Library, Yarmouth Branch
405 Main St, B5A 1G3
Tel: 902-742-5040

1. M-F, 12-9pm; Sa, 10-5
2. N/AP
3. G: English, 46; French, 6
4. 1
5. 64, including newspaper reels
6. Nova Scotia: Shelburne, Digby, Yarmouth Counties
7. Tel: yes, NC; letter: no. Refer to Yarmouth County Museum Library
8. No
9. No
10. Yes, to other Nova Scotia libraries through ILL
11. See #10
12. No
13. Library catalog
14. No
15. No

Yarmouth County Historical Society Archives, 22 Collins St, PO Box 39, B5A 4B1
Tel: 902-742-5539

1. Oct: M-Sa, 10-12, 2-5; Nov-Apr: T-Sa, 2-5; May: M-Sa, 10-12, 2-5; June-Sept: M-Sa, 9-5; Su, 1-5
2. Helen J. Hall, Librarian/ Archivist
3. English, 100; French, 5
4. 150
5. 50
6. Yarmouth County, western Nova Scotia
7. Tel: yes, NC; letter: yes, NC except 25¢/copy
8. No
9. Yes, $1 for adults
10. No
11. Yes
12. No
13. Finding aids, card files
14. Yes
15. N/AN

ATIKOKAN

Atikokan Public Library
Civic Center, P0T 1C0
Tel: 807-597-4406

1. M-F, 10:30-8:30; Sa, 12-5;
Su, 1-4
2. Doris B. Brown
3. English, 294
4. N/AN
5. 117
6. Atikokan; some Rainy River
District
7. Tel & letter: yes, NC
8. No
9. No
10. Yes
11. No
12. Yes
13. N/AN
14. No
15. N/AN

BARRIE

Barrie Public Library
37 Mulcaster St, L4M 3M2
Tel: 705-728-1010

1. M-F, 9:30-9; Sa, 9:30-5
2. Lynne Gibbon
3. English, 1,000. Library
also houses Simcoe County Branch
of Ontario Genealogical Society's
collection of 373 English titles
4. None
5. 253, plus 374 census reels
6. Simcoe County, with
emphasis on Barrie and townships
of Essa, Innisfil, Vespra, Oro
7. Tel & letter: yes, NC except
15¢/copy over 10 copies
8. No
9. No

10. No
11. No
12. No
13. Card index to Northern
Advance, 1847–1940; automated
index to local newspapers, 1984–;
index of births, marriages, and
deaths in Barrie newspapers,
1847–1907
14. No
15. N/AN
Books & Sets: 3

BEAMSVILLE

**Lincoln Public Library,
Fleming Branch**
PO Box 460, L0R 1B0
Tel: 416-563-7014

1. M-F, 9-9; Sa, 9-5
2. Lorene Sims
3. English, 70; other, 10
4. 140
5. 22
6. Town of Lincoln in Niagara
Peninsula
7. Tel & letter: yes, NC
8. No
9. No
10. No
11. No
12. No
13. N/AN
14. No
15. No

BELLEVILLE

Belleville Public Library
223 Pinnacle St, K8N 3A7
Tel: 613-968-6731

1. M,T,Th,F, 9:30-9; W,Sa,
9:30-5:30

2. Elizabeth Mitchell
3. English, 1,500
4. 20
5. 600, including local newspaper
6. Hastings, Prince Edward
Counties, Ontario, Canada
7. Tel & letter: yes, NC
8. No
9. No
10. No
11. No
12. No
13. Belleville Newspaper Index,
1860–79; Genealogical Sources
14. Yes
15. No
Periodicals: 2

BRADFORD

Bradford Public Library
35 John St W, PO Box 130,
L32 2A7
Tel: 416-775-3328

1. T,W,Sa, 10-5; Th,F, 1:30-
8:30
2. None
3. English, 20
4. N/AN
5. 20
6. Town of Bradford, Township of West Gwillimbury
7. Tel: yes, NC; letter: yes, NC
for brief queries
8. No
9. Yes, $5/person, or $10/
family only if books are checked
out
10. No
11. Yes, through CLA Interloan
Rules; 3-week loan except during
summer
12. No
13. N/AN

14. No
15. No

BRAMPTON

Brampton Public Library,
Chinguacousy Resource Branch
150 Central Park Dr, L6T 1B4
Tel: 416-793-4636

1. M-Th, 10-9; F,Sa, 10-5;
Su, 1-5
2. G. R. Deshpande
3. English, N/AP
4. None
5. 500
6. City of Brampton; former
township of Chinguacousy, Toronto Gore; Province of Ontario
7. Tel & letter: yes, NC
8. No
9. No
10. No
11. No
12. No
13. Local History Catalogue
14. No
15. No
Books & Sets: 24(v.1)
Periodicals: 2,4(1977–),5(1974–)

Region of Peel Archives
9 Wellington St E, L6W 1Y1
Tel: 416-457-3948

1. M-F, 8:30-4:30; Sa, 12-4:30
2. Ann ten Cate
3. English, LH, 300
4. LH: 2,000
5. LH: 200
6. Regional municipality of
Peel: includes Mississauga,
Brampton, Caledon
7. Tel & letter: yes, NC
8. No
9. No
10. No
11. No
12. No
13. N/AN
14. No
15. No

BRANTFORD

Brantford Public Library
73 George St, N3T 2Y3
Tel: 519-756-2220

1. Oct-May: M-Th, 9-8:30;
F,Sa, 9-5; Su, 1:30-5; June-Aug:
M-Th, 9-8; F,Sa, 9-5
2. Denise Kirk
3. English, 400
4. None
5. 900
6. Brant County, Ontario
7. Tel & letter: yes, NC except
for copies and postage
8. No
9. No
10. No
11. No
12. No
13. *Guide to the Local History*
Collection: Brantford Public
Library; also, free brochures
14. No
15. No
Books & Sets: 3
Periodicals: 2

BROOKLIN

Whitby Public Library,
Brooklin Branch
10 Vipond Rd, L0B 1C0
Tel: 416-655-3191

1. Winter: M-F, 2-9; Sa, 10-4;
summer: M-Th, 2-9; F, 2-6
2. Linda Maw
3. English, 30
4. None
5. None
6. 20-mile radius of Brooklin
7. Tel & letter: yes, NC
8. No
9. No
10. Yes, duplicates only
11. N/AP
12. No
13. N/AN
14. No
15. No

BURLINGTON

Burlington Public Library
2331 New St, L7R 1J4
Tel: 416-639-3611, ext 137

1. M-F, 9-9; Sa, 9-5; Su
(Sept-May), 1-5
2. Reference Dept
3. English, 200
4. Figures not available
5. 25
6. Burlington, Halton (regional
municipality)
7. Tel: no; letter: yes, with
SASE
8. No
9. No
10. No
11. No
12. No
13. Census name index for
Nelson Township, 1851, 1861,
1871, 1881; local newspaper
index, 1982–86
14. Yes
15. No
Periodicals: 2

CHATHAM

Chatham Public Library
120 Queen St, N7M 2G6
Tel: 519-354-2940

1. M-W, 9:30-9; Th-Sa, 9:30-
5:30
2. Arlene L. Mason, Head of
Reference and Information
Services
3. English, 800–1,000
4. None
5. 700–800; includes Chatham
newspapers, 1841–
6. Primarily Kent County, City
of Chatham; some Essex, Lambton
Counties; Province of Ontario
7. Tel: yes, NC; letter: yes,
charge varies
8. Pamela Currie, Reference
Librarian
9. No

10. No
11. No
12. No
13. *Tracing Your Roots in Kent County* (1987), booklist
14. Yes
15. No
Books & Sets: 3(no suppls), 24(v.1,7)

COLBORNE

Colborne Public Library
PO Box 190, K0K 1S0
Tel: 416-355-3722

1. T,Th, 1-6; Sa, 2-5
2. N/AN
3. English, LH, 5
4. LH: 5
5. None
6. Colborne Village, Cobourg; Cramahe Township
7. Tel: N/AN; letter: yes, NC
8. No
9. Yes, $1/Colborne resident, $6/nonresident
10. Yes
11. N/AN
12. No
13. *Looking Backwards* (photographs); Perry L. Climo, *Those Early Years* and *Colborne from the Pages of the Past; The Colborne Centennial Booklet; Colborne's 125th Anniversary*
14. No
15. N/AN

DESERONTO

Deseronto Public Library
PO Box 302, 309 Main St, K0K 1X0
Tel: 613-396-2744

1. M,W,F, 3-5, 6-8
2. G. Greenfield, Librarian
3. English, 10
4. 15
5. 39
6. South Hastings County
7. Tel: yes, $5, if local call; letter: yes, $5 plus postage
8. No

9. No
10. Yes, 2-week loan
11. Yes, only to other libraries
12. No
13. Index in progress
14. No
15. No

DUNDAS

Dundas Public Library
18 Ogilvie St, L9H 2S2
Tel: 416-627-3507

1. M,T,Th, 10-9; W,F, 10-6; Sa, 9:30-5:30; Su (mid-Sept–mid-May), 2-5
2. Rita Bloch
3. English, 100
4. 3
5. 63: Dundas newspapers; 34: assessment; 21: census
6. Wentworth County
7. Tel & letter: yes, NC
8. No
9. No
10. No
11. No
12. No
13. Indexes to: Dundas news-papers, 1859–1884, 1894–1944, 1977–; T. Roy Woodhouse, *The History of the Town of Dundas;* Wm. Henry Moss, *Reminiscences of an Old Boy*
14. No
15. No

ETOBICOKE

Etobicoke Public Library, Richview Branch, Box 760, 1806 Islington Ave, M9C 5H8
Tel: 416-248-5681

1. M-F, 9-9; Sa, 9-5; Su (Sept-Apr), 1:30-5
2. Marjorie Bender, Local History Librarian
3. English, 800
4. 32: oral histories
5. 40
6. Etobicoke, metropolitan Toronto; some Mississauga-York Region

7. Tel: yes, NC for quick reference only; letter: yes, NC
8. No
9. No
10. No
11. No
12. No
13. N/AN
14. No
15. N/AN
Books & Sets: 19(incomplete)
Periodicals: 2

GLOUCESTER

Gloucester Public Library
2721 Bank St, K1T 1N1
Tel: 613-731-9907

1. Local History Room: Th, 4:30-7:30
2. Albert Picard
3. English, 300; other, 100
4. N/AN
5. None
6. City of Gloucester
7. Tel & letter: yes, NC
8. No
9. No
10. No
11. No
12. No
13. N/AN
14. No
15. No

GUELPH

Guelph Public Library
100 Norfolk St, N1H 4J6
Tel: 519-824-6220

1. M-F, 10-9; Sa, 9-5; July-Sept: M-F, 10-8; Sa, 9-5
2. Linda J. Kearns
3. English, several hundred
4. 10–15 collections, varying from 50–3,000+ items
5. Several hundred
6. Guelph; some Wellington County, other Province of Ontario
7. Tel & letter: yes, NC except 25¢/copy and postage
8. No
9. No

10. Yes, duplicates only

11. Yes, Guelph *Mercury* newspaper, 2-reel maximum

12. Yes

13. Inventories to collections; holdings list for newspapers; keyword index to print and photo collection of Guelph Public Library Archives

14. Yes

15. No

Books & Sets: 1,3

Periodicals: 2,7

KENORA

Kenora Public Library
24 Main St S, P9N 1S7
Tel: 807-468-7091

1. M-F, 10-9; Sa, 10-5; Su, 2-4

2. Mae Gascoigne

3. LH: English, not estimated; German, 21; French, 132; Ukrainian, 96; Italian, 12; Spanish, 8

4. None

5. 210: local newspaper, 1894–

6. Kenora and area

7. Tel & letter: no

8. No

9. Yes, membership fee for nontaxpayers

10. Yes, 3-week loan

11. No

12. No

13. Card catalog

14. No

15. No

KESWICK

Georgina Public Library
80 Queensway S, L4P 1Z3
Tel: 416-476-7233

1. Archives by appointment only: 416-722-5680

2. Nina Marden, Georgina Historical Society

3. English, 400

4. 10

5. 10

6. Georgina, North Gwillimbury Townships; villages of Sutton, Keswick, Pefferlaw, Belhaven,

Baldwin, Udora; Region of York

7. Tel & letter: yes, NC

8. No

9. No

10. No

11. No

12. No

13. Card catalog

14. No

15. No

KINGSTON

Kingston Public Library
130 Johnson St, K7L 1X8
Tel: 613-549-8888

1. M-F, 9-9; Sa, 9-5; Su (Oct-Apr), 1-5

2. Deborah Defoe

3. English, 1,000; French, 20

4. 500: MS material owned and administered by Ontario Genealogical Society, Kingston Branch

5. 30: local newspaper, 1810–

6. City of Kingston; Frontenac County

7. Tel: no; letter: yes, NC except for copies

8. No

9. No

10. No

11. No

12. *Kingston: A Selected Bibliography*, Kingston Public Library Board (1982), $8

13. *Readings on Genealogy at Kingston Public Library*

14. Yes

15. No

Books & Sets: 3,13,14,19,24,25

Periodicals: 2(v.1–, 1979–), 4(v.31–, 1971–),6(v.12–, 1955–),7

KITCHENER

Kitchener Public Library, Grace Schmidt Room of Local History
85 Queen St N, N2H 2H1
Tel: 519-743-0271, ext 252

1. M-Th, 10-9; F, 10-5:30; Sa, 9-5:30

2. None

3. English, 6,213; German, 500

4. 80

5. 768

6. Kitchener; Waterloo County/Regional municipality of Waterloo

7. Tel: yes, NC; letter: yes, $5/letter (Canadian dollars)

8. No

9. Yes, $25/nonresidents; Grace Schmidt Room, NC

10. No

11. Yes, certain newspapers

12. No

13. *Welcome—Grace Schmidt Room of Local History*

14. Yes

15. No

Books & Sets: 3

Periodicals: 2(v.4–, 1982–)

LEAMINGTON

Leamington Public Library
1 John St, N8H 1H1
Tel: 519-326-3441

1. M-F, 10-9 (8 in summer); Sa, 9-5

2. N/AN

3. English, 200

4. None

5. 100: local newspaper, 1907–86

6. Essex, Kent Counties, Ontario

7. Tel: yes, NC; letter: no. Refer to local historical society

8. No

9. Yes, $24/yr for transients; NC for residents

10. Yes, 2-week loan

11. No

12. No

13. Card catalog

14. No

15. No

LINDSAY

Victoria County Public Library
32 William St N, K9V 4A1
Tel: 705-324-9872

1. M-F, 8:30-4:30
2. N/AN
3. English, LH, 65
4. None
5. None
6. Victoria County
7. Tel & letter: yes, NC
8. No
9. No
10. No
11. N/AN
12. No
13. N/AN
14. No
15. N/AN
Books & Sets: 3

LONDON

**Ontario Genealogical Society,
London Branch Library**
Lawson Museum,
1017 Western Rd, PO Box 871,
Station B, N6A 4Z3
Tel: N/AN

1. Sept-June: Sa, 10-4; July-Aug: F, 12-4; Sa, 10-4
2. W. G. Brown, Chairman, Library Committee
3. English, 900
4. N/AP
5. 400
6. Middlesex County, other western Ontario
7. Tel: no; letter: yes, NC
8. Yes, amateurs
9. No
10. No
11. No
12. *London Branch, Ontario Genealogical Society Library Holdings* (1986), $2.25 plus $1 postage and handling
13. "Latest Acquisitions," published in *London Leaf*, Branch quarterly bulletin. Full list of latest acquisitions since April 1, 1986
14. No
15. No
Periodicals: 2,4(1967–)

MARKDALE

Markdale Public Library
21 Main St E, N0C 1H0
Tel: 519-986-3436

1. T,F, 11-5:30; W, 2:30-5:30; Th, 6:30-9; Sa, 2-5
2. Phyllis E. Armstrong
3. English, 16
4. 46: family histories, used in part for *Markdale-Flesherton, A Written Heritage*
5. 47: *The Markdale Standard*, 1880–1982, with corresponding obituary file
6. Grey County, Ontario; townships of Glenelg, Artémesia, Holland; villages of Markdale, Flesherton
7. Tel & letter: yes, NC
8. Phyllis E. Armstrong
9. No
10. No
11. Yes, through ILL
12. No
13. N/AN
14. No
15. N/AN

MISSISSAUGA

**Mississauga Library System,
Central Branch**
110 Dundas St W, L5B 1H3
Tel: 416-279-7002

1. M-F, 9-9; Sa, 9-5; Su, 1-5
2. Michael Jones
3. English, LH, 4,750
4. None
5. LH: 265
6. City of Mississauga; regional municipality of Peel. Collection specializes in Canadian art, Ontario history
7. Tel & letter: yes, NC
8. No
9. No
10. No
11. No
12. No

13. N/AN
14. No
15. No
Books & Sets: 3,5(2 v., 1846–51)
Periodicals: 2(v.1–5, 1979–83)

NAPANEE

Lennox and Addington County Museum, 97 Thomas E, K7R 3S9
Tel: 613-354-3027

1. Library hours: T,Th, 12-4:30
2. Jane Foster
   Cora Reid, Genealogy
3. English, 1,000+
4. 200+ shelf feet
5. 76
6. County of Lennox and Addington, Ontario
7. Tel & letter: yes, $25 basic fee (4 hrs)
8. Cora Reid
9. No
10. No
11. No
12. *Preliminary Inventory, Collections of the Lennox and Addington Historical Society* (1959)
13. Indexes to: photograph holdings (2 v.), church records, miscellaneous small record groups, secondary sources, Cartwright Papers, G. F. Smith Papers, W. H. Wilkison Papers, et al. Babcock and Charles Walters in preparation
14. No
15. No

NEPEAN

Nepean Public Library
1541 Merivale Rd, K2G 3J4
Tel: 613-224-7876

1. M-F, 10-9; Sa, 9-5
2. Marlene MacLean
3. English, 900; French, 50
4. None
5. 5

6. Carleton County; Canada
7. Tel & letter: yes, NC
8. No
9. No
10. No
11. No
12. N/AN
13. *Nepean Public Library Reference*
14. Yes
15. No
Books & Sets: 3
Periodicals: 2

NIAGARA FALLS

Niagara Falls Public Library
4848 Victoria Ave, L2E 4C5
Tel: 416-356-8080

1. M-F, 9-9; Sa, 9-5:30
2. Inge J. Saczkowski
3. English, 300
4. N/AN
5. 50
6. Niagara Peninsula; Welland County
7. Tel & letter: yes, NC
8. Inge J. Saczkowski
9. No
10. No
11. No
12. No
13. *What's Your Line?*, no charge
14. Yes
15. No
Periodicals: 2

NIAGARA-ON-THE-LAKE

Niagara-on-the-Lake Public Library, Box 430, L0S 1J0
Tel: 416-468-2023

1. T-F, 1-9pm; Sa, 9-5; Su (Nov-May), 2-5
2. Linda Gula
3. English, 300
4. (Library's collection is 90% microfilm)
5. 386

6. Niagara-on-the-Lake, surrounding area
7. Tel & letter: yes, NC except for copies and postage
8. No
9. No
10. No
11. Yes, through ILL; 2- or 3-book limit for 3-week loan
12. No
13. N/AN
14. No
15. No

NORTH YORK

North York Central Library, Gladys Allison Canadiana Room, 5120 Yonge St, M2M 5N7
Tel: 416-733-5623

1. M-Th, 9-8:30; F, 9-6; Sa, 9-5; Su (late Sept–mid-May), 1-5
2. Phyllis Wood
3. English, 1,890; German, 10. 1,000 titles belong to Ontario Genealogical Society (q.v. under Toronto)
4. 50
5. 1,150
6. Concentration on Canada; some North America, Great Britain, Ireland, Europe
7. Tel & letter: yes, NC
8. No
9. No
10. No
11. No
12. No
13. N/AN
14. Yes
15. N/AN
Books & Sets: 1,3–13,15,17, 19,22–26
Periodicals: 1(v.35–, 1959–),2,3(1 issue),4(v.6, 1932),5,6(v.10–, 1947–),7,8(v.16–, 1928–),9(v.72–, 1918–)

OAKVILLE

Oakville Public Library
120 Navy St, L6J 2Z4
Tel: 416-845-3405

1. M-Th, 9-9; F,Sa, 9-5; Su, 1-5
2. Christine St. Jacques
3. English, 160
4. None
5. 193 reels; 836 fiche
6. Halton County: Trafalgar Township, Oakville
7. Tel & letter: yes, NC
8. No
9. No
10. Yes, 3-week loan
11. No
12. No
13. Newspaper index; names index (1800–1900); microfilm index to access to local history
14. No
15. No
Books & Sets: 3(3v., 1981)
Periodicals: 2

OSHAWA

Oshawa Public Library
65 Bagot St, L1H 1N2
Tel: 416-579-6111

1. M-Th, 9-9; F, 9-6; Sa, 9-5
2. Vivian Lescisin
3. English, 100; French, 2
4. 29
5. 165
6. Ontario
7. Tel & letter: yes, NC
8. No
9. No
10. No
11. No
12. No
13. N/AN
14. No
15. No
Books & Sets: 3,10,19,24
Periodicals: 2

OTTAWA

National Archives of Canada
395 Wellington St, K1A 0N3
Tel: 613-995-5138

1. M-F, 8:30-4:45 (Reading Room open 24 hrs/day)

2. N/AN
3. English, no estimate;
French, no estimate
4. National Archives: approx
450 collections, including official
census records of Canada
5. No estimate
6. Canada
7. Tel & letter: yes, NC
8. Yes
9. N/AN
10. No
11. Yes
12. Kennedy & Roy, *Tracing
Your Ancestors in Canada* (1984,
and 1986 Addendum); *Introduction to the National Archives of
Canada* (1987); *The Archivist*, bi-
monthly; *Publications*, updated
periodically
13. In-house finding aids
14. Yes
15. No
Books & Sets: 3,6,9–12,24,25
Periodicals: 1,2,9

**National Library of Canada/
Bibliothèque Nationale du
Canada,** 395 Wellington St,
K1A 0N4
Tel: 613-995-9481

1. M-F, 8:30-5; reading rooms
open 24 hrs/day, 7 days/week
2. Section Head, Reference
Services
3. Figures not available
4. N/AN
5. N/AN
6. Primarily Canada; some US,
Great Britain, France
7. Tel & letter: yes, NC
8. No
9. No
10. Yes, through ILL
11. Yes, through ILL
12. No, although *Canadiana*,
the national bibliography, includes
Library's Canadian holdings
13. *National Library of Canada*,
booklet
14. Yes
15. No
Books & Sets: 1,3,9–14,18–20,
24–26

Periodicals: 2,9(v.1–15,17–112,
1847–1958)

OWEN SOUND

Owen Sound Public Library
824 First Ave W, N4K 4K4
Tel: 519-376-6623

1. M-F, 9-9; Sa, 9-5; Su, 2-5
2. Andrew Armitage, Library
Administrator
3. English, 1,200
4. None
5. 99 (does not include local
newspapers)
6. Grey, Bruce Counties of
Ontario; some Great Lakes history
7. Tel & letter: yes, NC except
for copies
8. No
9. No
10. No
11. Yes
12. No
13. N/AN
14. Yes
15. No
Periodicals: 2(v.4–, 1982–),
4(1979–)

PEMBROKE

Pembroke Public Library
237 Victoria St, K8A 4K5
Tel: 613-732-8844

1. M-F, until 9pm; Sa, until 5
2. N/AN
3. English, 300; other, 10
4. 5
5. 100: local newspapers
6. City of Pembroke; Renfrew
County; upper Ottawa Valley
7. Tel & letter: yes, NC for
brief search
8. No
9. No
10. No
11. Yes, to libraries only, 3
reels at a time
12. *Catalogue of the Pembroke
Public Library Local History Collection* (1985 ed)
13. N/AN

14. No
15. N/AN

PETERBOROUGH

Peterborough Public Library
345 Aylmer St N, K9H 3V7
Tel: 416-745-5382

1. Sept-May: M,T,Th,F,10-
8:30; W, 10-6; Sa, 9-5; June-Aug:
M,T,Th,F, 10-8; W,Sa, 10-5
2. James A. Pendergest
3. English, 1,300
4. 31 linear ft
5. 68
6. City of Peterborough,
Peterborough County; selective
histories of Durham, Northumberland, Hastings, Victoria, Hali-
burton, Prince Edward Counties;
Regional Municipality of Durham
7. Tel: yes, NC for brief
queries; letter: yes, $4 for brief
search and 20¢/copy
8. No
9. No
10. No
11. No
12. No
13. N/AN
14. No
15. No

PICKERING

**Town of Pickering Public
Library,** Box 368, 1400 Bayly
St, Unit 12, L1V 2R6
Tel: 416-831-6265

1. T-F, 10-8; Sa, 10-4
2. Elaine Bird
3. English, 30
4. 5
5. 20: local newspapers
6. Pickering Township, adjoining areas in Durham Region
7. Tel & letter: yes, NC
8. No
9. No
10. No
11. No
12. No
13. In-house lists

14. No
15. No

PORT ELGIN

Bruce County Public Library
Box 16000, 662 Gustavus St,
N0H 2C0
Tel: 519-832-9218

1. M-F, 8:30-5:30
2. Shirley Morningstar
3. English, 350–400
4. None
5. 15
6. Bruce County
7. Tel & letter: yes, NC
8. No
9. No charge for Bruce County residents
10. No
11. No
12. No
13. *Bibliography of Local History File at Bruce County Public Library* (1983)
14. No
15. N/AN

RICHMOND HILL

Richmond Hill Public Library
24 Wright St, L4C 4A1
Tel: 416-884-9288

1. T-F, 9-9; Sa, 10-5; Su (Oct-Apr), 2-5
2. Mary Lloyd
3. English, 800; French, 2
4. 500
5. 25
6. York County, Ontario; US, Great Britain
7. Tel & letter: yes, NC
8. No
9. No
10. No
11. No
12. No
13. *Genealogy and Local History: Great Britain, United States, Canada*, Richmond Hill Public Library (1978)
14. No
15. No

Books & Sets: 3,10,19,24,26
Periodicals: 2

SAINT CATHARINES

St. Catharines Public Library
54 Church St, L2R 7K2
Tel: 416-688-6103, ext 20

1. T-Th, 9-9; F, 9-6; Sa, 9-5
2. N/AN
3. English, not estimated; French, 7
4. 5,150
5. 1,191
6. St. Catharines; Niagara Peninsula; Ontario; Canada
7. Tel & letter: yes, NC except for copies and postage
8. No
9. No
10. No
11. Yes
12. No
13. Names index; index to St. Catharines *Constitutional*; index to *Thorold Post*
14. Yes, for in-house use only
15. No
Books & Sets: 3,5(v.1),9,11(1972–76),19,24(v.1)
Periodicals: 2(1979–85)

SAINT THOMAS

Elgin County Library
450 Sunset Dr, N5R 5V1
Tel: 519-633-0815

1. M-F, 9-4:30
2. Fran K. Clarke
3. English, 3,000
4. Very few
5. 1,300
6. Elgin and Middlesex Counties, Ontario
7. Tel: no; letter: yes, NC
8. No
9. No
10. Yes
11. Yes
12. No
13. N/AN
14. No

15. N/AN
Books & Sets: 3

St. Thomas Public Library
153 Curtis St, N5P 3Z7
Tel: 519-631-6050

1. M-Th, 9:30-8:30; F,Sa, 9:30-5
2. Terri McFadden
3. English, 600
4. N/AP
5. 400
6. Elgin County, Ontario
7. Tel: yes, NC; letter: yes, NC except for copies
8. No
9. No
10. No
11. Yes, will lend 2 reels at a time
12. No
13. N/AN
14. No
15. No
Books & Sets: 3

SAULT SAINTE MARIE

Sault Ste. Marie Public Library
50 East St, P6A 3C3
Tel: 705-759-5230

1. M-Th, 9-9; F, 9-6; Sa, 9-5; Su (Sept-June), 2-5
2. W. Eisenbichler
3. English, 250
4. N/AN
5. 1,100
6. Sault Ste. Marie and surrounding district
7. Tel: no; letter: yes, NC except 10¢/photocopy, 30¢/microcopy
8. No
9. No
10. No
11. No
12. *Genealogy at the Sault Ste. Marie Public Library*, $10
13. N/AN
14. No
15. No
Books & Sets: 3,19

SCARBOROUGH

City of Scarborough Public Library Board, Cedarbrae District Library, 545 Markham Rd, M1H 2A1
Tel: 416-431-2222

1. M-F, 9-8:30; Sa, 9-5
2. Bill Hamade
3. English, 700
4. 15
5. 5
6. Scarborough
7. Tel & letter: yes, NC
8. No
9. No
10. No
11. No
12. No
13. *Index of Material of the City of Scarborough Public Library Board Local Historical Collection; Historical Bibliography of Scarborough*
14. No
15. No
Periodicals: 2

SMITHS FALLS

Smiths Falls Public Library
81 Beckwith St N, K7A 2B9
Tel: 613-283-2911

1. M,T,Th,F, 1-5:30, 7-9; Sa, 9:30-11:30, 1-5
2. N/AP
3. English, 40
4. None
5. 50: local newspaper
6. Eastern Ontario
7. Tel: yes, NC; letter: yes, NC except 15¢/photocopy
8. No
9. No
10. No
11. Yes, only to other libraries
12. No
13. None
14. No
15. No

STRATFORD

Stratford-Perth Archives
24 St. Andrew St, N5A 1A3
Tel: 519-273-0399

1. M-Sa, 9-5
2. Lutzen H. Riedstra, Archivist
3. English, 800; German, 20
4. 1,400, including municipal and school records
5. 200
6. Perth County, Ontario, and other areas
7. Tel: yes, NC; letter: yes, NC, but donation appreciated
8. Lutzen H. Riedstra
9. No
10. No
11. No
12. No
13. Name and subject card file; newspaper indexes
14. No
15. No
Books & Sets: 3
Periodicals: 2,4((v.34–, 1980–)

SUDBURY

Sudbury Public Library
Information Services, Civic Square, 200 Brady St, P3E 5K3
Tel: 705-673-1155, ext 32

1. 64 hrs/week
2. Michaele Mueller
3. English, not estimated; some French
4. G: 100; LH: 250
5. 70
6. Sudbury and Manitoulin Districts
7. Tel: N/AN; letter: yes, NC
8. No
9. No
10. No
11. No
12. No
13. N/AN
14. No
15. No
Books & Sets: 3,9,24,25
Periodicals: 2

THOROLD

Thorold Public Library
14 Ormond St N, L2V 1Y8
Tel: 416-227-2581

1. M-F, 10-8; Sa, 10-5
2. Cheryl Bowman
3. English, 115
4. N/AN
5. 27
6. Thorold Town and Township; former Welland County, Ontario; St. Catharines, Ontario
7. Tel & letter: yes, NC
8. No
9. No
10. Yes, duplicates only
11. No
12. No
13. N/AN
14. No
15. No

THUNDER BAY

Lakehead University, Chancellor Paterson Library
Oliver Rd, P7B 5E1
Tel: 807-345-2121, ext 350

1. M-Th, 8:30am-9pm
2. Vivian Nyyssonen
3. English, 300
4. 6
5. 1
6. Northwestern Ontario
7. Tel & letter: yes, NC
8. No
9. No
10. No
11. No
12. No
13. Archives inventories
14. No
15. No
Books & Sets: 3

TIMMINS

Timmins Public Library
236 Algonquin Blvd E, P4N 2B1
Tel: 705-267-8451

1. M-Th, 10-9; F,Sa, 10-5
2. Position vacant
3. English, 359; French, 68
4. N/AN
5. 369
6. Northeastern Ontario
7. Tel & letter: yes, NC
8. No
9. No
10. No
11. No
12. No
13. UTLAS
14. No
15. N/AN
Books & Sets: 9,24

TORONTO

Metropolitan Toronto Reference Library, History Department
789 Yonge St, M4W 2G8
Tel: 416-393-7161

1. Sept-Apr: M-Th, 10-9; F,Sa, 10-6; Su, 1:30-5; summer: M-Th, 10-8; F,Sa, 10-6
2. David Kotin, Head, History Dept
3. Not estimated
4. Not estimated
5. 236+ reels; fiche not counted
6. Canada, Great Britain, US; some Eire, Germany, Italy, France, Poland, Australia
7. Tel: yes, NC; letter: yes, NC except for copies
8. B. M. Prout
9. No
10. No, but will photocopy pages or check indexes for requested surnames
11. No
12. No
13. "European Materials of Interest to Genealogists in the History Department of the Metropolitan Toronto Library," by Michael Pearson and Gwen Manning, in *Canadian Genealogist* 5(4), Dec 1983, 221-30
14. No. Refer to Ontario Genealogical Society
15. No

Books & Sets: 1,3–5,7,9–12, 17,19–26
Periodicals: 1,2,5,6,8,9

Ontario Genealogical Society Library, Canadiana Collection, North York Public Library, 6th Floor, 5120 Yonge St, M2N 5N9
Tel: 416-489-0734

1. M-Th, 9-8:30; F, 9-6; Sa, 9-5
2. D. Grant Brown, Ontario Genealogical Society Librarian; Diana Fink, Canadiana Librarian
3. English, 3,000 (includes family histories); French, 10–12
4. None
5. 3, plus 3 sets fiche
6. Canada, US (especially Eastern Seaboard), United Kingdom, Ireland, Western Europe, Australia, New Zealand
7. Tel & letter: yes, NC except for cost of materials
8. Yes, volunteer research assistants
9. No
10. Yes, through ILL, with exceptions
11. No
12. *Ontario Genealogical Society Library Holdings* (1984), $12.75
13. Family Chart Collection listing; Cemetery Recordings Holdings list; various card indexes
14. Yes
15. No
Books & Sets: 3,4,5(v.1–2), 10–12,19,26(10v.)
Periodicals: 2(v.36–41,1960–65), 4(v.6–29, 1968–75),5(1962–65, 1968–69), 6(1947–56,1960–73), 8(incomplete)

TRENTON

Trenton Memorial Public Library, 18 Albert St, K8V 4S3
Tel: 613-394-3381

1. M-F, 9:30-8; Sa, 9-5; summer: M-W, 9:30-8; Th,F, 9-6; Sa, 9-3

2. N/AN
3. English, 200
4. 50
5. 300 (mostly newspapers)
6. Prince Edward County, Hastings County, Brighton, City of Trenton, Northumberland County, Bay of Quinte
7. Tel: no; letter: yes, NC except for copies
8. No
9. No
10. Yes, only circulating materials
11. Yes, in-library use only; 1-month loan
12. No
13. N/AN
14. N/AN
15. N/AN

WALLACEBURG

Kent County Library, Wallaceburg Branch
209 James St, N8A 2A1
Tel: 519-627-5292

1. M,T,Th, 10-8; W, 12-8; F, 10-5:30; Sa, 10-5
2. Susan Irvin
3. English, 50
4. N/AN
5. 40 (includes local newspaper)
6. Kent County, Ontario, Canada
7. Tel & letter: yes, NC
8. No
9. No
10. Yes
11. Yes
12. No
13. Index to the *Wallaceburg News*, 1896–1955
14. No
15. No
Books & Sets: 3,4

WATERLOO

University of Waterloo Library
University Ave, N2L 3G1
Tel: 519-885-1211, ext 3122

1. M-F, 9-12, 1-4
2. Susan Saunders Bellingham, Head, Special Collection
3. English, 200; German, 20
4. 6
5. None
6. Counties of Waterloo, York, Brant
7. Tel & letter: no
8. No
9. No
10. Yes, to other Ontario university libraries
11. N/AP
12. No
13. N/AN
14. Yes
15. No

WHITBY

Whitby Public Library
405 Dundas St W, L1N 6A1
Tel: 416-668-6531

1. M-F, 9:30-9; Sa, 9-5; summer: closed F evenings and Sa
2. Genny Prentice
3. English: LH, 150; Whitby-Oshawa Branch, Ontario Genealogical Society, 229
4. LH: 5; Whitby-Oshawa Branch, OGS, 20
5. Ontario county census, 14; Canada West and Ontario census (Whitby-Oshawa Branch, OGS), 12; local newspapers, 1850–, 89
6. Whitby, Durham Region
7. Tel & letter: yes, NC
8. No
9. No
10. Yes, through ILL
11. Yes, through ILL
12. No
13. Whitby-Oshawa Branch, Ontario Genealogical Society card catalog holdings; local history newspaper index
14. No. Refer to Ontario Genealogical Society, Toronto
15. No
Books & Sets: 5(v.1),26(CT,RI, MD,PA)
Periodicals: 2

WINDSOR

Hiram Walker Historical Museum, 254 Pitt St W, N9A 5L5
Tel: 519-253-1812

1. T-Sa, 9-5; Su, 2-5
2. R. Alan Douglas, Curator
3. English, 10
4. 10
5. None
6. Essex County, Ontario
7. Letter: yes, NC
8. No
9. No
10. No
11. No
12. No
13. N/AN
14. No
15. No

Windsor Public Library
Main Branch, 850 Ouellette Ave, N9A 4M9
Tel: 519-255-6774

1. M-Th, 9-9; F, 9-6; Sa, 9-5; Su (Oct-Apr), 1-5
2. Ruth Vukadinov
3. English, no estimate; French, few
4. 1,365 linear ft of MSS at Municipal Archives, housed at Main Library (Mark Walsh, Archivist)
5. 1,950 films
6. Windsor, Essex County, Ontario
7. Tel & letter: yes, NC except for copies
8. No
9. No
10. Yes, only rarely; prefer to photocopy
11. Yes, 2 films per request, for 1-week loan
12. No
13. Index to newspaper, *The Windsor Star*; *How to Find Your Roots in Essex County*, free pamphlet
14. No. Refer to Essex County Branch, Ontario Genealogical

Society, PO Box 2, Station A, Windsor, N9A 6J5
15. N/AN
Books & Sets: 1,3,10,12,19, 22,24,25
Periodicals: 2,3(v.24–, 1960–)

WOODSTOCK

Oxford County Library
93 Graham St, N4S 6T5
Tel: 519-537-3322

1. M-F, 9-5
2. Jane Gamble, Chief Librarian
3. English, 200
4. 1,000
5. Microfilm, 108; all Ontario land records on microfiche
6. County of Oxford; Ontario, Canada
7. Tel: yes, NC; letter: yes, NC except for postage
8. No
9. No
10. Yes, 2-week loan
11. Yes
12. No
13. 1951 census, 1971 census; all cemeteries of Oxford; Tweedsmuir histories; marriages, deaths, and births; voters' lists; family histories
14. No
15. N/AN
Books & Sets: 3(1983 suppl),8
Periodicals: 2,4

WYOMING

Lambton County Library, Lambton Room Collection
546 Niagara St, N0N 1T0
Tel: 519-845-3324

1. M,T,Th,F, 9-9; W, 9-5; Sa, 12:30-5:30
2. Carol Gardiner
3. English, 475
4. 75
5. 50
6. Lambton County; neighboring counties of Middlesex, Kent, Essex, Elgin

7. Tel & letter: yes, NC
8. No
9. No
10. Yes, in-library use, 2 weeks

11. Yes, in-library use, 2 weeks
12. No
13. *User's Guide to the Lambton Room*

14. Yes
15. N/AN
Books & Sets: 3
Periodicals: 2,7

PRINCE EDWARD ISLAND

CHARLOTTETOWN

Confederation Centre Public Library, PO Box 7000, C1A 8G8
Tel: 902-368-4642

1. Sept-June: T-Th, 10-9; F,Sa, 10-5; Su, 1-5; July-Aug: M-Th, 10-9; F, 10-5
2. None
3. LH: English, 300; French, 10
4. None
5. LH: 30
6. Prince Edward Island
7. Tel & letter: yes, NC
8. No
9. No
10. No
11. No
12. No
13. Index to newspaper holdings
14. No
15. No

Prince Edward Island Museum and Heritage Foundation, Genealogical Research Room
2 Kent St, C1A 1M6
Tel: 902-892-9127

1. Winter: T-F, 10-12, 1:15-4; June-Oct: M-F, 9-12, 1:15-3
2. Orlo Jones
3. English, 700
4. 650
5. 60
6. Prince Edward Island
7. Tel & letter: charge varies with query
8. Orlo Jones
9. No
10. No
11. No
12. *Family History on Prince Edward Island: A Genealogical Research Guide*, $2 plus postage
13. *Information for Researchers*, free
14. Yes
15. N/AN
Books & Sets: 8(Scotland, Ireland),24(v.1)
Periodicals: 2,4(1980–83),6, 8(1980–),9(1972–, partial)

University of Prince Edward Island, Robertson Library
C1A 4P3
Tel: 902-566-0536

1. M-F, 8-5; longer hours at different times during year
2. M. B. Harris
   F. L. Pigot
3. English, 6,000
4. None
5. Microfilms of newspapers and census records
6. Prince Edward Island
7. Tel & letter: no. Might answer query, depending upon available time
8. No
9. No
10. No; occasionally lend duplicates
11. No
12. No
13. Card catalog
14. No. Refer to Prince Edward Island Museum and Heritage Foundation
15. No

QUEBEC

BROSSARD

Bibliothèque Municipale de Brossard, 3200 Boul. Lapinière, J4Z 2B4
Tel: 514-656-5960

   1. M,F, 1:30-9:30; T, Th, 9:30-9:30; Sa, 10-5; Su, 1:30-5
   2. Claire Séguin
   3. French, approx 50
   4. 1, plus 1 vertical file with newsclippings, letters, papers from local organizations
   5. 57: local newspaper, *Courrier du Sud*
   6. City of Brossard, surrounding area
   7. Tel: yes, NC; letter: no
   8. No
   9. No
  10. No
  11. No
  12. No
  13. Index for local newspapers and photographs, posters, maps, etc.
  14. No
  15. No
Books & Sets: 9,24

HULL

Bibliothèque Municipale de Hull
25 Rue Laurier, c.p. 1970, succ. B, J8X 3Y9
Tel: 819-777-4341

   1. Sept-June: M-Th, 10-9; F, 10-6; Sa, 9:30-5; Su, 1-5; July-Aug: M-Sa, 10-8
   2. None
   3. English, 25; French, 500
   4. None
   5. None

   6. Quebec Province area near Ottawa
   7. Tel & letter: no
   8. No
   9. No
  10. No
  11. No
  12. No
  13. None
  14. No
  15. No
Books & Sets: 9,24,25

KNOWLTON

Brome County Historical Society, Museum and Archives
130 Lakeside, J0E 1V0
Tel: 514-243-6782

   1. M-F, 10-5; appointment preferred
   2. Marion L. Phelps, Curator
   3. English, no estimate; French, 25
   4. No estimate
   5. 25: census and church records
   6. Brome County; some Canada, US
   7. Tel & letter: yes, small research fee, usually $5, plus copies
   8. No
   9. No
  10. No
  11. No
  12. *Preliminary Inventory* (1954), $2.50. *Secondary Inventory*, must be copied
  13. See #12
  14. Yes
  15. N/AN
Books & Sets: 26(VT,NY,PA, RI,MA only)
Periodicals: 2(partial),4

LEVIS

Collège de Lévis, Bibliothèque
9 Rue Mgr. Gosselin, G6V 5K1
Tel: 418-833-1249, ext 140

   1. M-F, 8:30-5
   2. Roger Audet, Librarian
   3. French, 225
   4. None
   5. None
   6. Lévis (Quebec) region
   7. Tel & letter: no
   8. No
   9. Yes, variable charge
  10. Yes
  11. No
  12. No
  13. N/AN
  14. No
  15. No

MONTREAL

Bibliothèque Municipale de Montréal, Salle Gagnon
1210 Sherbrooke E, H2L 1L9
Tel: 514-872-1631

   1. Summer: M-F, 9am-10pm; winter: T-F, 9am-10pm; Sa, 9-5; Su, 1-5
   2. Daniel Olivier
   3. English, 19,760; French, 27,344
   4. N/AN
   5. 3,278 microfilm; 13,164 microfiche
   6. Province of Quebec, other Canadian provinces, New England states where French Canadians settled
   7. Tel & letter: yes, NC for brief queries
   8. No
   9. No

10. No
11. No
12. No
13. Card indexes for parish histories, family histories, baptisms, marriages, burials
14. Yes
15. N/AN
Books & Sets: 1,3,5,8–12,17, 19,24,25
Periodicals: 1(v.61, 1985–),2, 3(v.49, 1985–),4(v.10, 1986–), 5(v.22, 1983–),8(v.73, 1985–), 9(v.33, 1879–)

Bibliothèque Nationale du Québec, 1700 Rue Saint-Denis, H2X 3K6
Tel: 514-873-4553

1. T-Sa, 9-5; summer: M-F, 9-5
2. N/AN
3. English, 3,000; French, 7,000
4. N/AN
5. 2,000
6. Québec; Acadie; French-speaking regions of Canada, US
7. Tel: no; letter: yes, NC
8. No
9. No
10. No
11. No
12. No
13. Card index of parish baptism, marriage, burial records; index of monographs on family histories
14. No
15. No
Books & Sets: 9,24,25
Periodicals: 2

POINTE-CLAIRE

Pointe-Claire Public Library
100 Douglas Strand, H9R 4V1
Tel: 514-630-1218

1. M-F, 10-9; Sa, 9-5
2. Carol Lacourte
3. English, 30; French, 30
4. 3
5. 15
6. Montreal; Pointe-Claire; Quebec Province
7. Tel & letter: yes, NC
8. No
9. No
10. Yes
11. No
12. No
13. N/AN
14. No
15. N/AN
Books & Sets: 9,24

QUEBEC

Société Historique de Québec
2 Rue de la Fabrique, G1R 4R7
Tel: N/AN

1. By appointment only
2. N/AN
3. French, 200
4. N/AN
5. 10
6. Eastern Canada
7. Tel & letter: no
8. Benoit Pontbriand
9. No
10. No
11. No
12. No
13. N/AN
14. No
15. No
Books & Sets: 9,24,25

SHERBROOKE

Société d'Histoire des Cantons de l'Est, 1304 Boulevard Portland, J1J 1S3
Tel: 819-562-0616

1. M-F, 9-12, 1-5
2. Andrée Ally, Archivist; Roger Blanchette, Archivist
3. English, 3,500; French, 8,000
4. 21 meters
5. None
6. Eastern districts of Canada
7. Tel: no; letter: yes, $10+/ letter (Canadian dollars)
8. N/AN
9. No charge for members; $5/nonmembers
10. No
11. No
12. No
13. *Catalogue des fonds privés de la SHCE*; *Répertoire numérique détaillé des fonds d'archives de la SHCE*
14. Yes
15. N/AN
Books & Sets: 24,25

STANBRIDGE EAST

Missisquoi Historical Society, Archives, Box 186, J0J 2N0
Tel: 514-248-3153

1. M-W, 9-4:30
2. Sabine De Groote
3. English, 100; French, 50
4. 900
5. 20
6. County of Missisquoi, Quebec
7. Tel & letter: yes, $10/first hr, $5/each hr thereafter
8. No
9. No
10. No
11. No
12. No
13. Index to archives holdings
14. No
15. No
Books & Sets: 25,26(VT,NY)

SASKATCHEWAN

REGINA

Regina Public Library
2311 12th Ave, Box 2311,
S4P 3Z5
Tel: 306-569-7591

1. M-W, 9:30-9; Th,F, 9:30-5;
Sa, 12-5; Su, 1:30-5
2. Kenneth G. Aitken
3. English, 5,364; French, 100
4. 2
5. 500 titles on microfiche
6. Saskatchewan, Manitoba,
Alberta, pre-1905 North West
Territories
7. Tel & letter: yes, NC
8. Kenneth G. Aitken
9. No
10. No
11. No
12. *Saskatchewan Local History
Directory*, $10
13. N/AN
14. No
15. No
Books & Sets: 1,3,10–12
Periodicals: 2,4

Saskatchewan Library
1352 Winnipeg St, S4P 3V7
Tel: 306-787-2984

1. M-F, 8-5
2. None
3. English, 950
4. None
5. None
6. Saskatchewan
7. Tel & letter: yes, NC
8. No
9. No
10. Yes, through ILL

11. No
12. No
13. N/AP
14. No
15. No
Books & Sets: 1,3,19,24,25
Periodicals: 2(1982–)

SASKATOON

**Saskatchewan Archives Board,
Saskatoon Office,** University of
Saskatchewan, S7N 0W0
Tel: 306-933-5832

1. M-F, 8:30-5
2. D'Arcy Hande, Acting
Director, Saskatoon Office
3. English, 900; German, 20;
French, 20; Ukrainian, 10; Yiddish, 1
4. 50
5. 10
6. Province of Saskatchewan
7. Tel & letter: yes, NC except
20¢/copy
8. D'Arcy Hande
9. No
10. No
11. Yes, 1-month loan
12. No
13. D'Arcy Hande, *Exploring
Family History in Saskatchewan*,
revised 1986
14. No
15. No

Saskatoon Public Library
311 23rd St E, S7K 0J6
Tel: 306-975-7578

1. Local History Room: M-Th,
9am-9:30pm; F, 9-6; Sa, 1:30-6;
Su, 1-5:30

2. Arlean McPherson, Local
History Librarian
3. English, LH, 4,000
4. N/AN
5. LH: 190 local city newspapers to date
6. City of Saskatoon and
environs; western Canada
7. Tel & letter: yes, NC, LH
only
8. No
9. No
10. No
11. Yes, LH, through ILL
12. No
13. N/AN
14. N/AN
15. N/AN
Books & Sets: 1,3,24
Periodicals: 4(v.32, 1978–)

YORKTON

Parkland Regional Library
95A Broadway W, S3N 0L9
Tel: 306-783-7022

1. N/AN
2. N/AN
3. English, 1,000
4. None
5. 300
6. Saskatchewan; Parkland
area
7. Tel: no; letter: yes, NC
8. No
9. No
10. No
11. No
12. No
13. N/AN
14. No
15. No

YUKON
TERRITORY

WHITEHORSE

Yukon Archives
Box 2703, 2nd Ave &
Hawkins St, Y1A 4Z6
Tel: 403-667-5321

   1. T-F, 9-5

2. N/AP
3. English, 49
4. 3
5. 28; also, 177: local newspapers
6. Yukon Territory; some AK,
Northwest Territory
7. Tel & letter: yes, NC

8. No
9. No
10. No
11. No
12. No
13. *Genealogy Sources Available at Yukon Archives*
14. Yes
15. No

NO COLLECTIONS

*Libraries Not Holding Genealogy or Local History Collections**

UNITED STATES

ALABAMA

Birmingham, University of Alabama at Birmingham, Mervyn H. Sterne Library
Columbiana, Harrison Regional Library
Cullman, Cullman County Public Library
Florence, University of North Alabama, Collier Library
Montevallo, University of Montevallo, Carmichael Library
Montgomery, Alabama Historical Commission
Tuscaloosa, American College of Heraldry Library

ALASKA

Anchorage, Alaska Historical Society

CALIFORNIA

Altadena, Altadena Public Library
Belmont, College of Notre Dame Library
Beverly Hills, Beverly Hills Public Library
Fairfield, Solano County Library System
Glendale, Glendale Public Library
Independence, Inyo County Free Library
Mariposa, Mariposa Museum and History Center
Monterey, Monterey Public Library
Napa, Napa County Historical Society
Oxnard, Oxnard Public Library
Palo Alto, Palo Alto City Library
Redondo Beach, Redondo Beach Public Library
San Marino, Huntington Library

---

*These libraries returned questionnaires stating that they do not hold any genealogy or local history collections.

COLORADO

Denver, Colorado Genealogical Society
Wray, Northeast Colorado Bookmobile Services

CONNECTICUT

Bethel, Bethel Public Library
Bloomfield, Prosser Public Library
Fairfield, Fairfield Public Library
Hamden, Hamden Public Library
New Canaan, New Canaan Library
New Haven, Yale University Library
Trumbull, Trumbull Library

DELAWARE

Newark, Newark Free Library

DISTRICT OF COLUMBIA

Smithsonian Institution, National Museum of American Art/National Portrait Gallery

FLORIDA

Brooksville, Hernando County Library System
Delray Beach, Delray Beach Library
Key West, Florida Keys Community College, John S. Smith Learning Resources Center
Key West, Key West Art and Historical Society Library
Orlando, Municipal Reference Service—City of Orlando

GEORGIA

Atlanta, Georgia Genealogical Society
Cartersville, Bartow County Library System

HAWAII

Honolulu, Department of Land and Natural Resources, Bureau of Conveyances

IDAHO

Idaho Falls, Idaho Falls Public Library
Pocatello, Pocatello Public Library

ILLINOIS

Alsip, Alsip-Merrionette Park Library
Broadview, Broadview Public Library District
Carbondale, Carbondale Public Library
Chicago, Chicago Historical Society Library
Godfrey, Lewis and Clark Community College

Hodgkins, Hodgkins Public Library District
Joliet, Joliet Public Library
Northbrook, Northbrook Public Library
Prospect Heights, Prospect Heights Public Library
Roselle, Roselle Public Library District
Villa Park, Villa Park Public Library
Willowbrook, Willowbrook Public Library

INDIANA

Hanover, Hanover College, Duggan Library

KANSAS

Saint Marys, Pottawatomie-Wabaunsee Regional Library

KENTUCKY

Frankfort, Paul Sawyier Public Library

MAINE

Portland, Portland Public Library

MARYLAND

Hagerstown, Western Maryland Public Libraries Regional Library

MASSACHUSETTS

Billerica, Billerica Public Library
South Dartmouth, Southworth Library
Swampscott, Swampscott Public Library

MICHIGAN

Ann Arbor, Historical Society of Michigan
Ann Arbor, Huron Valley Library System
Canton, Canton Public Library
Jenison, Georgetown Township Library
Kalamazoo, Kalamazoo Institute of Arts Library
Muskegon, Muskegon County Library
Pontiac, Oakland County Reference Library
Pontiac, Waterford Township Public Library
Southfield, Southfield Public Library
Vestaburg, Richland Township Library

MINNESOTA

Blaine, Anoka County Library
Fergus Falls, Viking Library System
Marshall, Marshall-Lyon County Library

South Saint Paul, South Saint Paul Public Library

MISSISSIPPI

Clinton, Mississippi College Library

MISSOURI

Columbia, Daniel Boone Regional Library

MONTANA

Columbus, Stillwater County Library
Helena, Montana State Library

NEVADA

Las Vegas, Las Vegas-Clark County Library District

NEW HAMPSHIRE

Salem, Kelley Library

NEW JERSEY

Bergenfield, Bergenfield Free Public Library
Berkeley Heights, Free Public Library
East Brunswick, East Brunswick Public Library
Glen Rock, Glen Rock Public Library
Matawan, Matawan-Aberdeen Public Library
New Providence, New Providence Memorial Library
Orange, Free Public Library of the City of Orange
Princeton, Princeton University Library
Sewell, Gloucester County Library
Vineland, Vineland Public Library

NEW MEXICO

Santa Fe, Santa Fe Public Library

NEW YORK

Amityville, Amityville Public Library
Bellmore, Bellmore Memorial Library
Chappaqua, Chappaqua Library
East Islip, East Islip Public Library
Endicott, George F. Johnson Memorial Library
Franklin Square, Franklin Square Public Library
Hamburg, Hamburg Public Library
North Babylon, North Babylon Public Library
Ossining, Ossining Public Library
Pittsford, Pittsford Library
Sayville, Sayville Library

Setauket, Emma S. Clark Memorial Library
Shirley, Mastics-Moriches-Shirley Community Library
Uniondale, Nassau Library System
Uniondale, Uniondale Public Library
Yonkers, Yonkers Public Library

NORTH CAROLINA

Burgaw, Pender County Library
Chapel Hill, Chapel Hill Public Library
Greenville, East Carolina University, Joyner Library
Montreat, Montreat-Anderson College, L. Nelson Bell Library

OHIO

Columbus, Upper Arlington Public Library
North Canton, North Canton Public Library
Rocky River, Rocky River Public Library
Rossford, Rossford Public Library
Stow, Stow Public Library
Washington Court House, Fayette County Genealogical Society
Worthington, Worthington Public Library

OREGON

Pendleton, Blue Mountain Genealogical Society

PENNSYLVANIA

Ambler, Wissahickon Valley Public Library
Bethel Park, Bethel Park Public Library
Chester, Widener University, Wolfgram Memorial Library
Lancaster, Lancaster Newspapers Inc.
Pittsburgh, Northland Public Library
Pittsburgh, Upper Saint Clair Township Library

RHODE ISLAND

Cranston, Cranston Public Library
Pawtucket, Pawtucket Public Library
Providence, Rhode Island State Law Library

SOUTH CAROLINA

Columbia, South Carolina State Library

TENNESSEE

Clinton, Clinch-Powell Regional Library
Martin, Reelfoot Regional Library Center
Morristown, Nolichucky Regional Library
Sparta, Caney Fork Regional Library Center

TEXAS

Dallas, Dallas County Public Library
Houston, Harris County Public Library System
Richardson, Richardson Public Library

UTAH

Murray, Murray Public Library
Salt Lake City, Association of Professional Genealogists

VIRGINIA

Fairfax, Fairfax Genealogical Society
Lynchburg, Lynchburg Public Library
Radford, John Preston McConnell Library
Richmond, County of Henrico Public Library

WASHINGTON

Renton, Renton Public Library
Spokane, Spokane County Library District
Vancouver, Fort Vancouver Regional Library

WISCONSIN

Brown Deer, Brown Deer Library
Jefferson, Jefferson Public Library
Monroe, Wisconsin State Genealogical Society
Muskego, Muskego Public Library
New Berlin, New Berlin Public Library
Shawano, Shawano City-County Library

CANADA

ALBERTA

Athabasca, Athabasca University Library
Edmonton, Alberta Culture and Multiculturalism Library Services Branch
Rockyford, Rockyford and District Municipal Library
Strathmore, Marigold Library System
Tofield, Tofield Municipal Library

BRITISH COLUMBIA

North Vancouver, North Vancouver City Library
Terrace, Northwest Community College
Victoria, Legislative Library of British Columbia

MANITOBA

Winnipeg, Hudson's Bay Company Library

NEW BRUNSWICK

Edmundston, Bibliothèque Regionale du Haut Saint-Jean
Fredericton, New Brunswick Library Service

NORTHWEST TERRITORIES

Yellowknife, Yellowknife Public Library

ONTARIO

Frankford, Frankford Public Library
Kingston, Frontenac County Library, Kingston Township Days Road Branch
Saint Marys, Saint Marys Public Library
Stratford, Stratford Public Library
Val Caron, Valley East Public Library
Warkworth, Northumberland County Public Library

QUEBEC

Kirkland, Kirkland Municipal Library

INDEX

*Index of Libraries with Significant Out-of-State Collections**

Organized by State, Region and Ethnic Group, Province, or Country to Which a Collection Pertains

UNITED STATES

Collections Pertaining to ALABAMA

Pine Bluff and Jefferson County Library System   **Pine Bluff, Arkansas**
Polk County Historical and Genealogical Library   **Bartow, Florida**
West Florida Regional Library   **Pensacola, Florida**
Lake Blackshear Regional Library   **Americus, Georgia**
West Georgia Regional Library   **Carrollton, Georgia**
Satilla Regional Library   **Douglas, Georgia**
Vernon Parish Library   **Leesville, Louisiana**
Jefferson Parish Library   **Metairie, Louisiana**
Carnegie Public Library of Clarksdale   **Clarksdale, Mississippi**
Lowndes County Library System   **Columbus, Mississippi**
Washington County Library System   **Greenville, Mississippi**
Greenwood-Leflore Public Library   **Greenwood, Mississippi**
Meridian Public Library   **Meridian, Mississippi**
Ozarks Genealogical Society Library   **Springfield, Missouri**
Forsyth County Public Library, North Carolina Room   **Winston-Salem, North Carolina**
Bryan Public Library   **Bryan, Texas**
Cameron Public Library   **Cameron, Texas**
Kurth Memorial Library, Ora McMullen Room   **Lufkin, Texas**

Collections Pertaining to ALASKA

Vancouver Public Library   **Vancouver, British Columbia**

---

*Libraries holding genealogy or local history collections within their own state are not listed.

University of Washington, Suzzallo Library   **Seattle, Washington**
Yukon Archives   **Whitehorse, Yukon Territory**

Collections Pertaining to ARKANSAS

Huntsville-Madison County Public Library   **Huntsville, Alabama**
Polk County Historical and Genealogical Library   **Bartow, Florida**
Shawnee Library System   **Carterville, Illinois**
Carnegie Public Library of Clarksdale   **Clarksdale, Mississippi**
Joplin Public Library   **Joplin, Missouri**
Ozarks Genealogical Society Library   **Springfield, Missouri**
Oklahoma Historical Society   **Oklahoma City, Oklahoma**
Amarillo Public Library   **Amarillo, Texas**
Kurth Memorial Library, Ora McMullen Room   **Lufkin, Texas**
Sherman Public Library   **Sherman, Texas**
Temple Public Library   **Temple, Texas**
Texarkana Public Library   **Texarkana, Texas**

Collections Pertaining to COLORADO

Amarillo Public Library   **Amarillo, Texas**

Collections Pertaining to CONNECTICUT

Tama County Historical Museum Library   **Toledo, Iowa**
Maine State Library   **Augusta, Maine**
Maryland State Law Library   **Annapolis, Maryland**
Agawam Public Library   **Agawam, Massachusetts**
Lynnfield Public Library   **Lynnfield, Massachusetts**
Joint Free Public Library of Morristown   **Morristown, New Jersey**
Port Chester Public Library   **Port Chester, New York**

Onondaga County Public Library   Syracuse, New
   York
Stark County District Library   Canton, Ohio
Marysville Public Library   Marysville, Ohio
Firelands Historical Society   Norwalk, Ohio
Wayne County Public Library   Wooster, Ohio
Westerly Public Library   Westerly, Rhode Island

Collections Pertaining to DELAWARE

Valparaiso Public Library   Valparaiso, Indiana
Maryland State Law Library   Annapolis, Maryland
Wicomico County Free Library   Salisbury, Maryland
Gloucester County Historical Society Library   Wood-
   bury, New Jersey
Middletown Public Library   Middletown, Ohio
Wayne County Public Library   Wooster, Ohio
Haverford College Library, Quaker Collection   Haver-
   ford, Pennsylvania
Chester County Historical Society   West Chester,
   Pennsylvania
Roanoke City Public Library, Virginia Room
   Roanoke, Virginia

Collections Pertaining to DISTRICT OF COLUMBIA

Valparaiso Public Library   Valparaiso, Indiana

Collections Pertaining to FLORIDA

Satilla Regional Library   Douglas, Georgia

Collections Pertaining to GEORGIA

Public Library of Anniston and Calhoun County
   Anniston, Alabama
Houston-Love Memorial Library   Dothan, Alabama
Florence-Lauderdale Public Library   Florence,
   Alabama
Tuscaloosa Public Library   Tuscaloosa, Alabama
H. Grady Bradshaw-Chambers County Library   Valley,
   Alabama
Craighead County-Jonesboro Public Library   Jonesboro,
   Arkansas
Pikes Peak Library District   Colorado Springs, Colorado
Polk County Historical and Genealogical Library   Bartow,
   Florida
Suwannee River Regional Library   Live Oak, Florida
West Florida Regional Library   Pensacola, Florida
Bradford County Public Library   Starke, Florida
Valparaiso Public Library   Valparaiso, Indiana
Murray State University, Forrest C. Pogue Library   Murray,
   Kentucky
Washington Parish Library System   Franklinton, Louisiana
Vernon Parish Library   Leesville, Louisiana
Maryland State Law Library   Annapolis, Maryland
Carnegie Public Library of Clarksdale   Clarksdale, Missis-
   sippi
Lowndes County Library System   Columbus, Mississippi

Washington County Library System   Greenville, Mississippi
Greenwood-Leflore Public Library   Greenwood, Mississippi
Pike-Amite-Walthall Library System   McComb, Mississippi
Meridian Public Library   Meridian, Mississippi
Ozarks Genealogical Society Library   Springfield, Missouri
Catawba County Library   Newton, North Carolina
Forsyth County Public Library, North Carolina Room
   Winston-Salem, North Carolina
Jackson-Madison County Library   Jackson, Tennessee
Cameron Public Library   Cameron, Texas
Kurth Memorial Library, Ora McMullen Room   Lufkin,
   Texas
Gladys Harrington Public Library   Plano, Texas
Temple Public Library   Temple, Texas
Hampton Public Library   Hampton, Virginia
Roanoke City Public Library, Virginia Room   Roanoke,
   Virginia

Collections Pertaining to IDAHO

Butte-Silver Bow Public Library   Butte, Montana
Missoula Public Library   Missoula, Montana
University of Washington, Suzzallo Library   Seattle,
   Washington

Collections Pertaining to ILLINOIS

Craighead County-Jonesboro Public Library   Jonesboro,
   Arkansas
Genealogical Center Library   Atlanta, Georgia
Alexandrian Public Library   Mount Vernon, Indiana
Valparaiso Public Library   Valparaiso, Indiana
Davenport Public Library   Davenport, Iowa
Keokuk Public Library   Keokuk, Iowa
Tama County Historical Museum Library   Toledo, Iowa
Kansas State Historical Society Library   Topeka, Kansas
University of Kentucky, Margaret I. King Library   Lexing-
   ton, Kentucky
Murray State University, Forrest C. Pogue Library   Murray,
   Kentucky
Owensboro-Daviess County Public Library   Owensboro,
   Kentucky
Jefferson Parish Library   Metairie, Louisiana
Cape Girardeau Public Library   Cape Girardeau, Missouri
Mid-Continent Public Library   Independence, Missouri
Joplin Public Library   Joplin, Missouri
St. Louis Mercantile Library Association   Saint Louis,
   Missouri
Ozarks Genealogical Society Library   Springfield, Missouri
St. Louis Genealogical Society Library   University City,
   Missouri
Rowan Public Library, Edith M. Clark History Room
   Salisbury, North Carolina
Rutherford B. Hayes Presidential Center Library   Fremont,
   Ohio
Brigham Young University, Harold B. Lee Library   Provo,
   Utah
Genealogical Institute   Woods Cross, Utah

Collections Pertaining to INDIANA

Shawnee Library System **Carterville, Illinois**
Danville Public Library **Danville, Illinois**
South Suburban Genealogy and Historical Society Library
   South Holland, Illinois
Illinois State Historical Library **Springfield, Illinois**
Evans Public Library **Vandalia, Illinois**
Tama County Historical Museum Library **Toledo, Iowa**
Kansas State Historical Society Library **Topeka, Kansas**
Kentucky Department for Libraries and Archives **Frankfort,**
   Kentucky
University of Kentucky, Margaret I. King Library **Lexing-**
   ton, Kentucky
Owensboro-Daviess County Public Library **Owensboro,**
   Kentucky
Genealogical Association of Southwestern Michigan **Saint**
   Joseph, Michigan
Sturgis Public Library **Sturgis, Michigan**
Cape Girardeau Public Library **Cape Girardeau, Missouri**
Mid-Continent Public Library **Independence, Missouri**
Ozarks Genealogical Society Library **Springfield, Missouri**
Rowan Public Library, Edith M. Clark History Room
   Salisbury, North Carolina
Forsyth County Public Library, North Carolina Room
   Winston-Salem, North Carolina
Ross County Genealogical Society **Chillicothe, Ohio**
Rutherford B. Hayes Presidential Center Library **Fremont,**
   Ohio
Smith Library of Regional History, Lane Public Library
   Oxford, Ohio
Genealogical Institute **Woods Cross, Utah**

Collections Pertaining to IOWA

Huntsville-Madison County Public Library **Huntsville,**
   Alabama
Winnetka Public Library District **Winnetka, Illinois**
Valparaiso Public Library **Valparaiso, Indiana**

Collections Pertaining to KANSAS

Valparaiso Public Library **Valparaiso, Indiana**
Joplin Public Library **Joplin, Missouri**
Amarillo Public Library **Amarillo, Texas**

Collections Pertaining to KENTUCKY

Pikes Peak Library District **Colorado Springs, Colorado**
Polk County Historical and Genealogical Library **Bartow,**
   Florida
Volusia County Library Center **Daytona Beach, Florida**
Genealogical Center Library **Atlanta, Georgia**
Satilla Regional Library **Douglas, Georgia**
Ohoopee Regional Library **Vidalia, Georgia**
Shawnee Library System **Carterville, Illinois**
Danville Public Library **Danville, Illinois**
Gail Borden Public Library District **Elgin, Illinois**
Granite City Public Library **Granite City, Illinois**
Suburban Library System **Oak Lawn, Illinois**

Illinois State Historical Library **Springfield, Illinois**
Lincoln Library-Sangamon Valley Collection **Springfield,**
   Illinois
Evans Public Library **Vandalia, Illinois**
Bluffton-Wells County Public Library **Bluffton, Indiana**
Bartholomew County Public Library **Columbus, Indiana**
Crawfordsville District Public Library **Crawfordsville,**
   Indiana
Frankfort Community Public Library **Frankfort, Indiana**
Johnson County Historical Museum **Franklin, Indiana**
Indiana State Library **Indianapolis, Indiana**
Kokomo-Howard County Public Library **Kokomo, Indiana**
Madison-Jefferson County Public Library **Madison,**
   Indiana
Alexandrian Public Library **Mount Vernon, Indiana**
Tipton County Public Library **Tipton, Indiana**
Valparaiso Public Library **Valparaiso, Indiana**
Wabash Carnegie Public Library **Wabash, Indiana**
Maryland State Law Library **Annapolis, Maryland**
St. Mary's County Historical Society Library **Leonardtown,**
   Maryland
Wicomico County Free Library **Salisbury, Maryland**
Library of Michigan **Lansing, Michigan**
Carnegie Public Library of Clarksdale **Clarksdale, Missis-**
   sippi
Lowndes County Library System **Columbus, Mississippi**
Greenwood-Leflore Public Library **Greenwood, Mississippi**
Iuka Public Library **Iuka, Mississippi**
Cape Girardeau Public Library **Cape Girardeau, Missouri**
State Historical Society of Missouri **Columbia, Missouri**
Mid-Continent Public Library **Independence, Missouri**
Joplin Public Library **Joplin, Missouri**
Kansas City Public Library **Kansas City, Missouri**
Ozarks Genealogical Society Library **Springfield, Missouri**
Catawba County Library **Newton, North Carolina**
Rowan Public Library, Edith M. Clark History Room
   Salisbury, North Carolina
Forsyth County Public Library, North Carolina Room
   Winston-Salem, North Carolina
Ohio University, Alden Library **Athens, Ohio**
Stark County District Library **Canton, Ohio**
Ross County Genealogical Society **Chillicothe, Ohio**
State Library of Ohio **Cleveland, Ohio**
Dayton and Montgomery County Public Library **Dayton,**
   Ohio
Preble County District Library, Eaton Branch **Eaton, Ohio**
Marysville Public Library **Marysville, Ohio**
Middletown Public Library **Middletown, Ohio**
Firelands Historical Society **Norwalk, Ohio**
Sandusky Library **Sandusky, Ohio**
Oklahoma Historical Society **Oklahoma City, Oklahoma**
Bryan Public Library **Bryan, Texas**
Kurth Memorial Library, Ora McMullen Room **Lufkin,**
   Texas
Gladys Harrington Public Library **Plano, Texas**
Sherman Public Library **Sherman, Texas**
Buchanan County Public Library **Grundy, Virginia**
Hampton Public Library **Hampton, Virginia**
Roanoke City Public Library, Virginia Room **Roanoke,**
   Virginia

Tazewell County Public Library **Tazewell, Virginia**
Cabell County Public Library **Huntington, West Virginia**
Marshall University, James E. Morrow Library **Huntington, West Virginia**
Parkersburg and Wood County Public Library **Parkersburg, West Virginia**

Collections Pertaining to LOUISIANA

Huntsville-Madison County Public Library **Huntsville, Alabama**
Polk County Historical and Genealogical Library **Bartow, Florida**
Carnegie Public Library of Clarksdale **Clarksdale, Mississippi**
Greenwood-Leflore Public Library **Greenwood, Mississippi**
Cape Girardeau Public Library **Cape Girardeau, Missouri**
American-Canadian Genealogical Society Library **Manchester, New Hampshire**
Public Library of Cincinnati and Hamilton County **Cincinnati, Ohio**
Tyrrell Historical Library, Beaumont Library System **Beaumont, Texas**
Bryan Public Library **Bryan, Texas**
Kurth Memorial Library, Ora McMullen Room **Lufkin, Texas**

Collections Pertaining to MAINE

Maryland State Law Library **Annapolis, Maryland**
Lynn Historical Society **Lynn, Massachusetts**
Lynnfield Public Library **Lynnfield, Massachusetts**
Newburyport Public Library **Newburyport, Massachusetts**
Salisbury Public Library **Salisbury, Massachusetts**
Dover Public Library **Dover, New Hampshire**

Collections Pertaining to MARYLAND

Pikes Peak Library District **Colorado Springs, Colorado**
Delaware State Archives **Dover, Delaware**
Historical Society of Delaware **Wilmington, Delaware**
Polk County Historical and Genealogical Library **Bartow, Florida**
Lake Blackshear Regional Library **Americus, Georgia**
Clayton County Library System Headquarters **Jonesboro, Georgia**
Illinois State Historical Library **Springfield, Illinois**
Bartholomew County Public Library **Columbus, Indiana**
Madison-Jefferson County Public Library **Madison, Indiana**
Valparaiso Public Library **Valparaiso, Indiana**
Tama County Historical Museum Library **Toledo, Iowa**
Kentucky Department for Libraries and Archives **Frankfort, Kentucky**
University of Kentucky, Margaret I. King Library **Lexington, Kentucky**
Murray State University, Forrest C. Pogue Library **Murray, Kentucky**
Owensboro-Daviess County Public Library **Owensboro, Kentucky**

Washington Parish Library System **Franklinton, Louisiana**
Sturgis Public Library **Sturgis, Michigan**
Greenwood-Leflore Public Library **Greenwood, Mississippi**
Cape Girardeau Public Library **Cape Girardeau, Missouri**
Mid-Continent Public Library **Independence, Missouri**
Ozarks Genealogical Society Library **Springfield, Missouri**
Joint Free Public Library of Morristown **Morristown, New Jersey**
Gloucester County Historical Society Library **Woodbury, New Jersey**
Currituck County Library **Barco, North Carolina**
Cumberland County Public Library **Fayetteville, North Carolina**
New Bern-Craven County Public Library **New Bern, North Carolina**
Catawba County Library **Newton, North Carolina**
Rowan Public Library, Edith M. Clark History Room **Salisbury, North Carolina**
Forsyth County Public Library, North Carolina Room **Winston-Salem, North Carolina**
Stark County District Library **Canton, Ohio**
Ross County Genealogical Society **Chillicothe, Ohio**
Preble County District Library, Eaton Branch **Eaton, Ohio**
Marysville Public Library **Marysville, Ohio**
Middletown Public Library **Middletown, Ohio**
Firelands Historical Society **Norwalk, Ohio**
Sandusky Library **Sandusky, Ohio**
Wayne County Public Library **Wooster, Ohio**
Public Library of Youngstown and Mahoning County **Youngstown, Ohio**
Centre County Library and Historical Museum **Bellefonte, Pennsylvania**
Haverford College Library, Quaker Collection **Haverford, Pennsylvania**
Chester County Historical Society **West Chester, Pennsylvania**
Bryan Public Library **Bryan, Texas**
Kurth Memorial Library, Ora McMullen Room **Lufkin, Texas**
Hampton Public Library **Hampton, Virginia**
Eastern Mennonite College, Menno Simons Archives **Harrisonburg, Virginia**
Roanoke City Public Library, Virginia Room **Roanoke, Virginia**
Waynesboro Public Library **Waynesboro, Virginia**
Old Charles Town Library **Charles Town, West Virginia**
Martinsburg-Berkeley County Public Library **Martinsburg, West Virginia**
Jackson County Library **Ripley, West Virginia**

Collections Pertaining to MASSACHUSETTS

Pikes Peak Library District **Colorado Springs, Colorado**
Starved Rock Library System **Ottawa, Illinois**
Illinois State Historical Library **Springfield, Illinois**
Tama County Historical Museum Library **Toledo, Iowa**
Auburn Public Library **Auburn, Maine**
Maine State Library **Augusta, Maine**
Waterville Public Library **Waterville, Maine**
Maryland State Law Library **Annapolis, Maryland**

Lowndes County Library System **Columbus, Mississippi**
Greenwood-Leflore Public Library **Greenwood, Mississippi**
Dover Public Library **Dover, New Hampshire**
Joint Free Public Library of Morristown **Morristown, New Jersey**
Onondaga County Public Library **Syracuse, New York**
Stark County District Library **Canton, Ohio**
Firelands Historical Society **Norwalk, Ohio**
Westerly Public Library **Westerly, Rhode Island**
Rockingham Free Public Library **Bellows Falls, Vermont**

Collections Pertaining to MICHIGAN

Bluffton-Wells County Public Library **Bluffton, Indiana**
Valparaiso Public Library **Valparaiso, Indiana**
Berkshire Athenaeum **Pittsfield, Massachusetts**
Rutherford B. Hayes Presidential Center Library **Fremont, Ohio**
Monroe, Juneau, Jackson County Genealogy Workshop **Black River Falls, Wisconsin**

Collections Pertaining to MINNESOTA

Huntsville-Madison County Public Library **Huntsville, Alabama**
Winnetka Public Library District **Winnetka, Illinois**
Alexander Mitchell Public Library **Aberdeen, South Dakota**

Collections Pertaining to MISSISSIPPI

Craighead County-Jonesboro Public Library **Jonesboro, Arkansas**
Polk County Historical and Genealogical Library **Bartow, Florida**
Washington Parish Library System **Franklinton, Louisiana**
Vernon Parish Library **Leesville, Louisiana**
St. James Parish Library **Lutcher, Louisiana**
Tulane University, Howard-Tilton Memorial Library **New Orleans, Louisiana**
Lafourche Parish Library **Thibodaux, Louisiana**
Ozarks Genealogical Society Library **Springfield, Missouri**
Bryan Public Library **Bryan, Texas**
Kurth Memorial Library, Ora McMullen Room **Lufkin, Texas**

Collections Pertaining to MISSOURI

Huntsville-Madison County Public Library **Huntsville, Alabama**
Craighead County-Jonesboro Public Library **Jonesboro, Arkansas**
Shawnee Library System **Carterville, Illinois**
Southern Illinois University, Lovejoy Library **Edwardsville, Illinois**
Winnetka Public Library District **Winnetka, Illinois**
Valparaiso Public Library **Valparaiso, Indiana**
Keokuk Public Library **Keokuk, Iowa**
Kansas State Historical Society Library **Topeka, Kansas**

Kentucky Department for Libraries and Archives **Frankfort, Kentucky**
University of Kentucky, Margaret I. King Library **Lexington, Kentucky**
Murray State University, Forrest C. Pogue Library **Murray, Kentucky**
Owensboro-Daviess County Public Library **Owensboro, Kentucky**
Jefferson Parish Library **Metairie, Louisiana**
Catawba County Library **Newton, North Carolina**
Rowan Public Library, Edith M. Clark History Room **Salisbury, North Carolina**
Public Library of Cincinnati and Hamilton County **Cincinnati, Ohio**
Kurth Memorial Library, Ora McMullen Room **Lufkin, Texas**
Sherman Public Library **Sherman, Texas**

Collections Pertaining to MONTANA

Boise Public Library **Boise, Idaho**
Alexander Mitchell Public Library **Aberdeen, South Dakota**
University of Washington, Suzzallo Library **Seattle, Washington**

Collections Pertaining to NEBRASKA

Alexander Mitchell Public Library **Aberdeen, South Dakota**

Collections Pertaining to NEVADA

California State Railroad Museum Library **Sacramento, California**
California State Library, California Section **Sacramento, California**

Collections Pertaining to NEW HAMPSHIRE

Auburn Public Library **Auburn, Maine**
Maine State Library **Augusta, Maine**
Waterville Public Library **Waterville, Maine**
Old York Historical Society Library **York, Maine**
Maryland State Law Library **Annapolis, Maryland**
Chelmsford Public Library **Chelmsford, Massachusetts**
Lynn Historical Society **Lynn, Massachusetts**
Lynnfield Public Library **Lynnfield, Massachusetts**
Newburyport Public Library **Newburyport, Massachusetts**
Salisbury Public Library **Salisbury, Massachusetts**
J. V. Fletcher Library **Westford, Massachusetts**
Joint Free Public Library of Morristown **Morristown, New Jersey**
Firelands Historical Society **Norwalk, Ohio**
Rockingham Free Public Library **Bellows Falls, Vermont**

Collections Pertaining to NEW JERSEY

Delaware State Archives **Dover, Delaware**
Danville Public Library **Danville, Illinois**

Middletown Public Library **Middletown, Ohio**
Firelands Historical Society **Norwalk, Ohio**
Putnam County District Library **Ottawa, Ohio**
Flesh Public Library **Piqua, Ohio**
Sandusky Library **Sandusky, Ohio**
Tiffin-Seneca Public Library **Tiffin, Ohio**
Troy Historical Society **Troy, Ohio**
Wayne County Public Library **Wooster, Ohio**
Public Library of Youngstown and Mahoning County
Youngstown, Ohio
Muskingum County Genealogical Library **Zanesville, Ohio**
W. Walworth Harrison Library **Greenville, Texas**
Kurth Memorial Library, Ora McMullen Room **Lufkin,
Texas**
Gladys Harrington Public Library **Plano, Texas**
Genealogical Institute **Woods Cross, Utah**
Bridgewater College, Alexander Mack Memorial Library
Bridgewater, Virginia
Hampton Public Library **Hampton, Virginia**
Eastern Mennonite College, Menno Simons Archives
Harrisonburg, Virginia
Roanoke City Public Library, Virginia Room **Roanoke,
Virginia**
Staunton Public Library **Staunton, Virginia**
Waynesboro Public Library **Waynesboro, Virginia**
Marshall University, James E. Morrow Library **Huntington,
West Virginia**
Martinsburg-Berkeley County Public Library **Martinsburg,
West Virginia**
Parkersburg and Wood County Public Library
Parkersburg, West Virginia
Jackson County Library **Ripley, West Virginia**
Monroe, Juneau, Jackson County Genealogy Workshop
Black River Falls, Wisconsin

Collections Pertaining to RHODE ISLAND

Maine State Library **Augusta, Maine**
Maryland State Law Library **Annapolis, Maryland**
Joint Free Public Library of Morristown **Morristown, New
Jersey**

Collections Pertaining to SOUTH CAROLINA

Florence-Lauderdale Public Library **Florence, Alabama**
Tuscaloosa Public Library **Tuscaloosa, Alabama**
Pine Bluff and Jefferson County Library System **Pine Bluff,
Arkansas**
Polk County Historical and Genealogical Library **Bartow,
Florida**
West Florida Regional Library **Pensacola, Florida**
Bradford County Public Library **Starke, Florida**
Lake Blackshear Regional Library **Americus, Georgia**
West Georgia Regional Library **Carrollton, Georgia**
Satilla Regional Library **Douglas, Georgia**
Clayton County Library System Headquarters **Jonesboro,
Georgia**
LaFayette-Walker County Library **LaFayette, Georgia**
Statesboro Regional Library **Statesboro, Georgia**
South Georgia Regional Library **Valdosta, Georgia**

Ohoopee Regional Library **Vidalia, Georgia**
Shawnee Library System **Carterville, Illinois**
Illinois State Historical Library **Springfield, Illinois**
Evans Public Library **Vandalia, Illinois**
Bartholomew County Public Library **Columbus, Indiana**
Johnson County Historical Museum **Franklin, Indiana**
Madison-Jefferson County Public Library **Madison,
Indiana**
Valparaiso Public Library **Valparaiso, Indiana**
Tama County Historical Museum Library **Toledo, Iowa**
Kentucky Department for Libraries and Archives **Frankfort,
Kentucky**
University of Kentucky, Margaret I. King Library **Lexing-
ton, Kentucky**
Murray State University, Forrest C. Pogue Library **Murray,
Kentucky**
Owensboro-Daviess County Public Library **Owensboro,
Kentucky**
Washington Parish Library System **Franklinton, Louisiana**
Jefferson Parish Library **Metairie, Louisiana**
Maryland State Law Library **Annapolis, Maryland**
Wicomico County Free Library **Salisbury, Maryland**
Carnegie Public Library of Clarksdale **Clarksdale, Missis-
sippi**
Lowndes County Library System **Columbus, Mississippi**
Washington County Library System **Greenville, Mississippi**
Greenwood-Leflore Public Library **Greenwood, Mississippi**
Pike-Amite-Walthall Library System **McComb, Mississippi**
Cape Girardeau Public Library **Cape Girardeau, Missouri**
Mid-Continent Public Library **Independence, Missouri**
Kansas City Public Library **Kansas City, Missouri**
Ozarks Genealogical Society Library **Springfield, Missouri**
Public Library of Charlotte and Mecklenburg County
Charlotte, North Carolina
Cumberland County Public Library **Fayetteville, North
Carolina**
Scotland County Memorial Library **Laurinburg, North
Carolina**
Robeson County Public Library **Lumberton, North
Carolina**
Union County Public Library **Monroe, North Carolina**
Catawba County Library **Newton, North Carolina**
Robersonville Public Library **Robersonville, North
Carolina**
Rowan Public Library, Edith M. Clark History Room
Salisbury, North Carolina
Forsyth County Public Library, North Carolina Room
Winston-Salem, North Carolina
Wayne County Public Library **Wooster, Ohio**
Oklahoma Historical Society **Oklahoma City, Oklahoma**
Jackson-Madison County Library **Jackson, Tennessee**
McKenzie Memorial Library, Gordon Browning Room
McKenzie, Tennessee
Bryan Public Library **Bryan, Texas**
Cameron Public Library **Cameron, Texas**
Kurth Memorial Library, Ora McMullen Room **Lufkin,
Texas**
Gladys Harrington Public Library **Plano, Texas**
Temple Public Library **Temple, Texas**
Hampton Public Library **Hampton, Virginia**

305

U.S. REGIONS AND ETHNIC GROUPS

Kalamazoo Public Library **Kalamazoo, Michigan**
Library of Michigan **Lansing, Michigan**
Mount Clemens Public Library **Mount Clemens, Michigan**
Hoyt Public Library, Eddy Historical Collection **Saginaw, Michigan**
Northwestern Michigan College **Traverse City, Michigan**
Minneapolis Public Library, History Collection **Minneapolis, Minnesota**
Waseca-LeSueur Regional Library **Waseca, Minnesota**
Gulfport-Harrison County Library **Gulfport, Mississippi**
Pike-Amite-Walthall Library System **McComb, Mississippi**
Kansas City Public Library **Kansas City, Missouri**
Ozarks Genealogical Society Library **Springfield, Missouri**
New Hampshire Historical Society **Concord, New Hampshire**
New Hampshire State Library **Concord, New Hampshire**
American-Canadian Genealogical Society Library **Manchester, New Hampshire**
Manchester City Library, New Hampshire Room **Manchester, New Hampshire**
New Jersey State Library, Dept of Education **Trenton, New Jersey**
Vineland Historical and Antiquarian Society **Vineland, New Jersey**
Westfield Memorial Library **Westfield, New Jersey**
Gloucester County Historical Society Library **Woodbury, New Jersey**
New York State Library, Humanities/History **Albany, New York**
Richmond Memorial Library **Batavia, New York**
Buffalo and Erie County Public Library **Buffalo, New York**
East Hampton Library, Long Island Collection **East Hampton, New York**
Crandall Library **Glens Falls, New York**
Ogdensburg Public Library **Ogdensburg, New York**
Rochester Public Library, Local History Division **Rochester, New York**
Smithtown Library, Long Island History Room **Smithtown, New York**
Troy Public Library **Troy, New York**
New Bern-Craven County Public Library **New Bern, North Carolina**
State Library of Ohio **Cleveland, Ohio**
Rutherford B. Hayes Presidential Center Library **Fremont, Ohio**
Hudson Library and Historical Society **Hudson, Ohio**
Lorain Public Library **Lorain, Ohio**
Middletown Public Library **Middletown, Ohio**
Sandusky Library **Sandusky, Ohio**
Worthington Historical Society Library **Worthington, Ohio**
Public Library of Youngstown and Mahoning County **Youngstown, Ohio**
Centre County Library and Historical Museum **Bellefonte, Pennsylvania**
Annie Halenbake Ross Library **Lock Haven, Pennsylvania**
Bibliothèque Municipale de Montréal, Salle Gagnon **Montreal, Quebec**
Newport Historical Society Library **Newport, Rhode Island**
Westerly Public Library **Westerly, Rhode Island**

University of South Carolina, South Caroliniana Library **Columbia, South Carolina**
Sioux Falls Public Library **Sioux Falls, South Dakota**
Kurth Memorial Library, Ora McMullen Room **Lufkin, Texas**
McAllen Memorial Library **McAllen, Texas**
Waco-McLennan County Library **Waco, Texas**
Brigham Young University, Harold B. Lee Library **Provo, Utah**
Genealogical Institute **Woods Cross, Utah**
Bennington Museum, Genealogy Library **Bennington, Vermont**
Brooks Memorial Library **Brattleboro, Vermont**
Vermont State Archives **Montpelier, Vermont**
Rutland Free Library **Rutland, Vermont**
Springfield Town Library **Springfield, Vermont**
Hampton Public Library **Hampton, Virginia**
Tacoma Public Library, Special Collections **Tacoma, Washington**
Monroe, Juneau, Jackson County Genealogy Workshop **Black River Falls, Wisconsin**
Superior Public Library **Superior, Wisconsin**
Park County Library **Cody, Wyoming**

Collections Pertaining to NEW NETHERLAND

Holland Society of New York Library **New York, New York**

Collections Pertaining to NORTHEASTERN STATES

Society of Mayflower Descendants **Oakland, California**
Pequot Library **Southport, Connecticut**
Volusia County Library Center **Daytona Beach, Florida**
New England Historic Genealogical Society **Boston, Massachusetts**
Gulfport-Harrison County Library **Gulfport, Mississippi**
Lauren Rogers Museum of Art Library **Laurel, Mississippi**
Montana Historical Society **Helena, Montana**
New Hampshire State Library **Concord, New Hampshire**
Hempstead Public Library **Hempstead, New York**
New York Genealogical and Biographical Library **New York, New York**
Onondaga County Public Library **Syracuse, New York**
Metropolitan Library System, Downtown Branch **Oklahoma City, Oklahoma**
Herman Brown Free Library **Burnet, Texas**
Milwaukee Public Library **Milwaukee, Wisconsin**
Oshkosh Public Library **Oshkosh, Wisconsin**

Collections Pertaining to NORTHWESTERN STATES

University of Idaho Library **Moscow, Idaho**
Eastern Oregon State College, Walter M. Pierce Library **La Grande, Oregon**
Oregon Historical Society **Portland, Oregon**
Oregon State Library **Salem, Oregon**
Springfield Public Library **Springfield, Oregon**
Washington State Library **Olympia, Washington**

Collections Pertaining to SOUTHEASTERN STATES

Public Library of Anniston and Calhoun County **Anniston, Alabama**
Auburn University, Ralph Brown Draughon Library **Auburn , Alabama**
Harwell G. Davis Library **Birmingham, Alabama**
Florence-Lauderdale Public Library **Florence, Alabama**
Gadsden-Etowah County Public Library **Gadsden, Alabama**
Mobile Public Library **Mobile, Alabama**
Alabama Department of Archives and History **Montgomery, Alabama**
Chattahoochee Valley Community College **Phenix City, Alabama**
Jacksonville Public Library **Jacksonville, Florida**
West Florida Regional Library **Pensacola, Florida**
St. Petersburg Public Library **Saint Petersburg, Florida**
Bradford County Public Library **Starke, Florida**
Florida State Archives, Genealogy Collection **Tallahassee, Florida**
Tampa-Hillsborough County Public Library **Tampa, Florida**
Dougherty County Public Library **Albany, Georgia**
Georgia Department of Archives and History **Atlanta, Georgia**
Northeast Georgia Regional Library **Clarkesville, Georgia**
Cobb County Public Library **Marietta, Georgia**
Sara Hightower Regional Library **Rome, Georgia**
Chatham-Effingham-Liberty Regional Library **Savannah, Georgia**
Georgia Historical Society **Savannah, Georgia**
Shawnee Library System **Carterville, Illinois**
Johnson County Library **Shawnee Mission, Kansas**
Western Kentucky University, Kentucky Library **Bowling Green, Kentucky**
Louisiana State University, LeDoux Library **Eunice, Louisiana**
New Orleans Public Library **New Orleans, Louisiana**
Lincoln County Public Library **Brookhaven, Mississippi**
Gulfport-Harrison County Library **Gulfport, Mississippi**
Hattiesburg Public Library System **Hattiesburg, Mississippi**
Mississippi Department of Archives and History **Jackson, Mississippi**
Lauren Rogers Museum of Art Library **Laurel, Mississippi**
Meridian Public Library **Meridian, Mississippi**
Jennie Stephens Smith Library **New Albany, Mississippi**
Lee County Library **Tupelo, Mississippi**
Public Library of Charlotte and Mecklenburg County **Charlotte, North Carolina**
North Carolina Department of Cultural Resources **Raleigh, North Carolina**
University of South Carolina, South Caroliniana Library **Columbia, South Carolina**
Pickens County Library **Easley, South Carolina**
Chattanooga-Hamilton County Bicentennial Library **Chattanooga, Tennessee**
Knox County Public Library, Calvin McClung Collection **Knoxville, Tennessee**
Tennessee State Library and Archives **Nashville, Tennessee**

Moore Memorial Public Library **Texas City, Texas**
University of Virginia, Alderman Library **Charlottesville, Virginia**

Collections Pertaining to SOUTHWESTERN STATES

Mobile Public Library **Mobile, Alabama**
Flagstaff City-Coconino County Public Library **Flagstaff, Arizona**
Mohave County Historical Society Library **Kingman, Arizona**
Palm Springs Public Library **Palm Springs, California**
Thomas Branigan Memorial Library **Las Cruces, New Mexico**
University of Texas, Eugene C. Barker Texas History Center **Austin, Texas**
El Paso Public Library **El Paso, Texas**
Grapevine Public Library **Grapevine, Texas**
San Antonio Public Library **San Antonio, Texas**

Collections Pertaining to UNITED STATES

Calgary Public Library, W. R. Castell Central Library **Calgary, Alberta**
South Western Alberta Genealogical Library **Lethbridge, Alberta**
British Columbia Genealogical Society Library **Vancouver, British Columbia**
Greater Victoria Public Library **Victoria, British Columbia**
Manitoba Genealogical Society Library **Winnipeg, Manitoba**
Winnipeg Public Library, Centennial Library **Winnipeg, Manitoba**
Eastern Counties Regional Library **Mulgrave, Nova Scotia**
North York Central Library, Canadiana Room **North York, Ontario**
National Library of Canada **Ottawa, Ontario**
Richmond Hill Public Library **Richmond Hill, Ontario**
Metropolitan Toronto Reference Library, History Department **Toronto, Ontario**
Ontario Genealogical Society Library, Canadiana Collection **Toronto, Ontario**
Brome County Historical Society **Knowlton, Quebec**
Bibliothèque du Québec **Montreal, Quebec**

Collections Pertaining to WESTERN STATES

California State Railroad Museum Library **Sacramento, California**
Alameda May Petzinger Library of Californiana **Stockton, California**
University of the Pacific Libraries **Stockton, California**
Ricks College, McKay Library **Rexburg, Idaho**
State Historical Society of Missouri **Columbia, Missouri**
St. Louis Mercantile Library Association **Saint Louis, Missouri**
Oklahoma Historical Society **Oklahoma City, Oklahoma**
South Dakota State Historical Society Library **Pierre, South Dakota**
University of Texas, Eugene C. Barker Texas History Center

INTERNATIONAL

Surrey Public Library **Surrey, British Columbia**
British Columbia Genealogical Society Library **Vancouver, British Columbia**
Capitol Area Joint Genealogical Library **Carmichael, California**
El Segundo Public Library **El Segundo, California**
Los Angeles Public Library, History and Genealogy Department **Los Angeles, California**
El Dorado County Library **Placerville, California**
Porterville Public Library **Porterville, California**
Augustan Society Library **Torrance, California**
Weld Public Library **Greeley, Colorado**
Lakewood Library **Lakewood, Colorado**
North Brevard Public Library **Titusville, Florida**
Belleville Public Library **Belleville, Illinois**
Newberry Library **Chicago, Illinois**
Wheaton Public Library **Wheaton, Illinois**
Grout Museum of History and Science **Waterloo, Iowa**
Northwest Kansas Library System **Norton, Kansas**
Jefferson County Genealogical Society **Oskaloosa, Kansas**
Topeka Genealogical Society Library **Topeka, Kansas**
New Orleans Public Library **New Orleans, Louisiana**
Manitoba Genealogical Society Library **Winnipeg, Manitoba**
New England Historic Genealogical Society **Boston, Massachusetts**
Minneapolis Public Library, History Collection **Minneapolis, Minnesota**
University of Minnesota **Minneapolis, Minnesota**
Waseca-LeSueur Regional Library **Waseca, Minnesota**
Kansas City Public Library **Kansas City, Missouri**
Lewis and Clark Public Library **Helena, Montana**
Bethlehem Public Library **Delmar, New York**
North York Central Library, Canadiana Room **North York, Ontario**
Ontario Genealogical Society Library, Canadiana Collection **Toronto, Ontario**
Cottage Grove Genealogical Society Library **Cottage Grove, Oregon**
Carnegie Library of Pittsburgh, Pennsylvania Department **Pittsburgh, Pennsylvania**
University of South Carolina, South Caroliniana Library **Columbia, South Carolina**
Montgomery County Library **Conroe, Texas**
Dallas Public Library, Genealogy Section **Dallas, Texas**
Deer Park Public Library **Deer Park, Texas**
Houston Public Library, Clayton Library **Houston, Texas**
Oshkosh Public Library **Oshkosh, Wisconsin**

Collections Pertaining to FRANCE

Mesa Arizona Branch Genealogical Library **Mesa, Arizona**
Arizona State Library, Genealogy Library **Phoenix, Arizona**
Quincy Public Library **Quincy, Illinois**
National Library of Canada **Ottawa, Ontario**
Metropolitan Toronto Reference Library, History Department **Toronto, Ontario**

Collections Pertaining to GERMANY

Mesa Arizona Branch Genealogical Library **Mesa, Arizona**
Arizona State Library, Genealogy Library **Phoenix, Arizona**
R. H. Johnson Library **Sun City West, Arizona**
Fayetteville Public Library **Fayetteville, Arkansas**
Krans-Buckland Family Association Library **North Highlands, California**
Palm Springs Public Library **Palm Springs, California**
Genealogical Society of Santa Cruz County Library **Santa Cruz, California**
Denver Public Library **Denver, Colorado**
Library of Congress **Washington, District of Columbia**
Selby Public Library **Sarasota, Florida**
Brigham Young University, Joseph F. Smith Library **Laie, Hawaii**
Idaho State Historical Society **Boise, Idaho**
Belleville Public Library **Belleville, Illinois**
Morris Public Library **Morris, Illinois**
Suburban Library System **Oak Lawn, Illinois**
Quincy Public Library **Quincy, Illinois**
Indiana State Library **Indianapolis, Indiana**
Jefferson Parish Library **Metairie, Louisiana**
Kalamazoo Public Library **Kalamazoo, Michigan**
Troy Public Library **Troy, Michigan**
Concordia College, Carl B. Ylvisaker Library **Moorhead, Minnesota**
St. Joseph Public Library **Saint Joseph, Missouri**
American Historical Society of Germans from Russia **Lincoln, Nebraska**
Western New York Genealogical Society Library **Hamburg, New York**
Germans from Russia Heritage Society **Bismarck, North Dakota**
Cleveland Public Library **Cleveland, Ohio**
Sandusky Library **Sandusky, Ohio**
Ponca City Library, Genealogy Department **Ponca City, Oklahoma**
Metropolitan Toronto Reference Library, History Department **Toronto, Ontario**
Heritage Quest Research Library **Orting, Washington**
Yakima Valley Genealogical Society Library **Yakima, Washington**
Monroe, Juneau, Jackson County Genealogy Workshop **Black River Falls, Wisconsin**

Collections Pertaining to GUATEMALA

North Brevard Public Library **Titusville, Florida**

Collections Pertaining to HAITI

North Brevard Public Library **Titusville, Florida**

Collections Pertaining to HOLLAND

Herrick Public Library **Holland, Michigan**
Selby Public Library **Sarasota, Florida**

Collections Pertaining to SCOTLAND (SEE ALSO BRITISH ISLES)

Fayetteville Public Library **Fayetteville, Arkansas**
Genealogical Society of Santa Cruz County Library **Santa Cruz, California**
Denver Public Library **Denver, Colorado**
Selby Public Library **Sarasota, Florida**
Washington Memorial Library **Macon, Georgia**
Morris Public Library **Morris, Illinois**
Quincy Public Library **Quincy, Illinois**
Allen County Public Library **Fort Wayne, Indiana**
Western New York Genealogical Society Library **Hamburg, New York**
Muskingum County Genealogical Library **Zanesville, Ohio**
Genealogical Forum of Oregon **Portland, Oregon**
Belton City Library **Belton, Texas**
Genealogical Institute **Woods Cross, Utah**

Collections Pertaining to SWEDEN

Mesa Arizona Branch Genealogical Library **Mesa, Arizona**
Krans-Buckland Family Association Library **North Highlands, California**

Selby Public Library **Sarasota, Florida**
Quincy Public Library **Quincy, Illinois**

Collections Pertaining to SWITZERLAND

Idaho State Historical Society **Boise, Idaho**
Quincy Public Library **Quincy, Illinois**

Collections Pertaining to VOLGA-GERMANS

Hays Public Library, Kansas Room **Hays, Kansas**

Collections Pertaining to WALES (SEE ALSO BRITISH ISLES)

Fayetteville Public Library **Fayetteville, Arkansas**
Genealogical Society of Santa Cruz County Library **Santa Cruz, California**
Selby Public Library **Sarasota, Florida**
Washington Memorial Library **Macon, Georgia**
Quincy Public Library **Quincy, Illinois**
Allen County Public Library **Fort Wayne, Indiana**

Sample Questionnaire for the
Directory of American Libraries
with Genealogy or Local History Collections
Part 1

1. Days and hours open to the public.

2. Name of the head of your genealogy or local history section.

3. Approximate number of books by language in your genealogy or local history section.

4. Approximate number of manuscript collections concerning genealogy or local history in your library.

5. Approximate number of reels concerning genealogy or local history in your microfilm collection.

6. What geographical areas does your collection cover?

7. Do you answer questions by telephone or letter concerning genealogy or local history?

8. Is there a qualified genealogist on your staff?

9. Is there a charge for the use of your library?

10. Do you lend books from your genealogy or local history collection?

11. Do you lend microforms from your genealogy or local history collection?

12. Is there a published guide to your holdings?

13. List any unpublished indexes or other guides to your collection.

14. Have you a list of professionals who will research for a fee?

15. Is your collection on OCLC? Is your collection on RLIN?